# Lecture Notes in Computer Science 4148

*Commenced Publication in 1973*
Founding and Former Series Editors:
Gerhard Goos, Juris Hartmanis, and Jan van Leeuwen

Johan Vounckx   Nadine Azemard
Philippe Maurine (Eds.)

# Integrated Circuit and System Design

## Power and Timing Modeling, Optimization and Simulation

16th International Workshop, PATMOS 2006
Montpellier, France, September 13-15, 2006
Proceedings

 Springer

Volume Editors

Johan Vounckx
IMEC
Kapeldreef 75, 3001 Heverlee, Belgium
E-mail: vounckx@imec.be

Nadine Azemard
Philippe Maurine
LIRMM
161 Rue Ada, 34392 Montpellier Cedex 5, France
E-mail: {nadine.azemard,philippe.maurine}@lirmm.fr

Library of Congress Control Number: 2006931894

CR Subject Classification (1998): B.7, B.8, C.1, C.4, B.2, B.6, J.6

LNCS Sublibrary: SL 1 – Theoretical Computer Science and General Issues

ISSN        0302-9743
ISBN-10     3-540-39094-4 Springer Berlin Heidelberg New York
ISBN-13     978-3-540-39094-7 Springer Berlin Heidelberg New York

Springer is a part of Springer Science+Business Media

springer.com

© Springer-Verlag Berlin Heidelberg 2006

Typesetting: Camera-ready by author, data conversion by Scientific Publishing Services, Chennai, India
Printed on acid-free paper      SPIN: 11847083      06/3142      5 4 3 2 1 0

# Preface

Welcome to the proceedings of PATMOS 2006, the 16th in a series of international workshops. PATMOS 2006 was organized by LIRMM with CAS technical co-sponsorship and CEDA sponsorship.

Over the years, the PATMOS workshop has evolved into an important European event, where researchers from both industry and academia discuss and investigate the emerging challenges in future and contemporary applications, design methodologies, and tools required for the development of upcoming generations of integrated circuits and systems. The technical program of PATMOS 2006 contained state-of-the-art technical contributions, three invited talks, a special session on hearing-aid design, and an embedded tutorial. The technical program focused on timing, performance and power consumption, as well as architectural aspects with particular emphasis on modeling, design, characterization, analysis and optimization in the nanometer era.

The Technical Program Committee, with the assistance of additional expert reviewers, selected the 64 papers presented at PATMOS. The papers were organized into 11 technical sessions and 3 poster sessions. As is always the case with the PATMOS workshops, full papers were required, and several reviews were received per manuscript.

Beyond the presentations of the papers, the PATMOS technical program was enriched by a series of speeches, offered by world class experts, on important emerging research issues of industrial relevance. Giovanni De Micheli spoke on "Nanoelectronics: Challenges and Opportunities", Christian Piguet spoke on "Static and Dynamic Power Reduction by Architecture Selection", Peter A. Beerel spoke on "Asynchronous Design for High-Speed and Low-Power Circuits" and Robin Wilson spoke on "Design for Volume Manufacturing in the Deep Submicron Era".

We would like to thank the many people who voluntarily worked to make PATMOS 2006 possible, the expert reviewers, the members of the technical program and steering committees, and the invited speakers, who offered their skill, time, and deep knowledge to make PATMOS 2006 a memorable event. Last but not least we would like to thank the sponsors of PATMOS 2006, ATMEL, CADENCE, Mentor Graphics, STMicroelectronics, CNRS, and UM2 for their support.

September 2006
Johan Vounckx
Nadine Azemard
Philippe Maurine

# Organization

## Organizing Committee

General Co-chairs: Nadine Azemard, LIRMM, France
Philippe Maurine, LIRMM, France

Technical Program Chair: Johan Vounckx, IMEC, Belgium

Secretariat: Céline Berger, LIRMM, France

Proceedings: Johan Vounckx, IMEC, Belgium

## PATMOS Technical Program Committee

B. Al-Hashimi, Univ. of Southampton, UK
M. Alioto, University of Sienna, Italy
A. Alvandpour, Linkoping Univ., Sweden
N. Azemard, LIRMM, France
D. Bertozzi, Univ. di Bologna, Italy
L. Bisdounis, INTRACOM, Greece
A. Bogliolo, Univ. di Urbino, Italy
J.A. Carballo, IBM, USA
N. Chang, Seoul National Univ., Korea
J. Figueras, Univ. Catalunya, Spain
E. Friedman, Univ. of Rochester, USA
C.E. Goutis, Univ. Patras, Greece
E. Grass, IHP, Germany
J.L. Güntzel, Univ. Fed. de Pelotas, Brazil
P. Girard, LIRMM, France
R. Hartenstein, Univ. Kaiserslautern, Germany
R. Jakushokas, Univ. of Rochester, USA
J. Juan Chico, Univ. Sevilla, Spain
N. Julien-Talon, Lester, France
K. Karagianni, Univ. of Patras, Greece
S. Khatri, Univ. of Colorado, USA
P. Larsson-Edefors, Chalmers T. U., Sweden
P. Marchal, IMEC, Belgium
P. Maurine, LIRMM, France
V. Moshnyaga, Univ. Fukuoka, Japan
W. Nebel, Univ. Oldenburg, Germany
D. Nikolos, Univ. of Patras, Greece
J.A. Nossek, T. U. Munich, Germany
A. Nunez, Univ. Las Palmas, Spain

V.G. Oklobdzija, U. California Davis, USA
V. Paliouras, Univ. of Patras, Greece
M. Papaefthymiou, Univ. Michigan, USA
F. Pessolano, Philips, The Netherlands
H. Pfleiderer, Univ. Ulm, Germany
C. Piguet, CSEM, Switzerland
M. Poncino, Univ. di Verona, Italy
R. Reis, Univ. Porto Alegre, Brazil
M. Robert, Univ. Montpellier, France
A. Rubio, Univ. Catalunya, Spain
D. Sciuto, Politecnico di Milano, Italy
D. Soudris, Univ. Thrace, Greece
J. Sparsø, DTU, Denmark
A. Stauffer, EPFL, Switzerland
T. Stouraitis, Univ. Patras, Greece
A.M. Trullemans, Univ. LLN, Belgium
J. Vounckx, IMEC vzw, Belgium
R. Zafalon, STMicroelectronics, Italy

## PATMOS Steering Committee

A.J. Acosta, U. Sevilla/IMSE-CSM, Spain
Nadine Azemard, University of Montpellier, France
Joan Figueras, Universitat Politècnica de Catalunya, Spain
Reiner Hartenstein, Technische Universität Kaiserslautern, Germany
Bertrand Hochet, Ecole d'Ingenieurs du Canton du Vaud (EIVD), Switzerland
Jorge Juan-Chico, Instituto de Microelectrónica de Sevilla, Spain
Enrico Macci, Politecnico di Torino (POLITO), Italy
Philippe Maurine, University of Montpellier, France
Wolfgang Nebel, University of Oldenburg, Germany
Vassilis Paliouras, University of Patras, Greece
Christian Piguet, CSEM, Switzerland
Bruno Riccò, Università di Bologna, Italy
A. Rubio, Universitat Politècnica de Catalunya, Spain
Dimitrious Soudris, Democritus University of Thrace (DUTH), Greece
Jens Sparsø, Technical University Denmark, Denmark
Annemie Trullemans, Université Catholique de Louvain (UCL), Belgium
Johan Vounckx, IMEC, Belgium
Roberto Zafalon, ST Microelectronics, Italy

## Executive Steering Sub-committee

President:        Wolfgand Nebel, University of Oldenburg, Germany
Vice-president:   Enrico Macii, Politecnico di Torino (POLITO), Italy
Secretary:        Vassilis Paliouras, University of Patras, Greece

# Table of Contents

## Session 4 – Low-Power Digital Circuits

## Session 5 – Busses and Interconnects

## Session 6 – Low Power Techniques

## Session 7 – Applications and SoC Design

# Session 8 – Modeling

# Session 9 – Digital Circuits

# Session 10 – Reconfigurable and Programmable Devices

# Poster 1

## Poster 2

## Poster 3

# Keynotes

# Industrial Session

# Design of Parallel Implementations by Means of Abstract Dynamic Critical Path Based Profiling of Complex Sequential Algorithms

Anatoly Prihozhy and Daniel Mlynek

[1] Signal Processing Institute, Swiss Federal Institute of Technology,
LTS3/ELB-Ecublens, Lausanne, CH-1015, Switzerland
[2] Telecommunication Systems Software Department, HSCC,
F. Skarina St., 8/2, 220114, Minsk, Belarus
prihozhy@yahoo.com, daniel.mlynek@epfl.ch
http://lts3www.epfl.ch/

**Abstract.** This paper presents a methodology of parallel implementations design that starts with abstract sequential descriptions of complex systems when no any parallel solutions have been taken and solves dynamically at real input data very complex tasks that are typical for system-level design. Critical path and parallelization potential based profiling of large sequential algorithms on data flow execution graphs is the kernel of methodology that enables to search for optimal (sub-optimal) parallel implementation solutions at very abstract level of design flow. Experimental results obtained on the critical path and parallelization potential based profiling of MPEG4 video codec and subsequent performance analysis of possible parallel implementations prove usefulness and effectiveness of the developed methodology and tool.

## 1 Introduction

Existing approaches to automated design of parallel systems by means of partitioning, scheduling, allocation, and design space exploration usually start from task or event graphs which assume the existing of preliminary partitioning of whole behavior into large partitions or tasks [1-3]. Critical path analysis [4-9] is an efficient mechanism used at several design levels. Critical path profiling is a metric developed for parallel programs [9] and proved to be useful for several optimization goals. The critical path profile is a list of procedures and the time each procedure contributed to the length of the critical path. Critical path profiling is an effective metric for tuning parallel programs and is especially useful during the early stages when load imbalance is a significant bottleneck. Paper [9] describes a runtime non-trace-based algorithm to compute the critical path profile of the execution of message passing and shared-memory parallel programs. This work also presents an online algorithm to compute a variant of critical path, called critical path zeroing that measures the reduction in application execution time that improving a selected procedure will have. In paper [7], the critical path profiling is presented as a method for detailed understanding of when and how delays are introduced in data transfers in the Internet. By constructing and profiling the critical path, it is possible to determine what fraction of the total transfer latency is due to packet propagation, delays at the server and at the client, network variation etc.

J. Vounckx, N. Azemard, and P. Maurine (Eds.): PATMOS 2006, LNCS 4148, pp. 1–11, 2006.

Papers [5-6] present metrics, model, and tool for the evaluation of critical paths in parallel implementations defined on data flow execution graphs of sequential algorithms. In this paper, we propose a methodology of sequential algorithm data dependences based critical path and parallelization potential profiling, which helps to search for optimal parallel implementations starting from consideration of simple basic operations and scalar variables of programming languages and solving such complex tasks as critical path reduction, partitioning, scheduling, and allocation.

The paper is organized as follows. Section 2 formulates main principles of our parallelization methodology. Section 3 defines the model and key concepts of dynamic profiling of sequential preliminary partitioned algorithms based on data flow execution graphs and parallelization potential evaluation. Section 4 presents solutions for critical path reduction and parallelization potential enhancement by means of equivalent transformation of algorithm description driven by profiling results. Section 5 briefly explains our approach to design of efficient parallel implementations and in particular to solving the partitioning, scheduling, and allocation tasks. Section 6 presents our tool that implements the critical path profiling model and supports complex parallel solution space exploration for a given sequential C-code. Experimental results obtained during the generation of possible parallel implementations of a MPEG4 video codec are reported in Section 7 while conclusions are reported in Section 8.

## 2   Methodology of Abstract Sequential Algorithm Parallelization Through Critical Path Based Profiling

The key difference of methodology we propose in the paper compared with the majority of existing models and tools [2,3,8,9] is that it starts with a very abstract sequential description of a system when no any parallel solution has been taken and solves dynamically at real input data very complex tasks that are typical for system-level hardware/software co-design. Critical path and parallelization potential based profiling of large sequential algorithms on data flow execution graphs (DFEG) represented with basic operations and scalar variables of such programming languages as C (compared with the profiling of existing parallel programs represented by event graphs on basic machines) is the kernel of our methodology which enable searching for optimal (sub-optimal) parallel implementation solutions at very abstract levels of design flow. Key steps of the design flow we propose are presented in Fig.1: 1) dynamic profiling of a sequential algorithm with respect to data dependences based critical path and parallelization potential with and without taking into account the code partitioning and communications among partitions; 2) reduction of the critical path and enhancement of the parallelization potential by means of transforming the sequential code; 3) dynamic partitioning of the sequential algorithm code and data with minimization of the overall critical path at given constraints on implementation cost; 4) dynamic scheduling of operations in the algorithm partitions including the memory access and communication operations and serialization of operations in each partition; 5) allocation of parallel resources; 6) generation of a parallel implement-tation description. The code decomposition defined by a programmer being rather of sequential nature than of parallel one is a good partitioning for the profiling and

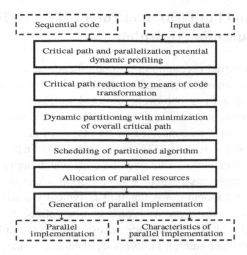

**Fig. 1.** Parallel implementation design flow

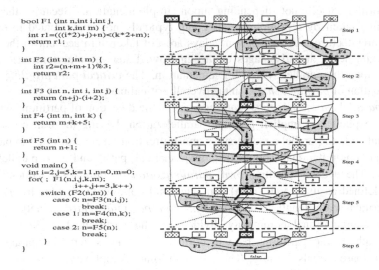

```
bool F1 (int n,int i,int j,
         int k,int m) {
  int r1=(((i*2)+j)+n)<(k*2+m);
  return r1;
}

int F2 (int n, int m) {
  int r2=(n+m+1)%3;
  return r2;
}

int F3 (int n, int i, int j) {
  return (n+j)-(i+2);
}

int F4 (int m, int k) {
  return m+k+5;
}

int F5 (int n) {
  return n+1;
}

void main() {
  int i=2,j=5,k=11,n=0,m=0;
  for( ;  F1(n,i,j,k,m);
          i++,j+=3,k++)
    switch (F2(n,m)) {
      case 0: n=F3(n,i,j);
              break;
      case 1: m=F4(m,k);
              break;
      case 2: n=F5(n);
              break;
    }
}
```

**Fig. 2.** Partitioned DFEG derived from example C-code function tree execution, partition subgraphs are in shadow

reduction of critical path. Code repartitioning is needed before the parallel system implementation, which reduces the overall critical path in term of basic, memory, and communication operations at given constraints on resources. True control structures of the sequential code are an obstacle in the implementation of parallelization potential. In [10] one basic block model (OBBM) and appropriate transformations breaking the true sequential control flow and merging the data flows of separate basic blocks in one basic block which preserve potential parallelism and possible acceleration are proposed. Based on the extended OBBM, our dynamic partitioning-scheduling-allocation algorithm is much more flexible and efficient.

## 3    Critical Path and Parallelization Potential Based Dynamic Profiling of Sequential Algorithm

*DFEG* derived from a partial execution of sequential code at a set of input data does not include true control flow elements and can be considered as an expansion of DFG. DFEG is represented as a finite non-cyclic directed weighted graph constructed on two types of nodes: 1) name-, address-, and scalar value-nodes and 2) operation-nodes. The graph nodes may be connected by two types of arcs: 1) data dependence arc and 2) conditional dependence arc. There are initial and final nodes on the graph. Function tree is the most natural *partitioning* of a code which implies a decomposition of DFEG onto sub-graphs associated with partition executions. In algorithms presenting branching and looping, one function is typically associated with several sub-graphs. A *computational complexity profile* can be defined on partitioned DFEG in terms of complexity of basic, memory access, and communication operations [5,6,13]. The *overall critical path* on DFEG is defined as a sequence of graph nodes with the maximum sum of weights, connecting an initial node with a final node. Any partition has its *own critical path*. Critical path of an abstract algorithm is a feature of the algorithm itself not depending upon implementation. Because the initial partitioning taken by a programmer is being typically not implemented in the final parallel architecture, communication delays are not taken into account in the overall critical path delay at early stages of design flow. Later the algorithm critical path depends upon the parallel system implementation. The *critical path profiling* aims at the evaluation of *partition shares* in the overall critical path.

The *parallelization potential profiling* aims at the detection of partitions with high and low explicit and implicit possible parallelization. During the transition from a sequential code to parallel code versions, most attention must be devoted to partitions with high computational complexity, long critical path, and low parallelization potential. The *overall* (partition *own*) *parallelization potential* of a sequential code can be defined as its overall (own) computational complexity divided by its overall (own) critical path length. The *parallelization potential share* is defined as the partition computational complexity divided by the partition share in the overall critical path. If the partition share in critical path equals zero the parallelization potential share equals infinity. The computational complexity, critical path, and parallelization potential based profiles of a sequential code are computed dynamically during the algorithm execution at typical input data.

An example partitioned C-code and its DFEG decomposed into sub-graphs associated with function executions are presented in Fig.2. The overall computational complexity and critical path (shown in bold) equal 81 and 42 basic operations respectively, while the parallelization potential equals 1.93. The C-code profile is represented by the shares of F1, F2, F3, F4, and F5 functions in the overall complexity (critical path): 44.4% (33.3%), 18.5% (35.7%), 9.9% (14.3%), 3.7% (7.2%) and 4.9% (9.5%) respectively. The parallelization potential of F1 and F3 functions equals 1.5 and 1.33 respectively, while the other functions cannot be parallelized as they are.

# 4 Reduction of Critical Path and Enhancement of Parallelization Potential

The algorithm transformation methodology is an efficient mechanism of critical path reduction and parallelization potential enhancement [6,10]. During the enhancement no communication has to be taken into account because there is no still partitioning that is intended for the generation of parallel solutions. The partitioning defined by a programmer can be mostly used for the localization of transformations capable of reducing the critical paths. Two types of transformations help in the extraction of parallelism from the sequential code: control and data flow transformations, including transformations of data dependent expressions, extractions of computations from control structures, split and possibly elimination of control structures and others.

The overall critical path profiling helps in detecting partitions to which transformations should be applied. The partitions with large shares in the critical path are preferable candidates for transformation. However, we need to know in which degree reductions in the own critical path lengths could reduce the overall critical path length. To measure the degree we have developed a partition zeroing technique. The difference between the critical path length before partition zeroing and the critical path length after zeroing is called a *critical path zeroing*. If the critical path zeroing equals zero, other long paths exist whose length is close to the critical path length. The transformation of partitions with the large critical path zeroing can reduce the overall critical path essentially.

# 5 Partitioning, Scheduling and Allocation for Abstract Parallel Implementations

We propose a new dynamic parallel partitioning-scheduling-allocation algorithm that does all work during the sequential execution of instrumented C/C++-code at typical input data. Our algorithm performs the partitioning of data and code, scheduling of operations through dynamic evaluation and minimization of the critical path on DFEG extended with memory and communication operations, and performs the allocation of resources with minimization of data exchanges. Fig.3 presents the parallel solution space exploration by various models at the same task size and input data.

The bottom curve describes the overall execution time versus the implementation cost when no parallel partitioning and communications are taken into account. The low time, $T_{min}$, implies the high cost, $C_{max}$, and the low cost, $C_{min}$, implies the high time, $T_{max}$. The top curve takes into account communications. The minimum time, $T'_{min}$, is achieved at the cost $C'_{min}$. The utilization of additional processors cannot reduce the overall execution time because it implies the increase in data exchanges and communication delays. The middle curve explains effectiveness of our algorithm. Additional resources can be involved by our algorithm in parallel implementations, which reduce the time from $T'_{min}$ to $T_{opt}$ with increase in the cost from $C'_{min}$ up to $C_{opt}$, be means of: the code profiling with consecutive lessening in the critical path and enhancement of the parallelization potential, the reduction of data exchanges among processors due to our flexible partitioning scheme and efficient resource

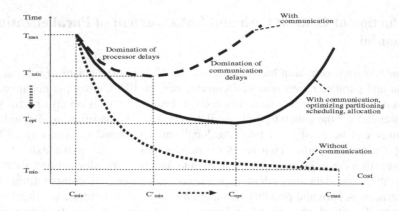

**Fig. 3.** Parallel code version execution time versus parallel system implementation cost

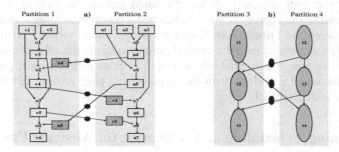

**Fig. 4.** Operation-based a) and thread-based b) algorithm partitioning on DFEG incorporating communication

allocation, and the generation of efficient schedules minimizing dynamically at typical input data the overall critical path in multiprocessor implementations. Our goal is to reduce up to twice the critical path length when a system is being decomposed into two parallel sub-systems.

We consider both the code partitioning and the data partitioning. Given code partitions, our algorithm performs profiling taking into account communications. Given constraints on the parallel resources, it searches for an optimal code and data partitioning while minimizing the overall critical path. The effectiveness of code partitioning depends upon which of two schemes is used: either operation-based or thread-based (Fig.4). We could associate threads with basic blocks, but this solution is not a good one because there is low correlation between the basic blocks and the efficient decomposition of data dependences graphs. All operations within one thread (partition) are serialized, which leads to losses in the algorithm parallelization potential. After serialization, the order of operations is essential for the reduction of delays associated with waiting operations [3].

# 6   Parallel Implementation Profiling and Optimization Tool

In order to be able to profile and optimize the complex parallel implementations derived from a sequential C-code, we have been developing a tool (Fig.5) that is capable of: 1) taking into account the parallel model and architecture constituting a basis for the implementation generation through using abstract weights for various types of operations; 2) instrumentation of the sequential code [13,5,6] with C++ in such a way as to be able to solve all the evaluation, profiling, optimization and generation tasks; 3) critical path and parallelization potential based profiling of complex sequential (possibly partitioned) algorithms; 4) enhancement of the parallelization potential by means of critical path reduction during code transformations; 5) partitioning of the sequential code with minimization of the overall

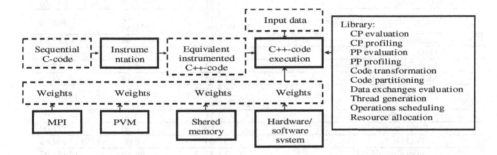

**Fig. 5.** General structure of parallelization tool, CP is critical path and PP is parallelization potential

critical paths in parallel implementations; 6) scheduling of operations and allocation of resources. The tool computes the true output data of the source code and dynamically executes the optimizing algorithms and computes additional values that are used during solving the listed tasks.

# 7   Results for a MPEG4 Video Codec

The complex algorithm that is under parallelization in the paper is an implementation of MPEG4 Video tools as specified by the Video standard ISO/IEC 14496-2 reference software [14-16]. This is an optimized enhanced compression codec based on the simple profile for representing visual data. H.263 is a video-conferencing codec depending upon two basic algorithms. Block discrete cosine transforms reduce spatial redundancy (intra coding). Motion-compensated coding uses block-based motion vector estimation and compensation to remove temporal redundancies (inter coding). At the early stages of parallelization process the detail analysis of critical path and parallelization potential should be performed in terms of basic operations and scalar variables. Experimental results are obtained on 100 frames of *foreman* video sequence.

**Table 1.** Complexity and critical path distribution on sub-functions, and parallelization potential of intra encoding functions (1 frame)

| Function | Complexity distribution, % | Critical path distribution, % | Own parallelization potential |
|---|---|---|---|
| CodeBaseVol | 99.91 (28034960) | 100.00 (152066) | 184.36 |
| ReadVopGeneric | 2.71 | 0.00 | 7.50 |
| GetVopBounded | 5.52 | 0.00 | 15.22 |
| WriteVopGeneric | 4.89 | 100.00 | 9.02 |
| VopProcess | 86.87 (24354565) | 0.00 (101383) | 240.22 |
| SetUpRecVop | 3.12 | 99.99 | 7.50 |
| VopCode | 96.88 (23593967) | 0.01 (54761) | 430.85 |
| VopPadding | 4.71 | 0.00 | 865.46 |
| VopCodeShapeTextIntraCom | 93.70 (22106556) | 50.14 (27459) | 805.08 |
| FindCBP | 2.69 | 0.00 | 4187.83 |
| DoDCACpred | 7.93 | 0.20 | 122.18 |
| Bits_CountMB_combined | 0.14 | 8.63 | 12.65 |
| MB_CodeCoeff | 15.65 | 90.65 | 138.58 |
| CodeMB | 72.05 (15928186) | 0.50 (210) | 75848.50 |
| MblockPredict | 3.24 | 0.00 | 14344.00 |
| BlockPredictUV | 1.89 | 0.00 | 8371.00 |
| BlockDCT | 37.05 | 0.00 | 113499.69 |
| BlockQuantH263 | 13.32 | 66.19 | 14942.97 |
| BlockDequantH263 | 7.50 | 8.57 | 8413.34 |
| BlockIDCT | 24.83 | 19.05 | 34993.26 |
| MBBlockRebuild | 8.22 | 2.38 | 33578.77 |
| BlockRebuildUV | 3.80 | 0.00 | 15933.79 |

Table I describes the distribution of complexity and critical path on direct sub-functions as well as the own parallelization potential of each intra encoding function. The overall complexity equals 28034960 operations. Composite function CodeMB is the most complexity consuming, 56.76% in overall complexity. Basic functions with the largest share in overall complexity are BlockDCT, BlockIDCT, and MB_CodeCoeff. The critical path length of WriteVopGeneric function equals 152065 operations and is the largest one. Conversely, the critical path length of CodeMB results the shortest one (210 operations and 0.14% in overall critical path). Critical paths of MB_CodeCoeff and Bits_CountMB_combined functions have to be reduced first. The overall parallelization potential is 184, although the parallelization potential of CodeMB is much larger, 75848, which is sufficient for efficient parallelization.

Table II describes three inter encoding profiles for the computational complexity, critical path, and parallelization potential. The overall computational complexity equals 9930773442 basic operations. The function shares are reported in comparison with the overall computational complexity. The MotionEstimation composite function has 69.89% in the overall complexity. Basic functions with the largest complexity share are FindSubPel, VopShapeMotText, and SAD_Block. The overall critical path

**Table 2.** Inter encoding function shares in overall complexity and critical path, and function own parallelization potentials (99 frames)

| Function | Complexity share, % | Critical path share, % | Own parallelization potential |
|---|---|---|---|
| CodeBaseVol | 100.00 (9930773442) | 100.00 (6054211) | 1640.3 |
| ReadVopGeneric | 0.76 | 0.00 | 742.5 |
| GetVopBounded | 1.54 | 1.68 | 1506.6 |
| WriteVopGeneric | 1.37 | 0.00 | 892.9 |
| VopProcess | 96.33 (9566444136) | 98.32 (5952722) | 1581.1 |
| VopCode | 99.21 (9491144637) | 98.32 (5952722) | 1568.7 |
| VopShapeMotText | 19.74 | 11.81 | 847.6 |
| VopMotionCompensate | 2.48 | 0.01 | 26353.8 |
| SubVOP | 2.06 | 0.00 | 1235.1 |
| RCQ2_MB_init | 1.32 | 0.13 | 4051.7 |
| VopPadding | 1.16 | 0.00 | 7068.9 |
| MotionEstimation | 73.12 (6940357262) | 83.42 (5050491) | 1192.5 |
| InterpolateImage | 9.97 | 0.00 | 309934.6 |
| MotionEstimatePicture | 89.96 (6243294170) | 83.42 (5050287) | 1072.8 |
| FindSubPel | 46.41 | 37.21 | 1143.8 |
| FindMB | 1.12 | 0.00 | 125.3 |
| FullPelMotionEstMB | 52.43 (3273115389) | 44.81 (2712966) | 994.2 |
| ChooseMode | 7.92 | 1.13 | 3399.0 |
| MBMotionEstimation | 92.06 (3013192869) | 43.23 (2617335) | 945.0 |
| SAD_Block | 61.06 | 4.60 | 5866.6 |
| SAD_Macroblock | 32.57 | 18.57 | 684.2 |
| ObtainRange8 | 0.31 | 1.61 | 83.9 |

length equals 6054211 operations. MotionEstimation has the largest share in critical path, 83.42%. Basic functions with the largest share in the overall critical path are FindSubPel, SAD_Macroblock, and VopShapeMotText. The overall parallelization potential depends upon the number of encoded frames and is in the range from 626 (1 frame) to 1640 (99 frames). The own parallelization potential of functions varies from 84 (ObtainRange8) to 309934 (InterpolateImage).

Table III helps by means of function zeroing results to enhance the algorithm parallelization potential. In the table, column 3 presents the share of a function in the overall critical path compared in percentages with the function own critical path and column 4 reports the difference between the overall critical path lengths before and after zeroing of the function. Three functions VopShapeMotText, FindSubPel, and FullPelMotionEstMB have the total critical path share of 93.83%. Transformations of only these functions imply the reduction in the overall critical path by 3.5, as a result the total abstract parallelization potential can be increased up to several thousands. Due to the time consuming memory and communication operations, the possible acceleration in encoder parallel implementations can constitute hundreds and tens.

**Table 3.** Own critical path, critical path share and critical path zeroing of inter encoding functions (99 frames)

| Function | Own critical path | Critical path share % | Critical path zeroing % |
|---|---|---|---|
| CodeBaseVol | 6054211 | 100.00 | 100.00 |
| GetVopBounded | 101732 | 99.72 | 0.35 |
| VopCode | 6050357 | 98.39 | 97.55 |
| VopShapeMotText | 2209971 | 32.35 | 7.56 |
| VopMotionCompensate | 7417 | 5.96 | 2.58 |
| RCQ2_MB_init | 57979 | 14.05 | 10.85 |
| MotionEstimation | 5819926 | 86.78 | 49.47 |
| InterpolateImage | 2233 | 4.25 | 0.00 |
| MotionEstimatePicture | 5819849 | 86.78 | 49.47 |
| FindSubPel | 2533334 | 88.92 | 64.64 |
| FullPelMotionEstMB | 3292285 | 82.40 | 68.05 |
| ChooseMode | 76274 | 89.67 | 89.61 |
| MBMotionEstimation | 3188680 | 82.08 | 68.50 |
| SAD_Block | 313592 | 88.83 | 88.19 |
| SAD_Macroblock | 1434231 | 78.37 | 71.02 |
| ObtainRange8 | 109719 | 88.86 | 62.09 |

## 8    Conclusion

The paper has presented a methodology and a tool for the design and optimization of complex parallel implementations at abstract levels by means of the dynamic critical path and parallelization potential based profiling of sequential algorithms represented with data flow execution graphs. Experimental results on a MPEG4 video codec prove usefulness and efficiency of the proposed methodology.

## References

1. E. Juarez, M. Mattavelli and D. Mlynek, A System-on-a-chip for MPEG-4 Multimedia Stream Processing and Communication, IEEE International Symposium on Circuits and Systems, May 28-31 2000, Geneva, Switzerland.
2. Y. Cho, K. Choi, N.-E. Zergainoh, A.A. Jerraya, Scheduler Implementation in MP SoC Design, Asia South Pacific Design Automation Conference, Shangai, China, 2005.
3. R. Gupta, G. De Micheli, Constrained Software Synthesis for Embedded Applications, EUROMICRO Journal, vol.43, pp.557-586, 1997.
4. L. Liu, D. Du, and H.-C. Chen, An Efficient Parallel Critical Path Algorithm, IEEE Trans. on Computer Aided Design, vol. 13, No. 7, 1994, pp. 909-919.
5. A. Prihozhy, M. Mattavelli, and D. Mlynek, Data Dependences Critical Path Evaluation at C/C++ System Level Description, in Book "Integrated Circuit and System Design", LNCS 2799, Springer, 2003, pp.569-579.
6. A. Prihozhy, M. Mattavelli, and D. Mlynek, Evaluation of Parallelization Potential for Efficient Multimedia Implementations: Dynamic Evaluation of Algorithm Critical Path, IEEE Trans. on Circuit and Systems for Video Technology, Vol. 15, No. 5, May 2005.
7. P. Barford, M. Crovella, Critical Path Analysis of TCP Transactions, IEEE/ACM Transactions on Networking, vol. 9, No. 3, 2001, pp. 238-248.

8.  L. Lucke, K. Parhi, Data-Flow Transformations for Critical Path Time Reduction in High-Level DSP Synthesis, IEEE Trans. on Computer Aided Design, vol. 12, No. 7, 1993, pp. 1063-1068.
9.  J. Hollingsworth, Critical Path Profiling of Message Passing and Shared-Memory Programs, IEEE Trans. on Parallel and Distr. Systems, vol. 9, No. 10, 1998, pp. 1029-1040.
10. A. Prihozhy, High-Level Synthesis through Transforming VHDL Models, in book "System-on-Chip Methodologies and Design Languages", Kluwer Academic Publishers, pp.135-146, 2001.
11. A. Prihozhy, Net Scheduling in High-Level Synthesis, IEEE Design & Test of Computers, 1996 spring, pp. 24-33.
12. A. Prihozhy, D. Mlynek, M. Solomennik and M. Mattavelli, Techniques for Optimization of Net Algorithms, Parallel Computing in Electrical Engineering, IEEE CS Press, 2002, pp. 211-216.
13. M. Ravasi and M. Mattavelli, High Abstraction Level Complexity Analysis and Memory Architecture Simulations for Multimedia Algorithms, IEEE Trans. on Circuits and Systems for Video Technology, vol. 15, No 5 May 2005.
14. M. Mattavelli and S. Brunetton, Implementing Real-Time Video Decoding on Multimedia Processors by Complexity Prediction Techniques, IEEE Trans. Consumer Electron., vol. 44, no. 3, pp. 760-767, Aug. 1998.
15. A.Prihozhy, M.Mattavelli, D.Mlynek, Analyses of Critical Path and Parallelization Potential of MPEG-4 Reference Software, Technical Report, Swiss Federal Institute of Technology, LTS3, No D108, September 2004, 60 p.
16. ISO/IEC, "Information technology – Coding of audio visual objects – Part 2 Visual", ISO/IEC International Standard 14496-2 (MPEG-4).

# Software Simultaneous Multi-Threading, a Technique to Exploit Task-Level Parallelism to Improve Instruction- and Data-Level Parallelism

Daniele Paolo Scarpazza[1,2], Praveen Raghavan[1,3], David Novo[1,3],
Francky Catthoor[1,3], and Diederik Verkest[1,3,4]

[1] IMEC vzw, Kapeldreef 75, Heverlee, Belgium - 3001
{scarpaz, ragha, novo, catthoor, verkest}@imec.be
[2] Dipartimento di Elettronica e Informazione, Politecnico di Milano, Italy
[3] ESAT, Kasteelpark Arenberg 10, K. U. Leuven, Heverlee, Belgium-3001
[4] Electrical Engineering, Vrije Universiteit Brussels, Belgium

**Abstract.** The search for energy efficiency in the design of embedded systems is leading toward CPUs with higher instruction-level and data-level parallelism. Unfortunately, individual applications do not have sufficient parallelism to keep all these CPU resources busy. Since embedded systems often consist of multiple tasks, task-level parallelism can be used for the purpose. Simultaneous multi-threading (SMT) proved a valuable technique to do so in high-performance systems, but it cannot be afforded in system with tight energy budgets. Moreover, it does not exploit data-level parallel hardware, and does not exploit the available information on threads.

We propose software-SMT (SW-SMT), a technique to exploit task-level parallelism to improve the utilization of both instruction-level and data-level parallel hardware, thereby improving performance. The technique performs simultaneous compilation of multiple threads at design-time, and it includes a run-time selection of the most efficient mixes.

We have applied the technique to two major blocks of a SDR (software-defined radio) application, achieving energy gains up to 46% on different ILP and DLP architectures. We show that the potentials of SW-SMT increase with SIMD datapath size and VLIW issue width.

## 1 Introduction

With the growing trends in mobile markets and the demand of more functionalities, power consumption is emerging as the fundamental design criterion of most embedded systems. In search of energy efficiency, designers are increasing the hardware support for instruction level parallelism (ILP) and data level parallelism (DLP). Designers equip their CPUs with more issue slots and wider SIMD (single-instruction multiple-data) datapaths. Examples of the trend towards large ILP-based architectures are Silicon Hive [1], ADRES [2], while others [3,4,5] advocate wide DLP support for signal processing applications.

J. Vounckx, N. Azemard, and P. Maurine (Eds.): PATMOS 2006, LNCS 4148, pp. 12–23, 2006.

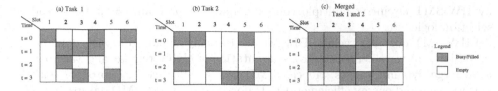

**Fig. 1.** Example: reclaiming horizontal ILP waste by merging tasks

An individual task can hardly exploit this abundance of CPU resources, due to insufficient parallelism. On the other hand, applications often consist of multiple portions that can execute in parallel. This makes available a good amount of task-level parallelism (TLP). In contexts where performance is the primary objective, this TLP is exploited directly via multiprocessor systems and chip multiprocessing. These approaches improve the system's throughput by providing more CPUs, but they do not increase the utilization of each CPU and, therefore, its energy efficiency.

It is common to distinguish the waste of CPU resources between vertical and horizontal waste. Vertical waste occurs when one or more cycles go completely unused, e.g. because of a memory miss during instruction issue. Horizontal waste occurs when some of the issue slots go unused, due to insufficient parallel instructions available. Figure 1 gives an informal depiction of horizontal waste in ILP systems, and how it could be reduced by merging tasks.

Fine-grain multi-threading (FGMT) was proposed [6] to reduce vertical waste. In FGMT, a single CPU executes multiple threads, by switching among them at cycle boundaries. When one thread is stalled, the processor switches to another, which is not stalled. Hardware support is added for keeping multiple contexts, so that a context switch causes no latency. Still, FGMT does not prevent horizontal waste, and can indeed increase it.

Simultaneous multi-threading (SMT) was proposed [7] to fight both horizontal and vertical waste. In SMT, at each cycle, instructions can be selected from all the threads. When threads have low ILP, SMT can truly execute them in parallel, reclaiming horizontal and vertical waste. To avoid confusion, we call this technique hardware SMT, or HW-SMT for short. HW-SMT is a way to convert TLP to ILP.

Although HW-SMT is valuable for high performance systems, it is not viable in extremely low-power systems: it is not affordable in terms of energy and area, it does not exploit DLP, and it does not take advantage of task knowledge available in advance. We motivate the above claims in detail.

(1) HW-SMT is oriented to high-performance systems (e.g. desktops, servers). They employ CPUs with deep pipelines, out-of-order execution, branch prediction, predication, speculation and register renaming, which are complex and power-hungry. In these systems, the added HW-SMT logic occupies a negligible relative area (<5% of the die area [8]), and has acceptable energy costs (24% energy overhead [9]). But low-power embedded CPUs pursue energy efficiency by minimizing hardware, and they cannot afford the additional energy required

by HW-SMT circuitry: multiple contexts, multiple program counters, thread selection logic, etc.

(2) HW-SMT does not reclaim DLP waste. In many signal processing domains (e.g. SDR, software-defined radio), computation is highly regular and variables have large dynamic ranges. Hence, SIMD is very effective in improving both performance and energy efficiency [10]. Unfortunately, wide SIMD datapath can easily go partly unused (i.e. DLP waste), due to application constraints like data dependencies. HW-SMT does not help in addressing this DLP waste.

(3) HW-SMT does not exploit knowledge about the tasks. HW-SMT was designed for general purpose systems, where little information is known in advance on task mix and individual task features. On the other hand, even in embedded systems with a high degree of dynamism, the possible task mixes and the nature of each task are often known in advance. A good multi-threading strategy must exploit this information to achieve higher energy efficiency.

Optimal CPU utilization could be achieved by statically merging and scheduling all the tasks, but this is unfeasible for most embedded applications, because of their dynamic nature. For example, the control flow of multimedia decoders depends more and more on the contents of their streams. Applications in many other domains (wireless, gaming, biomedical) show the same trends. The highly variable workload makes static techniques unfit for the purpose.

Summarizing the above considerations, currently no general approach exploits TLP to reclaim ILP and DLP waste in dynamic contexts. This paper presents the potentials of Software-SMT (SW-SMT), an approach which exploits thread level parallelism to achieve better CPU utilization (and therefore, better performance) addressing all the above shortcomings. SW-SMT consists of a design-time and a run-time phase, and it is oriented to low power systems. It has the following advantages: it does not require any hardware support; it allows to fill both ILP and DLP holes; it exploits the knowledge about the tasks; it does not require an operating system.

The remainder of this paper is organized as follows. We present the details of our technique with an example in Sec. 2. We present a motivating example in Sec. 3. We discuss the related work in Sec. 4. We present the details of our experiments in Sec. 5, discussing the results in Sec. 6. We draw the conclusions in Sec. 7.

## 2   How Software-SMT Works

We consider embedded system specified as multiple dynamic tasks. We adopt a *multi-thread* model, which consists of multiple *tasks, threads and nodes*. Figure 2 shows two sample tasks, containing threads and nodes. Now, we define these terms, because they are often used with different meanings by different communities:

- a **node** is a block of sequential statements which shows a limited variability between its minimum and maximum execution time;

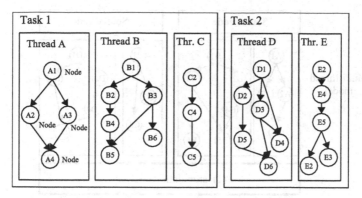

**Fig. 2.** An example of nodes, threads and tasks

- a **thread** is a dependence graph of nodes. A thread is started in response of an asynchronous event, either external or internally-generated. Such an event may be the reception of a symbols in a wireless receiver, the decoding of a frame in a video decoder, etc.;
- a **task** is a designer-defined group of threads.

Note that in our model, multiple nodes could be executed in parallel within the same thread (e.g. nodes A2 and A3). This model was extensively described in [11], and employed in [13] to optimize scheduling density at the task and thread level. The original contribution of SW-SMT is the ability to exploit TLP at a much finer granularity, i.e. within the node.

When modeling existing applications, the above definitions allow degrees of freedom, e.g. in setting the boundaries between nodes. Research is ongoing on how to perform this task optimally and automatically.

Our approach, SW-SMT, consists of the following 3 steps (Figure 3).

(1) we analyze the multi-thread model, analytically and/or using realistic stimuli, to determine which threads (and which nodes inside them) occur often at the same time, and how many instances are involved per each node. This results in a set of thread node mixes. Each mix consists in multiple nodes, which may come from any original thread and task. We apply appropriate heuristics to select mixes which are large enough to ensure sufficient DLP and ILP for the current architecture, and contain integral nodes, but not any larger. These heuristics can trade off quality of result with analysis time, in order to attack large-scale problems. Examining the possibilities of these trade-offs is beyond the purpose of this paper.

(2) we individually compile each of the mixes. Mixes are constructed by loop transformations across different nodes (e.g. unrolling, merging, morphing, etc.). Each mix provides, by construction, enough parallelism to ensure good utilization of VLIW or SIMD slots. The above stimuli analysis only considers the frequently needed mix, thus avoiding combinatorial explosion.

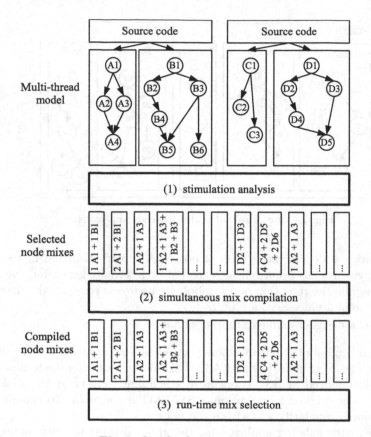

**Fig. 3.** Our fundamental approach

(3) at run time, a small software layer selects which mixes to launch, depending on the external stimuli. When infrequent mixes are needed, they are rendered as sequences of frequent mixes, trading off performance with space, as did in [13].

The energy efficiency of SW-SMT resides in moving to compile time the computational burden of instruction scheduling, which HW-SMT performs this task at run-time, in hardware. On the other hand, most previous approaches in TLP assume that the different tasks are pre-compiled, and use them as a black box to perform scheduling and assignment.

## 3   A Motivational Example

The remainder of this paper provides experimental quantification of the energy gains which SW-SMT can provide. As a benchmark we consider a software-defined radio (SDR) design of a MIMO WLAN receiver. MIMO (multiple-input multiple-output) communications are rapidly gaining diffusion, due to their ability to increase the channel capacity by employing multiple antennas. A block diagram of our 2-antenna MIMO receiver is depicted in Figure 4:

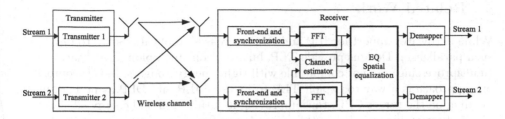

**Fig. 4.** Block diagram of the MIMO receiver used as an example

The transmitter outputs 2 streams of 64-carrier OFDM (Orthogonal Frequency-Division Multiplexing) symbols. Each antenna transmits one of the them. The streams experience different delay, fading and inter-stream interference while traveling. At the receiver, both antennas receive both streams mixed together. The receiver performs channel estimation and recovers the original streams.

Although our general approach is able to target dynamic applications, this example presents an application which is entirely known at static time. In fact, the example is designed to illustrate the potentials of software-SMT due to the unexploited parallelism, which is an orthogonal feature with respect to dynamism. With regard to the overhead of phase (3), previous work [13] has shown that the overhead of a run-time task scheduler similar to the one described above can be as small as 0.55% of the overall execution time for realistic examples.

We have selected for the example the two blocks which most contribute to the overall computational requirements (based on profiling on the target architectures, see Section 5): FFT and EQ, marked with a thick frame in the figure above. FFT is a 64-point Fast Fourier Transform. EQ, the spatial equalizer, is a matrix multiplication which inverts the effects of the channel over the transmitted symbols. EQ and FFT use quantized, fixed point values and contain significant data-level parallelism, but not enough to saturate the DLP slots offered by wide-SIMD architectures. Since each symbol can be processed independently, there is a great amount of thread-level parallelism which can be used for the purpose. Stimulation analysis reveals that there are exactly two executions of FFT nodes per each EQ node, therefore it is a wise choice to create a 1 EQ + 2 FFT node mix.

Even more TLP could be available on other SDR designs, since multiple standards could be running simultaneously on the platform [14], provided that the maximum processing latency keeps within the real-time constraints of the application.

The experiments of Sec. 5 and 6 show how SW-SMT improves the efficiency of executing the above blocks (EQ and FFT) both on ILP and DLP hardware. On a 256-bit wide SIMD CPU, the better utilization provided by SW-SMT saves 34% of the energy consumed by all the processor. On VLIW CPUs, SW-SMT can save 26% (4 issue slots) and 46% (6 to 12 issue slots) of the energy consumed by the instruction memory hierarchy.

## 4    Related Work

While hardware support for ILP and DLP increases, applications fail to provide such parallelism. Designs provide TLP, but solutions to exploit TLP "natively" (multiprocessing) are not compatible with tight energy budgets. In this context, our approach is a way to exploit TLP to increase ILP and DLP as needed, depending on the target CPU, thus improving its utilization and energy efficiency. To the best of our knowledge, this paper is the first to present this approach.

We also show that exploiting TLP at compile time before the regular compilation is either beneficial or neutral, i.e. it never reduces the ability of subsequent steps to find good scheduling solutions. Therefore it should be done *before* regular VLIW/SIMD compilation. To the best of our knowledge, this paper is also the first to discuss this so-called *phase-coupling* problem.

Sasanka [15] attempted an analysis of the different types of parallelism, but did not address phase coupling and his work is aimed at a general purpose domain rather than embedded systems. Tullsen et al. [7,16,17] discuss architectural enhancements like SMT and CMP, and compare them. Corbal et al. [18] present potential DLP and TLP available in multimedia applications on a SMT processor. Lo et al. [19] show the trade-off between TLP and ILP on SMT processors. Li et al. show [9] that SMT comes with a large penalty in energy efficiency which is not acceptable for embedded systems, where the energy-delay ($ED$) product is more important than $ED^2$. Other works [20, 21, 22] show how TLP can be exploited in VLIWs (which are rich in ILP) using SMT.

We are not aware of any work which addresses DLP, taking into account the idle slots inside a wide SIMD datapath at a task level.

## 5    Experimental Setup

We have conducted two experiments. The first experiment shows the energy gains achieved by exploiting TLP to reclaim ILP waste. The second one exploits TLP to reclaim DLP waste. For the two experiments, we have employed different architectures and simulation frameworks, but the same power models. The complete details are given below.

### 5.1    Architecture Setup for the ILP Experiment

The architecture chosen for the experiment is a VLIW with 4 to 12 slots, similar to the TI C64x processor. We have modeled it with CRISP [23], a cycle accurate VLIW compiler/simulator built on Trimaran [24]. We clustered the register file in 2 portions, as in Figure 5. We have included a loop buffer which improves energy efficiency by keeping entire small loops in a dedicated, small memory. This avoids the instruction fetch and decode costs for most inner loops. The loop buffer used has a depth of 32 instructions (sufficient to fit all inner loops of the benchmarks used). The details of loop buffering are outside the scope of this paper; to learn more on this, see [25, 26].

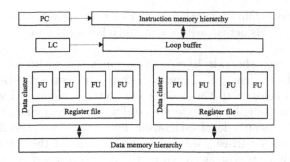

**Fig. 5.** Architecture setup for the ILP experiment

## 5.2 Architecture Setup for the DLP Experiment

The architecture chosen for the experiment is a basic SIMD-based RISC processor, also enhanced with a loop buffer (see Figure 6). We have chosen SIMD datapath sizes of 64, 128 and 256 bits. We have employed a 3-ported register file with a depth of 32 words, and a proprietary 32KByte memory with data widths of 64, 128, 256 bits respectively. The simulation of the benchmark for exploiting TLP to improve DLP was done using an extended version of the *e3tools* framework [27]. The flow works at the source-level, therefore it can yield accurate estimates for a specific platform (given datapath width, scratchpad width and length, ...) even when the build tool-chain is not available for it. In this research, we have extended the flow to estimate the consumption of the datapath, scratchpad, data memory and instruction memory hierarchy of a single-core or a multi-core architecture.

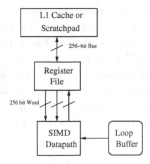

**Fig. 6.** Architecture setup for the DLP experiment

## 5.3 Power Modeling

We have employed the model presented here for both the experiments (see Figure 7). We have coded in VHDL the components of the processor (SIMD datapath, register files, clock trees, loop buffers, etc.) and synthesized them with Synopsys Physical Compiler, with UMC 130nm, 1.2V technology, DesignWare components, considering the worst-case design corner for the power estimation.

We extracted layouts from Physical Compiler to a gate-level netlist. We have simulated in ModelSim this netlist, with a testbench having the worst-case switching activity.

We have then used the gate-level netlist, annotated with this switching activity, to compute the energy consumed per component activation. With the above 130nm technology, All the leakage energies (as computed with Physical Compiler) resulted negligible, therefore we did not include them in the estimates.

For use with the source-level estimation flow, we have determined the cost of intrinsics. For each intrinsic, we determined the list of the components activated, and computed its cost as the sum of energy consumed by each activated component.

# 6    Results and Discussions

In this section we present and discuss the results of the above experiments. In both cases, we compare the energy consumed by 1 EQ and 2 FFT nodes (individually compiled, and run sequentially), with the energy consumed by a node-mix of 1 EQ + 2 FFT (compiled simultaneously, step (2) in Sec. 2). In all benchmarks, we have employed all the available compiler optimizations. In both cases, we observe a significant energy gain.

## 6.1    Applying the Approach on a ILP Architecture

To observe the effects of SW-SMT on ILP, we run the benchmarks on the VLIW architecture of Sec. 5.1. Since the number of operations per node did not change, there is no change in the energy consumed by functional units, register files and data memory hierarchy. On the other hand, for the instruction memory hierarchy (loop buffer, fetch and decode) the energy costs decrease, since the instructions of both threads are fetched and decoded simultaneously.

Figure 8 shows how SW-SMT decreases the energy costs of the instruction memory hierarchy as the VLIW issue slots are varied from 4 to 12. With 4 slots, SW-SMT decreases the energy cost from 1.81 nJ to 1.34 nJ (−26%). With 6,8,10 and 12 slots, the relative gains are higher (−46% in all the cases). For example, with 8 slots the energy cost decreases from 8.77 nJ to 4.76 nJ.

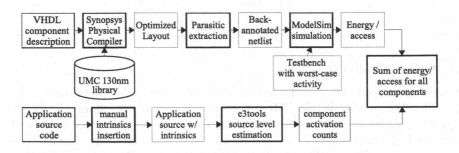

**Fig. 7.** The power estimation framework we have employed

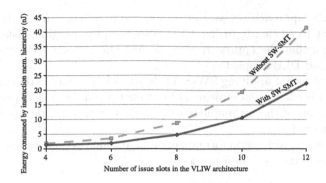

**Fig. 8.** Energy costs of SW-SMT on a ILP architecture

## 6.2 Applying the Approach on a DLP Architecture

To show the ability of SW-SMT to convert TLP into DLP, we have run the benchmarks on the SIMD processor presented in Sec. 5.2. We consider the energy cost of the entire processor, because the size of the SIMD datapath impacts on the consumption of all the parts of the processor (register file, instruction memory, data memory, functional units). The overhead due to pack/unpack operations across the nodes was observed to be negligible in this case.

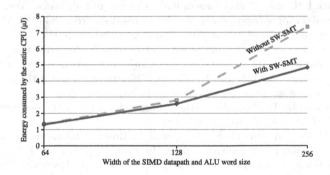

**Fig. 9.** Energy costs of SW-SMT on a DLP architecture

Figure 9 shows the increasing effectiveness of SW-SMT with growing datapath size. With a 64-bit datapath, the consumed energy decreases from 1.34 $\mu$J to 1.31 $\mu$J ($-1.8\%$). With a 128-bit datapath, a significant amount of waste appears which SW-SMT can reclaim, decreasing consumption from 2.80 $\mu$J to 2.58 $\mu$J ($-7.7\%$). With a 256-bit datapath, the gain is evident from 7.36 $\mu$J to 4.83 $\mu$J ($-34\%$).

## 7  Conclusions

We have introduced a new approach to improve the utilization of ILP and DLP features of modern processors, called software simultaneous multi-threading

(SW-SMT). The approach allows to increase the parallelism inside tasks, when it is insufficient to efficiently utilize CPU resources, by merging tasks together. We have proved that the approach is viable and effective on architectures with inherent ILP and DLP support.

We have shown that applying SW-SMT *before* VLIW and SIMD regular compilation phases is effective in improving both energy efficiency and performance, and that the gains of the technique increase when even wider datapath or issue slots are considered.

We are currently working on formalizing and automating the stimulation analysis and the node mix selection phases.

# References

1. Philips Research, http://www.siliconhive.com. *Philips SiliconHive Avispa Accelerator.*
2. B. Mei, S. Vernalde, D. Verkest, H. D. Man, and R. Laurereins. ADRES: An architecture with tightly coupled VLIW processor and coarse-grained reconfigurable matrix. In *Proc. of FPL*, 2003.
3. L. Y., Y. Harel, M. Woh, N. Baron, H. Lee, S. Mahlke, T. Mudge, and K. Flautner. A system solution for high-performance, low-power SDR. In *SDR Forum*, 2005.
4. H. Lee, Y. Lin, Y. Harel, M. Woh, S. Mahlke, T. Mudge, and K. Flautner. Software defined radio - a high performance embedded challenge. In *Proc. HiPEAC*, 2005.
5. K. V. Berkel, F. Heinle, P. Meuwissen, K. Moerman, and M. Weiss. Vector processing as an enabler for software-defined radio in handsets from 3G+WLAN onwards. In *Proc. Software Defined Radio Tech. Conf.*, p. 125–130, 2004.
6. R. Alverson, D. Callahan, D. Cummings, B. Koblenz, A. Porterfield, and B. Smith. The Tera computer system. In *Proc. Intl. Conf. on Supercomputing*, p. 1–6, 1990.
7. D. M. Tullsen, S. J. Eggers, and H. M. Levy. Simultaneous multithreading: Maximizing on-chip parallelism. In *Proc. ISCA*, p. 392–403, 1995.
8. D. Koufaty and D. T. Marr. Hyperthreading technology in the netburst microarchitecture. *IEEE Micro*, 23(2):56–65, 2003.
9. Y. Li, D. Brooks, Z. Hu, K. Skadron, and P. Bose. Understanding the energy efficiency of simultaneous multithreading. In *Proc. ISLPED*, p. 44–49, 2004.
10. M. van der Horst, K. van Berkel, J. Lukkien, and R. Mak. Recursive filtering on a vector DSP with linear speedup. In *Proc. ASAP*, p. 23–25, 2005.
11. F. Thoen and F. Catthoor. *Modeling, Verification and Exploration of Task-level Concurrency in Real-time Embedded Systems.* Kluwer Academic Publishing, 1999.
12. Z. Ma, F. Catthoor, and J. Vounckx. Hierarchical task scheduler for interleaving subtasks on heterogeneous multiprocessor platforms. In *Proc. ASP-DAC*, 2005.
13. Z. Ma. *Interleaved sub-task scheduling on multi-processor SoC.* PhD thesis, Katholieke Universiteit Leuven, 2006.
14. A. Parssinen. System design for multi-standard radios. In *Proc. ISSCC*, 2006.
15. R. Sasanka. *Energy Efficient Support for All levels of Parallelism for Complex Media Applications.* PhD thesis, University of Illinois at Urbana-Champaign, 2005.
16. H. Hirata, K. Kimura, S. Nagamine, Y. Mochizuki, A. Nishimura, Y. Nakase, and T. Nishizawa. An elementary processor architecture with simultaneous instruction issuing from multiple threads. In *Proc. ISCA*, p. 136–145, 1992.
17. J. S. Seng, D. M. Tullsen, and G. Z. Cai. Power-sensitive multithreaded architecture. In *Proc. ICCD*, p. 199–208, 2000.

18. J. Corbal, R. Espasa, and M. Valero. DLP+TLP processors for the next generation of media workloads. In *Proc. HPCA*, p. 219–228, 2001.
19. J. Lo, S. Eggers, J. Emer, H. Levy, R. Stamm, and D. Tullsen. Converting thread-level parallelism into instruction-level parallelism via simultaneous multithreading. *ACM Transactions on Computer Systems*, 15(5):322–354, 1997.
20. E. Özer, T. M. Conte, and S. Sharma. Weld: A multithreading technique towards latency-tolerant vliw processors. In *Proc. HiPC*, p. 192–203, 2001.
21. V. M. G. Ferreira and H. Yasuura. Simultaneous multithreading vliw processor architecture. Technical report, Dept. of Computer Science and Communication Engineering, Kyushu University, Japan, 2001.
22. S. Kaxiras, G. Narlikar, A. D. Berenbaum, and Z. Hu. Comparing power consumption of an smt and a cmp dsp for mobile phone workloads. In *Proc. CASES*, p. 211–220, 2001.
23. P. Op de Beeck, F. Barat, M. Jayapala, and R. Lauwereins. CRISP: A template for reconfigurable instruction set processors. In *Proc. FPL*, 2001.
24. *Trimaran: An Infrastructure for Research in Instruction-Level Parallelism.* http://www.trimaran.org, 1999.
25. S. Cotterell and F. Vahid. Synthesis of customized loop caches for core-based embedded systems. In *Proc. ICCAD*, 2002.
26. M. Jayapala, F. Barat, T. V. Aa, F. Catthoor, H. Corporaal, and G. Deconinck. Clustered loop buffer organization for low energy VLIW embedded processors. *IEEE Transactions on Computers*, 54(6):672–683, 2005.
27. D. P. Scarpazza. *A Source-Level Estimation and Optimization Methodology for the Execution Time and Energy Consumption of Embedded Software.* PhD thesis, Politecnico di Milano, May 2006. http://www.scarpaz.com/phd.

# Handheld System Energy Reduction
# by OS-Driven Refresh

Vasily G. Moshnyaga[1], Hoa Vo[2], Glenn Reinman[2], and Miodrag Potkonjak[2]

[1] Department of Electronics Engineering and Computer Science, Fukuoka University
8-19-1, Nanakuma, Jonan-ku, Fukuoka 814-0180, Japan
[2] Computer Science Department, University of California, Los Angeles,
3532 Boelter Hall, Los Angeles, CA 90095-1596

**Abstract.** Emerging portable devices relay on DRAM/flash memory system to satisfy requirements on fast and large data storage and low-energy consumption. This paper presents a novel approach to reduce energy of memory system, which unlike others, lowers energy of refresh operation in DRAM. The approach is based on two key ideas: (1) DRAM-based flash cache that keeps dirty pages to reduce the number of accesses to flash memory; and (2) OS-controlled page allocation/aging to stop the refresh operations in banks, whose pages are clean and not accessed for a long time. Simulations show that by using this technique we can decrease the overall energy consumption of DRAM/flash memory on video applications by 8-26% while reducing the DRAM refresh energy by 59-74%.

## 1 Introduction

### 1.1 Motivation

Modern battery-operated handheld devices, such as mobile phones, incorporate 128Mb-512Mb SDRAM as main storage and 256MB-1GB solid-state flash memory as non-volatile secondary storage to satisfy performance and memory demands of data-intensive multimedia applications. In 2.5-3G cell phones [1], flash (mainly NAND) memory stores OS, application programs, and data. During boot time, the OS and application programs are copied from the flash memory to the main memory in a process referred to as "memory shadowing". To reduce both the program download delay and the DRAM size, recent systems employ "demand paging" which swaps pages of code/data between memories according to processor's requests. This memory organization leads to a smaller DRAM, less loading time, but requires memory management unit that ensures both high performance and low energy page swapping.

In cell-phones, energy is consumed during active operation as well as on idling, i.e. periods of inactivity. The memory system takes almost 30% of total device power during program execution [2], and more than half of total energy consumed by phone over a day [3] with almost 20% of the energy spent for data retention. Clearly, reducing of energy consumed by memory can significantly extend mobile phone battery life.

J. Vounckx, N. Azemard, and P. Maurine (Eds.): PATMOS 2006, LNCS 4148, pp. 24–35, 2006.

The main goal of this paper is to develop a memory management technique capable of lowering energy consumed not only by data accesses, but also by DRAM refresh and data retention.

## 1.2 Background

(a) **Flash Memory:** Flash memory is a non-volatile device. It has higher storage density than DRAM. However, its content is not randomly accessed. Usually, a NAND flash contains a fixed number of blocks each of which consists of 16-64 pages. A page normally includes 512B of main data and 16B of spare data. So, a typical 32MByte NAND flash has 4K blocks of 16 pages each [4].

Using flash memory has two main limitations. The first one is a potential durability problem. The flash memory cells have a limited number of write/erase accesses for which performance is guaranteed. After about 10,000 cycles, subsequent accesses begin to take longer. After 100,000 write/erase cycles, flash cells begin fail and become unusable. The second limitation of flash memory is the need to erase data before it can be overwritten. The flash memory manufacturer determines how much memory is erased in a single operation. Usually, erase is performed on a *block* basis, while read and write are conducted based on a *page* basis.

There are three important aspects to erasure: *flash cleaning*, *performance* and *power*. When the size of data block is larger than transfer unit, any block data that are still needed must be copied elsewhere. Cleaning flash memory is thus analogous to segment cleaning in a log-structured file system. The cost and frequency of segment cleaning is related in part to cost of erasure and in part to segment size. The larger the segment, the more data will likely to be moved before erasure can take place.

The second aspect to erasure is performance. In NAND flash memory, the time to erase and write a page is 8 times longer than the time of read (see Table 1) [4]. Because the erasure time is independent of the amount of data being erased, the cost of erasure is amortized over large erasure units. To avoid delaying writes for erasure it is important to keep a pool of erased memory available.

The third aspect to erasure is power. Erasing a page in NAND memory consumes as twice as more power than reading the page. Since a write with erase takes almost 10 times more power than a read, page swapping policy must minimize the number of flash memory writes, even though it might incur additional read operations. One such policy is Clean-First-LRU [5], which swaps clean (i.e. unmodified pages first) while keeping dirty pages in the DRAM as long as possible. If there are no clean pages in a predefined time window, a standard LRU is used. To further reduce the number of flush memory writes, the Clean-first-LRU can be combined with selective compression and caching [6]. Because of compression and decompression overhead (248us and 216us, respectively), the compression is applied only to those pages, whose compression ratio exceeds a predefined threshold. The other pages are stored in un-compressed form.

(b) **DRAM:** Dynamic Random Access Memory (DRAM) contains a number of components: cell array, decoders, sense amplifiers and controller. Each DRAM cell consists of one transistor and one capacitor. A write operation of a DRAM cell is performed by charging the capacitor via an on-state cell transistor, while the cell transistor is in an off-state during the charge retention period. DRAM cell retention time is limited by charge leakage from the capacitor through an off-state transistor channel and/or

**Table 1.** Energy and delay parameters of 512b NAND flash (per 4KB access) [4]

| Operation | Energy(μJ) | Time(ns) |
|-----------|-----------|----------|
| Read      | 9.44      | 1180     |
| Write     | 76.08     | 7160     |
| Erase     | 16.49     | 1950     |

a p-n junction. Also, the process of retrieving, or reading, data from the memory array tends to drain these charges, so the memory cells must be precharged before reading the data. Therefore, a periodical re-write operation, called a *refresh* operation, is necessary in DRAM.

Normally, the refresh operation in modern DDR SDRAMs is initiated by the system's memory controller, but some chips are designed for "self refresh." This means that the DRAM chip has its own refresh circuitry and does not require intervention from the CPU or external refresh circuitry. Self refresh dramatically reduces power consumption and is often used in portable computers. Conventional DRAMs can refresh either one bank at a time or all banks simultaneously within a fixed time interval. The refresh period usually is larger than the DRAM access time; so many read/write accesses are stalled while refreshing. Since the DRAM power is proportional to the number of accesses and the number of refreshes, optimizing the number of refreshes is necessary.

Furthermore, to reduce power consumption, modern DRAMs incorporate a number of power saving modes, such as active (or read/write), idle (or standby) and self-refresh [7]. In the *active mode,* normal operation is activated. The *idle mode* moves memory to a power down mode, reactivating it only when a refresh is required. Once a refresh is issued, the memory is returned to power-down mode again. In the *self-refresh mode* the controller does not actively issue any commands. In this mode, additional logic can be used to control partial array refresh for additional power savings; the clock to memory is gated off. Obviously, to service a request the DRAM must be in the active mode, because the low-power modes increase time to transition back to active (see Table 2).

## 1.3 Related Reseach

A number of architectural approaches have been proposed to increase energy efficiency of DRAM. Most studies use control algorithms that dynamically transition DRAM devices (or banks) to low power modes after they are idle for a certain threshold period of time. Lebeck, et al [8] studied DRAM power state transition policies in conjunction with software page placement policies. To improve transition decisions, they control the page allocation by working set locality. Fan, et al [9] further explored policies for manipulating DRAM power states in cache-based systems. They stated that an immediate transition of idling DRAM chip to a lower power state might work better than a more sophisticated policy that tries to predict idling time. Delauz, et al [10] suggested various threshold predictors to determine idling time after which the DRAM should transition to a low-power state. However, predicting the transitions correctly is not easy even with different thresholds because the time of DRAM idling varies with power states and applications. Due to lack of long idling, deep power-saving states are rarely explored; so the efficiency of power management is low. To

**Table 2.** Characteristics of SDRAM @66MHz  (4 word burst access)[8]

| Operation | Energy(nJ) | Time ns) |
|---|---|---|
| Read | 70.2 | 120 |
| Write | 51.6 | 120 |
| Refresh op | 99.2nJper refresh | - |
| Active mode | 100 mW | - |
| Idle mode | 45.1 mW | - |
| Self-refresh mode | 1.8 mW | - |
| Idle→ Act | 15 mW | +6 ns |
| SelfRefresh→Act | 160 mW | +6000 ns |

prolong idling, Huang et al [11] advocated reshaping input traffic to DRAM by making memory accesses less random and thus more controllable. To save DRAM refresh energy, Ohsawa, et al. [12] used two schemes: a selective refresh with data allocation optimization and a variable period refreshing. The *selective* refresh scheme adds a valid bit to each memory row and only refreshes rows with valid bit set. The *variable* refresh scheme allocates a refresh counter to each row. When the number of cycles between the previous refresh exceeds the pre-defined threshold, the line is refreshed. As reported in [12], the selective refresh saves 5%-60% of energy while the variable refresh can save up to 75%. Hwang, et al. [13] proposed to apply array self-refresh operation partially, i.e. on a portion (e.g.1/2, 1/4, 1/8) of one or more selected memory banks. The operation is performed by (1) controlling the generation of row addresses during self-refresh operation, and (2) controlling a self-refresh cycle generating circuitry. Reduction in self-refresh current is achieved by blocking the activation of a non-used block in a memory bank. The partial array self-refresh is already supported by Mobile DRAM [14], Cellular RAM, etc. The main problem is how to distinguish the unused blocks in array? Since the currently unused blocks might be used in the future, the prediction policy is non-trivial.

## 1.4  Contribution

In this paper we propose an OS-based approach to reduce energy consumption of DRAM/flash memory system. Unlike related methods, the approach utilizes history of page accesses to improve energy efficiency of DRAM refresh.

This paper is organized as follows. Section 2 presents our approach. Section 3 shows the experimental results. Section 4 summarizes our findings and outlines future work.

# 2  The Proposed Approach

## 2.1  Main Idea

The approach we propose is based on observation that as DRAM memory size increases, more and more memory becomes unused at any given time. Because unused memory does not need to be refreshed, we can save energy by intelligently controlling which pages get refreshed. The system OS knows which pages are used and unused, so given the opportunity it could disable refresh on selected pages.

The main idea of our approach is simple and consists in disabling from refresh operations all individual banks which have not been referenced in given time-window *and* have no dirty (or modified) pages. If a non-referenced bank has dirty pages, we move the pages to the swap cache (see Fig.1) to keep them in DRAM as long as possible and thus minimize the number of writes to the flash storage. The swapping takes place either when the cache becomes full (in this case the LRU dirty page is moved from the cache to flash), or when the requested page is not in DRAM (in this case, the page is loaded from the flash memory to active DRAM bank).

In our approach, we exploit the fact that the OS not only has physical page allocation information for each executing process but also has information of pages that are actually being referenced (by sampling the reference bits in the page table and TLB). By compacting physical pages into minimum number of memory banks (using page coloring algorithm), we potentially eliminate refresh for entire DRAM banks in which there are no dirty pages. Modern memory systems swap out pages when the memory space is full. In our refresh-oriented page allocation, the OS starts swapping out pages when writing a page to the flash memory becomes less energy consuming than keeping the page refreshed in DRAM.

## 2.2 Assumptions

We take the following assumptions:

1.  Each DRAM bank can be in two modes: refresh and non-refresh (i.e. power down). The refresh mode can be further partitioned into active, nap, and standby, as it done in conventional DRAM, however, we do not address this issue for the simplicity of explanation.
2.  The banks are controlled separately, so each bank can be refreshed (if it in the refresh mode) or shut down (i.e. non-refreshed) independently of the others.
3.  Each page can be either active (i.e. open) or closed. Any access to a close page makes it active. Refresh banks may have as open as close pages, but non-refresh banks have no active pages (all their pages are closed).
4.  As in [5], the higher order banks in DRAM are allocated for flash cache to minimize the number of writes to the flash memory. Dirty pages are dropped into the cache banks unless these cache banks are full.

## 2.3 Algorithm

The proposed refresh-oriented page allocation scheme implements the following algorithm. After a given period of time, *t1*, it detects pages, which have not been accessed and closes them. Next, after a time, *t2*, the algorithm checks status of refreshed banks. If all pages in a bank are closed, the bank is put into a non-refresh mode, while dirty pages of this bank are moved to the flash cache. Finally, after a time, *t3*, the algorithm determines the least-recently used page in the swap-cache and moves it out onto the flash-memory. After dropping the content to flash memory, the cache page is considered empty, and hence can be used to store other dirty pages. If a requested page resides in the flash and DRAM is full, the algorithm applies "clean-page-first" [5] policy to allocate the DRAM page to be swapped with the requested page. If there are no clean pages in DRAM, the algorithm moves the LRU dirty page from DRAM to the swap-cache. The code below shows the algorithm in details.

*Algorithm:*

```
Initialization: all banks are in refresh mode, the last bank is the
                flash cache; all pages in DRAM are inactive;
At t = t2,
   find minimum number of memory banks that allocate all active pages;
   move other banks to non-refresh mode;
for each access to a page AP
   if page is in DRAM, access AP directly;
   else
   { find an inactive page (RP) in (non-cache) DRAM refresh-banks;
     if no inactive pages
     then
     if there is a non-refresh bank;
     then move it to refresh mode;
     let RP be the first page in this bank;
     else
     { find CFLRU page (CFP),
       if CFP is dirty,
       then move CFP to cache
            load demand page to RP(or CFP) page
     }
   }
do page & bank aging
 end

  move page to cache:
    find an empty page (EP) in cache;
    if EP is not found
       find a non-refresh bank (NRB) in DRAM;
       if NRB exists, then move NRB to cache;
            let EP be first page in this bank;
       Else
         {find LRU cache page (LP) ;
            store content of LP to the flash memory;
            empty page LP;
         }
    Drop page to empty page EP (or LP)

  page & bank aging:
   for each cache bank do
    {for each cache page do
       { if page is not accessed in t3, drop page to flash, empty page;
          else if a cache bank has only empty pages
             then move the bank to the non-refresh mode
       }
    }
   for each refresh non-cache bank do
    { for each refresh page (RP) do
        { if RP is not accessed in t1
            then if RP is dirty, then move RP to cache;


            move RP to the inactive mode;
        if bank has no active pages, move it to the non-refresh mode
        }
    }
```

## 3   Experimental Evaluation

### 3.1   Energy Modeling

The energy consumed by memory system is modeled by the sum of energies consumed by DRAM and flash memory:

$$E_{total} = E_{DRAM} + E_{flash.} \tag{1}$$

The energy consumed by each DRAM bank is directly proportional to the number of reads ($N_{read}$) and writes ($N_{write}$) and the unit access energy per read ($E_{read}$) and write ($E_{write}$), respectively. Further, SDRAM consumes idle power ($P_{idle}$) and refresh power ($P_{refresh}$) power during program execution. If there is no memory access, the memory stays in the power down state consuming only retention power ($P_{retention}$). Thus, assuming that SDRAM consists of N banks, the energy consumed by DRAM can be calculated by,

$$E_{DRAM} = E_{read}*N_{read} + E_{write}*N_{write} + t_{active}*(P_{idle} + P_{refresh}) + t_{inactive}*P_{retention}\}. \tag{2}$$

Similarly, the energy consumption of flash memory is modeled as,

$$E_{flash} = E_{fread}*N_{fread} + (E_{fwrite} + E_{erase})*N_{fwrite}. \tag{3}$$

where, {$E_{fread}$ and $E_{fwrite}$} are values of energy consumed by flash per read, write and erase operation, respectively, {$N_{fread}, N_{fwrite}$} are the number of flash reads and writes, respectively.

### 3.2   Experimental Setup

To collect data we augmented the SimpleScalar simulator [17] with our DRAM simulation program. The SimpleScalar simulated a 400MHz 32-bit RISC processor (similar to StrongARM-110 [18]), with 32 set-associative caches (16KB inst. and 16KB data), 32B cache block size, 1 clock cycle cache hit and 3 clock-cycle cache miss, 5 clock-cycle instruction miss-prediction penalty.

Four DRAM sizes (4, 8, 16, 32, 64, and 128) MB, respectively, have been tested. The energy parameters of DRAM and flash memory are given in Tables 1-2. The values of DRAM refresh power and retention power utilized in the experiments were 7mW and 1.8 mW, respectively [4]. We assumed that DRAM has 8 banks, page has 4KB, and refresh is performed every 15.6µsec per row.

**Table 3.** Benchmarks and descriptions

| Program | Description | Dataset | Symbol | Inst.(x10⁶) |
|---------|-------------|---------|--------|-------------|
| *Mpeg_dec* | A Mpeg2 video decoding | *tennis* | Mc | 62 |
| *Mpeg_enc* | A Mpeg2 video encoding | *tennis* | Md | 667 |
| *Jpeg_com* | JPEG image compression | *testimg* | Jc | 577 |
| *Jpeg_dec* | JPEG image decompression | *testimg* | Jd | 48 |
| *gcc* | C code compiler | *gcc* | gcc | 1,497 |

We assumed that DRAM has 8 banks, page has 4KB, and refresh is performed every 12.6μsec. The data retention energy is 1.8mJ/sec.

Five benchmark programs (Table 3) have been used in the experiment: *gcc* from the SPEC2000 suite and the rest from MediaBench [19]. To model user interactions, we ran each video program 10 times with a 30 second-gap between the runs. The input video contained 100 frames and no delay between the frames. Each program was run to completion. The results have been measured in terms of the total energy consumed by the memory system, the DRAM refresh energy and the total execution time. The energy consumption of L1benchmark programs have been used in experiment: *gcc* from the SPEC2000 suite and *Mpeg2decode*, *Mpeg2encode* programs from MediaBench [19].

To model user interactions, we have run each video program 10 times with a 30 second-gap between the runs. The input video contained 100 frames and no delay between the frames. Each program was run to completion. The results have been measured in terms of the total energy consumed by the memory system, the DRAM refresh energy and the total execution time. The energy consumption of L1 (D- and I-) caches and the energy of MMU have not been considered. Also, it was assumed that OS consume 16MB and this amount of memory was not available to application programs. Therefore, the memory size the applications could freely use was limited to 16MB, unless otherwise explicitly stated.

## 3.3 Results

Figure 1 shows the breakdown in energy consumption and the execution time achieved by the proposed approach on *gcc* benchmark and normalized to conventional method [5]. Based on the results obtained at fixed $t2$, $t3$ and variable $t1$ (see Fig. 1,a), we conclude that a small $t1$ increases both the energy and the delay due to very frequent page closing/opening and mode changing. Also, due to small size of DRAM, the amount of page swapping between DRAM and flash is large, so the flash access energy is high. As $t1$ increases, both the number of page mode changes and page swapping decreasing; so the total energy also goes down. According to the results, the best value of t1 ranges between 1625ms and 3200ms. The rightmost point represents the case when $t1=t3$. As we fix $t1$ and $t3$ at 3250ms, and vary $t2$, we see that the smaller $t2$, the better (see Fig.1, b). At 0.0125ms, for example, the refresh energy can be as much as 10%. Finally, as we expected, small $t3$ leads to fast page aging which extra page swapping and so increase of both DRAM access energy and flash energy (see Fig.1,c). For t3 larger than 375ms the figures do not change.

Figure 1(d) shows the impact of DRAM size on energy and execution time. During execution, the *gcc* program accesses 2196 different pages, which require little more than 8MB of DRAM. When the DRAM size is small, the refresh energy reduction achieved by our approach is diminished by energy consumed on page swapping. Therefore, the energy savings are small when memory is 4MB and 8MB. As memory grows, more energy can be saved. At 128MB DRAM, for example, the proposed technique can save up to 55% of the total energy without affecting the execution time.

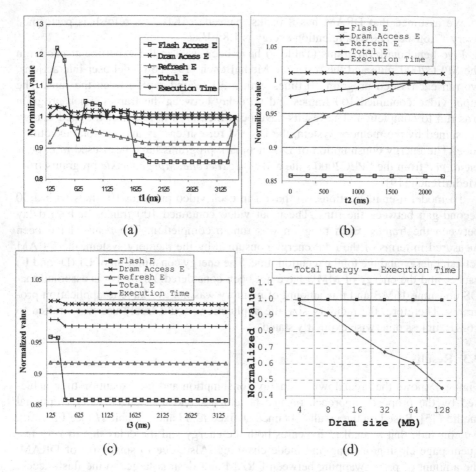

(a)                                    (b)

(c)                                    (d)

**Fig. 1.** (a-c) dependence of the results on t1, t2, and t3, respectively;(d) dependence of the results on the DRAM size

Figures 2, 3 show the performance of proposed technique in perspective to the related (conventional) technique [5] for 8- and 16-MB DRAM. In this figures, bars marked by $C$ show results of [5]; bars marked by $P$ depict results of the proposed technique. Symbols in parentheses denote the tested programs. We observe that the proposed technique lowers the refresh energy, while leaving the other energy components almost unchanged. Due to large variation in the number of pages accessed in DRAM (114 for $Mc$, 53 for $Md$, and 286 for $Jc$, 157 for $Jd$, and 2196 for $gcc$), number accesses (3535730 for $Mc$, 1374440 for $Md$, 16546151 for $Jc$, 1377033 for $Jd$, and 215594 for $gcc$), the results along the benchmarks as well memory size. We see that the proposed technique over performs the conventional method on all the benchmarks.

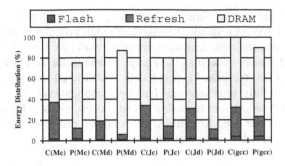

**Fig. 2.** Results obtained for 8MB DRAM

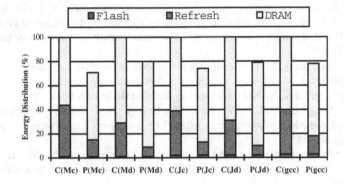

**Fig. 3.** Results obtained for 16MB DRAM

Table 4 summarizes the results in terms of energy reduction achieved by the proposed approach. The larger the memory size, the larger reduction ratio. For 16MB DRAM, for example, our approach reduces the DRAM refresh energy by 59-74% while lowering the total energy consumed by the tested applications by 8-26%.

**Table 4.** Energy reduction ratio observed for benchmarks

| Benchmarks | Jc | | Jd | | Mc | | Md | | gcc | |
|---|---|---|---|---|---|---|---|---|---|---|
| DRAM size (MB) | 8 | 16 | 8 | 16 | 8 | 16 | 8 | 16 | 8 | 16 |
| Refresh energy (%) | 62 | 71 | 64 | 72 | 68 | 70 | 72 | 74 | 32 | 59 |
| Total energy (%) | 20 | 26 | 21 | 23 | 24 | 28 | 14 | 20 | 10 | 21 |

## 4 Conclusion

In this paper we proposed a refresh-driven page allocation technique to lower the energy consumption of memory system in handheld devices. According to experiments, the proposed technique can decrease the total energy consumption of memory system significantly (by 14-26%) on standard image and video processing applications without affecting the execution time. In this preliminary work, we have not considered the energy overhead of busses as well as the energy consumption of OS and the memory management unit. Also, the investigation has been restricted to a small set of benchmarks which only lightly represent real handheld applications. To evaluate the approach on tasks such as internet browsing, word processing, MS PowerPoint, Adobe Acrobat Reader, etc., we need to perform an extensive profiling of the applications. This work will be conducted in the near future.

# References

[1] Weldon, T., Memory subsystems for 2.5G cellular handsets, Micron Techn. Inc., Jedex, San Jose, 2004 http://www.micron.com/products/dram/ddr2sdram/presentation.html

[2] Vargas, O., Minimum power consumption in mobile phone memory systems, Portable Design, 2006.

[3] Lee, H.G, and Chang, N., Low-energy heterogeneous non-volatile memory systems for mobile systems, J. of Low-Power Electronics, Vol.1, no.1, pp.52-62, 2005.

[4] Samsung Electronics. NAND flash memory & SmartMedia data book, 2002.

[5] Park, C., Kang,J.U., Park, S.,Y., Kim, J.S., Energy aware demand paging on NAND flash-based embedded systems, Proc. ACM/IEEE Int. Symp. Low-Power Electronics and Design, pp.338-343.

[6] Park, S., Lim, H., Chang, H., Sung, W., Compressed swapping or NAND flash memory based embedded systems, Proc. the IEEE Workshop on Signal Processing Systems (SiPS), 2003.

[7] Samsung Electronics, 128Mb DDR SDRAM Specification, Version 1.0, Rev.1.0, Nov.2, 2000.

[8] Lebeck, A.R., Fan, X., Zeng, H., Ellis, C., Power-aware page allocation, Proc. 9th Int. Conf. on Architectural Support for Programming Languages and Operation System (ASPLOS IX), Nov. 2000

[9] Fan, X., Zeng, H., Ellis, C., Lebeck, A.R., Memory controller policies for DRAM power management, Proc. ACM/IEEE Int. Symp. Low-Power Electronics and Design, 2001.

[10] Delauz, V., et al., Scheduler-based DRAM energy power management, 39th ACM/IEEE DAC, pp.697-702, 2002.

[11] Huang, H., Shin K., Lefurgy, C. Keller, T., Improving Energy efficiency by making DRAM less randomly accessed, Proc. ACM/IEEE Int. Symp. Low-Power Electronics and Design, 2005.

[12] Ohsawa, T., Kai, K., Murakami, K., Optimizing the DRAM refresh count for merged DRAM/logic LSIs, Proc. ACM/IEEE Int. Symp. Low-Power Electronics and Design, 1998, pp. 82-87.

[13] Hwang, H-R., Choi, J-H, Jang, H-S., Sysem and method for performing partial array self-refresh operation in a semi-conductor memory device, US Patent, no.20050041506, 02/24/2005.

[14] Takahashi M., et al., A 60-MHz 240-mW MPEG-4 videophone LSI with 16-Mb embedded DRAM. IEEE J. Solid-State Circuits, vol.35, no.11, pp.1713-1721, 2000

[15] Mobile DRAM: The secret to longer life, MicronTechn. Inc, http://download. micron. com/pdf/flyers/mobile_sdram_flyer.pdf

[16] Huang, H., Pillai, P., and Shin, K.G., Design and implementation of power-aware virtual memory, Proceedings of the 2003 USENIX Annual Technical Conf., June 2003.
[17] Burger D., Austin, T., Bennet, S., Evaluating future microprocessors- the superscalar tool set. Technical Report 1306, Univ. of Wisconsin-Madison, CSD, July 1996
[18] SA-110 Microprocessor, Technical Reference Manual, Intel Corporation, Dec.2000.
[19] Lee, C., Potkonjak, M., and Mangione-Smith, W-H., MediaBench: a tool for evaluating and synthesizing multimedia and communication systems, Proc. the IEEE Int. Symp. on Microarchitecture, 1997.

# Delay Constrained Register Transfer Level Dynamic Power Estimation*

Sriram Sambamurthy[1], Jacob A. Abraham[1], and Raghuram S. Tupuri[2]

[1] Computer Engineering Research Center, The University of Texas at Austin, USA
{sambamur, jaa}@cerc.utexas.edu
[2] Advanced Micro Devices Inc., USA
raghuram.tupuri@amd.com

**Abstract.** We present a top-down technique to estimate the average dynamic power consumption of combinational circuits at the register transfer level. The technique also captures the power-delay characteristics of a given combinational circuit. It uses the principles of logical effort to estimate the variation in capacitance, and a combination of existing techniques to estimate the variation in activity, over the delay curve of operation of the circuit. The technique does not involve post-estimation characterization and is applicable across technology nodes. The estimated power obtained from our method shows good accuracy with respect to the power obtained from a commercial gate-level power estimation tool.

## 1  Introduction

High demand for low power embedded and mobile microprocessors and the advance to sub-nanometer technology make power dissipation an important design constraint. Power estimation tools serve as design aids to reduce the optimization turnaround time and help achieve a faster time to market.

Power estimation tools are used at various stages of the design cycle. At the Register Transfer Level (RT-Level), the power estimation tools can be categorized into bottom-up and top-down techniques. In bottom-up techniques, the gate-level implementation of the circuit is known from previous design data [1]. Top-down techniques do not assume any circuit implementation structure and involve estimating the circuit capacitance of the implementation and the activity factor of the design [2]. The implementation of the design varies with the delay, power and area constraints to which the design is subjected. Therefore, at the RT-Level, it is difficult to estimate dynamic power in a top-down manner as very little information is available about the implementation and hence the capacitance. The activity factor depends on the functionality of the design which is available at the RT-Level. However, the total dynamic power is dependent on the switching activity at the gate nodes in the implementation and this information needs to be abstracted to the RT-Level. These factors make top-down power estimation at the RT-Level a challenging problem.

---

* This research was supported by Advanced Micro Devices, Inc.

J. Vounckx, N. Azemard, and P. Maurine (Eds.): PATMOS 2006, LNCS 4148, pp. 36–46, 2006.
© Springer-Verlag Berlin Heidelberg 2006

With RT-Level sign-offs becoming popular with embedded and ASIC chips, the designer needs to explore different trade-offs before assembling his design. It is essential that the designer evaluate the RT-Level modules at various points of operation before choosing the best one suited for the design. Analyzing the power consumption of a design at the target delay or frequency is essential in such a situation. The same RT-Level circuit can be used by different designers for operation at different frequency points. For example, a RT-Level circuit of a previous design may be evaluated for use in a next generation design that is designed for a higher frequency. In such cases, it is important that the Power Estimation Technique (PET) has the capability to estimate power over a range of target delays.

The RT-Level modules are composed of various functions implemented using macros, gates and multiplexers. Each macro is a combination of gates and multiplexers and its structure is known (e.g., adder, multiplier). Constraining the PET to particular macros limits its range and accuracy, as the number of macros that can be formed out of gates and multiplexers is limitless. Hence the PET must be generic so as to account for any type of logic structure that is present in the RT-Level modules [3].

Another constraint on the PET is that it needs to be tunable to any technology. In other words, a desirable characteristic of a PET is that it should estimate the power dissipation of a circuit for any technology with minor or no modifications. Such a PET can be used for evaluating designs for different technologies. Designers work at different levels of abstraction like the RT-Level, behavioral, transaction level, etc. For portability over multiple levels of abstraction, the PET should be extendable to the higher levels of design abstraction. This requires a PET to have as minimal links as possible with the underlying low level implementations and at the same time to give results of good accuracy.

In this paper, we present a dynamic power estimation technique which estimates the average dynamic power consumption of a synthesizable RT-Level combinational design for various delay points. The technique does not involve post-estimation characterization and can be merged into existing power oriented design frameworks for early stage power estimation.

The gate level technique of logical effort [4] is widely used for obtaining the transistor sizes of the different gate topologies being evaluated, for minimum delay. We abstract this technique to the RT-Level and use it in our algorithm to estimate the capacitance variation with respect to the target delays and loads to which the design is constrained. The advantage of this technique is that it requires only information of logical and parasitic efforts of the gates which can be easily obtained from the technology gate library. This provides an effective link with the technology and enables capture of the change in the average dynamic power in a systematic manner.

The total activity factor is composed of the unit or block level activity factor and the local switching factor. Estimation of the block level activity factor of the design is an architectural issue and can be obtained through existing architectural tools. The more complex problem of estimating the local switching factor has been a subject of extensive research in the past [5]. We use a combination of existing techniques to estimate the zero-delay switching factor in a *static* fashion. The glitch component of switching factor can be obtained by techniques proposed in [6] and we do not include it in our power model. Our capacitance estimation method can also be used in conjunction with a dynamic activity factor estimator to estimate power.

The paper is organized as follows. In Section 2, we discuss the related research in this field. In Section 3, we describe our methodology and the algorithms developed to estimate dynamic power. The experiments performed to validate our technique and the results obtained are presented in Section 4. Finally, we summarize our contribution in Section 5.

## 2   Related Work

To aid early design decisions, many tools and techniques have been developed to estimate dynamic power at the RT-level [5]. Methods based on bottom-up macro-modeling estimate power to a very good accuracy [1], [7]. In bottom-up macromodeling, the power for individual components is characterized for each technology or library in terms of various parameters like input signal probability, input activity, output activity, etc. Another method of power estimation is to perform a quick mapping of the logic to generic primitives to estimate the capacitance complexity and combine it with activity factor obtained from simulation to estimate power [8]. Analytical or top-down macromodeling is another way of estimating power which involves extracting parameters from code written in Hardware Description Languages (HDL). These parameters are used to build a model whose coefficients are determined through characterization for a particular technology library [2], [7]. The technique in [2] can be applied for different delay points. However, it involves characterization for every delay point and is applicable for structural verilog based designs. In [9], the authors estimate power for the mimimum delay and minimum area implementations of a RT-Level design. However they do not address the problem of estimating power at the intermediate delay points and their method involves characterization for the technology under consideration.

A way of classifying the existing power estimation tools is according to the switching factor estimation methods. Simulation based activity factor calculation is *dynamic* and gives accurate activity for a specific workload [10], [5]. *Static* approaches are probability based and compute activity through propagation of input signal statistics [5]. Analyzing the design space for different input activity with static techniques involves very little overhead. In this work, we follow a static approach for switching factor estimation.

## 3   Power Estimation Approach

The dynamic power consumption of a design is given by the sum of active power and short circuit power.

$$P = (V_{dd}^2 * f * \sum_{i=1}^{n} C_i * sf_i) + (I_{sc} * V_{dd}) \qquad (1)$$

where $C_i$ denotes the capacitance at node $i$, $sf_i$ denotes the switching factor at node $i$, $f$ denotes the frequency of the clock, $I_{sc}$ denotes the direct-path short-circuit current and $V_{dd}$ denotes the supply voltage. In this paper, we do not model the short-circuit power consumed by the design. So we use the term dynamic power to refer to the zero-delay dynamic power without the short circuit power component. In our proposed method, we tackle the problems of estimating capacitance and switching factor separately.

## 3.1  Capacitance Estimation

The circuit capacitance of a design varies with the way in which the design is implemented. The implementation in turn, varies with the gate library and the area, delay and power constraints. In this section, we present a top down approach to estimate the capacitance of the design with respect to its delay target. We discuss the method of logical effort briefly before describing how we use it to estimate the capacitance.

**Logical effort:** Logical effort [4] is widely used in the implementation world to compare alternative circuit topologies and to obtain the gate topology that corresponds to minimum delay. The delay of a path is estimated as the sum of the effort of each stage and its internal parasitic delay.

$$\frac{D}{\tau} = N \times F^{(\frac{1}{N})} + P \qquad (2)$$

where $N$ denotes the number of stages in the path, $\tau$ denotes the technology constant, $P$ denotes the sum of the parasitic efforts of the gates in the path and $F$ denotes the product stage effort of the gates in the path.

The stage effort of the path is given by,

$$F = G \times B \times H \qquad (3)$$

where $G$ denotes the product logical effort of the gates in the path, $H$ denotes the output to input capacitance ratio of the path and $B$ denotes the product branching efforts of the gates in the path. The delay of the path is minimum when the stage effort driven by each gate is the same.

**Capacitance estimation at the RT-Level:** At the higher level of abstraction, say RT-Level, we do not have the exact knowledge of the gates used in the implementation at every delay point. So the idea is to not constrain ourselves to specific gates. We model every gate as a blackbox with certain logical and parasitic efforts and use the term "virtual gate" to denote this structure. A path is represented by a string of virtual gates connected together. For a delay target, equation (2) can be rewritten to obtain the fanout that each virtual gate in the path should drive to meet the delay target.

$$f = F^{\frac{1}{N}} = \frac{(\frac{D}{\tau}) - P}{N} \qquad (4)$$

If g is the logical effort and p is the parasitic effort of the virtual gate, then the capacitance of the path is approximated by

$$Cp = C_{out} + C_{out} \times in_{avg} \times (\frac{(1 - \frac{g}{f}^{N+1})}{(1 - \frac{g}{f})} - 1) \qquad (5)$$

where $in_{avg}$ is the average number of inputs of the virtual gate and $C_{out}$ is the output capacitance of the path.

**Capacitance estimation of a generic combinational design:** The capacitance of a generic combinational RT-Level design is obtained by extending the theory of capacitance of a path. The algorithm to estimate the capacitance for a multiple-output combinational design is given in Figure 1.

First, we parse the RT-Level HDL code and convert it to a Control-flow Data-Flow Graph (CDFG). The mapping of HDL code to CDFG is performed based on the HDL structures present in the code. Next, we associate each node in the CDFG with an approximate value of the minimum number of stages needed for its implementation. This corresponds to the number of stages needed to implement the logic associated with the node for unconstrained delay. The nodal expression is converted to sum-of-products or product-of-sums format and the number of stages is estimated based on the number of inputs of the largest common gate available in the library. In the library considered for our experiments, the largest NAND is a 4-input gate. No other information from the library is needed to estimate the number of stages. Then, we process the CDFG and associate every primary output with the number of stages ($N$) in the critical path from its inputs.

---

**Input:**    The RT-Level circuit, worst case delay targets $D_i$
**Output:** Total Capacitance ($T_C$) of the function at $D_i$
**Algorithm**
(1) Map RT-Level structures to a CDFG form
(2) For every delay point $D_i$
 (A) For every output ($o$),
   (a) Find the associated number of inputs
   (b) Estimate the minimum number of stages needed to implement every node in the CDFG
   (c) Compute the capacitance of the function as in the algorithm given in Figure 2
   (d) Add the capacitance to $T_C$ for this delay point
   (e) Consider the next delay point
     (i) Calculate the average efforts, maximum and minimum capacitances.
     (ii) Check for validity of the number of stages
     (iii)If the number of stages is valid, then repeat step (2); else increment the
        number of stages and repeat step (ii)

**Fig. 1.** Algorithm to estimate capacitance at various delay points

The steps listed in the algorithm in Figure 2 are then executed to obtain the capacitance associated with the functions of every primary output. Each primary output is modeled as an uniform tree with number of inputs $i$ and a depth of $N$. Each node in the tree corresponds to a virtual gate. The average input size of every node in the tree is then calculated. The average of the logical and parasitic efforts of the common gates (inverter, nand, nor, xor, xnor, and, or, aoi, oai) present in the library are considered as the logical and parasitic efforts of the virtual gate. The stage effort computed using equation (4) for the current delay target is then used to size the virtual gates in the uniform tree, for a given output load. When the delay target is huge, the stage effort is very large and hence the sizing ratio $(g/f)$ is very small. The circuits are hardly sized in this case. As the delay target is decreased, the circuit are sized accordingly. Sizing for speed is performed by sizing up the gates from the output side of the fanin tree till the delay target is satisfied. By adding the capacitances at the individual nodes of the tree, we obtain the total capacitance and the level-by-level capacitances corresponding to each primary output. Since this sizing process is performed according to the stage effort requirement, our method implicitly considers the effect of area recovery for non-critical parts of the circuit.

The capacitance so obtained from the algorithm in Figure 2 is added to the total capacitance $T_C$ corresponding to the delay point $D_i$ as in step (d) in Figure 1. In the next step, the delay target is decreased to the next delay point and the average logical and parasitic efforts for the current value of $N$ for output $o$ are calculated. If the input capacitance of the virtual gate goes beyond the maximum capacitance for current value of $N$, $N$ is incremented and step (e) of Figure 1 is executed again. If the capacitances are acceptable, then execution is repeated from step (c) of Figure 1. This process is performed for all the delay points under consideration to obtain the capacitance associated with every primary output.

**Input:**    The function $(f)$, its number of inputs $(i)$, logical and parasitic efforts of the gates

**Output:** Total Capacitance $(C)$ and level-by-level capacitance $(LCi)$ of the function

**Algorithm**
  (1) Form a uniform tree with number of inputs $i$ and number of stages $N$
      (a) Calculate the average input size $(in_{avg})$
      (b) Calculate the average logical effort $(g)$, parasitic effort $(p)$, weighted maximum and minimum capacitances
  (2) Calculate the stage effort $(F^{\frac{1}{N}})$ for the delay $(D)$ using equation (4)
  (3) Size the critical path and hence the tree
  (4) Add the capacitances at each node to give the total capacitance $(C)$ and level-by-level capacitance $(LCi)$ of the fan-in tree

**Fig. 2.** Algorithm to estimate capacitance of a multiple-input single-output function

It is important to include the capacitance of the interconnects in the capacitance model since it is a major contributor to node capacitance in the deep sub-micron and sub-nanometer technologies. The interconnect capacitance from the wire-load models of the technology library is considered during the sizing process in step (3) of the algorithm shown in Figure 2. In the next subsection, we describe the method of estimating the switching factor for the given design at various delay points.

## 3.2   Switching Factor Estimation

The switching factor of a circuit can be determined either in a dynamic way using simulation or in a static way by propagating signal probabilities and transition densities. The block level activity factor of the circuit can be estimated using existing architectural techniques. The problem of estimating the local switching factor of a combinational design at the RT-Level in a top-down fashion has been addressed in [11] and [12]. These methods of calculating switching factor are based on entropy and informational energy of the module. The entropy of a module is calculated from the switching factors of the input and output ports. The total switching factor in [11] is approximated to be half the total entropy value of the module. Also it is shown empirically that on an average, the activity varies quadratically with respect to the circuit depth.

$$sf_i = (sf_{in} - sf_o) \cdot (1 - \frac{i}{N})^2 + sf_o \qquad (6)$$

where $sf_{in}$ denotes the input switching factor, $sf_o$ denotes the output switching factor, $i$ denotes the ith level and $N$ denotes the total number of levels in the circuit. We next describe how we compute the switching activity of the circuit.

The first step involves obtaining a generic description of the RT-Level code from Synopsys Design Compiler. This generic description is an unoptimized representation of the RT-Level code in terms of basic primitives like and, or, xor, select, mux and is independent of the technology. Another RT-Level power estimation approach uses a similar front-end for the switching factor calculation [7] in its topdown mode. The next step involves applying the Boolean Approximation Method (BAM) [13] to propagate the input statistics to the primary output nodes of the circuit. The advantage of this method is that it does not require constructing a Binary Decision Diagram (BDD). Since we do not have any knowledge of the internal nodes and gates, we approximate the switching factors at the intermediate levels by using equation (6). Combining the capacitance and the switching factor at each level gives a more accurate power estimate than that obtained by combining the entire capacitance of the circuit with the total activity estimate. The total dynamic power consumed by an output is,

$$P = V_{dd}^2 * f * \sum_{i=1}^{n} C_i * sf_i \qquad (7)$$

where $i$ denotes the level number, $C_i$ denotes the capacitance and $sf_i$ denotes the switching factor at level $i$. The sum of the active power components of the individual outputs gives the total power consumed by the circuit. However, the total power calculated does not take into account the effect of the shared logic in the circuit. This effect of signal fanouts is accounted for by using a branching factor and the total power is given by,

$$TP = (\sum_{j=1}^{m} P_{o_j})/bf \qquad (8)$$

where $TP$ denotes the total power of the RT-Level circuit and $bf$ denotes the branching factor which is given by,

$$\frac{\sum_{o_j} (num\_inputs + num\_outputs + num\_branching\_wires)}{tot\_sig} \qquad (9)$$

where $num\_inputs$ and $num\_outputs$ denote the number of input and output nodes associated with the output $o_j$, $num\_branching\_wires$ denotes the wires with fanout greater than one which $o_j$ depends on and $tot\_sig$ denotes the sum of all inputs, outputs and branching nodes in the circuit. When the output nodes of the circuit do not share any logic, $bf$ equals one.

We prefer the static method of estimating switching factor since input vectors for the module being designed may not be available and getting a representative set in the early stages of the design is difficult. Alternatively, if a representative input vector set can be obtained, the activity at the output nodes can be noted through simulation and equation (6) can be applied to get the switching factor at the intermediate levels.

## 4 Results

Our methodology has been validated on synthesizable RT-Level combinational designs derived from the OR1200 processor [14], the Floating-point co-processor from [14] and on the high-level combinational models from [15]. The experiments were performed using the 0.18um Artisan TSMC technology library. The estimated zero-delay power numbers using our technique were compared against the gate-level zero-delay power estimated using Synopsys Power Compiler. A signal probability of 0.5 and a transition density of 0.5 were assumed at the primary inputs of the circuits for modeling input activity.

The power estimation results are presented in Table 1. The technology gate library used for obtaining the reference power numbers for this experiment was composed of one and two-input gates. The target delay specified in the second column denotes the worst-case delay target used for estimating the capacitance of the circuits. The delay targets were chosen depending upon the size of the circuits. The third column lists the power estimates obtained from our technique and the fourth column lists the gate-level power numbers obtained from Synopsys Power Compiler. The gate level reference circuits were

**Table 1.** Power estimation results

| RT-Level circuit | Target delay in ns | Estimated power in mw | Reference power in mw | Absolute Error in % |
|---|---|---|---|---|
| | 1.25 | 1.546 | 1.705 | 9.33 |
| Circuit-1 | 1.00 | 1.881 | 2.069 | 9.09 |
| | 0.75 | 2.277 | 2.596 | 12.29 |
| | 5.00 | 2.334 | 3.204 | 27.15 |
| Circuit-2 | 3.50 | 2.376 | 3.225 | 26.33 |
| | 2.00 | 4.272 | 5.898 | 27.57 |
| | 2.00 | 1.193 | 1.779 | 32.94 |
| Circuit-3 | 1.50 | 1.576 | 1.884 | 16.35 |
| | 1.00 | 2.179 | 2.782 | 21.68 |
| | 1.30 | 1.239 | 1.285 | 3.58 |
| Circuit-4 | 1.00 | 1.275 | 1.325 | 3.77 |
| | 0.70 | 2.006 | 1.799 | 11.56 |
| | 0.75 | 1.177 | 0.955 | 23.24 |
| Circuit-5 | 0.58 | 1.269 | 1.423 | 10.82 |
| | 0.40 | 2.249 | 1.858 | 21.04 |

obtained by synthesizing the RT-Level circuits for the listed delay targets using Synopsys Design Compiler. Circuit-1 is the combinational part of the exceptions module of the OR1200 processor [14], circuit-2 is the c432b interrupt controller [15], circuit-3 is the 74181 4-bit ALU [15] and circuits 4 (combinational part of exceptions unit) and 5 (part of combinational portion of prenormalization unit) were extracted from the Floating-point co-processor [14]. The average power estimation error across these circuits (for minimum load) is 17.12% over their delay curve of operation. The relative accuracy of the estimated power at various delay points was calculated with respect to the estimated power at the maximum delay point. The average relative error with respect to the minimum power across the circuits was observed to be 8.04%. The error results are encouraging considering the fact that these are early stage estimates and that we do not perform statistical characterization to arrive at the power estimates.

The power variation with respect to a different output load was captured and the results are presented in Table 2 for circuit-1. The average power estimation

**Table 2.** Power variation with output load for circuit-1

| Output load in #flip-flops | Delay target in ns | Estimated power in mW | Reference power in mW | Abs. Error in % |
|---|---|---|---|---|
| | 1.25 | 1.545 | 1.705 | 9.38 |
| 1 | 1.00 | 1.881 | 2.069 | 9.09 |
| | 0.75 | 2.277 | 2.596 | 12.29 |
| | 1.25 | 1.604 | 1.705 | 5.92 |
| 4 | 1.00 | 1.940 | 2.268 | 14.46 |
| | 0.75 | 2.341 | 2.720 | 13.93 |

Table 3. Power estimation for different libraries

| Target gate library | Number of gate-types in the library | Number of gate-types used by the technique | Avg. abs. error% |
|---|---|---|---|
| one and two-input gates | 6 | 6 | 17.12 |
| one, two and three-input gates | 15 | 15 | 18.95 |
| entire library | 52 | 19 | 19.60 |

error across the five circuits for the increased output load was 16.79%. It can be observed that our technique gives consistent power estimates with variation in output load as well as over different delay targets.

The power consumed by a circuit strongly depends on the gates present in the library used for its implementation. In Table 3, the power estimation results are presented for various target gate libraries. Our power estimation technique considers only the basic gates for computing the average logical and parasitic efforts. These average efforts were used to estimate the power consumed by the circuits. The results were compared against the power estimates from Synopsys Design and Power Compilers which used the gate libraries listed in column two of Table 3. It can be observed that our technique gives results of good accuracy even in this case. Overall, the method is robust with respect to variations in output load and gate libraries and gives power estimates of good accuracy over various delay targets.

## 5   Conclusion

In this work, we have presented a top-down technique to estimate the average zero-delay dynamic power of RT-Level combinational designs at various delay points. The proposed technique works at the synthesizable RT-Level and has minimal, but effective connections with the technology. The method is not based on statistical characterization, estimates the dynamic power accurately and can be applied as part of a power oriented design framework for early stage power estimation.

We plan to improve the absolute and relative accuracy in the future by utilizing the activity factor at the RT-Level visible nodes. Since short-circuit and glitch power form a substantial part of total dynamic power [6], [16] we plan to include them in our future studies.

## Acknowledgements

The authors acknowledge Sankar Gurumurthy and Ramtilak Vemu for their helpful reviews and suggestions.

# References

1. G. Bernacchia and M. C. Papaefthymiou, "Analytical Macromodeling for High-Level Power Estimation," in *Proceedings of the International Conference on Computer-Aided Design*, pp. 280–283, 1999.
2. K. M. Buyuksahin and F. N. Najm, "Early Power Estimation for VLSI Circuits," *IEEE Transactions on Computer-Aided-Design of Integrated Circuits and Systems*, vol. 24, no. 7, pp. 1076–1088, 2005.
3. M. Bruno, A. Macii, and M. Poncino, "A Statistical Power Model for Non-synthetic RTL Operators," in *Proceedings of the International Workshop on Power and Timing Modeling, Optimization and Simulation*, pp. 208–218, 2003.
4. I. Sutherland, R. Sproull, and D. Harris, *Logical Effort: Designing Fast CMOS Circuits*. San Francisco, CA: Morgan Kaufmann, 1999.
5. E. Macii, M. Pedram, and F. Somenzi, "High-Level Power Modeling, Estimation and Optimization," *IEEE Transactions on Computer-Aided-Design of Integrated Circuits and Systems*, vol. 17, no. 11, pp. 1061–1079, 1998.
6. A. Raghunathan, S. Dey, and N. K. Jha, "Register-Transfer Level Estimation Techniques for Switching Activity and Power Consumption," in *Proceedings of the IEEE/ACM International Conference on Computer-Aided Design*, pp. 158–165, 1996.
7. R. Zafalon, M. Rossello, E. Macii, and M. Poncino, "Power Macromodeling for a High Quality RT-level Power Estimation," in *Proceedings of the International Symposium on Quality of Electronic Design*, p. 59, 2000.
8. R. P. Llopis and K. Goossens, "The Petrol Approach to High-Level Power Estimation," in *Proceedings of the International Symposium on Low Power Electronics and Design*, pp. 130–132, 1998.
9. C. Chen and C. Tsui, "Towards the Capability of Providing Power-Area-Delay Trade-off at the Register Transfer Level," in *Proceedings of the International Symposium on Low Power Electronics and Design*, pp. 24–29, 1998.
10. S. Ravi, A. Raghunathan, and S. Chakradhar, "Efficient RTL Power Estimation for Large Designs," in *Proceedings of the International Conference on VLSI Design*, pp. 431–439, 2003.
11. M. Nemani and F. N. Najm, "Towards a High-Level Power Estimation Capability," *IEEE Transactions on Computer-Aided-Design of Integrated Circuits and Systems*, vol. 15, no. 6, pp. 588–598, 1996.
12. D. Marculescu, R. Marculescu, and M. Pedram, "Information Theoretic Measures of Energy Consumption at Register Transfer Level," in *Proceedings of the International Symposium on Low Power Electronic Design*, pp. 81–86, 1995.
13. T. Uchino, F. Minami, T. Mitsuhashi, and N. Goto, "Switching Activity Analysis using Boolean Approximation Method," in *Proceedings of the IEEE/ACM International Conference on Computer-Aided Design*, pp. 20–25, 1995.
14. "OR1200 processor and Floating-point co-processor," *http://www.opencores.org/*.
15. M. C. Hansen, H. Yalcin, and J. P. Hayes, "Unveiling the ISCAS-85 Benchmarks: A Case Study in Reverse Engineering," *IEEE Design and Test*, vol. 16, no. 3, pp. 72–80, 1999.
16. C. Baena, J. Juan-Chico, M. J. Bellido, P. R. de Clavijo, C. J. Jiminez, and M. Valencia, "Measurement of the Switching Activity of CMOS Digital Circuits at the Gate Level," in *Proceedings of the International Workshop on Power and Timing Modeling, Optimization and Simulation*, pp. 353–362, 2002.

# Circuit Design Style for Energy Efficiency: LSDL and Compound Domino

Xiao Yan Yu[1,4], Robert Montoye[2], Kevin Nowka[3],
Bart Zeydel[4] , and Vojin Oklobdzija[4]

[1] IBM Poughkeepsie
2455 South Rd
Poughkeepsie, NY 12601, USA
xianyu@us.ibm.com
[2] IBM T.J. Watson Research Center
1101 Kitchawan Rd, Route 134
Yorktown Heights, NY 10598, USA
montoye@us.ibm.com
[3] IBM Austin Research Laboratory
11501 Burnet Rd
Austin, TX 78758, USA
nowka@us.ibm.com
[4] ACSEL Laboratory
University of California
Davis, CA 95616, USA
{zeydel, vojin}@acsel-lab.com

**Abstract.** Introduction of sub-90nm technology has made a profound impact on circuit designs. Thus, it requires understanding of existing design styles for desired energy-efficiency. We compare adder designs in the energy-delay space, implemented with Limited Switch Dynamic Logic (LSDL) and Compound Domino Logic (CD) in a 65nm SOI technology. Evaluation results show that LSDL can provide more than 35% energy savings than CD with 25% switching activity at relaxed cycle times greater than 10.5 FO4.

## 1 Introduction

The emergence of sub-90nm poses several challenges to circuit designers. First, the interconnect delay is becoming more dominant compared to transistor delay as technology moves beyond 90nm. Traditionally, designs are created prior to physical implementation. Performance degradation due to interconnect parasitic has been considered as minor effect. Today, technology scaling provides higher levels of integration and smaller devices. As a result, delays due to interconnect parasitic can no longer be ignored. [7] Performance impact due to physical implementation must be analyzed at design time in order to guarantee optimality of the design.

As transistor length reduces beyond 90nm, gate oxide is reduced to a few atom layers. Sub-threshold and gate oxide leakage are increasing. This is especially true for low-$V_t$ transistors which have been intensively used in high-performance designs.

J. Vounckx, N. Azemard, and P. Maurine (Eds.): PATMOS 2006, LNCS 4148, pp. 47 – 55, 2006.
© Springer-Verlag Berlin Heidelberg 2006

Hence, it is desirable to use low-$V_t$ devices only on critical paths. As circuits approach the ultimate power limit, high performance application designs need to be energy-efficient. Therefore, it is very valuable to use energy efficient circuit design styles, especially when performance is not pushed to the limit. We need to know which circuit family can provide the desired speed while not consuming more energy than allowed by the energy budget. In this paper, we analyze two representative energy efficient logic families, namely, Limited Switch Dynamic Logic (LSDL) [3] and Compound Domino Logic (CD) [4]. Several adder topologies are implemented using these two families and are compared for their energy efficiencies. The evaluation of these implementations is based on delay characterizations at the nominal supply voltage. The rest of the paper is organized as follows. Section II briefly describes the operations of LSDL and CD. Section III provides details of the adder topologies used in the evaluation of these two logic families. Section IV discusses the evaluation results. Our goal here is show which of these two logic families is the best in the energy-delay space based on our analysis of adder implementations.

## 2 Preliminary

Based on the analysis of adder topologies in a 100nm technology, CD has been shown to be more energy efficient than conventional domino logic [1], [2]. Figure 1(a) shows a CD implementation of a function. It is composed of a dynamic gate followed by a static gate such as 2-input NOR or NAND instead of an inverter. When the clock signal is low, all dynamic nodes are pre-charged to logic "1" and all static nodes fall to logic "0".

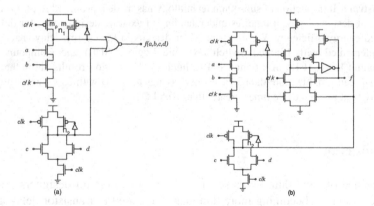

**Fig. 1.** (a) Compound Domino (b) Limited Switch Dynamic Logic

Figure 1(b) shows a LSDL implementation of the function, which is the complement of the function shown in Figure 1(a). It is composed of dynamic gates with a latch output. All dynamic nodes are pre-charged to logic "1" when the clock is low. Static nodes, on the other hand, preserve the value from the previous evaluation cycle. To improve performance, some logic may be merged into the latch. Since the latch is capable of producing outputs of both polarities, it eliminates the need to have dual-rail circuitry in LSDL.

# 3  Design Style Evaluation

We chose to evaluate the effectness of LSDL and CD on a class of parallel carry look-ahead schemes [9]. These schemes are extended from the idea of carry look-ahead computation and rely on recursive carry computation as follows:

$$(g, p) \bullet (g', p') = (g + p \cdot g', p \cdot p') \tag{1}$$

Thus,

$$(G_i, P_i) = \begin{cases} (g_0, p_0), if\ i = 0 \\ (g_i, p_i) \bullet (G_{i-1}, P_{i-1}), if\ 1 \le i \le n-1 \end{cases} \tag{2}$$

These adders are also known as recurrence solver adders. There are two properties of this recursive formulation:
$C_i = G_i \forall\ i$
The operator "$\bullet$" is associative

Adders implemented using these techniques are favorable due to their regular layout and fixed fan-out.

In this paper, we will be analyzing three representative adder topologies suitable for performance-demanding applications, namely, full tree prefix-4 carry look-ahead adder, sparse tree Ling adder with sparseness of 3 and sparse tree pseudo carry look-ahead adder with sparseness of 2.

## 3.1  Full Tree Prefix-4 Carry Look-Ahead Adder (Park Adder)

Park *et al* have proposed a 64-bit carry look-ahead and Prefix-4 Kogge-Stone hybrid adder in [11]. Figure 2 shows the prefix diagram of this adder. It has been implemented using CD. It has the shortest number of stages on the critical path among all previously published designs.

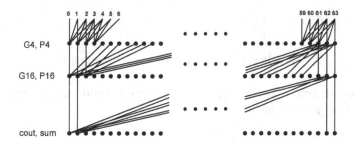

**Fig. 2.** Prefix diagram of Park adder

The advantages of this design over others are:
- Group-4 generate and propagate terms are produced directly from primary inputs
- Final carry generation at each bit is combined with sum generation

This scheme simplifies the conventional group generate and propagate term into:

$$G_{4_i} = \left( g_i + g_{i+1} + g_{i+2} + p_{i+2}g_{i+3} \right) \cdot \left( g_i + p_i p_{i+1} \right)$$

$$P_{4_i} = \left( g_i + g_{i+1} + g_{i+2} + p_{i+2}p_{i+3} \right) \cdot \left( g_i + p_i p_{i+1} \right)$$

(3)

by using the following properties:

$$\begin{cases} g_i = p_i \cdot g_i \\ p_i = p_i + g_i \end{cases}$$

(4)

where $p_i = a_i + bi$ and $gi = ai \cdot bi$. With the above mentioned advantages, a design with three stages of CDL gates on its critical path is produced.

## 3.2 Sparse Tree Ling Adder (Ling662 Adder)

Figure 3 shows the prefix diagram of a sparse tree Ling adder with sparseness of 3. This scheme is a variant of a Ling design that is proposed in [16], [17]. It has three stages on its critical path like the Park adder described previously. Group-6 pseudo generate (H6) and propagate (I6) bits are generated every three bits using Ling's carry scheme [10] in its first stage.

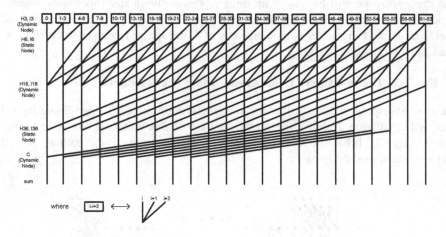

**Fig. 3.** Prefix diagram of sparse tree Ling 662 adder

The equations below show formulations of Ling's group-6 pseudo carry and propagate terms using primary inputs.

$$H_{3_i} = a_i \cdot b_i + a_{i+1} \cdot b_{i+1} + \left( a_{i+1} + b_{i+1} \right) \cdot \left( a_{i+2} \cdot b_{i+2} \right)$$

$$I_{3_i} = \left( a_{i+1} + b_{i+1} \right) \cdot \left( a_{i+2} + b_{i+2} \right) \cdot \left( a_{i+3} + b_{i+3} \right)$$

$and$

$$H_{6_i} = H_{3_i} + I_{3_i} \cdot H_{3_{i+3}}$$

$$I_{6_i} = I_{3_i} \cdot I_{i+3}$$

(5)

At end of the second stage, group-36 pseudo generate (H36) and propagate (I36) bits are generated. Final pseudo carry and its conversion to physical carry and sum generation are done in the third stage. This configuration has reduces input loading and wire complexity compared with other designs.

### 3.3 Sparse Tree Pseudo Carry Look-Ahead Adder (PCLA842)

Figure 4 shows the prefix diagram of a sparse tree pseudo carry look-ahead adder with sparseness of 2. It has the same number of stages on its critical path as other adders in this paper.

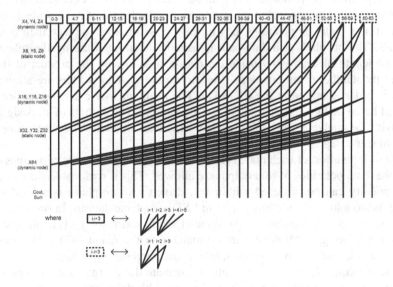

**Fig. 4.** Prefix diagram of sparse tree PCLA842

There are two key differences between this adder and others. First of all, it transmits pseudo carry (X), propagate (Y) and complementary (Z) terms so that the group-4 pseudo carry (X4) and propagate (Y4) terms can be generated from primary inputs using footed dynamic gates with the maximum transistor stack height of 4. If Ling's recursion is used, it would result in an implementation consisting of footed dynamic gates with the stack height of 5. Secondly, non-uniform prefix scheme is used in order to reduce branching at nodes on its critical path. Group-8 pseudo generation (X8), propagate (Y8) and complementary (Z8) bits are generated at every other bit in the static gate of the first stage. Final pseudo carry (X64) is generated in the dynamic gate in the third stage which is then used to select the correct sum. This approach reduces the complexity of the wiring and the loading caused by wires at later stages. Thus, it is more efficient than other published adder designs for performance-demanding applications.

## 4 Evaluation Results

We have implemented Park adder, Ling662 and PCLA842 using both CD and LSDL. Transistors with nominal threshold voltage are used for each design. All dynamic gates have maximum NMOS stack height of 4 and are footed to reduce leakage current. Each design is optimized for delay using Logical Effort [1, 2, 8] in a 65nm SOI CMOS technology with a nominal supply voltage at 85°C. The optimization points of each design are obtained by varying the transistor sizes of the input drivers. The wire lengths are estimated using 4 μm bit pitch. The bit pitch and bit stack arrangements are often determined during floorplanning after iterations of simulating critical path and logic repartition [18]. In a custom data-path design, the wires between two stages are generally placed orthogonal to the data signals. The length of these wires is then a function of how many bit positions they have to cross in order to reach their destination nodes. The bit pitch of a data-path is usually determined during floorplanning. Hence, the length of each wire inside the data-path is simply the product of the bit pitch and the number of bit positions it has to cross [6]. Wire widths are allowed to increase in order to minimize the RC delay. The resultant wire capacitances are then calculated based on the characteristic of the technology. The outputs of all designs are loaded with the equivalent of a 50 μm gate. This load simulates the actual loopback bus in a pipeline stage.

The branching effort of each node is calculated iteratively to assure correctness. We assume that both polarities of sum output are allowed. This is reasonable since conversion of polarity can be achieved within bus drivers. A two-phase non-overlapping clocking methodology is a preferred style in LSDL implementations. In order to maintain the fairness of this comparison, the same clocking methodology is applied to both LSDL and CD designs. All delays are normalized to the fanout-of-4 (FO4) inverter delay, which does not vary over process, temperature and supply voltage [5].

We use the equivalent transistor width to estimate the energy value at a performance point. Hence, the comparisons in transistor width-delay space are equivalent to comparisons in energy-delay space. To calculate the equivalent transistor width, we assume 100% clock activity rate for both LSDL and CD. Our experiences show that the data activity rate for CD gates is about 50% and the data activity rate for LSDL gates can be in the range of 10% to 25%. Our intention here is not to justify the data activity rate for our LSDL analysis but to provide a way to compare LSDL against CD. Thus, we have performed analysis on these LSDL implementations with data activity rate at both its lower and upper bounds, which corresponds to rates of 10% and 25%. For the simplicity of our analysis, we ignore any overheads in generating the clock phases. Figure 5 and Figure 6 show the transistor width vs. performance results with activity rate for LSDL to be 10% and 25% respectively. Solid curves show the results of CD implementations and dotted curves show the results of LSDL implementations. At the data activity rate of 10% for LSDL, it is evident that more than 50% energy saving is possible when using LSDL compared to CD. This is at the cost of having a stronger input driving source to achieve the same performance point as CD.

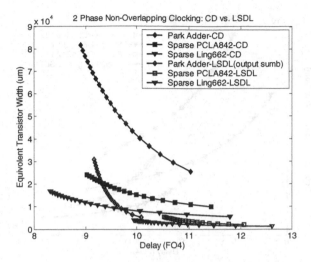

**Fig. 5.** Results assuming 10% data activity rate for LSDL

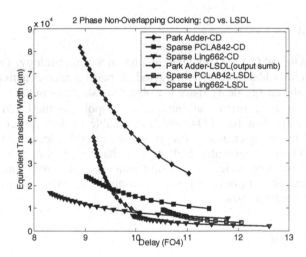

**Fig. 6.** Results assuming 25% data activity rate for LSDL

At 25% data activity rate, LSDL implementations of PCLA842 and Ling662 are more advantageous than their CD counterparts at speeds slower than 10 FO4 and 10.5 FO4 respectively. Figure 7 shows results of PCLA842 and Ling662 at upper bound data rate of for LSDL. It clearly demonstrates that significant energy savings can be achieved using LSDL.

The CD implementations of PCLA842 and Ling662 are capable of operating at speeds faster than 10 FO4. It is difficult for LSDL to reach this speed range without a strong input driving source. Hence, CD is more suitable for the critical paths in a design.

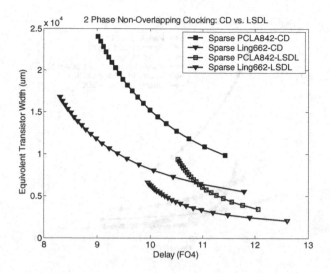

**Fig. 7.** Results of PCLA and Ling with 25% data rate for LSDL

## 5  Conclusion

In this paper, LSDL and CD are compared in a 65nm SOI technology. The evaluation is based on several adder topologies targeted at performance-demanding designs. Design points in the energy-delay space are obtained using a nominal supply voltage at 85°C. Estimations show that for all implemented topologies the LSDL is desirable at cycle times greater than 10.5 FO4, which is suitable for low power applications. CD can be used in timing-critical paths. However, careful selection of paths is required in order to keep power within budget. As technology continues to scale, power management will be more critical in a design than speed improvement. Careful implementation of circuit and placement may be required to provide an energy-efficient solution for future technologies.

## Acknowledgement

This work is supported by IBM Academic Learning Assistance Program.

## References

1. V. G. Oklobdzija, et. al, "Energy-Delay Estimation Technique for High-Performance Microprocessor VLSI Adders", Proceedings of the International Symposium on Computer Arithmetic, ARITH-16, Santiago de Compostela, SPAIN, June 15-18, 2003.
2. V. G. Oklobdzija, et. al, "Comparison of High-Performance VLSI Adders in Energy-Delay Space", IEEE Transaction on VLSI Systems, Volume 13, Issue 6, pp. 754-758, June 2005.

3. R. Montoye, et. al., "A Double Precision Floating Point Multiply", Digest of Technical Papers, 2003 IEEE International Solid-State Circuits Conference, San Francisco, Feb. 2003.
4. T. W. Houston, et. al., "Compound Domino CMOS Circuit", U.S. Patent No. 5,015,882, Issued: May 14, 1991.
5. Horowitz, M. "VLSI Scaling for Architects", Presentation slides, Computer Systems Laboratory, Stanford University.
6. Kevin J. Nowka, "Issues in High-Performance Processor Design", book chapter in The Computer Engineering Handbook, Vojin G. Oklobdzija (Ed.), CRC Press, Inc., 2002.
7. "Interconnect", International Technology Roadmap for Semiconductors (ITRS) 2005.
8. I.E. Sutherland and R.F. Sproull, "Logical Effort: Designing for Speed on the Back of an Envelope", in C.H. Sequin, Ed., Advanced Research in VLSI. Cambridge, MA: MIT Press, 1991.
9. P.M. Kogge and H.S. Stone, "A parallel algorithm for the efficient solution of a general class of recurrence equations", IEEE Trans. Computers, Vol. C-22, No. 8, 1973, pp. 786-793.
10. H. Ling, "High-Speed Binary Adder", IBM J. Res. Dev., vol.25, p.156-66, 1981.
11. J. Park, et. al, "470ps 64-bit Parallel Binary Adder", Digest of Technical Papers, of 2000 Symposium on VLSI Circuits, 2000.
12. S. K. Mathew, et. al, "Sub-500-ps 64-b ALUs in 0.18-μm SOI/bulk CMOS: design and scaling trends", IEEE Journal of Solid-State Circuits, Volume 11, Nov. 2001.
13. S. Mathew, et. al, "A 4-GHZ 130-nm address generation unit with 32-bit sparse-tree adder core", IEEE Journal of Solid-State Circuits, Volume 38, Issue 5, May, 2003.
14. S. Mathew, et. al, "A 4GHZ 300mW 64b Integer Execution ALU with Dual Supply Voltage in 90nm CMOS", Digest of Technical Papers of 2004 IEEE International Solid-State Circuit Conference, San Francisco, February, 2004.
15. Y. Shimazaki, et. al, " A shared-well dual-supply-voltage 64-bit ALU", IEEE Journal of Solid-State Circuits, Vol. 39, Issue 3, March, 2004.
16. Bart R. Zeydel et. al, "Efficient Mapping of Addition Recurrence Algorithms in CMOS", 17th IEEE Symposium on Computer Arithmetic, June 27-29, 2005.
17. G. Dimitrakopoulos and D. Nikolos "High Speed Parallel-Prefix VLSI Ling Adders", IEEE Transactions on Computers, Feb. 2005.
18. R. M. Averill, et. al, "Chip Integration Methodology for the IBM S/390 G5 and G6 Custom Microprocessors", IBM Journal of Research and Development, Vol. 43, No. 5/6, 1999.

# Accurate PTV, State, and ABB Aware RTL Blackbox Modeling of Subthreshold, Gate, and PN-Junction Leakage

Domenik Helms[1], Marko Hoyer[1], and Wolfgang Nebel[2]

[1] OFFIS Research Institute
[2] University of Oldenburg
D-26121 Oldenburg, Germany
{helms, hoyer, nebel}@offis.de

**Abstract.** We present a blackbox approach to model leakage currents of RTL data-path components. The model inputs are temperature, $V_{DD}$, body voltage of NMOS and PMOS and the bitvector at the input. Additionally, the model accepts a statistical Gaussian variation introduced by intra-die and systematic variation introduced by inter-die. Both variations can be given independently for each BSIM-level process parameter; in this work we evaluate variation of channel length, gate-oxide thickness and channel doping. Model output is the sum of subthreshold, gate, and pn-junction leakage. The evaluation of an RT component can be done in milliseconds and the result for the $45nm$ and $65nm$ BPTM technology is within 2% against single BSIM4.40 evaluation and within 5% against statistical BSIM4.40 evaluation assuming 1% variation of the process parameters.

## 1 Introduction

When working at the well established field of RTL modeling one will soon find out, that doing RTL leakage estimation is by no means a simple modification of a timing, area or dynamic power model. There are several factors, making leakage macro modeling a completely new challenge:

Leakage is barely state dependent from an RT level view. Instead, dynamic parameters highly influencing leakage are temperature $\vartheta$ (dominating subthreshold leakage) and supply voltage $V_{DD}$ (having highest influence on gate and pn-junction leakage). Process variations also are a new challenge for RT models. All leakage currents are highly dependent on variation of certain process parameters [1, 2].

Additionally, there are low leakage design techniques, as adaptive body biasing $ABB$ and power gating, both implemented at circuit level but controlled at system level. Thus complete RT-models also have to regard the influence of these techniques. Both techniques have influence not only on leakage but also on performance and area, and (in case of power gating) also on dynamic power. In this paper, we focus on the description of the leakage modeling aspect.

The important difference between leakage-models for power gating and ABB is, that power gating can be easily modeled by setting up a model for each power

J. Vounckx, N. Azemard, and P. Maurine (Eds.): PATMOS 2006, LNCS 4148, pp. 56–65, 2006.

gating implementation - typically only two. In contrast, ABB is controlled by a continuous parameter, the body voltage $V_{BB}$. Thus, ABB can hardly be modeled by model separation, but the body voltage has to enter the model as a further parameter.

Finally, we end up with the need for leakage models being aware of 4 dynamic (variable at system runtime) parameters and $2n$ static (variable at design time) parameters when regarding $n$ process parameters. The model evaluated in this contribution has $4+6$ parameters: temperature, supply and body voltage, state, and additionally inter- and intra-die variation of channel length $L$, gate oxide thickness $T_{ox}$, and channel doping $N$.

After the review of related work in Sec 2, we present the 2 stages, our model can be separated into: Modeling of reference transistors, presented in Sec 3, and abstracting a gate's and even an RT component's physical behavior by automatically generating an equivalent circuit of these reference transistors in Sec 4. In Sec 5, we evaluate the model, Sec 6 finally concludes this paper.

## 2    Related Work

Leakage estimation at circuit level, regarding all important parameters and returning all leakage currents can be done using the Berkeley transistor model BSIM [3], which is accurate, but slow. Using a GHz machine, a single transistor evaluation needs $10ms$, thus an RT-component is computed in minutes and a statistical Monte-Carlo evaluation of the variations needs hours.

Various approaches abstracting to high level exist. Intel presented a framework [4,5,6,7] with a focus on PTV variations, accurately modeling temperature and process variation. Neither optimization (ABB) nor gate and pn-junction leakage are supported.

The IBM work [8,9,10] introduces temperature and supply voltage derating and package models for temperature and $V_{DD}$-drop determination and a state dependent model for both, subthreshold and gate-leakage.

The University of Michigan work presents accurate PTV variation modeling of subthreshold leakage mainly for yield estimation purposes, and also not supporting bulk voltage [11,12,13,14,15]. In [16] they also present gate leakage estimation but with no PTV analysis.

The Purdue University work [1,17,18] gives deep insight to the device physics enabling estimation of subthreshold, gate, and pn-junction leakage under parameter variation. Their results are accurate, but hardly applicable to RT level.

Best to our knowledge, no holistic, monolithic and thus blackbox macro-modeling approach supporting all parameters and estimating all 3 leakage-currents has been published prior to this contribution.

## 3    Transistor Models

Fig 1 describes the bottom-up model construction flow. Our model can estimate an RT component's PTV dependence, when exactly knowing PTV dependence of 4 reference transistors under these PTV variations. Thus, in this section, we describe our PTV-aware subthreshold, gate and pn-junction leakage transistor model.

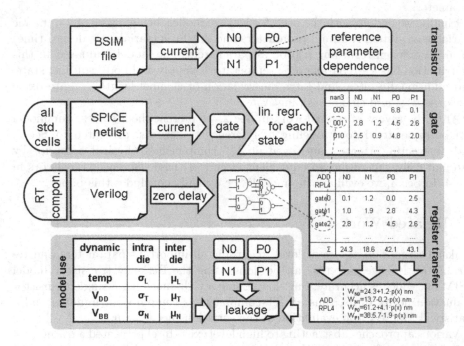

**Fig. 1.** Stages of the model. **Transistor:** 4 reference transistors are sampled and stored in tables. **Gate:** Using measurement of all gates in all states at different parameter settings, the linear parameter regression automatically finds equivalent transistor widths for the 4 reference transistors. **RT level:** The component mapped to standard cells is simulated, and the states obtained are used to set up a firm-macro of the component. Using measurements at different input bitvectors, the state dependence can be abstracted. **Model use:** Given the dynamic and static parameters, the 4 reference transistors can be evaluated. Knowing the signal probability, the effective widths of the reference transistors is known. The result is a leakage current estimation of an RT component, regarding the most relevant parameters.

### 3.1 Parameter Sampling

Modeling of varying temperature, $V_{DD}$ and body-voltage is straight-forward. For each transistor $N0$ (NMOS with low input - thus locking), $N1$ (NMOS conducting), $P0$ (PMOS conducting), and $P1$ (PMOS locking), we sample at equidistant parameter combinations within a typical parameter-space (Tab 1). Including transistor type ($\tau \in \{N, P\}$) and state ($s \in \{0, 1\}$), we have to regard $\approx 12000$ sampling points. For each point, we measure the sum of subthreshold, gate and pn-junction leakage.

When using interpolation between sampled values, the accuracy is raised by interpolating the exponent of the current and not the current itself. The

**Table 1.** Parameter selection of the sampling points and stride $\Delta$

| Parameter | min | max | $\Delta$ |
|---|---|---|---|
| $\vartheta$ [K] | 300 | 400 | 5 |
| $V_{DD}$ [mV] | 600 | 1200 | 50 |
| $V_{BB}$ [mV] | −200 | 200 | 20 |

**Table 2.** Std. dev. and max. error when sampling temperature, supply and body voltage

| technology | std [%] | max [%] |
|---|---|---|
| 70nm | 2.38 | 5.66 |
| 65nm | 0.67 | 1.92 |
| 45nm | 1.42 | 3.77 |

errors resulting from the sampling (Tab 2), are averaged over a complete set of measurements within the parameter range (Tab 1).

## 3.2 Modeling Variation of the Process Parameters

Our model supports estimation of two variations: Inter-die results in a systematic deviation of a process parameter, intra-die results in a random deviation of a process parameter between the transistors. The influence of inter-die is obvious, the influence of intra-die is introduced by a second order effect [18].

Our modeling methodology is as follows: For each sampling point we measure the leakage not only at nominal parameters, but also with a variation $\pm\Delta$ of each parameter. Regarding 3 process parameters, for each sampling point, we end up with 7 measurements: $I(L, T, N)$, $I(L \pm \Delta_L, T, N)$, $I(L, T \pm \Delta_T, N)$, and $I(L, T, N \pm \Delta_N)$, where $L$ is the nominal length, $T$ the nominal oxide thickness, and $N$ the nominal channel doping. Assuming separability[1] $I(l, t, n) = I_0 + f(l - L) + g(t - T) + h(n - N)$ with $l, t, n$ the actual parameters, and $L, T, N$ the nominal ones, and $f(0) = g(0) = h(0) = 0$, we can develop a $3D$, second order Taylor polynomial and compute the effect on the expectation value.

If the input parameters are statistically independent $(P(l, t, n) = P(l) \cdot P(t) \cdot P(n))$, we can use

$$E(I(l, t, n)) = I_0 + E(f(l)) + E(g(t)) + E(h(n)). \tag{1}$$

If Equation 1 is valid, the expectation value of each parameter $P$ can be computed separately. Using three measurements $I(P) = I_0$ and $I(P \pm \Delta) = I_\pm$, the Taylor polynomial results as

$$I(p) = I_0 + (p - P) \cdot \frac{I_+ - I_-}{2\Delta} + (p - P)^2 \cdot \frac{I_- - 2I_0 + I_+}{2\Delta^2}. \tag{2}$$

Assuming a Gaussian distribution of the parameter $p$ around the nominal value $P$ and a standard deviation of $\sigma_P$, the expectation value can be computed in closed form as

$$E(I(p)) = \frac{1}{\sigma_P \sqrt{2\pi}} \int_{-\infty}^{+\infty} I(p) \cdot e^{-(p-P)^2/2\sigma_P^2} = I_0 + \sigma_P^2 \cdot \frac{I_- - 2I_0 + I_+}{2\Delta^2}. \tag{3}$$

---

[1] Note, that the assumption of separability, and the higher order terms of the Taylor series both increase the errors of the variation model (ref. Sec 5).

For a linear dependent parameter $(I_- + I_+)/2 = I_0$ holds and thus $E(I(p)) = I_0$. As the expectation value of error term of the Taylor series is $\sigma_P^4/12\Delta^4$, we chose the measured deviation $\Delta$ larger than the typical variation $\sigma_P$ of this parameter to increase accuracy.

The linear part of the Taylor polynomial $(I_+ - I_-)/2\Delta$ does not contribute to the expectation value (for intra-die), but is giving the current variation for a systematic deviation for inter-die. In order to increase accuracy, we use $(I_0 - I_-)/\Delta$ for negative deviation and $(I_+ - I_0)/\Delta$ for positive ones.

The resulting transistor model supports all dynamic and static parameters described in Sec 1 for NMOS and PMOS in conducting and locking state. For characterization, we need to sample $\approx 84000$ single BSIM results of total leakage current. The simulation takes less than an hour, which is acceptable, as it has to done only once for each technology.

## 4   Gate and RTL Models

The transistor model, presented in Sec 3 accurately captures the dependence of the leakage to all physical parameters (dynamic and static). The basic idea (Fig 1) of this contribution, is that the physical behavior of a larger structure of transistors - gate or component - can only result from a linear combination of the transistor behavior.

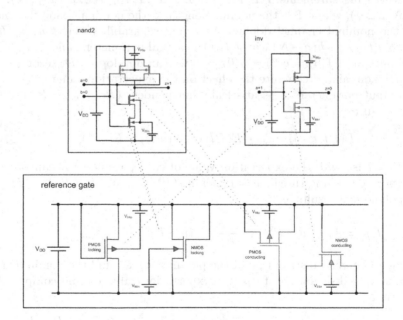

**Fig. 2.** Basic idea of this work is to use linear regression obtaining effective width of 4 reference transistors for each state of each gate. An $n$ input gate can be modeled by storing this $4 \cdot 2^n$ widths in a table (Tab 3). The reference transistors are identical for all gates being modeled.

**Example:** Let PMOS leakage double each $20K$ in temperature, and NMOS leakage doubles each $40K$. If we only know the leakage of a component is $10\mu A$ measured at $300K$ we can not identify, how much of this leakage was due to NMOS or PMOS. Thus we can not compute the leakage at $340K$ ($20\mu A \leq I \leq 40\mu A$). If we measure the component's current at a second temperature (e.g. $I(380K) = 76\mu A$) and we assume, that total current is a sum of NMOS and PMOS leakage currents, we can solve this example:

$$I(T) = 3\mu A \cdot 2^{(T-300K)/20K} + 7\mu A \cdot 2^{(T-300K)/40K} \qquad (4)$$

and thus also estimate $I(340K) = 26\mu A$.

## 4.1  Gate Modeling

Our gate model in principle is a high-dimensional extension of the example given above. We assume, that the leakage of each gate results as a linear combination of the leakage of the 4 reference transistors $N0$, $N1$, $P0$, and $P1$. For each gate, we model, we set up a spice-netlist and perform a series of BSIM evaluations at various combinations of the dynamic parameters. For each state we perform a linear parameter regression, fitting the scaling parameters of the 4 reference transistors to the measurement of the complete gate. The scaling parameters then can be interpreted as the effective widths of the reference transistors (Tab 3).

Without having transistors stacked, this approach obviously is correct and the scaling parameters obtained represent the physical width of the transistors (Tab 3, inverter). For more complex structures, the scaling parameters do not need to have a physical meaning.

The two parallel NMOS transistors of the NOR2 gate in Tab 3, behave like a single transistor of double width in terms of leakage, if both inputs lock or both conduct. In the mixed case, there is no $N0$ contribution, as the conducting $N1$ transistor short-circuits the subthreshold leakage dominated $N0$ contribution. The gate-leakage dominated $N1$ is in the order of the physical width of the conducting transistor.

The PMOS part behaves similarly for the 00 case. As $P0$ is gate-leakage dominated, the PMOS branch is equivalent to a single $P0$ transistor of double width. In the 11 state, the widths of both transistors do not add, as current passes them in series. Instead, due to the stacking effect [1], the effective width is far below the $220nm$, we would expect for resistors. The mixed states are asymmetrical as in the 10 case, the locking transistor cuts the gate leakage path. The small negative values are numerical artifacts stemming from the linear regression. Model accuracy is reduced by $\approx 0.1\%$ if the regression parameters are limited to positive values.

## 4.2  RTL Component Modeling

In the final step of the model, we generate firm-macros for each RT component; meaning (one model for each bitwidth). The gate level description of the

**Table 3.** Effective widths resulting from the linear parameter regression for 65nm INVD1 and NOR2D1. $N0$ is the locking NMOS transistor, $N1$ the conducting one, $P0$ is PMOS conducting and $P1$ PMOS locking.

|               | $N0$    | $N1$     | $P0$    | $P1$    |
|---------------|---------|----------|---------|---------|
| Inverter real | 195nm   |          | 390nm   |         |
| Regr. @0      | 187nm   | -0.05nm  | 389nm   | 0.08nm  |
| Regr. @1      | -0.10nm | 187nm    | 6.14nm  | 384nm   |
| Nor2 real     | 204nm/197nm |      | 456nm/441nm |     |
| Regr. @00     | 384nm   | -0.02nm  | 886nm   | 1.06nm  |
| Regr. @01     | -2.36nm | 196nm    | 425nm   | 452nm   |
| Regr. @10     | -16.1nm | 185nm    | 88.8nm  | 408nm   |
| Regr. @11     | -2.54nm | 364nm    | 405nm   | 117nm   |

component (e.g. Verilog) is zero-delay simulated using certain test pattern. The state of each gate is used to select the parameter-set of each gate. Assuming, that there is no interaction between leakage currents in two consecutive CMOS gates (SPICE analyses verify this assumption within 1% accuracy), the leakage current of the (simulation based) RT model results as

$$I_{\text{comp}} = \sum_{j}^{\text{gates}} I\left(\text{gate}_j\left(\text{state}_j\right)\right) = \sum_{j}^{\text{gates}} W_{N0}(j, s_j) \cdot I_{N0} + W_{N1}(j, s_j) I_{N1} + \dots \quad (5)$$

where $W_{N0}(j)$ is the width of the $N0$ obtained by regression for the gate $j$ at the state $s_j$. $I_{N0}$ is the $N0$ current which captures the dependence on $\vartheta$, $V_{DD}$, and $V_{BB}$, and the variation of process parameters. By summing up the widths of all gates before multiplying with the reference transistor $W_{\tau s}^{\text{tot}} = \sum_j^{\text{gates}} W_{\tau s}(j, s_j)$, the simulation results are abstracted to 4 effective width parameters. For a single input vector, the RTL and the gate model just differ in magnitude of the effective widths. Note, that this simplification is valid only, if all transistor models have the same $\vartheta$, $V_{DD}$, and $V_{BB}$:

$$I_{\text{comp}}\left(T, V, \sigma\right) = \sum_{\tau \in \{N, P\}} \sum_{s \in \{0,1\}} W_{\tau s}^{\text{tot}} I_{\tau s}\left(T, V, \sigma\right) \quad (6)$$

In order to abstract from the absolute data dependence, which would result in the need for $2^n$ models per $n$-bit component, we try to merge our data-abstraction approach, we proposed in [19][2]. Using the input signal probability $p(x)$ of the component, the final firm-macro for RT components results as:

$$I_{\text{comp}}\left(T, V, \sigma\right) = \sum_{\tau \in \{N, P\}} \sum_{s \in \{0,1\}} \left(W_{\tau s} + p(x) \cdot \delta W_{\tau s}\right) I_{ij}\left(T, V, \sigma\right), \quad (7)$$

---

[2] The result of this work is, that the leakage of RT components has a variation of 15%. With an error of only 5%, the signal probability at the input is a good predictor of this variation.

where $W_{\tau s}$ are the equivalent transistor widths, extracted at 0...0 input and $\delta W_{\tau s}$ the difference between the widths at 1...1 and 0...0.

## 5   Evaluation

All evaluation results are obtained using the SPICE simulator with the BSIM4.40 transistor model. Simulations of gates were done using our $45nm$ and $65nm$ technology [19]. RT-components were synthesized, using a commercial synthesis tool.

In Tab 4, accuracy of the model of the 4 reference transistors is analyzed, for randomly chosen dynamic parameters ($\vartheta$, $V_{DD}$, and $V_{BB}$) within the characterized range. Except for the $P1$, which has much lower total current, as it is dominated by PMOS gate-tunneling, the error of the transistor model is always below 1% at $65nm$ and 2% at $45nm$.

**Table 4.** Average leakage, standard deviation, and maximum error of the reference transistor models over all dynamic parameters due to sampling and interpolation. As the gate-tunneling of PMOS is orders of magnitude smaller [2], the regression of the $P1$ parameter becomes unstable.

**Table 5.** Comparison of the model to statistical SPICE simulation. With rising parameter variance, the influence of the higher order terms increases the error.

|  | 65nm | | | | 45nm | | | |
|---|---|---|---|---|---|---|---|---|
|  | N0 | N1 | P0 | P1 | N0 | N1 | P0 | P1 |
| Avg. [nA] | 125 | 76.8 | 77.8 | 1.1 | 1210 | 887 | 617 | 17.0 |
| Std. [%] | 0.63 | 0.81 | 0.49 | 7.51 | 1.76 | 1.50 | 0.49 | 7.46 |
| Max. [%] | 2.00 | 2.28 | 0.84 | 44.8 | 4.74 | 3.69 | 0.88 | 44.4 |

| $\sigma_P[\%]$ | 1 | 2 | 4 |
|---|---|---|---|
| Std. 65nm[%] | 0.8 | 1.2 | 3.8 |
| Max. 65nm[%] | 2.8 | 4.6 | 23.3 |
| Std. 45nm[%] | 1.7 | 2.3 | 6.6 |
| Max. 45nm[%] | 6.4 | 10.4 | 36.1 |

Tab 5 was obtained as follows: For a fixed set of dynamic parameters, 1000 sets of Gaussian distributed static parameters ($L, T_{ox}$, and $N$) are simulated with a relative variation of all parameters identically at 1%, 2%, and 4%. The result is averaged and stored as a single measurement. For 500 random sets of dynamic parameters, we repeat the *inner loop*, comparing our model to the result of a Monte-Carlo based statistical SPICE simulation. For small variations, the results are small, but with rising parameter variation, our model starts to consistently underestimate the effect of the variation.

For evaluation of the state dependent gate model, we compare to SPICE evaluation at random dynamic parameters (Tab 3). The effect of parameter variation was not regarded here. We present the regular structures of NAND and NOR as they have highest errors among all gates (e.g .the AOI211 gate has standard deviation of below 4% and maximum error below 17% ).

To evaluate the overall model, we compute the Monte-Carlo computation of an RT components, having individual variation in each transistor for a huge number of input states. As a single statistical SPICE evaluation of an RT component takes hours, we limited the evaluation to 3 small components (see Tab 6) and a variation of 1% in all parameters and to the $45nm$ technology. Using our model, the same RT component can be evaluated in $30ms$.

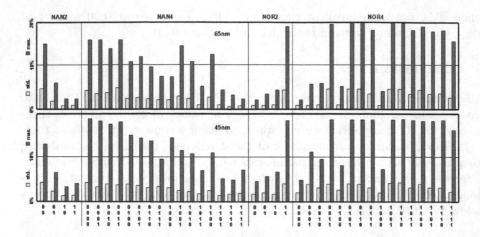

**Fig. 3.** Standard deviation and maximum error of the 45nm and 65nm technology: Standard deviation for all gates in technology is below 5% for all states, maximum error is always below 20%

**Table 6.** Evaluation of three $45nm$ RT components against statistical SPICE simulation and against the explicitly data dependent model. The std. dev. for the state abstraction and the overall model both seem to be smaller, the bigger the component is.

| Component | #gates | vs. SPICE std. [%] | max. [%] | vs. itself std. [%] | max. [%] |
|---|---|---|---|---|---|
| AddCla4 | 83 | 4.11 | 12.9 | 3.86 | 11.7 |
| AddRpl8 | 151 | 2.90 | 11.6 | 2.64 | 10.4 |
| MultWall8 | 767 | 2.33 | 11.1 | 2.00 | 9.65 |

# 6   Conclusion

We presented a blackbox firm-modeling approach, with high accuracy for moderate intra-die variations. The characterization of the RT components can be automated, no designer decision is needed. All parameters which are known to influence the leakage are regarded and all relevant leakage currents are estimated.

Future work will extend the model into 2 directions: Increasing the model accuracy, especially for large parameter variation, and embedding the model into an existing high level estimation flow. For flow integration, the models have to be made parameterizable in bitwidth, and the timing model has to be updated to also regard parameter variation and $V_{BB}$.

In order to increase estimation accuracy, we will evaluate 2 alternatives, using higher (4th order) Taylor approximation, and regard cross terms of the parameter variation like $I(L + \Delta, T, N - \Delta)$.

Additionally, the $P1$ which is orders of magnitude less leaking can be replaced by stacked $N0$ and $P0$ transistors, as the highest errors at gate level occur for large stacked structures.

# References

1. K Roy, S Mukhopadhyay, H Mahmoodi-Meimand: Leakage Current Mechanisms and Leakage Reduction Techniques in Deep-Submicrometer CMOS Circuits. *Proc. of the IEEE Vol.91 No.2*, 2003.
2. D Helms, E Schmidt, W Nebel: Leakage in CMOS circuits - An Introduction. *PATMOS*, 2004.
3. The Berkeley Device Group www-device.eecs.berkeley.edu
4. S Narendra, V De, S Borkar, D Antoniadis, A Chandrakasan: Full-Chip Subthreshold Leakage Power Prediction Model for sum-0.18$\mu m$ CMOS. *ISLPED*, 2002.
5. S Borkar, T Karnik, S Narendra, J Tschanz, A Keshavari, V De: Parameter Variations and Impact on Microarchitecture. *DAC*, 2003.
6. K Banerjee, S-C Lin, A Keshavarzi, S Narendra, V De: A Self-Consistent Junction Temperature Estimation Methodology for Nanometer Scale ICs with Implications for Performance and Thermal Management. *IEEE*, 2003.
7. M Ashouei, A Chatterjee, A D Singh, V De, T M Mak: Statistical Estimation of Correlated Leakage Power Variation and Its Application to Leakage-Aware Design. *VLSI Design*, 2006
8. R M Rao, J L Burns, A Devgan, R B Brown: Efficient techniques for gate leakage estimation. *ISLPED*, 2003.
9. H Su, F Liu, A Devgan, E Acar, S R Nassif: Full chip leakage estimation considering power supply and temperature variations. *ISLPED*, 2003.
10. E Acar, A Devgan, R Rao, Y Liu, H Su, S R Nassif, J L Burns: Leakage and leakage sensitivity computation for combinational circuits. *ISLPED*, 2003.
11. A Srivastava, R Bai, D Blaauw, D Sylvester: Modeling and analysis of leakage power considering within-die process variations. *ISLPED*, 2002.
12. R R Rao, A Srivastava, D Blaauw, D Sylvester: Statistical estimation of leakage current considering inter- and intra-die process variation. *ISLPED2005*.
13. R R Rao, A Srivastava, D Blaauw, D Sylvester: Statistical analysis of subthreshold leakage current for VLSI circuits. *IEEE Trans. VLSI Syst.*, 2004.
14. R R Rao, A Devgan, D Blaauw, D Sylvester: Parametric yield estimation considering leakage variability. *DAC*, 2004.
15. A Srivastava, S Shah, K Agarwal, D Sylvester, D Blaauw, S W Director: Accurate and efficient gate-level parametric yield estimation considering correlated variations in leakage power and performance. *DAC*, 2005.
16. D Lee, W Kwong, D Blaauw, D Sylvester: Analysis and minimization techniques for total leakage considering gate oxide leakage. *DAC*, 2003.
17. S Mukhopadhyay, A Raychowdhury, K Roy: Accurate Estimation of Total Leakage Current in Scaled CMOS Logic Circuits Based on Compact Current Modeling. *DAC*, 2003.
18. S Mukhopadhyay, K Roy: Modeling and Estimation of Total Leakage Current in Nano-scaled CMOS Devices Considering the Effect of Parameter Variation. *ISLPED*, 2003.
19. D Helms, G Ehmen, W Nebel: Analysis and Modeling of Subthreshold Leakage of RT-Components under PTV and State Variation, *ISLPED*, 2006.

# Leakage Power Characterization Considering Process Variations

Jose L. Rosselló, Carol de Benito, Sebastià Bota, and Jaume Segura

Electronic Technology Group, Universitat Illes Balears
Campus UIB, 07122, Palma de Mallorca, Spain
j.rossello@uib.es
http://omaha.uib.es

**Abstract.** We present a novel technique to accurately describe the leakage power in CMOS nanometer Integrated Circuits (ICs) considering process variations. The model predicts a leakage power increment due to process variations with high accuracy. It is shown that leakage increases considerably as channel length variations become larger due to technology scaling. The present work also describes accurately the dependence of leakage dispersion with process variations. The model developed shows that, even if channel length variations are kept small the leakage dispersion is considerably large. Finally, the concept of "Hot Gates" (HGs) is introduced, showing that HGs will be an important reliability factor in near future nanometer technologies.

## 1 Introduction

Power dissipation has become a major concern in IC design due to the increasing importance of portable devices and wireless communication systems, and to the heating problems that may arise in high-density/high-performance circuits.

Technology scaling rules based on constant field scaling dictate voltage supply reduction from generation to generation, forcing a consequent threshold voltage reduction to maintain performance. This has a side effect of a dramatic leakage current increase given its exponential dependence with threshold voltage. For 90nm process generations, the subthreshold leakage power can contribute as much as 42% of the total power [1]. Consequently, leakage power is no longer negligible in deep-submicron CMOS technologies and the development of accurate models for the estimation of this power component is a must.

As digital technologies scales down, process variations become larger leading to an appreciable increment of total leakage [2]. This is of special interest if we consider that leakage becomes the main contributor to the IC power in nanometer technologies. Different works have been developed to estimate leakage taking into account process variations. In [2] and [3] we find different studies for the estimation of static power considering channel length variation effects. The inclusion of other variation sources (like doping), with a clear impact on leakage, was not included in their analysis.

In this work we present an elaborated study of the leakage distribution dependence with process variations. Both total static power and leakage dispersion are analyzed

J. Vounckx, N. Azemard, and P. Maurine (Eds.): PATMOS 2006, LNCS 4148, pp. 66–74, 2006.
© Springer-Verlag Berlin Heidelberg 2006

when considering process variations effects. Compact analytical models for both leakage dispersion and total leakage are presented. Finally, the concept of *Hot Gates* (HGs) is introduced and analyzed. We show that HGs will be an important reliability problem in near future nanometer ICs due to the elevated operating temperatures that may be achieved by these gates.

## 2  Leakage Current Modeling

The leakage current of a MOS device in cutoff has an exponential dependence on the threshold voltage:

$$I_{OFF} = \frac{\omega}{L} I_0 e^{-\frac{V_{TH}}{nV_T}} \left( 1 - e^{-\frac{V_{DD}}{V_T}} \right) \tag{1}$$

where $\omega$ and $L$ are the channel width and length respectively, $I_0$ is a process-dependent parameter, and $V_T$, $V_{DD}$, and $V_{TH}$ are the thermal, supply, and threshold voltages respectively. The supply-voltage dependent term in (1) may be neglected when $V_{DD} \gg V_T$ (the thermal voltage is typically equal to 25mV at room temperature), and $n$ is a technology-dependent parameter with a typical value of 1.5.

For a CMOS gate, the OFF current is driven by a stack of serially-connected transistors. In this case, the $I_{OFF}$ current has a similar expression with respect to the channel length and supply voltage, that is:

$$I_{OFF} = \frac{\omega_{eff}}{L} I_0 e^{-\frac{V_{TH}}{nV_T}} \tag{2}$$

where $\omega_{eff}$ is an effective "channel width" that mainly depends on the channel widths of the transistors in the stack, and the supply voltage [4].

For the purpose of analyzing leakage with respect to variations of the main parameters as channel length or substrate doping we express threshold voltage in the next form:

$$V_{TH} = V_{TH_\mu} + \left. \frac{\partial V_{TH}}{\partial L} \right|_{L_\mu} \Delta L + \left. \frac{\partial V_{TH}}{\partial N_{SUB}} \right|_{N_{SUB_\mu}} \Delta N_{SUB} + \ldots = V_{TH_\mu} + \frac{\Delta L}{\lambda} n V_T + \Delta V'_{TH} \tag{3}$$

where $\lambda$ is related to the $V_{TH}$ derivative with respect channel length. Parameter $L_\mu$ and $N_{SUB\mu}$ are the nominal channel length and substrate doping respectively. Parameter $V_{TH\mu}$ refers to the nominal threshold voltage (evaluated at the nominal values for design and process parameters $L_\mu$ $N_{SUB\mu}$, ...). Expression (3) holds as long as $\Delta L \ll L_\mu$ and $\Delta N_{SUB} \ll N_{SUB\mu}$. Parameter $\Delta V'_{TH}$ in (3) refers to threshold voltage variations caused by other factors different than channel length variations.

From (3) the off-current of a CMOS gate is given by :

$$I_{OFF} = I_\mu \frac{e^{-\frac{\Delta L}{\lambda} - \frac{\Delta V'_{TH}}{nV_T}}}{1 + \Delta L/L_\mu} \tag{4}$$

where $I_\mu$ refers to the nominal leakage current.

## 3  Leakage Power Characterization Considering Process Variations

We assume a normal Probability Density Function (PDF) for channel length and $\Delta V'_{TH}$ distributions:

$$f(x) = \frac{e^{-\frac{(x-\mu)^2}{2\sigma^2}}}{\sigma\sqrt{2\pi}} \tag{5}$$

where x refers to the parameter under consideration while $\mu$ and $\sigma$ represent the mean and standard deviation. From (5) we calculate the mean value of any magnitude $g(x)$ as:

$$\langle g \rangle = \int g(x) f(x) dx \tag{6}$$

Therefore, the total leakage current in an IC containing $N$ gates is computed as:

$$\langle I_{LEAK} \rangle = N I_\mu \left\langle \frac{e^{-\frac{\Delta L}{\lambda} - \frac{\Delta V'_{TH}}{nV_T}}}{1 + \Delta L/L_\mu} \right\rangle \tag{7}$$

Assuming independence between channel length and the other mechanisms that induce threshold voltage fluctuation (as the substrate doping) we approximate (7) as:

$$\langle I_{LEAK} \rangle = N I_\mu \left\langle e^{-\frac{\Delta L}{\lambda}} \left(1 - \Delta L/L_\mu + (\Delta L/L_\mu)^2 + ...\right) \right\rangle \left\langle e^{-\frac{\Delta V'_{TH}}{nV_T}} \right\rangle \tag{8}$$

where the two mean values in (8) are extended over the distributions $f(L)$ and $f(\Delta V'_{TH})$. Assuming that $\Delta L \ll L_\mu$ and using the normal distribution for $f(L)$ and $f(\Delta V'_{TH})$ we get:

$$\langle I_{LEAK} \rangle \approx N I_\mu e^{\frac{(\sigma_L/\lambda)^2}{2}} \left(1 + \frac{\sigma_L^2}{\lambda L_\mu} + \frac{\sigma_L^2}{L_\mu^2} + \frac{\sigma_L^4}{(\lambda L_\mu)^2}\right) e^{\frac{(\sigma'_{V_{TH}}/nV_T)^2}{2}} \tag{9}$$

where $\sigma_L$ and $\sigma'_{VTH}$ are defined as the standard deviations of distributions $f(L)$ and $f(\Delta V'_{TH})$ respectively. If process variations are neglected, the total leakage current corresponds to $I_{LEAK} = N I_\mu$.

Eq.(9) indicates an exponential dependence of leakage with channel length and threshold voltage variations that produce a higher leakage with respect $NI_\mu$. This fact is mainly due to the exponential dependence of leakage with threshold voltage that leads to an asymmetry in the current PDF towards high leakage values as illustrated in Fig. 1.

The standard deviation may also be computed analytically using the previous procedure obtaining:

$$\sigma_I^2 = \big\rangle(I - I_\mu)^2\big\langle = \big\rangle I^2\big\langle - 2\big\rangle I\big\langle I_\mu + I_\mu^2 \approx I_\mu^2\left[e^{2(\sigma_L/\lambda)^2}\left(1+\frac{4\sigma_L^2}{\lambda L_\mu}\right)e^{2(\sigma'_{V_{TH}}/nV_T)^2} - \right.$$

$$\left. -2e^{\frac{(\sigma_L/\lambda)^2}{2}}\left(1+\frac{\sigma_L^2}{\lambda L_\mu}\right)e^{\frac{(\sigma'_{V_{TH}}/nV_T)^2}{2}}+1\right] \tag{10}$$

Eq. (10) provide an idea about the dispersion in leakage current distribution.

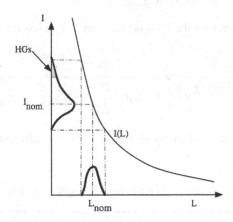

**Fig. 1.** Current and channel length PDF functions relationship. Hot gates are defined as those with higher current value.

## 4  Hot Gates Characterization

As shown in Fig.1, the leakage current PDF presents a deformation with respect to a normal distribution that results in an increased mean leakage current with respect the nominal current $I_\mu$, as is expressed in (9). Moreover, the leakage distribution is also highly influenced by process variations, as is shown by the previously developed expression (10) This deformation of the current PDF toward high currents implies an undesirable effect consisting in the existence of a small number of gates driving a high leakage current. These gates are defined as *Hot Gates* (HGs). In this section we present a study of the expected current driven by these gates to investigate their possible negative effects in high volume ICs.

We consider only channel length variations (with a greater influence on leakage with respect to $N_{SUB}$ variations [5]). We define the group of "Hot Gates" composed by the $N_{HGs}$ gates giving the higher leakage (with $N_{HGs} \ll N$). It may happen that HGs lie in physical clusters within the circuit due to possible spatial correlations of channel length variations. For an IC having N gates it is possible to estimate the channel length of the HGs devices (defined as $L-\kappa\sigma_L$). For the estimation of $\kappa$ we state that:

$$N \int_0^{L-\kappa\sigma_L} f(L)dL = N_{HGs} \tag{11}$$

From (11) we have that $\kappa$ is obtained from the solution of the next equation:

$$\frac{N}{2}\left[1 - erf\left(\frac{\kappa}{\sqrt{2}}\right)\right] = N_{HGs} \tag{12}$$

Unfortunately we cannot provide an exact solution for $\kappa$. For the special case of $N_{HGs}$ being equal to $10^2$, a good approximation for $\kappa$ is obtained with the next expression:

$$\kappa \approx 0.51 \log_{10}(N) + 0.63 \tag{13}$$

The total current driven by the HGs is therefore computed as:

$$I_{HTs} \approx I_\mu \frac{e^{\frac{k\sigma_L}{\lambda}}}{\left(1 - k\sigma_L/L_\mu\right)} = \frac{I_\mu N^{0.223\frac{\sigma_L}{\lambda}} e^{+0.63\frac{\sigma_L}{\lambda}}}{1 - 0.63\frac{\sigma_L}{L_\mu} - 0.51\frac{\sigma_L}{L_\mu}\log_{10}(N)} \tag{14}$$

We compute the current driven by HGs using (14) for different values of $\sigma_L$ and N. Those values are shown in Table 1.

Table 1. $I_{HS}/I_\mu$ dependence on channel length dispersion ($N_{HGs} = 10^2$)

| 0.13μm Tech. | $N=10^6$ | $N=10^7$ | $N=10^8$ |
|---|---|---|---|
| $\sigma_L = 0.005\mu m$ | 3.6 | 4.3 | 5.2 |
| $\sigma_L = 0.01\mu m$ | 13.5 | 20 | 28 |

For the 0.13μm technology that we use, $\sigma_L$ may be fixed to 0.005μm. For a one million gates IC, HGs alone would dissipate 3.6 times the static power dissipated by nominal gates. Therefore HGs do not represent a reliability problem for this technology. Although this, for scaled technologies the threshold voltage variation $\sigma(V_{TH})$ is expected to increase inversely proportional to the square root of the channel length, following the next expression [6]:

$$\sigma(V_{TH}) = \frac{A}{\sqrt{\omega L}} \tag{15}$$

where $\sigma(V_{TH})$ refers to the standard deviation of threshold voltage taking into account all parameter variation contributors (channel length, substrate doping, gate oxide thickness, etc). Parameter $\omega$ is the transistor's channel width and A is a technology-dependent parameter. From(3), and considering only channel length variations, we can relate $\sigma_L$ and $\sigma(V_{TH})$:

$$\sigma_L = \sigma(V_{TH})\frac{\lambda}{nV_T} \qquad (16)$$

Inserting the channel length dependence of $\sigma_L$ (16) in the $I_{HGs}$ expression (14) we can check the variation of $I_{HGs}/I_\mu$ with respect to the channel length.

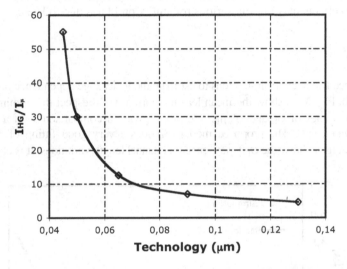

**Fig. 2.** Static power dissipation increment of Hot Gates with technology scaling

In Fig. 2 we show the HGs static power relationship to the nominal static power $I_\mu$ for an IC containing $10^7$ gates. Leakage current increment due to the self-heating of HGs (static power increases exponentially with temperature) is not taken into account in Fig. 2, and therefore represents a best case estimate of leakage increase with respect to nominal gates. We appreciate that the static power dissipated by HGs become critical for sub-50nm technologies, where the HGs contribution will be more than 50 X the nominal value $I_\mu$(that also increases with technology scaling following expression(2)). This has a direct impact on HGs operating temperature and circuit reliability since HGs are dissipating more power than the expected from the technology ($I_\mu$). A first-order approximation of HGs operating temperature with respect to nominal gates temperature (the majority of gates in the IC) for bulk technologies is done using the next expression: [7]:

$$T_i \approx T_{op} + 3.74\frac{P_i}{\sqrt{A_i}} \qquad (17)$$

where $T_i$ is the temperature of the circuit block containing the HGs, occupying a silicon area $A_i$ and dissipating a power $P_i$. Parameter $T_{op}$ is the temperature of operation of the whole IC that depends on the IC thermal resistance and the IC total power. Setting $I_\mu \approx 10^{-8}$A, $V_{DD}$=1.2V, and $A_i \approx 500\mu m^2$, we can estimate $T_i$ from (17) as being 2°C over the temperature of operation $T_{op}$. For a sub-50nm technology, the HG operating temperature can be more than one order of magnitude higher than the power dissipated by nominal devices. Taking from Fig. 2 a value of $I_{HGs}/I_\mu$=50 we get a temperature increment of $\Delta T_{HGs}$=100°C over the mean IC operating temperature. This high operating temperature value for HGs has a direct impact on circuit reliability. HGs may cause circuit malfunction due to increased gate delays [8], increase the voltage IR drop nearby the HGs area, or even cause thermal runaway of the whole circuit. Therefore, near future high density ICs with an expected increment of parameter variation effects may present serious reliability problems due to HGs.

## 5  Results

We performed Montecarlo simulations to estimate the IC leakage dependence on parameter variations. In Fig. 3 we show the mean leakage current with respect the nominal ($I_{mean}/I_\mu$) for different values of $\sigma_L$ and $\sigma'_{VTH}$. We also provide a comparison with a previously developed model [3]. The proposed model provides a very good fitting of Montecarlo simulations. Fig. 4 shows the $\sigma_I$ dependence on channel length variations. It is observed that

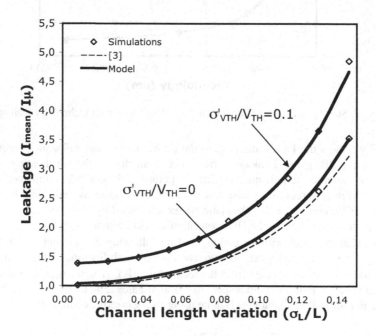

**Fig. 3.** Total leakage dependence with channel length variation

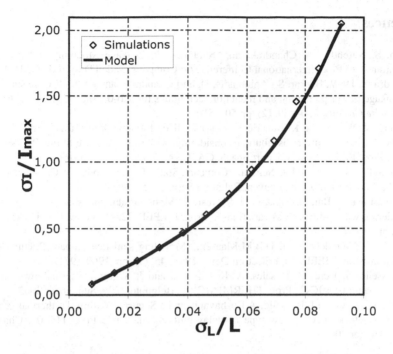

**Fig. 4.** Leakage current dispersion dependence with channel length dispersion

small channel length variations lead to high leakage variations. Again, the proposed model provides very good approximation with respect to the Montecarlo simulations.

## 6 Conclusion

We exposed a detailed study of leakage characterization of deep-submicron CMOS ICs taking into consideration channel length variation effects. An accurate model for the estimation of total static power is presented and evaluated. It is shown that parameter variations increase static power considerably and cannot be neglected when estimating total power. We also introduced a new IC reliability weakness that comes from the hottest gates present in the circuit (the so called *Hot Gates*). The power dissipated in HGs is estimated and compared to the nominal leakage value. Although HGs does not represent a problem for current technologies, they can represent a serious problem for next technology generations due to the high operating temperature achieved by these gates.

## Acknowledgment

This work has been partially supported by the Spanish Ministry of Science and Technology, the Regional European Development Funds (FEDER) from EU project TEC2005-05712/MIC.

# References

1. J. Jao, S. Narendra, A. Chandrakasan, "Subthreshold Leakage Modeling and Reduction Techniques" In Proc. International Conference on Computer-Aided Design (ICCAD'02).
2. Narendra, S, De,V, Borkar, S., Antoniadis, D, and Chandrakasan, A.: "Full-Chip subthreshold leakage power prediction and reduction techniques for sub-0.18mm CMOS", *IEEE J. of Solid-State Circuits*, 2004, 39, (2), pp.501-510
3. S.Zhang, V. Wason and K. Banerjee, "A probabilistic framework to estimate full-chip subthreshold leakage power distribution considering within-die and die-to-die P-T-V variations", Proc. ISLPED'04, Newport Beach, CA, USA, August 2004, pp. 156-161
4. J.L.Rosselló, S. Bota and J. Segura, "Compact Static Power Model of Complex CMOS Gates", Proc. PATMOS'05, Leuven, Belgium, Sept. 2005.
5. A. Srivastava, R. Bai, D. Blaauw, D. Sylvester, "Modeling and analysis of leakage power considering within-die process variations", Proc. ISLPED'02, Monterey, CA, USA, August 2002, pp. 64-67.
6. P. Stolk, F.P.Widdershoven, D.B.M.Klaasen, "Modeling statistical dopant fluctuations in MOS transistors", IEEE T. on Electron Dev., 1998, 45, (9), pp. 1960-1971.
7. J.L.Rosselló, S. Bota, M. Rosales, A. Keshavarzi, and J. Segura, "Thermal-aware design rules for nanometer ICs", Proc. THERMINIC'05, Belgirate, Italy, September 2005.
8. S.Bota, M.Rosales, J.L.Rosselló, A.Keshavarzi and J.Segura, "Within die thermal gradient impact on clock skew: a new type of delay-fault mechanism", Proc. ITC'04, Charlotte, USA, October 2004.

# Heuristic for Two-Level Cache Hierarchy Exploration Considering Energy Consumption and Performance

Silva-Filho, A.G.[1], Cordeiro, F.R.[1], Sant'Anna, R.E.[2], and Lima, M.E.[2]

[1] University of Pernambuco (UPE), Department of Computational Systems
Phone: (+55) 8134456015, Recife-PE, Brazil
{abel, frc}@dsc.upe.br
[2] Federal University of Pernambuco (UFPE) - Informatics Center
Phone: (+55) 8121268430, Recife-PE, Brazil
{res, mel}@cin.ufpe.br

**Abstract.** In this work is presented an automated method for adjusting two-level cache memory hierarchy in order to reduce energy consumption in embedded applications. The proposed heuristic, TECH-CYCLES (*Two-level Cache Exploration Heuristic considering* CYCLES), consists of making a small search in the space of configurations of the two-level cache hierarchy, analyzing the impact of each parameter in terms of energy and number of cycles spent for a given application. Experiments show an average reduction of about 41% in the energy consumption by using our heuristic when compared with the existing heuristic (TCaT), also for two-level caches. Besides the energy improvement, this method also reduces the number of cycles needed to execute a given application by about 25%. In order to validate the proposed heuristic, twelve benchmarks from the MiBench suite have been used.

## 1 Introduction

Currently, the energy consumed by microprocessor memory hierarchy can reach up to 50% of the total energy spent by the microprocessor [1][2]. This fact has driven many researchers and processor designers to analyze and to understand the relation between the various configurations and structures of memory and the involved energy consumption. Thus, many efforts have been made in order to find optimizations to reduce the consumption of energy. Adjusting cache parameters to the needs of a particular application can be a good solution to save energy.

No given cache configuration would be perfect for all applications, seeing as every application has different cache requirements. Thus, finding the best cache configuration for a particular application could save energy and time. However, it is not so easy, and exploring all possible cache configurations would not be a viable solution, due to the length of time involved.

For instance, if we consider only variations in the parameters in a one level cache such as: total cache size, line size, and associativity, the exploration space of dozens of configurations [3] will be need in order to find out the best one for a given application. In hierarchies that include a second level of cache, where both levels have separated

J. Vounckx, N. Azemard, and P. Maurine (Eds.): PATMOS 2006, LNCS 4148, pp. 75–83, 2006.

instruction and data caches, few hundreds of configurations [4] have to be tested. Also, for hierarchies that have a unified second-level cache (instructions and data), this number can reach thousands of configurations, owing to the interdependence between data and instructions in the second level [5].

Otherwise, the use of heuristics, associated with an environment capable of analyzing the behavior of the architecture can yield results that reduce the application exploration space. This is possible because of the highly predictable nature of cache and application behaviors. Caches are designed to exploit the temporal and spatial locality of applications and good heuristics can use this behavior to converge on an optimal cache configuration quickly.

Several heuristics have been developed based on cache parameters, aiming for reduction of the application's energy consumption. Zhang's heuristic [3] that is used for one-level-only hierarchies, manages to save about 40% of energy. Now considering the inclusion of a second level of cache where both levels have a separate instruction cache and data cache, the heuristic proposed by Ann Gordon (TCaT), based on Zhang's heuristic, succeeds in saving about 53% of energy [4].

In this work, a heuristic for adjusting two-level memory hierarchy called TECH-CYCLES (*Two-level Cache Exploration Heuristic considering* CYCLES) is proposed. This approach, different from most heuristics, doesn't worry only about the reduction in the energy consumption. It also tries to connect the architecture exploration with the number of cycles necessary to execute a given application. Twelve benchmarks from MiBench suite have been used to validate the proposed heuristic. The results have been compared with the TCaT heuristic, proving satisfactory. In the next section, we discuss some recent related work.

## 2  Related Work

Adjusting the parameters of an application's cache memory can save on average 60% of energy consumption [3]. By tuning these parameters, the cache can be customized to a particular application. However, no single cache configuration would be perfect for all applications. Thus, strategies to explore the cache parameters may be applied in order to customize the cache structure to a given application.

Some methods apply exhaustive search to find optimal cache configurations, however, the time required for an exhaustive search is often prohibitive. Platune [6] is an example of framework for adjusting configurable System-on-Chip (SoC) platforms that utilizes this exhaustive search method for one-level-only caches. It becomes suitable only in some cases when there are a small number of possible configurations. But for a large design space, a long exploration time may be necessary. For instance, considering a design space of $10^{14}$ configurations, it can take from one to three days to find the best option. Certainly, for the case above, a method based on an exploration heuristic could be more adequate.

Palesi et al. [7] reduces the possible configuration space by using a genetic algorithm and produces results quicker than Platune heuristics.

On the other hand, the heuristic developed by Zhang et al. [3] is based on the importance of the cache parameters (cache size, line size and associativity). In this method, a single level cache approach, two of the three cache parameters are fixed.

The third parameter is changed and each new configuration is analyzed in terms of miss rates and energy consumption. The three parameters are examined, generating a resultant set of possible configurations that aim for reduction in energy consumption for a given application. Since this heuristic is intended for one-level-only caches, Gordon-Ross [4] observed that for two-level caches the results were not so good. Based on these analyses Gordon-Ross extended her "initial heuristic", producing the TCaT heuristic [4]. The use of TCaT heuristic allows energy savings of 53% when compared with Zhang heuristic.

Preliminary results from TECH heuristic, also for two-level caches, proposed in [8][9] demonstrated that the order of exploration of the cache parameters can have a considerable impact in the determining of the cache configuration that better adapts to a given application in terms of decreasing the energy consumption.

A new heuristic for two-level caches called TECH-CYCLES is proposed, based on detailed studies performed over TCaT and TECH heuristics. This heuristic presents a new exploration approach that, different from previous ones, considers reducing the total number of cycles necessary to execute a given application and also the hierarchical cache energy consumption. This heuristic is discussed in detail in the next sections.

To the best of our knowledge, no previous work has explored and adjusted the whole cache using as an exploration criteria to reduce energy consumption and the number of cycles spent to execute a given application.

## 3 Experimental Environment

The proposed heuristic in this work is not based on the exhaustive exploration approach, but it was essential to better validate the heuristic. All benchmarks had been simulated into SimpleScalar [12] for each cache configuration to determine the numbers of misses, hits and accesses of the cache.

Twelve benchmarks from MiBench [10] benchmark suite, a free benchmark suite commercially representative for embedded applications, have been used.

The energy consumption of the hierarchy was determined using the eCACTI cache memory model [11], that models two energy components: static and dynamic. A few years ago only the energy dynamic component was needed to be modeled on the simulation tools. Nowadays, the exponential growth of the static component for recent technologies has changed the scenario. The static component now represents up to 30% of the energy in CMOS circuits [14].

The eCACTI is a recent cache memory model that was extended from the CACTI model [13], which doesn't consider the static component of energy. In the CACTI tool the transistor widths of various devices are assumed to be constant (except for *wordlines*) in the analyses for delay and power. However, nowadays, this assumption is incorrect [11] because the transistor widths in actual cache designs change according to their capacitive load. Another important point is the read/write control logic that is not modeled in CACTI model. These limitations lead to significant inaccuracies in the CACTI power estimates.

In this work, we considered the following space of exploration: from 2 Kb to 8 Kb for first level cache size, from 16k to 64k bytes for second level cache size, from 8 to 32 bytes for the cache line size of both cache levels, and 1 to 4 for associativity for both levels of the cache. Preliminary studies with respect to the heuristic exploration view have been done and are discussed in next section.

## 4 Preliminary Studies

The target architecture for the proposed TECH-CYCLES (*Two-level* Cache *Exploration Heuristic considering* CYCLES) heuristic considers two levels of cache, both levels having a separate instruction and data caches. The adjustable parameters consist of the cache size, cache line size and cache associativity. The target architecture for the proposed heuristic in this work considers all the possible configurations for the simulation environment, being limited only by the inclusion properties of multilevel cache hierarchies.

This heuristic was based on another approach, the TCaT, developed by Ann Gordon-Ross [4], applied for two-level caches. The TCaT heuristic adopts the following strategy: initially the cache parameters are minimal, after that it explores the size of the cache of the first level and then of the second level, followed by the exploration of the size of the line of cache of the first level and then second, after which it explores similarly both levels associativity. This procedure is done first for instruction caches and afterwards the procedure is repeated for data caches.

In-depth studies related to the mechanism of execution of the proposed heuristic TECH-CYCLES, have been conducted aiming not only at a better usage in terms of energy consumption, but also in the application performance. The essential factor was the inclusion in our studies of the number of cycles spent to execute an application.

Figure 1 shows the exploration space approach proposed by the heuristic. Now, not only with the energy consumption of the application, but also with the number of cycles necessary to execute the application are taking into account. For example, we assume that the exploration starts on point P ($C_P$, $E_P$) with energy $E_P$ and it executes the application with $C_P$ cycles. This approach allows us only to choose candidates who have energy lower than $E_P$ and that execute the application in fewer cycles (for example, points A, B or D). Both conditions must be satisfied for each new point chosen during heuristic execution. If a given cache configuration is analyzed, and its energy or number of cycles values are higher than previous cache configuration, then these configuration must be discarded (for example, points F, G and H). Note that, despite the fact that points to the right side of the graph have lower energy values (for example, point F and G), the proposed heuristic discards these samples. Once chosen a candidate, for instance the point A, the next candidate must have lower energy and lower number of cycles than previous candidate. It is done for each new candidate and the heuristic finish when all parameters are explored. This approach can provide points closer to the *Pareto-optimal*.

The TECH-CYCLES heuristic has been tested in this vision of space exploration considering twelve benchmarks of the MiBench benchmark suite [10]. The results we got have been encourage.

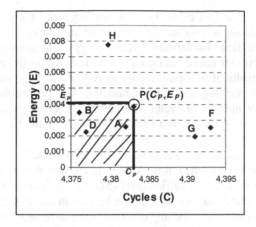

**Fig. 1.** TECH-CYCLES view

# 5  TECH-CYCLES Heuristic

The proposed heuristic, TECH-CYCLES (*Two-level Cache Exploration Heuristic considering* CYCLES), allows two-level-cache exploration, both levels having separate instruction and data caches. The proposed heuristic selects the cache parameters (cache size, cache line size and associativity) in a specific order based on its impact on energy consumption and in the total number of cycles necessary to execute the application. This heuristic also explores a parameter for both levels of the cache before exploring the next. The exploration is performed from the second level to the first level.

The cache architecture exploration flow can be showed in figure 2. Initially the designer considers an interval of parameters (S2: level two cache size, S1: level one cache size, L2: level two cache line size, L1: level one cache line size, A2: level two cache associativity and A1: level one cache associativity) with minimum and maximum values (MIN, MAX) within the configuration space, for all parameters. This heuristic considers that all the parameters are initialized with minimum values, except S2 with maximum value. In this manner the initial vector of parameters is defined.

The six-position vector shown in the exploration flow diagram indicates the current value of each parameter. The parameters of the vector are selected from the left to the right. The parameters initialized with MIN values vary from MIN to MAX and increase by powers of 2 within this interval. The parameters initialized with MAX values vary from MAX to MIN decreasing by powers of 2. The order is important to guarantee the correct use of the heuristic. While a parameter varies, all the others remain fixed. The heuristic is initially applied to instruction caches and after for data caches.

Initially, as depicted in figure 2, the *CurrConf* vector that contains the values of the current parameters of caches during the exploration of the architecture receives the initial parameter vector {S2,S1,L2,L1,A2,A1}. The best cache size is obtained for the two-level cache by varying its size (S2) decreasingly. That is made varying only the cache sizes of the second level, from a maximum (MAX) to a minimum (MIN) value. Before each simulation, the cache hierarchy is tested if it is a valid configuration. After, by using the SimpleScalar and eCACTI tools, the amount of energy spent and the number of cycles necessary to execute the application are found.

In case that it is the first simulation or, if the energy consumption and number of cycles values of the current cache configuration be lesser than the previous one configuration, then the results of this analysis are stored ($E_{MIN}$, $C_{MIN}$ and BestConf). The heuristic continues by varying the same parameter. The procedure stops when the energy consumption or number of cycles of a new cache configuration is bigger than a previous configuration. Then, the last sample is discarded and the next parameter is taken for analysis.

Once found the best cache configuration for the second cache level (*lesser energy consumption and number of cycles*), this value is fixed, and the exploration continues varying increasingly the cache size of first level (S1) until to find the best configuration. This configuration is found varying only the cache size of the first level from a minimum value to a maximum value. The stop criterion is the same as in the second level.

At this point, the first and second cache sizes are fixed. Now, in a second stage, the heuristic increases the cache line size of the second level (L2) initially, until find a new configuration with energy consumption or number of cycles inferior to previous configuration. The same procedure is carried out with cache of first level (L1).

Finally, the same procedure is carried out with cache associativity, for the two cache levels (A2 and A1 respectively). The heuristic finish when all parameters are explored.

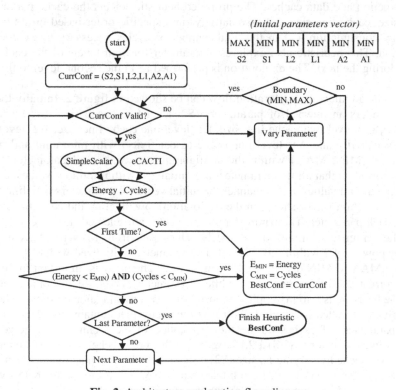

**Fig. 2.** Architecture exploration flow diagram

# 6 Case Study

In this case study, the TECH-CYCLES heuristic is applied for twelve benchmarks of the MiBench benchmark suite [10]. A MIPS architecture based on two-level memory hierarchy structure has been used (the instruction and data caches being separate for both levels). An input voltage of 1.7V is considered, with write-through writing method and transistor technology 0.08µm.

We applied the proposed heuristic using the experimental environment mentioned in section 3. We compare our results with the work [4] that used a similar exploration environment. All benchmarks were simulated using both heuristics (TCaT and TECH-CYCLES) in order to validate the proposed heuristic.

An analysis for twelve benchmarks in terms of percentage of energy reduction was performed. We got in average, a reduction in terms of energy of approximately 41% for cache of instructions in relation to the TCaT heuristic. The number of cycles spent in average is reduced around 25% when the same comparison is made. For all benchmarks analyzed, we had a reduction of energy and in some cases it exceeded 85%, as shown in figure 3 (*basicmath_small, patricia_small and patricia_large*).

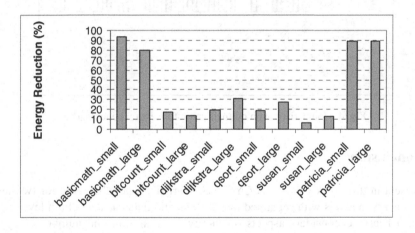

**Fig. 3.** Percentage of energy reduction compared to the TCaT

We also evaluated the impact of the number of configurations necessary to conclude the execution of the heuristic. We note that it had an average increase of 9% if compared with the TCaT heuristic. But when compared with the space of 458 configurations, it represents a percentile increase of 0.3%. A total of 4.4 hours was spent to simulate all *benchmarks* with the proposed heuristic, what makes it an attractive solution when compared to the 210 hours that would be necessary to simulate an exhaustive search on a Pentium IV machine.

The same analyses have also been made for data caches. The results received have not been as good in caches of instruction, getting an average reduction of energy of approximately 1% and an average reduction of cycles of 9%. The average number of configurations necessary for the execution of the heuristic remained the same.

In order to show the effectiveness of our cache tuning heuristic in reducing energy, we compare our results for instruction caches with optimal results. In order to normalize the data for comparison purposes, we have chosen a **base cache** hierarchy configuration defined by the 8 kByte, 4-way set associative level one cache with a 64 Byte line size, and a 64 kByte 4-way set associative level two cache with a 64 Byte line size – a reasonably common configuration. Five out of twelve analyzed benchmarks (*basicmath_small, bitcount_small, bitcount_large, susan_large and patricia_small*) reached the lowest energy consumption results for instruction caches as showed in Figure 4.

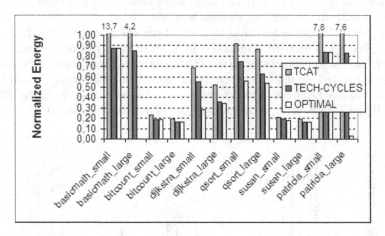

**Fig. 4.** Comparison with optimal value for several benchmarks

## 7 Conclusions

We present in this work the TECH-CYCLES heuristic, a new heuristic for two-level caches energy analysis with separated instructions and data caches in both levels. The proposed heuristic considers aspects of energy consumption and number of cycles used to execute an application. A total of twelve benchmarks have been used to analyze it and compare it with the TCaT heuristic in terms of energy consumption and application performance. An average reduction for instructions cache of 41% in energy use and 25% in the amount of cycles has been observed in relation to the TCaT heuristic. For data caches, the results have not been as satisfactory. However, we believe that minor variations in the heuristic mechanism can contribute to an improvement in the data cache efficiency. Considering the whole space of configurations, we also verified that it had an increase of 0.3% in the average number of configurations that are necessary for complete execution of the proposed heuristic when compared with the TCaT.

Five out of twelve analyzed benchmarks reached optimal energy values. Thus, we can conclude that the proposed heuristic can be a good option for instruction cache architecture exploration. New studies are being conducted with the objective of improving the efficiency of this heuristic for the data cache. Future works also include the creation of a framework based on SystemC in which the automatic mechanism of the proposed heuristic will be added.

## Acknowledgment

Our thanks to CNPq for supporting this work (142171/2003-4).

## Bibliography

1. Chang, H.; Code, L.; Hunt, M., Martin, G., McNelly, A.J. and Todd, L., "Surviving the SOC revolution: A guide to platform-based design"; Kluwer Academic Publishers, 1 ed., 1999.
2. Malik, B. Moyer and D. Cermak, "A Low Power Unified Cache Architecture Providing Power and Performance Flexibility", Int Symp. On Low Power Electronics and Design, June 2000, pp. 241-243.
3. Zhang, D., Vahid, F., Cache configuration exploration on prototyping platforms. 14th IEEE Interational Workshop on Rapid System Prototyping (June 2003), vol 00, p.164.
4. Gordon-Ross, Ann, Vahid, F., Dutt, Nikil, Automatic Tuning of Two-Level Caches to Embedded Aplications, DATE, pp.208-213 (Feb 2004).
5. Gordon-Ross, Ann, Vahid, F., Dutt, Nikil, Fast Configurable-Cache Tuning with a Unified Second-Level Cache, ISLPED05, (Aug 2005).
6. Givargis, T.; Vahid, F.; "Platune: A Tuning framework for system-on-a-chip platforms", IEEE Trans. Computer-Aided Design, vol 21, nov. 2002. pp.1-11.
7. Palesi, M., Givargis, T. Multi-objective design space exploration using genetic algorithms. Internacional Wordshop on Hardware/Software Codesign (May 2002).
8. Silva-Filho, A.G.; Lima, M.E.; A Heuristic for Energy Consumption Exploration Based on Two-Level Cache Hierarchy, Forum SoC2005, (dez 2005).
9. Silva-Filho, A.G.; Lima, M.E.; Nascimento, P.S.B.; Eskinazi, R.; An Energy-Aware Exploration Approach Based on Open Software Enviroment, IESS 2005, jul 2005, pp. 97-102.
10. Guttaus, M. R.; Ringenberg, J.S.; Ernst, D.; Austin, T.M.; Mudge, T.; Brown, R.B.; Mibench: A free, commercially representative embedded benchmark suite. In IEEE 4th Annual Workshop on Workload Characterization, pp.1-12, December 2001.
11. Dutt, Nikil; Mamidipaka, Mahesh; "eCACTI: An Enhanced Power Estimation Model for On-chip Caches", TR 04-28; set. 2004.
12. Burger, D.; Austin, T.M.; "The SimpleScalar Tool Set, Version 2.0"; Computer Architecture News; Vol 25(3), pp.13-25; June 1997.
13. Shivakumar, P.; Jouppi, N.P.;"Cacti 3.0: An Integrated Cache Timing, Power and Area model", WRL Research Report 2001/2.
14. Macii, E.; Benini, L.; Poncino, M.; "Energy-Aware Design of Embedded Memories: A Survey of Technologies, Architectures and Optimization Techniques", *ACM Transactions on Embedded Computing Systems*; Vol. 2, No. 1, February 2003, pp. 5-32.

# System Level Multi-bank Main Memory Configuration for Energy Reduction

Hanene Ben Fradj, Cécile Belleudy, and Michel Auguin

Laboratoire d'Informatique, Signaux et Systèmes de Sophia-Antipolis, Les Algorithme-bat.
Euclide 2000, route des Lucioles-BP 121, 06903 Sophia-Antipolis Cedex. France
{benfradj, belleudy, auguin}@i3s.unice.fr

**Abstract.** The main memory is one of the most energy-consuming components in several embedded system. In order to minimize this memory consumption, an architectural solution is recently adopted. It consists of multi-banking the addressing space instead of monolithic memory. The main advantage in this approach is the capability of setting individually banks in low power modes when they are not accessed, such that only the accessed bank is maintained in active mode. In this paper we investigate how this power management capability built into modern DRAM devices can be handled for real-time and multitasking applications. We aim to find, at system level design, both an efficient allocation of application's tasks to memory banks, and the memory configuration that lessen the energy consumption: number of banks and the size of each bank. Results show the effectiveness of this approach and the large energy savings.

## 1 Introduction and Related Work

According to ITRS prevision, embedded memory will continue to dominate SoC content in the next several years, approaching 94% of the die area by year 2014 [1]. This trend makes the power consumption of memories increases tremendously. The main memory is consuming an increasing proportion of this power budget and thus motivates efforts to improve DRAM energy efficiency. On the other hand, memories with multiple banks instead of a monolithic module appeared in several architectures to improve performance (bandwidth, density...). Recently, this kind of memory architecture was exploited to reduce energy dissipation by operating banks at different modes (Active, Standby, Nap, Power-Down...) for example RAMBUS-DRAM technology (RDRAM) [8], Mobile-RAM of Infineon (SDRAM) [9]. To service a memory request (read or write), a bank must be in active mode which consumes most of the power. When a bank is inactive, it can be put in any low power mode (Standby, Nap, Power-Down). Each mode is characterized by its power consumption and the time that takes to transit back to the active mode (resynchronization time). The lower the energy consumption of the low power mode is, the higher the resynchronization time is (see table 1 [8]). Several techniques, which exploit the low power modes of memories, were recently published. Those works can be classified in two categories. The first one tries to determine when to power down and into which low power mode it's possible to transit the memory banks. These memory controllers policies are either

J. Vounckx, N. Azemard, and P. Maurine (Eds.): PATMOS 2006, LNCS 4148, pp. 84–94, 2006.

hardware [6] or software [7] oriented. The second category focuses on data allocation (dynamically or passively) to memory banks to minimize energy. The paper [10] studied the impact of loop transformations (loop fission, loop splitting) on banked memory architecture; [4] proposed an automatic data migration to reduce energy consumption in multiple memory banks by exploiting the temporal affinity among data. Authors in [2] proposed an integer linear programming (ILP) based approach that returns the optimal non uniform bank sizes and the mapping of data to banks.

Our work is classified in the second category as we consider only one low power mode at once. We address the energy optimization in multi-bank memory architecture but unlike the previous quoted works, we choose to operate at the task system level of the co-design steps. In this level we can achieve larger energy savings. So the considered data granularity is the combined task's data and code. We noted that results in previous researches like [2,4,7,10] can be added to our approach by optimizing the data and code allocation of each task. The focus of this paper is to find the optimal allocation of tasks to banks based on several parameters: task size, number of times the task was executed during the hyperperiod ($N_{exeTi}$), number of main memory accesses, number of preemptions between tasks...) and the corresponding memory configuration that lessens the memory energy consumption (optimal number of banks and optimal size of each bank). The paper is structured as follow: section 2 presents the memory architecture and system model. In section 3 an estimation of multi-banked main memory consumption is presented. In section 4 we focus on searching the low power tasks allocation to banks and the associated memory configuration (number of banks and banks size). Section 5 shows experiments and results obtained with our approach. We close the paper in section 6 with concluding remarks and future works.

**Table 1.** Energy consumption (per cycle) and resynchronization times for different operating modes for 8 MB RDRAM bank size

| Operating modes | Energy consumption (nJ) | Resynchronization cost (cycles) |
| --- | --- | --- |
| Active | 3.57 | 0 |
| Standby | 0.83 | 2 |
| Nap | 0.32 | 30 |
| Power-Down | 0.005 | 9,000 |

## 2  Memory Architecture and System Model

For the architecture model, we consider multi-bank main memory architecture. Each bank can be controlled independently and placed into one of the available low power modes. Each low power mode is characterized by the number of components being disabled to save energy. This multi-bank main memory communicates with an embedded processor through a L1 SRAM cache (figure1).

We consider real-time and multitasking embedded application. This application is described by a set of N periodic tasks; each task is characterized by temporal parameters namely ($P_i$: period, $wcet_i$: worst case execution time), $M_i$: number of memory accesses and $S_{Ti}$: the task size (code and data). These tasks are scheduled according to the fixed priority and preemptive Rate Monotonic (RM) algorithm as shown in figure 2 for a task set described in table 2.

We define an allocation function noted φ; that associates each task $T_i$ belonging to a set of N tasks to a bank $b_j$ belonging to a set of k banks.

$$\varphi: \{T_1,T_2,...T_N\} \rightarrow \{b_1,b_2,...b_k\}$$
$$\varphi(T_i) = b_j$$

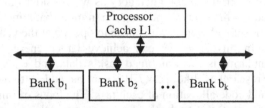

**Fig. 1.** Multi-bank main memory architecture

**Table 2.** Example of 3 task set

| Task | wcet$_i$ | $P_i$ |
|------|------|-------|
| $T_1$ | 1 | 3 |
| $T_2$ | 1 | 4 |
| $T_3$ | 2 | 6 |

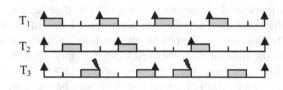

**Fig. 2.** RM schedule of the 3 task set during the hyperperiod

## 3 Energy Estimation and Models

### 3.1 Parameters Influencing Memory Consumption

**Bank size.** The energy consumption monotonically increases with the memory size. The analytical model given in [5] illustrates that the memory energy consumption increases with the number of lines and columns in the memory. For the multi-bank main memory, several papers consider that the energy values given in table 1 (active, low power mode, resynchronisation) increase by $\tau_1$= 30% when bank size is doubled [2, 4]. In our approach, we consider that the size $S_{bj}$ of bank $b_j$ is the sum of the size of all tasks $T_i$ allocated to this bank:

$$S_{bj} = \sum_{T_i / \varphi(T_i)=b_j} S_{T_i}$$

So in the same architecture, the banks can have different sizes (non uniform banks sizes). A mathematic formula was developed that traduces the 30% of increase in memory energies consumption when the bank size is doubled for RDRAM technology. So with equation 1, we can determine the energy values per memory cycle of a bank $b_j$ for a given size of $S_{bj}$.

$$E_\alpha = E_{0\alpha}(1.3)^{Log_2(\frac{S_{bj}}{8})} \qquad (1)$$

$\alpha$ = {active, lp-mode, resynchronization}, $E_{0\alpha}$: The energy values for the 8 MB bank size given in table 1.

**Number of banks and communication.** The multi-bank energy consumption depends also on the number of banks in the memory architecture. When we add a new bank, the sizes of banks decrease (less tasks per bank) as well as the energy values (active, low power mode and resynchronization). However, the energy consumption in the banks connecting increases. We assume that the energy consumption for communication increases by $\tau_2$ = 20% when we add a new bank to the architecture [3]. So for main memory architecture with k banks, the communication energy is described by equation 2.

$$E_{bus} = E_{0bus} (1.2)^{k-1} . \tag{2}$$

$E_{0bus}$: The bus consumption for one bank main memory architecture (monolithic memory). In our approach, $\tau_1$ and $\tau_2$ can be easily adjusted for different technologies.

**Successivity and preemption between tasks.** We call successivity between task $T_i$ and task $T_j$ noted $\sigma_{ij}$ when $T_j$ begins its execution just after the end of $T_i$ or when the higher priority task ($T_i$ or $T_j$) preempts the other one. The successivity parameters are deduced from the application's scheduling during the hyperperiod. They are exploited to minimize the number of resynchronisations of memory banks and making the idle period of banks longer. The resynchronizations number of a bank $b_j$ is computed as follows.

$$N_{resynchronization\_b_j} = \sum_{T_i / \varphi(T_i)=b_j} N_{exeTi} - \sum_{T_i,T_j / (\varphi(T_i),\varphi(T_j))=(b_j,b_j)} \sigma_{ij}$$

Where $N_{exeTi}$ is the number of execution of task $T_i$ in the hyperperiod.

From the RM schedule of figure 2, the successivity between the three tasks are: $\sigma_{12}$= 3, $\sigma_{13}$= 4, $\sigma_{23}$= 3. Considering the tasks allocation given in figure 3, the resynchronizations numbers of each bank are: $N_{resynchronization\_b1}$= $N_{exeT1}$+ $N_{exeT3}$ - $\sigma_{13}$ = 4, $N_{resynchronization\_b2}$ =$N_{exeT2}$ = 3.

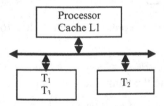

**Fig. 3.** Tasks allocation to 2 memory banks

By exploiting the successivity between tasks we can minimize the resynchronizations numbers of banks and the energy associated. However, reducing the energy of resynchronisation by grouping in the same bank the tasks having the maximum number of successivity, can increase other energy contributions due for example to the increase in the size of the banks. In conclusion, minimizing separately each memory energy contribution cannot usually minimize the total memory consumption because of the strong interdependence between the memory parameters relevant to energy consumption. The problem can be modeled as a problem of allocation of tasks to banks with an objective of energy optimization.

## 3.2 Energy Models for a Multi-bank Memory

The energy consumption of a memory composed of k banks and a given allocation of N tasks to these banks is evaluated with equation 3.

$$E_{memory} = E_{access} + E_{nonaccess} + E_{lpmode} + E_{resynchronization} + E_{preemption} + E_{bus} \tag{3}$$

Unlike [2] we separate the active mode given in table 1 into two different operating modes: the read/write mode (access) and active but idle mode (non-access).

$E_{access}$: the energy due to read or write accesses to the memory banks.

$$E_{access} = \sum_{b_j / j=1}^{k} \left( \sum_{T_i / \varphi(T_i)=b_j} N_{cycles\_access\_T_i} \; E_{0access} \; (1.3)^{Log_2(\frac{S_{b_j}}{8})} \right)$$

$E_{nonaccess}$: the energy consumption when the memory banks are active but not servicing any read or write operation. This energy is essentially due to the co-activation of the memory bank with the task execution by the processor.

$$E_{nonaccess} = \sum_{b_j / j=1}^{k} \left( \sum_{T_i / \varphi(T_i)=b_j} N_{cycles\_nonaccess\_T_i} \; E_{0nonaccess} \; (1.3)^{Log_2(\frac{S_{bj}}{8})} \right)$$

$E_{lpmode}$: the energy consumed by banks when they are in low power mode

$$E_{lp\,mode} = \sum_{b_j / j=1}^{k} N_{cycles\_lp\,mode\_bj} \; E_{0lp\,mode} \; (1.3)^{Log_2(\frac{S_{bj}}{8})}$$

$E_{resynchronization}$: the energy consumption due to the transition of memory banks from a low power mode to the active mode to service a memory request.

$$E_{resynchronization} = \sum_{b_j / j=1}^{k} N_{resynchronization\_bj} \; E_{0resynchronization} \; (1.3)^{Log_2(\frac{S_{bj}}{8})}$$

$E_{preemption}$: the energy induced by context switches due to the preemption between tasks on the processor.

$$E_{preemption} = N_{preemptions} \; E_{context\_switch}$$

$E_{bus}$: the energy consumption in the bank interconnection.

$$E_{bus} = E_{0bus} (1.2)^{k-1}$$

$N_{cycles\_access\_Ti}$ : the number of memory access cycles of task $T_i$ to the memory bank.

$$N_{cycles\_accessTi} = M_i \times t_{accessM} \times f_{memory}$$

$N_{cycles\_nonaccess\_Ti}$ : the number of memory cycles of Task $T_i$ when the memory bank is active but idle.

$$N_{cycle\_nonacessTi} = (wcet_i \times \frac{1}{f_{processor}} - M_i \times t_{accessM}) \times f_{memory}$$

$t_{accessM}$: the memory access time. $f_{memory}$, $f_{processor}$ are respectively memory and processor frequency.

$N_{cycles\_lpmode\_bj}$: the number of memory cycles the bank $b_j$ spent in low power mode.

$N_{resynchronization\_bj}$: the resynchronizations number of bank $b_j$ from low power mode to the active mode.

$N_{preemptions}$: the number of preemptions of tasks in the hyperperiod.

We note that $N_{cycles\_access\_Ti}$, $N_{cycles\_nonaccess\_Ti}$, $N_{preemptions}$ are application related constants, whereas $N_{cycles\_lpmode}$, $N_{resynchronization\_bj}$ are variables depending on the number of banks and the tasks' allocation.

$E_{0access}$, $E_{0nonaccess}$, $E_{0lpmode}$, $E_{0resynchronization}$ are the initial energy values per memory cycle.

$E_{context\_switch}$: the preemption energy due to the context switching.

# 4 Solution Exploration Algorithms

Our aim is to find both; an allocation $\varphi$ of tasks to a multi-bank memory and the number of banks and their respective sizes; so as to minimize the overall energy consumption due to the main memory structure. In this study, only a single low power mode is considered.

## 4.1 Exhaustive Explorations

The strong interdependence of the different parameters influencing memory consumption, as explained in the previous section, makes the problem NP-hard to solve. An exhaustive approach exploring all the configurations space was firstly adopted. This technique allows to find the optimal solution, to compare the energy of all the configurations and to observe the behavior of the memory consumption according to the variations of tasks and system characteristics.

First, the algorithm starts by finding all the banks configurations to arrange N tasks in a k memory bank structure with k = 1 to N. Each configuration is represented by a set of integers; the cardinal of the set (k) represents the number of banks in the memory architecture and the set's elements called tasks_$b_i$ represents the number of tasks in a bank $b_i$.

Considering for example a 4 tasks application, five bank configurations are possible : {4} ; {3, 1} ; {2, 2} ; {2, 1, 1} ; {1, 1, 1, 1}. For a number of banks equals to 2, there are two different configurations for arranging tasks in banks. In the first one {3, 1}: 3 tasks are allocated to the first bank and one task is in the second while in the second configuration {2, 2} two tasks are allocated to each bank.

In a second step, for each configuration, the algorithm enumerates all possible permutations of tasks in banks. For the configuration {3,1}, allocating tasks $T_1$, $T_2$ and $T_3$ in the first bank $b_1$ and task $T_4$ in $b_2$, i.e. {$(T_1,T_2,T_3)$ ; $(T_4)$} does not consume the same energy as if we allocate tasks $T_2$, $T_3$ and $T_4$ in the bank $b_1$ and task $T_1$ in bank $b_2$, i.e. {$(T_2,T_3,T_4)$ ; $(T_1)$}. This is due for example, to the different number of banks resynchronizations or to the different bank sizes. For the 4 tasks application example, there are 15 possibilities for arranging 4 tasks in a number of banks varying from 1 to 4. Once all tasks permutations are exhibited for all bank configurations; the energy consumption of each solution is estimated based on energy models developed in section 3.2. The optimal multi-banked memory configuration and the associated tasks' allocation are then returned. The total number of memory configurations is known as number of Bell ($B_N$), which is the sum of Stirling number of the second kind S (N, k). S(N, k) represents the number of memory configurations of N tasks in k banks.

$$B_N = \sum_{k=1}^{N} S(N,k) \quad and \quad S(N,k) = \frac{1}{k!}\sum_{j=1}^{k}(-1)^{k-j}\binom{k}{j}j^N$$

Some numbers of Bell are presented: $B_4 = 15$; $B_5 = 52$, $B_6 = 203$, $B_7 = 877$, $B_8 = 4140$, $B_9 = 21147$, $B_{10} = 115975 \dots B_{20} = 51724158235372$

## 4.2 Heuristic Approach Overview

Although the exhaustive approach returns the optimal solution, the exploration space increases exponentially with the numbers of tasks. The exhaustive approach becomes impractical exceeding a set of 20 tasks, so employing such approach to take into account for example additional tasks that appear on-line (sporadic tasks for example) is impractical. So we seek to propose an heuristic approach that is able to prune the configuration space, and to efficiently resolve, in polynomial time, the power aware multi-bank main memory configuration and the corresponding tasks allocation.

We use a two steps heuristic approach. Step1 generates an initial memory configuration that will be refined iteratively during step 2.

- Step1 : *initial solution generation*:

- Initially all tasks are allocated to a same initial bank.
- Then we isolate the task that produces the greatest energy reduction, when it is moved to an additional bank. Iteratively, we repeat this process on the remaining tasks. The choice of the task to be isolated in an additional bank is based on a *criteria* computed for each task $T_i$. The *criteria* is determined in such a way that it detects the most consuming task and expresses the energy benefit to isolate a task in a new bank.

$$criteria = N_{exeTi} \times N_{cycles\_acess\_Ti} \times E_{0access} + N_{exeTi} \times N_{cycles\_nonaccess\_Ti} \times E_{0nonaccess}$$

$$+ (N_{exeTi} - \sum_{\substack{j=1/\varphi(Tj)=b_i \\ j \neq i}}^{N} S_{ij}) \times E_{0resynchroi\,zation}$$

- An energy evaluation is done after each generation of a new solution: if a reduction in the memory consumption is detected in the new solution, we keep this memory configuration, update the criteria and re-iterate to isolate another task from the initial bank. Else, we reject the current solution and return to the previous memory configuration solution for an energy refinement with step 2.

- Step 2: *initial solution refinements*: a refinement step of the memory configuration obtained in step 1.

- Firstly banks are sorted by an increasing order of their energy consumption.
- We choose the task having the greater criteria to be allocated to the less consuming bank.

- An energy evaluation is done after each generation of a new solution: If a reduction in the memory consumption is detected in the new solution, we keep this memory configuration and update both the criteria of tasks in the initial bank and the banks consumption. This process is iterated while tasks can be isolated from the initial bank and moved to the less consuming bank. Otherwise we keep the previous memory configuration.

The complexity of the proposed heuristic is $O(N^3)$; a complexity of $N^2$ is detected for the energy evaluation.

## 5  Experiments and Results

In our experiments, we used some real-time benchmarks from [11]; table 3 gives the description of these benchmarks. To estimate the tasks parameters : wcet, size (code and data) and the number of L1 cache misses that represent also the number of main memory accesses ($M_i$); we used the SimpleScalar architectural simulation platform [12]. A 32kB 2-way set associative unified instruction/data cache with 2 cycles latency access time and a RDRAM main memory with 20 cycles latency and the Nap mode as low power mode are simulated.

We've considered two task sets, the first one with seven tasks described in table 4 and the second taken from [13] with four tasks described in table 5.

In our study, we take into account, in addition of the cold and intrinsic misses [14], the extrinsic misses due to multi-task effect. Extrinsic misses occur when blocks of different tasks are on conflict for the same cache line. DLite! debugger of SimpleScalar is used to insert breakpoints in the tasks' schedule at the beginning and at the end of each task's instance and to collect the number of misses between two breakpoints. We've obtained the number of misses of each task's instance in a multi-task execution system as depicted in Figure 4 (the bold numbers represent the number of cache misses).

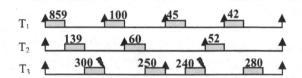

**Fig. 4.** Cache misses for a multi-task system

For each task, the average number of cache misses is used in our energy models. For example, the schedule in the figure 4 shows an average $M_1$ of 262 misses for the task $T_1$.

As first experiment, we plot the variation of the total main memory consumption versus the number of configurations for the task set 1, and versus the number of banks for task set 2 due to the important number of configurations (877). So we present for each number of banks, only the minimal energy consuming configuration. Figure 5 and figure 6 illustrate the energy efficiency of a multi-bank memory architecture compared to a monolithic module (single bank memory). The minimum consumption is obtained for architecture with 2 banks for task set 1 and with 3 banks for task set 2. Compared to the most consuming architecture, the energy savings is about 15% for both examples.

**Table 3.** Benchmarks' description

| Benchmarks | Description |
|---|---|
| CRC | Cyclic Redundancy Check program |
| FIR | FIR filter with Gaussian number generation |
| FFT | Fast Fourier Transform using Cooly-Turkey algorithm |
| LMS | adaptive signal enhancement |
| LUD | LU decomposition algorithm |
| Matmul | Matrix multiplication |
| ADPCM | CCITT G.722 Adaptive Differential Pulse Code Modulation |

**Table 4.** Task set 1

| Tasks | $P_i$ (cycles) | $wcet_i$ (cycles) | $S_{Ti}$ (kB) | $M_i$ |
|---|---|---|---|---|
| CRC | 1000,000 | 42,907 | 31 | 99 |
| Fir | 1000,000 | 33,983 | 152 | 47 |
| FFT | 5000,000 | 515,771 | 97 | 493 |
| LMS | 5000,000 | 365,893 | 32 | 123 |
| LUD | 5000,000 | 255,998 | 38 | 102 |
| Matmul | 1000,000 | 13,985 | 29 | 26 |
| ADPCM | 10000,000 | 2486,633 | 139 | 3387 |

**Table 5.** Task set 2 from [13]

| Tasks | $P_i$ | $wcet_i$ | $S_{Ti}$ (kB) | $M_i$ |
|---|---|---|---|---|
| FFT | 320,000 | 60,234 | 96 | 280 |
| LUD | 1120,000 | 255,998 | 38 | 364 |
| LMS | 1920,000 | 365,893 | 32 | 474 |
| FIR | 6000,000 | 557,589 | 152 | 405 |

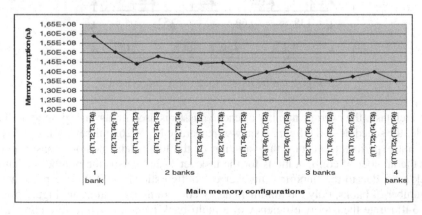

**Fig. 5.** Multi-bank memory consumption for all the memory configurations for task set 2; $T_1$=FFT; $T_2$=LUD; $T_3$=LMS; $T_4$=FIR

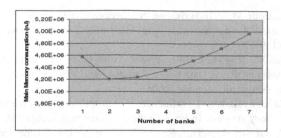

**Fig. 6.** Multi-bank memory consumption for task set 1

**Table 6.** Energy comparison of exhaustive algorithm and the heuristic approach

| | Optimal allocation | | Heuristic solution | | % |
|---|---|---|---|---|---|
| | configurations | Energy (nJ) | configurations | Energy (nJ) | gap |
| Set 1 | {(CRC,FIR,FFT,LUD,Matmul); (ADPCM, LUD)}; | $4.20\ 10^6$ | {(CRC, FIR, FFT, LUD, Matmul, LUD); (ADPCM)} | $4.23\ 10^6$ | 0.8 |
| Set 2 | {FFT; LUD; LMS; FIR} | $1.35\ 10^8$ | {(FFT,FIR);(LUD);(LMS)} | $1.35\ 10^8$ | 0.1 |

Table 6 shows a comparison of results produced by the exhaustive searching method and the heuristic approach for the two task sets. The results show a very weak energy gap compared to the optimal solution.

## 6   Conclusion and Future Works

For the multi-bank memory consumption problem, two approaches were proposed at system level and for real-time applications. An exhaustive algorithm that returns the optimal allocation of tasks to banks (the optimal number of banks and their optimal sizes) was firstly developed. This approach can reduce the memory consumption by up to 15% compared to the most consuming memory configuration. The exponential complexity and the important computational time of the exhaustive approach lead to the development of the heuristic approach. Experiments show the effectiveness of this approach. As the multi-bank memory increases the area especially for embedded DRAM [16], we plan to take into account the trade-off energy/area optimization.

## References

1. SIA: International Roadmap for Semiconductors, 2001.
2. Ozturk O., Kandemir M.: Nonuniform banking for reducing memory energy consumption. DATE'05 Munch, Germany 2005.
3. Benini L., Macci A., Poncino M.: A recursive algorithm for low-power memory partitioning. ISLPED, Rapallo, Italy 2000.
4. Delaluz V., Kandemir M., Kolcu I.: Automatic Data Migration for Reducing Energy Consumption in Multi-Bank Memory Systems. DAC, 2002.
5. Itoh K., Sasaki K., Nakagome Y.: Trends in Low-Power RAM Circuit Technologies. Proc. IEEE, vol. 83, no. 4 (April 1995): 524-543.

6.  Delaluz V., Kandemir M., Vijaykrishnan N., Sivasubramaniam A., Irwin M.J.: DRAM Energy Management Using Software and Hardware Directed Power Mode Control. HPCA, 2001 pp.159-170
7.  Lebeck A. R., Fan X., Zeng H., C. Ellis: Power Aware Page Allocation. ASPLOS, 2000.
8.  128/144 MBit Direct RDRAM Data Sheet, Rambus Inc. 1999.
9.  Mobile-RAM data sheet, infineon Inc, 2004.
10. Kandemir M., Kolcu I., Kadayif I.: Influence of loop optimizations on energy consumption of multi-bank memory systems. In Proc. Compiler Construction, April 2002.
11. Seoul National University Real-Time Research groups. SNU real-time benchmarks.
12. Burger D., Austin T.M.: The SimpleScalar Tool Set, Version 2.0. Univ. of Wisconsin-Madison Computer Sciences Dept. Technical Report #1342, June 1997.
13. Lee C., Lee K., Hahn J., Seo Y., Min S. L., Ha R., Hong S., Park C. Y., Lee M., Kim C.S.: Bounding Cache-Related Preemption Delay for Real-Time Systems. IEEE Transactions on Software Engineering, v.27 n.9, p.805-826, September 2001.
14. Agarwal A., Hennessy J., Horowitz M.: An analytical cache model. ACM Transactions on Computer Systems (TOCS), Vol. 7, Issue 2 (May 1989), pp 184 – 215.
15. Gajski D., Vahid F., Narayan S., Gong J.: Specification and Design of Embedded Systems. Prentice Hall, 1994.
16. Yamauchi T., Hammond L., Olukotun K.: The Hierarchical Multi-Bank DRAM: A High-Performance Architecture for Memory Integrated with Processors. In Advanced Research in VLSI, Ann Arbor, MI, USA, pp. 303--319. 1997.

# SRAM CP: A Charge Recycling Design Schema for SRAM

Ka-Ming Keung and Akhilesh Tyagi

Electrical and Computer Engineering
Iowa State University
Ames, IA 50011
{xskeung, tyagi}@iastate.edu

**Abstract.** An adiabatic charge-pump based charge recycling design was proposed in [1]. It was shown to save upto 15% energy on several DSP systems with no performance loss. In this paper, we illustrate new charge source multiplexing techniques that are especially targeted towards SRAM arrays. The trigger control mechanism for charge sharing, additionally, can be derived from the application level characteristics rather than from circuit level attributes. These two methods help minimize the charge sharing energy dissipation. The SPICE level simulation results show that the proposed scheme reduces energy consumption in L2 caches by 24.9% with no performance loss.

## 1 Introduction

The power consumption has become a critical design parameter in digital VLSI design. The ever-growing embedded consumer device market favors portability, significant computational power, and small physical dimensions. Some examples include 3rd generation phone with walkman and TV, Personal Digital Assistant with Global Positioning Systems. The limited energy supply on the portable computing unit limits its functionalities. The Internaional Technology Roadmap for Semiconductors(ITRS) has identified power dissipation as one of the technology barriers in the future. Low power design could be addressed at multiple abstraction and physical levels in a digital system including materials, algorithms, circuits, and architectures. This paper focuses on the circuit and architecture in the low power VLSI design. Manne & Tyagi [1] proposed a charge recycling scheme which recycles the dirty charges adiabatically with a charge pump. This scheme is applicable to the non-critical modules in a system. With smaller technology nodes, 65 nm to 45nm to 32 nm, the static leakage has become the dominant energy consumption mode. Many device level and high-threshold gating techniques have been proposed to limit the leakage current. This paper is an attempt to explore the utility of charge recycling techniques at leakage energy reduction. SRAM arrays account for a significantly large fraction of chip area in embedded computing systems in order to realize caches or other on-chip memory structures. Consequently, a large fraction of leakage energy of a system is due to SRAM arrays. We explore the integration of charge recycling into

J. Vounckx, N. Azemard, and P. Maurine (Eds.): PATMOS 2006, LNCS 4148, pp. 95–106, 2006.
© Springer-Verlag Berlin Heidelberg 2006

SRAM arrays. This technique seems to be well-suited to SRAM arrays because almost all of the array is idle during a typical computing phase. The spatial and temporal localities within the computation limit the working sets to be a few cache blocks.

We propose a more efficient charge pumping scheme targeted towards SRAM arrays. An architecture for integrating charge recycling into SRAM arrays is developed and presented. Our results show that SRAM with charge-pumps is able to save upto 24.9% energy consumption. The paper is organized as follows. Section 2 revisits the charge-pump design by Manne & Tyagi [1]. Section 3 introduces the new charge pumping scheme. The design of virtual supply rails is explained in Section 4. Section 5 shows the details of SRAM CP (SRAM with charge pump) and Section 8 concludes the paper.

## 2   Revisiting Charge Recycling Schema

Chargepump is commonly used for generating voltage higher than the supply voltage [2,3]. Instead, for low power purpose, Manne [1] proposed a charge pump to recycle the dirty charge. The recycled charge collected on a virtual $V_{DD}$ node then drives other modules with in the system. The delay of charge recycling through a charge pump is overlapped with some other computation. In general, charge recycling is applied to non-critical modules in the system so that the delay of the critical paths is not adversely affected. In Manne's design, three modules are chosen as charge producers/sources which serve to feed virtual ground nodes to collect the dirty charge. One module is chosen as the charge consumer/sink which forms a virtual $V_{DD}$ to supply the recycled charge.

Charge is collected on the virtual grounds over several switching operations. The charge at the virtual ground is transferred to the virtual $V_{DD}$ adiabatically through multiple charge pumping events. Each consecutive charge pumping event induces charge sharing and bootstrapping driven voltage boosting through an intermediate capacitor. Firstly, virtual ground 1 charge is shared with the virtual $V_{DD}$. Then the switch between virtual ground 1 and virtual $V_{DD}$ is closed. The sharing starts between virtual ground 2 and virtual $V_{DD}$. Finally, virtual ground 3 shares charge with virtual $V_{DD}$. Fig.1 shows these steps. After these charge sharing transfers, charge at the virtual $V_{DD}$ is pumped up through bootstrapping. The consumer node would use the virtual $V_{DD}$ instead of the real $V_{DD}$.

The shortcomings of this schema arise from the charge sharing between virtual ground and virtual $V_{DD}$. In this process, $E = N * C * \Delta V^2 = C * V^2 / N$ energy is dissipated for an $N$-step adiabatic charging. We have found that charge sharing between multiple spatially distributed virtual ground nodes and virtual $V_{DD}$ has higher energy overhead compared to a time multiplexed version of a single virtual ground. This is partly so due to the control logic energy overhead. The time-multiplexing of charge source along with a simplified design for the charge pump initiation control logic enable higher energy savings in the proposed design schema.

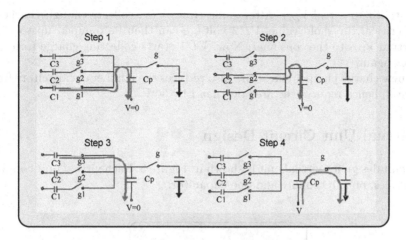

**Fig. 1.** V. Manne's pumping scheme

## 3   Efficient Charge Pump Architecture

We propose a new charge pump architecture specifically targeted for SRAM arrays. The proposed charge pump schema is illustrated in Figure 2.

Charge sharing event scheduling can be simplified by time multiplexing the virtual ground and virtual $V_{DD}$ nodes. The spatial multiplexing requires a sufficiently complex state machine to keep track of the spatial charge sharing schedule. In the new architecture, there is only one charge producer and one charge consumer. Two virtual units are introduced. These two identical units, $VU1$ and $VU2$, are responsible for collecting charge from the producer and supplying it to the consumer consecutively. $VU1$ is first used as a virtual ground. The unit $VU1$ will collect charge and its capacitor voltage will increase. When the voltage at $VU1$ reaches the critical voltage, $VU2$ is used as a virtual ground and $VU1$ is pumped up to serve as a virtual $V_{DD}$. Consumer node will be disconnected from the real $V_{DD}$ when supplied by a virtual $V_{DD}$. Charge at $VU1$ would constitute the virtual $V_{DD}$ for the consumer. When $VU1$ voltage drops to a critical value,

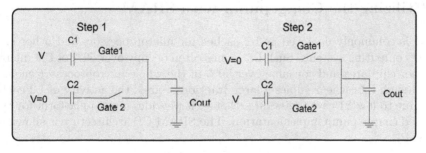

**Fig. 2.** New Stepwise Operation of the Charge Pump

it is switched to a real $V_{DD}$. After some time, $VU2$ collects enough charge to hit the critical threshold value. $VU2$ voltage can then be pumped up to serve as a virtual $V_{DD}$ to the consumer. Now, $VU1$ starts collecting charge from the producer again.

The new charge pump architecture also reduces the number of capacitors from 4 to 2 and, hence reduces the area overhead by 50%.

## 4 Virtual Unit Circuit Design

The circuit design for virtual unit is shown in Figure 3. Each virtual unit contains five switches, one DC supply and one capacitor.

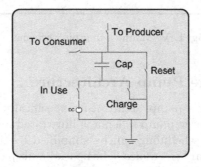

**Fig. 3.** Virtual Unit

The capacitor is connected to the producer and the charge switch is closed when the capacitor is collecting charge from the producer.

The capacitor is connected to the consumer node when the virtual unit serves as a virtual $V_{DD}$. At that time, other terminal of the capacitor is connected to a low DC voltage supply to bootstrap the charge voltage on this capacitor so as to serve the consumer.

The capacitor is connected to the ground when it is in reset state.

## 5 Utilizing the Chargepump with SRAM

SRAM is commonly deployed as L2 caches for microprocessors and other embedded computing systems. Such L2 caches often occupy over 50% of the microprocessor chip area and consume over 50% of the whole microprocessor energy. Even though L2 cache occupies a large fraction of area, the activity of L2 cache is low due to low L1 cache miss rate. Hence, it provides a good platform for the proposed charge pump implementation. The SRAM CP architecture is shown in Figure 4.

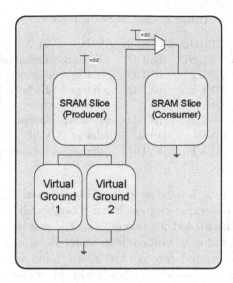

**Fig. 4.** Conceptual Description of the Proposed Architecture

## 5.1    Control Strategy for SRAM CP

We call our implementation schema SRAM CP. The SRAM CP virtual units are controlled by a control circuit, which we have designed and implemented. It ensures that the SRAM is operating at a proper voltage level.

In SRAM CP, the controller has 7 stages which are listed in Table 1. When the consumer or producer blocks are in active phase (actively accessed), the control circuit goes to the reset state. In the reset state, both virtual units are disabled. The producer is connected to the real ground ($RGND$) and the consumer is connected to the real $V_{DD}$ ($RVDD$).

Once the active access is over (as indicated by the word lines), the control system transitions to State 2, the virtual unit 1 starts collecting charge and virtual unit 2 is disabled. Virtual unit 1 takes 2 stages to charge upto the critical voltage.

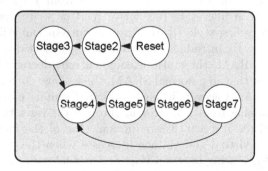

**Fig. 5.** Control State Machine

**Table 1.** Control State Table

|         | Producer | Consumer | VU1       | VU2       |
|---------|----------|----------|-----------|-----------|
| Reset   | RGND     | RVDD     | discharge | discharge |
| Stage 2 | VU1      | RVDD     | charge    | discharge |
| Stage 3 | VU1      | RVDD     | charge    | discharge |
| Stage 4 | VU2      | VU1      | Vdd       | charge    |
| Stage 5 | VU2      | RVDD     | discharge | charge    |
| Stage 6 | VU1      | VU2      | charge    | Vdd       |
| Stage 7 | VU1      | RVDD     | charge    | discharge |

At Stage 4, Virtual unit 1 is being pumped to Virtual $V_{DD}$. Virtual unit 2 is enabled and starts collecting charge. Even though unit 1 has collected the leakage current from the SRAM for two cycles, it is not be able to supply the consumer for two cycles due to voltage level differences, and the leakage from the virtual unit to the ground through the real ground versus virtual ground switch transistor. Hence, to avoid insufficient charge supply for the consumer, the Virtual $V_{DD}$ will only be used for 1 cycle.

At Stage 5, real $V_{DD}$ is used for the consumer and virtual unit 1 is set back to zero voltage to make it ready for the next charging cycle.

At Stage 6, virtual unit 2 has reached the critical voltage. It would be pumped up to Virtual $V_{DD}$. Virtual unit 1 is enabled and starts collecting charge again.

At Stage 7, real $V_{DD}$ is used for the consumer and virtual unit 2 is set back to zero voltage to make it ready for the next charging cycle. The control state machine would cycle between stages 4, 5, 6, 7 when both consumer and producer are idle.

The clock period of each stage depends on the time required for charging and discharging the capacitors. In an ideal situation, different stages may have different cycle length. For instance, at Stage 4, the charge at virtual unit 1 could be fully used instead of being discharged in Stage 5 too early.

## 6    Static Current Reduction

In a normal SRAM, static leakage current passes from $V_{DD}$ to ground even though the SRAM is in idle state (no active read or write operation). With the earlier charge recycling style [1], the leakage current can still leak through the control transistors. By introducing virtual unit to collect dirty charge at the ground node of the SRAM, the static leakage current decreases dramatically. Our simulations show that in a normal SRAM, the leakage current passing from $V_{DD}$ to gnd is 59.2uA. However, when the virtual unit is placed on the gnd path, the current passing from $V_{DD}$ to gnd through the reset transistor on the virtual unit is 0.387uA. It's a 99.3% reduction! One of the factors in leakage reduction is that the virtual gnd voltage increases when the capacitor charges up. It reduces the $V_{DD}$ swing between $V_{DD}$ and virtual gnd, and hence reduces leakage current. Recall that the sub-threshold leakage current can be modeled as [ [12], page 201] $I_{sub} = A * exp\langle \frac{q}{n'kT}(V_g - V_s - V_{th0} - \gamma'V_s + \eta V_{ds})\rangle * B$, where $A = \mu_0 C_{ox} \frac{W_{eff}}{L_{eff}} \langle \frac{kT}{q} \rangle^2 e^{1.8}$, and $B = 1 - exp(\frac{-qV_{ds}}{kT})$. Note that the leakage power decreases exponentially with respect to $V_{ds}$ due to the Drain Induced Barrier Leakage effect [12, 13]. This helps explain the leakage current reduction in part. Another cause for this reduction is due to the body effect induced by higher voltage at the virtual ground terminal. This effectively raises the threshold voltages for the $n$-channel transistors in the cross-coupled inverters of the SRAM array, which in turn reduces the leakage current.

Another factor at play is that a large fraction of the leakage current that still manages to go through is collected at the virtual ground capacitor helping to charge the capacitor. Note that a capacitor even in 32nm technology has very favorable leakage profile.

There still is a concern that a leakage path may exist from the virtual ground through the reset transistor. Simulations show that during the charging phase, 98.63% of the current goes into charging the capacitor, and only 1.37% of the current leaks through the reset transistor. Therefore, the virtual units effectively collect all the dirty charge.

## 6.1    Determining the Size of Virtual Ground Capacitance

The choice of capacitance is a critical parameter in energy reduction. If the capacitance is low, the area overhead would be smaller. However, the realized virtual $V_{DD}$ would have low capacitance and hence its voltage will drop sooner with few transitions. This will result in increased pumping frequency. It means a faster control circuit clock would be needed. Our target is to lower the frequency meanwhile keeping the area overhead to within 5%. Cacti [11] shows that the area of a 2MB L2 cache is $227mm^2$ using 30nm technology. Within 5% area overhead, we could build a capacitor which occupies $346.41um^2$ area. According to the NEC technology [10] ZrO2 parameters, the realizable capacitance values are $16fF/0.22um^2$. Assume the same ZrO2 dielectric material could be used on SRAM, $346.41um^2$ area would provide $24.6pF$ capacitance. We built the SRAM CP in 32nm BPTM technology [5]. The 32nm BPTM parameters are used to simulate the charging and discharging processes. The 32nm BPTM technology uses 0.7V supply voltage. We hereby assume that the SRAM circuit could tolerate the gnd terminal voltage upto $1/3 * V_{DD}$ and similarly tolerates the $V_{DD}$ terminal voltages upto $2/3 * V_{DD}$ voltage level. The results show that it takes 174ns to collect the charge from a SRAM slice to reach $1/3 * V_{DD}$ voltage level and it takes 163ns to discharge the capacitor from $V_{DD}$ to $2/3 * V_{DD}$ voltage when the capacitor is used for a virtual $V_{DD}$.

## 6.2    SRAM Access Time Performance

The SRAM read time depends on the $V_{DD}$ swing because the output of the sense amplifier depends on the difference between the two bitlines. In order to keep the read time unaffected, the SRAM slice modules should be connected back to

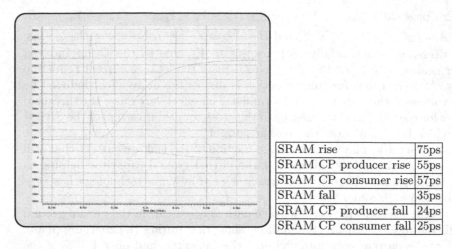

| SRAM rise | 75ps |
|---|---|
| SRAM CP producer rise | 55ps |
| SRAM CP consumer rise | 57ps |
| SRAM fall | 35ps |
| SRAM CP producer fall | 24ps |
| SRAM CP consumer fall | 25ps |

**Fig. 6.** SRAM CP write                    **Fig. 7.** Write Time

the real $V_{DD}$ and real ground when the SRAM is being accessed. This switching occurs as the wordline signal is asserted.

We performed the following experiment with HSPICE [6] based on 32nm BPTM technology [5]. Each wordline shares one charge-pump. Each wordline has 512 SRAM cells. 256 bits are chosen as producer and another 256 bits are grouped as consumer. The SRAM runs at 1GHz. The precharge voltage is set as 0.35V which is half of the $V_{DD}$. The decode time is calculated by CACTI [11]. Write Delay is measured between the time wordline is set and the time the voltage reaches 0.63V or 0.07V. Read Delay is measured between the time wordline is set and the time the output of the sense amplifier reaches 0.63V or 0.07V.

**Write Performance.** The results are shown in Table 7. This data shows that our design technique introduces no additional delay to the write operation. The rise time is less because the bit line is going from a non-zero value (already above ground) to $V_{DD}$ in SRAM CP. The fall time is also shorter because the voltage of a bitline A at SRAM CP is slightly higher than in a normal SRAM. It helps discharging the SRAM cell.

**Read Performance.** SRAM CP Consumer read time is close to rise time because of the fact that its ground is at zero during a read. The producer read delay penalty is increased by 39 ps. It would bring about a 3.9% delay to the cache read compared to the original 1ns cycle. However, the penalty can be hidden at architecture level. In some CPUs e.g. Alpha 21364 [7], the data block is read in a 4-cycle (stage) pipeline. It is desirable to set the producer as the data block to be read in the first 2 cycles and the consumer as the data block to be read in the last 2 cycles. In this case, the delay would be hidden by placing the consumer at the non-critical path.

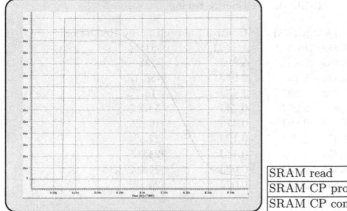

| SRAM read | 29ps |
| SRAM CP producer read | 68ps |
| SRAM CP consumer read | 28ps |

**Fig. 8.** SRAM CP read                    **Fig. 9.** Read Time

## 6.3   Determining the Size of SRAM Slice

Several SRAM cache blocks are grouped into a single SRAM slice to serve as a single charge source or consumer. The choice of SRAM slice size is another critical parameter in energy reduction. It is clear that if the SRAM slice is bigger, the whole SRAM would contain fewer charge pumps. Hence, the control circuit's energy consumption will be less. However, as the size of SRAM slice becomes bigger, the probability of accessing that SRAM slice at any given point in time also increases. If the probability of accessing an arbitrary wordline is $p$ (assuming it is uniformly distributed), the probability of accessing an SRAM slice which contains $k$ wordlines would be $kp$. Therefore, the number of switching events between real $V_{DD}$ and virtual $V_{DD}$ also increase. It reduces the saved energy due to increased control switching energy overhead.

We evaluate the energy savings for a microprocessor which has configuration similar to Alpha 21346 processor as listed in TABLE-I. The average number of cache accesses is captured by Simplescalar version 3.0 [8]. We executed SPEC2000 [9] integer benchmarks on this simulator to find out the best SRAM slice size. The programs include Bzip, Eon, Gcc, Mcf, Parser, Perlbmk, Twolf and Vpr. Each benchmark is executed for 1,000,000,000 instructions. The average energy consumption for each wordline settingis shown in Table 3. The SRAM column shows the energy spent on normal SRAM arrays. The SRAM CP column

**Table 2.** Simple Scalar Configuration

| Processor | Alpha out of order 4 way issue |
| L1-ICache | 64KB, 1-way, 64B line, 1 cycle access latency |
| L1-DCache | 64KB, 2-way, 64B line, 1 cycle access latency |
| L2-Unified | 2MB, 8-way, 64B line, 4 cycles access latency |

**Table 3.** Net Energy Saving

| # of Wordline | SRAM | SRAM CP | Control Energy | Energy Reduction |
|---|---|---|---|---|
| 8 | 3.45J | 14.29J | 11.78J | -315% |
| 16 | 3.45J | 8.40J | 5.89J | -143.8% |
| 32 | 3.45J | 5.46J | 2.94J | -58.4% |
| 64 | 3.45J | 3.99J | 1.47J | -15.7% |
| 128 | 3.45J | 3.25J | 0.74J | 5.62% |
| 256 | 3.45J | 2.89J | 0.37J | 16.2% |
| 512 | 3.45J | 2.71J | 0.19J | 21.5% |
| 1024 | 3.45J | 2.62J | 0.11J | 24.0% |
| 2048 | 3.45J | 2.59J | 0.07J | 24.9% |
| 4096 | 3.45J | 2.59J | 0.07J | 24.8% |

shows the energy spent on the SRAM CP array and the Control Energy column lists the energy spent on the control circuit of SRAM CP.

The results show that the group size of 2048 wordlines would save the energy consumption by 24.9%. If the slice size increases, the energy savings would decrease.

## 6.4    Temporal Locality Savings

The typical programs exhibit temporal locality wherein the same data object (at address $A$) is accessed many time in the near future (at times $T, T + \Delta T, T + 2\Delta T, \ldots, T + l\Delta T$) [14]. Such program or behavior level temporal locality results in SRAM level temporal locality. SRAM exhibits such temporal locality as repeated wordline access over many cycles within a time epoch (word line accessed in this cycle is accessed in near future). L1 cache has very strong temporal locality characteristic such that 74.31% of the accessed wordlines are accessed again within 50 cycles [17]. We try to exploit these characteristics to further extend energy savings. Whenever the cache is being accessed, the state machine would stay at reset state for $Y$ cycles before going back to the charging state. Such *hysteresis* approach reduces the energy used for switching MOSFET in the virtual unit. Table 4 shows the temporal locality of L2 caches.

The temporal locality characteristic is weaker in L2 caches (than L1 caches) because the data being accessed from L2 cache is already stored in L1 cache. A wordline at L2 cache will be reaccessed only if the data in L1 cache is replaced by other wordlines. We set up another simulation by setting the number of wordlines in one group as 2048 and by varying the reset cycle of the state machine. Our results, shown in Table 5, demonstrate that temporal locality does not give significant energy reduction for SRAM CP. Therefore, the SRAM CP should go back to charging state once the access is completed.

**Table 4.** Reaccess percentage W.R.T Cycles

| # of Cycles | Percentage |
|-------------|------------|
| 10          | 4.25%      |
| 20          | 5.75%      |
| 30          | 6.53%      |
| 40          | 8.22%      |
| 50          | 9.17%      |
| 60          | 10.68%     |
| 70          | 11.6%      |
| 80          | 12.2%      |
| 90          | 13.2%      |
| 100         | 13.6%      |

**Table 5.** Energy Reduction using temporal locality

| length of reset state | Energy Consumption |
|-----------------------|--------------------|
| 1                     | 2.5888165J         |
| 10                    | 2.5887928J         |
| 20                    | 2.5887844J         |
| 30                    | 2.5887800J         |
| 40                    | 2.5887704J         |
| 50                    | 2.5887649J         |
| 60                    | 2.5887565J         |
| 70                    | 2.5887515J         |
| 80                    | 2.5887482J         |
| 90                    | 2.5887427J         |
| 100                   | 2.5887405J         |

## 7  Future Work

Even though the charge pump based recycling strategy is able to save energy for SRAMs, the control units consume some of the energy saved. This hurts the net saving bottom line. We will explore the design of low power control units and charge pumping strategies for further energy reductions in the future. It is feasible to allow the program to control the charge pumping operation. Such control could be completely explicit to the programmer/compiler. We do not know of any existing research that exposes such low level control valves to the program. Alternately, such control could be transparent to the program, but could be microarchitecturally driven, as in drowsy caches [16]. Another concern for the SRAM CP is the leakage current flowing through the reset transistor to the ground. Even though our design has dramatically reduced the leakage current, a better design for this circuit could reduce the current even further. Gomathisankaran & Tyagi [17] suggested the use of a depletion mode transistor to reduce the leakage current from L1 SRAM cache. By replacing the reset transistor inside the virtual unit with a depletion mode transistor, we may be able to cut down the leakage current further.

## 8  Conclusions

The power consumption is a big concern in the next generation systems. The shifting trend in the smaller scale technology nodes [4] is from the switching power to the leakage power. The area dominating units tend to be the major leakage sources. The SRAM based memory units deployed as caches or register files or latches or look-up tables are becoming omni-present in the embedded systems on a chip. This drives a need for leakage power reduction in SRAMs. This paper proposed and verified an innovative way to apply the charge pump based charge recycling scheme to an SRAM. This method not only saves the energy of the SRAM blocks, it also reduces the leakage current flowing through the SRAM units. The experimental results show that there is a 26.56% energy reduction in L2 cache over SPEC2000 benchmarks.

# References

1. V.Manne, A. Tyagi *An Adiabatic Charge Pump Based Charge Recycling Design Style*, PATMOS 2003, Lecture Notes in Computer Science vol. 2799, p. 299-308, 2003
2. Pylarinos, L.: Charge Pumps: An Overview. Edward S. Rogers Sr. Department of Electrical and Computer Engineering, University of Toronto.
3. Dickson, J.: On-chip High-Voltage Generation in NMOS Integrated Circuits Using an Improved Voltage Multiplier Technique. IEEE Journal of Solid-State Circuits, Vol.11, No.6, June 1976. pp. 374-378.
4. International Technology Roadmap for Semiconductors, 2003 Edition (2004 Update), Executive Summary. URL: *http://public.itrs.net*
5. Berkeley Predictive Technology Model. URL: *http://www-device.eecs.berkeley.edu.*; Now known as Predictive Technology Model. URL: *http://www.eas.asu.edu/~ptm.*
6. Star-HSPICE 2001.4 Avant! Corporation.
7. Hp-Compaq Corporation
8. Doug Burger and Todd M. Austin. The SimpleScalar Tool Set, Version 2.0. Computer Sciences Department Technical report #1342. University of Wisconsin-Madison. June 1997.
9. Standard Performance Evaluation Corporation, URL: *http://www.specbench.org/ osg/cpu2000/*
10. NEC Electronics eDRAM Process Advantages URL: *http://www.necel.com/ process/en/edramprocess.html*
11. Steven J. E. Wilton and Norman P. Jouppi, *An Enhanced Access and Cycle Time Model for On-Chip Caches.* WRL Research Technical Report 93/5. July 1994.
12. Kaushik Roy and Sharat C. Prasad, *Low-Power CMOS VLSI Circuit Design.* John Wiley & Sons, INC. 2000.
13. Saibal Mukhopadhyay, Arijit Raychowdhury, Kaushik Roy. *Accurate Estimation of Total Leakage Current in Scaled CMOS Logic Circuits Based on Compact Current Modeling*, Proceedings of 40th Design Automation Conference (DAC'03), 2003. pp. 169-174.
14. John L. Hennessy and David A. Patterson, *Computer Architecture: A Quantitative Approach.* Morgan Kaufman, CA. 2003.
15. Jan Rabey and Anantha Chandrakasan and B. Nikolić, *Digital Integrated Circuits.* Prentice Hall, 2003.
16. K. Flautner, N. S. Kim, S. Martin, D. Blaauw, and T. Mudge, *Drowsy Caches: Simple Techniques for Reducing Leakage Power.* In Proceedings of 29th Annual International Symposium on Computer Architecture, pages 148-157. IEEE CS Press. 2002.
17. M.Gomathisankaran, A.Tyagi *WARM Sram: A novel scheme to reduce leakage energy in SRAM Arrays*, ISVLSI 2004.

# Compiler-Driven Leakage Energy Reduction in Banked Register Files

David Atienza[1,2], Praveen Raghavan[3,4], José L. Ayala[5], Giovanni De Micheli[1], Francky Catthoor[3,4], Diederik Verkest[3,6], and Marisa Lopez-Vallejo[5]

[1] Laboratoire des Systemes Integres (LSI)/Ecole Polytechnique Federale de Lausanne (EPFL), Switzerland
{david.atienza, giovanni.demicheli}@epfl.ch
[2] Computer Architecture and Automation Department (DACYA)/Universidad Complutense de Madrid (UCM), Spain
datienza@dacya.ucm.es
[3] Digital Design Technology Group (DDT)/Inter-University Micro-Electronics Center (IMEC) vzw, Heverlee, Belgium
{ragha, catthoor, verkest}@imec.be
[4] ESAT/Katholic University of Leuven (KUL), Heverlee, Belgium
[5] Depto. de Ingenieria Electronica (DIE)/Universidad Politecnica de Madrid (UPM), Spain
{jayala, marisa}@die.upm.es
[6] Electrical Engineering/Vrije Universiteit, Brussels, Belgium

**Abstract.** Tomorrow's embedded devices need to run high-resolution multimedia applications which need an enormous computational complexity with a very low energy consumption constraint. In this context, the register file is one of the key sources of power consumption and its inappropriate design and management can severely affect the performance of the system. In this paper, we present a new approach to reduce the energy of the shared register file in upcoming embedded VLIW architectures with several processing units. Energy savings up to a 60% can be obtained in the register file without any performance penalty. It is based on a set of hardware extensions and a compiler-based energy-aware register assignment algorithm that enable the de/activation of parts of the register file (i.e. sub-banks) in an independent way at run-time, which can be easily included in these embedded architectures.

## 1 Introduction

Current trends on communications, multimedia, networking, and other areas encourage the development of high-performance platforms that include structures to hold complex algorithms that cannot be supported by simple hardware. In this sense VLIW-like processors are the only solution that can provide a suitable performance-power trade-off for this kind of applications. Moreover, product complexity continues to increase making scalability a must of these complex architectures. Also, the time-to-market pressure provokes that a design group can no longer start from scratch. These assumptions make the use of heterogeneous multi-processor architectures the only solution to meet design goals in the

J. Vounckx, N. Azemard, and P. Maurine (Eds.): PATMOS 2006, LNCS 4148, pp. 107–116, 2006.

required time to market [1]. Several platforms have recently appeared from important semiconductor companies that confirm this tendency to multi-processor systems, e.g. ST Nomadik [2], Philips Nexperia [3] or TI OMAP [4].

On the other hand, most current systems require battery operation, which puts intense pressure on energy consumption. Given the impact that static power causes in current sub-micron technologies, as indicated by [5], energy consumption becomes a critical design metric. New embedded applications require an enormous computational performance (2 - 30 $GOPS$) that need to be executed with low energy consumption demands (0.3 - 2 $W$) for battery duration constraints [6]. Although new processors with multiple processing units can fulfill these performance figures, they consume too much power (10-100 $W$) as outlined by [7]. Therefore, while keeping the performance results, the power consumption needs to be at least two or three orders of magnitude lower to be used in embedded environments. Within this context, methods to reduce the power consumption of the new multi-processor embedded platforms are needed.

One of the main factors that affect performance and power consumption of the new embedded platforms is the memory hierarchy. As a matter of fact, an inappropriate design of the memory subsystem and the management of the data transfers between its levels can attain up to 70% of the total power consumed in the system and up to two orders of magnitude in performance for dynamic multimedia systems [6]. Moreover, very recently it has been found that in new proposed embedded platforms with several processing elements, the shared register file plays a very important role as part of the memory subsystem and it can heavily affect the cycle time and consumes a very significant portion of the aforementioned percentage of the total energy consumed by the memory hierarchy [4]. Furthermore, it has become one of the critical processor hot-spots, specially for VLIW architectures, as [8] have shown. The main reasons are similar to those found in other layers of the memory subsystem. The register file has to support concurrent access of the several present processors and continuous exchanges of information with the L1 memory caches, therefore it is large and multi-ported. These characteristics, as occurs with memory layers on top, lead to a large increase in the power dissipation (and indirectly temperature too) of the whole system [9]. Hence, it is crucial to reduce the energy spent on it.

In this paper we introduce a new hardware approach to reduce the energy of the shared register file in upcoming embedded architectures with several VLIW processors. This work relies on a set of special hardware extensions that are controlled by the compilers of these new embedded platforms. This complete hardware/software approach enables reducing the energy consumed in the register file of forthcoming embedded architectures with multiple processing elements without incurring in performance penalties. The experimental setup is built over the CRISP (Coarse-grained Reconfigurable Instruction Set Processor) framework [10], which provides the compilation and simulation capabilities.

The remainder of the paper is organized as follows. In Section 2 we describe some related work. In Section 3 we explain the proposed architectural extensions for these new embedded platforms, while the compiler modifications

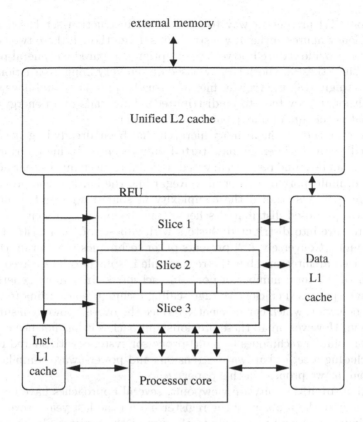

**Fig. 1.** CRISP: Overall emulated architecture

are explained in Section 4. Then, in Section 5, we shortly introduce the case studies and present the experimental results obtained with our proposed hardware/software approach. Finally, in Section 6 we draw our conclusions.

## 2   Related Work

Nowadays two major types of processing architectures have been proposed to achieve low power processing of multimedia and consumer applications. First, most forthcoming low power embedded architectures are typically customized to handle signal processing operations efficiently. Interesting domain-specific commercial DSP processors is the Coolflux Philips-PDSL [11]. Second, Application-Specific Instruction set Processors (ASIPs) have been presented as an alternative for low power embedded processing [12]. Good examples of commercially available ASIPs are Altera's NIOS [13] and Tensilica's Xtensa [14]. The academic research performed by [15] and [16] in the design of ASIPs has focused at the problem of identification and implementation of an efficient set of instruction set extensions. Although most of the work has focused on improving performance, not much work has been done specifically in the area of reducing energy consumption. [17] presents a way to extend the instruction set based on the energy-efficiency figures of the new instructions. Even though these two types of architectures provide reduced power consumption compared to general-purpose processors, since these are both largely based on the Very Long Instruction Word (VLIW) paradigm [18], the register files are usually quite large and have several of ports (although they tend to be distributed). This leads to an energy/power wastage that is the aim of our research in this paper.

However, even though the memory hierarchy has been already largely studied, work related to the register file has started only recently. In high performance processors it can be found research devoted to defining mechanisms that decrease the energy of multi-ported register files. Regarding the hardware approaches to the problem, [19] has studied the complexity of shared register files and [20] and [21] have proposed distributed schemes and techniques to split the global microarchitecture into distributed clusters with subsets of the register file and functional units. Conversely, [22] presents other techniques that retain the idea of a centralized architecture, but the register file is split into interleaved banks, which reduces the total number of ports in each bank. In a more general context, [23] have proposed efficient voltage scaling techniques according to the application's behavior, which can efficiently reduce the overall power consumption of the system. However, in all these previous approaches it has not been studied how to apply similar techniques to multi-processor systems with shared register files by including a set of hardware extensions and power-aware compilation to control them, as we propose in this paper.

In addition, from the software viewpoint, several approaches have been proposed to alleviate the problem of the register file. In the last years, several software pipelining strategies to distribute the use of the register file, targeted at reducing memory pressure in VLIW systems, have been outlined [24]. Also, [25] and [26] have recently presented different compiler techniques, including complex register renaming, to reduce the energy spent in the register file of in-order processors. Nevertheless, such techniques were not aimed to enable the use of voltage scaling mechanisms in multi-processor environments as we introduce in the present approach.

## 3   Proposed Architectural Extensions

In this work we have used the compilation and simulation capabilities provided by the cycle-accurate CRISP framework [10]. It is a re-targetable compiler and simulator framework based on Trimaran [27]. The baseline architecture described by CRISP in shown in Figure 1 and consists of a selectable number of processing elements (i.e. slices) as in VLIW processors , where the compiler and architecture can be adapted to each desired DSP instruction set to be simulated. To this end, the slices of the configurable VLIW processing part are mapped onto the CRISP's Reconfigurable Functional Unit (RFU) part [10]. The RFU allows extensive customization of the VLIW processing units for a certain instruction set and an operation can be issued every clock cycle. Thus, in order to provide enough bandwidth for the potential concurrent accesses of multiple operations, our baseline architecture includes two read and one write port of the register file, which are allocated to each slot of the VLIW processor. All functional units in one slot are connected to these three ports via a full crossbar. Regarding interconnections, the RFU part reads/writes data from/to the main shared register file. Also, CRISP includes a main processor core, which can be any type of processor, and which is used to schedule instructions that real-life VLIW systems cannot execute efficiently (e.g. control and non-parallel operations). In our experimental results (Section 5), all the real-life applications used are data-dominated and the main processor executes a very insignificant proportion of operations compared to DSP-like or loop operations (less than 5%). Thus, these figures are not considered in our reported results.

The baseline architecture described by CRISP has been extended and modified in several ways to support the power reduction mechanisms proposed in this paper. They are described in the following paragraphs of this section.

First, the register file shared among all processing elements has been split into several banks, which can be independently accessed by the processors. Then, a Dynamic Voltage Scaling (DVS) technique is applied to turn the unused banks into a low power state and thus save as much energy as possible in the system.

The register file architecture is split into independent banks and each sub-bank counts with the additional logic required to implement the DVS state. Since the low power consumption state is selected for the whole bank instead of a specific register, the overhead of the control logic is greatly minimized.

This hardware support is exploited by the compiler to power up banks of registers in the shared register file when they are needed by the several processing elements. In normal execution of the system, most banks of the shared register file are kept in a low power state thanks to our modified register assignment implemented in the compiler. In fact, only when needed, the register file banks are powered up to fulfill the register demands of the code, without performance degradation.

## 4   Compiler Optimizations

The complete hardware architecture depicted in the previous section has also been extended with the design of a specific compiler. The register allocation phase in the compiler of the CRISP framework was modified to exploit the new architectural feature.

The register assignment is the phase of any compiler that determines which register(s) to use for each program value selected during register allocation, while the register allocation is the phase that determines which values will be placed in registers. As a matter of fact, computer architectures (*out-of-order* processors) can destroy this first assignment by means of a hardware mechanism designed to avoid hazards, namely using *register renaming*, as was studied by [25].

Traditionally, the register assignment algorithm has been designed to choose registers from the whole pool of free registers without any other constraint. In the case of Trimaran, as many other compilers, when it tries to assign an architectural

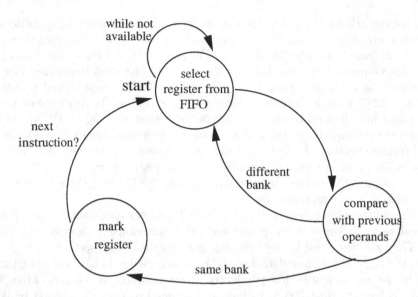

**Fig. 2.** Register assignment algorithm

register to the instruction operands, it retrieves the first available register from a First Input First Output (FIFO) list of free registers. In fact, the order of the registers inside the list is not representative and depends on the specific hardware architecture. Moreover, since Trimaran does not consider any restriction on assigning the registers, they are selected from the FIFO without a particular order. Therefore, the assigned registers can easily come from different register file banks if no modification to the register assignment algorithm is accomplished.

The register assignment policy we have implemented in the compiler modifies the aforementioned traditional assignment of Trimaran by promoting every operand in the instruction to the same register file bank. With this modification, most of the registers are selected from the first bank in the register file and the other banks can be kept in the low power state by turning down the voltage power supply. Instructions required for turning off the unused banks in each Basic Block was inserted by the compiler before the Basic Block.

The structure of the algorithm followed by the compiler to assign the architectural registers is shown in Figure 2. First, the first available register in the list of free registers is selected. This register is double-checked to be free and not system-reserved. Then, it is compared to the registers assigned to the other operands of the instruction. If the register file bank for the operand under assignment does not match any of the other operands of the instruction, this register is discarded and the procedure is repeated until a register belonging to the same bank is found. When the register is selected, the liveness of the register is calculated and the annotation is generated. It is important to remark that the compiler has been designed with enough flexibility to perform the register assignment algorithm with varying sizes of the register file bank, as the experimental results in Section 5 show.

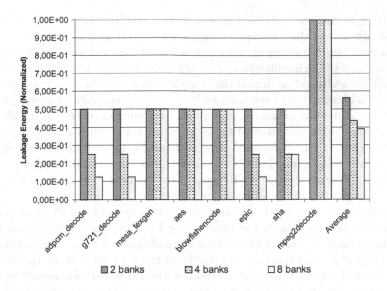

**Fig. 3.** Leakage Energy savings for the three configurations (normalized to non-banked register file)

Finally, when the register assignment is performed with our proposed algorithm, we can observe that in most of studied multimedia and encryption real-life applications, the registers can belong to the same bank and just few need to be selected from another register file bank (see Section 5 for more details).

## 5 Experimental Results

The CRISP framework detailed in Section 3 was used to simulate a VLIW processor. The processor chosen for our simulations was a 32-bit, 4-issue VLIW processor, trying to represent the forthcoming tendencies in commercial VLIW platforms for embedded multimedia applications. The register file was considered to have 12 ports (8 read and 4 write), 128 entries deep. Three cases were chosen for banking strategies: 8, 4 and 2 banks. However, the proposed architectural and compiler extensions are independent of the size of the VLIW, the ports of the register file or the number of banks. The *90*nm leakage model proposed by [28] has been used for the different register file architectures considered.

The simulator provides a trace from which the activation of each of the registers and the banks of the register file is computed. Based on the number of cycles each basic block was active and the leakage energy consumption of the bank, the net leakage energy that is consumed can be computed. The results are compared with respect to a case where no compiler modification was done. Hence, the base line case for the 4-banked register file experiment, would be a case where the compiler was not aware of such a banking.

During our first set of experiments we considered the simplest possible partition with respect to extra hardware overhead and its complexity for the management of the register file, namely, it was divided only in 2 banks. The results obtained regarding leakage energy are depicted in Figure 3. The results shown for each benchmark using our proposed hardware/software approach have been normalized to the baseline architecture considered where all the banks of the register file are switched on during the complete execution of the program. First of all, we can observe that even with such a simple two-banked register file, we can actually reduce the leakage energy in all benchmarks (except *mpeg2decode*) by 50% as one bank can be turned to low power mode roughly during the whole execution. In the case of *mpeg2decode*, after a careful analysis of the compilation and simulation results, we could verify that this particular application puts an extremely high register pressure. Hence, all the registers are used all the time during its execution and no bank can be turned off.

Then, during the second set of experiments we explored the effect of using a more complex partitioning of the register file by considering the options of 4-banked and 8-banked register files. The results obtained for our case studies are shown in Figure 3 and Figure 3 respectively. It can be seen that, as the number of banks defined for the register file increases, the gains improve as well in most of the studied embedded applications, since they do not use a large number of simultaneous registers. Thus, more banks can be turned into low power mode. In addition, after a careful study of the results, we can observe that the type of benchmarks that benefit more from the 8-banked partitioning of the register file are the embedded multimedia applications (e.g. *mesa_texgen*, *g721_decode*, etc.). Moreover, *adpcm_decode* shows that even though it requires a significant amount of main memory to process the incoming audio (in our experiments up to 1MB), it puts very little register pressure. Hence, it enormously benefits from the increase in the number of banks considered for the register file. Conversely, the benchmarks from the cryptography domain (e.g. *blowfishencode*, *sha*, etc.) utilize more registers concurrently and do not show any improvement beyond partitioning the register file in 4 banks (see Figure 3). In the case of the *mpeg2decode* benchmark, the pressure it generates in the register file does not enable any benefit of partitioning the register file in any number of banks. Thus, there is no gain in leakage energy for any of the studied configurations.

In addition, these trends in energy improvements achieved by bank-partitioning of the register file for both types of application domains are illustrated in Figure 3. It outlines that in most of the cases the 8-banked configuration saves more energy than 2-banked and 4-banked options since it keeps a larger area of the register file in the low-power state. On the other hand, this configuration presents more overhead of extra logic needed to turn the banks into the low power state. However, this extra logic has been found to be quite simple. As a result, the gains achieved at run-time due to the low-power state of a very significant part of the register file overcome the energy overheads of the extra logic. Therefore, most of the studied benchmarks still benefit from partitioning the register file in 8 banks.

Finally, we have calculated the area overhead in the register file needed to provide the architectural extensions presented, namely, the banked-registers and the DVS technique. Our results indicate that the area overhead is only 2.16% of the total area of the original register file respectively, which illustrates that the proposed HW/SW approach is not costly. Also, the cost of inserting the extra instructions required for the DVS was negligible, as it has to be done only for basic blocks where the execution count can be large (i.e. nested loops).

## 6    Conclusions

New consumer applications have recently increased in complexity and demand a very high level of performance in the next generation of low-power embedded devices. Therefore, new techniques and mechanisms that can provide solutions for an efficient mapping of these complex applications in such platforms are in great need. One of the most important factors of power consumption and performance penalty is the shared register file between all processing units. In this paper we have presented and shown in realistic examples the applicability of a new set of architectural extensions to enable the use of sub-banks in the register file, which achieves important reductions in the energy of the shared register file in upcoming embedded architectures with several VLIW processors. Our results indicate that this new integral approach enables on average a 60% reduction of the energy consumed in the register file of such forthcoming embedded architectures when they run real-life embedded multimedia, wireless network and cryptography applications without introducing performance penalties.

## Acknowledgements

This work is partially supported by the Swiss FNS Research Grant 20021-109450/1, and the Spanish Government Research Grants TIN2005-05619 and TIC2003-07036. Also, this research is partially sponsored by the contract number 910467 of the Funding Program for Research of UCM-Region of Madrid.

## References

1. Wayne Wolf. The Future of Multiprocessor Systems-on-Chips. In *Proceedings of DAC*, 2004.
2. ST Nomadik Multimedia Processor, 2004. http://www.st.com.
3. Philips Nexperia - highly integrated programmable system-on-chip (mpsoc), 2004. http://www.semiconductors.philips.com/products/nexperia.
4. TI's Omap platform, 2004. http://focus.ti.com/omap/docs/.
5. Nam Sung Kim, T. Austin, D. Blaauw, T. Mudge, K. Flautner, J. Hu, M. Irwin, M. Kandemir, and N. Vijaykrishnan. Leakage current: Moore's law meets static power. *Computer*, volume 36(12), December 2003.
6. M. Viredaz and D. Wallacha. Power evaluation of a handheld computer. *IEEE Micro*, volume 23(1), January 2003.
7. P. Bose, D. Brooks, A. uktosuno, et al., V. Zyuban, D. Albonesi, and S. Dwarkadas. Early-stage definition of LPX: A low power issue-execute processor. In *Proceedings of PACS*, November 2002.

8. A. Lambrechts, P. Raghavan, A. Leroy, M. Jayapala, T. Vander Aa, and F. Catthoor et. al. Power breakdown analysis for a heterogeneous noc platform running a video application. In *Proceedings of ASAP*, June 2005.

9. J. Abella and A. Gonzalez. On reducing register file pressure and energy in multiple-banked register files. In *Proceedings of ICCD*, 2003.

10. Pieter Op de Beeck, Francisco Barat, Murali Jayapala, and Rudy Lauwereins. Crisp: A template for reconfigurable instruction set processors. In *Proceedings of FPL*, 2001.

11. Philips PDSL. Coolflux dsp, 2005.

12. Tilman Glokler and Heinrich Meyr. *Design of Energy-Efficient Application-Specific Instruction Set Processors.* Kluwer Academic Publishers, AH Dordrecht, The Netherlands, 2002.

13. Altera. Nios embedded processor system developement, 2001.

14. R.E. Gonzalez. Xtensa: A configurable and extensible processor. In *IEEE Micro*, volume 20(2), 2002.

15. P. Biswas, V. Choudhary, K. Atasu, L. Pozzi, P. Ienne, and N. Dutt. Introduction of local memory elements in instruction set extensions. In *Proceedings of DAC*, June 2004.

16. P. Yu and T. Mitra. Characterizing embedded applications for instruction set extensible processors. In *Proceedings of DAC*, June 2004.

17. Kubilay Atasu, Laura Pozzi, and Paolo Ienne. Automatic application-specific instruction-set extensions under microarchitectural constraints. In *Proceedings of DAC*, 2003.

18. L. Benini, D. Bruni, M. Chinosi, C. Silvano, V. Zaccaria, and R. Zafalon. A power modeling and estimation framework for vliw-based embedded systems. In *Proceedings of PATMOS*, Yverdon Les Bains, Switzerland, September 2001.

19. V. V. Zyuban and P. M. Kogge. The energy complexity of register files. In *Proceedings of ISLPED*, 1998.

20. A. Seznec, E. Toullec, and O. Rochecouste. Reducing register ports for higher speed and lower energy. In *Proceedings of MICRO*, 2002.

21. V. V. Zyuban and P. M. Kogge. Inherently lower-power high-performance superscalar architectures. *IEEE Transactions on Computers*, volume 50(3), March 2001.

22. I. Park, M. D. Powell, and T. N. Vijaykumar. Reducing register ports for higher speed and lower energy. In *Proceedings of MICRO*, 2002.

23. Johan Pouwelse Koen, K. Langendoen, and H. J. Sips. Application-directed voltage scaling. *IEEE Transactions on Very Large Scale Integration (TVLSI)*, volume 11(5), October 2003.

24. Cagdas Akturan and Margarida F. Jacome. Caliber: A software pipelining algorithm for clustered embedded VLIW processors. In *Proceedings of ICCAD*, 2001.

25. J. L. Ayala, M. López-Vallejo, and A. Veidenbaum. Energy-efficient register renaming in high-performance processors. In *Proceedings of WASP*, 2003.

26. J. L. Ayala and M. López-Vallejo. Improving register file banking with a power-aware unroller. In *Proceedings of PARC*, 2004.

27. Trimedia Technologies Inc. Trimaran: An infrastructure for research in instruction-level parallelism, 1999. http://www.trimaran.org.

28. P. Raghavan, A. Lambrechts, M. Jayapala, F. Catthoor, and D.Verkest. Empirical power model for register files. In *Workshop on Media and Streaming Processors (with MICRO-38)*, 2005.

# Impact of Array Data Flow Analysis on the Design of Energy-Efficient Circuits

M. Hillers[1] and W. Nebel[2]

[1] OFFIS, Escherweg 2, 26121 Oldenburg, Germany
hillers@offis.de
[2] University of Oldenburg, 26129 Oldenburg, Germany
nebel@informatik.uni-oldenburg.de

**Abstract.** The grade of abstraction (specification level) for designing digital circuits has risen in the recent years from RT over algorithmic up to system level. An ambitious challenge of the EDA is to provide an efficient design space exploration with design-solutions comparable to hand-crafted optimisations. The accuracy of the legal design space directly influences the efficiency of automatically generable designs. Current Design-Tools do not exploit the freedom that is enabled by array data-flow analysis (ADFA). This paper shows the impact of our ADFA on behavioural synthesis and estimation for the metrics execution-time, area, and energy. Data-flow intensive benchmarks show improvements of up to 12% less energy and 30% less execution-time while area varies by ±15%.

## 1 Introduction

Algorithmic level specifications given in SystemC or C usually do not explicitly define the dataflow. In fact one benefit of high-level design languages is not being obliged to care about the exact sequence of calculations. Instead algorithms are specified in one of the possible sequences that preserve the functionality. High-level synthesis and estimation tools need to explore the design-space of semantically equivalent realizations and find the best solutions in terms of a given objective function. A well known and established representation of algorithms is the Control-Data-Flow-Graph (CDFG). Both, the dataflow and the control flow constrain the freedom of the design space, as an automated scheduling is extremely dependent on the movability resp. concurrency of operations. Constraints being too conservative restrict the search space to certain subspaces in terms of area, execution-time and energy.

In this paper[1] we focus on the dataflow analysis of array accesses in dataflow-intensive designs, like image processing algorithms. Arrays basically map single or multidimensional data structures onto memories. Memory accesses overconstrain the

---

[1] This work has been funded by the German Federal Ministry of Education and Research (BMBF) within the research project LEMOS (grant no. 01M3155). Further information is available on the project website: http://lemos.offis.de

J. Vounckx, N. Azemard, and P. Maurine (Eds.): PATMOS 2006, LNCS 4148, pp. 117–126, 2006.

design space if an inappropriate analysis of data dependencies between array accesses is done. While the data flow analysis is trivial for accesses to scalar variables, the application of the same techniques to arrays will most likely enforce a sequential schedule of the specification. Thus array accesses need special techniques optimised for the necessary data-flow.

The ADFA has been a research topic for decades in the domain of optimising compilers. We will examine its applicability to improve high-level synthesis as well as architecture prediction. By providing a more precise view on data dependencies, the ADFA uncovers parts of the design space that provide higher parallelism in data-flow between array accesses. Higher parallelism can be exploited to construct shorter schedules, which in turn decreases static energy consumption. Further it can enable or increase utilization of memory ports, such that multi-ported memories might become efficient alternatives.

The difficulty of the ADFA is to statically analyse, whether two accesses are dependent on each other in terms of data. Further the accesses may be multi-dimensional, non-perfectly nested, and of arbitrary expressiveness. Consider the following code-fragment and the corresponding CDFG translations of the loop body:

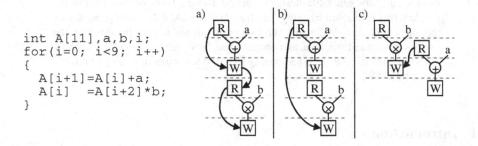

```
int A[11],a,b,i;
for(i=0; i<9; i++)
{
   A[i+1]=A[i]+a;
   A[i]  =A[i+2]*b;
}
```

**Fig. 1.** A simple example of code with loop CDFGs using a) scalar dependence analysis, b) ADFA plus slow schedule and c) ADFA plus fast schedule

Figure 1 shows a simple example code to illustrate the effect of both types of data-flow analysis. Fig. 1a) depicts the CDFG using a scalar dependence analysis. The blocks R and W represent read resp. write accesses to an array with an assumed duration of 1 clock cycle, the circles contain arithmetic operations, the straight lines are non-array data flows and the arcs show the data flow between array operations of the same loop iteration. Assuming a single-ported memory to contain the array A, we see an extremely sequential, constrained graph. The horizontal lines between the operations indicate a shortest possible schedule of 6 cycles. Fig. 1b) shows the CDFG after application of ADFA. None of the dependencies from the latter graph was necessary but a new edge has to be added. Still a schedule of the prior length is possible but the scheduler can now exploit more freedom. Fig. 1c) shows one of the shortest possible schedules with 4 cycles. Thus the higher degree of freedom can be exploited for reducing static energy consumption. Further, by preserving the value written to A[i+1] for the next iteration, a memory access reduction could be achieved, which in turn reduces dynamic energy. While a multi-ported memory would not have been usable with scalar analysis, the graph using ADFA allows more schedules with increased utilization of the memory ports. Of course real world algorithms can be more complicated to analyse. E.g. subscripts could contain multiple index variables which operate between undefined loop bounds. An important question is what should be the appropriate analysable expressiveness to handle common code complexities. We answer this question in the following chapters and give experimental results.

The paper is organized as follows: In the next chapter we provide related work and further background to the topic. In Chapter 3 we present our approach for an efficient analysis. Chapter 4 gives experimental results obtained by a prototypic evaluation and a conclusion summarizes this work.

## 2  Terminology and Related Work

Existing work on ADFA focuses on compiler based software optimisation on processor architectures [3], [8]. The impact of an ADFA on energy, execution time, and area has not yet been examined for the application domain of ASIC design. In the next paragraphs we give an overview to the terminology and prior work on ADFA.

A *subscript expression* describes the accessed array cells, e.g. A[i-1][j+1] has two subscript expressions (short: *subscripts*). A subscript using index variables is typically surrounded by a *nested loop* structure. All index variables of the nested loop form an *index vector*. The domain of index vectors, called *iteration space*, is defined by the loop borders of each particular index variable. If all bounds are constant, the iteration space of a nested loop is called *rectangular*. If the stride of each loop is 1 or -1, the iteration space is called *dense*. A loop nest of depth n may be represented as a finite convex polyhedron in the iteration space bounded by the loop bounds [13].

Assuming we would like to test the dependence of two array accesses, we have to find legal solutions to the *subscript equation system* (SES). If we assume i, j to be integer index vectors, array accesses $A_{s,i} = A[s_1(i)]...[s_m(i)]$ and $A_{t,j} = A[t_1(j)]...[t_m(j)]$. Then the SES $A_{s,i} = A_{t,j}$ is defined by the subscript equations (SE) $s_1(i) = t_1(j)$, ..., $s_m(i) = t_m(j)$. A *solution* is an iteration tuple (i,j), i.e. an integer assignment of i and j, such that the equation system is satisfied.

Generally spoken, with growing expressiveness of the subscripts to be handled, a more complex methodology for testing is necessary. Unfortunately the subscript expressions, loop bounds and loop strides are arbitrary and may even contain undefined symbols or they are conditionally dependent on these symbols. Thus the problem in general (if analysed statically) is undecidable [11]. To approach this problem, commonly the expressiveness and conditionality is restricted. Everything violating these restrictions has to be handled pessimistically, i.e. a data edge may and thus must exist to preserve semantic correctness. A widely used compromise between implementation effort and coverage of practical cases are the *affine expressions*. These have the common form $c_0 \cdot 1 + c_1 \cdot v_1 + c_2 \cdot v_2 + ... + c_N \cdot v_N$, where N represents the number of variables, $c_i$ the coefficients, and $v_i$ the (index) variables.

The simplest subdomain of the affine expressions which considers subscripts is the *ZIV* domain. ZIV is the short form of "zero index variables" and assumes that no (index) variable is contained in the affine expressions. For a pair of accesses the disproval of the dependence of a single dimension is sufficient to ensure independence of all *array dimensions*. E.g. A[i][1] could never meet A[i][0]. Affine expressions with N>0 are called *SIV* (single index variable, N=1), *DIV* (dual index variables, N=2) and *MIV* (multiple index variables, N>1).

A data dependence test is *exact*, if it provides a definite answer in its domain, whether there is dependence between two accesses or not. Inexact tests assume dependences, if they cannot disprove the existence of a solution.

A *dependence relation* summarises the common accesses by integer tuple relations [9]. Due to large or partially unknown iteration spaces, a static analysis methodology has to abstract from the full tuple information. These abstractions are in ascending grade of abstraction the dependence distance vectors [7], dependence polyhedra, dependence cones [14], dependence direction vectors [7], and dependence levels [6]. For our needs the following descriptions are sufficient. A *forward dependence* denotes a loop-independent dependence, i.e. no matter how the index variables are set, the dependence exists in each iteration. The second type of dependence is the *backward dependence* which corresponds to loop-carried dependences, i.e. two different iterations of the nested loop visit the same array address.

Subscripts or equations of a SES are called *coupled* if at least one index variable appears in different SE. So, computing the solution of a SES in sequence of the array dimensions (subscript-by-subscript) might construct a solution that is right for each individual equation but not valid for the entirety of the equations (e.g. in A[i][0] and A[1][i]). If no equation of the SES is coupled, it is called *separable*.

## 3 Description of Work

This section describes our new ADFA approach. Its goal is to combine known methods for dependence analysis to maintain a large analysable expressiveness of the algorithmic description with an acceptable computational effort. For the purpose of evaluation, our methodology was implemented into the power estimation and optimisation tool ORINOCO [4]. The tool is able to read algorithmic system level descriptions in the languages SystemC and C. A description is represented as a CDFG, which is the entry point for our framework. In short our contribution analyses the CDFG, removes unnecessary edges derived by scalar interpretation of arrays and inserts the new analysis results into the graph.

Next a scheduling incorporating the new dependence information is generated. An allocation of multiported memories allows exploiting parallelism of data paths. Finally estimation is performed through the ORINOCO flow that continues with generating instrumented code, a simulation with application specific input data and eventually the calculation of the consumed energy.

For an efficient approach solving this task, we need to answer the following questions: What is the complexity of known approaches? What amount of expressiveness is sufficient to handle real life problems? What is an efficient strategy to manage the dependence tests? The next sections will respectively answer these questions.

## 3.1  Selection of the Dependence Test Set

Of course, for ASIC design the ADFA has to be static, i.e. valid for all applicable input data streams. In other words, from simulation we cannot prove the general absence of any dependence, and dynamic concepts would bring along expensive additional hardware requirements and would complicate scheduling. Though static analysis can never handle arbitrary expressions.

Different dependence tests vary in application domain, complexity of calculation and effort of implementation. To decide which set of tests is sensible to apply, we refer to Table 1 showing the domains of well known dependence tests. The term exactness of a dependence test is always related to its individual domain. By combining several techniques into one framework, we can extend the domain until it complies with our needs concerning the application domain.

**Table 1.** Properties of dependence tests, observed appearance of subscripts and test results

| Test | restriction to AE | coupled | loop bounds | exact | complexity | relative occurrence | relative success |
|------|------|------|------|------|------|------|------|
| ZIV | $n=0$ | | | | | | |
| simple test | none | - | const. | + | $O(1)$ | 44.8 | 19.7 |
| SIV | $n \le 1$ | | | | | | |
| strong | $c_1=d_1$ | - | const. | + | $O(1)$ | 34.0 | 33.0 |
| weak-zero | $c_1=0 \vee d_1=0$ | - | const. | + | $O(1)$ | 6.8 | 4.9 |
| weak-crossing | $c_1=-d_1$ | - | const. | + | $O(1)$ | 0.8 | 0.4 |
| MIV | $n \in \mathbb{N}$ | | | | | | |
| GCD | none | - | const. | - | $O(\log n)$ | | |
| gGCD | none | + | const. | - | $O(n)$ | | |
| Banerjee Ineq | none | + | affine | - | $O(\text{poly } n)$ | 13.6 | n.a. |
| Simplex IPT. | none | + | const. | + | $O(\text{poly } n)$ | | |
| Omega | none | + | affine | + | $O(\exp n)$ | | |
| | | | | | Sum: | 100 | 58.0 |

The column "restriction to AE" of Table 1 denotes the working domain of the according test. Indented conditions conjunct with the above non-indented restrictions. All conditions assume the SEs $s(i) = t(j)$ of the SES to be of the form: $c_0 + c_1 \cdot i_1 + ... + c_n \cdot i_n = d_0 + d_1 \cdot j_1 + ... + d_n \cdot j_n$, where $c_0,...,c_n$ and $d_0,...,d_n$ are integer coefficients of the index variables $i_1,...,i_n$ and $j_1,...,j_n$. The index variables $i_1,...,i_n$ are the same as $j_1,...,j_n$, with the difference that $i_x$ might be another assignment of the same index $j_x$ ($x \in \{1,...n\}$). The attributes coupled, loop bound, and exact, correspond to the terms in Chapter 2. The complexity is only a rough estimate of its runtime dependence on the number of index variables n.

The last two columns summarize the following examination. The occurrences of different expressive classes and effectiveness of simple tests were discussed in [6]. The empirical examination bases on four classes of benchmarks with scientific application[2]. 6% of the 74889 SEs were non-linear such that we pragmatically restrict on the remaining affine part for further considerations.

The column "occurrence" shows that the majority of equations have a complexity below MIV domain. Solvers for ZIV, strong SIV, weak-zero SIV and weak-crossing SIV apply to 86.4% of the problems remaining SEs. The last column denotes the net success of the simple tests. A success means that the test could be applied and it returned either dependence for the subscript position or independence for the accesses. So the net success rate over the applied ZIV and SIV tests is 58%.

Due to their simplicity the ZIV and SIV tests are fast, yet incomplete over the entire domain. MIV tests like Banerjee's Inequality Test, GCD, gGCD, Simplex IPT and Omega test solve more complex problems, but require a high worst case runtime complexity and more extensive programming effort. We leave out details here and refer to [1], [10], [6], [9], [2], [5], and [12].

We decided to restrict on test complexities below linear, to avoid linear growing runtimes when analysing large memory traversals. The appropriate tests cover 86% of the affine problem domain. Additionally to these approaches from literature, we added two methods to solve common SIV problems (enhSIV) and forward dependences of DIV problems (fwdDIV). Both use a 2 variable equation solver similar to the GCD approach. Therefore we are able to analyse affine expressions with $n \leq 2$. We are further restricted to rectangular iteration spaces, but these do not need to be dense.

## 3.2  Integration into the Toolflow

In the following paragraphs we briefly describe the pseudo code of our approach.

**Generation of potential edges.** Dependences of accesses may be analysed in sequence array-by-array. Initially we assert the whole Cartesian product of array accesses to the same array. To some combinations, like self edges or accesses between different control paths, pruning of dependence types can be applied.

**Extraction of definitions, conversion to affine expressions and simplification.** Each dependence test needs expressions for the subscripts and possibly loop bounds as input. Every access expression has to be derived from the CDFG through forward expression substitution and constant propagation. Though control structures can induce multiple definitions, if e.g. an involved value is redefined in an if-statement. We organize these multiple definitions in a tree, where each path from the root to a leaf represents one possible definition of the expression. So far we restrict to uniquely defined expressions because otherwise the test effort would rise exponentially.

After extraction of the first or unique definition path we generate an affine expression over index variables and symbols. By arithmetic simplification we obtain expressions with each variable or symbol occurring just once.

---

[2] RiCEPS, Perfect, SPEC, Eispack and Lapack (libraries for Eigensystems and linear algebra). Even though these benchmarks are written in FORTRAN, the observations are transferable to the C world, since the classification of subscripts is similar in both languages.

For performance issues we implemented a simple database that stores evaluated subscripts, index variables with their borders and strides, or other variables of the CDFG for succeeding tests. Further we integrated lazy evaluation techniques, such that information is derived only when it is explicitly needed.

Pseudo-code for ADFA as integrated into the high level power estimation methodology

```
ADFA( cdfg ) {
   foreach (array in cdfg) {
      potentialEdges = cartesianProd(accessesTo(array));
      foreach (edge in potentialEdges) {
         disproveByDFG( edge, cdfg );
         result[dimensions(array)] = [unknown,…,unknown];
         while (result contains unknown) {
            foreach (test in DependenceTestSet) {
               foreach (dim in dimensions(array)) {
                  if (result[dim]==unknown) {
                     dimres = test(dim, edge); // extracts if
                        // needed further affine expressions
                     if (dimres==disproved) edge=disproved;
                     else result[dim]=dimres;
      } } } }
         updateGraph( CDFG, edge )
} } }
```

**Application of dependence tests.** The dependence tests are applied in lowest domain first order, to reduce testing time to a minimum because simple domains have higher probability of appearance. Analysis for the edge may stop if a single dimension can be disproved. Therefore, to lower effort again, each undetermined dimension is tested using the same test.

The tests themselves decide, which set of expressions (e.g. loop bounds, strides of occurring index variables) have to be derived. Inapplicable or pessimistically dependent dimensions are passed to tests with higher expressiveness. A test is inapplicable if its restrictions are exceeded. If all dimensions are dependent or inapplicable to the given set of tests, the edge is and has to be assumed as dependent respectively. Each test registers new dependence-information with the potential edge.

**Modification of the graph.** The results of the ADFA have to be integrated into the CDFG. For speed purposes usually only a scalar analysis on the array accesses is applied. Updating the graph corrects this initial step by removing the disproved set of edges and inserting the potential edges that could not be disproved. Further we need to close any dangling control data flow caused by deletion of edges.

ADFA removes edges between successive accesses, but in common adds even more non-successive edges because its analysis is made address-based instead of value-based. The additional edges through the ADFA will cause the scheduler to require more time to consider these edges. In principle no modification to an existing scheduling algorithm is necessary, but the runtime of the scheduler will surely increase.

## 4 Experimental Results

We evaluated our approach using the high-level power estimation tool ORINOCO. It estimates the energy consumption of a SystemC/C specification under consideration of the data activity. For showing our ADFA's impact to the examined designs we will provide the relative change of the metrics energy, execution time, and area. To point out the benefit of our ADFA against a scalar analysis, we deactivated ORINOCO's built-in ADFA. All experiments were performed using a 0.18μm technology.

**Graph changes.** In order to evaluate the effectiveness of the ADFA, we applied it to several different scientific algorithms. Primarily, just the edges of the graph change. This we classified into changes to scalar edges, i.e. edges between successive operations from the specification, and additional non-scalar edges. We divided each class into forward and backward edges.

Forward edges (iteration distance 0) define the data-flow inside an iteration, while backward edges (iteration distance >0) describe the flow between different iterations of loops or the whole algorithm. Backward edges become important when source transformations are applied. Using e.g. loop unrolling by factor 4, all backward edges with an iteration distance below or equal 4 would become forward edges.

The change of edges is given in Table 3. For each edge type the column "prior" denotes the number of existing edges due to scalar analysis prior the ADFA. Column "red." holds the number of redundant edges.

**Table 3.** Change of edges by ADFA

| Benchmark | scalar edges | | | | additional edges | | covered | |
|---|---|---|---|---|---|---|---|---|
| | Forward | | backward | | for- | back- | expressiveness | |
| | prior | red. | prior | red. | ward | ward | edges | rate |
| Heat2d | 25 | 20 | 12 | 12 | 22 | 13 | 225 | 82% |
| Viterbi | 119 | 67 | 163 | 118 | 58 | 141 | 2814 | 96% |
| FDCT | 86 | 84 | 17 | 17 | 36 | 28 | 2172 | 100% |
| FFT | 80 | 28 | 37 | 11 | 808 | 838 | 3150 | 20% |

Note that a disproved scalar dependence is more valuable in terms of relaxing scheduling or binding constraints than a non-scalar one. Scalar edges enforce a sequential schedule of the specification. The more scalar edges can be proved redundant, the less tight constraints have to be considered while scheduling. The table shows that in general the ADFA creates in sum more edges.

To evaluate to what extend a more sophisticated analysis could further improve the ADFA, we analysed the amount of edges that were assumed dependent, because of the ADFA's inability to prove or disprove them. This examination relies on the set of tests denoted in subsection 3.1. We see a high coverage of analysable expressions except in the FFT benchmark. The reason for this exception is an implementation which uses symbolic variables in many subscripts. Nevertheless around a third of the scalar edges could still be disproved. The resulting count of additional edges is comparable high and thus enforces small movabilities of array accesses. As we will see, the grade of coverage corresponds to the improvements of the benchmark designs.

**Modification of energy dissipation.** As a direct consequence of the graph changes the increased solution space for a scheduler may result in faster and less energy consuming designs. We present this observation in Table 4. Compared to scalar analysis, in average ADFA saves 7% of energy. Further exploitation of the dependence information increases that result as we will explain for the modified Heat2d benchmark. The area varies by 15% and the amount of executed cycles is reduced by up to 30%. For each of the solutions allocation and binding were heuristically optimized incorporating also register binding optimization.

The reduction of the design's executed cycles enables other methodologies to decrease energy consumption, e.g. voltage scaling, power management, or component selection of slower but less energy consuming components. Of course circuit technology has influence on the correlation between runtime and energy consumption. It rises due to increasing leakage effects in smaller structures. Hence more potential for energy savings can be expected for the designs Viterbi and FDCT.

**Table 4.** Runtime and energy dissipation change through ADFA

| Benchmark | executed cycles | Energy | Area |
|---|---|---|---|
| Heat2d | 0.0% | -3.4% | -0.4% |
| Viterbi | -5.7% | -12.3% | -15.1% |
| FDCT | -30.2% | -11.9% | 15.5% |
| FFT | 0.0% | -2.3% | 2.0% |
| Heat2d, mod | -30.6% | -30.4% | -12.4% |

For the last row (Head2d, mod) we manually applied two source transformation techniques. After unrolling of the inner loop by factor 2, more array accesses are inside one iteration, which can partially be shared by privatisation in one and consequent iterations. Our ADFA allows by far more effective scheduling optimisations on this array access dominated transformation.

Note that in all presented energy values the memory energy is not incorporated due to two reasons. The number of accesses using ADFA remains the same as without its application, and the static power of the SRAM memories is small, such that the reduction of runtime does not induce a noteworthy amount of energy change.

Our framework has been designed for rapid results and long-term extendibility regarding dependence tests, and dependence abstraction. The runtime aware implementation techniques pay off in runtime speedups of factor 2 thus consuming less than 2 seconds on an 1 GHz PC for each of the benchmarks.

We demonstrated the design-space could be enlarged to perform better in number of executed cycles and energy. From the benchmarks, different improvements were obtained dependent on the test-coverage and the structure of array accesses in the control flow. The application of ADFA is efficient where many accesses inside one basic block do access disjunctive address sets.

## 5  Conclusion

The presented ADFA approach addresses the restrictions on memory intensive designs induced by scalar dependence analysis of array accesses, which is the state of the art in many high-level synthesis tools.

We compared various ADFA methodologies, from simple tests to complex frameworks, concerning runtime complexity and coverage of the application domain. An appropriate set of dependence tests has been chosen, implemented and evaluated.

Finally the impact has been evaluated by prototypic integration into a high-level power estimation tool. We measured energy savings by 2% up to 12% and achieved runtime savings up to 30% while the area varied by ±15%. As we showed, techniques that transpose runtime by energy promise even better energy reductions.

Concluding, we proved the ADFA methodology has significant impact on energy, time, and area and therefore should not be neglected in high-level design flows or tools. Extensions to the coverage, like e.g. handling multiple defined expressions, as well as dependence motivated code transformations promise even higher impact on design metrics. Our ongoing research addresses these topics.

## References

1. U. Banerjee: Loop Transformations for Restructuring Compilers: The Foundations. Kluwer Academic Publishers, 1993.
2. W. Blume, R. Eigenmann: Non-Linear and Symbolic Data Dependence Testing. IEEE Transactions on Parallel and Distributed Systems, vol. 9, no. 12, 1998.
3. D. Brooks, V. Tiwari, and M. Martonosi: Wattch: A framework for architectural-level power analysis and optimizations. 27th Annual Intl. Symp. on Computer Architecture, 2000.
4. ChipVision Design Systems AG, Webpage, http://www.chipvision.com
5. Goumas, Athanasaki, Koziris: Code Generation Methods for Tiling Transformation. Journal of Information Science and Engineering 18, 2002.
6. G. Goff, K. Kennedy, C. Tseng: Practical Dependence Testing. Proc. of the ACM, SIGPLAN '91, Conference on Programming Language Design and Implementation, 1991.
7. D. Kulkarni, M. Stumm: Loop and Data Transformations: A Tutorial. Technical Report CSRI-337, Computer Systems Research Institute, 1993.
8. Kandemir, M. And Vijakrishnan N., Irwin M.J. and Ye, W.: Influence of Compiler Optimizations on System Power, Proc. of the 37th Design Automation Conference, 2000.
9. W. Pugh: Uniform techniques for loop optimisations. International Conference on Supercomputing, 341-352, 1991.
10. Petersen, P. M. and Padua, D. A.: Static and Dynamic Evaluation of Data Dependence Analysis Techniques. IEEE Trans. Parallel Distrib. Systems, vol. 7, no. 11, 1996.
11. M.J. Wolfe: High Performance Compilers for Parallel Computing. Addison-Wesley Publishing Company, 1996.
12. D. Wonnacott: Constraint-Based Array Dependence Analysis. PhD thesis, University of Maryland, 1995.
13. Wolf, M. E. and Lam, M. S.: A Loop Transformation Theory and an Algorithm to Maximize Parallelism. IEEE Transactions on Parallel Distrib. Systems, vol. 2, no. 4, 1991.
14. Y.-Q. Yang, C. Ancourt, F. Irigoin: Minimal Data Dependence Abstractions for Loop Transformations. In Proc. Languages and Compilers for Parallel Computing, 1994.

# Methodology for Energy-Efficient Digital Circuit Sizing: Important Issues and Design Limitations*

Bart R. Zeydel and Vojin G. Oklobdzija

Advanced Computer Systems Engineering Laboratory
University of California, Davis,
One Shields Ave, Davis, CA 95616, USA
{zeydel, vojin}@acsel-lab.com
http://www.acsel-lab.com

**Abstract.** This paper analyzes the issues that face digital circuit design methodologies and tools which address energy-efficient digital circuit sizing. The best
known techniques for resolving these issues are presented, along with the
sources of error. The analysis demonstrates that input slope independent models
for energy and delay and stage based optimization are effective for analyzing and
optimizing energy-efficient digital circuits when applied correctly.

## 1 Introduction

For several years, the semiconductor industry has been facing a power crisis. Much of
the work addressing this issue has focused on system level approaches to reducing
power [4][5] or on optimization tools [7]. While these advances have helped to reduce
energy in digital circuits, they do not offer insight into how the savings is achieved.
Additionally it is not known whether a different realization of the same function
would yield better results or how that modification should be made. The opportunity
for energy reduction is still significant in digital circuits where even in adders an
energy savings of up to 50% without delay degradation has recently been shown [5].

In this work we examine the issues facing digital circuit design methodologies for
the analysis and design of energy-efficient circuits. As the intent of a design methodology is to enable short design times, we impose the constraint that the delay and
energy of each logic gate must be calculated solely from its output load and size. This
inherently limits the types of energy and delay models to those that do not account for
input slope variation.

The analysis is organized as follows: Section 2 presents the energy and delay models used for circuit sizing analysis; Section 3 presents the logic families which can be
efficiently optimized using these models; Section 4 examines approaches to digital
circuit sizing and identifies issues and limitations; Section 5 presents comparison results of different approaches to circuit sizing optimization; Section 6 presents a summary of the analysis.

---

* The work was supported in part by California MICRO.

J. Vounckx, N. Azemard, and P. Maurine (Eds.): PATMOS 2006, LNCS 4148, pp. 127–136, 2006.
© Springer-Verlag Berlin Heidelberg 2006

## 2 Logic Gate Delay and Energy Models

### 2.1 Delay and Energy Models

In this section the input slope independent models for delay and energy are presented. To simplify discussion, Logical Effort (LE) terms will be used [1][2]. The delay of a logic gate can be expressed using an RC-model [3]. One such model is the normalized LE form:

$$Td = (gh + p) \cdot \tau$$

The limitation of this model is that it does not account for the dependence of delay on input slope.

Energy can be computed directly from the gate size and output load. The model presented in [11] performs a best fit for energy due to changes in gate size and output load, where $E_p$ and $E_g$ are the fitting terms and $E_{leakage}$ is a function of cycle time:

$$E = E_p C_{in} + E_g C_{out} + E_{leakage}$$

The limitation of this type of energy model is that the change in short-circuit current due to input slope variation is not accounted for. Each of the parameters for the delay and energy models can be obtained from either hand estimation or simulation.

### 2.2 Effect of Relative Input Arrival Time on Model Parameters

The impact of relative input arrival time on the delay of a logic gate is widely known, however it is ignored in digital circuit sizing optimization and static timing analysis tools [10]. A comparison of LE parameters obtained from hand estimates with those obtained from HSPICE simulation for single input switching and worse case input switching is shown in Table 1.

**Table 1.** LE parameters obtained using different approaches in a 130nm CMOS technology

| Circuit | LE Hand Estimates ($\mu_n = 2.5\mu_p$) | | Single Input Switching HSPICE | | Worst Case Input Switching HSPICE | |
|---|---|---|---|---|---|---|
| | $g_{avg}$ | $p_{avg}$ | $g_{avg}$ | $p_{avg}$ | $g_{avg}$ | $p_{avg}$ |
| inv | 1 | 1 | 1.0 | 1.04 | 1.0 | 1.04 |
| nand2 | 1.29 | 2 | 1.13 | 1.72 | 1.28 | 1.95 |
| nand3 | 1.57 | 3 | 1.29 | 2.68 | 1.57 | 3.21 |
| nor2 | 1.71 | 2 | 1.69 | 2.46 | 1.87 | 2.67 |
| nor3 | 2.43 | 3 | 2.36 | 4.65 | 2.74 | 5.06 |

The values of $g$ and $p$ are 10-20% larger for worst-case input switching compared to the values obtained from single input switching analysis. Interestingly, the hand estimates for $g$ fall in between the single input switching and worst case input switching values, making the values obtained from hand analysis reasonable for use in design methodologies for circuit sizing and analysis. The appropriate characterization environment depends on the goal of the designer. If static timing analysis is acceptable, single input switching can be used. However if the desire is to bound the worst possible delay, worst case input switching should be used. The impact of input arrival time on circuit sizing will be demonstrated in Section 5.

## 3 Logic Families Included in Analysis

To be compatible with the models in Section 2, digital circuit sizing will only be allowed on an entire logic gate. That is, if the size of a logic gate changes by a factor $\alpha$, the size of each transistor in the logic gate will also change by the same factor $\alpha$. To achieve the best possible circuit sizing using these models, a logic gate will be defined as a group of transistors with the following characteristics: each input is attached to the gate of a transistor (i.e. no input can be attached to the source/drain of a transistor), for each valid combination of inputs there exists a path to $V_{dd}$ or $V_{ss}$, and no source/drain can be connected to the gate of a transistor within the logic gate. The following sub-sections describe the issues (if any) that commonly used logic families have with meeting these criteria, along with techniques for resolving these issues.

### 3.1 Static and Domino CMOS Logic Families

Static CMOS logic gates require no modification to meet the logic gate definition. Domino gates are similar to static CMOS, except they have a keeper which violates the source/drain connection to the gate of a transistor within the logic gate. To handle the keeper, a separate inverting logic gate which does not drive the output is used for feedback to the keeper. The size of the inverting gate and the keeper scale directly with $\alpha$, resulting in extra parasitic delay for the gate. *Note: The dynamic gate is treated as an individual gate separate from the static gate that follows it.*

### 3.2 Static CMOS with Pass-Gates

Since pass-gates are commonly used in digital circuits for implementing MUX's and XOR's it is essential that they can be analyzed and sized using the models of section 2. One of the problems with pass-gates arises from the fact that they are often treated

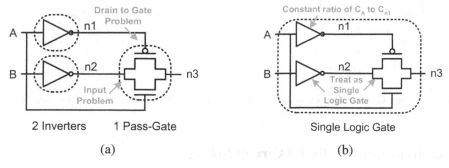

**Fig. 1.** (a) Logic Gate definition issues when separating pass-gates from static CMOS gates (b) Modifications required to handle as a single Logic Gate

as a logically separate entity from a static CMOS logic gate (Fig. 1a). This issue can be resolved by treating the pass gate as part of the logic gate that is driving it as is the case with the path through input B in Fig. 1b. Input A is more difficult to handle. Since the pass-gate begins to turn on when input A arrives, it is impossible to treat input A and n1 as independent inputs to the logic gate. As a result, a fixed ratio of $C_{n1}$ to $C_A$ must be chosen to create a roughly constant relative arrival time of signal A and n1. This exception to the logic gate definition constrains the circuit sizing optimization by fixing the relative arrival of A to n1, regardless of delay target. To achieve the best results, this relative arrival time should be selected based on the expected performance of the circuit (larger for low-speed and smaller for high-performance).

A pass-gate implementation of an XOR logic gate creates further complications as seen in Fig. 2. The issues associated with input A can be handled as in Fig. 1. Accurate handling of input B requires that the input of a logic gate be allowed to connect to the source/drain of a transistor. The drawback of this approach is that the output load of a gate is potentially a mix of gate capacitance and a pass-gate connection, making modeling complex. Instead of increasing the complexity, an approximation can be made. The worst case delay for input B is through the inverter and upper pass-gate (which can be handled in the same fashion as in Fig. 1). However, the load that is presented to input B depends on the state of input A. Assuming only a single input switches at a time, it is seen that only one pass-gate can be "on" at a time. Therefore the load presented to input B for the worst case delay of the gate is the sum of the input capacitance of the inverter and capacitance of the lower pass-gate. To allow this approximation, the upper and lower pass-gates must be sized to guarantee that the path from B through the lower pass-gate will be faster than the path from B through the upper pass-gate regardless of the logic gate driving input B or the load at the output.

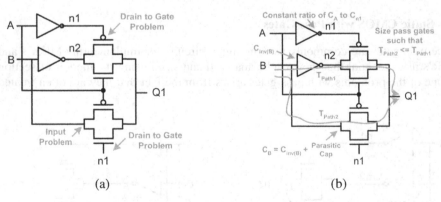

(a)    (b)

**Fig. 2.** (a) Pass-Gate XOR logic gate definition issues. (b) Modifications and approximations required to treat as a single Logic Gate.

## 4  Optimization of Digital Circuit Sizing

In this section, the input slope independent energy and delay models are used to examine the optimization of digital circuit sizing.

## 4.1 Optimization of a Chain of Logic Gates

Sutherland and Sproull developed Logical Effort based on the characteristic that the optimal sizing for a chain of gates occurs when each gate has the same stage effort [1][2]. They demonstrated this using a RC-delay model which does not account for delay variation due to changes in input slope. From this the optimal stage effort, $f_{opt}$, could be found by taking the $N^{th}$ root of the product of stage efforts (where N is the number of stages), which by definition yields equal stage effort. This solution allows for input slope independent energy and delay models to be very accurate for a chain of identical gates.

In simulation it is observed that the delay of a logic gate is approximately linear with respect to $h$ when the ratio of input slope to output slope is constant [2][8]. As a result, the delay and energy models are accurate for each gate in the chain because equal $f$ corresponds to equal $h$ in a chain of identical gates. If the types of gates in a chain differ, the parasitic capacitance will differ resulting in different slopes which introduce error into the delay estimate.

The delay optimal sizing is not always the minimum energy solution for a circuit. Depending on the system that a circuit is used in, it is possible that the optimal solution might occur at a relaxed delay target (while still maintaining the same input size and output load) [6]. The energy optimization of a chain of digital circuits for a fixed delay, input size, and output load can be performed by redistributing the stage efforts from the delay optimal solution [8][6]. The error introduced by this optimization to the input slope independent energy and delay models is best observed by comparing

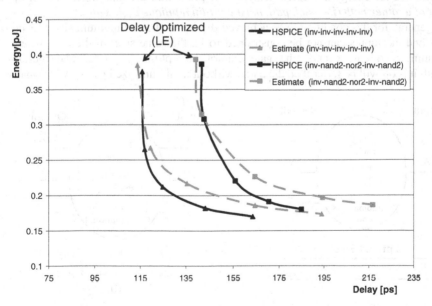

**Fig. 3.** Estimated Energy and Delay vs. HSPICE for two chains of logic gates optimized for different performance targets with a fixed output load and input size

the energy minimized sizing to the delay optimal sizing of a circuit with a smaller input size. In order for the energy minimized case to have the same delay as the delay optimized sizing the summation of the stage efforts must be the same, resulting in some stage efforts that are larger and some that are smaller than the delay optimized stage efforts. From this it can be seen that the error introduced is not additive.

In Fig. 3, a comparison of estimated minimum energy points for different delay targets versus HSPICE simulation is shown for two different chains of gates. Each circuit has the same output load and input size (with $C_{out} = 32C_{in}$). The energy error is small, demonstrating that the change in short circuit energy due to changes in input slope does not constitute a large portion of the total energy. The delay error on the other hand grows as the performance target is relaxed from delay optimal.

## 4.2 Optimization of Multiple-Output Digital Circuits

The exact optimization of digital circuit sizing for digital circuits with branching and multiple inputs is a complex problem. While recent advances have been made in computing power and numerical methods, such as the application of geometric programming [7], no commercial tools are available which solve this problem exactly or quickly. However, characteristics of the optimal solution are known. It is possible to simplify the optimization process using the characteristics of the optimal sizing solution. In a circuit optimization with a fixed output load and fixed maximum input size, the delay from input to output of each dependent path in the circuit should be equal [10]. This is true whether the circuit has a single input (Fig 4a) or multiple inputs (Fig. 4b). The condition holds whether the circuit is being optimized for delay or optimized for energy at a fixed delay. *Note: paths that are equalized can not be a subset of another path (i.e. each path must contain a unique logic gate).*

In general, for this condition to be achieved there must be no minimum size gate constraint and the inputs can not be constrained to be the same size. In the case where a minimum sized gate occurs, the gate cannot be optimized further and therefore the path it is on will be faster than the paths without minimum sized gates. Additionally,

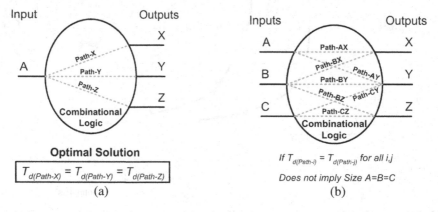

**Fig. 4.** Unconstrained delay optimal sizing solutions for (a) Single input multiple-output circuit and (b) Multiple input and multiple output circuit

the critical path will be slower when minimum gate sizes occur as the off-path loading can not be reduced further. The case of having all inputs the same size is similar. By forcing the inputs to be the same size, certain paths are overdriven. As a result, these paths will be faster than the paths that require the largest input (which is used as the input size for all paths). In practice these two constraints do occur, minimum sizes because of physical limitations of technology and equal input sizes because of a desire to create a regular layout.

The optimization of a path that branches to multiple gates is examined on the circuit structure shown in Fig. 5 for a fixed output load, $C_{out}$, and fixed input size $C_1$. To allow for application of LE, the parasitic delay difference between paths is ignored (this is why the hand estimate for parasitic delay does not need to be very accurate, as it does not affect circuit sizing when using LE, it only affects the reported delay). The optimality of the solution depends on the parasitic delay difference between the paths. If the delay difference is small, the circuit sizing solution will be close to optimal however as the delay difference grows, the optimality of the solution degrades. It is important to note that the calculation of branching can be prohibitively complex in multi-stage circuits. Often a simplification is made where the branch value is treated as the number of paths attached to a node. The problem with this simplification is that it does not relate to a physical sizing, resulting in inaccurate energy estimates.

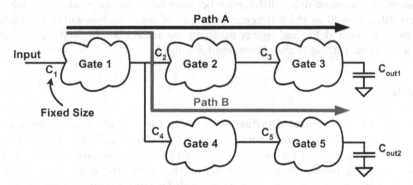

**Fig. 5.** Multiple output circuit with equal number of stages on each branch

Another issues arises when the length of branches differ (i.e. if another gate were added at the end of path A in Fig. 5). In this case, LE's solution of equal effort per stage is not optimal (even when parasitic delay difference of paths is ignored). Clearly if each gate had the same stage effort, the delay associated with stage effort of Path A and B would differ. Additionally, the optimal solution does not occur when the stage effort of Gate 1 is equal to the stage effort of Gate 2 or 4. The exact solution to this case, even when ignoring the parasitic delay difference of paths, must be found using numerical methods. As larger circuits are analyzed, the complexity of this type of optimization becomes prohibitive for use in design methodologies and even CAD tools. To reduce complexity, the analysis and circuit size optimization are often decoupled in modern CAD tools, where the critical path of the circuit is identified using static timing analysis and the sizes of the circuits along that path are optimized. This process is repeated until the result converges.

### 4.3 Stage-Based Optimization

Instead of optimizing each logic gate individually in a circuit, the sizes can be optimized based on logic stages. The following steps describe the setup.

1) Each gate is assigned to the earliest possible logic stage.
2) Delay is equalized by assigning the same stage effort to each logic gate in the stage.
3) For logic gates that are attached only to an output, yet are not in the last stage of the circuit, the stage efforts of subsequent stage are added to the stage effort of the logic gate in order to equalize the delay of each path.

The stage assignment equalizes the delay associated with stage effort of each path except for in the following cases: an input is attached to a logic gate that is not in the first logic stage; the output of a logic gate attaches to multiple logic stages; minimum gate sizes occur; input sizes are constrained to be equal; and wires. Proper handling of these cases requires additional constraints on the optimization.

Once stage assignment is complete and additional constraints are added, the circuit can be optimized for delay or energy at a fixed delay using numerical optimization of the N variables (where N is the number of stages). The optimality of the result is dependent on the parasitic delay differences between the logic gates along a path and between paths as well as the difference in length of the branches within the circuit. Using this approach, delay and energy estimate can always be obtained which correspond to a physical sizing of the circuit, unlike with LE.

## 5   Results

A comparison of the optimal delay and total width for several chains of logic gates using the characterization parameters of Table 1 is shown in Table 2. The results demonstrate an increase in optimal delay of 13-18% for worst case input switching compared to single input switching. The sizing (shown by total width) does not vary significantly for each setup. The sizing does not differ much because $f = gh$. Thus, for a chain of identical gates, regardless of the value of g, the delay optimal sizing of the chain will be the same. Differences in sizing occur because of differences in g per stage (as seen in the third and fourth cases).

**Table 2.** Comparison of Delay results and sizing of paths sized for delay optimization using the characterization parameters for $g$ and $p$ in Table 1 ($C_{out} = 12C_{in}$ for all paths)

| Circuit | Hand Estimates ($\mu_n = 2.5\mu_p$) | | Single Input Switching | | Worst Case Input Switching | |
|---|---|---|---|---|---|---|
| | Delay ($\tau$) | Width ($C_{in}$) | Delay ($\tau$) | Width ($C_{in}$) | Delay ($\tau$) | Width ($C_{in}$) |
| nand3-nand3-nand3 | 19.78 | 8.53 | 16.9 | 8.53 | 20.41 | 8.53 |
| nor3-nor3-nor3 | 25.69 | 8.53 | 30.16 | 8.53 | 34 | 8.53 |
| nand3-nor3-nand3 | 21.47 | 8.18 | 20.84 | 8.08 | 24.46 | 8.11 |
| nand2-nand3-nor2 | 17.39 | 7.49 | 16.14 | 7.21 | 18.51 | 7.22 |

A comparison of gate based optimization and stage based optimization is shown in Table 3. The comparison is performed on a circuit with an inverter driving two branches (similar to Fig. 5). One branch has 8 inverters, while the other branch ranges from 2 to 8 inverters creating a path length difference of 6 to 0 inverters respectively. The output of each path is loaded the same for all cases, with $C_{out} = 128C_{in}$.

**Table 3.** Comparison of Gate Based Optimization and Stage Based Optimization

| Path Length Difference | Gate Based Optimization | | Stage Based Optimization | | % worse for Stage Based | |
|:---:|:---:|:---:|:---:|:---:|:---:|:---:|
| | Delay [$\tau$] | Energy [pJ] | Delay [$\tau$] | Energy [pJ] | Delay | Energy |
| 6 | 27.03 | 2.57 | 28.25 | 2.90 | 5% | 13% |
| 5 | 25.71 | 2.72 | 26.82 | 3.15 | 4% | 16% |
| 4 | 25.31 | 2.88 | 26.15 | 3.28 | 3% | 14% |
| 3 | 25.19 | 3.01 | 25.78 | 3.35 | 2% | 11% |
| 2 | 25.23 | 3.16 | 25.57 | 3.39 | 1% | 7% |
| 1 | 25.38 | 3.34 | 25.51 | 3.43 | 0% | 3% |
| 0 | 25.67 | 3.52 | 25.67 | 3.52 | 0% | 0% |

As can be seen in the table, the delay error of stage based optimization compared to gate based optimization is relatively small, regardless of the path length difference. The energy error can be up to 16%. If the path length difference is only 2 gates, the energy result is only 7% worse. Typically in digital circuits the difference in lengths of branches is only large when the off-path circuit is minimum size. In that case the stage based optimization will yield similar energy as gate based optimization. As a result, for many digital circuits, stage based optimization gives comparable results to gate based optimization. The case when stage based optimization suffers is when the resulting sizing gives off-path gate sizing that is not minimum size and the path length difference between the branches is large.

# 6  Conclusion

It is shown that the error introduced using delay and energy models that do not account for input slope variation is relatively small. The true challenge facing design methodologies is that the accurate application of these models requires the analysis of the entire circuit. Since system optimization requires energy and delay values for each input size and output load of a digital circuit [6], it is essential that the reported energy and delay of a design methodology have a one-to-one correlation with the resulting circuit sizing (meaning that LE branching simplifications can not be used). The analysis also showed that stage based optimization yields comparable results to gate based optimization, while reducing the complexity of the optimization. Stage based optimization also appears promising for future technologies where circuits will have a more regular layout [9] (i.e. each logic gate in a logic stage has the same size). Under this condition, it is possible to use a stage based optimization approach where the size of each logic stage is used as the variable instead of the stage effort.

# References

1. R. F. Sproull, and I. E. Sutherland, "Logical Effort: Designing for Speed on the Back of an Envelop," IEEE Adv. Research in VLSI, C. Sequin (editor), MIT Press, 1991.
2. I. E. Sutherland, R. F. Sproull, and D. Harris, "Logical Effort: Designing Fast CMOS Circuits," Morgan Kaufmann Publisher, c1999.
3. M. Horowitz, "Timing Models for MOS Circuits," PhD Thesis, Stanford University, December 1983.
4. V. Zyuban, P. N. Strenski, "Balancing Hardware Intensity in Microprocessor Pipelines", IBM Journal of Research and Development, Vol. 47, No. 5/6, 2003.
5. B. R. Zeydel, T.T.J.H. Kluter, V. G. Oklobdzija, "Efficient Energy-Delay Mapping of Addition Recurrence Algorithms in CMOS", International Symposium on Computer Arithmetic, ARITH-17, Cape Cod, Massachusetts, USA, June 27-29, 2005.
6. H. Q. Dao, B. R. Zeydel, V. G. Oklobdzija, "Energy Optimization of Pipelined Digital Systems Using Circuit Sizing and Supply Scaling", IEEE Transaction on VLSI Systems, to appear, 2006.
7. S. Boyd, S. -J. Kim, D. Patil and M. Horowitz, "Digital Circuit Sizing via Geometric Programming," Operations Research, Nov.-Dec. 2005, Vol. 53, Issue 6, pp.899-932.
8. H. Q. Dao, B. R. Zeydel, V. G. Oklobdzija, "Energy Optimization of High-Performance Circuits", Proceedings of the 13th International Workshop on Power And Timing Modeling, Optimization and Simulation, Torino, Italy, September 10-12, 2003.
9. P. Gelsinger, "GigaScale Integration for Teraops Performance -- Challenges, Opportunities, and New Frontiers", 41st DAC Keynote, June 2004.
10. S. Sapatnekar, "Timing," Kluwer Academic Publishers, Boston, MA, 2004.
11. V. G. Oklobdzija, B. R. Zeydel, H. Q. Dao, S. Mathew, R. Krishnamurthy, "Comparison of High-Performance VLSI Adders in Energy-Delay Space", IEEE Transaction on VLSI Systems, Volume 13, Issue 6, pp. 754-758, June 2005.

# Low-Power Adaptive Bias Amplifier
# for a Large Supply-Range Linear Voltage Regulator

Stefan Cserveny

CSEM SA, Neuchâtel, CH
stefan.cserveny@csem.ch

**Abstract.** A multiple stage adaptive bias error amplifier has been developed for a linear voltage reducer that should regulate for a very large and continuous supply-voltage range between 1.2 and 3.6 V. It uses both the 3.3 V high voltage transistors available in the considered generic 0.18 µm logic process to allow above 1.8 V functioning and the normal transistors needed to reach the desired performance at the lowest supply voltages. The proposed multiple stage approach solves the contradictory requirements for low and high supply voltages, reduces the amplifier power consumption to less than 1.35 % of the load current and shows good regulator stability in spite of an increased number of poles.

## 1 Introduction

The power consumption optimization is a major issue for complex Systems-on-Chips. As the power management has become a critical part for their realization, efficient DC-DC converters are required [1-3]. This is particularly important for battery powered portable electronic equipments. Standard products to be used in such equipments for several specific applications must be capable to work with different energy sources and, in the same time, bias each internal functional block with its desired optimum supply voltage. Therefore large supply-range voltage reducers are needed that can satisfy all the specified performance requirements. Among them, the linear Low Drop-Out (LDO) regulator is still widely used [1-4].

The major problem in realizing high performance linear regulators is to obtain a good stability in the whole working range of the supply voltage and the load current. Adapted to the specific application requirements, innovative frequency compensation techniques are continuously proposed in the literature [3-6].

Power consumption reduction is also an important requirement for most voltage reducers: they must have a high efficiency and small standby power consumption. One most interesting power efficient approach is to use adaptive bias transconductance amplifiers [7] in LDO regulators [6, 8].

In order to satisfy the large supply range requirement and to improve even more the power efficiency while guaranteeing good regulator stability, a novel multiple-stage adaptive bias error amplifier is proposed in this paper.

J. Vounckx, N. Azemard, and P. Maurine (Eds.): PATMOS 2006, LNCS 4148, pp. 137 – 147, 2006.

## 2  The Considered Linear Regulator and Its Requirements

The principle of a linear LDO regulator is schematically presented in Fig. 1.

The output voltage $V_L$ on the load absorbing a variable load current $I_L$ is regulated to the specified value by the voltage drop in the output driver ballast transistor. The ballast transistor gate is controlled in a closed loop with the error amplifier. The divider made by $R_1$ and $R_2$ realize the ratio between the reference voltage $V_{REF}$ and the desired output voltage.

The large value filter capacitance $C_L$ is an external element. This capacitor's equivalent series resistance (**esr**) and equivalent series inductance (**esl**) must also be taken into account, together with the parasitic elements of the connection between $C_L$ and the pad **L**.

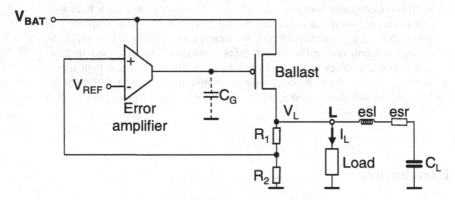

**Fig. 1.** Linear regulator block diagram

The foreseen working values for the $V_{BAT}$ supply are in a continuous range between 1.2 V and 3.6 V.

In the same time, it has been required to use the generic 0.18 µm logic process in which all the other building blocks were already realized. In this process, besides the normal 1.8 V devices, high voltage 3.3 V devices are also available; however, these high voltage transistors have different sizes and characteristics, in particular they have longer minimum channel length and higher threshold voltages.

In such a design, whenever a transistor can encounter a voltage above 1.98 V, the high voltage transistors, specified up to 3.63 V, must be used. This is in particular the case for the PMOS ballast transistor directly connected to $V_{BAT}$. However, the W/L ratio of this PMOS has to be sufficiently large in order to obtain the desired low voltage drop at the smallest supply voltage and for the maximum load current, which has been specified at 20 mA. As a result, with the almost two times longer high voltage transistors, the gate area will be about four times larger than with a normal PMOS, therefore a large gate capacitance $C_G$ has to be taken into account in the design.

The use of low and high voltage transistors in the error amplifier gain stage has to be considered carefully to find the best trade-off between the opposing requirements at the lowest and highest supply voltages. In the same time, the demanded performance concerning the voltage regulation characteristic, speed, start-up time, PSRR, power efficiency and standby consumption have to be satisfied in the entire supply range.

## 3 The Multiple-Stage Adaptive Bias Amplifier

In general, it is intended in the Fig. 1 linear regulator to obtain good stability by imposing as dominant pole the pole related to the output node **L** with the large external capacitor $C_L$. In this case, the poles related to the relatively large gate capacitance of the ballast transistor $C_G$ and all the internal poles of the error amplifier have to be at much higher frequencies.

However, as this dominant pole varies with the load current $I_L$, the adaptive bias amplifier becomes a very interesting approach to be considered; besides its low power characteristics, it allows the tracking of the load current by the non-dominant poles.

The simplest implementation of this approach is given in Fig. 2; this basic configuration has been used successfully in many realized regulators at normal limited supply voltage ranges, such as those for a given battery.

The error signal detecting differential pair M1 and M2 has a tail current containing an adaptive bias component in the transistor MS and a small fixed $I_0$. In the positive feedback loop containing MP, MPM, MNM and MS, the tail current in MS is approximately $k$ times the current in the branch with M1 and MP. With M2 and M1 having the same size, $k$ should be about 2.

In the same time, MP is made $x$ times smaller than the ballast transistor MB, therefore the currents in the differential pair are a fraction of the load current $I_L$.

For a larger load current, therefore higher dominant pole, the node **G** pole is also higher; the equivalent conductance related to the MP current is larger, even if not as much as its $g_m$ because of the positive feedback loop. A large $x$ ratio is wanted for good power consumption efficiency, however for normal stable functioning it is usually about 20 or 40, maximum 100.

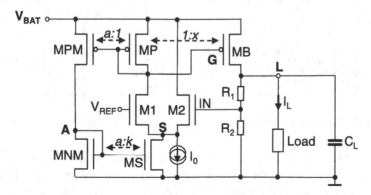

**Fig. 2.** Basic linear regulator configuration using an adaptive bias amplifier

At high $V_{BAT}$ values, most transistors in this configuration can see voltages above 1.98 V, therefore should be high voltage devices. However, with such devices, the lowest $V_{BAT}$ for which the amplifier can work is well above 1.2 V, especially when the load current $I_L$ is high. With a voltage drop well above 1 V in the worst process and temperature corner, the diode connected high threshold MP is the largest contributor to the lowest acceptable $V_{BAT}$ value. The threshold voltage of the high voltage NMOS is not only higher, it has also a larger process corner spread. With such transistors, M1 and M2 can have a large $V_{GS}$, therefore $V_{REF}$ should be high enough to keep the MS transistor saturated, well above the about 0.6 V of the considered band gap reference. Moreover, the large size of the high voltage devices, especially when the mentioned voltage drops are to be minimized, results in very high capacitances on the nodes **A** and **S**, which is bad for the corresponding internal poles.

In order to reduce the smallest acceptable supply voltage and keep the given $V_{REF}$ value, the M1/M2 differential pair and the MP diode have to be normal threshold devices. High voltage NMOS cascode transistors can protect the drains of M1 and M2. The diode connected MP does not see the high voltage, but in this case it cannot be matched any more with the high voltage ballast transistor MB. High $V_{DS}$ can occur on the MPM loop transistor, which also has to be matched with MP, therefore the normal threshold MPM drain should also be protected with a high voltage PMOS cascode.

Such an implementation, using both high and normal threshold transistors, requires at least one additional stage to close a well matched adaptive bias loop. The proposed new adaptive bias configuration shown in the Fig. 3 has two additional stages, MPB matched with MP (normal threshold) and MPO matched with MB (high threshold).

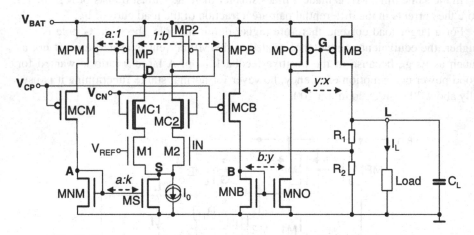

**Fig. 3.** Three stage adaptive bias amplifier for the considered linear regulator

The MP to MB ratio $x$ is the result of the multiplication of $x/y$, $y/b$ and $b/1$ ratios: moderate values for each of these ratios allow for a much higher $x$, therefore for a much lower current in the differential pair. The $y$ time larger current in the MPO diode pushes up the critical node **G** pole frequency; the equivalent conductance for this pole is the $g_m$ of MPO, which is directly related to that of MB.

Small values for $a$ and $b$ limit the additional capacitive load on the node **D**, which is now replacing the node **G** as most important pole, closest to the dominant pole.

A two stage solution has also been considered, without the node **B** branch and with a current mirror between MNO and MNM with the mirror ratio $y/a$; in order to avoid a too large capacitance on the node **A**, this ratio cannot be very large, therefore the current in the differential pair should be larger than in the Fig. 3 three stage approach.

The amplifier current consumption is approximately $(2+a+b+y)/x$ time the load current $I_L$; in the present design with $x = 2000$, $y = 20$ and $a = b = 1$, it is only 1.2%, a very good efficiency, 2.5 to 6 times better than without this multistage approach.

High voltage native NMOS transistors were used for the MC1 and MC2 cascode transistors. This was needed to allow enough $V_{DS}$ for M1, M2 and MS to keep them in saturation at the 1.2 V low $V_{BAT}$ limit for all corners; a too large $V_{GS}$ does not allow the use of the high threshold NMOS without boosting their gates above such a low $V_{BAT}$. Unfortunately no native high voltage PMOS are available in the process to be used as cascode for MCM and MCB; even if the design constraints are less severe than for the NMOS cascode, the sizing of the PMOS transistors had to deal with a very difficult trade off between the amplifier PSRR and gain in the opposite process and temperature corners.

Because the native NMOS are not in saturation at $V_D = V_G$, an additional voltage drop given by a normal threshold NMOS diode biased by a current source $I_{DN}$ is used to generate the native NMOS cascode voltage $V_{CN}$ (Fig. 4).

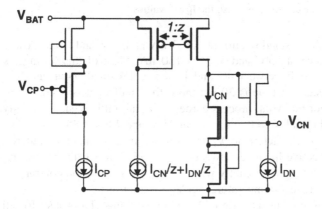

**Fig. 4.** Cascode gate voltage generation for the high-voltage PMOS and native NMOS

# 4   Simulation Results

For standby, enabling switches pull up the **G** and **D** nodes to $V_{BAT}$ and cut off the fixed bias currents, i.e. the I0 fixed amplifier tail current and the three current sources needed for cascode gate voltage generation as shown in the Fig. 4.

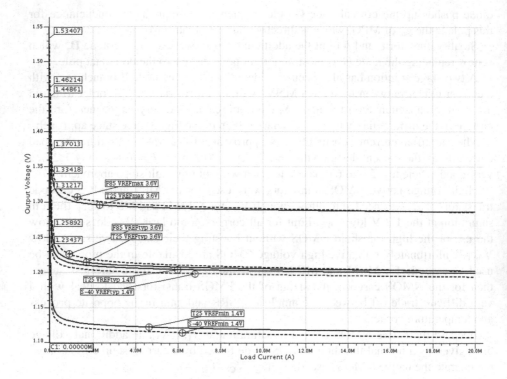

**Fig. 5.** Regulation characteristics for typical and extreme process and temperature corner, $V_{REF}$ and $V_{BAT}$ values; the cursor shows also the $I_L = 0$ values

Typical regulator standby current is 0.3 nA at 1.4 V and 0.42 nA at 3.6 V while worst corner value at 85°C and 3.6V is 130 nA. Most of this leakage is due to the large MB ballast; only between 4% and 4.7% is OTA standby current.

The typical start up time is 30 μs; more than half of it is needed to establish the bias currents. For the worst process corner, with an unlikely small resistive load as if $I_L = 20$ mA and initial $V_L = 0$, it is 43μs at 25°C and 70μs at 85°C.

The regulation characteristic $V_L$ ($I_L$) shows an equivalent output resistance less than 1 Ω in the active $I_L$ range between 1 mA and 20 mA (Fig. 5). The regulated output voltage $V_L$ varies significantly with the $V_{REF}$ value; on the contrary, it is not very sensitive to the process, temperature and $V_{BAT}$ variations.

There is an important increase of $V_L$ when $I_L$ drops. To protect for all conditions the load containing circuits realized with normal 1.8 V devices, the resistive divider $R_1 + R_2$ has been reduced to about 125 kΩ; this limits the maximum worst case $V_L$ value for zero load current at 1.534 V, well below the 1.98 V limit.

The simulated active mode OTA consumption is near 1% of $I_L$ at 1.4 V and 1.3% at 3.6V, not far from the estimated 1.2% in the simple theory. At very low $I_L$, when the MB current reaches the smallest values (near 10 μA) limited by $R_1$ and $R_2$, the OTA consumption is 0.5 ± 0.1 μA in which 0.3 μA are for the cascode bias.

The open loop ac analysis results show the good phase margin and the load current tracking obtained with the designed adaptive bias OTA (Fig.6).

For the miniature $C_L$ = 2.2 µF filtering capacitor the equivalent series inductance **esl** = 0.49 nH and the frequency dependent series resistance **esr** were included, however this resistance had little effect. The additional external connection resistance *rce* and inductance *lce* were also considered.

In Fig. 6 different effects on the Bode plot are compared. Reducing $I_L$ 20 times, so do the dominant pole and also the internal poles. The first internal pole is always high enough for a near -20 dB/dec slope at the 0 dB crossing.

The additional poles in this multistage approach are high enough to avoid any effect on the phase margin. Notice the esl inductance resonance with $C_L$ near 5 MHz; an additional *lce*, estimated as ≤ 2 nH, will move this resonance to an even lower frequency. Notice also the beneficial effect of series resistance *rce*, estimated between 0.1 and 0.3 Ω even for a carefully made PCB; however, the corresponding zero occurs after the 0 dB crossing, not as in the pole-zero frequency compensation methods.

Significant results for the open loop phase margin and low frequency gain are shown in the Fig. 7.

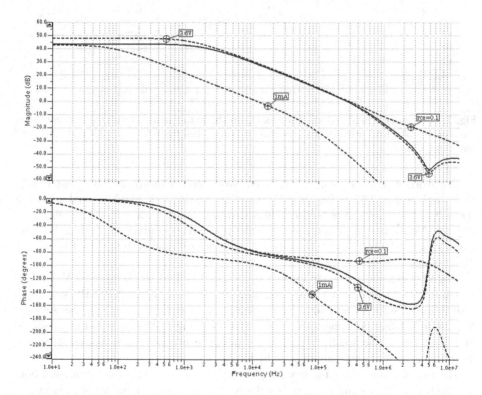

**Fig. 6.** Open loop Bode plot for $I_L$ = 20mA $V_{BAT}$ =1.4 V *rce* = 0 *lce*=0 typical corner (solid line) and with modified values for either $I_L$ at 1mA or $V_{BAT}$ at 3.6 V or *rce* at 0.1Ω

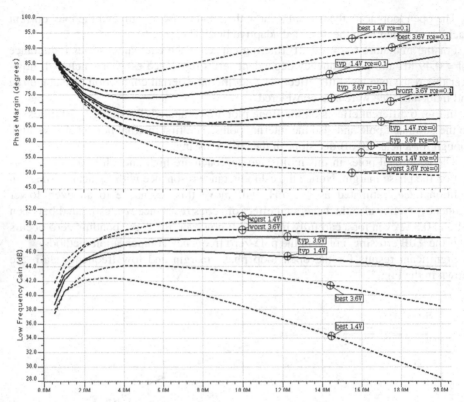

**Fig. 7.** Phase margin (top) and low frequency gain (bottom) variations with the load current $I_L$ for typical (solid line) and extreme process corners (dashed line), for $V_{BAT}$ 1.4 and 3.6 V and *rce* 0 and 0.1 Ω

The worst case phase margin, i.e. in the worst corner (normal NMOS fast PMOS slow, high voltage PMOS fast, at -40 °C), for the maximum $I_L$ and $V_{BAT}$ and assuming *rce* = 0, is 50 degrees. The typical values with the smallest rce = 0.1 Ω are above 70 degrees. Notice that the worst corner for the phase margin gives the highest low frequency gain, which is lowest in the opposite corner (normal NMOS slow PMOS fast, high voltage PMOS slow, at 85 °C).

One very important requirement was for a PSRR at least 30 dB up to 16 MHz. This was not easy to obtain in all corners. The low frequency value PSRR0 with both PMOS in the slow corner and at low temperature increases at low $V_{BAT}$ because the $V_{CP}$ cascode bias can clamp to zero. The PMOS sizing that could avoid this resulted in a total loss of the amplifier gain in the opposite process and temperature corner; therefore a narrow compromise had to be found.

The Fig. 8 results show the low temperature worst corner PSRR degradation both at a high $I_L$ = 20 mA and at a low $I_L$ = 1mA. This degradation occurs already at low frequency and dominates up to 16 MHz. For $I_L$ = 1 mA the full 16 MHz range PSRR

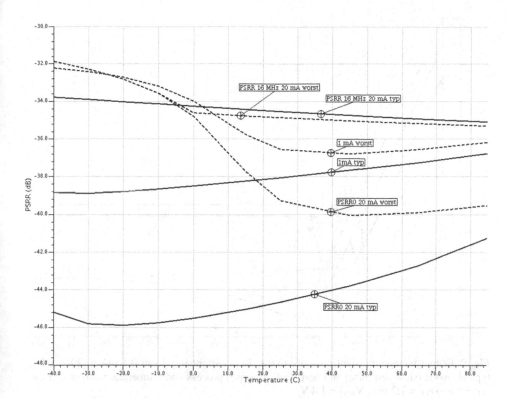

**Fig. 8.** PSRR at low frequency (PSRR0) and up to 16 MHz as a function of temperature for typical and worst process corners and for $I_L$ 1 mA and 20 mA and $V_{BAT} = 1.4$ V

is the same as the PSRR0 both in the typical and the worst cases. At $I_L = 20$ mA the smallest PSRR occurs at 16 MHz, except for the worst corner at low temperature.

Transient simulations with abrupt 0.1 to 20 mA load current steps show stable behavior in all worst cases, as can be seen in the Fig. 9. Results are shown for the typical process at 25 °C, for the slowest response "worst" corner (normal NMOS slow PMOS fast, high voltage NMOS and PMOS slow, at 85 °C) and for the fastest response "best" corner (normal NMOS fast PMOS slow, high voltage NMOS fast PMOS slow, at - 40 °C).

At the beginning, the output voltage drops linearly as long as the 2.2 µF capacitor delivers the 20 mA load current before it can flow through the ballast transistor.

In the presence of a series resistor *rce*, there is also an initial abrupt *rce* * $\Delta I_L$ voltage drop.

The total voltage drop goes down to less than 20 mV under the new equilibrium value reached at the end of the transient.

This initial voltage drop is followed by a quite fast settling with almost no ringing. The total settling time is about 10 µS typical, less than 22 µS in the worst case.

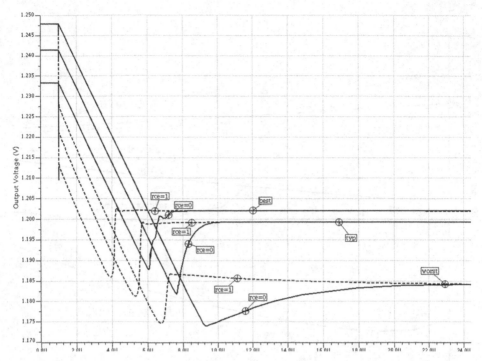

**Fig. 9.** Output voltage transient response to a $I_L$ load current step from 0.1 mA to 20 mA for typical, worst (slow response) and best (fast response) process and temperature corner and for *rce* = 0 and *rce* = 1Ω with $V_{BAT}$ = 1.4 V

## 5  Conclusions

A multiple stage adaptive bias amplifier has been proposed and designed in a generic 0.18 μm logic process for a linear dissipative regulator working continuously in the 1.2 to 3.6 V supply range. The input stage uses normal threshold transistors for the NMOS differential pair and for the PMOS diode to satisfy low supply voltage requirements. As their current is a very small fraction (1/2000) of the load current, they remain in moderate inversion even at the highest load current with reasonable device sizes; as a result the necessary $V_{DS}$ drops and the internal node capacitances are small. The worst case OTA consumption is less than 1.35% of the load current, 2.5 to 6 times better than without the proposed multiple stage approach.

The low voltage devices are protected at supply voltages above 1.98 V by high voltage cascode transistors. A native high voltage NMOS allows further reduction of the minimum acceptable supply voltage, however, in order to stay in saturation, it needs a special cascode gate voltage generation configuration.

In spite of the addition of two more nodes with the additional stages, good regulator stability is obtained; this is demonstrated by open loop ac analysis and closed loop transient simulations for abrupt load current steps. The dominant pole is on the output node with its 2.2 μF external filtering capacitor, the first internal pole is high enough for a near -20 dB/dec slope at 0 dB gain, and all other poles are at much higher frequencies. All poles track the load current. No frequency compensation is needed; nevertheless the very small series resistance on the capacitor further improves the phase margin. The worst case PSRR is better than 30 dB.

# References

[1] G. Patounakis, Y. W. Li, K. Shepard, "A Fully Integrated On-Chip DC-DC Conversion and Power Management System", *IEEE J. Solid-State Circuits*, vol. 39, pp. 443-451, March 2004

[2] P. Hazucha, T. Karnik, B. A. Bloechel, C. Parsons, D. Finan, S. Borkar, "Area-Efficient Linear Regulator with Ultra-Fast Load Regulation", *IEEE J. Solid-State Circuits*, vol. 40, pp. 933-940, April 2005

[3] X. Fan, C. Mishra, E. Sanchez-Sinencio, "Single Miller Capacitor Frequency Compensation Technique for Low-Power Multistage Amplifiers", *IEEE J. Solid-State Circuits*, vol. 40, pp. 584-592, March 2005

[4] J.-F Perotto, S. Cserveny, "Power Management for Low-Power Battery Operated Portable Systems Using Current Mode Techniques", in *V.Paliouras, J. Vounckx and D.Verkest (Eds.): PATMOS 2005, LNCS 3728*, pp. 197-206, Springer 2005

[5] C. Chava, J. Silva-Martinez, "A Frequency Compensation Scheme for LDO Voltage Regulators" *IEEE Trans. Circuits and Systems-I, vol.51*, pp. 1041-1050, June 2004

[6] G. Rincon-Mora, P. Allen, "A Low-Voltage, Low Quiescent Current, Low Drop-Out Regulator", *IEEE J. Solid-State Circuits*, vol. 33, pp. 36-44, Jan. 1998

[7] M. Degrauwe, J. Rijmenants, E. Vittoz, H. DeMan, "Adaptive Biasing CMOS Amplifiers", *IEEE J. Solid-State Circuits*, vol. 17, pp. 522-528, June 1982

[8] V. Balan, "A Low-Voltage Regulator Circuit with Self-Bias to Improve Accuracy", *IEEE J. Solid-State Circuits*, vol. 38, pp. 365-368, Feb. 2003

# Circuit Sizing and Supply-Voltage Selection for Low-Power Digital Circuit Design

Milena Vratonjic, Bart R. Zeydel, and Vojin G. Oklobdzija

Department of Electrical and Computer Engineering,
University of California, Davis, CA 95616
{milena, zeydel, vojin}@acsel-lab.com
http://www.acsel-lab.com

**Abstract.** This paper analyzes energy minimization of digital circuits operating at supply voltages above threshold and in the sub-threshold region. Circuit sizing and supply-voltage selection are simultaneously analyzed to determine where the minimum energy solution occurs. In this work we address the effects of architectural modifications on the design choices in different regions of operation. Two new architectural parameters are introduced that can be used for fast design comparison in the low power region of operation.

## 1 Introduction

Modern wireless handheld devices utilize signal processing algorithms with complex computational demands, requiring hardware implementations that support high-speed computing yet maintain low-power levels. To extend battery life, the optimal design for these devices is the one which achieves the lowest energy consumption at the desired performance target. In order to find the optimal design, circuit designers must understand the impact of circuit sizing, supply voltage and technology limitations on the energy and delay of their designs.

In the fields of sensor networks and medical devices, speed is not as important as energy consumption. Reducing the amount of energy per computation allows for extended operation or smaller form factor. For ultra-low power, circuit designers have proposed operating with sub-threshold supply voltages.

This paper analyzes how circuit sizing and supply voltage should be used to achieve minimum energy consumption at the desired performance. Two design approaches are used: (1) starting from the highest-performance point (Logical Effort [7]) we show the best way to trade delay relaxation for energy reduction; (2) from the point corresponding to the minimum sizing of the circuit, we show how up-sizing, supply-voltage scaling and architectural modifications lead to the best trade-offs in energy and delay.

Finally, we introduce two architectural parameters which can be used to quickly find the most energy-efficient circuit design.

J. Vounckx, N. Azemard, and P. Maurine (Eds.): PATMOS 2006, LNCS 4148, pp. 148–156, 2006.

## 2  Energy Components

The total energy consumption of a circuit can be expressed as the sum of three components: dynamic energy ($E_{dyn}$), short-circuit energy ($E_{sc}$) and leakage energy ($E_{lkg}$). Until recently, dynamic energy dominated energy consumption in digital circuits. However, as CMOS technology advances into sub-100nm, leakage energy is becoming as important as dynamic energy.

Short-circuit, or so-called crowbar current, occurs only when both pMOS and nMOS are conducting at the same time. For low supply-voltage values, when $V_{dd} < 2V_T$, short-circuit energy component is eliminated. When supply-voltage falls below the threshold voltage, $V_T$, we enter the sub-threshold region of operation where the transistor current is given by:

$$I_{sub} = I_{off}e^{(V_{GS}-V_T)/nV_{th}} \, , I_{off} = \mu_o C_{ox} \frac{W}{L}(n-1)V_{th}^{\ 2} \tag{1}$$

with n corresponding to the sub-threshold slope and $V_{th}$=kT/q.

## 3  Optimization for Minimum Energy

In this section we examine the optimization of circuit sizing and supply voltage selection to minimize energy at a desired performance target. For analysis we use a 130nm technology with a fixed threshold voltage ($V_T$). The optimization process is therefore reduced to the design space exploration for finding circuit sizing and supply-voltage. It was shown previously in [2] how balancing sensitivities of a design to the sizing and supply-voltage gives the optimal solution on the energy-efficient curve.

### 3.1  Circuit Sizing

Dynamic energy is directly proportional to the equivalent switched capacitance at the output of the logic gate:

$$E_{dyn} = \alpha C_{tot} V_{dd}^{\ 2} \tag{2}$$

where $\alpha$ is activity factor and $C_{tot}$ is the total gate capacitance (total transistor width). Mathematically and intuitively from equation (2), the minimum sized circuit would provide the minimum energy point. This is the case when the supply-voltage is above the threshold voltage. The solution becomes less obvious at the sub-threshold region of operation where minimum sized devices have failure point at higher supply-voltages comparing to the devices sized-up for functionality at lower supply-voltages. It was shown in [1] that due to the shallow nature of the optimum point corresponding to the energy minima, reaching the minimum possible supply-voltage through the up-sizing of the devices does not allow for any significant energy savings comparing to the minimum sized solution. Therefore, using minimum sized devices is a good approach when designing in the sub-threshold region.

It was shown by Zyuban et. al [2] that every design point on the energy-efficient curve obtained through the circuit sizing corresponds to the certain value of hardware intensity (η). Hardware intensity is defined as the percentage of energy increase per percentage of delay improvement on the energy-efficient curve attainable through the circuit sizing. At the point where this percentage corresponds to the value of 1%, the hardware intensity (η) equals to one and this is indeed the energy-delay product (EDP) point.

A good starting point for circuit sizing is the delay optimized sizing of a circuit for a fixed input size and output load using Logical Effort [7] (LE point). There are two possible approaches to lowering energy consumption of the circuit starting from LE point: 1) if it is allowed to increase the input size of the circuit, the techniques proposed in [3] give solution for energy minimization by redistributing the stage efforts among the stages and keeping the delay fixed at lower energy level; 2) if change in input is not possible, we can trade the delay increase by either circuit sizing or through the use of lower supply-voltages.

## 3.2  Supply-Voltage Scaling

Supply-voltage reduction is often considered the most effective technique for low-power design. Similar to the hardware intensity, we can express voltage intensity (θ) as the tradeoff between the energy and delay of the circuit due to the supply-voltage, as shown by Zyuban et. al [2].

As supply-voltage decreases, total energy decreases until the sub-threshold region is reached. In the sub-threshold region, propagation delay increases exponentially with respect to supply-voltage reduction resulting in diminishing returns in energy savings due to the increase in leakage energy. Therefore, minimum voltage operation point does not coincide with the minimum energy point. Minimum energy point occurs at the supply-voltages higher then the minimum supply-voltage points where the design is still operational.

## 3.3  Minimum Circuit Sizing with Supply-Voltage Scaling

Recently, we have shown that more complex high-performance structures combined with supply-voltage scaling outperform traditional low-power oriented designs in the low- and ultra-low power domains [4]. The designs were sized for minimum energy

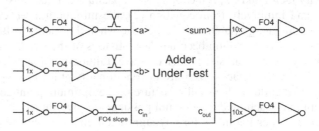

**Fig. 1.** Simulation test bench

operation such that the minimum energy point is initially obtained through the minimum circuit sizing and then supply-voltage was varied from 1.2V to 0.6V.

The results are obtained from simulations in a 130nm technology under nominal process conditions. The simulation test bench is shown in Figure 1.

Fig. 2. shows the voltage intensity, $\theta$, and energy of the minimum sized Sparse Carry-Lookahead adder design (SCL) [4, 5] with supply-voltages scaled below 0.6V. The adder is functional in sub-threshold voltage region even at 0.1V (the threshold voltage is 220mV in the 130nm technology used for analysis).

It is also shown in Fig. 2. how the voltage intensity of the design changes as supply-voltage is varied. The point where no further savings in energy is possible through supply-voltage reduction ($E_{min}$) corresponds to the supply-voltage for which the voltage intensity is zero.

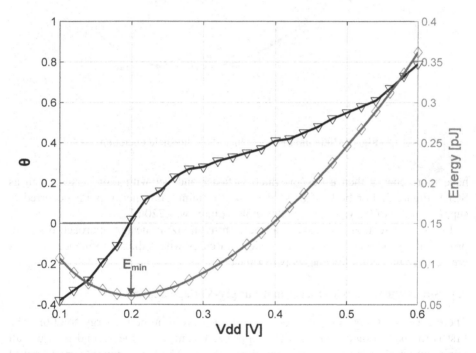

**Fig. 2.** Energy-Delay curve of the minimum-sized Sparse Carry-Lookahead adder (SCL) with supply-voltages scaling from 0.6V to 0.1V

The minimum energy operation point occurs in the sub-threshold region at 0.2V (Figures 2, 3). The effect of supply-voltage on the energy and delay of the minimum-sized Sparse Carry-Lookahead Adder (SCL) and Ripple-Carry Adder (RCA) is plotted in Figure 3, for supply-voltages ranging from 0.6V to 0.1V. The two examples, SCL and RCA, are representatives of high-performance and low-power designs.

Dynamic energy consumption of a design depends on the size and switching activity of the circuits; while leakage energy depends on the size of the circuits and the cycle time. Design with fewer devices and longer cycle time (such as RCA adder) can

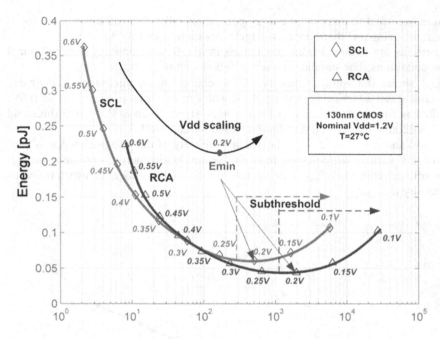

**Fig. 3.** Minimum Energy point at Sub-threshold operation

have more energy then a design which is faster and yet with more gates (such as SCL), Figure 3. For both of these designs, the minimum energy point occurred at supply-voltage of 0.2V, where the threshold voltage was 220mV.

In the next section, we show that the minimum sizing design approach does not provide the most energy-efficient solutions in cases where the performance target is greater then the minimum energy performance.

### 3.4  Simultaneous Device Sizing and Supply-Voltage Scaling

There exist two ways  for circuit designers to achieve minimum energy solution. The first is to obtain Logical Effort (delay optimized sizing) and the second is to use all minimum sized circuits (energy minimized sizing). These two points correspond to the left and right ends of the minimum energy-delay bound (curve) for the solution space obtained from circuit sizing. The minimum energy points on this curve can be obtained by either down-sizing the circuit from the LE point or up-sizing the circuit from minimum sizes. Down-sizing from LE is most effective for performance targets near the LE solution, while upsizing from minimum is better to apply for slow performance targets. Minimum energy-delay curves of the Sparse Carry-Lookahead adder (SCL) for supply voltages 1.2V, 1.1V, and 1V are shown in Figure 4. The points on each curve are obtained by minimizing energy through circuit sizing from the LE point to the minimum size limit.

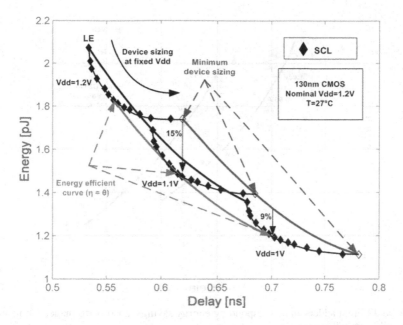

**Fig. 4.** Energy-Delay curve obtained through sizing and supply-voltage scaling

The minimum energy for each performance target is obtained by jointly optimizing circuit sizing and supply voltage. A compound energy-delay curve is created by selecting the minimum energy points from the combined energy-delay curves. At each of these points on the compound energy-delay curve hardware and voltage intensities are balanced [2]. If, for example, we need to meet the performance target of 0.62ns we have the following choices: using minimum sizing of SCL at nominal voltage of 1.2V, or reducing the supply-voltage to the value of 1.1V and up-sizing the design to meet the target performance. As seen from Figure 4, the second design approach results in 15% energy saving compared to the minimum sized SCL design at nominal voltage. If our performance demands were not so severe, i.e. delay is increased, we see that the energy savings decrease from 15% at 0.62ns to 9% at 0.7ns until the point where further voltage reduction and upsizing of the devices would not provide additional savings. This is the region where minimum sizing of the devices is the correct approach for reducing energy while still meeting the target performance.

## 4 Choices for Energy-Delay Optimization

In this section we investigate the consideration of different topologies in combination with device-sizing and supply-voltage scaling for energy-delay optimization.

Figure 5. illustrates example of two different adders as test cases, Variable-Block Adder (VBA) [6] and Ripple-Carry Adder (RCA) over a range of supply-voltages.

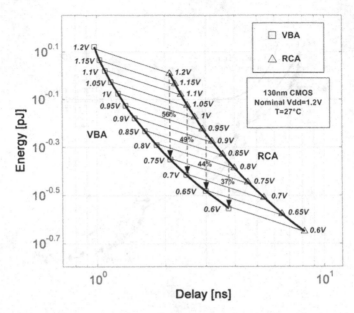

**Fig. 5.** Two different adders and corresponding energy savings at iso-performance with supply-voltage scaling @ minimum sizing

At the low-power region where the performance target is met even with the simplest and slowest topology, such as RCA is, using more complex structures at reduced supply-voltage levels results in significant energy savings, 56% at 2ns up to 37% at 3.8ns target delay. To expand on this analysis, we were interested in analyzing the relative energy-delay relationship of complex circuits over the wide range of supply-voltages.

We use the property of the constant energy-delay relationship versus supply-voltage observed in complex circuits [2, 3] to explore the tradeoffs between different designs. This property is not satisfied at lower supply-voltages where leakage energy is comparable to the dynamic energy consumption, Figure 3, and where the designs have cross-points in the energy-delay space.

The lines in Figures 5 and 6 connect the design points of the two topologies at iso-voltage. In the figures it can be seen that the relationship between the circuits remains constant, thus each circuit behaves the same with supply voltage. We use this property to introduce two new parameters, $\lambda$ and $\rho$, that we are defining here as:

$$\lambda = \sqrt{\partial e^2 + \partial d^2}, \text{ where } \partial e = const \text{ and } \partial d = const \text{ @ } \forall \text{ Vdd} \tag{2}$$

$$\rho = \tan\frac{\partial e}{\partial d}, e = \log E, d = \log D \tag{3}$$

Knowing these two parameters and the data-sets of one topology, $\{(D_1',E_1'), (D_2', E_2'), \ldots , (D_k', E_k')\}$, we can easily obtain the design points of the second topology, $\{(D_1'',E_1''), (D_2'', E_2''), \ldots , (D_k'', E_k'')\}$, for k-values of supply-voltage, which can then be used for quick design space exploration, eq. (4).

$$D_i'' = D_i'10^{\frac{\lambda}{\sqrt{1+\rho^2}}}, \quad E_i'' = E_i'10^{-\frac{\lambda\rho}{\sqrt{1+\rho^2}}}, \quad i=1, ..., k \tag{4}$$

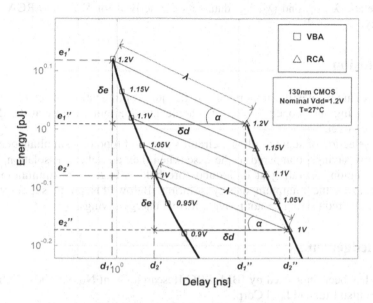

**Fig. 6.** Introducing parameters $\lambda$ and $\rho$

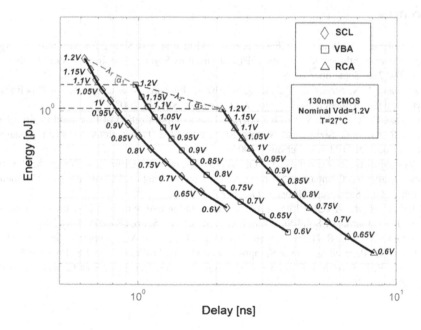

**Fig. 7.** Design space exploration with different adder topologies

Above defined parameters could be found based on the (E, D) points at nominal supply-voltage values. Knowing how one design behaves with the supply-voltage scaling, we can obtain the whole set of data points for a different one. Presented in Figure 7. are the data-sets of three topologies obtained from SCL data-set and, knowing parameters $(\lambda_1, \rho_1)$ and $(\lambda_2, \rho_2)$, data-sets are derived for VBA and RCA adders respectively.

## 5  Conclusion

This work demonstrates the importance of the joint optimization of supply-voltage and circuit sizing and proper topology for achieving minimum energy at the desired performance target.

Careful selection of supply-voltage, circuit sizing and topology simultaneously has bigger energy savings, compared to the case when they are taken in isolation. In the low-power region, operating at or around threshold voltage using minimum sized devices achieves the minimum energy solution. Below this point, supply-voltage reduction and circuit sizing do not provide further energy savings.

## Acknowledgements

This work has been supported by IBM, SRC Research Grant No. 931.001, California MICRO, Fujitsu Ltd. and Intel Corp.

## References

1. B. H. Calhoun, A. Wang, A. Chandrakasan, "Modeling and Sizing for Minimum Energy Operation in Subthreshold Circuits", IEEE Journal of Solid-State Circuits, Vol. 40, No. 9, pp. 1778-1786, September 2005.
2. V. Zyuban, P. N. Strenski, "Balancing Hardware Intensity in Microprocessor Pipelines", IBM Journal of Research and Development, Vol. 47, No. 5/6, 2003.
3. H. Q. Dao, B. R. Zeydel, V. G. Oklobdzija, "Energy Optimization of Pipelined Digital Systems Using Circuit Sizing and Supply Scaling", IEEE Transactions on VLSI Systems, Vol.14, No. 2, pp. 122-134, February 2006.
4. M. Vratonjic, B. R. Zeydel, V. G. Oklobdzija, "Low- and Ultra Low-Power Arithmetic Units: Design and Comparison", Proceedings of the International Conference on Computer Design, ICCD, San Jose, California, October 2-5, 2005.
5. S. Mathew, et. al, "A 4GHz 130nm Address Generation Unit with 32-bit Sparse-Tree Adder Core", IEEE Journal of Solid-State Circuits, Vol. 38, No. 5, pp. 689-695, May 2003.
6. V. G. Oklobdzija, E. R. Barnes, "Some Optimal Schemes for ALU Implementation in VLSI Technology", Proceedings of the Symposium on Comp. Arithmetic, pp.2-8, June 1985.
7. D. Harris, R. F. Sproull, I. E. Sutherland, "Logical Effort: Designing Fast CMOS Circuits", M. Kaufmann, 1999.

# Power Modeling of a NoC Based Design for High Speed Telecommunication Systems

Philippe Grosse[1], Yves Durand[1], and Paul Feautrier[2]

[1] CEA Léti, Grenoble F-38000, France
[2] ENS de Lyon/LIP, Lyon F-69364 , France

**Abstract.** Considering the complexity of the future 4G telecommunication systems, power consumption management becomes a major challenge for the designers, particularly for base-band modem functionalities. System level low-power policies which optimize dynamically the consumption, achieve major power savings compared to low level optimisations (e.g gated clock or transistor optimisation). We present an innovative power modeling methodology of a 4G modem which allows to accurately qualify such low power solutions. Then, we show the energy savings attended by these power management methods considering silicium technology.

## 1 Introduction

Managing the complexity of the future 4G telecommunication protocols within the energy constraints of a mobile terminal, is a major challenge for systems designers. In particular, the base-band modem is 10 times more complex in 4G applications compared to current 3G systems. Assuming that the consumption part due to base-band will increase as well (30% in 3G chips), power management of such processing parts must be considered carefully. Whereas low level optimisations (gated clock, low power transistor design...) reduce the consumption by 15 to 45 % [13], higher level methods, by dynamically optimising power consumption, improve further energy savings. But, these optimisations influence the system latency and are constrained by the application. To qualify such low power policies, we require an accurate consumption model which takes into account the real temporal profile of the application. Gate level power analysis is a mature and accurate way to evaluate the power consumption of digital SoC but requires long simulation times and is unpractictable for actual systems. The use of existing power models for circuits like CPU, bus, memories [10][11][12], is another solution. But none exists for such heterogeneous and complex design. Therefore, the first step of our study is to build a consumption model of a base-band modem which would be a trade-off between accuracy and simulation performance.

In this paper, we first expose our modeling methodology and then, evaluate the impact of well known low power policies at logical and system level. The paper is organized as follows: section 2 presents the base-band design under consideration

J. Vounckx, N. Azemard, and P. Maurine (Eds.): PATMOS 2006, LNCS 4148, pp. 157–168, 2006.

and the specific consumption issues encountered; section 3 details the modeling method and simulations scenarios; the results of the application low power policies are presented on section 4 and we conclude in section 5 by indicating future works.

## 2  Power and Energy Consumption of a 4G Modem

Our study and modeling works is focused on the power consumption of a 4G MC-CDMA base band modem. The design under consideration is based on a set of independents hardware fonctionnal units linked by an innovative asynchronous Network On Chip detailed below[1],[2],[3].

### 2.1  Design Overview

Compared to data rates targeted by 3G systems (1 to 2 Mbps), the 4G transmission systems address higher data rates (100 Mbps and more) and so drastically increase the data traffic in the chip itself. Whereas computing power of DSPs or general purpose processors was sufficient for 3G modulations techniques, latency constraints and data rates of MC-CDMA transmission requires the design of dedicated and powerful hardware blocks (FFT, channel estimation) tailored to support such data flows [2]. The design is also constrained by the on-chip connections throughput and traditional bus solutions are no longer appropriate for such applications. [2][3] To satisfy these constraints, the FAUST project (Flexi-

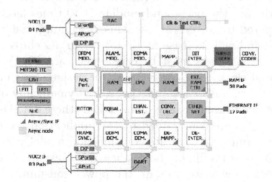

**Fig. 1.** Architecture of FAUST Chip

ble Architecture of Unified Systems for Telecom), started on 2003, proposes an innovative architecture of an OFDM base-band modem which can be used for 4G transmissions. FAUST consists of a set of independent and re-configurable hardware blocks, which performs the MC-CDMA base-band tasks, controlled by a CPU (ARM 946) and interconnected by an asynchronous network on chip (NoC) as depicted on Fig. 1.

## 2.2   Problematic of Power Modeling

In this paragraph, we recall briefly the main consumption parameters that we consider meaningful in our context. Next, we describe the main instruments that we use to reduce consumption, called here "low power policies".

**State of the Art.** Power consumption estimation is the purpose of numerous tools and studies. Physical models deduced from architecture and technology exist for memories or on-chip connections [11]. For CPU, models deduced from instructions profiling are common for embedded processors [10][14]. These models are accurate but specific. Thus, adapting and combining them to build a consumption model of our chip does not guarantee consistent results.

CAD tools propose others solutions to perform accurate power analyses at each step of the design. SPICE [15] (transistor level) and SYNOPSYS "Prime-Power" (gate level) [7] relate the power dissipation with the activity by using activity files coming from behavioral simulations. CADENCE "SoC Encounter"[17] integrates statistical analysis functionnalities to quickly evaluate the power dissipation of a whole SoC. Qualify low power managements methods implies numerous iterations and simulation times becomes unpracticable for real design.

Hereafter, we identify the main characteristics of our base-band consumption in order to build a model which can be a trade-off between accuracy and simulation performance.

**Power Consumption of a 4G Modem.** Power consumption of such architecture corresponds to the summation of the functionnal units contributions (which performs MC-CDMA base-band functions), NoC consumption, IO pads and CPU. Like any digital architecture, the consumption of theses design units corresponds to the sum of their static (leakage) and dynamic (switching) power dissipation which is given by [6]:

$$P_{tot} = P_{leak} + P_{switch} = V_{dd} * I_{sub} + \frac{1}{2} * \alpha * C_{load} * Vdd^2 * f_{clock} \qquad (1)$$

Where $\alpha$ represents the switching activity; $C_{load}$ is the output capacitive load; linked with the technology and the number of gates, $V_{dd}$ is the supply voltage and $f_{clock}$ the frequency of the unit. $I_{sub}$ represents the major source of static power dissipation, the sub-threshold leakage, and is given by [5]:

$$I_{sub} = k * e^{\frac{-Q*Vt}{a*kT}} \qquad (2)$$

Thus, $Vt$ represent the threshold voltage which is a technology linked parameter. Power dissipation of our base-band modem is so function of :

- **Technology** $Vt, C_{load}$
- **Runtime parameters** $f_{clock}$, $V_{dd}$, $\alpha$

We consider two low power policies, usually applied on system level, for our base-band modem.

**System Level Low Power Policies.** Two common ways are used to reduce power consumption dynamically: *resource shut down* (Dynamic Power Management) and *resource slow down* (Dynamic Voltage scaling)[5][6].

DPM techniques avoid static and dynamic dissipation by shutting down all supply sources during idle states. These methods may be tailored to our design and save the static and dynamic energy wasted during idle states. But they have two major consequences on the timing of the application :

- Reconfiguration after shut down is needed
- Response time of the supply source must been considered (almost $5\mu s$ for our blocks)

DVS, is a well known method to reduce the quadratic contribution of $Vdd$ into $P_{switch}$. However, reducing this supply voltage increases the gate traversal delay (and thus the global delay) $D$ as given by [4]:

$$D \propto \frac{Vdd}{(Vdd - Vt)^2} \tag{3}$$

Considering this delay $D$, frequency must be decreased linearly with the supply voltage in first order approximation ($f \propto V_{dd}$). This, in turn, increases the computation time, inversely proportional to the voltage supply. Moreover, $Vt$ is also reduced in new technologies and causes an exponential growing of the standby current (Equ. 2) [6]. Energy savings of a DVS policy will be also both function of application (computation times and timing constraints) and technology ($Vt$ scaling).

These power management methods, usually applied on the CPU [15] [16], may as well apply to our design considering our set of hardware units as a set of "task" schedulable by our central processing unit.

To summarize, we identify keys parameters of the power dissipation of our architecture:

- **Technology** ($Vt, C_{load}$)
- **Architecture** (reconfiguration times)
- **Temporal consumption profiles and run time parameters** (idle time, active time, $f_{clock}$, $V_{dd}, \alpha$)
- **Real time constraints**

At this stage, it should be noted that the two first parameter are technological, whereas the two others require the knowledge of the actuel run-time profile of the application.

## 3   Modeling the Consumption of the Base-Band Modem

We base our model on two complementary analysis: a gate power analysis, which links our model with the technology, and a functional analysis which gives an accurate image of the activity profile of our application.

## 3.1   Modeling Methodology

We run the gate level analysis with a real MC-CDMA transmission/reception scenario on the gate-level netlists of each functionnal unit, synthesized on the current technology of the chip (130nm). We use for that a commercially available tool, SYNOPSYS Prime-Power [7]. To evaluate the impact of the technology scaling on the consumption (dynamic and static), we run a similar analysis on the same units synthesized in other technologies (65 nm). These simulations, based on real scenario, give us an accurate timing profile of the architecture power dissipation and its consumption results will be the basis of our model. In a second time, we characterize the main consumption phases and correlate them with the algorithms to build a functional model of the architecture with PTOLEMY [8]. This software, developed by Berkeley University, is designed to model embedded systems. With this software we build components simulating the consumption of each blocks of FAUST architecture.

The figure below summarizes the modeling flow:

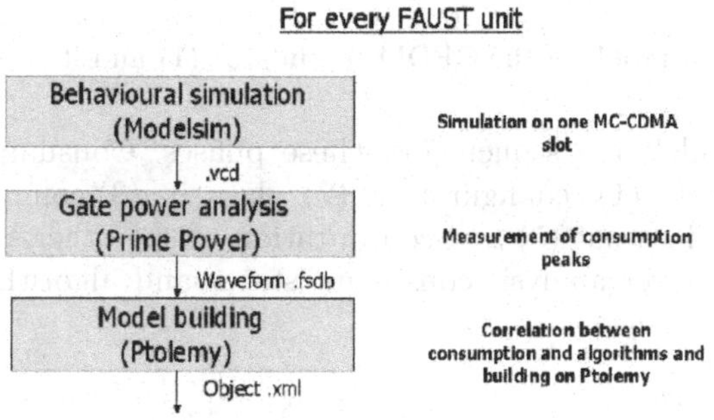

**For every FAUST unit**

| Behavioural simulation (Modelsim) | Simulation on one MC-CDMA slot |
| --- | --- |

.vcd

| Gate power analysis (Prime Power) | Measurement of consumption peaks |
| --- | --- |

Waveform .fsdb

| Model building (Ptolemy) | Correlation between consumption and algorithms and building on Ptolemy |
| --- | --- |

Object .xml

**Fig. 2.** Modeling flow

In the next section we detail the application of this methodology on FAUST architecture.

## 3.2   The FAUST Consumption Model

As we mentioned in section 2, FAUST architecture can be considered like a set of hardware blocks connected by a NoC and controlled by a CPU.

- **Modeling hardware blocks:** In order to build a functional model of the digital blocks consumption, we simulate every processing units by a Finite State Machine (FSM) built with PTOLEMY. The exhaustive modeling of each unit considering the consumption of each arithmetical operation (sum,division ...) is time-consuming and implies long simulation time. To avoid this drawback we build an abstracted model of each functionnal unit consumption. From the gate analysis, we identify different phases of consumption which correspond to a set of macroscopic events of our block activity, such CPU configuration burst, computation of the core or incoming data (Fig. 3).

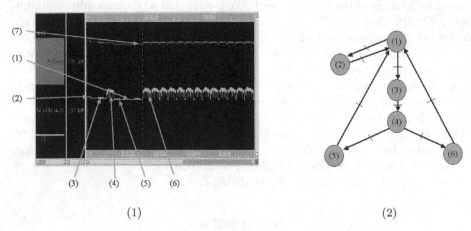

(1)                                                    (2)

**Fig. 3.** Consumption profile of the OFDM modulator (1) and its FSM model (2)

The FSM models the sequence of these phases. Consumption "events" (Fig. 3) (idle state (1), configuration (2), data in (3),computation of the first symbol(4), data out (5) and computation of the other symbol (6)) derived from the power analysis constitute states and algorithmic execution conditions, transitions.

*DVS instrumentation*

From gate power analysis, we extract $\beta_{phase,tech}$ such as, for each phase:

$$P_{switch} = \beta_{phase,tech} * V_{dd}^2 * f_{clock} \tag{4}$$

$\beta_{phase,tech}$ depends on the technology of our base-band design (one value for the 130 nm design and one for the 65 nm model). For each consumption phase, we calibrate this parameter with the initial conditions of the gate power analysis (supply: 1.2V, fclock : 200 Mhz). In order to instrument our model for DVS, each unit have a modifiable $V_{dd}$ and $f_{clock}$ value. Then, modify these parameters shows the impact of a voltage scaling on the power dissipation.

Each FSMs is synchronized by its own model of variable clock initialized at the normalized frequency of each block ($\frac{f_{clock}}{200Mhz}$) and linked with the supply voltage of the unit ($f_{clock} \propto V_{dd}$). A watch-dog monitors the global duration of transmission, which shall not exceed $666\mu s$. Then, we guaranteed the fulfillment of our application's timing constraints.

*DPM instrumentation*

In our base-band design, each block independently adheres to a DPM policy. When units are idle, i.e. neither computing nor awaiting data, we shut their core down. Our abstract model reproduces this policy by setting the FSM on a non-consumptive state as soon as all pending data transfers are cleared. Therefore, data traffic regulation is explicitly simulated in each unit: it is based on a credit mechanism which used the exchange of signaling message between destination and source.

– **NoC consumption model:** The FAUST's NoC is based on the Globally Asynchronous Locally Synchronous (GALS) concept [7]. Nodes (routing units of the FAUST NoC) communicate via an asynchronous handshake protocol whereas fonctionnal units execute their task in a synchronous way. This asynchronous design avoid the power associated with the NoC's clock distribution network. Our model simulates the power dissipated at the flit level, the elementary network data (32 bit), in an asynchronous node. In FAUST, since the NoC is based on a deterministic routing protocol, the number of node and the latency between two units is known *a priori*. Therefore, we

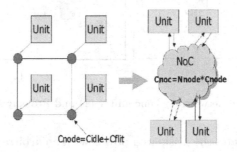

**Fig. 4.** Faust Noc (1) and its Ptolemy representation (2)

model our network with a "routing" table (Fig. 4), which indicates the number of asynchronous nodes that must be traversed between two units. Flit latency through the node is simulated by an event initialized at the crossing time of a node (deduced from the gate simulation).

– **Memories consumption:** We based our RAMs models on data sheets avaiable for the 130nm technology. We relate power dissipation with the size and the state of the memories units (enable, write/read, selected...) and simulate their activity with a FSM.

– **Power model of the CPU:** FAUST integrates a CPU (ARM 946) which manages the configuration of each blocks (telecom protocol used, frequency, timing constraint). To compensate the absence of gate model we based our model on a bibliographic study which give us average consumption values of an ARM integrated in a HIPERLAN/2 and 802.11a modem [9]. In our application, the CPU is only utilized to configure the base-band modem and its activity has a limited impact on the consumption (less than 10 %). However, we can assume that an average value is sufficient to our model.

– **Final mapping:** These design units are finally assembled and form the complete consumption model of the FAUST architecture. Silicon technology, timing constraints and telecom standards are used as global parameters and are applied on all units (by modifying $\beta$ for each consumption phase of each unit). Finally, all consumption values of each block are linked with a sequence plotter which give a temporal representation of the power dissipation.

### 3.3  Validation

In order to check the validity of our model, we compare the average results of our simulation (transmission/reception of one MC-CDMA slot [19]) to a statistical analysis performed by a commercial tool (CADENCE SoC Encounter).

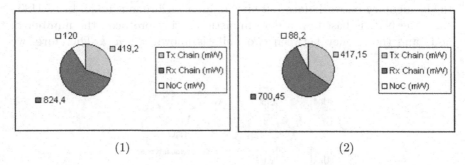

(1)                                              (2)

**Fig. 5.** Comparison between SoC encounter (1) and Ptolemy simulations (2)

SoC Encounter relates the dissipated power with an arbitrary activity parameter (20% in our simulation) and, unlike our model, has no knowledge of the application. This explains why results of our two analysis differ notably. However, both results are similar enough to asses the consistency of our model (30 % of relative variation for Tx, 15% for Rx and 26% for the NoC). This, in turn, justifies its use for qualifying the low power policies on our design.

## 4  Impact of Low Power Policies Combined with Technological Improvements

We have used our model to compare the results of different power optimization methods at each step of the design. On a first time we compare the influence of two low power policies (DPM and DVS) on a non optimized design. Then, we show the influence of one low level optimization (gated clock) on the savings performed by these high level methods. As energy is the main characteristic of batteries supply in mobile applications, our simulations are characterized in term of dissipated $\mu$joules (mW*ms).

### 4.1  Energy Savings of System Level Policies on a Non Low Level Optimized Design

Gate power analysis of our initial design (130 nm) have shown that the power consumption during idle states are equivalent, in average, to 80% of the dissipated power of the computation phases. Therefore, save energy during idle phases by shutting down the units is a tempting solution compared to a voltage scaling.

This table represent the comparison between DPM and DVS policies during the transmission of one MC-CDMA slot (the macro unit of an 4G transmission duration : 666 $\mu$s) detailed by each transmission chain units. For each block the scenario is functionnally equivalent but the temporal profile, and so results of power optimizations, may vary for one to another.

**Table 1.** Comparison between DVS and DPM on a 130 nm non optimized base-band modem

| Unit | Eref($\mu$j) | Energy savings DVS | Energy savings DPM |
|---|---|---|---|
| Encoder | 10.34 | 49% | 99% |
| Bit interleaving | 24.40 | 54.8% | 99.5% |
| Mapping | 24.40 | 54.8% | 99.5% |
| Fast Hadamard Transform | 33.5 | 6.1% | 38.8% |
| Ofdm modulation (IFFT) | 202 | 14.45% | 0% |
| **Total** | **294.64** | **15.48%** | **24.38%** |

$E_{ref}$ is the reference energy dissipated by the base-band modem (130nm implementation) without any optimization and the energy savings corresponding to $\frac{E_{ref} - E_{optim}}{E_{ref}}$ with $E_{optim}$ the energy dissipated after the use of one low power management method.

For a non low level optimized base-band design, a DPM policy appears more efficient than a DVS policy given to the timing constraint of the transmission. In particular, shutting down the first blocks of the transmission chain (encoding, interleaving and mapping units) , is an easy way to save energy. Apply DPM on these units saves almost 99% of their dissipated energy. Moreover, these units represent just 20% of our transmission chain consumption, so savings performed by a DPM represent just 24% of the initial energy dissipation.

The most consuming unit (OFDM modulator), receives data request permanently during one slot transmission and can not be shut down. The only way to save energy on this functionnal unit is to scale its supply voltage (DVS). Thus, we adopt this methodology:

- On a first time, we slow our OFDM modulator frequency (and supply) to reach the minimum admissible througput in established mode
- Then we adjust the speed of the other transmission units in accordance to our block througput

In this case, timing constraints and technology allows just a small scaling (90% of the initial value). Therefore energy savings of a DVS policy represent just 15% of our reference dissipated energy. For a non low level optimized design, DPM is so more efficient than DVS. This conclusion depend on the application and is only valid for the current power dissipation profile of the non-saturated blocks (i.e the first units).

However, technology scalings and low level optimization have an huge influence on the power dissipation profile. In the next section, we show how these low level modifications impact the choice of high level policies.

### 4.2   Low Level Optimization and Consequence on the Choice of Low Power Policies

Conclusions presented above are only valid for the non power-optimized librairies used for the first release of the chip. We have to actualize this comparison between DVS and DPM for the 65nm libraries used for the second release. Netlist utilized to perform the gate power analysis were optimized with a gated clock policy generated by the synthesis tool with a low leakage 65nm library. Gated clock, by avoiding useless gate commutation, reduce the dynamic idle power dissipation by a factor of 10. Use of low power libraries allow us to neglect the leakage power dissipated (less than 5% in our application).

These low level optimizations implies less energy waste during idle state and so decrease the influence of a DPM policy. Another aspect of the technology scaling is the reduction of $Vt$ and transistor delay which increases the maximum speed of the architecture. Considering these evolutions, a DVS applied on such architecture become more interesting. Table 2 presents the results of the comparison between DPM and DVS on our base-band optimized design.

**Table 2.** Low level optimization and influence on system level policies;(1):Initial dissipated energy 130 nm without Gated-Clock during slot transmission;(2):Initial energy for a 65nm Low level optimized base band design during slot transmission;(3):% of energy savings achieved by technology scaling and low power optimization;(4):% of energy savings achieved by DPM methods on low level optimized design;(5):% of energy savings achieved by DVS on low level optimized design

| Unit | (1) | (2) | (3) | (4) | (5) |
|---|---|---|---|---|---|
| Encoder | 10.34 | 1.02 | 90.2% | 97.46% | 49% |
| Bit interleaving | 24.40 | 2.37 | 90.3% | 97.46% | 54.8% |
| Mapping | 24.40 | 2.37 | 90.3% | 97.47% | 54.8% |
| Fast Hadamard Transform | 33.5 | 11.03 | 67.4% | 13.56% | 54.8% |
| Ofdm modulation (IFFT) | 202 | 116.4 | 42.37% | 0% | 50.5% |
| Total | 294.64 | 133.19 | 54.79% | 21.26% | 51% |

We optimize the power consumption regarding the more consuming unit, and adhere to the DVS methodology described in the precedent section. The 65nm technology allows better scaling capabilities and so better results. Table. 2 shows that, if DVS achieves less energy savings than DPM on the first blocks of the MC-CDMA chain (50% of their initial dissipated energy compared to 97%), the global savings are more significant due to the OFDM block consumption which is the critical unit of our transmission chain. From these studies and comparisons we conclude that:

- A DPM policy is only useful for blocks which are in idle state a long period of time, i.e first units performing binary treatments in our base-band.
- Low power optimizations by reducing idle power consumption, decrease the influence of a DPM policy
- Consumption of our transmission chain is conditioned by the OFDM block. An adequate DVS policy must be optimized for this critical block to achieve the higher energy savings.

Clearly,the optimal power management method consist to associate DPM and DVS, on a first time we adjust frequency and supply voltage in order to saturate the timing constraints of all blocks. In a second time, we shut down the first block of the transmission chain at the end of their treatment.

Such power management applied on a low level optimized design can reduce the consumption by 60%.

## 5    Conclusion and Future Works

Our methodology is an easy way to obtain an accurate and technology linked model of a complex SoC. With our model based on a gate power analysis, we have been able to qualify low power system level solutions on our 4G modem. Results of simulations shows how energy savings performed on computation units with system policies are dependent to the algorithm and the technology of the initial architecture and allows to target an optimal power management method. We have progressed in the exploration of low power policies for high speed telecommunication designs, but our approach remains exploratory and not very practical for industrial applications. Futures work will adress analytical tools to improve the accuracy ouf our model and methodology.

## References

1. **Stefan Kaiser and al.** "4G MC-CDMA Multi Antenna SoC for Radio Enhancements", IST summit Lyon June 2004
2. **Yves Durand and al.** "FAUST: On chip distributed Architecture for a 4G Baseband Modem SoC", IP-SOC Grenoble 2005
3. **Fabien Clermidy and al.** "A NoC based communication framework for seamless IP integration in Complex Systems", IP-SOC Grenoble 2005
4. **Yann-Hang Lee, C.M Krishna** "Voltage-Clock Scaling for Low Energy Consumption in Real Time Embedded Systems" Proceedings of the Real-Time Computing Systems and Applications Conference IEEE,december 1999
5. **Ravindra Jejurika, Rajesh Gupta** "Dynamic Voltage Scaling for Systemwide Energy Minimization in real time embedded Systems", ISLPED IEEE, Newport beach 2004
6. **Kamal S. Khouri** "Leakage Power Analysis and Reduction During Behavioral Synthesis", IEEE Transactions on VLSI systems, December 2002

7. **Synopsys** "Prime Power" website : http://www.synopsys.com/products/power/
8. **Berkeley University** "The Ptolemy Project" website :http://ptolemy.eecs.berkeley.edu/
9. **Easy project team** "The EASY project design story 4", Easy Project IST 2004
10. **Amit Sinha ,Anantha Chandrakasan** "JouleTrack A web based Tool for Software energy Profiling", DAC IEEE, June 2001
11. **Dake Liu and Christer Svensson** "Power Consumption Estimation in CMOS VLSI Chips" , IEEE Journal of Solid State Circuits, June 1994
12. **Tajana Simunic and al.** "Cycle Accurate Simulation of Energy Consumption in Embedded Systems", DAC IEEE, New Orleans 1999
13. **David Chillet** "Basse consommation dans les systèmes embarqués", Roscoff-Ecole thématique, avril 2003
14. **Vivek Tiwari and al** "Power analysis of Embedded Software : A first Step Towards Software Power Minimization", Transactions on VLSI systems IEEE, december 1994
15. **Gupta R** "Formals Methods for Dynamic Power Management",ICCAD IEEE, November 2003
16. **Woonseok Kim and al** "Performance Comparison of Dynamic Voltage Scaling Algorithms for Hard Real Time Sytems", Proceedings of the Real-Time Computing Systems and Applications Conference IEEE,2002
17. **CADENCE CAD Tools** "SoC Encounter design tools" website: http://www.cadence.com/products/digital_ic/soc_encounter/index.asp
18. **Vivet Pascal and Beigne Edith** "Design of On-chip and Off-chip Interfaces for a GALS NoC Architecture"', Proceedings of the ASYNC Conference IEEE,Grenoble 2006
19. **Lemaire Romain and al** "Performance evaluation of a NoC based design for MC-CDMA Telecommunication using NS2"', Proceedings of the RSP Conference IEEE,Montreal 2005

# Partial Bus-Invert Bus Encoding Schemes for Low-Power DSP Systems Considering Inter-wire Capacitance

T. Murgan, P.B. Bacinschi, A. García Ortiz, and M. Glesner

Institute of Microelectronic Systems,
Darmstadt University of Technology
Karlstr. 15, D-64283 Darmstadt, Germany

**Abstract.** In this work, we develop simple yet very effective bus encoding schemes that dramatically reduce both self and coupling transition activity in common DSP signals. We show that, efficient low-power codes must cope with the different statistical characteristics of the most and least significant bits. On one hand, the high correlation in the most significant bits can be exploited by employing a simple non-redundant code. On the other hand, Bus Invert based codes are very efficient when applied only on the poorly correlated uniformly distributed least significant bits. The latter should not be employed on the most significant bits in order to preserve their high correlation. Additionally, we show that low-power codes can be easily compared by means of a simple graphical method.

## 1 Introduction

With technology advancements, the on-chip interconnection structures increasingly affect the overall chip power consumption. Therefore, various signal encoding schemes have been proposed as an efficient way to reduce the transition activity and thus the power consumption in buses. Moreover, with increasing wire aspect ratios, coupling capacitances are dominating line capacitances. Thus, an efficient low power signal encoding scheme has to reduce mainly the coupling transition activity and not only the self transition activity.

The first main objective of this work is to show that by exploiting the temporal and spatial correlation typical for the most significant bits of common DSP signals, simple yet very effective coding schemes based on Bus Invert can be developed. The second goal is to construct simple partial codes based on BI and Odd/Even Bus Invert (OEBI). For this purpose, we analyze the bit level transition activity in DSP signals and show that especially when combined with a certain non-redundant code, the developed codes dramatically reduce both self and coupling activity. The main idea is to preserve the high correlation in the most significant bits and apply the classic BI low-power codes only for the least significant ones which are poorly correlated and uniformly distributed.

This work is organized as follows. In Sec. 2, we briefly discuss the notions of coupling and self transition activity and also analyze the bit-level transition

J. Vounckx, N. Azemard, and P. Maurine (Eds.): PATMOS 2006, LNCS 4148, pp. 169–180, 2006.

activity in DSP signals. Sec. 3 presents the developed POEBI codes and the modified PBI schemes. Further, Sec. 4 presents and discusses the results obtained on both synthetic and real DSP data. In Sec. 5, we compare the effectiveness of the proposed schemes in reducing the total equivalent transition activity and illustrate a graphical method to choose among the best alternatives. The work ends with some concluding remarks.

## 2   Power Consumption and Transition Activity in Buses

Classically, for power consumption analysis, on-chip buses have been modeled with a capacitance between bus lines and ground, $C_{gnd}$, and the dynamic energy dissipated by the bus drivers has been considered to be proportional to the number of bit transitions in the bus. However, due to the increase in aspect ratio of on-chip interconnects, the coupling capacitance, $C_{cpl}$, increased significantly and tends to dominate the total bus capacitance [3]. Therefore, one has to consider not only the transition activity related to the ground capacitances (the so-called self activity), but also the transition activity associated to the coupling capacitances (coupling activity).

Let $T_c$ and $T_s$ denote the total coupling and self transition activity, respectively. Consequently, the dynamic power drawn by interconnects and their drivers in a bus consisting of identical and equally spaced lines can be defined as [6]:

$$P_d = (T_c C_{cpl} + T_s C_{gnd}) V_{dd}^2. \tag{1}$$

The total self and coupling activities are the sum of the corresponding bit-level activities [9,5,4], $t_{s_i}$ and $t_{c_i}$, respectively. The bit-level transition activities for line $i$ are defined by employing the expectation operator $\mathbf{E}[\cdot]$:

$$t_{s_i} = \mathbf{E}[b_i^+ \Delta b_i], \tag{2}$$

$$t_{c_i} = \mathbf{E}[b_i^+ (2\Delta b_i - \Delta b_{i+1} - \Delta b_{i-1})], \tag{3}$$

where $b_i^+$ and $b_i^-$ denote the current and previous values on line $i$ respectively, while $\Delta b_i$ represents the transition in line $i$ [2]. In order to reduce the transition activity, one has to efficiently decrease the activity at bit level.

After analyzing the shape of the bit-level transition activity in common DSP signals that are generally represented in 2's complement (K2), Landman and Rabaey showed in [5] that the self transition activity can be represented by a continuous piece-wise linear model, called Dual-Bit Type (DBT) model. The model consists of three regions corresponding to the least significant bits (LSBs), the intermediate ones, and the most significant bits (MSBs). The regions are delimited by two breakpoints, namely the LSB breakpoint, $BP_0$, and the MSB one, $BP_1$, defined as:

$$BP_0 = \log_2(\sigma), \tag{4}$$

$$BP_1 = \log_2(|\mu| + 3\sigma), \tag{5}$$

$$\Delta BP_0 = \log_2(\sqrt{1 - \rho^2} + |\rho|/8), \tag{6}$$

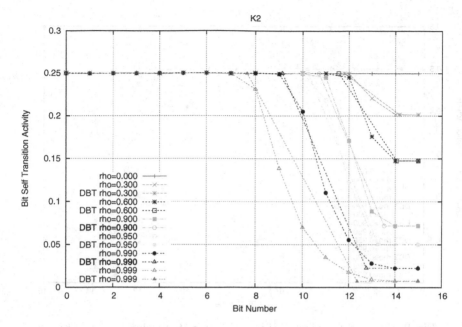

**Fig. 1.** Bit Level Self Activity: K2, $B = 16$, varying $\rho$, $\sigma_n = 0.12$

where $\rho$ and $\sigma$ denote the correlation and standard deviation of the signal, while $\Delta BP_0$ represents a correction factor for $BP_0$. To be noticed, that instead of $\sigma$, one can use the normalized standard deviation, $\sigma_n = \sigma/2^{B-1}$, where $B$ is the width of the bus. The normalized standard deviation is a measure of the relative value of $\sigma$ with respect to the total signal range.

The self activity in the LSB region is 0.25, while that of the MSB region should be simulatively determined. Another drawback of the DBT is that in the presence of high correlations, the accuracy decreases significantly, especially for the intermediate bits. In order to overcome these shortcomings, Ramprasad et al introduced in [9] closed form solutions for the bit-level correlation in the intermediate bits and for $t_m$:

$$t_m = \frac{acos(\rho)}{2\pi}. \tag{7}$$

Further, it can be shown that the accuracy of the DBT can also be improved by defining correction factors for both breakpoints in a more general fashion:

$$\Delta BP_k = log_2\left(\frac{\sqrt{1-\rho^2}}{\alpha_k} + \frac{|\rho|}{\beta_k}\right), \text{ for } k = 1, 2. \tag{8}$$

The coefficients $\alpha_k$ and $\beta_k$ are functions of $\rho$ and $\sigma_n$ and can be derived empirically in a similar way as indicated in [5]. The main advantage of this extended DBT model is that it is also applicable to the coupling activity, as seen in the

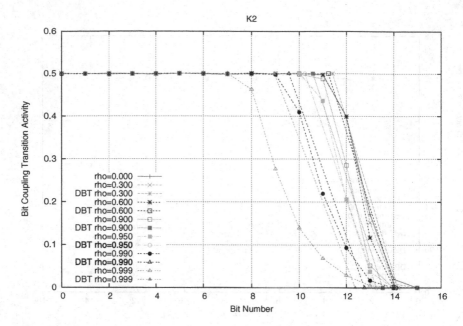

**Fig. 2.** Bit Level Coupling Activity: K2, $B = 16$, varying $\rho$, $\sigma_n = 0.12$

sequel. Although the DBT was derived mainly for Gaussian signals, the formulae for the breakpoints are robust for uni-modal distributions [5, 9].

Figures 1 and 2 illustrate the self and coupling activity for a fixed $\sigma_n$ and varying $\rho$. We can see that the self activity in MSB region is accurately defined by $t_m$, and that the coupling activity in the MSBs is zero even for small correlation factors. It can also be observed that the breakpoints are sufficiently accurate for correlation factors between 0 and 0.99.

Consequently, in order to reduce the coupling activity, low-power codes should focus on reducing the activity in the LSB region and not destroy the spatial correlation of the MSBs. In the case of self activity however, the problem is slightly more complex. For very high values of $\rho$, the activity in the MSBs is close to zero. Encoding schemes have to focus on the LSBs while not affecting the MSBs. When $\rho$ decreases, the self activity in the MSB approaches that of the LSBs and low-power codes should also try to reduce this activity. Nonetheless, this problem can be alleviated by employing a non-redundant code.

Let us define the so-called K0 code. In this code, the transmitted bit is computed as the XOR of two neighboring bits, i.e. $b_i' = b_i \oplus b_{i+1}$. The MSB is left unchanged. This code profits better from the spatial correlation between neighboring bits, though the decoding is slower, as it requires a cascade of XOR gates. As shown in Fig. 3, when applying K0, the self activity in the MSBs is reduced to zero also for small correlation factors. The coupling activity is also reduced, though by far not as much as the self activity.

Consequently, when applying K0, we can state that the activity in the MSBs is zero and that the LSBs are uncorrelated and uniformly distributed. Therefore,

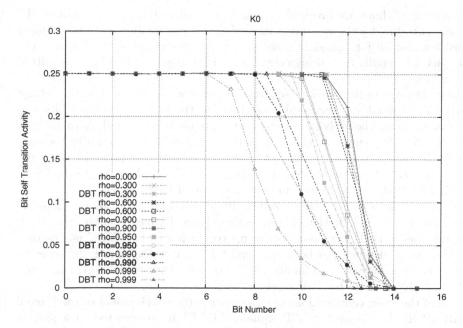

**Fig. 3.** Bit Level Self Activity: K0, $B = 16$, varying $\rho$, $\sigma_n = 0.12$

any efficient encoding scheme for typical DSP signals should focus on reducing the activity in the LSBs and preserve the correlation in the MSBs.

## 3    Partial Bus-Invert Based Coding Schemes

In order to reduce the self and coupling transition activity, numerous encoding schemes have been proposed. One of the most popular low-power codes, the Bus-Invert (BI) [12] can be applied to encode buses for reducing self activity without prior knowledge of data statistics. BI is especially efficient when transmitting low-correlated uniformly distributed data. To encode signals with highly correlated access patterns several methods have been developed: T0, working zone, PBM, VBM, etc. For a brief review, the interested reader is referred to [1,8,13]. In [10], partial bus-invert (PBI) was proposed to meet the requirement of application-specific systems and avoid unnecessary inversions in highly correlated bits. To minimize coupling transitions, Sotiriadis and Chandrakasan proposed in [11] the so-called Transition Pattern Coding (TPC). Nevertheless, because of its complex codec architecture, the application domain of this scheme is rather limited.

A more simple yet very efficient scheme to reduce coupling activity, called Odd/Even Bus Invert (OEBI), has been proposed in [14]. The main idea behind that scheme is to handle the odd and even lines separately. Somewhat similar to the original BI scheme, OEBI introduces two extra lines to indicate four possible cases: no bus lines are inverted, only odd lines are inverted, only even lines are inverted, or all lines are inverted. Unlike the regular BI case, determining the optimal encoding for the two invert-lines of OEBI is more difficult. The coupling transitions for all four possible cases are explicitly computed. Afterwards, the case with the smallest resulting coupling activity is selected to be transmitted on the bus.

As mentioned in the previous section, an efficient low-power code should not destroy the spatial and temporal correlation in the highly correlated bits and focus on reducing the activity in those which are lowly correlated. Actually, this is rather easy to achieve in the case of DSP signals. Let us consider the case of PBI. Basically, we have to estimate the regions of the MSBs and that of the LSBs. Once the regions have been identified, BI can be applied only to the LSBs. In this way, PBI becomes very simple in the case of DSP signals.

We have implemented PBI for self activity and adapted it for coupling activity. For instance, PBIH4 means that the classic BI based on the Hamming distance (hence BIH) has been applied up to the fourth bit. PBIC means that the Hamming distance has been replaced with a coupling metric in order to reduce coupling activity, and finally, K0PBI denotes the conjunction of the non-redundant K0 code with a PBI scheme.

One of the main contributions of this paper is the development of the Partial OEBI (POEBI) scheme for DSP signals. POEBI is constructed in a similar fashion as PBIC. Basically, the coupling activity is reduced only in the LSBs by applying OEBI. Compared to PBI, POEBI is more flexible and due to these higher degrees of freedom, we can expect it to be more efficient.

## 4    Interpretation of Results

In order to analyze the effectivenes of the proposed encoding schemes, we have performed extensive simulations with large sets of synthetic and real data from various DSP applications. Like explained in [9], signals obtained from sources such as speech, audio, and video can be modeled using ARMA (Auto-Regressive Moving Average) models. Therefore, we have employed these ARMA models to generate zero-mean Gaussian distributed data with varying standard deviation and correlation factor.

The coupling and self transition activity for synthetic data represented on 8 bits are illustrated in Fig. 4 and Fig. 5, respectively. We first discuss the behavior of the PBI-based schemes and afterwards that of the POEBI-based ones.

We can see that for $T_s$, BIH and K0BIH behave best at very small values of $\rho$ and become less efficient when $\rho$ increases. This can be explained as follows. For $\rho = 0$, we have $t_m = 0.25$, which actually means that there is no breakpoint and thus, no temporal correlation to take advantage of. For high $\rho$-s, K0BIH slightly improves the temporal correlation by exploiting the spatial correlation in the MSBs. However, the improvement is rather insignificant (less than 2%) because the temporal correlation in the MSBs is poorly exploited. On the contrary, the PBI-based schemes are able to efficiently exploit the high temporal and spatial correlation for high $\rho$-s. As expected, in terms of reducing $T_s$, the PBIH schemes

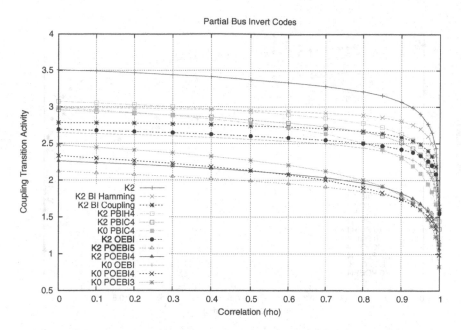

**Fig. 4.** Coupling Transition Activity for fixed $\sigma$ and varying $\rho$

perform better than the PBIC ones and KOPBI manage to achieve better results than K2PBI. Similarly, the codes tailored for reducing $T_s$ behave better than those designed for decreasing $T_s$. We also observe that K0 helps the encoding schemes to better exploit the spatial and temporal correlation. In the represented case, K2BIC and K2PBIC4 reduce $T_c$ by around 14% and 19%, respectively. With the proposed K0PBIC4, we achieve a reduction of more than 27%.

Even more interesting results are obtained when applying OEBI and POEBI. We analyze first the results from the perspective of $T_s$. It can be observed that OEBI behaves poorly for DSP signals, especially for high values of $\rho$. Nevertheless, POEBI schemes behave better than PBIC. The reason behind that is that in order to reduce the coupling activity, POEBI inverts fewer bits than PBI, affecting thus less the self activity. Furthermore, K0POEBI4 is basically as efficient as the best BI-based scheme and for $\rho \geq 0.96$, K0POEBI3 becomes also very effective. Consequently, we can say, that POEBIs significantly reduce $T_s$.

Nonetheless, OEBI has been developed for reducing mainly $T_c$. In Fig. 4, we can see that the POEBI-based schemes dramatically improve the efficiency of the classic OEBI scheme for any $\rho$ and clearly outperform the more simple PBIs, although they introduce a supplementary redundancy bit. Let us first consider the case of highly correlated data, f.i. $\rho = 0.95$. The classic OEBI reduces $T_c$ by 19% and K0PBIC4 (the best PBIC) by more than 27%. In contrast, the POEBI-based schemes achieve improvements of more than 40%, with K0POEBI3 and K0POEBI4 reaching almost 45%. The ameliorations are also remarkable for

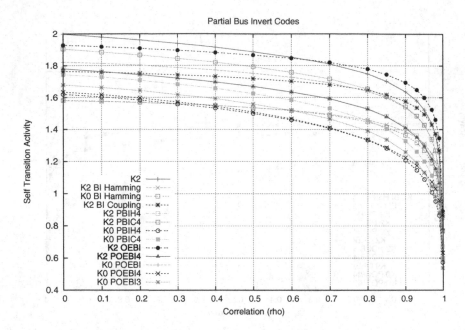

**Fig. 5.** Self Transition Activity for fixed $\sigma$ and varying $\rho$

poorly correlated signals. For example, when $\rho = 0.4$, K0POEBI4 reduces $T_c$ by more than 35% while OEBI and K0PBIC achieve reductions of around 23% and 17% respectively. We can also notice that K0 allows OEBI to exploit more efficiently the spatial correlation in the MSBs.

The above mentioned comments can be resumed as follows. As previously mentioned, we can consider the MSBs spatially and temporally highly correlated and the LSBs uncorrelated and uniformly distributed. The non-redundant K0 code efficiently exploits the spatial correlation existing in the MSBs of typical DSP signals reducing thus the self activity, especially for smaller values of $\rho$. The temporal correlation is preserved and in some cases (depending on $\sigma$ and $\rho$) even slightly reduced. Than, the PBI-based schemes exploit this temporal correlation by applying BI only on the LSBs. As these bits are uncorrelated and uniformly distributed, BI behaves in the case of self-activity optimally among 1-bit redundant low-power codes [12]. Similarly, POEBI is taking advantage of the high temporal and spatial correlation in the MSBs by not destroying it. Due to the extra-bit, these schemes have more degrees of freedom than the PBIs. In contrast to the PBIs, in the POEBI codes, the LSBs can be inverted completely or only partly. This offers higher optimization capabilities. Moreover, as the lower and upper breakpoints for $T_s$ and $T_c$ are practically the same, the POEBI schemes are in general as efficient as the PBI codes, especially when the breakpoints have higher values. In this case, we have more LSBs and the effect of having an extra-bit is decreased.

**Table 1.** Self and Coupling Transition Activities for Real DSP Data

| | $K2$ | $BIH$ | $BIC$ | $OEBI$ | $PBIH$ | $PBIC$ | | $POEBI$ | |
|---|---|---|---|---|---|---|---|---|---|
| $v_1$ | | | | | $K0PBIH2$ | $PBIC2$ | $K0PBIC2$ | $POEBI2$ | $K0POEBI2$ |
| $T_c$ | 1.26 | 1.25 | 1.15 | 1.22 | 0.86 | 0.97 | 0.81 | 0.77 | 0.68 |
| $T_s$ | 0.72 | 0.58 | 0.81 | 0.75 | 0.40 | 0.68 | 0.45 | 0.61 | 0.43 |
| $v_2$ | | | | | $K0PBIH2$ | $PBIC4$ | $K0PBIC3$ | $POEBI3$ | $K0POEBI3$ |
| $T_c$ | 1.71 | 1.67 | 1.53 | 1.57 | 1.21 | 1.36 | 1.18 | 1.00 | 0.92 |
| $T_s$ | 0.97 | 0.79 | 1.02 | 1.02 | 0.61 | 0.90 | 0.66 | 0.85 | 0.63 |
| $v_3$ | | | | | $K0PBIH2$ | $PBIC2$ | $K0PBIC2$ | $POEBI2$ | $K0POEBI2$ |
| $T_c$ | 1.03 | 1.03 | 0.95 | 0.98 | 0.71 | 0.79 | 0.70 | 0.65 | 0.60 |
| $T_s$ | 0.63 | 0.47 | 0.68 | 0.66 | 0.35 | 0.60 | 0.39 | 0.56 | 0.37 |
| $v_4$ | | | | | $K0PBIH6$ | $PBIC8$ | $K0PBIC8$ | $POEBI7$ | $K0POEBI3$ |
| $T_c$ | 4.84 | 2.86 | 2.83 | 1.92 | 2.17 | 2.77 | 1.85 | 1.24 | 1.81 |
| $T_s$ | 2.21 | 1.67 | 1.78 | 2.43 | 1.14 | 1.79 | 1.85 | 2.05 | 1.97 |
| $v_5$ | | | | | $K0PBIH6$ | $PBIC6$ | $K0PBIC5$ | $POEBI5$ | $K0POEBI5$ |
| $T_c$ | 3.60 | 3.22 | 2.91 | 2.90 | 3.16 | 2.89 | 2.99 | 2.22 | 2.34 |
| $T_s$ | 2.17 | 1.75 | 1.97 | 2.11 | 1.60 | 2.02 | 1.77 | 1.94 | 1.69 |
| $v_6$ | | | | | $K0PBIH4$ | $PBIC6$ | $K0PBIC5$ | $POEBI5$ | $K0POEBI4$ |
| $T_c$ | 3.61 | 3.14 | 2.78 | 2.86 | 2.99 | 2.89 | 2.83 | 2.22 | 2.26 |
| $T_s$ | 2.25 | 1.66 | 1.94 | 2.12 | 1.50 | 2.10 | 1.61 | 2.03 | 1.53 |

The developed codes have been also applied on a set of real DSP signals. Due to their varying statistical characteristics, we have chosen the following data:

$v_1$ Classic music: 1300000 samples, $B = 8$, $\sigma_n = 0.0448$, $\rho = 0.984$,

$v_2$ Modern punk rock music: 1000000 samples, $B = 8$, $\sigma_n = 0.0804$, $\rho = 0.975$,

$v_3$ Poem recitation: 800000 samples, $B = 8$, $\sigma_n = 0.0369$, $\rho = 0.961$,

$v_4$ Pressure measurement in an ignition knock detector: 23000 samples, $B = 10$, $\sigma_n = 0.1288$, $\rho = 0.389$,

$v_5$ Real part of an FFT output of an IEEE 802.11g OFDM transmitter using a 64QAM modulation: 700000 samples, $B = 9$, $\sigma_n = 0.1072$, $\rho = 0.271$, and

$v_6$ Imaginary part of an FFT input of an IEEE 802.11g OFDM receiver using a 64QAM modulation: 700000 samples, $B = 9$, $\sigma_n = 0.1118$, $\rho = -0.001$.

Tab. 1 shows the transition activity for BI and OEBI as well as for the best PBI and POEBI. The coding scheme for which the optimum has been achieved is also indicated.

In the case of typical audio signals, i.e. $v_1$, $v_2$, and $v_3$, we can see that K0POEBI is improving the self activity by almost the same amount as the best PBIH. For instance, $T_s$ of $v_3$ is reduced with K0PBIH2 and with K0POEBI2 by 44.44% and 41.27%, respectively. Further, K0POEBI is more effective in reducing $T_c$ than any other scheme. For example, in the case of $v_1$, K0POEBI2 reduces $T_c$ by 46.03%, while OEBI and BIC only by 3.17% and 8.73%, respectively. On the contrary, K0PBIC2 significantly reduces $T_c$ by 35.71%. It is worth mentioning, that while OEBI generally reduces $T_c$ by merely 5%, POEBI manages to improve the coupling activity by more than 40%.

**Table 2.** Analysis of Total Equivalent Transition Activity for Different Bus Types

|  | $T_c$ | $T_s$ | $T_{eq}$ | | |
|---|---|---|---|---|---|
|  |  |  | $\lambda=2.76$ | $\lambda=2.09$ | $\lambda=0.65$ |
| K2 | 6.01 | 3.17 | 19.78 | 15.74 | 7.08 |
| K2 BIH | 5.69 | 2.87 | 18.60 | 14.78 | 6.58 |
| K2 BIC | 5.17 | 3.23 | 17.51 | 14.04 | 6.60 |
| K2 PBIH10 | 5.16 | 2.74 | 16.99 | 13.53 | 6.10 |
| K2 PBIC11 | 4.86 | 2.87 | 16.30 | 13.04 | 6.03 |
| K2 OEBI | 5.05 | 3.30 | 17.24 | 13.86 | 6.58 |
| K2 POEBI10 | 3.79 | 2.75 | 13.24 | 10.69 | 5.22 |
| K0 | 5.72 | 2.86 | 18.65 | 14.81 | 6.57 |
| K0 BIH | 5.53 | 2.81 | 18.09 | 14.38 | 6.41 |
| K0 BIC | 5.24 | 3.02 | 17.49 | 13.98 | 6.43 |
| K0 PBIH10 | 4.86 | 2.43 | 15.87 | 12.61 | 5.60 |
| K0 PBIC10 | 4.64 | 2.58 | 15.41 | 12.30 | 5.60 |
| K0 OEBI | 4.94 | 3.10 | 16.75 | 13.44 | 6.31 |
| K0 POEBI9 | 3.63 | 2.47 | 12.50 | 10.06 | 4.83 |

Things are similar in the case of $v_5$ and $v_6$. There are only two differences mainly because the correlation in OFDM communication systems is close to zero and thus, the breakpoints have higher values. On one hand, there is less temporal correlation in the MSBs to take advantage and the achieved improvement is slightly smaller than in the previous cases. On the other hand, POEBI and PBI use more bits for coding. The results confirm those obtained with synthetic data.

In the case of signal $v_4$, which is poorly correlated and is characterized by a large $\sigma_n$, there is a behavioral discrepancy between the coding schemes that achieve the best results for $T_c$ and $T_s$, respectively. While K0PBIH6 reduces $T_s$ by 48.41%, the best OEBI brings an improvement of 10.86%. However, POEBI7 manages to reduce $T_c$ by an incredible 73.38% while K0PBIH6 improves the coupling activity by 55.15%. This shows that, in order to choose the optimal low-power code, designers need in the early stages of the design flow information about the statistical characteristics of the data.

## 5    High-Level Analysis of Low-Power Codes

We have seen that the low power codes may have a different impact on $T_s$ and $T_c$. By introducing the bus aspect factor $\lambda = C_{cpl}/C_{gnd}$, we can define the total equivalent transition activity $T_{eq} = T_s + \lambda T_c$. Thus, the consumed power can also be written as:

$$P_d = (T_s + \lambda T_c)C_{gnd}V_{dd}^2 = T_{eq}C_{gnd}V_{dd}^2. \tag{9}$$

Consequently, in order to efficiently analyze at higher levels of abstraction different alternatives for low-power codes, the only required technological information is related to the bus geometry. For a given geometry, in order to determine

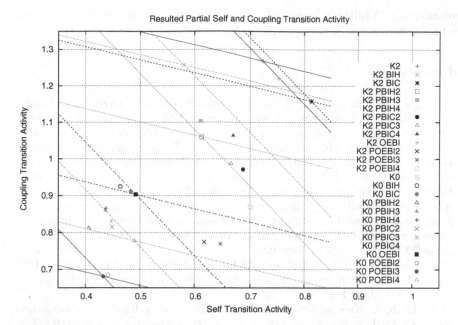

**Fig. 6.** Graphical Figure of Merit for Low-Power Codes as a Function of $\lambda$

$\lambda$, the ground and coupling capacitances can be either computed by means of closed form formulae or extracted with field solvers.

Tab. 2 shows the effectiveness of different codes in a projected 65nm technological node for $v_1$ when applied in typical local ($\lambda$=2.76), intermediate ($\lambda$=2.09), and global wires ($\lambda$=0.65). Capacitances and bus aspect factor have been computed by employing the interconnect formulae offered by [7].

As shown in Fig. 6, by representing each encoding scheme as a point in the $\{T_s,T_c\}$ plane, we can easily define a graphical figure of merit. For a given $\lambda$, we draw for each $(T_s,T_c)$ pair the lines defined by $y = (Ts + \lambda T_c - x)/\lambda$. The best code is determined by finding the line that is closest to the origin.

## 6    Concluding Remarks

In the case of DSP signals, we have shown that on one hand, efficient low-power bus encoding techniques must take advantage of the temporal and spatial correlation in the MSBs. On the other hand, the uncorrelated uniformly distributed LSBs are perfect candidates for schemes like BI and OEBI. Based on these observations and by analyzing the breakpoints of the extended DBT model, we have constructed several simple yet powerful PBI and POEBI based schemes. Furthermore, by applying first the non-redundant K0 code, the temporal and spatial correlation characteristic for MSBs is exploited in order to reduce significantly the self activity. As the breakpoints are extremely close, the developed PBI and especially POEBI dramatically improve self and coupling activity simultaneously. Additionally, we have shown that low-power codes can be compared for different bus geometries by means of a simple graphical method.

# References

1. L. Benini, A. Macii, E. Macii, M. Poncino, and R. Scarsi. Architectures and Synthesis Algorithms for Power-Efficient Bus Interfaces. *IEEE Trans. on Computer-Aided Design (CAD) of Integrated Circuits and Systems*, 19(9):969–980, September 2000.
2. A. García Ortiz, T. Murgan, L. D. Kabulepa, L. S. Indrusiak, and M. Glesner. High-Level Estimation of Power Consumption in Point-to-Point Interconnect Architectures. *Journal of Integrated Circuits and Systems*, 1(1):23–31, March 2004.
3. International Technology Roadmap for Semiconductors, 2005 Edition. *Interconnect.* http://www.itrs.net/, Jan. 2006.
4. P. E. Landman and J. M. Rabaey. Power Estimation for High-level Synthesis. In *European Conf. on Design Automation with the European Event in ASIC Design*, pages 22–25, Paris, France, Feb. 1993.
5. P. E. Landman and J. M. Rabaey. Architectural Power Analysis: The Dual Bit Type Model. *IEEE Trans. on Very Large Scale Integration (VLSI) Systems*, 3(2):173–187, June 1995.
6. C.-G. Lyuh, T. Kim, and K.-W. Kim. Coupling-Aware High-level Interconnect Synthesis for Low Power. In *Intl. Conf. on Computer-Aided Design (ICCAD)*, pages 609–613, San Jose, California, Nov. 2002.
7. Nanoscale Integration and Modeling (NIMO) Group, Arizona State Univ. Predictive Technology Model. http://www.eas.asu.edu/ptm/, Dec. 2005.
8. S. Ramprasad, N. R. Shanbag, and I. N. Hajj. A Coding Framework for Low-Power Address and Data Busses. *IEEE Trans. on Very Large Scale Integration (VLSI) Systems*, 7(2):212–221, June 1999.
9. S. Ramprasad, N. R. Shanbhag, and I. N. Hajj. Analytical Estimation of Signal Transition Activity from Word-Level Statistics. *IEEE Trans. on Computer-Aided Design (CAD) of Integrated Circuits and Systems*, 16(7):718–733, July 1997.
10. Y. Shin, S.-I. Chae, and K. Choi. Partial Bus-Invert Coding for Power Optimization of Application-Specific Systems. 9(2):377–383, April 2001.
11. P. P. Sotiriadis and A. P. Chandrakasan. Low Power Coding Techniques Considering Inter-Wire Capacitance. In *Custom Integrated Circuits Conf.*, pages 507–510, Orlando, Florida, May 2000.
12. M. R. Stan and W. P. Burleson. Bus-Invert Coding for Low-Power I/O. *IEEE Trans. on Very Large Scale Integration (VLSI) Systems*, 3(1):49–58, March 1995.
13. M. R. Stan and W. P. Burleson. Low-Power Encodings for Global Communication in CMOS VLSI. *IEEE Trans. on Very Large Scale Integration (VLSI) Systems*, 5(4):444–455, December 1997.
14. Y. Zhang, J. Lach, K. Skadron, and M. R. Stan. Odd/Even Bus Invert with Two-Phase Transfer for Buses with Coupling. In *Intl. Symp. on Low Power Electronics and Design (ISLPED)*, pages 80–83, Monterey, California, August 2002.

# Estimation of Power Reduction by On-Chip Transmission Line for 45nm Technology

Kenichi Okada, Takumi Uezono, and Kazuya Masu

Tokyo Institute of Technology, Yokohama 226-8503, Japan

**Abstract.** This paper evaluates the feasibility of on-chip transmission-line interconnect at 45nm CMOS technology. Circuit performances tend to depend heavily on global interconnects, and power and delay of global interconnects are increased due to the miniaturization of process technology. On-chip transmission line has been proposed, which can improve such the large delay and large power consumption of the long RC interconnects. The improvement has been evaluated only for a single interconnect. In this paper, the total power reduction of the entire circuit is evaluated for 45nm technology, which is based on the measurement results at 180nm technology. As an example, the power consumption of global interconnects is improved by 6.6% on a circuit designed for 45nm process.

## 1  Introduction

International Technology Roadmap for Semiconductors (ITRS) shows that circuit performance becomes dependent on resistance and capacitance in long interconnects, and the global interconnect delay becomes much larger than gate delay year by year. To obtain faster circuits in future technologies, it is indispensable to reduce the global interconnect delay.

Conventional global interconnect is usually divided by several repeaters to reduce delay. More repeaters are required for longer global interconnect. Delay and power consumption tend to be proportional to the number of repeaters and the line length. Then, on-chip transmission line as a global interconnect has been proposed to improve such the problem [1,2,3,4]. The on-chip transmission line achieves electromagnetic-wave transmission. The transmission-line interconnect can propagate signal faster than an RC interconnect, and the transmission line consumes lower power than the RC line in the long interconnects [1,2,3]. The transmission line can be realized using the inductance of interconnects in Si ULSI. In recent technologies, interconnect has larger inductance than before because of increase of signal frequency, so transmission lines can easily be realized in Si ULSI. For example, 4 Gbps signal propagation using the on-chip transmission line is reported at $0.35\mu$m technology [2,3]. It is also predicted that 10 times smaller delay and 5 times lower power for 5mm-length interconnect can be achived by the on-chip transmission-line interconnect at 45nm process technology [1].

Figure 1 shows an RC interconnect and a transmission-line interconnect. The transmission-line interconnect shown in Fig. 1 consists of a driver, a differential transmission line, and a receiver, and it is used to replace the RC interconnects.

J. Vounckx, N. Azemard, and P. Maurine (Eds.): PATMOS 2006, LNCS 4148, pp. 181–190, 2006.

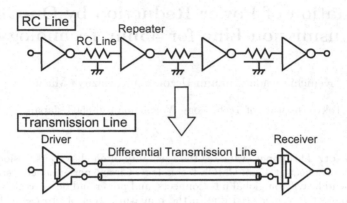

**Fig. 1.** An RC interconnect and a transmission-line interconnect

The driver and the receiver consist of differential amplifiers. Power consumption of the transmission-line interconnect does not depend on signal frequency and line length because power consumption of the differential amplifier is constant [1, 2, 3].

As a disadvantage of the transmission line, the transmission line requires larger wiring area than the RC line [4]. It is not feasible to replace all the RC lines with the transmission lines. Line-to-line capacitance will become extremely large if too many transmission-line interconnects are used. There is a trade-off between the increase of capacitance and the improvement by the transmission-line interconnects. The transmission-line interconnect has been evaluated only for a single interconnect. Therefore, this paper presents estimation results for the entire circuit about power reduction by the on-chip transmission lines [5, 6].

The transmission-line interconnect can improve delay and power of long interconnects. The increase of line-to-line capacitance caused by the insertion of transmission-line interconnects also causes degradation of delay and power, so an optimization method is required. There are two optimizing objects, delay and power. To improve delay, longer interconnect on critical paths should be replaced with transmission-line interconnects [5]. To improve power, just longer interconnect should be replaced with transmission-line interconnects [6]. An interconnect that has higher switching frequency should be replaced for the power reduction. Ref. [6] presents a design methodology using the on-chip transmission-line interconnects for $0.18\mu m$ technology. In this paper, we focus on the power improvement method and show estimation results of power reduction for the entire circuit at 45nm technology [1, 3]. In this paper, Wire Length Distribution (WLD) is utilized to estimate a statistical relationship between wire length and the number of wires [7]. It is derived from Rent's rule, which is a relationship between the number of gates and pins [8], and the WLD can be extracted from a gate-level netlist. The WLD can estimate an appropriate wire length over which the transmission line should be used.

This paper is structured as follows. Advantages for a single interconnect are discussed for 45nm technology. Next, the WLD is explained. We show the method to replace RC lines with transmission lines. Finally, we demonstrate experimental results for delay and power consumption at 45nm technology.

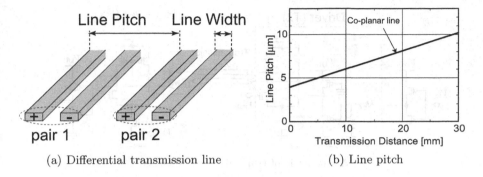

(a) Differential transmission line          (b) Line pitch

**Fig. 2.** Structure of differential transmission line

## 2   On-Chip Transmission Line Interconnect

In this section, the characteristics for on-chip transmission line is discussed, and the effectiveness of transmission line is evaluated as compared with RC lines [1,3]. The differential signal is transmitted using transmission line shown in Fig. 2(a). Transmission line structure is determined by interconnect loss and crosstalk, so the line pitch is proportional to the transmission distance as shown in Fig. 2(b).

The line pitch is the sum of line space, line widths and gap between lines in differential pair. A wider line width is required to transmit a longer distance because signal is attenuated, and the signal attenuation caused by the resistance is estimated by 2-dimensional electromagnetic simulator. The line space between differential pairs is determined according to the crosstalk coefficient [4]. We assume that the attenuation margin is 20 dB at frequency $f_{sig} = 0.34/t_r$, where $t_r$ is the rise time [9], and $t_r = 0.10 \times t_{period}$, where $t_{period}$ is the clock period. The line space is determined to have less than 0.05 of the crosstalk coefficient as shown in Fig. 2(b).

Figure 3(a) shows driver and receiver circuits of transmission-line interconnect. Delay and power consumption for the transmission-line interconnect of 45nm technology have been reported [1,3], which are estimated using mearement results of $0.35\mu$m and $0.18\mu$m technologies [1,2,3]. As an example, Fig. 3(b) shows micrograph of the on-chip transmission-line interconnect fabricated using 180nm process [3].

Delay of RC interconnect is estimated by the following equation [8].

$$T_{delay} = 2.5\sqrt{R_{int}C_{int}R_oC_o}\,\ell_{int} \tag{1}$$

where $R_{int}$ is interconnect resistance per unit length, $C_{int}$ is interconnect capacitance per unit length, which is calculated by [10], $R_o$ is gate output resistance, $C_o$ is gate input capacitance, and $\ell_{int}$ is interconnect length. We assume that track utilization is 10% in this example. The optimal number of repeaters $k$ and the repeater size coefficient $h$ are calculated to reduce delay as follows [8].

$$k = \sqrt{\frac{0.4R_{int}C_{int}}{0.7R_oC_o}}, \tag{2}$$

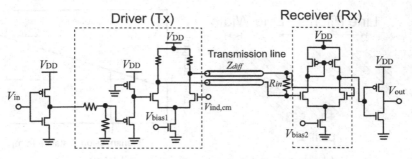

(a) A schematic of transmission-line circuit

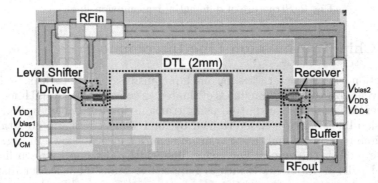

(b) Micrograph of differential transmission line interconnect

**Fig. 3.** Differential transmission line interconnect fabricated using 180nm process

$$h = \sqrt{\frac{R_{\mathrm{o}} C_{\mathrm{int}}}{R_{\mathrm{int}} C_{\mathrm{o}}}} \tag{3}$$

Repeater size are determined from the following equation.

$$W_{\mathrm{n}} = h W_{\mathrm{n_{unit}}}, W_p = h W_{\mathrm{p_{unit}}}$$

where $W_{\mathrm{n}}$ and $W_{\mathrm{p}}$ are nMOS and pMOS gate widths, respectively. $W_{\mathrm{n_{unit}}}$ and $W_{\mathrm{p_{unit}}}$ are unit inverter sizes, and both are $0.125\mu$m.

Figure 4 shows delay and power consumption of a single interconnect using RC line and transmission line. Power consumption and delay are proportional to the number of repeaters and line length in RC lines. On the other hand, transmission line interconnect consumes power in driver and receiver circuit [1, 2, 3]. The transmission line interconnect has offset delay caused by the driver and receiver circuit. However, transmission line can carry signal faster than RC lines because voltage swing transmits at an electromagnetic-wave speed. At 45nm technology, transmission line has advantage over 0.7mm and 2.5mm for delay and power consumption, respectively.

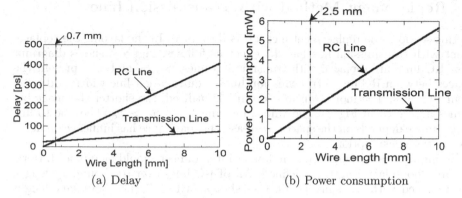

(a) Delay                          (b) Power consumption

**Fig. 4.** Delay and power consumption at a single interconnect using co-planar structure

# 3 Wire Length Distribution

Figure 5 shows the analytical expression of the WLD, where $\ell$ is interconnect length per unit of gate pitch and $i(\ell)$ is the number of interconnects at length of $\ell$. This expression has been derived from Rent's empirical rule [7,8], which gives the relationship between the number of pins $T$ and the number of gates $N$.

$$T = kN^p \tag{4}$$

where $k$ and $p$ are Rent's constants, representing the average number of pins and a constant related to the complexity of the circuit, respectively. In this case, these parameters are extracted from the actual data in Fig. 5. In general, complex circuits tend to have large $p$ and small $k$, while simple circuits tend to have small $p$ and large $k$ [8]. The WLD can predict the number of pins and wires for the future technology by simple equations.

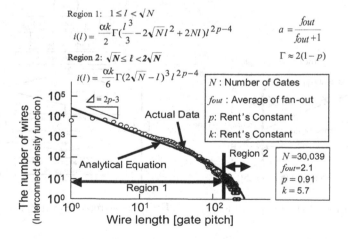

**Fig. 5.** Wire length distribution

## 4    Replacement Method with Transmission Line

In this section, the replacement method is described. In the layout, the replacement with transmission line has the effect as follows. Figure 6 shows diagrams that RC lines are replaced with transmission lines. $S_a$, $S_b$ and $S_c$ represent the spaces between RC lines. Transmission lines require larger line width and pitch than RC lines. The more transmission line is utilized, the shorter the space becomes as shown in Fig. 6. The values become $S_a > S_b > S_c$. The line-to-line capacitance depends on the spaces. Increase of capacitance has influence on delay and power consumption.

To improve power consumption, longer interconnect should be replaced. Here, a word "boundary length" is defined. All of RC lines over the boundary length are replaced with transmission lines as shown in Fig. 7. The boundary lenght should be optimized. In this method, power is reduced, and delay and area are not varied. The appropriate boundary length is derived using the WLD.

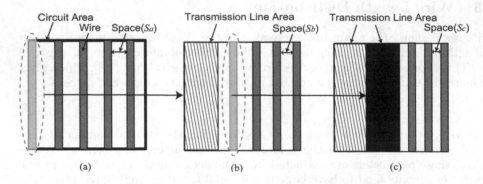

**Fig. 6.** Diagrams that RC lines are replaced with transmission lines

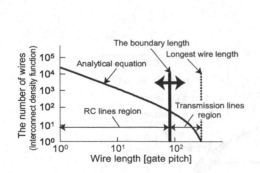

**Fig. 7.** Position of the boundary length

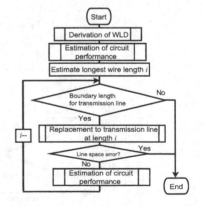

**Fig. 8.** The replacement flow with transmission line

Figure 8 shows the replacement flow with transmission lines. First, the WLD is derived, and circuit performance is estimated for a circuit consisting of only RC lines. The space between RC lines is calculated from the RC-line width and the total wiring area for RC lines. Line-to-line capacitance is calculated from the space, and delay is estimated using Eq.(1). Next, longer interconnects are replaced with transmission-line interconnects in order of length. Delay and power are estimated again. If delay becomes larger, replacement is finished. The replacement is also stopped if the space is less than that limited by the process design rule, Then, the appropriate boundary length is determined.

## 5    Experimental Results

In this section, circuit performance compared with a single interconnect is estimated using the proposed replacement method. In Sec. 5.1, the delay is estimated considering wire density for RC lines. In Sec. 5.2, total power consumption for long wire length is estimated. Power consumption for only the RC lines is compared with that for transmission line.

### 5.1    Estimation of Circuit Delay

In this section, the influence on the entire circuit by the replacement is described. In this case, the estimation of line-to-line capacitance is important. The capacitance is estimated on the WLD, and the appropriate boundary length is determined. Circuit configuration is assumed as listed in Table 1. We assume a typical 45nm CMOS process technology. Figure 9 shows interconnect cross section and process parameters taken from ITRS.

Figure 10 shows a relationship between capacitance per unit length and the boundary length. Total interconnect length is long on large $p$ circuit. It requires large wiring area, so capacitance per unit length increases as the boundary length becomes short. Delay and power consumption of transmission line does not depend on wire density [1, 2, 3].

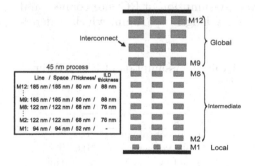
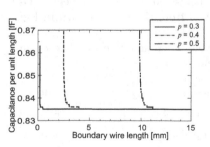

**Fig. 9.** Interconnect cross section for 45nm technology

**Fig. 10.** Capacitance per unit length for each $p$

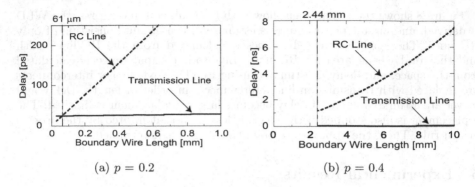

(a) $p = 0.2$                                    (b) $p = 0.4$

**Fig. 11.** A relationship between boundary wire length and delay for circuit complexity $p$

Figure 11 shows a relationship between a boundary wire length and delay for each circuit complexity $p$. In case $p$ is 0.2, delay of RC interconnect intersects with that of the transmission-line interconnect as shown in Fig. 11(a), and the boundary length have to be longer than $61\mu m$ not to degrade delay. In case $p$ is 0.4, the density of RC lines is too high where the boundary length is shorter than 2.44mm. Moreother, geometorical wiring structure has to fulfill physical design rules. Figure 12 shows a relationship between circuit complexity $p$ and boundary wire length. At less than 0.25 of $p$, the boundary length is constant. At more than 0.25 of $p$, the boundary length becomes longer and the only longer wires have to be replace with transmission lines.

## 5.2   Estimation of Circuit Power Consumption

This section reports a simple estimation for power consumption for the circuit with and without transmission line for 45nm technology. The assumption listed in Table 2 is employed for power estimation. The number of gates, average fanout, average pins and chip size are listed in Table 1. Figure 13 shows a relationship between wire length and power consumption of RC interconnect and transmission-line interconnect. The boundary length is 5.4mm, which is determined from the result shown in Fig. 11.

**Table 1.** Assumption of delay estimation

| Factors | Value |
|---|---|
| Number of gates | 240M gates |
| Chip size | 3.1cm$^2$ |
| Number of average fanout | 3 |
| Number of average pin | 4 |
| Gate output resistance | 6.3k$\Omega$ |
| Gate input capacitance | 0.43fF |

**Table 2.** Assumption of Power Estimation

| Factors | Value |
|---|---|
| Circuit complexity $p$ | 0.4 |
| Supply voltage | 0.6[V] |
| Frequency | 15[GHz] |
| Activity factor | 0.5 |

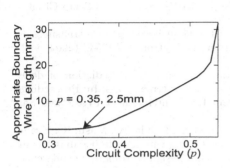
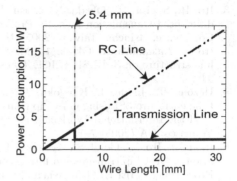

**Fig. 12.** A relationship between circuit complexity and boundary wire length

**Fig. 13.** Power consumption of the circuit with and without transmission lines

The global-interconnect power can be calculated with the WLD and the relationship shown in Fig. 13. The global-interconnect power with and without transmission lines is 41.6[W] and 38.8[W], respectively. In this case, power reduction with the transmission-line interconnects is 6.6% for a circuit of 45nm technology.

## 6  Summary and Conclusions

The advantage of transmission line for global interconnect at 45nm technology is demonstrated, and the replacing method with the transmission line is presented. The boundary length becomes longer for complex circuits, so only long interconnects should be replaced with transmission lines. In the experimental results for 45nm technology, the transmission-line interconnects can improve the power consumption of global interconnects by 6.6%. It is expected that the transmission line becomes more advantageous as the transistor characteristics are improved [1], so the proposed methodology will become more important in the future process technologies.

## Acknowledgements

This work was partially supported by MEXT.KAKENHI, JSPS.KAKENHI, STARC, and VDEC in collaboration with Synopsys, Inc.

## References

1. Ito, H., Inoue, J., Gomi, S., Sugita, H., Okada, K., Masu, K.: On-Chip transmission line for long global interconnects. In: IEEE International Electron Devices Meeting Technical Digest, San Francisco, CA (2004) 677–680
2. Gomi, S., Nakamura, K., Ito, H., Okada, K., Masu, K.: Differential transmission line interconnect for high speed and low power global wiring. In: Proceedings of IEEE Custom Integrated Circuits Conference, Orlando, FL (2004) 325–328

3. Ito, H., Sugita, H., Okada, K., Masu, K.: 4 Gbps on-chip interconnection using differential transmission line. In: Proceedings of IEEE Asian Solid-State Circuits Conference, Hsinchu, Taiwan (2005) 417–420
4. Ito, H., Nakamura, K., Okada, K., Masu, K.: High density differential transmission line structure on Si ULSI. IEICE Transaction on Electronics **E87-C** (2004) 942–948
5. Uezono, T., Inoue, J., Kyogoku, T., Okada, K., Masu, K.: Prediction of delay time for future LSI using On-Chip transmission line interconnects. In: Proceedings of IEEE International Workshop on System Level Interconnect Prediction, San Francisco, CA (2005) 7–12
6. Inoue, J., Ito, H., Gomi, S., Kyogoku, T., Uezono, T., Okada, K., Masu, K.: Evaluation of On-Chip transmission line interconnect using wire length distribution. In: Proceedings of IEEE/ACM Asia and South Pacific Design Automation Conference, Shanghai, China (2005) 133–138
7. Davis, J.A., De, V.K., Meindl, J.D.: A stochastic wire length distribution for gigascale integration (GSI): Part I: Derivation and validation. IEEE Transactions on Electron Devices **45** (1998) 580–589
8. Bakoglu, H.B.: Circuits, Intreconnections, and Packaging for VLSI. Reading. MA: Addision-Wesley (1990)
9. Cheng, C.K., Lillis, J., Lin, S., Chang, N.: Interconnect Analysis and Synthesis. A Wiley-Interscience Publication (2000)
10. Sakurai, T., Tamaru, K.: Simple formulas for two- and three-dimensional capacitances. TED **ED-30** (1983) 183–185

# Two Efficient Synchronous ⇔ Asynchronous Converters Well-Suited for Network on Chip in GALS Architectures

A. Sheibanyrad and A. Greiner

The University of Pierre and Marie Curie
4, Place Jussieu, 75252 CEDEX 05, Paris, France
abbas.sheibanyrad@lip6.fr, alain.greiner@lip6.fr

**Abstract.** This paper presents two high-throughput, low-latency converters that can be used to convert synchronous communication protocol to asynchronous one and vice versa. These two hardware components have been designed to be used in Multi-Processor System on Chip respecting the GALS (Globally Asynchronous Locally Synchronous) paradigm and communicating by a fully asynchronous Network on Chip (NoC). The proposed architecture is rather generic, and allows the system designer to make various trade-off between latency and robustness, depending on the selected synchronizer. These converters have been physically implemented with the portable ALLIANCE CMOS standard cell library and the architecture has been evaluated by SPICE simulation for a 90nm CMOS fabrication process.

## 1 Introduction

NoCs (Network on Chip) are a new design paradigm for scalable, high throughput communication infrastructure, in Multi-Processor System on Chip (MP-SoC) with billions of transistors. The idea of NoC is dividing a chip into several independent subsystems (or clusters) connected together by a global communication architecture which spreads on the entire chip.

Because of physical issues in nanometer fabrication processes, it is not anymore possible to distribute a synchronous clock signal on the entire wide chip area. The Globally Asynchronous Locally Synchronous (GALS) addresses this difficulty. In this approach, each subsystem is a separated synchronous domain running with its own local clock signal.

**Table 1.** Timing Dependency Methods

| Type | Δ Frequency | Δ Phase |
|---|---|---|
| Synchronous | 0 | 0 |
| Pseudochronous | 0 | Constant |
| Mesochronous | 0 | Undefined |
| Plesiochronous | ε | ε |
| Heterochronous | Rational | Undefined |
| Multi-synchronous | Undefined | Undefined |
| Asynchronous | - | - |

J. Vounckx, N. Azemard, and P. Maurine (Eds.): PATMOS 2006, LNCS 4148, pp. 191–202, 2006.

Several solutions have been proposed to resolve the problems of clock boundaries between different clusters, and the risk of synchronization failures (metastability). The proposed solutions depend on the constraints that must be respected by the clock signals in different clusters: The mesochronous, plesiochronous, pseudochronous (or quasi synchronous) and heterochronous approaches correspond to various hypothesis regarding the phases and frequencies of clocks signals. Table 1 summarizes these conditions.

The Globally Pseudochronous Locally Synchronous scheme (GPLS) is proposed in [1]. In [2], [3] and [4] the authors have proposed plesiochronous solutions which rely on exact or nearly exact frequency and phase matching of the clocks. Mesochronous solutions are described in [4], [5] and [6]: it is argued that maintaining the same frequency in several clock domains is not too difficult. The main problem is the skew between clock phases. In heterochronous solutions ([4], [7], [8] and [9]) all clock signals can have different frequencies, but with fixed and integer ratios.

In MP-SoC design, a fundamental challenge is the capability of operating under totally independent timing assumptions for each subsystem. Such a multi-synchronous system contains several synchronous subsystems clocked with completely independent clocks.

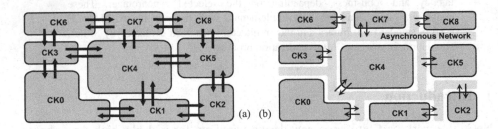

**Fig. 1.** Multi-Synchronous System in 2D Mesh Topology

In a two dimensional mesh respecting the multi-synchronous approach (Fig. 1a) we must solve the problem of communication between two neighbors clusters clocked with two fully asynchronous clocks. In [4], [5], [10] and [11] several authors have proposed different types of bi-synchronous FIFOs which can be used as a robust interface between neighbors. But this type of architecture implies one possibility of synchronization failure (metastability) at each clock boundary between neighbors.

We illustrate in Fig. 1b an alternative solution: The global interconnect has a fully asynchronous architecture. As an example we can denote the *MANGO* architecture presented in [26] which was one of the first asynchronous NOC. This type of NoC respects the GALS approach by providing synchronous ⇔ asynchronous interfaces to each local subsystem. In this case, the synchronization failure can only happen in the two synchronous ⇔ asynchronous converters located in the destination and source clusters. Providing a robust solution for those hardware interfaces is the main purpose of this paper. The *MANGO*'s designers have proposed in [27] an OCP Compliant Network Adapter (NA) interfacing local systems to NOC. The synchronization in NA has a minimized overhead.

The design of various architectures that can be used to interface an asynchronous domain with a synchronous one, are presented in [10], [14], [15], [16] and [17]. We present in this paper two converters architectures which can be used to convert a Four Phase Bundled Data asynchronous protocol to a synchronous FIFO protocol and vice versa. Using FIFOs to interface mixed timing systems couple two fundamental issues which need to be considered in designing such interfaces: flow control (high level issue) and synchronization (low level issue). This coupling reduces the need of hardware synchronizer to the handshake signals that are used for the flow control.

Some of the published solutions for interfacing asynchronous and synchronous domains are strongly dependent on synchronizer choice. In [15] and [16] the designs of various types of synchronizers using pausible clocking methods ([12]), are proposed and in [17] the authors have suggested to generate a stoppable clock for local systems.

In [14] a pipelined synchronizing FIFO is proposed. This FIFO requires that the producer produces data at a constant rate. The latency of this design is proportional to the number of FIFO stages and requires the use of a specific synchronizer.

In [10] various FIFOs are used to interface four possible combinations of independent mixed timing environments. These four FIFOs have the same basic architecture. The small differences in FIFO designs are simple adaptation to the consumer and the producer interface type. There is at least two weak points in this proposal: the architecture is dependent on a specific synchronizer (the cascaded Flip-Flops), and the use of a more conservative synchronizer (with latency larger than one clock cycle), can decrease the throughput to a value less than one data transfer per cycle. Furthermore, the authors of [10] didn't said anything about silicon area, but we believe that the architecture proposed in the present paper has a smaller foot-print.

We discuss the synchronizer issue in section 2. We present the general architecture of the synchronous ⇔ asynchronous converters in section 3. The detailed schematic is described in section 4. The system architecture is briefly illustrated in section 5. The hardware implementation is presented in section 6. The main conclusions are summarized in the last section.

## 2 Synchronizer: The Latency / Robustness Trade-Off

Transferring data between different timing domains requires safe synchronization. The main goal of the synchronization is the prevention of metastability (synchronization failure). The metastability can happens, for example, when an asynchronous signal A, connected to the input of a Flip-Flop controlled by a clock signal CK, is sampled when it has an intermediate value between VDD and VSS. It means when A doesn't respect Setup and Hold time to the sampling edge of CK; the Flip-Flop can enter a metastable state. As the duration of this metastable state is not predictable, the Flip-Flop output will have itself an asynchronous behavior and metastability can propagate in the synchronous part of the circuit, resulting generally in loss of functionality.

Some authors recommended stretching the clock signal (modifying the cycle time). In these methods, instead of synchronizing asynchronous inputs to the clock, the clock is synchronized to the asynchronous inputs. The synchronizer must be able to detect that it will be in the metastable situation and it stretches the clock cycle of the local system until the probability of metastability is zero. For more than one asynchronous input, the clock must be stretched until all the synchronizers are sure that the metastable states don't occur. Consequently, as it is said in [7] and [18], these solutions are not well suited for high speed designs with IP cores having large clock buffer delays.

Some others suggested modifying the Flip-Flop design to avoid propagation of metastable state values ([19]). Although the output of such circuit has well defined values (VDD or VSS), and undesirable values are prevented to propagate, this does not solve the problem: the precise duration of the metastable state being not predictable. The transition of the Flip-Flop output signals is asynchronous compared with the clock signal of the next Flip-Flop...

The metastability in multi-synchronous systems can not be totally suppressed, but as it is explained in [21], the synchronization failure probability (typically expressed in terms of Mean Time Between Failures or MTBF) can be bounded to an acceptable value by a carefully designed synchronizer ([22] and [23]). The simplest and safest solution is to use several cascaded Flip-Flops. According to [21], with two cascaded Flip-Flops with 200 MHz clock frequency and 20 MHz input data rate, for the 0.18 μm technology MTBF can be estimated to about $10^{204}$ years. For three consecutive Flip-Flops in the same condition, MTBF will be $10^{420}$ years!

Increasing synchronization delay is a penalty for obtaining extra safety: When synchronization latency is not an issue, the MTBF can be improved by using conservative synchronizers. We believe that the synchronizer choice must be a design decision depending on the application requirements. The general architecture of our converter will support trade-off between latency and robustness.

## 3   General Architecture of the Converters

The design of any synchronous ⟺ asynchronous protocol converter must satisfy two main requirements: minimizing the probability of metastability, and maximizing the throughput (data transfer rate). Fig. 2 illustrates how these two aims can be achieved.

The Four-Phase, Bundled Data, asynchronous protocol, is a sequence of REQ+, ACK+, REQ- and ACK- events, where REQ and ACK are the asynchronous flow control signals. Data is valid when REQ is in the positive state. The high level of ACK indicates that the request of data communication is accepted.

In the synchronous FIFO protocol, the producer and the consumer share the same clock signal, and the protocol uses two handshake signals: ROK (correspondingly WOK) and READ (correspondingly WRITE). The ROK signal (or not empty) is set by the producer at each cycle where there is a valid data to be transferred. The READ signal is set by the consumer at each cycle where the consumer wants to consume a data on the next clock edge. Both the ROK and READ signals are state signals that can be generated by Moore FSMs.

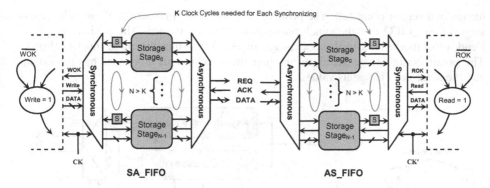

**Fig. 2.** Synchronizing FIFOs with Maximum Throughput

We call AS_FIFO, the asynchronous to synchronous converter, and SA_FIFO, the synchronous to asynchronous converter. The task of protocol converting is the responsibility of the storage stages of the FIFOs. The signals that have a risk of metastability (and must use a synchronizer) are the handshake signals transmitted from the asynchronous side to the synchronous side.

As it is said in previous section, the synchronizer design is a trade-off between robustness (i.e. low probability of metastability) and latency (measured as a number of cycles of the synchronous domain). If the synchronization cost is K clock cycles, the FIFO must have at least K+1 stages, if we want a throughput of one data transfer per cycle. In such pipelined design, the effect of synchronization latency is different in the two FIFO types. In the asynchronous to synchronous converter (AS_FIFO), it is visible only when the FIFO is empty. In the synchronous to asynchronous converter (SA_FIFO), it is visible when the FIFO is full. The latency between the arrival of data to an empty AS_FIFO and its availability on the output (typically named FIFO Latency) is about K clock cycles. For a full SA_FIFO, the latency between the consumption of a data and the information of the availability of an empty stage on the other side is about K clock cycles. For a data burst these latencies are just the initial latencies.

## 4 Detailed Architecture

The Fig. 3a and 4a show the internal architecture of the SA_FIFO and AS_FIFO converters, with a depth of 2 storage stages. Clearly, these two architectures can be generalized to n-stage FIFOs.

We present in Fig. 3b and Fig. 4b the FSM of the synchronous side controllers. These controllers are Mealy Finite State Machines. The state $W_i$ means that the next WRITE event will be done to stage i. Similarly, the state $R_i$ means that data will be read in stage i at the next READ event. Consequently, the WOK and ROK signals depend on both the FSM state and the asynchronous stage content (signals $WOK_i$ or $ROK_i$). A synchronous Hazard free command is generated ($WRITE_i$ or $READ_i$) when there is a synchronous request (WRITE or READ signals) and the current asynchronous stage is ready to accept. $ROK_i$ means that stage i is not empty. $WOK_i$

means that stage i is not full. The positive edge of $Write_i$ indicates to $i^{th}$ asynchronous stage of SA_FIFO that the synchronous data must be written. The positive edge of $Read_i$ informs the $i^{th}$ asynchronous stage of AS_FIFO that the stage must be freed. The positive edge of $wasRead_i$ means that the synchronous consumer has read data and the stage can change its value.

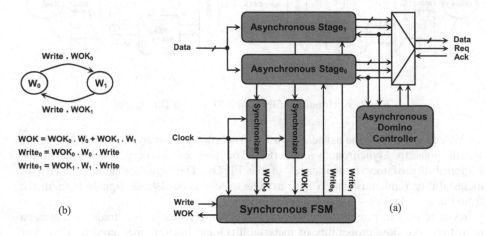

**Fig. 3.** Synchronous to Asynchronous Converter (SA_FIFO)

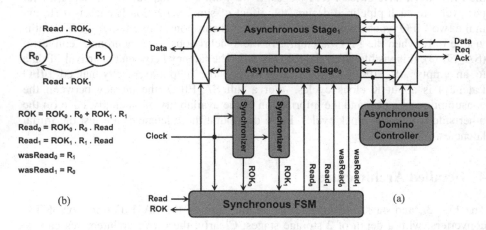

**Fig. 4.** Asynchronous to Synchronous Converter (AS_FIFO)

The asynchronous side of the design includes an asynchronous controller and an asynchronous Multiplexer in SA_FIFO. It includes an asynchronous controller and an asynchronous Demultiplexer in AS_FIFO. The design of the asynchronous Multiplexer and Demultiplexer using four phase bundled data protocol ([13]) are respectively shown in Fig. 5a and Fig. 5b. These circuits need to do a handshake with their controller module controlling the Select signals ($S_i$). This handshaking brings out with the sequence of $S_i+$, $Ack_i+$, $S_i-$ and $Ack_i-$. After $Ack_i-$ indicating the end of the current four phase sequence, the controller can select another set to multiplexing or demultiplexing.

The asynchronous controller used in AS_FIFO and SA_FIFO is named Domino Controller. It is an asynchronous One-Hot counter providing required handshake protocol to the asynchronous multiplexer and demultiplexer. As an instance, the block diagram of a 3-bit Domino Controller is illustrated in Fig. 5c. Each cell of i has 2 outputs $S_i$ and $A_i$ ($i^{th}$ bit of the counter) and 4 inputs $Ack_{i-1}$, $Ack_i$, $Ack_{i+1}$ and $A_{i-1}$. The one bit is moved from cell to cell in a ring topology. At the initial state, $A_2$ and $S_0$ are 1 and the other outputs are 0. The High value of $S_0$ means that the first asynchronous event will be performed in $stage_0$.

The functionality of Domino Controller could be understood by looking the cell STG (Signal Transition Graph) demonstrated in Fig. 5d. The synthesized circuit of the STG is presented in Fig. 5e. $Ack_i+$ means $S_i+$ has done and is seen. So, the one bit that is in the previous cell (i-1) can be transferred to current cell. The handshake protocol continues by $S_i-$ when the one transferring is ended.

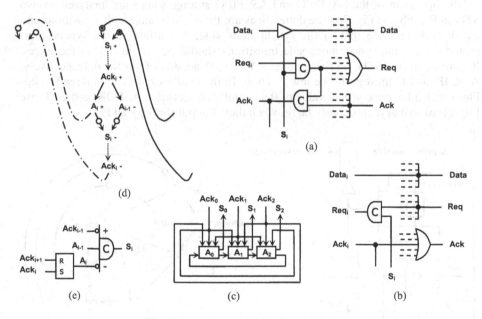

**Fig. 5.** Asynchronous Side Components

As we said before, the pipelined stages in AS_FIFO and SA_FIFO have two main functionalities: storing data and converting communication protocol. As it is demonstrated in Fig. 6a and Fig. 7a illustrating the schematics of the SA_FIFO and AS_FIFO stage circuits, data storage is done by the latches sampling on high value of $WOK_i$ and of L. The transition to 0 of $WOK_i$ means that this stage contains valid data and no more writing is permitted. So data sampling must be ended at this time. When the value of L on rising edge of $wasRead_i$ intending the content of the stage was read, is changed to 1 a new data can be written.

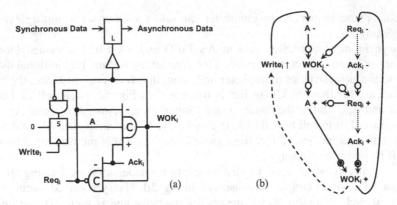

**Fig. 6.** Asynchronous Storage Stage of SA_FIFO

The operation of the SA_FIFO and AS_FIFO storage stages are analyzed as two STG in Fig. 6b and Fig. 7b. The dotted lines are the asynchronous side transitions and the dashed lines are that of the synchronous side. According to the synchronous protocol base, the synchronous side transitions should be considered on the edges. Regarding to two STG, on rising edge of $Write_i$, $Read_i$ and of $wasRead_i$ respectively, A, $ROK_i$ and C must go to the low position. In the synthesized circuits three D Flip-Flops which have a constant value of 0 as input data, generate A, $ROK_i$ and C. These Flip-Flops will asynchronously be set when their S input (Set) signal is 1.

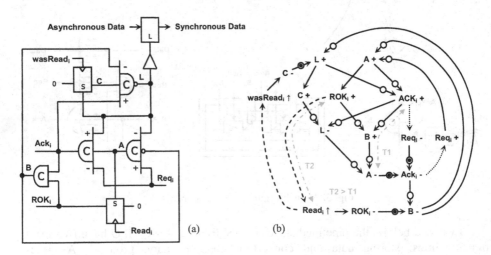

**Fig. 7.** Asynchronous Storage Stage of AS_FIFO

The synthesized circuit of the AS_FIFO stage shown in Fig. 7a has a time constraint: before rising edge of $Read_i$ where $ROK_i$- must be done, the value of A should be returned to 0; because, while A (as a set signal of Flip-Flop) has high value, $ROK_i$ (as an output signal of the Flip-Flop) is hold at 1. The transition of $ROK_i$+ causes $Read_i$ to rise. Regarding to the AS_FIFO architecture (Fig. 4) the time between

$ROK_i+$ and rising edge of $Read_i$ (T2) is more than K clock cycles where K is the synchronizer latency. In the other side, A- happens after $Ack_i+$ occurring simultaneous with $ROK_i+$, by propagation delay of two gates (T1). Evidently a two gate propagation delay is less than the latency of a robust synchronizer. The latency of a two cascaded Flip-Flops is one clock cycle. But really it is true that if a designer uses a miraculous synchronizer (!) which has very low latency, this time constraint express a bother of functionality for the design.

## 5  System Architecture

As mentioned in the previous sections, the goal of this paper is to define a new design to robustly interface an asynchronous network to the synchronous subsystems on a chip. In the architecture presented in Fig. 8, SA_FIFO and AS_FIFO are instantiated between Network Wrapper and Asynchronous NOC. The Network Wrapper translates the local interconnect protocol (such as VCI or OCP) to the network protocol. The Network Interface Controller (NIC) is composed of one AS_FIFO, one SA_FIFO and one Network Wrapper. In fact, NIC provide local interconnect protocol compliant packets at the synchronous side and the asynchronous network compatible packets at the asynchronous ports. Required by Multisynchronous GALS approach, each subsystem may have its synchronous clock domain dependent neither on the frequency nor on the phase.

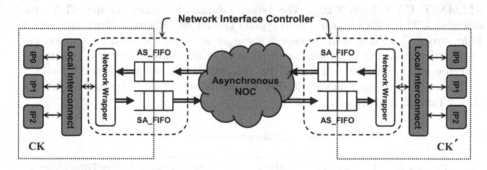

**Fig. 8.** AS_FIFO and SA_FIFO used in a Network Interface Controller

## 6  Implementation

We developed a generic converter generator, using the *Stratus* hardware description language of the *Coriolis* platform ([25]). This generator creates both a netlist of standard cells and a physical layout. The two parameters are the number of storage stages (depth of FIFO) and the number of data bits. In this implementation the synchronizer uses two cascaded Flip-Flops. As a standard cell library, we used the portable *ALLIANCE* CMOS standard cell library ([24]). The physical layout of the 32-bit converters with depth of 8, 3 and 2 stages are presented in Fig. 9. The silicon area of the 2-stage SA_FIFO is $12.15 \times 216$ µm$^2$ for a 90 nm fabrication process.

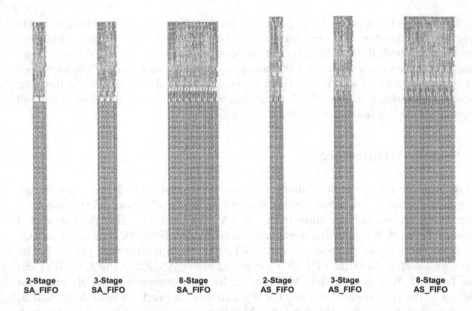

**Fig. 9.** Physical Layouts of Converters

From the physical layout, we extracted SPICE models of the converters, using *ALLIANCE* CAD Tools ([20]). The target fabrication process is the ST-Micro-electronics 90 nm LVT transistors in typical conditions. Electrical simulation under *Eldo* proved that the aim of maximum throughput of one event (data transfer) per cycle is attained, and these low-area FIFOs have low initial latencies. Due to the asynchronous event entrance time, the AS_FIFO has various latencies with a difference of about one clock cycle. The simulation results are presented in Table 2. In this Table, T is the clock cycle time.

**Table 2.** Simulation Results

| Converter | Surface | Min Latency | Max Latency | Max Throughput |
|---|---|---|---|---|
| **2-Stage SA_FIFO** | 2624 $\mu m^2$ | 177 pS | | 2.39 GEvents/S |
| **3-Stage SA_FIFO** | 3791 $\mu m^2$ | 181 pS | | 2.36 GEvents/S |
| **8-Stage SA_FIFO** | 9623 $\mu m^2$ | 192 pS | | 2.22 GEvents/S |
| **2-Stage AS_FIFO** | 2679 $\mu m^2$ | 271 pS + T | 271 pS + 2T | 1.50 GEvents/S |
| **3-Stage AS_FIFO** | 3870 $\mu m^2$ | 275 pS + T | 275 pS + 2T | 2.61 GEvents/S |
| **8-Stage AS_FIFO** | 9823 $\mu m^2$ | 290 pS + T | 290 pS + 2T | 2.56 GEvents/S |

The throughput value is related to the asynchronous handshake protocol. The low throughput value of 2-stage AS_FIFO compared with 3-stage and 8-stage AS_FIFOs, is because of existence of another constraint if maximum throughput of one word per cycle is required: In 2-stage AS_FIFO, $Ack_i+$ and $Req_{i+1}+$ must be happened in the same clock cycle. For 8-stage and 3-stage AS_FIFO, the time between these two transitions, respectively can be seven and two clock cycles.

Due to the inability of 2-stage AS_FIFO to reach the maximum throughput (comparing 1.5 GEvents/Sec with 2.61 of 3-stage AS_FIFO), in order to sustain the throughput, one could opt for 3-stage AS_FIFO. Its area (3870 $\mu m^2$) is not negligible, but it should not be forgotten that this component has another advantage: providing a storage place with a FIFO behavior. As we know, in order to obtain minimum overhead of data communication between two different timing domains, having a FIFO in the interface is not eliminable. So, we suppose that using an AS_FIFO or SA_FIFO with the storage stages of more than three may also be reasonable!

## 7  Conclusion

Two new converter architectures for interfacing asynchronous NoCs and synchronous subsystems in MP-SoCs have been presented. The designs can be used to convert asynchronous Four-Phase Bundled-Data protocol to synchronous FIFO protocol. The synchronizer used in the architectures can be arbitrarily chosen by the system designer, supporting various trade-off between latency and robustness. The Converters (FIFOs) can achieve the maximal throughput of one word per cycle, even if the selected synchronizer has a large latency. The designs have been physically implemented with the portable *ALLIANCE* CMOS standard cell library. The throughputs and latencies have been proved by SPICE simulation from the extracted layout.

## References

1. Nilsson E., Öberg J., *"Reducing power and latency in 2-D mesh NoCs using globally pseudochronous locally synchronous clocking,"* 2nd IEEE/ACM/IFIP international Conference on Hardware/Software Codesign and System Synthesis (Stockholm, Sweden, September 08 - 10, 2004)
2. L.R. Dennison, W.J. Dally, D. Xanthopoulos, *"Low-latency plesiochronous data retiming,"* arvlsi, p. 304, 16th Conference on Advanced Research in VLSI (ARVLSI'95), 1995
3. W.K. Stewart, S.A. Ward, *"A Solution to a Special Case of the Synchronization Problem,"* IEEE Transactions on Computers, vol. 37, no. 1, pp. 123-125, Jan., 1988
4. Ajanta Chakraborty, Mark R. Greenstreet, *"Efficient Self-Timed Interfaces for Crossing Clock Domains,"* async, p. 78, 9th IEEE International Symposium on Asynchronous Circuits and Systems (ASYNC'03), 2003
5. Yaron Semiat, Ran Ginosar, *"Timing Measurements of Synchronization Circuits"* async, p. 68, 9th IEEE International Symposium on Asynchronous Circuits and Systems (ASYNC'03), 2003
6. Ran Ginosar, Rakefet Kol, *"adaptive Synchronization,"* iccd, p. 188, IEEE International Conference on Computer Design (ICCD'98), 1998
7. Joycee Mekie, Supratik Chakraborty, D.K. Sharma, Girish Venkataramani, P. S. Thiagarajan, *"Interface Design for Rationally Clocked GALS Systems,"* async, pp. 160-171, 12th IEEE International Symposium on Asynchronous Circuits and Systems (ASYNC'06), 2006

8. U. Frank, R. Ginosar, *"A Predictive Synchronizer for Periodic Clock Domains,"* PATMOS 2004
9. L.F.G. Sarmenta, G.A. Pratt, S.A. Ward, *"Rational clocking [digital systems design],"* iccd, p. 271, IEEE International Conference on Computer Design (ICCD'95), 1995
10. S. M. Nowick, T. Chelcea, *"Robust Interfaces for Mixed-Timing Systems with Application to Latency-Insensitive Protocols,"* dac, pp. 21-26, 38th Conference on Design Automation (DAC'01), 2001
11. J. Jex, C. Dike, K. Self, *"Fully asynchronous interface with programmable metastability settling time synchronizer,"* US Patent 5 598 113, 1997
12. Kenneth Y. Yun, Ryan P. Donohue, *"Pausible Clocking: A First Step Toward Heterogeneous Systems,"* iccd, p. 118, IEEE International Conference on Computer Design (ICCD'96), 1996
13. Jens Sparsoe, Steve Furber, *"Principles of Asynchronous Circuit Design – A Systems Perspective,"* Kluwer Academic Publishers, 2001
14. Jakov N. Seizovic., *"Pipeline synchronization,"* International Symposium on Advanced Research in Asynchronous Circuits and Systems, pages 87--96, November 1994
15. Simon Moore, George Taylor, Peter Robinson, Robert Mullins, *"Point to Point GALS Interconnect,"* async, p.69, 8th International Symposium on Asynchronous Circuits and Systems (ASYNC'02), 2002
16. David S. Bormann, Peter Y. K. Cheung, *"Asynchronous Wrapper for Heterogeneous Systems,"* iccd, p. 307, IEEE International Conference on Computer Design (ICCD'97), 1997
17. A. E. Sjogren, C. J. Myers, *"Interfacing Synchronous and Asynchronous Modules Within a High-Speed Pipeline,"* arvlsi, p.47, 17th Conference on Advanced Research in VLSI (ARVLSI '97), 1997
18. Rostislav (Reuven) Dobkin, Ran Ginosar, Christos P. Sotiriou, *"Data Synchronization Issues in GALS SoCs,"* async, pp. 170-180, 10th IEEE International Symposium on Asynchronous Circuits and Systems (ASYNC'04), 2004
19. S. Ghahremani, *"Metastable Protected Latch,"* US Patent 6 072346, 2000
20. Greiner A., F. Pêcheux, *"ALLIANCE. A Complete Set of CAD Tools for Teaching VLSI Design,"* 3rd Eurochip Workshop on VLSI Design Training, pp. 230-37, Grenoble, France, 1992
21. Ran Ginosar, *"Fourteen Ways to Fool Your Synchronizer,"* async, p. 89, 9th IEEE International Symposium on Asynchronous Circuits and Systems (ASYNC'03), 2003
22. C. Dike, e. Burton, *"Miller and Noise Effects in A synchronizing flip-flop,"* IEEE J. Solid-state circuits, 34(6), pp. 849-855, 1999
23. D.J. Kinniment, A. Bystrov, A.V. Yakovlev, *"Synchronization Circuit Performance,"* IEEE Journal of Solid-State Circuits, 37(2), p. 202-209, 2002
24. http://www-asim.lip6.fr/recherche/alliance/
25. http://www-asim.lip6.fr/recherche/coriolis/
26. Tobias Bjerregaard, Jens Sparsø, *"A Router Architecture for Connection-Oriented Service Guarantees in the MANGO Clockless Network-on-Chip,"* Proceedings of the Design, Automation and Test in Europe Conference, IEEE, March 2005
27. Tobias Bjerregaard, Shankar Mahadevan, Rasmus Olsen, Jens Sparsø, *"An OCP Compliant Network Adapter for GALS-based SoC Design Using the MANGO Network-on-Chip,"* Proceedings of the International Symposium on System-on-Chip, IEEE, November 2005

# Low-Power Maximum Magnitude Computation for PAPR Reduction in OFDM Transmitters*

Th. Giannopoulos and V. Paliouras

Electrical & Computer Engineering Department
University of Patras
25600 Patras, Greece

**Abstract.** Increased Peak-to-Average Power Ratio (PAPR) is a serious drawback in an Orthogonal Frequency Division Multiplexing (OFDM) system, leading to inefficient amplification of the transmitted signal. Partial Transmit Sequences (PTS) approach is a distortionless PAPR-reduction scheme which imposes low additional complexity to the overall system. This paper introduces a new version of the PTS algorithm which selects weighting factors from a different set than the ones commonly used. Furthermore, this paper proposes a new PAPR estimation method that reduces the implementation complexity. The proposed architecture reduces the power consumption of the complete transmitter by up to 22% in comparison to OFDM systems where no PAPR reduction method is employed, depending on the power consumption of the power amplifier.

## 1 Introduction

OFDM is a very attractive technique for high-bit-rate transmission in wireless applications, as it provides increased immunity to multipath fading and impulse noise. Two major drawbacks of OFDM systems are the great sensitivity to time and frequency synchronization errors, and the high PAPR. Due to high PAPR, the amplified signal suffers from distortion and out-of-band noise when passed through nonlinear devices, such as a Power Amplifier (PA). For that reason the use of highly linear Power Amplifiers (PA) is required. High linearity normally implies low efficiency, since large back off needs to be applied. Therefore, the use of a PAPR reduction method is essential.

A number of PAPR reduction schemes have been proposed to alleviate this problem [1][2][3]. All PAPR reduction techniques impose additional processing in the digital part of the transmitter in order to reduce signal distortion and the power consumption of the analog part of the transmitter. Two promising and distortionless techniques for improving the statistics of the PAPR are the Selective Mapping approach [4] and the PTS approach [5][6]. The PTS approach combines signal subblocks, phase-shifted by constant weighting factors to form

---

* We thank the European Social Fund (ESF), Operational Program for Educational and Vocational Training II (EPEAEK II), and particularly the Program PYTHAGORAS, for funding the above work.

J. Vounckx, N. Azemard, and P. Maurine (Eds.): PATMOS 2006, LNCS 4148, pp. 203–213, 2006.

the signal to be transmitted. PTS-based PAPR reduction can be exploited to achieve system-level low-power operation in cases of practical interest [7].

This paper introduces an alternative VLSI implementation of PTS using different values for the weighting factors. Furthermore a new estimation method of the magnitude of the transmitter samples is presented. The proposed estimation method implies no performance loss while reduces significantly the area and the power consumption of the circuit needed for the implementation of PTS. The digital realization cost and the corresponding power savings on PA are compared with results previously reported [7]. In order to evaluate the trade-off between the additional processing, required to reduce PAPR, and the corresponding power savings in the analog part of the transmitter, three different new architectures are evaluated:

- Architecture-I utilizes the $\{1, j\}$ weighting factor set. The maximum magnitude of each sequence is evaluated as in [7].
- Architecture-II utilizes the $\{1, -1\}$ weighting factor set. The maximum magnitude of each sequence is evaluated by the new estimation method.
- Architecture-III utilizes the $\{1, j\}$ weighting factor set and employees the new magnitude estimation method.

For all the proposed architectures the initial OFDM symbol is partitioned into four subblocks.

The digital realization cost of PTS application is evaluated in terms of area, latency, and power consumption for various data wordlengths. To quantify the impact of the PAPR reduction architecture at the analog-digital system level, the expected reduction of power consumption for the complete digital-analog transmitter is evaluated, for different types of PA. The proposed architecture reduces the power consumption of the complete digital-analog system by even 9% in comparison to results in [7] and 22% in comparison to OFDM systems where no PAPR reduction method is employed.

The remainder of the paper is as follows: Section 2 discusses the basics of OFDM transmission, defines PAPR, the efficiency of a class-A power amplifier and its relationship to PAPR reduction. Section 3 outlines the PTS approach. In section 4 the first proposed architecture, resulting by the application of the new set of weighting factors is presented. Subsequently section 5 summarizes the proposed PAPR estimation method and the other two proposed architectures. Section 6 presents the simulation results and explores the implementation complexity of the proposed architectures, while section 7 discusses conclusions.

## 2    Basic Definitions

Initially the binary input data are mapped onto QPSK or QAM symbols. An IFFT/FFT pair is used as a modulator/demodulator. The $N$-point IFFT output sequence is $x_k = \frac{1}{\sqrt{N}} \sum_{n=0}^{N-1} X_n e^{j\frac{2\pi nk}{N}}$, where $X_n$ is the transmitted symbol sequence and $N$ is the block size.

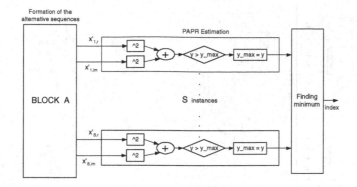

**Fig. 1.** Block Diagram of the optimize block for Architecture-I. Block A is depicted in Fig. 2.

The PAPR of the signal $x_k$ is defined as square of the ratio of the peak power magnitude and the square root of the average power of the signal; i.e.,

$$\text{PAPR} = \frac{(\max |x_k|)^2}{E[|x_k|^2]}, \qquad (1)$$

where $E[\cdot]$ is the expected value operator.

Power consumption is a critical factor in PA design. Signals with time-varying amplitudes impose time-varying efficiencies. In this case, a useful measure of performance is the average output power, $P_{outAVG}$ to the average DC-input, power ratio $P_{inAVG}$:

$$n = P_{outAVG}/P_{inAVG}. \qquad (2)$$

Assuming that a PAPR reduction method is used and the PAPR value is reduced from the value $\xi$ to the value $\xi'$, the average DC-input power, required to give the same output power, is [8][7]

$$P'_{inAVG} = \frac{\xi'}{\xi} P_{inAVG}, \qquad (3)$$

and the power gain in the analog part of the transmitter is

$$P_{an} = P_{inAVG} - \frac{\xi'}{\xi} P_{inAVG} \qquad (4)$$

$$P_{an} = \frac{\Delta\xi}{\xi} P_{inAVG}, \qquad (5)$$

where $\Delta\xi = \xi - \xi'$ is the achieved PAPR reduction.

The application of any PAPR reduction method, imposes additional processing onto the digital part of transmitter, and additional power, $P_{dig}$, is consumed. Hence, the power gain for the complete transmitter is

$$P_g = P_{an} - P_{dig}. \qquad (6)$$

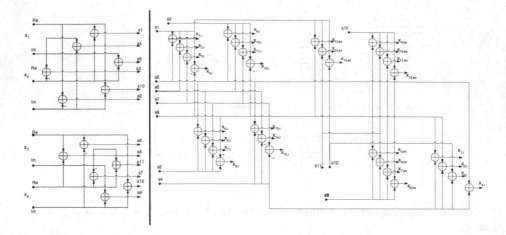

**Fig. 2.** Formation of PTSs when $b_i \in \{1, j\}$ (Architecture-I)

## 3   Partial Transmit Sequences Method

In the PTS approach [5][6], the input data block is partitioned into disjoint
subblocks of equal size, each one consisting of a contiguous set of subcarriers.
These subblocks are properly combined to minimize the PAPR. Let the
data block, $\{X_n, n = 0, 1, \cdots, N-1\}$, be represented as a vector, $X =
[X_0 \ X_1 \ \ldots \ X_{N-1}]^T$. Then $X$ is partitioned into $V$ disjoint sets, represented
by the vectors $\{X_v, \ v = 1, 2, \ldots, V\}$, such as $X = \sum_{v=1}^{V} X_v$. The objective of
the PTS approach is to form a weighted combination of the $V$ subblocks,

$$X'_s = \sum_{v=1}^{V} b_w X_v, \tag{7}$$

where $\{b_w, v = 1, 2, \cdots, W\}$ are the weighting factors and $X'_s, s = 1, 2, \ldots, V^W$
are alternative sequences which represent the same information with the initial
OFDM symbol, for a particular choice of $b_w$. The objective of PTS algorithm is
to choose the appropriate combination of $b_w$ from a specific set of values, such
that the PAPR corresponding to $x'_s = IDFT\{X'_s\}$ is minimized. In order to
calculate $x'_s$ the linearity of the IDFT is exploited. Accordingly, the subblocks
are transformed by $V$ separate and parallel IDFTs yielding

$$x'_s = IDFT\{\sum_{v=1}^{V} b_w X_v\} = \sum_{v=1}^{V} b_w IDFT\{X_v\} = \sum_{v=1}^{V} b_w x_v. \tag{8}$$

The application of PTS algorithm requires the following steps:

1. Calculation of $x_v = IDFT\{X_v\}$. If the block partitioning of the initial
   OFDM symbol is performed with respect to the computational structure
   of FFTs and taking into account the fact that most of the points of the

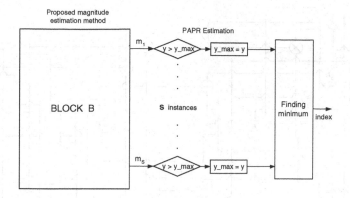

**Fig. 3.** Block Diagram of the optimize block employing the new magnitude estimation method (Architectures II and III). Block B is detailed in Fig. 4.

sequence, on which the IFFT is applied, are zero, the implementation complexity of the $V$ parallel IFFTs is reduced to the complexity of the classic OFDM (OFDM without the application of PTS) [9].

2. Formation of all Partial Transmit Sequences according to (8).
3. Choice of optimum weighting factors, such that [5]:

$$\mathbf{b} = [b_1, b_2, \ldots, b_W] = \arg \min \left( \max \left\| \sum_{u=1}^{V} b_w x_v \right\| \right), \qquad (9)$$

resulting in the optimum transmitting sequence $x'$ in terms of low PAPR.

The norm $\| \cdot \|$ denotes the magnitude of each sample of each alternative sequence. For a particular sequence the maximum value of norm $\| \cdot \|$ is used as the PAPR of the corresponding sequence. The calculation of the exact symbol PAPR requires the computation of the magnitude of each sample of the symbol and symbol's average power. However, PTS algorithm does not seek the actual PAPR value; instead the vector $x'$ with the lowest PAPR is sought. Therefore, assuming that the average power remains almost the same for all symbols, (9) is a very good approximation of the optimal weighting factors [5].

In this paper the proposed Architecture-I utilizes the norm $\|x\| = \Re\{x\}^2 + \Im\{x\}^2$. Architectures II and III utilize a new magnitude estimation method which decreases the implementation complexity without loss of efficiency, as detailed in section 5.

## 4   New Set of Weighting Factors

In [7] a VLSI architecture of PTS algorithm using the set $\{\pm 1\}$ as weighting factors is detailed. Applying the particular PTS architecture in the digital part of the transmitter, the power consumption of the complete digital-analog system is reduced by 12.6%, due to the PAPR reduction. In this section we present

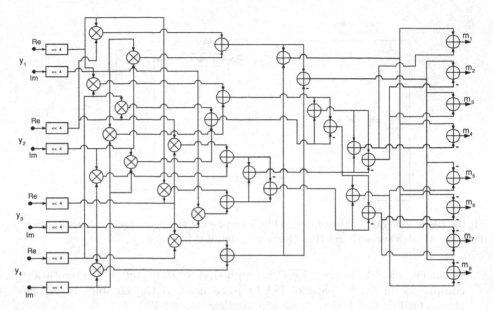

**Fig. 4.** Block Diagram of the new magnitude estimation method for PTS with $b_i \in \{1, -1\}$ (Architecture-II)

a VLSI architecture for the PTS algorithm where the permissible values for weighting factors belong to set $\{1, j\}$. In [10] it is proven that when using this set of parameters the PTS algorithm reduces PAPR by almost 3 dB, instead of 1.9 dB when the employed by PTS weighting factors are $\{\pm 1\}$ [7]. Hence, according to (3), the power consumption of PA is decreased by 25% when the new set of weighting factors is used, instead of 15.8% in [7]. Furthermore with the proposed weighting factors set the required resolution of DAC can be decreased by one bit [10].

The number of alternative sequences explored in order to obtain the one of lowest PAPR are fifteen. All the possible combinations of the four subblocks with the two weighting factors are sixteen. But the alternative sequences resulting by the application of $\mathbf{b_1} = [1, 1, 1, 1]$ and $\mathbf{b_{16}} = [j, j, j, j]$, have exactly the same PAPR value. Hence one of $\mathbf{b_1}$ and $\mathbf{b_{16}}$ can be omitted, without any performance loss. The corresponding VLSI architecture (architecture-I) resembles [7], is depicted in Figs. 1 and 2.

Due to the different values of weighting factors the formation of alternative sequences is implemented in a different way. Taking into account the common subexpressions for the computation of all PTSs a significant reduction of the required computational complexity is achieved. For example when $\mathbf{b} = [1, j, 1, 1]$ the corresponding PTS is

$$x_6' = x_{1,r} - x_{2,im} + x_{3,r} + x_{4,r} + j(x_{1,im} + x_{2,r} + x_{3,im} + x_{4,im}). \quad (10)$$

This sequence is not computed in a straightforward way. The partial sums $x_{1,r} - x_{2,im}$, $x_{4,r} + x_{3,r}$, $x_{1,im} + x_{2,r}$, $x_{4,im} + x_{3,im}$ are initially calculated.

Subsequently the partial sums are added to form (10). The particular partial sums are formed because the same partial sums are employed in other alternative sequences as well. For all PTSs, 12 partial sums are computed in a first stage and are subsequently combined to create the 15 PTSs. A detailed block diagram of the circuit which formulates the PTSs is depicted in Fig. 2. Architecture-I requires 42 real additions instead of 24 in [7]. In addition the proposed architecture requires 30 squarers for the calculation of the norm $\| \cdot \|$ instead of 16 in [7]. The increase in the number of required squarers results in a significant increase in the area and power consumption of the digital implementation of PTS algorithm. Section 6 presents a detailed analysis of the implementation cost of Architecture-I and the expected power saving. Also there is a comparison with the other two architectures proposed in the next section.

## 5   Proposed PAPR Estimation Method

This section explores a different architecture for the implementation of PTS algorithm, and particularly for the estimation of each sample magnitude. Each sample $x_v(k), k = 0, 1, 2, \ldots, N - 1$, where $N$ is the number of carriers, of the sequences $x_v$ is of the form $x_v(k) = x_{v,r}(k) + j x_{v,im}(k)$. The corresponding sample of PTSs will have the value,

$$x'_v(k) = \sum_{v=1}^{4} b_w(x_{v,r}(k) + j x_{v,im}(k)). \tag{11}$$

In Architecture-I (5) is initially computed and subsequently the norm of (9) is evaluated. In order to reduce the computational complexity the magnitude of $x'_v(k)$ is computed as follows,

$$x'_v = \sum_{v=1}^{4} b_v(x_{v,r} + j x_{v,im}) \tag{12}$$

$$x'_v = b_1 x_{1,r} + b2 x_{2,r} + b_3 x_{3,r} + b_4 x_{4,r} + \ldots$$
$$+ j(b_1 x_{1,im} + b_2 x_{2,im} + b_3 x_{3,im} + b_4 x_{4,im}). \tag{13}$$

Assuming that the weighting factors assume values from the set $\{1, -1\}$, the magnitude of each sample of any sequence is sum of specific products of the form,

$$\|x'_v\| = x_{1,im}^2 + x_{1,r}^2 + x_{2,r}^2 + x_{2,im}^2 + x_{3,r}^2 + x_{3,im}^2 + x_{4,r}^2 + x_{4,im}^2 + \ldots$$
$$\pm 2 \, x_{1,im} \, x_{2,im} \pm 2 b_1 b_2 x_{1,r} x_{2,r} \pm 2 b_1 b_3 x_{1,im} x_{3,im} \pm 2 b_2 b_3 x_{2,im} x_{3,im} \cdots$$
$$\pm 2 b_1 b_3 x_{1,r} x_{3,r} \pm 2 b_2 b_3 x_{2,r} x_{3,r} \pm 2 b_1 b_4 x_{1,im} x_{4,im} \pm 2 b_2 b_4 x_{2,im} x_{4,im} \cdots$$
$$\pm 2 b_3 b_4 x_{3,im} x_{4,im} \pm 2 b_1 b_4 x_{1,r} x_{4,r} \pm 2 b_2 b_4 x_{2,r} x_{4,r} \pm 2 b_3 b_4 x_{3,r} x_{4,r}. \tag{14}$$

From (14) it is obvious that the sum

$$S = x_{1,im}^2 + x_{1,r}^2 + x_{2,r}^2 + x_{2,im}^2 + x_{3,r}^2 + x_{3,im}^2 + x_{4,r}^2 + x_{4,im}^2, \tag{15}$$

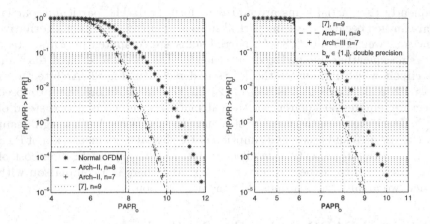

**Fig. 5.** CCDF for the the two versions of PTS and for input wordlength $n = 7, 8$

is a common term for all the PTSs, therefore it is omitted from every calculation without any performance loss. Hence no squarer is needed. Instead 12 multipliers are required, which in general are more complicated circuits than squarers. The actual gain from the proposed estimation method of magnitude is the fact of that the length of the data input is substantially smaller. From experimental results it is derived that 7 bits for the real and 7 bits for the imaginary part are enough for the fixed-point implementation of PTS algorithm to achieve the same performance with the double-precision floating point implementation. Thus, with the proposed magnitude estimation method 12 7-bit multipliers are required instead of 16 11-bit squarers. On the other hand the proposed magnitude estimation method requires signed numbers to be compared, while in [7] unsigned numbers are compared. As it is demonstrated by the synthesis results in the next section, the application of the proposed estimation method results in significant reduction of the occupied area and power consumption of Architecture-II.

The same simplification is employed in Architecture-III. Resembling the case of Architecture-II the computation of the term S of (15) can be omitted, without any performance degradation. Also Architecture-III requires the same reduced wordlength. In that case 24 7-bit multipliers are required instead of 30 11-bit squarers. The block diagram of Architectures II and III is depicted in Fig. 3, while Fig. 4 demonstrates a more detailed diagram of the proposed magnitude estimation block for Architecture-II. The corresponding block diagram for Architecture-III is similar and is omitted due to lack of space.

## 6   Simulation Results

In an OFDM symbol the large peaks occur with very low probability, therefore for characterizing the PAPR of OFDM signals, the statistical distribution of the PAPR should be taken into account [11]. For that reason, the complementary

**Table 1.** Synthesis results

| PTS architecture | input wordlength | Digital Part | | | Analog Part |
| | | area ($\mu m^2$) | delay ($ns$) | power ($mW$) | DC-input Power Reduction (%) |
|---|---|---|---|---|---|
| [7] | 9 | 216474 | 3.50 | 53.20 | 15.8 |
| ArchitectureI | 9 | 353996 | 3.10 | 148.06 | 25 |
| ArchitectureII | 7 | 130064 | 3.16 | 39.88 | 15.8 |
| ArchitectureIII | 7 | 227630 | 3.85 | 60.22 | 25 |

cumulative distribution function $CCDF = Pr(PAPR > PAPR_o)$ is used. In the following results, 100000 random OFDM symbols were generated to obtain the CCDF. Each symbol includes 64 carriers, each one QPSK modulated. Cyclic Prefix is restricted to the 25% of the OFDM symbol. The transmitted signal is oversampled by a factor of 4 [6], in order to better approximate the continuous-time PAPR.

Fig. 5 compares the achieved PAPR reduction of architectures II and III, when fixed-point two's complement representation is employed instead of floating-point double precision. The real and imaginary part of the complex-valued input of the optimization block, have wordlengths of $n$ bits, each. During optimization, the word length remains constant at the output of the multiplier and increases by one bit at the output of each adder. By simulation results $n = 7$ bits is sufficient for both architectures II and III. The performance of PTS method does not improve when the input data word length increases to more than 7 bits.

Table 1 tabulates the implementation cost of PTS method in the digital part and the corresponding reduction of power consumption in the analog part for all the implemented circuits. The digital implementation cost is evaluated by the the area, the latency and the total, including dynamic and leakage, power dissipation of the optimization block. The corresponding results are obtained using Synopsys Design Compiler using an $0.18\mu m$ ASIC library. The power consumption is estimated assuming a 4 nsec clock. The reduction of PA power consumption is evaluated by (5).

When PTS algorithm employs the set of weighting factors $\{1, j\}$ instead of $\{1, -1\}$ the achieved PAPR reduction is increased resulting in further reduction of the power consumption of the PA. On the other hand there is a significant increment on the occupied area and power consumption of the digital circuit required for the application of PTS. The application of the proposed magnitude estimation method doesn't affect the performance of PTS algorithm, but reduces the implementation cost of PTS for both sets of weighting factors. Comparing the four architectures summarized in Table 1, the most efficient, in terms of power consumption is architecture-III; i.e., the application of PTS algorithm employing the weighting factors $\{1, j\}$ and utilizing the proposed magnitude estimation method. Architecture-III occupies slightly more area and consumes about 14% more power than the architecture presented in [7]. However the reduction of the

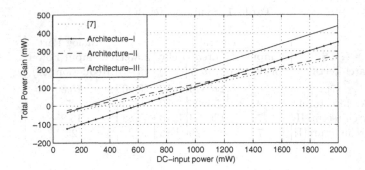

**Fig. 6.** Power gain for the complete digital-analog system

PA power consumption is increased from 15.8% to 25%, which, as the following analysis demonstrates, is very important.

Fig. 6 demonstrates power savings in the complete digital-analog transmitter in relation to the average DC-input power required to give the same output power in comparison to normal OFDM; i.e., when no PAPR reduction method is used. The range of PA power consumption is extended from 100 mW to 2 W [12]. Fig. 6 shows that the most efficient architecture is the Architecture-III. For power amplifiers with average DC-input power less than 200 mW, Architecture-II becomes slightly more efficient. For large values of average DC-input Architecture-I outperforms the Architecture-II and the architecture proposed in [7]. Nevertheless Architecture-III is still more efficient.

Fig. 6 suggests that for OFDM systems for which the power amplifier requires low DC-input power, the PAPR reduction should be of low complexity because the power consumption in digital part is a crucial factor. On the other hand when the power amplifier requires high DC-input power, its power consumption becomes a dominant factor for the complete system and the complexity of extra digital processing needed for PAPR reduction could be increased significantly, thus following the PAPR reduction algorithm to achieve better performance.

## 7   Conclusions

This paper presents a new version of PTS algorithm which uses a different set of weighting factors. The proposed Architecture-I offers increased PAPR reduction on the penalty of increased digital complexity. For that reason a new estimation method of the magnitude of each sample is proposed. Applying the proposed magnitude estimation method the area of the digital circuit required for PAPR reduction (architecture-III) remains almost the same in comparison to architecture in [7]. The power consumption of the whole digital-analog system is reduced by even 9% in comparison to results in [7] and 22% in comparison to OFDM systems where no PAPR reduction method is employed.

# References

1. Li, X., Cimini Jr., L.J.: Effects of clipping and filtering on the performance of OFDM. IEEE Comm. Letts. **2** (1998) 131–133
2. Jones, A.E., Wilkinson, T.A., Barton, S.K.: Block coding scheme for reduction of peak to mean envelope power ratio of multicarrier transmission scheme. Elec. Letts. **30** (1994) 2098–2099
3. Kang, H.W., Cho, Y.S., Youn, D.H.: On compensating nonlinear distortions of an OFDM system using an efficient adaptive predistorter. IEEE Trans. on Comm. **47** (1999)
4. Bäuml, R.W., Fischer, R.F.H., Hüber, J.B.: Reducing the peak-to-average power ratio of multicarrier modulation by selective mapping. Elec. Letts. **32** (1996) 2056–2057
5. Müller, S.H., Bäuml, R.W., Fischer, R.F.H., Hüber, J.B.: OFDM with reduced peak-to-average power ratio by multiple signal representation. In: Annals of Telecommunications. Volume 52. (1997) 58–67
6. Cimini Jr., L., Sollenberger, N.R.: Peak-to-average power ratio by optimum combination of partial transmit sequences. In: Proc. of ICC'99. (1999) 511–515
7. Giannopoulos Th., Paliouras, V.: Low-power VLSI architectures for OFDM transmitters based on PAPR reduction. In: 15th International Workshop on Power and Timing Modeling, Optimization and Simulation, PATMOS 2005. (2005) 177–186
8. Razavi, B.: RF Microelectronics. Prentice Hall (1998)
9. Giannopoulos Th., Paliouras, V.: An efficient architecture for peak-to-average power ratio reduction in OFDM systems in the presence of pulse-shaping filtering. In: Proc. of ISCAS'04. Volume 4. (2004) 85–88
10. Giannopoulos Th., Paliouras, V.: A novel technique for low-power D/A conversion based on PAPR reduction. In: Proc. of ISCAS'06. (2006)
11. Ochiai, H., Imai, H.: On the distribution of the peak-to-average power ratio in OFDM signals. IEEE Trans. on Comm. **49** (2001)
12. Wight, J.: The OFDM challenge. (In: http://www.commsdesign.com/showArticle.jhtml?articleID=16503621)

# Dynamic Management of Thermally-Induced Clock Skew: An Implementation Perspective

A. Chakraborty, K. Duraisami, A. Sathanur, P. Sithambaram,
A. Macii, E. Macii, and M. Poncino

Dipartimento di Automatica e Informatica, Politecnico di Torino, Torino-10129, Italy

**Abstract.** High performance VLSI designs require strict control over clock skew since skew directly impacts the cycle time calculation. For nano-meter CMOS designs, clock-skew and signal integrity are tremendously affected by process and temperature variations. A successful high performance VLSI design should not only aim to minimize the clock skew, but also control it while the chip is running. The issues rising out of temperature variations are particularly tough to tackle because of its dynamic, run-time nature. Although techniques for clock skew management/tuning due to temperature do exist in literature, they have mainly focused on how to solve skew issues, and have usually regarded the implementation of the thermal management scheme as a secondary problem.

In this work we focus on the implementation issues involved in the implementation of a thermal management unit (TMU) relative to a skew management scheme based on the insertion of *variable delay buffers (VDBs)*. We demonstrate the feasibility of the VDB-based methodology, and compare different implementation styles, showing that the most efficient TMU can be implemented with negligible overhead in various physical level metrics (0.67% in area, 0.62% in wire-length, 0.33% in power, and 0.37% in via-number).

## 1 Introduction

Integration densities in nanometer CMOS designs have dramatically increased over the last thirty years, resulting in a continuous increase in power density. Microprocessors are a striking example of this trend: Their power density has doubled every three years [1]. Decreasing the power consumption of a chip is the most intuitive way to reduce power density; unfortunately, typical techniques to reduce power consumption tend to produce temperature gradients across the chip. (e.g., dynamic power management, clock-gating) tend to increase the variance of power dissipation over the chip area, which generally translates into many areas with different power densities.

These time and space power dissipation variations cause temperature gradients in the substrate and, as a consequence, non-uniform substrate temperature: Gradients of $50^o$ C have been measured across the substrate in high-performance ICs [2]. Temperature variations over time are even more insidious, as it is much harder to characterize them off-line at design time. In fact, these variations

J. Vounckx, N. Azemard, and P. Maurine (Eds.): PATMOS 2006, LNCS 4148, pp. 214–224, 2006.

depend on a number of environmental conditions and on thermal transients that have time constants much longer than the typical simulation times used for design-time power estimation. For this reason a number of closed-loop techniques (e.g. clock throttling, thermal shutdown) have been developed for run-time temperature sensing and temperature-aware power management [3,4,5].

In [7] a technique for the design of a temperature-aware zero-skew clock distribution network was proposed that addresses the drawbacks of traditional clock-tree routing that assume a uniform thermal profile. This method was extended in [8] to deal with non-zero skew, thus achieving clock trees with smaller total wire-length. Even though these approaches take into account temperature variations across various regions of the chip, they do not account for *variations over time*. In other words, they optimize clock distribution for a given (non uniform) temperature profile, but they cannot account for the fact that such a profile can greatly change during system operation, depending on environmental conditions and workloads. Dynamically tunable clock trees have been proposed by several authors in the literature, to boost yield under increasing process variations [10,11]. In this paper we propose the use of an on-chip CMOS controller to generate appropriate signals which dynamically allow clock skew correction.

This paper is organized as follows: Section 2 surveys the state-of-the-art. In Section 3 we outline the motivation for this paper. Section 3 highlights our main contributions in this work. We present our *VDB* characterization flow and various implementation flavors of VDB in Section 4. Section 5 explains our experimental setup and physical design steps. We report our results in Section 6 and conclude with remarks and future work in Section 7.

## 2   Previous Work

Previous works in this area of research can be classified into two broad categories: appropriate clock tree Generation, and management of skew given a Clock Tree. Traditional approaches for the design of the clock network focused on generating a clock tree with minimum wire-length, with zero [12,13] or bounded skew [14,15], and possibly combined with wire sizing and/or with buffer insertion [16,17]. All these approaches assume a constant temperature along the clock network. For current and future nano-meter VLSI designs, this assumption is not anymore realistic, and the effects of substrate temperature variations over time and space must be taken into account to guarantee proper operations of a circuit.

The work of [7] was the first one proposing an adaptation of the basic Deferred-Merge-Embedding algorithm [13] that accounts for skew variations due to *spatial* temperature gradients along a clock network. That work was improved in [8], in which a more general approach was proposed that allows for a non-zero skew bound. None of these approaches, however, deal with *temporal* temperature variations. In fact, they optimize the clock network starting from a given (non-uniform) temperature profile, without considering that the thermal profiles may change over time, i.e., in response to workloads and environmental changes. Accounting for such temporal temperature variations implies having a clock network that is dynamically able to adjust delay or skew variations. A widely used solution for online, post-silicon tuning of delays is the use of *tunable delay buffers* (TDBs). In [10] TDBs are used to implement a post-silicon clock optimization technique for reducing timing violations induced by process variations, through a statistical timing driven clock scheduling algorithm. A similar solution was proposed in [18,19], where TDBs are inserted into the clock network for redistributing slacks and correcting timing failures through post-silicon clock tuning.

Recently, [9] dealt with the issue of clock skew violations due to the *deterministic* source of temperature variation over the die using a variant of TDBs referred to as Variable Delay Buffer(VDB). A *VDB* has a more general application as compared with TDBs, since a VDB can be tuned at *runtime* as opposed to the onetime post-silicon tuning mechanism of TDBs as used in [10]. Figure 1 pictorially depicts how a VDB looks like. The buffer, which is implemented as two inverters in sequence, is split up and the extra tunable capacitance added in the middle loads the inverter I1 leading to higher/lower delay values. The authors have used Linear Programming formulation to calculate the value of delay for each buffer in the clock network that will satisfy the skew condition while minimizing (the cost function) the number of buffers in the clock tree that need to be made *VDB*.

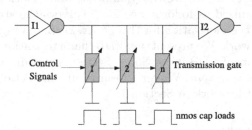

**Fig. 1.** Variable Delay Buffer

## 3  Motivation

In the approach of [9], three main questions remain un-answered: Who is incharge of driving the proper tuning calculated by the underlying algorithm? What are the penalties associated with such a technique? Is it possible to integrate such a unit in the top-down design flow? A realistic validation of the *VDB*-based approach requires in fact addressing all of the above issues, which in fact constitutes the motivating factor of this work.

The primary contribution of this work is therefore that of providing answers to these questions; in particular, we:

- Propose to use a hardware control unit to manage *VDB*s;
- Present the implementation issues for the physical implementation of this unit using two different alternative styles: *Centralized* and *distributed* standard cell block;
- Discuss impact of insertion of this unit on metrics such as power consumption, area, wire-length penalty, increase in number of vias.

This work will be useful for VLSI designers to understand the various possibilities of clock skew management due to on-chip temperature variations. The result reported in this paper will further allow her/him to make a smart choice regarding which implementation to pick.

## 4   Characterization Flow

Figure 2 describes the flow used by the VDB-based methodology. The layout information in Design Exchange Format (DEF) and the temperature profile of the die are used to generate the nominal and thermal delays of each path of the clock tree from the root to the sink.

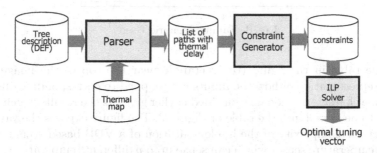

**Fig. 2.** Flow of the VDB-Based Methodology

Thermal delays for all the paths have two components: Temperature dependent interconnect delay and temperature dependent buffer delay. Temperature dependent interconnect delay is calculated by using the methodology in [6] and temperature dependent buffer delays are obtained from empirical delay model of the buffers corresponding to the target library used to map the design. We then calculate the resulting value of skew for each temperature profile. In case the calculated skew violates the skew bound supplied to the clock tree synthesis tool, we generate the least cost tuning using an ILP formulation, for all the buffers such that the skew constraint is satisfied. We call an instance of such a tuning as a tuning vector as it can be visualized as a sequence of numbers which tell each buffer how many taps to allow in the clock signal flow to increase/decrease the delay in the element. The tuning vector is computed for each thermal profile, and combined to form a single maximum tuning vector which is the maximum number of taps required for any buffer, under all profiles. This then determines how many buffers will be converted to *VDB*s and the number of taps supported by each of them.

We define an abstract on-line unit called Thermal Management Unit (TMU) that provides information regarding the number of taps to be enabled in each *VDB* for a given temperature profile. This is pictorially depicted in Figure 3, where for the given clock tree, the *TMU* reads in temperature values from sensors distributed across the chip and provides as output the tuning assignment of each

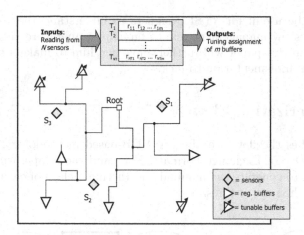

**Fig. 3.** Tuning Scenario Used

*VDB.* The table in the figure (the rectangle near the top of the image) is a possible representation of how the inputs get mapped to corresponding outputs. The off-line characterization flow outlined earlier gives us the results which are in principle to be stored into the table of Figure 3. The figure exposes the variables that affect the complexity of the implementation of a VDB-based scenario.

For a temperature sensor which can sense upto $p$ different temperature values, $log_2p$ wires are required to transfer this data to the *TMU*. Assuming a total of $N$ temperature sensors, the *TMU* will have a total of $N * log_2p$ inputs. Because of their implementation, conversely, the controlling inputs of VDBs are one-hot encoded. Therefore, for each *VDB* having $r$ taps as tunable range, we need exactly $r$ inputs, each one to turn on a tap. Thus, assuming a total of $m$ *VDBs*, the fanout of the *TMU* is $\sum_{1,...,m} r_i$, where $r_i$ denotes the number of taps in the $r$-th *VDB*,. These values indicate that the wiring overhead of such a scheme can easily become very large, depending on the number of VDBs and the number of sensors. Therefore, a practical assessment of its feasibility is mandatory.

For the implementation of the VDB, we extracted the input-output characteristics of the *TMU* in PLA format using the above flow for each temperature profile. This PLA was optimized in a technology independent fashion and then mapped onto our target library using Synopsys Design Compiler.

## 4.1   TMU Implementation Styles

Two different methodologies were used for implementing the TMU: Centralized and distributed. The difference between these two styles lies in whether the controller's components are spread out over the die or appear as a block in the layout. Both these implementation styles have their own benefit. Whereas the distributed components facilitate reduction in wirelength of the nets connecting the TMU and the VDBs, the centralized unit has the attractive benefit of being ECO friendly, i.e., if the controller needs to be changed at a later time of design cycle, the placement of the new controller can be done without modifying the placement/routing of the rest of the part of the die. Other design styles such as memory-based LUT and custom decoder designs were also considered, but since the TMU for our designs was very simple, standard cell based design proved by far the most efficient design technique. Nevertheless, it is important to note that for a complex TMU implementation, it might be the case that other implementation styles prove better.

## 5   Experimental Steps/Setup

### 5.1   Temperature Sensors

We assumed a total of 3 temperature sensors over the die of our benchmarks, which is in line with current trends, e.g. Intel's Montecito based Itanium 2 processor has 4 on-chip sensors. Since the scale of the sensor reading impacts the complexity, we discretized the readings according to 4 different temperature ranges: a) $\leq 40^oC$, b) $40-60^oC$, c) $60-80^oC$, and d) $80-100^oC$. These 4 states are captured via 2 nets which connect these sensors with our *TMU*. The above settings are quite generic and can be changed based on the design our flow has to deal with. The ranges were chosen as a middle ground in terms of accuracy of the readings as it has direct impact on the design of the control unit.

### 5.2   Benchmarks and Temperature Profiles

We chose three designs for benchmarking: *WishBone* (A portable SOC IP core), *i8051* (an Intel I8051 family micro-controller variant), and *vga* (a VGA LCD Controller). These benchmarks were downloaded from an online repository of open source IP cores [20]. The benchmarks selected were based on their increasing level of complexity and respective sizes. All the benchmarks mentioned above have a single clock domain. We divided our die into three regions, each of which was assumed to contain one temperature sensor described in Section 5.1. This means an overall 6 nets which originate from the 3 on-chip sensors. We ran our experiments for all possible set of 64 (=26) different temperature profiles (the *thermal states* of the design). Note that a careful analysis may help to reduce the number of temperature profiles to be considered, by means of a profiling of the switching activities thus ruling out some infeasible temperature profiles.

### 5.3   Physical Design

We used a 90nm STMicroelectronics standard $V_t$ cell library containing 700 cells to synthesize the designs. We chose the 90nm library owing to temperature characteristics exhibited by the buffers in it's library. The physical design was generated using Cadence Silicon Ensemble and CTGen tools followed by delay calculation using the Standard Delay Format (SDF) file after parasitics extraction. The SDF file along with the DEF file of the design was then used to determine the number of buffers that had to be replaced by *VDB*s along with the number of taps required for each of them. The design's DEF was modified accordingly to account for the newly introduced *VDB*s and re-placed using QPlace's ECO capability, after fixing the position of the already placed cell. The placement of these cells again is necessary because our *VDB*s have different (bigger) footprint than the existing buffer cells. Finally, additions were made to the DEF file to mirror the connections required between the *TMU* and the *VDB*s and Wroute was used to incrementally route these extra nets without touching the existing routed wires. The steps of not modifying the existing cells (nets) during incremental placement (routing) was done to make sure that the analysis of the design does not change, which otherwise might render the whole aim of skew management based on geometrical information useless.

### 5.4    TMU Insertion

After the DEF of design was annotated with the *VDB*s information, we inserted the *TMU* made specifically for the design. As outlined in Section 4, we experimented with two implementation flavors.

- Centralized TMU - In this implementation, we made a dummy group containing all the cells which implement the *TMU* and use Silicon Ensemble's region-based placement which places all these cells as a block in close vicinity of each other.
- Distributed TMU - In this implementation, we modified the DEF of the routed design to insert the cells which make up the *TMU* as un-placed cells and ran QPlace again to place only these un-placed cells. This gives QPlace freedom to distribution the *TMU's* cells at any part of the chip for reducing the additional interconnect lengths.

### 5.5    Metrics of Interest

Using the minimally intrusive technique outlined in Section 5.3, we could guarantee the correct-by-construction insertion of our *VDB*s, and *TMU*. However, to judge its impact, we measured the following metrics: Area penalty, Via Impact, Power Penalty, and Wirelength Penalty. We believe that since our flow requires routing the additional nets without disturbing the existing nets, number of vias provide us with a good measure of the meandering in the design.

## 6    Results

The main features of the benchmarks are presented in Table 1. Column 2 shows the number of sinks (i.e., registers) in the design; the total number of buffers inserted by the clock synthesis tool is shown in Column 3. In Column 4, the number of buffers which need to be changed to *VDB*s is shown. The total number of taps required in the design (sum of all tunable ranges of VDBs) is reported in Column 5 (which corresponds to the number of fan-outs of the *TMU*).

We observe that only a small fraction of the buffers are converted to *VDB*s. Furthermore, the total number of taps is also quite low, with an average of only 2 taps per *VDB*. Column 7 exposes the problem we are trying to solve. We notice that the worst case skew is much higher than the allowed skew bound (Column 6). Without our technique, the design would suffer from skew violations. The last column indicates the meager power penalty for the clock network incurred due to insertion of extra switching capacitance in the VDB (Figure 1).

**Table 1.** Benchmark Description

| Benchmark | Sinks # | Buffers # | VDB # | Taps # | Orig Skew (ps) | Temp Skew (ps) | New Skew (ps) | Penalty Power% |
|-----------|---------|-----------|-------|--------|----------------|----------------|---------------|----------------|
| I8051     | 325     | 9         | 4     | 5      | 30             | 43.8           | 30            | 3.57           |
| Vga       | 1523    | 67        | 19    | 25     | 55             | 100.4          | 55            | 3.4            |
| WishBone  | 690     | 33        | 8     | 14     | 110            | 142.2          | 110           | 2.85           |

Table 2 shows the various penalties resulting from the centralized control unit insertion. We observed that the active area penalty was 0.67% averaged over all benchmarks. The average wirelength penalty was found to be around 0.62% with overall 0.37% increase in the number of vias. The increase in power due to the *TMU* was found to be only 0.33%.

Notice that power has been measured by assuming that the TMU activated at every cycle. This is an extremely worst-case assumption, since the TMU would be activated at a much smaller frequency, namely, when a relevant variation of temperature is detected by the sensors. Since temperature has much larger time constants we can expect the TMU very occasionally. The power overhead figures are therefore extremely pessimistic, and we can safely say that the power overhead due to the TMU cells is in practice zero.

**Table 2.** Centralized standard cell Implementation of TMU

| Benchmark | Area Original mm2 | Area Incr % | Power Orig mW | Power Incr % | Wire Orig um | Wire Incr % | Via Orig | Via Incr % |
|-----------|-------------------|-------------|---------------|--------------|--------------|-------------|----------|------------|
| I8051     | 36306             | 0.34        | 0.642         | 0.40         | 190549       | 0.15        | 50256    | 0.20       |
| Vga       | 54492             | 1.13        | 1.958         | 0.43         | 241495       | 1.27        | 44648    | 0.84       |
| WishBone  | 227129            | 0.53        | 3.483         | 0.18         | 2981089      | 0.44        | 325057   | 0.07       |

**Table 3.** Distributed standard cell implementation of TMU

| Benchmark | Area Original mm2 | Area Incr % | Power Orig mW | Power Incr % | Wire Orig um | Wire Incr % | Via Orig | Via Incr % |
|-----------|-------------------|-------------|---------------|--------------|--------------|-------------|----------|------------|
| I8051     | 36306             | 0.34        | 0.642         | 0.40         | 190549       | 0.13        | 50256    | 0.19       |
| Vga       | 54492             | 1.13        | 1.958         | 0.43         | 241495       | 0.55        | 44648    | 0.76       |
| WishBone  | 227129            | 0.53        | 3.483         | 0.18         | 2981089      | 0.26        | 325057   | 0.04       |

Table 3 shows the various penalties resulting from the distributed control unit insertion. We notice that area and power overhead are identical to the case of a centralized unit. This is because the area figure refers to *active* area, that is, only the area of the cells (in fact, the TMU implementation is identical). For the same argument, power overhead is also identical in the two cases (figures refer to the power consumed by cells only).

In the distributed implementation, however, the placement tool has the flexibility to reduce the interconnect length by placing the individual parts of the controller close to the VDB they are supposed to drive. The average wirelength penalty was found to be only 0.2%, about half of the penalty observed for the centralized controller placement. Further, we observed an increase of 0.33% in the total number vias which also smaller than that for centralized controller placement, since the the interconnect has to hop lesser vias to connect its endpoint pins.

Overall, we found out that although both the *TMU* implementations have a very low impact on the metrics of interest for our benchmark designs, the distributed *TMU* is the most efficient of the two implementations.

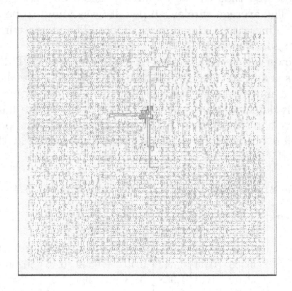

**Fig. 4.** Layout of the i8051 Benchmark with TMU

As a visual example of the actual impact of the TMU insertion in a layout, Figure 4 shows the layout of the i8051 benchmark when the controller was placed as a block. Light lines denote nets, while light boxes delimit the controller's standard cell implementation. Other nets of the layout are omitted for the sake of clarity. The placement of the block was decided by searching for an under-utilized layout area in the vicinity of the *VDB* positions so as to minimally affect the already placed cells.

# 7  Conclusions

In this paper, we have demonstrated the use of an on-chip thermal management unit for thermally induced clock skew violation correction. We presented two different implementation strategies for the controller and quantitatively measured the overhead incurred in using such a scheme over different metrics such as wirelength, power, via increase, and area. The controller insertion leads to extremely low penalties (0.67% in area, 0.62% in wire-length, 0.33% in power, and 0.37% in via-number) and guarantees correct operation over all possible temperature profiles. The future work in this direction of research includes incorporating thermal aware clock skew simulator within the clock tree synthesis tool to generate a clock tree which is more resilient to temperature variations.

# References

1. K. Skadron et al., "Temperature-Aware Computer Systems: Opportunities and Challenges," IEEE Micro, Vol. 23, No.6, Nov-Dec 2003, pp. 52-61.
2. S. Borkar et al., "Parameter Variation and Impact on Circuits and Microarchitectures," *DAC'03*, IEEE Design Automation Conference, 2003, Jun. 2003, pp. 338-342.
3. D. Brooks, M. Martonosi, "Dynamic thermal management for high-performance microprocessors" *HPCA'01*, High-Performance Computer Architecture, Jan. 2001, pp. 171-182.
4. J. Srinivasan, S. V. Adve, "Predictive Dynamic Thermal Management for Multimedia Applications," *ICS'03*, International Conference on Supercomputing, June 2003.
5. K. Skadron, "Hybrid architectural dynamic thermal management," *DATE'04* Design Automation and Test in Europe Conference, Feb. 2004, pp. 10–15.
6. Amir H. Ajami, Kaustav Banerjee, Massoud Pedram, "Modeling and Analysis of Nonuniform Substrate Temperature Effects on Global ULSI interconnects.", *IEEE Transactions on CAD*, Vol. 24, No. 6, June 2005, pp. 849–861.
7. M. Cho, S. Ahmed, D. Z. Pan, "TACO: Temperature Aware Clock-tree Optimization," *ICCAD'05*, International Conference on Computer-Aided Design, Nov. 2005, pp. 582-587.
8. A. Chakraborty, P. Sithambaram, K. Duraisami, M. Poncino, A. Macii, E. Macii, "Thermal Resilient Bounded-Skew Clock-Tree Optimization Methodology", *DATE-06: IEEE Design Automation and Test in Europe*, Munich, Germany, March 2006.
9. A. Chakraborty, P. Sithambaram, K. Duraisami, M. Poncino, A. Macii, E. Macii, "Dynamic Thermal Clock Skew Compensation using Tunable Delay Buffers", *Accepted for publication ISLPED 2006*, Tegernsee, Germany, October 2006.
10. J.-L. Tsai, D. Baik, C. C.-P. Chen, K. K. Saluja, "A Yield Improvement Methodology Using Pre- and Post-silicon Statistical Clock Scheduling," *ICCAD'04*, International Conference on Computer-Aided Design, Nov. 2004, pp. 611-618.
11. J.-L. Tsai, L. Zhang, C. Chen, "Statistical Timing Analysis Driven Post-Silicon-Tunable Clock-Tree Synthesis," *ICCAD'05*, International Conference on Computer-Aided Design, Nov. 2005, pp. 575-581.
12. R. S. Tsay, "Exact Zero Skew Clock Routing" *ICCAD'91*, International Conference on Computer-Aided Design, Nov. 1991, pp. 336-339.

13. T. H. Chao, Y-C.Hsu, J-M.Ho, K.D.Boese, A.B. Kahng, "Zero Skew Clock Routing with Minimum Wirelength," *IEEE Transactions on Circuits and Systems II*, Vol. 39, No. 11, Nov. 1992, pp. 799 - 814.
14. J. Cong, C. K. Koh, "Minimum-Cost Bounded-Skew Clock Routing," *ISCAS'95*, IEEE International Symposium on Circuits and Systems, May 1995, pp. 215-218.
15. D. J. H. Huang, A. B. Kahng, C.-H. A. Tsao, "On the Bounded-Skew Clock and Steiner Routing Problems," *DAC'95*, IEEE Design Automation Conference, Jun 1995, pp. 508–513.
16. Y.P. Chen, D.F. Wang, "An algorithm for Zero-Skew Clock Tree Routing with Buffer Insertion," *EDTC'96*, Mar. 1996, pp. 230–236.
17. Jeng-Liang Tsai, Tsung-Hao Chen, Chen, C.C.-P, "Zero Skew Clock Tree Optimization with Buffer insertion/sizing and wire sizing.", *IEEE Transactions on CAD*, Vol. 23, No. 4, Jun 2004, pp. 565-572.
18. S. Tam et al., "Clock generation and distribution for the first IA-64 microprocessor," *IEEE Journal of Solid-State Circuits*, Vol. 35, No. 11, Jun 2000, pp. 1545–1552.
19. E. Takahashi, Y. Kasai, M. Murakawa, T. Higuchi, "A post-silicon clock timing adjustment using genetic algorithms," *VLSI'03* Symposium on VLSI circuits, pp. 13–16.
20. http://www.opencores.org

# A Clock Generator Driven by a Unified-CBiCMOS Buffer Driver for High Speed and Low Energy Operation

Toshiro Akino and Takashi Hamahata

Program in Electronic System and Information Engineering
The Graduate School of Biology-Oriented Science and Technology
Kinki University
930 Nishi-Mitani, Kinokawa, Wakayama, 649-6493 Japan
akino@info.waka.kindai.ac.jp

**Abstract.** A new operation mode for a lateral unified-complementary BiCMOS (hereafter abbreviated as U-CBiCMOS) buffer driver based on a partially depleted CMOS/SOI process is proposed. The scheme utilizes a gated npn or pnp BJT inherent to a n- or p-channel MOSFET. Forward current is applied to the base terminal of the channel MOSFET, with a normal pull-up or pull-down MOSFET as a current source, where each drain terminal is connected to the corresponding base terminal of the buffer. A new logic scheme is designed to feed an input signal to the gates of the pull-up and pull-down MOSFETs, rather than to those of the n- and p-channel MOSFETs as in our previous work, while also keeping both the n- and p-channel MOSFETs inactive and activating either the lateral npn or pnp BJT. A clock generator composing of the ring oscillator with a 21-stage CMOS inverter driven by the U-CBiCMOS buffer driver is designed. Circuit simulation using 0.35μm BSIM3v3 model parameters for the MOSFETs and a current gain of $\beta_F = 100$ for the BJTs revealed the speed of the U-CBiCMOS buffer driver to be more than 4 times faster than that of an equivalent 4-stage CMOS (4SCMOS) inverter designed on the basis of logical effort for driving a load capacitance of 1.417 pF at $V_{dd} = 1$ V.

## 1 Introduction

An important feature of complementary metal-oxide semiconductor (CMOS) circuits is that their switching power density per unit area remains almost unchanged under constant-field scaling. However, as the design size of CMOS circuits becomes smaller, high performance becomes more difficult to achieve due to the effect of velocity saturation. At a short channel length $L$, the drain current per channel width ($W$) is no longer proportional to $(V_{gs} - V_t)^2/L$, where $V_{gs}$ is the gate-to-source voltage and $V_t$ is the threshold voltage. As the drain current tends to be proportional to $v_{sat}*(V_{gs} - V_t)$, where $v_{sat}$ is the saturation velocity [1], this value becomes independent of $L$ and constant at $V_{gs}=V_{dd}$. Thus, the signal propagation delay driven by the current required for large interconnect capacitance is a major limitation on the performance of CMOS circuits.

An alternative solution to the problem of driving large capacitive loads can be provided by merging CMOS and bipolar devices (BiCMOS) on chip [2, 3]. Taking advantage of the low static power consumption of CMOS circuits and the high current

J. Vounckx, N. Azemard, and P. Maurine (Eds.): PATMOS 2006, LNCS 4148, pp. 225–236, 2006.
© Springer-Verlag Berlin Heidelberg 2006

driving capability of two vertical npn bipolar transistors connected in series, the BiCMOS configuration can combine the best of both devices. However, the most significant drawback of the BiCMOS circuits lies in the increased complexity of the fabrication process. Along similar lines, the even more complicated vertical CBiCMOS fabrication process has been developed [4, 5].

A hybrid-mode device has been fabricated based on standard bulk CMOS technology. The device is essentially a MOSFET with an effective channel length of $0.25\mu m$ in which the gate and well are connected internally to form the base of the lateral BJT. This device can achieve a current gain, $\beta_F$, of higher than 1,000 at a substrate bias of less than 0.6 V, and a gain of around 100 at 0.7 V [6]. A double-diffused lateral npn BJT with peak $\beta_F$ of 120 was fabricated in a simple CMOS-like process using SIMOX SOI substrates [7].

To extend the CMOS driving capability in the switching state, our group has investigated the use of high charge/discharge currents using a lateral npn or pnp BJT. Here, the BJT is inherent to the corresponding n- or p-channel MOSFET in a partially depleted CMOS inverter on SOI substrates. Our group proposed a new operation mode of applying forward current to the base terminal of each n-channel or p-channel MOSFET to achieve hybrid operation of a lateral-BJT (LB) CMOS inverter [8]. The LB-CMOS inverter was designed such that each inverter had normal pull-up and pull-down MOSFETs as current sources and had drain terminals connected to the corresponding base terminals [9].

A logic scheme to control the gates of the pull-up or pull-down MOSFET as a base current source in the switching state has been proposed [10, 11]. This scheme enhances the driving capability of the collector current when the forward base current is drained and the n-channel (p-channel) MOSFET is on while discharging (charging) by using two output signals generated by two CMOS inverters with difference resistance ratios.

In this paper, a new circuit scheme is proposed to feed an input signal to the gates of the pull-up and pull-down MOSFETs as a U-CBiCMOS buffer, rather than to those of the n- and p-channel MOSFETs in the LB-CMOS as in our previous work [8, 9, 10, 11], while keeping both the n- and p-channel MOSFETs inactive and activating either the lateral npn or pnp BJT. Using a circuit simulator with $0.35\mu m$ BSIM3v3 model parameters for MOSFETs and $\beta_F=100$ for the BJTs, the speed and energy of the U-CBiCMOS buffer in a clock generator composing of the ring oscillator with a 21-stage inverter are compared with a 4-stage CMOS (4SCMOS) inverter designed based on logical effort [12] in the same oscillator assuming a $V_{dd}$ of about 1 V and capacitive loads of around 1.417 pF, which allows $256 \times 5.534$ fF, where the value 5.534 fF is taken as the smallest inverter gate capacitance.

## 2    DC Characteristics of U-CBiCMOS Buffer Driver

A cross-sectional view of the partially depleted MOSFETs on a SOI substrate which makes up the U-CBiCMOS buffer driver is shown in Fig. 1, where each MOSFET includes the corresponding BJT. Although a symmetric structure is employed for the drain (collector) and source (emitter), the lateral BJTs are capable of high current gain, $\beta_F$, and can achieve high performance as a result of the SOI substrates. The n-channel MOSFET with a lateral npn BJT has the drain, source, and substrate terminals of the MOSFET connected to the corresponding collector, emitter, and base terminals of the BJT.

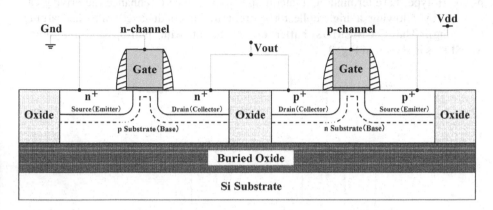

**Fig. 1.** Cross-sectional view of U-CBiCMOS buffer driver

Circuit diagrams for the hybrid devices comprising an n-channel MOSFET and lateral npn BJT are shown in Fig. 2. When the gate terminal of the n-channel (p-channel) MOSFET is fixed at the voltage level of $Gnd$ ($Vdd$) for a p-type (n-type) substrate, both MOSFETs are off and thus the hybrid circuit consists of the lateral CBJTs. The minimum width is $W_n = 6\lambda = 1.05\mu m$ ($W_p = 6\lambda = 1.05$ $\mu m$), and the p-type base resistance is $R_{bp} = 62$ $\Omega$ ($\cong R_{bn}$) based on a $2\lambda = 0.35$ $\mu m$ design.

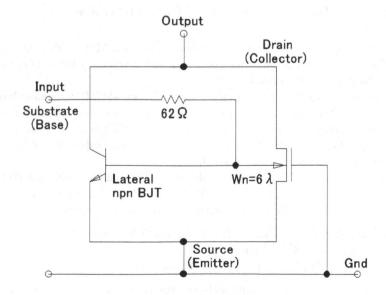

**Fig. 2.** Lateral npn BJT

Using only the active complementary BJTs, a U-CBiCMOS buffer driver that drains the forward base current through either of two base terminals in the switching state is proposed. The buffer scheme utilizes the instantaneous forward current supplied to the p-type (n-type) base terminal in a lateral npn (pnp) device to enhance the driving capability by allowing a high collector current to be conducted while discharging (charging). The U-CBiCMOS buffer driver circuit with pull-up and pull-down MOSFETs is shown in Fig. 3.

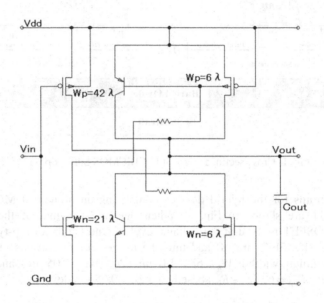

**Fig. 3.** Circuit diagram of U-CBiCMOS buffer driver

Fig. 4 shows a cross-sectional view of several n-channel MOSFETs in an ordinary CMOS circuit with a p-well substrate connected at the voltage level of $G$nd on SOI. The converse system is not shown.

Fig. 5 shows the benchmark circuit of a 4-stage CMOS (4SCMOS) inverter based on a normal CMOS/SOI process designed based on the concept of logical effort with fan-out 4 to maximize the speed of 4 inversions. This 4SCMOS inverter was designed for a load capacitance $C_{out}$ of $256 \times 5.534$ fF = 1.417 pF, where the value of 5.534 fF is taken as the smallest inverter gate capacitance.

The circuit simulator T-Spice was employed for the analysis using the BSIM3v3 model parameters for a 0.35 μm CMOS/SOI process. The BSIM3v3 model parameters used for the n-channel MOSFET with lateral npn BJT were as follows:

(1) n-channel MOSFET: $V_{t0}(n) = 0.287$ V, $K_1 = 0.47$ V$^{1/2}$, $K_2 = -0.057$, $\varphi_S = 0.80$ V, $\mu_0 = 550$ cm$^2$/(V s), $t_{OX} = 7$ nm.
(2) npn BJT: $\beta_F = 100$, $\beta_R = 1$, $I_S = 2 \times 10^{-15}$ A, Area = 1.

The value of the current gain, $\beta_F$, represents the worst case scenario. The parameters for a p-channel MOSFET with lateral pnp BJT were as follows:

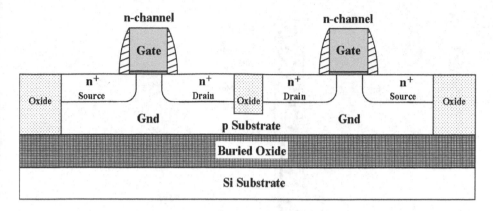

**Fig. 4.** A cross-sectional view of two n-channel MOSFETs in ordinary CMOS circuits at a p-well substrate connected to Gnd

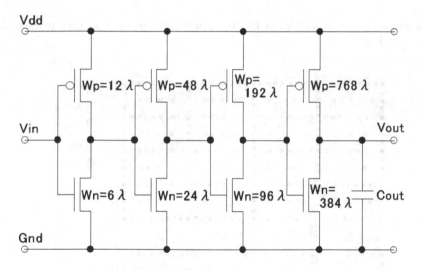

**Fig. 5.** Circuit diagram of 4-stage CMOS (4SCMOS) benchmark inverter circuit

(3) p-channel MOSFET: $V_{t0}(p) = -0.355$ V, $K_1 = 0.45$ $V^{1/2}$, $K_2 = -0.03$, $\varphi_S = 0.82$ V, $\mu_0 = 220$ cm$^2$/(V s), $t_{OX} = 7$ nm.

(4) pnp BJT: $\beta_F = 100$, $\beta_R = 1$, $I_S = 2\times10^{-15}$ A, Area = 1.

Fortunately, the proposed U-CBiCMOS buffer driver cell, which utilizes hybrid operation to drive a high load capacitance at the output stages for all standard cells of the building blocks, can be easily added to a CMOS/SOI standard cell library. It is natural to employ ordinary CMOS/SOI circuits with two kinds of substrate terminals Vdd and Gnd (as shown in Fig. 4) for normal logical operations in the core parts for all standard cells of the building blocks as this allows minimal energy consumption for the CMOS/SOI circuits in the switching state.

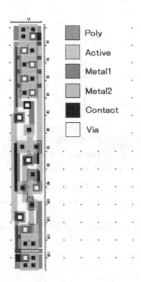

**Fig. 6.** Standard cell layout for U-CBiCMOS buffer driver corresponding to the circuit as shown in Fig. 3

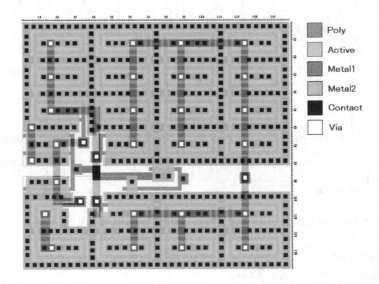

**Fig. 7.** Standard cell layout for 4SCMOS inverter corresponding to the circuit as shown in Fig. 5

The standard cell layout of the U-CBiCMOS buffer driver corresponding to the circuit shown in Fig. 3 is given in Fig. 6. Fig. 7 shows the layout of the 4SCMOS inverter benchmark circuit shown in Fig. 5.

The results of a direct current (DC) circuit simulation for the proposed U-CBiCMOS buffer driver are shown in Fig. 8.

The buffer driver circuit exhibits a rapid transition at around $Vin = Vdd/2$ due to the two strong BJT currents. The DC circuit simulation revealed that the U-CBiCMOS buffer driver could achieve the sharp transition characteristics found in BJT circuits in the switching state, as well as low power consumption by the collector currents in stationary states. However, although only a little, some forward n-type (p-type) base current inside the buffer driver is drained as shown in Fig. 8.

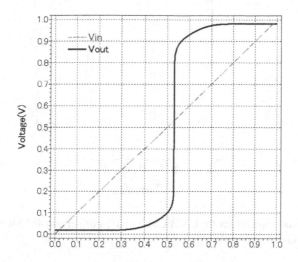

**Fig. 8.** DC circuit simulation results for U-CBiCMOS buffer driver

# 3   Transient Characteristics of U-CBiCMOS Buffer Driver

By comparing with the benchmark circuit of the 4SCMOS inverter in Fig. 5, we try to evaluate the delay, power, and energy characteristics of the U-CBiCMOS buffer driver shown in Fig. 3.

The results of transient simulation for the U-CBiCMOS buffer driver and 4SCMOS inverter are shown in Fig. 9 for driving at a load capacitance of 1.417 pF at $Vdd = 1$ V. We design the ring oscillator with a 21-stage CMOS inverter. The frequency of an input pulse $Vin$ is about 300 MHz as shown in Fig. 9. The figure clearly shows that the U-CBiCMOS buffer driver has an overwhelmingly high speed compared to the 4SCMOS inverter. However, there is a small voltage drop from $Vdd$ and correspondingly also a small voltage rise from $Gnd$.

The delay, power, and energy characteristics of the U-CBiCMOS buffer driver and 4SCMOS inverter are shown versus load capacitance in Figs. 10, 11, 12, respectively.

The delays for both the U-CBiCMOS buffer driver and 4SCMOS inverter are nearly proportional to the load capacitance. The key characteristics of the U-CBiCMOS buffer driver are a high drive capability and the more than 4 times higher speed available compared with the ordinary 4SCMOS inverter in driving a load capacitance from 0.708 pF to 2.125 pF at $Vdd = 1$ V. In addition, the energy of the U-CBiCMOS buffer driver

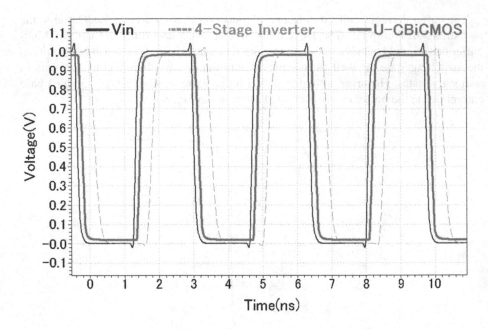

**Fig. 9.** Transient simulation results for U-CBiCMOS buffer driver and 4SCMOS inverter under the input pulse of ring oscillator with 21-stage inverters

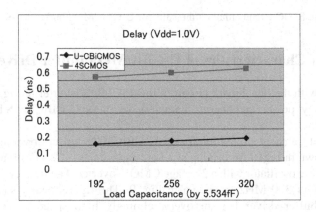

**Fig. 10.** Delay of U-CBiCMOS buffer driver and 4SCMOS inverter versus load capacitance

is about 40 % lower than that of the ordinary 4SCMOS inverter over the same range of load capacitance, as shown in Figs. 10, 11, 12.

The delay, power, and energy characteristics of the U-CBiCMOS buffer driver and 4SCMOS inverter are shown versus Vdd in Figs. 13, 14, 15. A reduction in the value of Vdd gives a decrease in the energy of the U-CBiCMOS buffer driver and 4SCMOS inverter, because the power rather than the delay strongly dominates the energy characteristics.

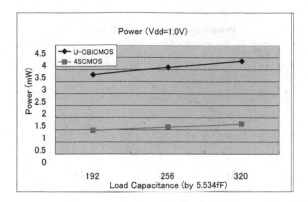

**Fig. 11.** Power of U-CBiCMOS buffer driver and 4SCMOS inverter versus load capacitance

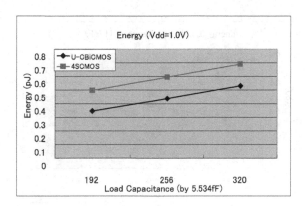

**Fig. 12.** Energy of U-CBiCMOS buffer driver and 4SCMOS inverter versus load capacitance

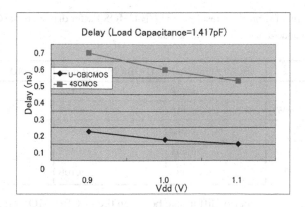

**Fig. 13.** Delay of U-CBiCMOS buffer driver and 4SCMOS inverter versus *Vdd*

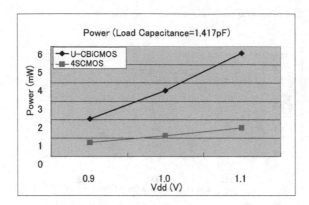

**Fig. 14.** Power of U-CBiCMOS buffer driver and 4SCMOS inverter versus Vdd

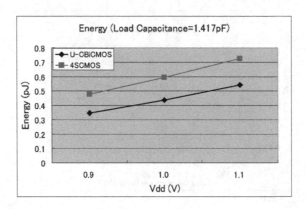

**Fig. 15.** Energy of U-CBiCMOS buffer driver and 4SCMOS inverter versus Vdd

**Table 1.** Comparison of simulation results for U-CBiCMOS buffer driver and 4SCMOS inverter for driving a load capacitance of 1.417 pF at Vdd = 1 V

|  | 4SCMOS Inverter | U-CBiCMOS Buffer | 4SCMOS/U-CBiCMOS |
|---|---|---|---|
| Switching Delay (ns) | 0.548 | 0.125 | 4.38 |
| Switching Power (mW) | 1.113 | 3.587 | 0.31 |
| Average Power (mW) | 0.613 | 0.847 | 0.72 |
| Switching Energy (pJ) | 0.594 | 0.437 | 1.36 |
| Average Energy (pJ) | 0.336 | 0.106 | 3.17 |

On the other hand, the energy difference between the U-CBiCMOS buffer driver and 4SCMOS inverter becomes larger versus Vdd.

The circuit simulations results for the U-CBiCMOS buffer driver and 4SCMOS inverter assuming a load capacitance of 1.417 pF and Vdd of 1 V are summarized in Table 1.

In conclusion, the proposed U-CBiCMOS buffer driver is shown to be more than 4 times faster than that of the 4SCMOS inverter for a load capacitance of 1.417 pF at Vdd = 1 V. And, the energy consumption of the buffer is about 36 % lower than that of the 4SCMOS inverter.

# 4 Conclusions

A logic scheme for controlling the gates of pull-up and pull-down MOSFETs as current sources in a unified-complementary BiCMOS (U-CBiCMOS) buffer driver is proposed. The design enhances the driving capability of the collector current when the forward base current is drained and the n-channel (p-channel) MOSFET is off while discharging (charging) through direct application of the input signal to the pull-up and pull-down MOSFETs. T-Spice simulation of the circuits using 0.35μm BSIM3v3 model parameters for the MOSFETs and $\beta_F = 100$ for the BJTs revealed that the proposed U-CBiCMOS buffer driver could achieve a sharp transition in BJTs in the switching state as well as low energy consumption. Based on transient circuit simulation, the speed of the proposed U-CBiCMOS buffer driver was found to be more than 4 times faster than the 4-stage CMOS (4SCMOS) inverter at Vdd = 1 V. Furthermore, the U-CBiCMOS buffer driver consumes about 36 % less energy which is almost comparable to the 4SCMOS inverter. Here, we assume a load capacitance of 1.417 pF which allows $256 \times 5.534$ fF, where the value 5.534 fF is taken as the smallest gate capacitance of a latch. Thus, the U-CBiCMOS buffer driver can feed the clock pulse to the 256 smallest latches at the same time.

Further investigations of this circuit will address the problem of including a dynamic domino CMOS circuit for high speed and low energy operation.

# References

[1] Y. Taur and T. H. Ning, "Fundamentals of Modern VLSI Devices," *Cambridge University Press*, 1998.
[2] S.-M.K. Kang, and Y. Leblebici, "CMOS Digital Integrated Circuits: Analysis and Design, 2nd Edition," *WCB/McGraw-Hill*, 1999.
[3] M. Kubo, I. Masuda, K. Miyata and K. Ogiue, "Perspective on BiCMOS VLSI's," *IEEE Journal of Solid-State Circuits*, vol. 23, no. 1, pp. 5-11, 1988.
[4] S. W. Sun, P. G. Y. Tsui, B. M. Somero, J. Klein, F. Pintchovski, J. R. Yeargain and B. Pappert, "A 0.4-micron fully complementary BiCMOS technology for advanced logic and microprocessor applications," in *IEEE IEDM Tech. Dig.*, pp. 85-88, 1991.
[5] C. Kim and K. D. Wise, "Low-voltage electronics for the stimulation of biological neural networks using fully complementary BiCMOS circuits," *IEEE Journal of Solid-State Circuits*, vol. 32, no. 10, pp. 1483-1490, 1997.

[6]  S. Verdonckt-Vandebroek, S. Wong, J. Woo, and P. Ko, "High-gain lateral bipolar action in a MOSFET structure," *IEEE Trans. Electron Devices*, vol. Ed-38, pp. 2487-2496, Nov. 1991.

[7]  S. A. Parke, C. Hu and P. K. Ko, "A high-performance lateral bipolar transistor fabricated on SIMOX," *IEEE Electron Device Letters*, vol. 14, no. 1, pp. 33-35, 1993.

[8]  T. Akino, "Driving capability by lateral BJT-CMOS inverter," in *Proceedings of SASIMI2003*, pp. 265-271, April 2003.

[9]  T. Akino, "High speed and low energy CMOS inverter powerfully driven by lateral BJT," in *Proceedings of Karuizawa Workshop on Circuits and Systems*, pp. 79-84, April 2003 (in Japanese).

[10]  T. Akino, "High speed and low energy lateral BJT-CMOS inverter," in *Proceedings of SASIMI2004*, pp. 73-76, October 2004.

[11]  T. Akino, K. Matsuura, A. Yasunaga, "A high-speed domino CMOS full adder driven by a new unified-BiCMOS inverter," in *Proceedings of ISCAS2005*, pp.452-455, Kobe, May 2005.

[12]  I. Sutherland, B. Sproull, and D. Harris, "Logical Effort - Designing Fast CMOS Circuits," *Morgan Kaufmann Publishers, Inc.*, 1999.

# Gate-Level Dual-Threshold Static Power Optimization Methodology (GDSPOM) Using Path-Based Static Timing Analysis (STA) Technique

B. Chung[*] and J.B. Kuo[**]

School of Eng Science, SFU,
Burnaby, Canada V5A 1S5
jbkuo@sfu.ca

**Abstract.** This paper describes a novel gate-level dual-threshold static power optimization methodology (GDSPOM), which is based on the static timing analysis technique for designing high-speed low-power SOC applications using 90nm MTCMOS technology. The cell libraries come in fixed threshold – high $V_{th}$ for good standby power and low $V_{th}$ for high-speed. Based on this optimization technique using two cell libraries with different threshold voltages, a 16-bit multiplier using the dual-threshold cells meeting the speed requirement has been designed to have a 50% less leakage power consumption when compared to the one using only the low-threshold cell library.

## 1 Introduction

SOC systems implemented by CMOS VLSI circuits using nanometer transistors have been evolving quickly [1]. Low power consumption has become a significant requirement [1]. For achieving low static power consumption, multi-threshold CMOS (MTCMOS) circuits have been proven to be an effective approach [2] [3]. Various algorithms of minimizing static power consumption using dual-threshold techniques have been proposed [4]-[6]. However, static power optimization of a multi-million gate design using MTCMOS technology at the transistor level is difficult, while at the gate level it is much easier to implement.

In this paper, a gate-level dual-threshold static power optimization methodology (GDSPOM) using path based static timing analysis (STA) is described. It will be shown that via two cell libraries with different threshold voltages, the design of a 16-bit multiplier circuit has been optimized based on GDSPOM, which has a 50% less leakage power consumption in comparison with the all-low threshold voltage one at the operating frequency of 500MHz. In the following sections, characters and usages of timing and power models are introduced first, the principle of GDSPOM is presented next, followed by the performance of the test multiplier circuits, discussion and conclusion.

---

[*] B. Chung is with PMC Sierra, Canada.
[**] J. B. Kuo is on leave from NTUEE.

J. Vounckx, N. Azemard, and P. Maurine (Eds.): PATMOS 2006, LNCS 4148, pp. 237 – 246, 2006.
© Springer-Verlag Berlin Heidelberg 2006

## 2  Timing Models

A cell is a fundamental logic block and it is the basic element in a gate-level netlist. A cell built with all high threshold voltage transistors has a longer signal propagation delay and blocks more unwanted leakage current; a cell built with all low threshold voltage transistors has a faster signal transition time but suffers from generating a large amount of sub-threshold leakage current [7] [8].

A cell may have multiple timing arcs. A timing arc defines a timing relationship between one input pin and one output pin of a cell. Different timing arcs have different cell propagation delays [9]. As shown in Fig. 1 (a), a two-input XOR gate has four arcs: A to Z when B is 0, A to Z when B is 1, B to Z when A is 0, and B to Z when A is 0. In the case when a pin is assigned a constant value as shown in Fig. 1 (b), when input A is assigned a constant value of 0, there is only one arc between input B to output Z available for analysis.

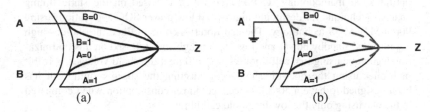

**Fig. 1.** XOR cell timing arcs

Arc delay calculation formula can be simplified as a function of the input transition time and the output load capacitance. Timing lookup table like the one shown in Fig. 2 is recorded in the cell technology library [9]. Using the example in Fig. 2, a cell delay time from input B to output Z is 8.8 ns when the input transition time is 100 ps and the output load capacitance is 0.4 fF. When values of the input transition time and the output load capacitance are between the table points or outside the table range, we use the interpolation or the extrapolation approach to estimate the delay.

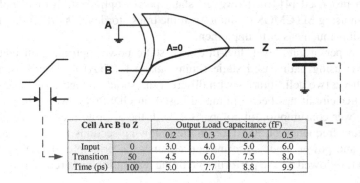

| Cell Arc B to Z | | Output Load Capacitance (fF) | | | |
|---|---|---|---|---|---|
| | | 0.2 | 0.3 | 0.4 | 0.5 |
| Input | 0 | 3.0 | 4.0 | 5.0 | 6.0 |
| Transition | 50 | 4.5 | 6.0 | 7.5 | 8.0 |
| Time (ps) | 100 | 5.0 | 7.7 | 8.8 | 9.9 |

**Fig. 2.** Arc timing lookup table

Arc delay is the cell internal signal propagation time. Net delay is the total time for a signal to travel between two cells. Knowing cell and net delays as well as input latency, path arrival time can be calculated as following:

$$AT_{path} = D_{clk} + D_{clk\_net} + \sum D_{cell} + \sum D_{net} \tag{1}$$

$AT_{path}$ is path arrival time; $D_{clk}$ is clock source latency, $D_{clk\_net}$ is clock network latency; $D_{cell}$ is cell delay; $D_{net}$ is net delay.

Assuming that source clock latency is 2 ns, clock network latency is 3 ns, sequential and combinational cell delays are 3 ns, and net delay is 2 ns, the path shown in Fig. 3 has arrival time of 20 ns.

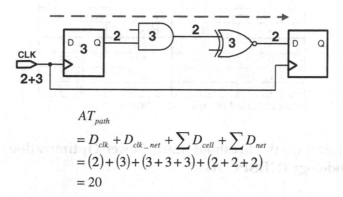

$$AT_{path}$$
$$= D_{clk} + D_{clk\_net} + \sum D_{cell} + \sum D_{net}$$
$$= (2) + (3) + (3 + 3 + 3) + (2 + 2 + 2)$$
$$= 20$$

**Fig. 3.** Path arrival time calculation example

Furthermore, required setup time of a path can be calculated using the following formula:

$$RT_{path\_setup} = T_{clk} + D_{clk} + D_{clk\_net} - T_{clk\_uncertainty} - T_{setup} \tag{2}$$

$RT_{path\_setup}$ is setup required time; $T_{clk}$ is clock period; $D_{clk}$ is clock source latency; $D_{clk\_net}$ is clock network latency; $T_{clk\_uncertainty}$ is clock uncertainty; $T_{setup}$ is capture flop setup time.

When a path's arrival time is shorter or equal to its required time, this path meets the setup timing constraint. On the other hand, when a path's arrival time is longer than its required time, this path does not satisfy its timing constraint and has setup timing violation. The difference between path arrival and required time is called path slack and can be calculated with the formula:

$$S_{path\_setup} = RT_{path\_setup} - AT_{path} \tag{3}$$

Positive slack indicates that the path meets timing and negative slack tells that the path has a timing violation. Because all timing checks are done per path bases, this type of STA is characterized as path based STA approach.

## 3  Leakage Power Models

Leakage power is cell state dependent. As shown in Table 1, cell leakage current can vary in more than 5 orders of magnitude. Leakage current varies because transistors inside a cell have different on and off combinations in different state. As a result, the drain source voltages VDS of each transistor varies. In VLSI design, the impact of different cell states on the total leakage current is ignorable. Therefore, average leakage value is recorded in the technology library.

**Table 1.** 90nm NAND2 Leakage Current

| NAND2 Input Value | | Leakage Current (nA) | |
|---|---|---|---|
| A | B | High $V_{th}$ | Low $V_{th}$ |
| 0 | 0 | 1.49 | 3.72 |
| 0 | 1 | 2.56 | 14.93 |
| 1 | 0 | 3.57 | 18.95 |
| 1 | 1 | 4.61 | 21.77 |

Source: Based on Spice simulation

## 4  Gate-Level Dual-Threshold Static Power Optimization Methodology (GDSPOM)

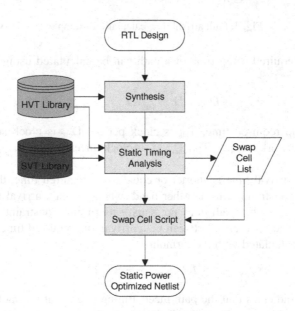

**Fig. 4.** Flow chart of the gate-level dual-threshold static power optimization methodology (GDSPOM)

Fig. 4 shows the flow chart of GDSPOM used for designing high-speed low-power SOC applications using MTCMOS technology. As shown in the figure, a Register Transfer Language (RTL) design is synthesized into gate-level netlist of cells using CMOS devices with a high-threshold voltage (HVT). Then, static timing analysis is performed to report a list of cells that are required to swap from HVT type to the low-threshold voltage (SVT) type to meet timing constraints. Finally, cell-swapping script is executed to create the netlist built with dual-threshold HVT/SVT cells.

In the synthesis step, 25% slower operation speed is applied. In the example of 500MHz 16-bit multiplier, 400MHz frequency is targeted when converting the multiplier's RTL design to HVT gate-level netlist. The additional 100MHz speed will be caught up in the cell swapping step, which replaces slow HVT cells with fast SVT ones. Comparing speeds of HVT and SVT cells in the 90nm technology library, SVT ones are about 30% faster than HVT ones. This is the reason why 25% slower speed is chosen to create the initial HVT gate-level netlist and why it is possible to achieve the final speed target by changing cell types without altering design architecture and increasing area overhead.

STA breaks a design into a group of timing paths and calculates the signal propagation delay of each path individually. Fig. 5 illustrates three timing violated paths labeled green, blue, and purple. The number of timing violating paths through one cell defines this cell's cost value. For instance, AND gate has the cost value of 1; bottom NAND gate has the cost value of 2, middle NAND and OR gates have the cost value of 3. The cells with the highest cost value such as middle NAND gate and OR gates will be targeted for cell type change. After changing these bottleneck cells to SVT type, STA is performed again to recalculate cell cost values. This STA process continues until all the timing paths meet the required timing constraints.

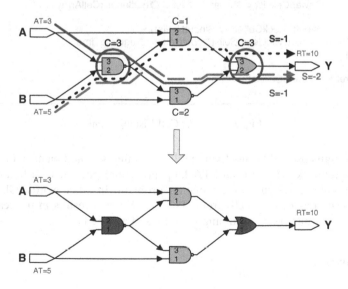

**Fig. 5.** GDSPOM cell swapping example

Fig. 6 explains how cost values are assigned to cells and Fig. 7 shows the STA iterating process.

```
procedure getBottleneckCells ($inputNetlist, $requiredTime) {
        @pathArray = all paths in $inputNetlist
        %cellCostHash = all cells in $inputNetlist with initial cost value 0

        foreach $path (@pathArray) {
            $arrivalTime = calculated $path arrival time

            if ($arrivalTime > $requiredTime) {
                foreach $cell in $path {
                    incr $cellCostHash{$cell}
                }
            }
        }

        sort %cellCostHash by cost value
        @bottleneckCellArray = first n cells with positive cost value in %cellCostHash
        $outputNetlist = $inputNetlist after @bottleneckCellArray cell type change

        return (@bottleneckCellArray, $outputNetlist)
}
```

**Fig. 6.** Get Bottleneck Cells algorithm

```
procedure getSwapCellList ($originalNetlist, $requiredTime) {
        (@bottleneckCellArray, $inputNetlist) =
            &getBottleneckCells ($origianlNetlist, $requiredTime)

        while (@bottleneckCellArray != NULL) {
            @swapCellList = @swapCellList + @bottleneckCellArray

            (@bottleneckCellArray, $inputNetlist) =
                &getBottlenetCells($inputNetlist, $requiredTime)
        }

        return @swapCellList
}
```

**Fig. 7.** Get Swap Cell List algorithm

Fixing a high cost cell means fixing multiple timing violated paths at once. Always targeting bottleneck cells in each STA loop procedure guarantees a highly efficient solution of solving design timing violation problem. In other words, GDSPOM replaces minimum amount of cells from HVT to SVT and results in the least leakage power increase while fixing all timing violations in a design.

## 5 Performance

In order to assess the effectiveness of GDSPOM for designing low-power high-speed SOC applications using a 90nm MTCMOS technology, three 16-bit multipliers with

Wallace tree reduction architecture [10] have been implemented. All of them are generated based on the same RTL source except that one multiplier uses all HVT cells, another has all SVT cells, and the third one contains both types of cells optimized via GDSPOM. Targeting operating frequency is set to be 500MHz and 90nm cell libraries are used in this experiment. A 16-bit multiplier has 7320 unity gates and it contains approximately 30000 transistors.

As shown in Fig. 8, with the 500MH clock frequency constraint, thousands of paths in the HVT multiplier fail the speed test. This result is expected because the HVT multiplier was synthesized with 400MHz timing constraint, which is 25% slower than the targeting speed performance. Fig. 8 also indicates that 15 paths have the longest delay time and these 15 paths define the operating speed of 16-bit multipliers.

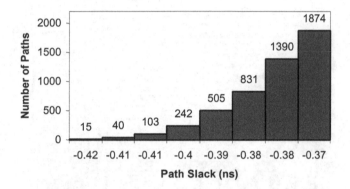

**Fig. 8.** Number of timing violated paths in the all-HVT multiplier

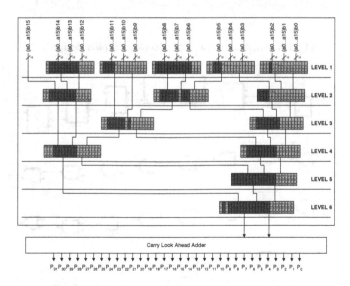

**Fig. 9.** Block diagram of the 16-bit multiplier design

In this experiment, GDSPOM reassigned 352 out of total 1715 cells from HVT to SVT to satisfy the 500MHz speed constraint. Fig. 9 shows the block diagram and Fig. 10 shows the schematic view of the 16-bit dual-$V_t$ multiplier design optimized by GDSPOM to have HVT (blue) and SVT (red) cells. Note that yellow paths in Fig. 10 are originally timing violated paths.

A path between input $IN2_8$ (the 8th multiplicand bit) and output $P_{23}$ (the 23rd product bit) is randomly selected to demonstrate how the swapping of the cell types has been used to resolve the timing violation. Fig. 11 shows this path in the HVT multiplier, whose data arrival time is 2.21 ns, which does not meet the 500MHz operating

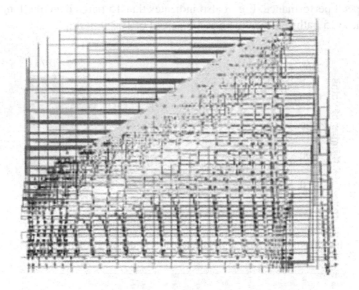

**Fig. 10.** Schematic view of the 16-bit multiplier design

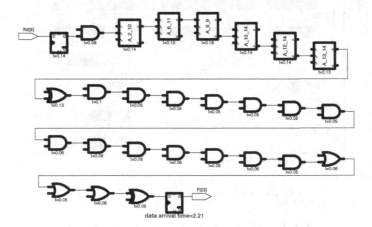

**Fig. 11.** Timing path from IN28 to P23 in an all-HVT multiplier

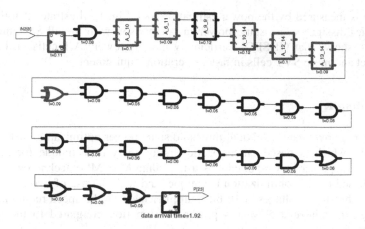

**Fig. 12.** Timing path from $IN2_8$ to $P_{23}$ in a dual-threshold multiplier

frequency specification. The arrival time of each cell shown in the figure includes net delay time. Fig. 12 shows the same path in the dual-$V_t$ multiplier. After performing GDSPOM flow, seven cells have been swapped from HVT to SVT. The data arrival time of this path becomes 1.92 ns, which meets the operating frequency constraint.

Among three multipliers using all-HVT, all-SVT, and dual-threshold HVT/SVT cells, the all-HVT one has the least leakage power consumption of 51 uW, but can only operate in 400MHz frequency. All-SVT multiplier has the highest leakage power of 280 uW. Using the dual-threshold HVT/SVT cells adopting the GDSPOM flow, the power consumption of dual-$V_t$ multiplier is 139 uW, which is 50% less than the all-SVT one, and meets the operating frequency constraint.

## 6  Discussion

To further assess the performance of this dual-threshold voltage design flow, multipliers meeting different operating frequencies are generated, and their static power

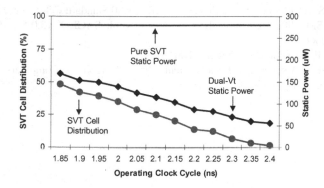

**Fig. 13.** Power consumption of the 16-bit multiplier using all-HVT cells, all-SVT cells, and dual-threshold HVT/SVT cells operating at different frequencies

dissipation is measured by the power estimation tool. Fig. 13 illustrates that the dual-$V_t$ multiplier dissipates less static power in comparison with the all-SVT multiplier one. It also shows that GDSPOM efficiently assigns fewer SVT cells in the lower speed target and more SVT cells in faster operation requirement.

# 7  Conclusion

In this paper, a novel gate-level dual-threshold static power optimization methodology (GDSPOM), which is based on the static timing analysis technique for designing high-speed low-power SOC applications using 90nm MTCMOS technology has been reported. Based on this optimization technique, and with the use of two cell libraries of different threshold voltages, a 16-bit multiplier meeting the speed requirement has been designed to have a 50% less power consumption compared to the all low-threshold voltage one.

# References

1.  J. Kuo & J. Lou, "Low-Voltage CMOS VLSI Circuits," Wiley, New York, 1999
2.  J. Kao, S. Narendra, A. Chandrakasan, "MTCMOS Hierarchical Sizing Based on Mutual Exclusive Discharge Patterns," Design Automation Conference Proc, pp. 495-500, June 1998
3.  K. Usami, N. Kawabe, M. Koizumi, K. Seta, T. Furusawa, "Automated Selective Multi-Threshold Design for Ultra-Low Standby Applications," Low Power Electronics and Design Conference Proc, pp. 202-206, 2002
4.  L. Wei, Z. Chen, M. Johnson, K. Roy, and V. De, "Design and Optimization of Low Voltage High Performance Dual Threshold CMOS Circuits," Design Automation Conference Proc, pp. 489-494, June 1998
5.  D. Samanta, A. Pal, "Optimal Dual-VT Assignment for Low-voltage Energy-Constrained CMOS Circuits," International Conference on VLSI Design, pp. 193-198, January 2002
6.  Q. Wang, S. Vrudhula, "Algorithms for Minimizing Standby Power in Deep Submicrometer, Dual-Vt CMOS Circuits," IEEE Trans. Computer-Aided Design of IC and Systems, Vol. 21, No. 3, pp.306-318, March 2002
7.  Artisan, "TSMC 90nm CLN90G Process SAGE-X v3.0 Standard Cell Library Databook."
8.  Artisan, "TSMC 90nm CLN90G HVt Process 1.0-Volt SAGE-X v3.0 Standard Cell Library Databook."
9.  Synopsys, "PrimeTime User Guide," v2004.12
10.  C. S. Wallace, "A suggestion for a fast multiplier", IEEE Trans. Computers, Vol. EC-13, pp. 14-17, February 1964

# Low Power Distance Measurement Unit for Real-Time Hardware Motion Estimators

Tiago Dias[2,3], Nuno Roma[1,3], and Leonel Sousa[1,3]

[1] IST / [2] ISEL / [3] INESC-ID
Rua Alves Redol, 9
1000-029 Lisboa, Portugal
{Tiago.Dias, Nuno.Roma, Leonel.Sousa}@inesc-id.pt

**Abstract.** Real-time video encoding often demands hardware motion estimators, even when fast search algorithms are adopted. With the widespread usage of portable handheld devices that support digital video coding, low power consideration becomes a central limiting constraint. Consequently, adaptive search algorithms and special hardware architectures have been recently proposed to perform motion estimation in portable and autonomous devices. This paper proposes a new efficient carry-free arithmetic unit to compute the minimum distance in block matching motion estimation. The operation of the proposed unit is independent of the adopted search algorithm and of the used prediction error metric, simultaneously speeding up motion estimation and significantly reducing the power consumption. Moreover, its low latency is particularly advantageous when partial distance techniques are applied to further reduce the power consumption. Experimental results show that the proposed unit allows to reduce the computation time in about 40% and it consumes 50% less power than commonly adopted architectures.

## 1 Introduction

Motion Estimation (ME) is a central operation in video encoding, in order to exploit temporal redundancy in sequences of images. However, it is also by far the most computationally costly part of a video CoDec [1]. Among the several algorithms that have been proposed, the Block-Matching Motion Estimation (BME) is the most adopted method. Using this strategy the distance between each block of the reference frame and a set of candidate prediction blocks, defined within reduced areas of the previous frame (search areas), is computed to obtain the corresponding motion vector (MV). Nevertheless, even though the complexity of this method depends on the adopted distance metric and on the selected search algorithm, only hardware solutions are usually able to fulfill the real-time requirement.

In the last few years, it has been widely claimed that the first generation of search algorithms often reveals to be inadequate for portable devices, powered by batteries. Examples of these algorithms are the optimal Full-Search Block-Matching (FSBM) and other non-optimal but faster search algorithms, such as

J. Vounckx, N. Azemard, and P. Maurine (Eds.): PATMOS 2006, LNCS 4148, pp. 247–255, 2006.

the Three-Step-Search (3SS) [2], the Four-Step-Search (4SS) [3] and the Diamond Search (DS) [4]. Therefore, more efficient search algorithms have been developed by taking advantage of temporal and spacial correlations of the MVs in order to adapt and optimize the search pattern, thus avoiding unnecessary computations and memory accesses. Examples of these recent fast search techniques are the Motion Vector Field Adaptive Search Technique (MVFAST) and the Enhanced Predictive Zonal Search (EPZS) [5,6].

At the same time, several specific architectures have also been proposed to implement the different search algorithms [7,8]. Very recently, an Application Specific Instruction Set Processor (ASIP) was proposed for adaptive video motion estimation [9]. The common feature of all these hardware architectures is that they all use, at their processing core, an arithmetic unit specially designed to compute the distance metric between the current block and the considered prediction blocks, as well as to compare these distances in order to find the best match.

The investigation of efficient hardware units for estimating MVs has been mainly focused either on the implementation of the overall algorithms [7] or on the computation of the distance metrics (such as the Sum of Absolute Differences (SAD) [10] or the Mean Square Error (MSE)). However, it has not yet been proposed any efficient structure that avoids the usage of carry-propagate type adders to compute and compare the obtained values of the distance measure, in order to obtain the minimum distance value and thus the best match. This issue presents several drawbacks, since carry-propagate type adders are rather slow units with a high cost. Furthermore, the application of the usual alternative accelerating techniques, such as the application of pipelining, can often be disadvantageous for fast BME, since the data dependency in fast and adaptive algorithms implies sequentiality in the processing.

In this paper it is proposed a very efficient hardware unit that avoids the usage of carry-propagate units to compute and compare any considered distance metric. This unit exhibits null latency, reduced cost and power consumption, speeding up the evaluation of the BME condition by using carry-free arithmetic. Due to its null latency, the proposed unit can also be directly used to apply some of the power-saving techniques that have been proposed in the last few years, which evaluate the partial measures and disable a sub-set of the architecture modules in order to further reduce the power consumption [11].

## 2    Block-Matching Motion-Estimation Algorithm

In the widely adopted BME algorithm, for each macroblock of $N \times N$ pixels of the current image $(z)$ it must be found the best matching prediction block in a reference frame $(\hat{z})$, according to the considered search algorithm and the used matching criterion. The MSE and the SAD are the most frequently used matching metrics. For a given distance metric $(D)$, eq. 1 is computed for each candidate MV $v$ and the set of pixels $\gamma$ in a macroblock:

$$D = \sum_{(i,j)\in\gamma} f(z_{i,j} - \hat{z}_{v_i+i,v_j+j}) \; ; \; f : | \; | \; (\text{SAD}), \; [\;]^2 \; (\text{MSE}) \left(z_{i,j} - \hat{z}_{v_i+i,v_j+j}\right)^2$$

(1)

The BME algorithms then determine the MV corresponding to the "best match" ($V$) for a given search region ($\zeta$) and a specific metric:

$$V(\zeta,\gamma) = \underset{v\in\zeta}{\arg\min}\; \{D(v,\gamma)\}.$$

(2)

By considering a single iteration, i.e., a single candidate block $t$, this condition can be stated as:

$$V(\zeta^t,\gamma) = \begin{cases} V(\zeta^{t-1},\gamma) & \text{if } D(v^t,\gamma) > D(v^{t-1},\gamma) \\ v^t(\gamma) & \text{otherwise.} \end{cases}$$

(3)

The optimal solution of this algorithm, given by the FSBM approach, is provided by searching over all possible candidate macroblocks in $\zeta$ and by using a metric that considers all pixels ($\gamma$) of the macroblock. To achieve fast BME, not only can the search range be restricted to a subset of vectors, but also can the matching criteria be simplified by only computing partial metrics [12]. Partial-distance search techniques [13] are particular cases of these fast schemes.

## 3    Proposed Architecture

The traditional hardware architecture of a generic block matching motion estimator is presented in fig. 1. Such structure is usually composed by:

- an arbitrary *metric computation unit*, where either the SAD, MSE or any other distance metric is computed using the input pixels of both the current and previous frames;
- an *accumulation unit*, that accumulates, one at a time, the computed partial values for the considered metric;
- a *best-match detection unit*, which compares the value of the considered metric for the prediction macroblock under processing with the value obtained for the best matching macroblock that was found up to the current instant.

As it is presented in this block diagram, carry-save adder structures are often used in the implementation of the *accumulation unit*, in order to avoid the introduction of carry-propagation delays in the accumulation critical path, thus maximizing the operating frequency. In fig. 2 it is presented the hardware structure that is traditionally adopted to update the MV in each iteration of the BME algorithm. Such structure is usually composed by a fast carry-propagate adder (e.g.: carry-look-ahead structure), to add the sum ($S^t$) and the carry ($C^t$) bit-vectors obtained from the *accumulation unit*, and a fast carry-propagate subtracter, to compare the current distance metric with the best one previously obtained. This subtracter issues the "Greater or Equal" (GE) signal, that will be used by the state machine to update the Best-Metric Register, corresponding to the current MV.

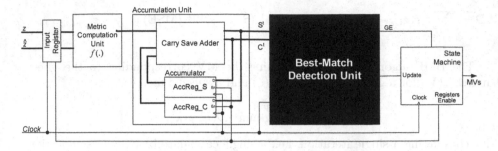

**Fig. 1.** Traditional hardware architecture of a generic block matching motion estimator

Nevertheless, this solution still reveals to be somewhat inefficient, since it does not prevent the need to use a carry-propagate adder structure in the best-match detector in order to compare the current metric value with the best one previously obtained. As an example, if power-saving techniques that abort the computation of the distance measure as soon as the partial value of the distance metric is greater that the one corresponding to the best matching macroblock [11] are applied, the carry-propagate structures present at the best-match detector will introduce a significant delay in the overall data-path, thus greatly conditioning the operation frequency.

To derive more efficient hardware structures to compute eqs. 1 and 2 in real-time, the following two specific properties of BME can be applied:

**Property 1** - the distance $D$ is a natural number, non-fractional and always positive;

**Property 2** - the ultimate goal of BME is to compute the MV $V$ (eq. 2) corresponding to the minimum distance measure ($D$), and not the value of $D$ itself.

*Property 1* can be used to simplify the comparison in each iteration $t$ of eq. 3 provided that the strategy proposed in [10] to compare two $m$-bit numbers is also applied. By adopting a simplified notation, with $D^t \equiv D(v^t, \gamma)$, it can be shown that:

$$D^t - D^{t-1} > 0 \iff 2^m - 1 - D^{t-1} + D^t > 2^m - 1 \iff \overline{D^{t-1}} + D^t \geq 2^m \quad (4)$$

To perform this comparison, it can be easily shown that only the carry out of the most significant bit ($m-1$) must be computed, which corresponds to a much faster and simpler logic circuit than any carry-propagate subtracter required by the traditional architecture (see fig. 2).

On the other hand, *Property 2* provides the possibility to choose a representation for $D$ that is more suitable to evaluate the condition stated in eq. 2. In fact, if the carry-save representation is also used to compute eq. 4, a single and unique representation can be applied to compute both eqs. 1 and 2, thus avoiding the inevitable penalty associated with carry-propagate operations.

Consequently, by storing the pair of carry-save $(m-1)$ bit vectors $\{C^{t-1}, S^{t-1}\}$, representing $D^{t-1}$, eq. 4 can be rewritten using the corresponding bit vectors

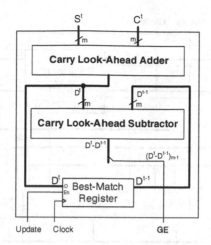

$S^t$    $C^t$

**Fig. 2.** Traditional hardware structure of the *best-match detection unit*

computed at iteration $t$:

$$D^t - D^{t-1} > 0 \tag{5}$$

$$\Leftrightarrow \{C^t, S^t\} > \{C^{t-1}, S^{t-1}\} \tag{6}$$

$$\Leftrightarrow 2^m - 1 - (S^{t-1}) + 2^m - 1 - (2 \times C^{t-1}) + S^t + 2 \times C^t \geq 2^{m+1} - 1 \tag{7}$$

By replacing each multiplication by a left shift ($<< 1$) and each subtraction by the corresponding one's complement value, eq. 7 can be written as:

$$1\#\overline{S^{t-1}}_{m-2:0} + \left(\overline{C^{t-1} << 1}\right)_{m-1:1} \#1 + (C^t << 1)_{m-1:1}\#1 + S^t \geq 2^{m+1} \tag{8}$$

where $\#$ denotes the concatenation operation and $(Z)_{y:x}$ the extraction of bits $x$ to $y$ of a binary number $Z$.

Hence, if the result of the left hand-side of inequality 8 is represented in the carry-save format ($\{C, S\}$), it can be shown that only bitwise logic operations and carry-free arithmetic are required for its evaluation. Once again, to perform the comparison only the carry-out of the most significant bit $m$ must be computed, instead of the full sum value ($S + 2 \times C$).

In fig. 3 it is depicted the proposed hardware structure for the *best-match detection unit*, directly obtained from the previous equations. With this new architecture, the carry-propagate type adder and subtracter of fig. 2 are replaced by two carry-save adders and a simple carry-out detector. This detector computes the carry-out signal that will be used to obtain the "Greater or Equal" (GE) signal, supplied to the main state machine of the motion estimator. It can be implemented using only the carry-generate descending branch of a carry-look-ahead adder structure, which provides a fast computation of the carry-out bit of two operands addition without actually computing the addition result.

It is also worth noting that the proposed architecture can still be applied with increased advantages to compare the partial computed distance metrics

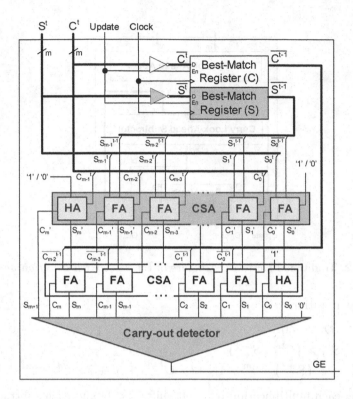

**Fig. 3.** Proposed carry-free hardware structure for the *best-match detection unit*

with a predefined threshold $(T)$. This feature is particularly useful in the implementation of some of the last generation partial-distance search algorithms and techniques with strict power restrictions [13], which have been recently proposed to perform ME in portable and handheld devices:

$$\overline{T}_{m-1:0} + (C^t << 1)_{m-1:0} + S^t \geq 2^m \Rightarrow \boldsymbol{V}(\zeta^t, \gamma) = \boldsymbol{V}(\zeta^{t-1}, \gamma) \qquad (9)$$

The amount of hardware that is required for this approach is approximately one half of the original one, since only the components corresponding to the shaded blocks in fig. 3 are used.

## 4    Performance Evaluation

The performance evaluation of the proposed arithmetic unit for computing the minimum distance in BME was assessed using experimental results obtained for ASIC implementations of the considered structure. To do so, both the traditional and the proposed architectures of such unit were specified in the IEEE-VHDL hardware description language using fully structural and parameterizable descriptions of their structure and circuits based only on three simple 2-input logic gates: AND, OR and EX-OR. The fast carry-propagate adder and subtracter of

**Table 1.** Implementation results obtained using the StdCell library based on a $0.18\mu$m CMOS process

(a) Traditional architecture

| Structure | F [$MHz$] | Area [$\mu m^2$] | Power [$mW$] |
|---|---|---|---|
| Datapath | 294.99 | 12269 | 12.75 |
| Best-Match Detection Unit | 363.64 | 7025 | 14.47 |

(b) Proposed architecture

| Structure | F [$MHz$] | Area [$\mu m^2$] | Power [$mW$] |
|---|---|---|---|
| Datapath | 416.67 | 14213 | 13.78 |
| Best-Match Detection Unit | 497.51 | 8968 | 14.62 |

the traditional architecture, see fig. 2, were implemented using carry-look-ahead adders with binary tree architectures [14].

The implementation in ASIC was performed using Synopsys synthesis tools and a high performance StdCell library from Virtual Silicon Technology Inc., which is based on a $0.18\mu$m CMOS process from UMC [15]. The two architectures were synthesized for the typical operating conditions, $V_{dd} = 1.8V$ and $T = 25\,^oC$, and using the "suggested 20k" wire model. Moreover, some constraints were also imposed to the synthesis tool in order to achieve a minimum area solution.

The obtained experimental results for the two implementations demonstrate the superiority of the proposed architecture over the traditional structure. From table 1 it can be seen that the proposed architecture allows for a reduction of about 40% in the computation time with a modest increase of the implementation area, about 16%. Nevertheless, despite such increase the two circuits present very similar power consumption requirements. In fact, when operating at its maximum operating frequency (416.67 MHz) the proposed architecture consumes only more 8% than the traditional circuit, also operating at its maximum operating frequency (294.99 MHz). However, such high operating frequencies are not required for low power digital video coding applications, such as mobile and portable handheld devices that use non-optimal search algorithms [2,3,4,5,6]. For example, to encode a CIF frame in real-time using the 4SS [3] algorithm the ME circuit does not need to operate at a frequency higher than 150 MHz. Consequently, by considering the proposed and the traditional architectures operating at the same frequency, the maximum allowed operating frequency of the traditional one, it can be shown that the proposed structure allows a significant reduction in the power consumption requirements, as depicted in table 2. The power consumption of the *best-match detection unit* is reduced by more than 60% and the reduction for the complete datapath is about 50%.

The proposed architecture is able to provide even greater power saving rates when used as a control mechanism to avoid needless calculations in the computation of the best match for a macroblock [13]. Such computations can be avoided by disabling all the logic and arithmetic units used in the computation of the adopted matching metric as soon as the partial value of the distance metric for the candidate block under processing exceeds the one already computed for the

**Table 2.** Comparative evaluation of the power consumption of the traditional and of the proposed architectures

| Structure | Traditional Architecture | Proposed Architecture | |
|---|---|---|---|
| Datapath | $12.75mW$ | $6.83mW$ | 54% |
| Best-Match Detection Unit | $14.47mW$ | $5.38mW$ | 37% |

current macroblock. On average, this technique allows to avoid up to 50% of the required computations [11]. Consequently, a ME circuit using such technique and the proposed architecture for the *best-match detection unit* is able to reduce in up to 75% its power consumption requirements.

## 5    Conclusions

By analyzing the particular computational characteristics of block-matching motion-estimation, a complete carry-free arithmetic formulation was derived and an improved architecture was proposed for computing the minimum distance in block-matching motion-estimation algorithms. Experimental results show the practical importance of this novel structure in the design of efficient real-time motion estimators, regardless of the search algorithms and the matching metrics adopted by such circuits. By using the proposed arithmetic unit, it is not only possible to reduce the computation time in about 40%, with only a modest penalty in the cost of about 16%, but also to maintain similar power consumption requirements. Moreover, for low power digital video coding applications, such as mobile and portable handheld devices, where fast and adaptive search algorithms are used, the proposed architecture provides a very significant reduction of about 50% in the power consumption of the motion estimators. Since the proposed arithmetic unit exhibits no latency, it can also be directly used to avoid unnecessary calculations in the computation of the minimum distance value, by using partial distance values to disable specific hardware blocks of the motion estimators. In such cases, the proposed architecture is expected to reduce even further, to a minimum of 25%, the power consumption requirements of motion estimators for real-time video encoding.

## References

1. Richardson, I.: H.264 and MPEG-4 Video Compression: Video Coding for Next Generation Multimedia. Wiley (2003)
2. Li, R., Zeng, B., Liou, M.L.: A new three-step search algorithm for block motion estimation. IEEE Transactions on Circuits and Systems for Video Technology 4(4) (1994) 438–442
3. Po, L.M., Ma, W.C.: A novel four-step search algorithm for fast block motion estimation. IEEE Transactions on Circuits and Systems for Video Technology 6(3) (1996) 313–317
4. Zhu, S., Ma, K.K.: A new diamond search algorithm for fast block-matching motion estimation. IEEE Transactions on Image Processing 9(2) (2000) 287–290

5. Tourapis, A., Au, O., Liou, M.: Predictive motion vector field adaptive search technique (PMVFAST) - enhancing block based motion estimation. In: Proceedings of SPIE - Visual Communications and Image Processing (VCIP), San Jose, CA (2001) 883–892
6. Tourapis, A.: Enhanced predictive zonal search for single and multiple frame motion estimation. In: Proceedings of SPIE - Visual Communications and Image Processing (VCIP), San Jose, CA (2002) 1069–1079
7. Roma, N., Sousa, L.: Efficient and configurable full search block matching processors. IEEE Transactions on Circuits and Systems for Video Technology **12**(12) (2002) 1160–1167
8. Saponara, S., Fanucci, L.: Data-adaptive motion estimation algorithm and VLSI architecture design for low-power video systems. IEE Proceedings Computers and Digital Techniques **151**(1) (2004) 51– 59
9. Momcilovic, S., Dias, T., Roma, N., Sousa, L.: Application specific instruction set processor for adaptive video motion estimation. In: 9th Euromicro Conference on Digital System Design: Architectures, Methods and Tools - DSD'2006. (2006)
10. Vassiliadis, S., Hakkennes, E., Wong, S., Pechanek, G.: The sum-absolute-difference motion estimation accelerator. In: Proc. of the 24th Euromicro Conference. (1998) 559–566
11. Sousa, L., Roma, N.: Low-power array architectures for motion estimation. In: Workshop on Multimedia Signal Processing - MMSP'99, IEEE (1999) 679–684
12. Lengwehasatit, K., Ortega, A.: Probabilistic partial-distance fast matching algorithms for motion estimation. IEEE Trans. on Circuits for Video Techn. **11**(2) (2001) 139–152
13. Sousa, L.: A general method for eliminating redundant computations in video coding. IEE Electronics Letters **36**(4) (2000) 306–307
14. Roma, N., Dias, T., Sousa, L.: Fast adder architectures: Modeling and experimental evaluation. In: Proc. of the Conference on Design of Circuits and Integrated Systems (DCIS'03). (2003) 367–372
15. Virtual Silicon Technology Inc., Tech. Rep. v2.4: eSi-Route/11$^{TM}$ High Performance Standard Cell Library (UMC 0.18$\mu$m). (2001)

# Reducing Energy Dissipation of Wireless Sensor Processors Using Silent-Store-Filtering MoteCache

Gurhan Kucuk and Can Basaran

Department of Computer Engineering, Yeditepe University,
34755 Istanbul, Turkey
{gkucuk, cbasaran}@cse.yeditepe.edu.tr

**Abstract.** Wireless sensor networks (WSNs) gained increasing interests in recent years; since, they allow wide range of applications from environmental monitoring, to military and medical applications. As most of the sensor nodes (a.k.a. motes) are battery operated, they have limited lifetime, and user intervention is not feasible for most of the WSN applications. This study proposes a technique to reduce the energy dissipation of the processor component of the sensor nodes. We utilize a tiny cache-like structure called MoteCache between the CPU and the SRAM to cache the most recently used data values as well as to filter silent-store instructions which write values that exactly match the values that are already stored at the memory address that is being written. A typical WSN application may sense and work on constant data values for long durations, when the environmental conditions are not changing rapidly. This common behavior of WSN applications considerably improves our energy savings. The optimal configuration of MoteCache reduces the total node energy by 24.7% on the average across a variety of simulated sensor benchmarks. The average lifetime of the nodes is also improved by 46% on the average for processor-intensive applications. Using the proposed technique, the lifetime of the nodes that run communication-intensive applications, such as TinyDB and Surge, is also improved as much as 14%.

## 1 Introduction

Wireless sensor networks (WSNs) became a leading research and development area arose from the field of ad hoc networking research. Increased research activity is due to the potential for significant monitoring applications on various properties of matter such as heat, humidity, pressure, acceleration, smoke and light. This new technology combines sensing, computation, and communication into a tiny device (a.k.a. mote) which is typically provided with an embedded microprocessor and a small amount of memory. Consequently, the most difficult resource constraint to meet becomes energy consumption of these devices, since the energy is directly related to many critical parameters such as lifetime, scalability, response time and effective sampling frequency of the network.

The introduction of a small-scale operating system (TinyOS [1]) and more complex applications considerably increased the energy consumption of the processor and

J. Vounckx, N. Azemard, and P. Maurine (Eds.): PATMOS 2006, LNCS 4148, pp. 256–266, 2006.

the memory system of these tiny devices. In [2], the authors show that the processor/memory component constitutes 35% of the total energy budget of the MICA2 platform while running *Surge*, a TinyOS monitoring application. In [3], the authors estimate similar energy values when running a TinyDB query reporting light and accelerometer readings once every minute. In [4], the researchers study the data compression algorithms for saving energy in sensor nodes, and find that the energy consumption of the processor/memory component for running the compression algorithms is so high that sending raw data without any compression instead is a much more feasible solution. Similarly, today most of the applications available in the sensor networks domain avoid extensive computations and choose to transfer raw data to server machines to increase the lifetime of the sensor nodes.

Moreover, the applications that are executed by sensor nodes have periodic behavior. Especially, monitoring applications, such as *Surge*, may sense and work on constant data for long durations. Similarly, a continuous TinyDB query may initiate sensor nodes to work on data with temporal and spatial locality for a long time. In this paper, we propose *MoteCache* architecture to exploit these types of characteristic behavior. By caching commonly used data in a small number of latches (*MoteCache*), we show that we can considerably reduce the energy dissipation of the WSN processors. In this study, we mainly focus on MICA2 platform; however, the proposed technique is platform-independent, and can be easily applied to other sensor platforms such as TelosB, Tmote Sky and EYES sensor nodes.

We begin by presenting an overview of current processor/memory architecture of MICA2 sensor nodes in Section 2. We present the details of MoteCache design in Section 3. The simulation methodology is given in Section 4 followed by the presentation and the discussion of the results in Section 5. Finally, we discuss the related work in Section 6, and conclude our study in Section 7.

## 2 Related Work

In the literature, there are various proposals that target energy-efficient microprocessors for wireless sensor nodes [5, 6, 7]. However, to our best knowledge, this is a unique study that proposes architecture-independent extensions to the existing commercially available, general-purpose microcontrollers that are used by sensor nodes.

In [5], the authors present SNAP/LE, an event-driven microprocessor for sensor networks. They avoid the TinyOS overhead by their asynchronous, event-driven approach. In [6], the authors seek to fully leverage the event-driven nature of applications. They study the application domain of sensor networks and they seek to replace the basic functionality of a general-purpose microcontroller with a modularized, event-driven system.

In [8], the authors reveal that significant benefits can be gained by detecting and removing silent store instructions. They propose free silent store squashing and successfully increase the processor performance by 11%, on the average. In this study, on the other hand, we choose to move to a completely different direction, and utilize a similar mechanism to reduce the energy consumption of the microcontrollers that are used in wireless sensor devices.

## 3 Current State of the Art

In this paper, we study the MICA2 platform manufactured by Crossbow Inc. [9]. The platform includes an AVR-RISC processor, ATmega128L. The AVR architecture has two main memory spaces, 4Kx8 bytes of SRAM data memory and 64Kx16 bytes of flash program memory space. Additionally, the Atmega128 features an EEPROM memory for data storage. All three memory spaces are linear and regular [10]. Up until now, there are only a few applications making use of EEPROM memory. Therefore, in this paper, we mainly focus on the energy reduction of SRAM storage component.

Figure 1 shows the timing diagram of memory read/write operations for the SRAM structure of the AVR. Each memory read or memory write operation takes two cycles to complete. In the first clock cycle, T1, the memory address is computed, and in the second clock cycle, T2, the actual memory access takes place.

The AVR architecture does not contain a cache structure. The reason behind this cacheless architecture becomes very clear, when we examine the timing diagram in Figure 1 in detail. The main idea to include a cache structure in any design is to increase the processor performance, and it is obvious that no cache structure may improve upon a 1-cycle-access SRAM. On the other hand, a cache structure may be beneficial from the energy/power point of view. A tiny cache structure may reduce the memory access energy by filtering most of the accesses to the main memory. In this study, we propose such cache structure, called MoteCache, for the same purpose. Moreover, we show that with a very small, additional complexity we can also use this cache structure to filter silent-store instructions which write values that exactly match the values that are already stored at the memory address that is being written.

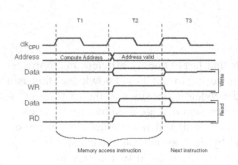

**Fig. 1.** On-chip Data SRAM access cycles

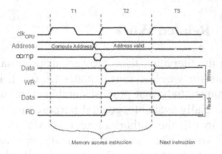

**Fig. 2.** Modified On-chip Data SRAM and MC access cycles

## 4 Memory with MoteCache

We now briefly review the design of memory with MoteCache (hereafter MC). In a memory with MC, each row consists of data buffers and an associative CAM (content-addressable memory) for holding the addresses or the tags (parts of the addresses) corresponding to the contents of these buffers. The idea is to cache data values of the N most recently accessed addresses. The design presented here is a generalization of the designs of [11, 12]. By using independent CAMs for more than one way, we can improve the hit ratio of the MC. In this paper, we study three types of MC configuration:

**1) Direct-Mapped MoteCache (DMMC):** This configuration mimics the behavior of an ordinary direct-mapped cache. Since, the data SRAM of AVR microcontroller contains a single byte at each line, the direct-mapped cache is organized to contain a single byte at each of its sets. In this configuration, we do not need to have a CAM structure, since we can locate the required line using a small line decoder. Consequently, the corresponding tag comparator of that line may be activated to find if it is a cache hit (MC-hit) or a miss (MC-miss).

**2) Set-Associative MoteCache (SAMC):** In order to reduce the possible conflict misses of DMMC configuration; we also decided to try the set associative cache configuration. This configuration is similar to a standard set-associative cache configuration, and requires the activation of more comparators in a single access. Since, this configuration requires less number of lines compared to the DMMC configuration for the same buffer size, it enables us to utilize a smaller decoder.

**3) Fully-Associative MoteCache (FAMC):** This configuration is the extreme cache configuration that activates all the tag/address comparators for each memory access. In this configuration, a MC-miss results in no-match situation in all of these tag comparators. Incase of a MC-hit, only one of the comparators will have a full-match situation. After careful observation of this phenomena, for this configuration, we prefered to use Dissipate-on-Match Comparators (DMCs) proposed in [13]. Basically, DMCs dissipate power when there is a full-match situation, whereas traditional comparators dissipate power when there is a mismatch situation. The rest of the match cases dissipate negligible amount of power in both types of comparators.

### 4.1   Access to MoteCache

A read access in the MC structure proceeds as follows:

**Step 1. MoteCache Tag Comparison:** After the address computation, the address number issued by the CPU is compared associatively with the address numbers associated with the contents of the MoteCache. If an associative match is detected ("MC-hit"), the scheduled readout of the memory, for the next clock cycle, is cancelled, potentially saving energy wasted in reading out the row (again) from the memory. Again, for the DMMC configuration, there is a single comparison at the selected MC set.

When the associative match using the CAM fails, the memory access continue in the next cycle and the data is read out into a MC entry selected as a victim, based on some replacement policy. In our simulations, we studied least recently used (LRU) replacement policy, since it is feasible to implement it for small number of entries.

**Step 2. Data Steering:** On a tag match, the desired data is steered out from the corresponding MC entry. On a mismatch, a row from a victim way is eventually replaced with the tag and data value corresponding to the target. Of course, if we use DMMC configuration, there is no victim selection (i.e., the conflicted line automatically becomes the victim line).

Writing to a MC entry has analogous steps, followed by a step that installs the update into the tag and data part of the corresponding MC entry. Here, we only study the writeback policy, since our initial experiments showed that write-through policy is not suitable for an energy-aware design.

Figure 2 shows the modified timing diagram for the proposed architecture. Notice that, at the end of the first clock cycle, T1, there is a comparison latency that compares all the tags of the MC set with the computed address[1]. According to the outcome of the tag comparison process, either MC or SRAM is accessed.

Energy savings result in the MC as locality of reference guarantees that there is a good chance of producing a MC-hit. As our result section shows later, using just 8 entries for a 4-way SAMC, the hit rate is in excess of 82% (see Section 5) on the average.

## 4.2  Silent-Store Filtering

A recent study notes that many store instructions write values that actually match the values that are already stored at the memory address that is being written [8]. These store instructions are called *silent stores*, since they have no effect on machine state. Detecting and filtering silent stores may considerably improve the lifetime of WSNs. Our experiments show that WSN applications have a high potential for introducing silent store instructions, since they generally work on sensed data that may stay constant for long durations. Figure 3 shows the percentages of silent store instructions in our simulated benchmarks. Across all simulated WSN benchmarks, the average percentage of silent stores is 80.5%.

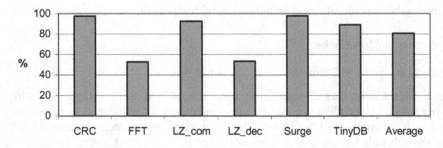

**Fig. 3.** Percentages of silent stores in WSN benchmarks

We propose to add another functionality to the *dirty-bit* in our writeback Mote-Cache for detecting and filtering silent stores. Therefore, the *dirty-bit* is renamed to *dirty&noisy-bit* (or DN-bit in short.) Hereafter, we writeback data value to SRAM

---

[1] Notice that, we assume that the address computation process may be completed a little earlier than the original design. This is possible, since the microprocessors used by the sensor nodes have very low frequency (approx. 7 MHz). Therefore, we assume large clock cycle periods provided by these processors make small tasks such as tag comparison possible in the same clock cycle. However, this is not a strict requirement for the success of our solution. Actually, WSNs may easily tolerate a small increase in processor cycle time for serializing address computation and MoteCache tag comparison in cycle T1, since performance is not their major concern, anyways.

when the data is *dirty* (i.e. it is modified) and also *noisy* (i.e. if the new data value is different than the one that was stored before.) To set the DN-bit, we need additional 8-bit data value comparators at each line of MoteCache structure.

A write access in the silent-store filtering MC structure proceeds as one of the two ways described below:

**1. MC-hit and Silent Store Detection:** After an MC-hit (i.e. when the MC has a copy of the data stored in the requested address), the data value to be written is compared with the data value of the corresponding MC line. If there is no match, we set the DN-bit of that MC line to indicate that this store instruction is not silent but *noisy*. On the other hand, if there is a match situation, then the corresponding DN-bit stays clean.

**2. MC-miss and MoteCache Writeback:** After a MC-miss, we select a victim line. Before replacing the victim line, we check its DN-bit to see if it is set. If it is so, we continue with the standard MC writeback procedure. Otherwise, we just replace the MC line and cancel the rest of the writeback process. This prevents us from executing an energy-hungry SRAM write operation, since we already know that MC and SRAM data are in sync.

## 5 Simulation Methodology

We chose Avrora, The AVR Simulation and Analysis Framework, [14] as our simulation platform, since it accurately models ATmega128L processor of MICA2 platform, and also simulates sensor networks in various topologies. For network-based benchmarks (Surge and TinyDB), a three node network topology is used. Table 1 gives the details of the benchmarks used for this study:

Table 1. WSN benchmarks details

| Benchmark | Size in ROM (bytes) | Size in RAM (bytes) | Execution Time (mins) |
|---|---|---|---|
| CRC | 1072 | 1492 | 5 |
| FFT | 3120 | 1332 | 5 |
| LZ77 Compression | 2700 | 486 | 5 |
| LZ77 Decompression | 1228 | 356 | 5 |
| Surge | 17120 | 1928 | 50 |
| TinyDB | 65050 | 3036 | 50 |

- CRC benchmark is a simple CRC32 algorithm continuously ran on 448 byte data. It contains send/receive operations triggered every 2 seconds to imitate typical WSN applications.
- FFT benchmark is a discrete Fourier Transform on 256 bytes of data. This transformation is executed within an infinite loop [15]. This benchmark also contains periodic send/receive calls.
- LZ77 compression is again enclosed in an infinite loop and works on 448 bytes of data taken from the header file of an *excel* file.
- LZ77 decompression is the decompression of the compressed data obtained from the LZ77 compression. This data is 330 bytes long. LZ77 applications do not use radio communication, and, therefore, represent CPU-intensive applications.

- Surge application ran on three nodes using Avrora sensor network simulation and the average of the result values is taken.
- TinyDB application is used to execute the query "select light from sensors". Two sampling periods were used: 128 and 1024 milliseconds.

### 5.1 Calculation of MC Energy Dissipation

The simulator records transitions at the level of bits for the processor/memory components. Coupled with energy per transition measurements obtained from the SPICE simulations of the actual component layouts for 0.35u CMOS technology (SRAM and MC, this allows us to estimate the overall energy dissipated within the processor. We modified the energy model of Avrora to accurately model very fine-grain, instruction-level energy dissipation of the processor, and we test our benchmarks against MC configurations implemented using Dissipate-on-Match (DMC) comparators [13]. For accurate energy savings estimations, we consider detailed energy dissipations from such additional comparators (both for tag and data values), line decoders and LRU replacement logic.

## 6   Results and Discussions

Figure 4 shows the average energy savings on memory read/write operations in MC without the silent store filter. Note that, when we increase the MC size in both FAMC (first five configurations) and DMMC (configurations from 4x1 to 64x1), either comparator energy (in FAMC configurations) or decoder energy (in DMMC configurations) becomes the dominant factor and reduces our energy savings. In *LZ77_comp* benchmark, 1x64 configuration dissipates considerably more energy (31% more, to be exact) than the baseline case. Again, this is due to the activation of 64 comparators at each memory access.

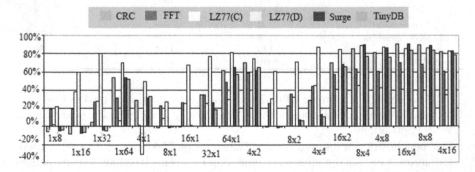

**Fig. 4.** Average savings on memory access energy dissipation for various MC configurations without the silent store filter (s x a, s: set no, a: associativity)

Figure 5 shows our energy savings for MC configurations with the silent store filter. Notice that, after enabling the silent store filter, even the smallest MC configurations

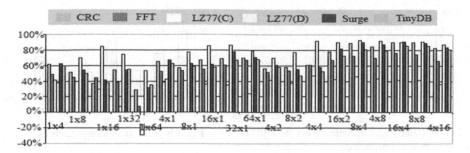

**Fig. 5.** Average savings on memory access energy dissipation for various MC configurations with the silent store filter (s x a, s: set no, a: associativity)

(1x4 and 4x1) save more than 52% of the memory access energy on the average. The optimal configuration is found to be the 8x4 configuration, since it gives similar savings compared to the MC configurations with twice of its size (78.7% of 8x4 vs. 79.2% of 16x4.)

In Figure 6, we show the hit rates to each MC configurations. The lowest hit rate is observed in the smallest FAMC configuration (i.e. 1x4) as 5.6%, on the average. On the other hand, the highest hit rate is again observed in the FAMC configuration with maximum size (i.e. 1x64) as 95.9%, on the average. The hit rate for the optimal configuration chosen above (i.e. 8x4) is 81.7%, on the average.

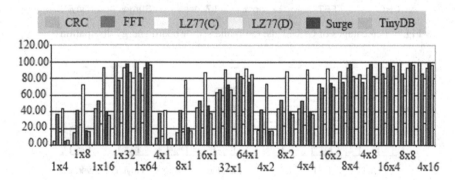

**Fig. 6.** MC hit rates to various MC configurations

As a result, SAMC (8x4) configuration yields to 78.7% energy savings (average) on memory access operations. However, although energy saving results of memory read/write operations provide means to identify the most effective MC configuration, they do not give the details about total processor energy savings. This consideration requires more figures such as percentage of memory read/write operations. Figure 7.a shows that, on the average, 36% of total instructions are memory read/write instructions. When we apply these figures to our optimal configuration, we found that the total processor energy savings turn out to be 49.7%, on the average (Figure 7.b)

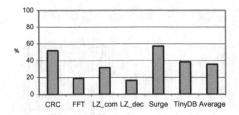

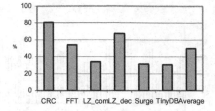

**Fig. 7.a.** Percentages of memory access instructions over total instructions

**Fig. 7.b.** Processor energy savings

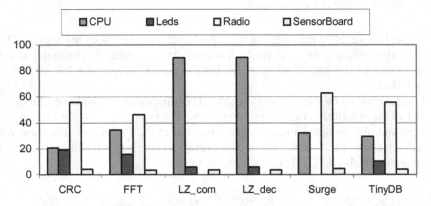

**Fig. 8.** Percentages of CPU, leds, radio and sensor board energy dissipation

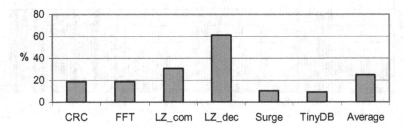

**Fig. 9.** Node-level energy savings and lifetime improvement percentages

Next, we identify the percentage of CPU energy dissipation over total energy dissipation of a sensor node to compute the possible lifetime increase with MC architecture. Figure 8 shows that, CPU energy constitutes 49.6% of the total energy dissipation across the simulated benchmarks, on the average. Using the percentages given in this graph, we computed the percentages of total energy savings of individual WSN nodes. We present the results in Figure 9. Notice that, for communication-intensive applications (*CRC, FFT, Surge* and *TinyDB*), the savings are 14.2%, on the average. Unfortunately, both *Surge* and *TinyDB* do not utilize low power listening mode; therefore, the results can be further improved through utilizing this mode in these applications. For computation-intensive applications (*LZ77_comp* and *LZ77_decomp*), the savings are 45.9%, on the average. The significant difference between LZ// compress and decompress applications is due to the significant hit rate difference between those applications. Notice that, these energy savings percentages are directly related to lifetime improvement of the node running that specific application.

## 7  Concluding Remarks

In this study, we proposed the architecture-independent MoteCache structure for reducing the energy dissipation of the processor/memory component of wireless sensor nodes. We studied various MoteCache configurations and found that 8-byte 4-way set-associative, silent-store-filtering configuration shows the best energy/lifetime characteristics. This optimal configuration reduces the node energy by 24.7% on the average across a variety of simulated sensor benchmarks. For the CPU-intensive applications, the lifetime of the nodes can be improved by 46%, on the average. The lifetime of the nodes that run communication-intensive applications, such as TinyDB and Surge, is also improved as much as 14%. We also believe that the savings will be greatly improved when low-power listening modes are utilized for these applications.

## References

1. Hill J., Szewczyk, R., Woo, A., Hollar, S., Culler, D., and Pister, K., "System Architecture Directions for Networked Sensors", in Proc. of the 9th Int'l. Conf. on Architectural Support for Programming Languages and Operating Systems (2000), ACM Press, pp. 93-104
2. Conner, W.S., Chhabra, J., Yarvis, M., Krishnamurthy, L., "Experimental Evaluation of Synchronization and Topology Control for In-Building Sensor Network Applications", in Proc. of WSNA'03, Sep. 2003
3. Madden, S., Franklin, M.J., Hellerstein, J.M., and Hong, W., "TinyDB: An Acquisitional Query Processing System for Sensor Networks", in ACM TODS, 2005
4. Polastre, J.R., "Design and Implementation of Wireless Sensor Networks for Habitat Monitoring", Research Project, University of California, Berkeley, 2003
5. .Ekanayake, V. et al, "An Ultra Low-Power Processor for Sensor Networks", in Proc. ASPLOS, Oct. 2004
6. Hempstead, M. et al, "An Ultra Low Power System Architecture for Sensor Network Applications", in the Proc. of 32nd ISCA'05, Wisconsin, USA, 2005
7. Warneke, B.A. and Pister, K.S., "An Ultra-Low Energy Microcontroller for Smart Dust Wireless Sensor Networks", in Proc. ISSCC, Jan. 2005
8. Lepak, K.M., Bell, G.B., and Lipasti, M.H., "Silent Stores and Store Value Locality", in IEEE Transactions on Computers, (50)11, Nov. 2001
9. Crossbow Technology, Inc., http://www.xbow.com
10. Atmel 8-bit AVR Microcontroller with 128K Bytes In-System Programmable Flash, http://www.atmel.com/dyn/resources/prod_documents/doc2467.pdf
11. Ghose, K. and Kamble, M., "Reducing Power in Superscalar Processor Caches Using Subbanking, Multiple Line Buffers and Bit-Line Segmentation", in ISLPED'99, 1999, pp.70-75
12. Kucuk, G. et al, "Energy-Efficient Register Renaming", in PATMOS'03, Torino, Italy, September 2003. Published as Lecture Notes in Computer Science, LNCS 2799, pp.219-228

13. Ponomarev, D. et al, "Energy-Efficient Comparators for Superscalar Datapaths", in IEEE Transactions on Computers, vol.53, No. 7, July 2004, pp.892-904
14. Titzer, B. et al, "Avrora: Scalable Sensor Network Simulation with Precise Timing", In 4th International Conference on Information Processing in Sensor Networks, 2005
15. Numerical recipes in C, Cornell University, Online book, http://www.library.cornell. edu/ nr/cbookcpdf.html

# A Comparison of Two Approaches Providing Data Encryption and Authentication on a Processor Memory Bus

Reouven Elbaz[1,2], Lionel Torres[1], Gilles Sassatelli[1],
Pierre Guillemin[2], Michel Bardouillet[2], and Albert Martinez[2]

[1] LIRMM UMR University of Montpellier II/ CNRS C5506,
34392 Montpellier, France
{elbaz, torres, sassatelli}@lirmm.fr
http://www.lirmm.fr
[2] STMicroelectronics, Advanced System Technology,
13106 Rousset, France
{pierre.guillemin, michel.bardouillet,
albert.martinez}@st.com
http://www.st.com

**Abstract.** This paper presents a comparison of two engines providing encryption and authentication of data exchanged between a System on Chip (SoC) and its external memory. The first engine is based on a generic composition scheme, meaning that each required security service, confidentiality and authentication, is guaranteed by a dedicated algorithm i.e. respectively AES (Advanced Encryption Standard) and CBC-MAC (Message Authentication Code). The second one, called PE-ICE (Parallelized Encryption and Integrity Checking Engine), uses AES encryption to provide both properties to data by adding the authentication capability to block cipher. Performance evaluations show that our scheme PE-ICE always outperforms the combination of AES encryption and CBC-MAC.

## 1 Introduction

The development of pervasive computing increases the need of security because the underlying private data and intellectual properties are usually transmitted over unsecured channel. Moreover today's embedded computing systems are considered as untrustworthy hosts since the owner, or anyone else who manages to get access, is a potential adversary.

One of the weakest points of such systems is the bus between the System on Chip (SoC) and the external memory which contains sensitive data (end users private data, software code…). Those data are usually exchanged in clear over the bus during software loading and execution. Therefore an adversary may probe this bus in order to read private data or retrieve software code (data privacy concern). Another possible attack relies on code injection (data integrity concern). A relevant example combining those two kinds of attacks is the one performs by Markus Kuhn [1], which consists in modifying the behavior of a software execution to obtain the plaintext version of the ciphered data stored in the off-chip memory.

J. Vounckx, N. Azemard, and P. Maurine (Eds.): PATMOS 2006, LNCS 4148, pp. 267–279, 2006.

Hardware protection must be provided to prevent such attacks and to guarantee a Private and authenticated Tamper Resistant (PTR) environment for application execution. This implies ensuring the data confidentiality and authenticity. In our context, the confidentiality security service is to prevent any useful information leaking from off-chip, whereas the authentication security service is to forbid execution of intentionally altered memory content.

In the domain of the security of the processor-memory communications, most of proposed engines in the literature [2] [3] [4] are based on generic composition schemes, i.e. one dedicated hardware-core (algorithm) per security property along with its own key. As a consequence, both processes are serialized which introduces an additional performance overhead.

Several new block encryption modes performing Authenticated Encryption (AE) were presented to the NIST (National Institute of Standards and Technology) standardization process [5]. Authenticated encryption scheme refers to a shared-key based transform whose goal is to provide both privacy and authenticity [9]. However, as for generic composition schemes such modes require two passes over the data (one for each security service). Moreover, no implementation or evaluation of authenticated encryption modes exists concerning our application domain.

The proposed engine, PE-ICE [6] [7] for Parallel Encryption and Integrity Checking[1] Engine, is not a new authenticated encryption mode but a dedicated solution to processor-memory bus transactions. It has been designed to optimize latencies introduced by the hardware security mechanisms on all kinds of read and write operations. The key aspect of this engine is the adding of the integrity checking capability to an existing block encryption algorithm.

This paper presents a comparison of a generic composition scheme i.e. AES (Advanced Standard Encryption) encryption and CBC-MAC (Cipher Block Chaining Message Authentication Mode) with PE-ICE. It is organized as follows:

Section 2 presents the considered threat model. Pre requisites and schemes proposed in the state of the art in order to provide the confidentiality-and-authenticity property to data are discussed in section 3. Section 4 describes the two evaluated engines. Simulation results are given and discussed through a comparison with an encryption-only engine in section 5. Finally, perspectives and improvements are exposed in section 6.

## 2  Threat Model

The System on Chip (SoC) is considered as trusted. Only board level attacks with processor-memory bus probing are taken into account (Figure 1). Such attacks allow to perform reads (passive attacks) or to inject data (active attacks) on the bus. We are particularly concerned by the "Man in the middle" attacks. The corresponding protocol consists in observing processor-memory communications, intercepting the data on the bus (confidentiality issue), and sending to the processor or storing in memory a chosen text – called in the following "fake" text (integrity issue). The choice of this

---

[1] In this paper we use the terms authentication and integrity checking, and authenticity and integrity interchangeably.

"fake" by the attacker leads us to define three kinds of attack that the integrity checking engine must detect:

- *Spoofing attacks*: The adversary exchanges a memory block transmitted on the bus with a random fake one. The attacker mainly alters program behavior but cannot foresee the results of his attack if the data are encrypted.
- *Splicing or relocation attacks:* the attacker swaps a memory block transmitted on the bus by another one previously recorded in the external memory. Such an attack may be viewed as a spatial permutation of memory blocks. When data are ciphered, the advantage of using a memory block copy as a fake is the knowledge of its behavior if this one was previously observed.
- *Replay attacks*: As with splicing attacks, an attacker records on the bus a ciphertext at a specified address. Then this recorded value may be reuse later on at the same address (current data value replaced by an older one). Such an attack may be viewed as a temporal permutation of memory blocks at a specific address location.

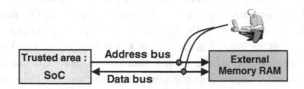

**Fig. 1.** Board level attack with bus probing

# 3 State of the Art

This section first presents the general principles ensuring data confidentiality and integrity separately and then describes the conventional ways to provide both security properties.

## 3.1 Pre Requisites

Hardware mechanisms guaranteeing data confidentiality and authenticity are usually inserted between the cache memory and the memory controller to i) prevent any CPU (Central Processing Unit) modification which could lead to performance degradations ii) keep data in clear in the cache memory iii) remain on the trusted area (SoC). For the same security reason, secret values like encryption keys, needed for those mechanisms are stored on-chip.

**Confidentiality** is usually ensured by using symmetric encryption algorithms, which are divided in two families: stream cipher algorithms – encryption is done bit per bit - and block cipher algorithms - the plaintext is first split into blocks, and then each block is ciphered separately. For more details on encryption techniques refer to [8].

**Data authenticity** is guaranteed by checking that read data has not been tampered with during external storage or transmission over the bus. In the following, the term "chunk" is used to define the size of the atomic memory block loaded from the off-chip memory, decrypted and verified by the integrity checking engine on read operations. As Load/Store processor architectures fetch memory blocks of a cache line size on a cache miss, a chunk is usually of this size.

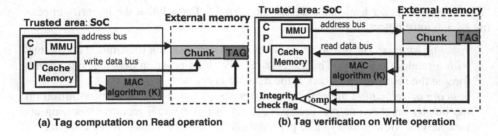

(a) Tag computation on Read operation          (b) Tag verification on Write operation

**Fig. 2.** Integrity checking principle

To fulfill the integrity checking objective, a value is appended to each chunk stored in the external memory. The goal of this value called tag is to give a compact representative image of the data and its source. It is computed on-chip with MAC (Message Authentication Code) algorithms [8] on write operations (Figure 2a). Such algorithms based on hash functions or on symmetric primitives [8] accept as inputs the chunk data and a key. Theoretically they create a unique Chunk/Tag pair. Only the SoC is capable to compute the tag as the secret key is stored on-chip. On read operations (Figure 2b), the integrity of the loaded chunk is checked: the tag is recomputed on the loaded data and compared to the one retrieved from off-chip memory along with the data. If the tag matching process fails, an integrity checking flag informs the CPU, which in turn adopts an adequate behavior (for instance a HALT instruction to stop processor execution).

### 3.2  Confidentiality-and-Authenticity: The Conventional Way

The conventional way to satisfy the confidentiality-and-authenticity property is to make two passes on data. A first pass is dedicated to encryption and a second one is done to compute a tag with a MAC algorithm. Three different schemes defined in [9] are depicted in Figure 3. Encrypt-then-MAC (Figure 3a) encrypts the plaintext to get a ciphertext C, and then appends to C a tag computed with a MAC algorithm over C. MAC-then-Encrypt (Figure 3b) calculates a tag over the plaintext P, appends the resulting tag to P and then encrypts them together. The third scheme, Encrypt-and-MAC (Figure 3c) encrypts the plaintext P to get a ciphertext C and append to C a tag computed over P. The main drawback of such techniques is the non-parallelizable property of the two security mechanisms (encryption and MAC computation) on read or on write operations or on both. On write operations, for the Encrypt-then-MAC scheme, the tag computation starts only at the end of the encryption process while for the MAC-then-Encrypt, encryption starts after the completion of the tag calculation. Concerning read operations, for Encrypt-and-MAC and MAC-then-Encrypt schemes, the tag matching process begins only when the decryption process is completed.

In the specific processor/memory context, proposed engines [2][3][4] are based on one of the conventional way schemes (two passes on the data) to satisfy both authenticity and confidentiality properties. Such engines belong to the *generic composition* [9] family as they use a different algorithm for each security service. They usually use Encrypt-then-MAC approach. The cost to achieve data confidentiality-and-authenticity is then the cost to encrypt plus the cost of MAC computation on write operations.

In order to thwart replay attacks hash or Merkle trees [10] are proposed in [2][3][11]. Such a technique is a strong solution. However it is unaffordable for an embedded computing system since it implies a huge performance loss due to multiple hash computations and external memory accesses.

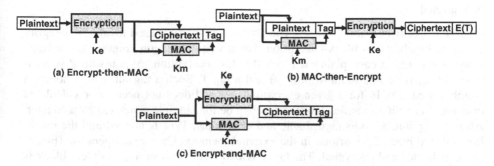

**Fig. 3.** The conventional way to provide the confidentiality-and-authenticity property

In addition, there are several *authentication modes* which have been proposed to the NIST (National Institute of Standard and Technology) standardization process [5]. Authenticated encryption is defined as a shared-key transform whose goal is to guarantee data privacy and authenticity [9]. However, they do not imply one pass on data to provide both properties and most of the AE modes still require to chain two computations on read or on write operations. The most relevant AE modes for our application domain seem to be OCB (Offset CodeBook) and GCM (Galois Counter Mode) [5] in term of computation performance. Unfortunately, no implementation or evaluation exists of such modes for our application domain.

## 4  The Evaluated Encryption-and-Authentication Engines

This section describes the two encryption-and-authentication engines that were evaluated and compared. First we start with an overview of our solution, PE-ICE – for a detailed view, refer to [6] [7]. Then we present the generic composition scheme based on AES [12] (Advanced Encryption Standard) encryption – to provide confidentiality - and on CBC-MAC [14] – for data authentication.

### 4.1  PE-ICE (Parallelized Encryption and Integrity Checking Engine)

PE-ICE is a dedicated solution providing strong encryption and integrity checking to data transferred on the processor-memory bus of an embedded computing system.

Data confidentiality is provided by AES encryption. AES is a block cipher algorithm processing 128-bit blocks with a 128-bit key.

In order to verify the integrity of data, PE-ICE relies on the diffusion property identified by Shannon [13] for block ciphers to be considered as secure: the redundancy in the statistics of the plaintext is dissipated in the statistics of the ciphertext. Therefore once a block encryption is performed, the position and the value of all bits in a ciphertext block C are influenced by each bit of the corresponding plaintext block P. Suppose that P is composed of two distinct data ($P_L$ and T), after ciphering, it is impossible to distinguish the $P_L$ ciphered part from the T one in C. Moreover if one bit is modified in C, after decryption all bits of the corresponding plaintext block will be impacted.

*PE-ICE integrity checking process:* The previous property is used to add the integrity checking capability to block-encryption. On a write operation (Figure 4a), a "tag" value is inserted in each plaintext block P before encryption. As a result, P is composed of a payload $P_L$ (data to protect) and a tag T. Such a tag must be a nonce, a Number used ONCE, for a given encryption key and does not need to be calculated over the data with a specific algorithm; it may be for example generated by a counter. After encryption, an indistinguishable and unique pair $P_L/T$ is created and the resulting ciphered block C is written in the external memory. On a read operation (Figure 4b) C is loaded and decrypted. The tag T issued from the resulting plaintext block is compared to an on-chip regenerated tag called the tag reference T'. If T does not match T', it means that at least one bit of C has been modified (spoofing attack) then PE-ICE raises an integrity checking flag to prevent further processing.

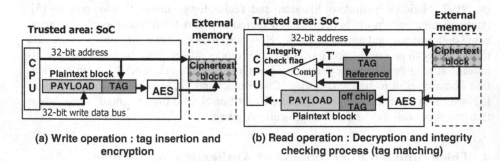

(a) Write operation : tag insertion and encryption

(b) Read operation : Decryption and integrity checking process (tag matching)

**Fig. 4.** PE-ICE principle

*The tag generation:* In the processor-memory communications context, the SoC is alone achieving both the encryption and the decryption process. Therefore, the SoC has to hold the tag value T of each ciphered block between the encryption and the decryption or must be able to regenerate it on read operations and perform the integrity checking process. The challenge is to reach this objective by storing as less as possible tag information on the SoC to optimize on-chip memory usage. Moreover T may be public because an adversary needs the secret encryption key to create an accepted $P_L/T$ pair. A CPU processes two kinds of data, Read Only (RO) data and Read/Write data. The composition of the tag is different for each kind of data and depends on their respective properties. RO data are only written once in external memory and are not modified during program execution. In addition, the secret encryption key is changed for each application downloaded in the external memory. Hence, the tag can be fixed for each plaintext block of RO data for a given application. PE-ICE uses the most significant bits of the ciphered block address as tag. If an attacker performs a splicing attack, the address used by the processor to fetch a block and by PE-ICE to generate the tag reference T' will not match the one loaded as tag T. RW data are modified during software execution and are consequently sensitive to replay attacks. Using only the address as tag is not enough to prevent such attacks because the processor cannot verify that the data stored at a given address is the most recent one (temporal permutation). For that reason the tag is composed of the most significant bits of the address of each ciphered block, concatenated with a random value for each plaintext block. This random value is changed on each write operation and is stored on-chip to be able to re-generate the tag reference on read operations.

*Example of implementation:* The targeted processor for PE-ICE implementation is a Load / Store RISC (Reduced Instruction Set Computer) architecture, meaning that on a cache miss, the CPU loads a payload of a cache line size. PE-ICE has been configured to encrypt and to check the integrity of such a payload. In the following PE-ICE configuration is given considering 256-bit cache lines.

The memory block M (payload + tags) loaded by the processor on a cache miss must be a multiple of the ciphered-block length. As a consequence, the minimum size of all tags needed for a payload of a whole 256-bit cache line is one AES block (128-bit). The resulting memory block M to load is three AES blocks long (384-bit) and therefore requires three tags. The tags distribution among plaintext blocks composing M is depicted in Figure 5. Tags storage take up to 33% of the external memory. Concerning RO data, the 32-bit address of each ciphered block address is used as tag (Figure 5a). For RW data, the tag is composed of (at minimum) the 24 most significant bits of the ciphered block address plus an 8-bit random value (Figure 5b).

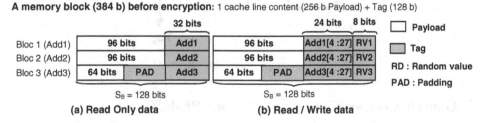

**A memory block (384 b) before encryption:** 1 cache line content (256 b Payload) + Tag (128 b)

**Fig. 5.** Tag distribution over a memory block (for a cache line of 256-bit)

## 4.2 The Generic Composition Scheme: AES Encryption and CBC-MAC

The generic composition engine, GC, defined in this paper for comparison with PE-ICE is the combination of AES encryption – for the confidentiality service - and of a CBC-MAC algorithm [14] – for the authentication service.

AES modes of operation implemented for such an engine are the same as the one used for PE-ICE [7] i.e. CBC mode for RO data and ECB mode for RW.

The tag required for the integrity checking process (Figure 2) is computed over a chunk of a cache line size with a CBC-MAC algorithm as depicted Figure 6. Such a

MAC algorithm uses block cipher encryption in CBC mode. In our implementation of CBC-MAC, the underlying block cipher $E_k$ is AES which uses a different key than the one required for encryption. The Encrypt-then-MAC scheme is chosen as it is the most secured conventional method [9]; therefore the tag is computed over the cipher-text composed of two AES blocks C1 and C2 and over a nonce N. The goal of N is to thwart splicing and replay attacks by allowing to produce a different tag on each write operation. Hence N must be different for each cache line and unpredictable from an adversary point of view. In order to respect those requirements the 128-bit nonce is divided into two parts. The first one is a counter and is dedicated to thwart splicing attacks. This counter is initialized with an $m$-bit random value generated and stored on-chip and it is then incremented with the data address. By this way, a different nonce is attributed to each memory location. The second part of the nonce is a coun-termeasure against replay attacks. For RW data, as in PE-ICE, an $n$-bit random value is generated and stored on-chip. Thus it can be retrieved for integrity checking on read operations while making it inaccessible from adversaries. For RO data, this part of the nonce is padded since such kind of data are not sensitive to replay attacks.

In our implementation the tag is 128-bit long, $n$ is equal to 24 and therefore $m$ is equal to 104. By this way PE-ICE and GC have the same on-chip and off-chip mem-ory cost which allow us to perform a fair comparison regarding security robustness.

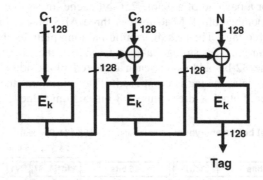

**Fig. 6.** Tag computation with CBC-MAC

## 5    Generic Composition Scheme Versus PE-ICE

This section first evaluates the robustness of each encryption-and-authentication scheme in term of security and then compares their performance.

### 5.1    Security Considerations

In the following, the robustness of the studied engines is evaluated regarding the at-tacks presented in the threat model.

Concerning spoofing attacks, the strength of PE-ICE depends on the size of the in-serted block. The chance for an adversary to succeed is a function of the number of AES blocks impacted by the attack and of the size of the corresponding tag. It is equal to $1/2^p$ with $p = 32 * 2^{(b-1)}$ - the size of the corresponding tag - and $b$ the number AES blocks impacted ($1 \leq b \leq 3$). For CBC-MAC, the chance to succeed is always of $1/2^{128}$. However the level of security provided by PE-ICE remains sufficient since an adversary has in the worst case only $1/2^{32}$ to succeed such an attack.

In order to perform replay or splicing attacks, an adversary must replay a previously recorded data with its corresponding tag. The granularity[2] of integrity checking is smaller for PE-ICE than for CBC-MAC - respectively one AES block and a cache line - therefore the size of the corresponding tag which defines the level of security is smaller too. While the tag is always of 128-bit long for a cache line with CBC-MAC, it is between 32-bit and 64-bit long for an AES block with PE-ICE. Hence, for a given application, 4GB of memory is immune against splicing attack with CBC-MAC, whereas 256MB and 4GB of external memory dedicated to respectively RW data (the tag contains minimum 24 addr. bit addressing 128-bit blocks $\Leftrightarrow 2^{28}$) and RO data (the tag contains the 32-bit address $\Leftrightarrow 2^{32}$) are protected with PE-ICE. Concerning replay attacks the strength of PE-ICE depends on the number of AES blocks replayed. The chance for an adversary to succeed is equal to $1/2^{8b}$ where $b$ is the number of AES blocks replayed ($1 \leq b \leq 3$). For CBC-MAC this probability is always of $1/2^{24}$.

The robustness is slightly better for GC than for PE-ICE due to the different granularity of integrity checking. However the security level of PE-ICE remains high and such an advantage for GC become a great drawback from a performance point of view as exposed in section 5.2.

Concerning the encryption schemes, AES block cipher is used for PE-ICE and for GC. Therefore the robustness of each engine regarding encryption depends on the modes of operation chosen. In order to perform a fair comparison of both schemes in term of performance, the modes of operation selected for GC are the same as the ones used for PE-ICE – ECB mode for RW data and CBC for RO data. However it is not recommended to use ECB mode since with such a mode a plaintext block encrypted twice always results in the same ciphertext block. For PE-ICE, this security weakness is circumvented by inserting a random value in each plaintext block (Figure 5b). For GC, a way to solve such a drawback is to use CBC mode for RW data too. However this would imply a significant performance overhead on write operations since encryption is done in series with such a mode.

## 5.2  Performance Comparison

In this section, performance of both encryption-and-authentication engines are evaluated and discussed through a comparison with an encryption-only engine using AES.

PE-ICE and AES encryption engines have been designed in VHDL on a 32-bit AMBA-AHB [15] bus from ARM. AES engine encryption modes are the same for PE-ICE and GC. We have performed RTL simulation to obtain the penalties introduced by PE-ICE and by the AES engine on all kind of external memory accesses requested by an ARM9 core [15]. We can deduce those introduced by GC since it uses the same hardware. Results[3] are given in cycles in Table 1 with the overhead of both encryption-and-authentication engines compared to the AES one.

---

[2] Meaning the size of the atomic memory block loaded from the off-chip memory and verified by the integrity checking engine on read operations.

[3] Write operations of RO data in CBC are not considered since they are not involved during run-time.

PE-ICE outperforms GC on all kinds of operation. The reason comes from the fact that the granularity of integrity checking is smaller for PE-ICE than for GC and that GC performs two computations over the data to provide both security services (confidentiality and authentication). On all read operations, whatever the size of the data to read (8 to 256 bits), GC loads a memory block of a cache line size to re-compute the tag whereas PE-ICE only loads the matching AES blocks. Concerning write operations, encryption and tag computation are not parallelizable for GC. Moreover when writing a data smaller than a chunk, the following operations are required (Read Modify Write (RMW) operation [7]): load the chunk, check its integrity (tag computation and tag matching process), decrypts the corresponding AES block, re-encrypts it and re-computes the tag for the whole chunk. The same process is required for PE-ICE however the operations are only performed on the AES blocks concerned by the write operation, and no tag computation is necessary.

**Table 1.** Latencies introduced by AES encryption, PE-ICE and GC on an ARM AMBA-AHB bus for all operations performed by an ARM9 core

| Operation | AES Ext. memory Latencies (Cycles) | PE-ICE Ext. memory Latencies (Cycles) | PE-ICE Overhead Vs AES | GC (AES + CBC-MAC) Ext. memory Latencies (Cycles) | GC (AES + CBC-MAC) Overhead Vs AES |
|---|---|---|---|---|---|
| 8 to 32-bit write | 37 | 37 | 0% | 67 | +81% |
| 8 to 32-bit read | 15 | 15 | 0% | 34 | +126,6% |
| 4-word write | 15 | 38 | +153% | 47 | +213,3% |
| 4-word read | 15 | 17 | +13,3% | 34 | +126,6% |
| 8-word write | 15 | 18 | +20% | 41 | +173,3% |
| 8-word read | 15 | 17 | +13,3% | 34 | +126,6% |

When comparing with AES encryption engine, PE-ICE is only penalizing for 4-word write operations (+153%) since the 128-bit payload is spread in two AES blocks. Hence, for PE-ICE, such an operation implies a RMW: first load the two AES blocks, then decrypt them, compare tag, modify the payload and re-encrypt the two blocks. For the AES engine, only the direct encryption of the 4-word provided by the processor is performed since ECB mode is used. Concerning GC, it introduces an overhead of at least 126% on all operations when compared to the AES engine except for 8 to 32-bit write (81% of overhead) for which the latency of encryption alone is already high[4].

As exposed in section 3.1, data are stored in clear in the cache memory and therefore latencies of Table 1 only occurs on external memory access i.e. on cache misses or for operations on non-cacheable data. In order to estimate the global performance overhead of such engines during software execution, we have used the cycle accurate simulator SoCDesigner from ARM (MaxSim technology) [15] with four benchmarks developed for embedded systems. Those benchmarks are ADPCM (Adaptive Differential Pulse Code Modulation), DES (Data Encryption Standard), FingerPrint (Fingerprint skeletization) and MP2Audio (MPEG2 audio encoder).

---

[4] 8 to 32-bit data write implies a RMW operation for the AES engine since it is required to first load the matching AES block and then decrypts it before being able to write the data.

Figure 7 shows simulation results in Normalized IPC (Instruction Per Cycle) for two different sizes of data cache memory (4KB and 128KB). Encryption introduces an overhead comprised between 5 and 23% with a cache memory of 4KB. Increasing the size of the cache decreases the encryption cost except for the DES benchmark. Indeed, such an application requests successive write operations which lock the bus (write through cache policy).

Concerning the encryption-and-authentication engine, Figure 7 shows that contrary to GC, the overhead of PE-ICE compared to AES encryption is almost negligible. Figure 8 focuses on this overhead and clearly highlights that the integrity checking mechanism of PE-ICE is less expensive in terms of performance than CBC-MAC. For PE-ICE, it is equal to 3,2% of NIPC (Normalized Instruction Per Cycle) in the worst case (DES) - which is due to successive the 4-word writes - whereas for GC it reaches up to 21% for ADPCM. Increasing the data cache memory size decreases the

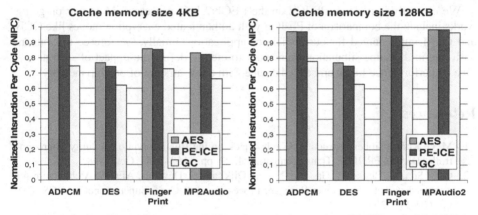

**Fig. 7.** Run-time performance overhead of AES encryption engine, PE-ICE and GC (AES + CBC-MAC) for two different data cache sizes with cache lines of 256-bit

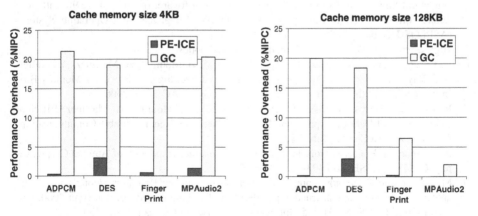

**Fig. 8.** Performance overhead of the Encryption-and-Authentication engine, PE-ICE and GC, compared to AES encryption only

performance overhead of the integrity checking mechanisms. However if external memory accesses are mainly relatives to write operations (ADPCM and DES) it remains almost the same.

## 6 Conclusion

The previous comparison shows that PE-ICE offers a better trade-off between security and computing performance than the generic composition scheme (AES + CBC-MAC). Our engine guarantees a strong encryption with the AES algorithm and allows data authentication at low cost – between 0,1% and 3,2% of overhead- by using the same encryption algorithm. Therefore, for commercial devices using block cipher for data confidentiality, PE-ICE implementation seems to be more realistic than using an additional scheme dedicated to data authentication.

We currently implement PE-ICE on the LEON2 [16] processor. Moreover on-going works include the comparison of PE-ICE with authenticated encryption modes like OCB and GCM implemented for our domain of application. Finally, we foresee to evaluate hash tree in the same simulation framework to clearly define the impact of such an engine on performance for an embedded device with a low amount of on-chip memory.

## References

1. M. G. Kuhn: Cipher Instruction Search Attack on the Bus-Encryption Security Microcontroller DS5002FP, IEEE Trans. Comput., vol. 47, pp. 1153–1157, Oct. 1998.
2. G. E. Suh, D. Clarke, B. Gassend, M. van Dijk, and S. Devadas, AEGIS: Architecture for Tamper-Evident and Tamper-Resistant Processing, Intl Conf. Supercomputing (ICS '03), pp. 160–171, 2003.
3. G. E. Suh and al, Efficient Memory Integrity Verification and Encryption for Secure Processors, 36th IEEE/ACM Intl. Symposium on Microarchitecture, p.339, 2003.
4. D. Lie, C. Thekkath, M. Mitchell, P. Lincoln, D. Boneh, J. Mitchell, and M. Horowitz. Architectural Support for Copy and Tamper Resistant Software. In Proc. of the 9th Intl Conference on Architectural Support for Programming Languages and Operating Systems (ASPLOS-IX), pages 169-177, 2000.
5. http://csrc.nist.gov/CryptoToolkit/modes/proposedmodes/
6. R. Elbaz, L. Torres, G. Sassatelli, P. Guillemin, M. Bardouillet, A. Martinez. A Parallelized Way to Provide Data Encryption and Integrity Checking on a Processor-Memory Bus. In Proceedings of the Design Automation Conference (DAC), July 2006.
7. R. Elbaz, L. Torres, G. Sassatelli, P. Guillemin, M. Bardouillet, A. Martinez. Efficient Combination of Data Encryption and Integrity Checking. Reconfigurable Communication-Centric SoCs (ReCoSoC) July 2006
8. A. J. Menezes, P. C. van Oorschot, and S. A. Vanstone. Handbook of Applied Cryptography. CRC Press, ISBN 0-8493-8523-7, 1996.
9. M. Bellare and C. Namprempre. Authenticated encryption: Relations among notions and analysis of the generic construction paradigm. In T. Okamoto, editor, Asiacrypt 2000, volume 1976 of LNCS, p. 531-545. Springer-Verlag, Berlin Germany, Dec. 2000.
10. R. C. Merkle. Protocols for public key cryptography. In IEEE Symp. on Security and Privacy, pages 122–134, 1980.

11. B. Gassend, G. E. Suh, D. Clarke, M. v. Dijk, and S. Devadas, Caches and Hash Trees for Efficient Memory Integrity Verification, in Proc. of the 9th Intl Symposium on High Performance Computer Architecture (HPCA9), February 2003.
12. N. I. of Standards and Technology. FIPS PUB 197: Advanced Encryption Standard (AES), November 2001.
13. C. Shannon. Communication Theory of Secrecy Systems, Bell System Technical Journal, vol.28(4), page 656–715, 1949
14. W. Dent, C.J. Mitchell, Cryptography and Standards, Artech House, ISBN 1-58053-530-5, 2004
15. http://www.arm.com/products/
16. http://www.gaisler.com/

# Methodology for Dynamic Power Verification of Contactless Smartcards

Julien Mercier[1,2], Christian Dufaza[1], and Mathieu Lisart[2]

[1] L2MP, UMR CNRS 6137, Technopôle de Château Gombert,
13451 Marseille Cedex 20, France
{Julien.Mercier, Christian.Dufaza}@l2mp.fr
[2] STMicroelectronics, Division DSA, Zone Industrielle de Rousset,
13106 Rousset Cedex, France
{Julien.Mercier-rou, Mathieu.Lisart}@st.com

**Abstract.** Considering the SmartCards (SC) family, two products types can be defined: contact and contactless ones. For contactless SC, analysis of power consumption is essential. While functioning, energy for these products is supplied by electromagnetic waves and value of stored energy depends directly on the distance between the emitter and the card. Then, for each defined product operations, and at any time, the stored energy must be higher than the required energy. If not, the product will not operate correctly. This paper presents a methodology to survey the dynamic power of contactless SC by current analysis, and so to verify safe operation mode of the product.

## 1 Introduction to Contactless SC

Today, the SC market is in full expansion. SCs execute and save data in embedded Systems on Chip (SoC) and their main differences with magnetic cards is the possibility to execute operations and data processing in silicon. Main applications are in high secure and authentication processes like: bank transfers, mobile communications, health, passport, pay TV, etc [1].

There are mainly two SC products categories: contact and contactless ones. For contact product, card reader supplies energy to the product, while for contactless application, energy is supplied by an electromagnetic wave. Then, a secure design of contactless products necessitates accurate analysis of the dynamic power consumption.

In the following, operation mode for contactless SC is given and relative ISO14443 norm is introduced. Then, a basic methodology for the analysis of the dynamic power consumption in contactless SC is described in Section 2. Section 3 presents the main verifications steps and simulations models of a real SC product. Finally, conclusions and perspectives are given.

### 1.1 Contactless SC Power Consumption

Basic architecture of a SC product includes: a processor, clock, memories, data busses, inputs/outputs and a DC-DC converter. The difference between contact and contactless products is located on $V_{PS}$ node, see Fig. 1. For a contact product, voltage on

J. Vounckx, N. Azemard, and P. Maurine (Eds.): PATMOS 2006, LNCS 4148, pp. 280–291, 2006.

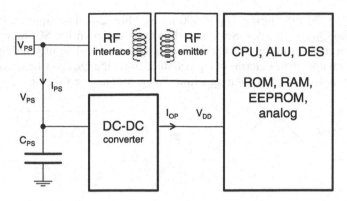

**Fig. 1.** RF energy provider of a contactless SC

this node is provided by the card reader while for a contactless product, the RF interface supplies it. The associated current is named $I_{PS}$.

$V_{PS}$ voltage value, most often equal to 3 V, is essential for a contactless product fine working since, if $V_{PS}$ decreases under a threshold voltage, reset of the product may be activated. The DC–DC converter transforms the $V_{PS}$ voltage into a supplied voltage $V_{DD}$ for the circuit [2].

According to the nature of data sent by the card emitter, an operation is going to be executed by the SC processor: cryptographic keying, non volatile memory programming, data reading, etc. Each potential operation consumes a specific current, named $I_{OP}$. If this current value is lower than $I_{PS}$, the leftover current will be discharged by a Zener diode. Nevertheless, $I_{OP}$ may be higher than $I_{PS}$, especially in the case where the physical distance between the SC and the card emitter is excessive, resulting in a low electromagnetic field and low $V_{PS}$ amplitude. So, a dynamic overconsumption will appear in the product, and if too long or too high, the storage capacitance $C_{PS}$ cannot maintain its charge. Then, the $V_{PS}$ voltage will decrease under a critical threshold voltage value and reset of the product and fail of the desired operation appear.

## 1.2  ISO Norms

ISO norms specify several criteria, such as mechanical, electric, temporal, etc., parameters that ensure products compatibility in a domain. Norm ISO14443 is dedicated to contactless SC [3] and specifies for power consumption that safe operations must be guaranteed for electromagnetic field values H in the range [$H_{MIN}$=1,5 A/m to $H_{MAX}$=7,5 A/m].

Then, simulations concerning the RF interface allow traducing these electromagnetic field values in terms of DC and AC consumption characteristics [4]. In our case, main focus is given in $H_{MIN}$ since it corresponds to the lowest $V_{PS}$ and to the minimal current value $I_{PS}$.

Concerning an AC criterion, previous electromagnetic values do not provide any specification about the maximal allowed current variation $I_{OP-AC}$. So, we look for others ISO norms that indicate tolerances for dynamic current. Norm ISO7816, that concerns contact SC but not contactless SC [5], specifies a current consumption peak

$I_{OP\text{-}AC} = I_{MAX} = 30$ mA during $T_{DIS} = 400$ ns, see Fig. 2-a. The equivalent maximal charge is then $Q_{MAX} = 6$ nA.s. Since no other norm exists in the SC domain for dynamic current, our definition of AC criterion in Section 2 will be inspired by the term $Q_{MAX}$. One can note that, in terms of equivalent charge, the $Q_{MAX}$ value is also equivalent to a current $I_{MAX} = 15$ mA during a time $T_{DIS} = 400$ ns, see Fig. 2-b.

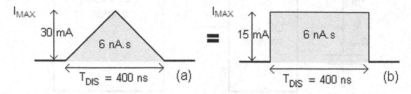

**Fig. 2.** Contact smartcard AC criterion

Today, SC products must be certified for the minimal electromagnetic field value $H_{MIN} = 1.5$ A/m, but things are undergoing with new products. The next step in norms specifications will be probably to decrease $H_{MIN}$ to 0.8 A/m and even 0.5 A/m. The main target with these values is to increase the physical distance between the SC and the card reader emitter. Of course, it will impact drastically the static (DC) and dynamic (AC) power consumptions authorized for these products, then the need of an accurate verification methodology.

## 2   Methodology for AC Criterion Definition

In this section, we will define for contactless SC products a new AC power consumption criterion based on ISO7816 contact SC specifications.

### 2.1   AC Criterion for Contactless SC

Concerning $C_{PS}$ capacitance, that represents both the RF capacitance as well as the internal parasitic capacitances, let us describe its current variation. Assuming $I_{OP\text{-}DC}$, the static current consumption of the product at any time, the maximal available current value to charge the $C_{PS}$ capacitance will be $(I_{PS} - I_{OP\text{-}DC})$, see Fig. 3. Note also that $I_{OP\text{-}DC}$ value is quite always the same whatever is the SC operation.

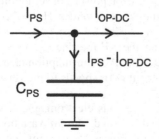

**Fig. 3.** DC currents for $C_{PS}$

Concerning the AC criterion, as seen previously, we assume a maximal charge $Q_{MAX} = 6$ nA.s. However, in this case for contactless products, we consider a larger time window T, greater than $T_{DIS}$ and whose value depends on currents $I_{OP-DC}$ and $I_{PS}$.

Let us formulate now an expression for T in the most compliant case where a maximal dynamic current $I_{OP-AC} = I_{MAX}$ is required by the SC product during a time window $T_{DIS}$, see Fig. 4. Also note that the total current $I_{OP}$ for a SC operation is the sum of the static current and of the dynamic current: $I_{OP} = I_{OP-AC} + I_{OP-DC}$.

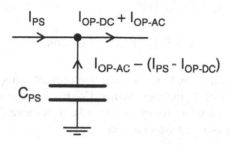

**Fig. 4.** AC currents for $C_{PS}$ during $T_{DIS}$

During a time window $T_{DIS}$ and for maximal dynamic current $I_{OP-AC} = I_{MAX}$, the corresponding capacitance discharge $Q_{DIS}$ is given by Equation 1:

$$Q_{DIS} = \left[ I_{MAX} - \left( I_{PS} - I_{OP-DC} \right) \right] \times T_{DIS}. \tag{1}$$

Equation 1 is valid both for contact and contactless SC products. However, a contact SC product is authorized to loose the charge $Q_{DIS}$ for any time value $T_{DIS}$, while for a contactless SC product, the capacitance $C_{PS}$ may retrieve it initial maximal charge before being re-used. Then, we can define the time window T as the sum of the time $T_{DIS}$ (time for discharge) and of the time $T_{CHA}$ (time for charge). Since an expression for $T_{CHA}$ using $Q_{DIS}$ is straight, the time period T is given by Equation 2:

$$T = T_{DIS} + T_{CHA} = T_{DIS} + \frac{Q_{DIS}}{\left( I_{PS} - I_{OP-DC} \right)}. \tag{2}$$

This expression for T shows clearly that the time required by capacitance $C_{PS}$ to restore its initial charge depends on the product static current $I_{OP-DC}$ and on $I_{PS}$. The smaller $I_{OP-DC}$ and higher $I_{PS}$ will be, the fastest the capacitance will retrieve its maximal charge. So, previously defined AC criterion indicates that the charge variation for capacitance $C_{PS}$ over a time T, must at least, not exceed $Q_{MAX} = 6$ nA.s. Now, our objective will be to define a methodology to calculate this charge variation.

## 2.2 Charge Variation Analysis

Let us consider two theoretical examples to describe this methodology, see Fig. 5 and Fig. 6. For both examples, we assume that the initial charge of the capacitance $C_{PS}$ is maximal.

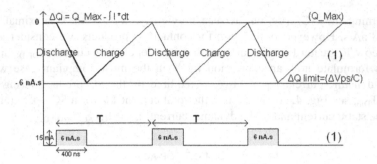

**Fig. 5.** 1$^{st}$ Theoretical example

In Fig. 5, we show a maximal charge variation of 6 nA.s over a time period T. In this case, for this value of T, the capacitance $C_{PS}$ has sufficient time to accumulate energy between two successive discharges, that is, to retrieve its initial charge. The limit value $Q_{MAX}$ = 6 nA.s is not crossed over.

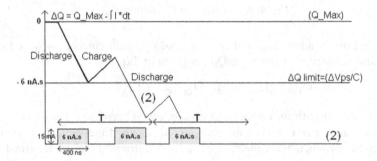

**Fig. 6.** 2$^{nd}$ Theoretical example

In the 2$^{nd}$ example of Fig. 6, the time T between two consumption requests is too short and the capacitance $C_{PS}$ has no sufficient time to retrieve its initial charge. The limit value $Q_{MAX}$ = 6 nA.s is crossed over; the SC product will not operate.

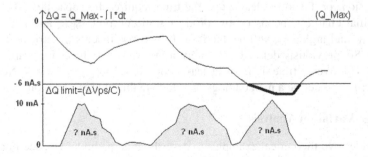

**Fig. 7.** Shapes of charges in real SC example

Of course, these examples remain theoretical and the shape of a real SC product consumption current is not a constant value but rather a pseudo-random erratic wave that depends on the nature of the functional operation executed by the SC, see Fig. 7. In addition, an accurate value for the $C_{PS}$ capacitance is hard to determine in practice.

So in practice, only two potential candidates: verification (see Section 3) and debugging measures on silicon may deal with the problem of charges analysis.

Assuming some current data for all the SC components, these values being extracted from electrical simulation results, our objective is now to verify that the discharge $Q_{PS}$ of the capacitance $C_{PS}$ will never exceed $Q_{MAX} = 6$ nA.s. In this case, we consider only the dynamic current $I_{OP-AC}$. This is justified by the fact that the static current $I_{OP-DC}$ is constant whatever the AC functional operation is.

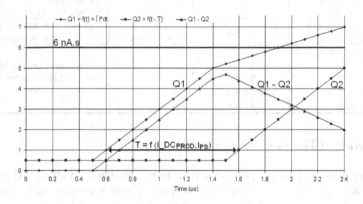

**Fig. 8.** Technique to verify $C_{PS}$ discharge in real SC

From this dynamic current $I_{OP-AC}$, curve Q1 in Fig. 8 represents the dynamic cumulated charge consumed in a SC product $Q1 = \int I_{OP-AC} \times dt$. The curve Q2 is the same as Q1 curve, but shifted by the time window T, so that $Q2(t) = Q1(t-T)$. The 3rd curve (Q1-Q2) is simply their difference and allows to verify that, for any two time points separated by a time window value T, the discharge $Q_{PS}$ of the capacitance $C_{PS}$ do not exceed $Q_{MAX}$.

## 2.3  Summary of Terms

Let us summarize the various terms and their significations:

$V_{PS}$    Voltage defined by the SC product team (e.g. 3 V).

$I_{PS}$    Maximal DC current available, depends on the electromagnetic field H and RF Interface.

$C_{PS}$    Storage capacitance value on node $V_{PS}$.

$T_{DIS}$    Elementary discharge time, defined in norm ISO7816 (= 400 ns).

$I_{MAX}$    Maximal static (DC) current allowed during $T_{DIS}$, defined in norm ISO7816 (= 15 mA).

$Q_{MAX}$    Maximal charge allowed during $T_{DIS}$ (= $I_{MAX} \times T_{DIS} = 6$ nA.s).

$I_{OP}$    Total current for a SC product functional operation.

$I_{OP-DC}$    Static (DC) current of the SC product (= for all SC operations).
$I_{OP-AC}$    Dynamic current (AC) for a SC product functional operation.
$Q_{DIS}$    Charge loosed for $I_{MAX}$ during $T_{DIS}$.
T    Time required by capacitance $C_{PS}$ to restore its initial charge after a discharge
$Q_{DIS}$.
Q1-2    Equivalent dynamic discharge assumed for a real SC product instruction.

Table 1 below summarizes the specific consumption criteria for ST products:

**Table 1.** ST consumption criteria

|  | Current / Energy | Time Window | Comment |
|---|---|---|---|
| ST RF product DC criterion | $I_{PS}$ | 1 ms | Depend on electromagnetic field H and RF interface |
| Contact AC criterion (ISO7816 norm) | 6 nA.s | $T_{DIS}$ = 400 ns | 15 mA average on 400 ns Time window |
| ST RF product AC criteria 1.5 A/m 0.8 A/m 0.5 A/m | 6 nA.s 3 nA.s 2 nA.s | T | Based on Contact AC criterion and RF macros simulation |

## 3   RF Product Development Verification

The ultimate goal of complete product verification is to check-up all the SC potentials operations and specifically to verify their respective power consumption. Especially, the dynamic criterion, e.g. ST RF product AC criterion, must be guaranteed for each operation.

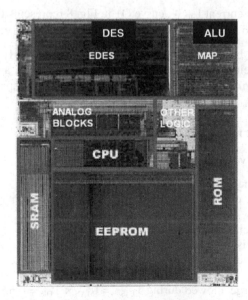

**Fig. 9.** Contactless SC Architecture

Before to detail the SC instructions set and their respective simulations for power consumption determination, let us precise a generic SC architecture, see Fig. 9. A contactless SC is composed of hard macrocells: ROM, RAM, EEPROM, analog blocks, etc., but also of digital macrocells: CPU, ALU (Arithmetic Logic Unit), DES (Data Encryption Standard cryptographic block), etc. For any operation of the SC instruction set, we will use such kind of cutting to analyse the elementary dynamic current consumption of all the functional blocks. Then, we will sum these currents to verify the previously defined AC criterion

Let start now by listing the set of functional operations of a SC, see Table 2. In this table, a cross indicates that, for a functional operation, a macrocell has a significant contribution in the overall dynamic consumption.

**Table 2.** Macrocells and Functional Operations of a SC

| Operations | Hard Macros | | | | Digital Macros | | |
|---|---|---|---|---|---|---|---|
| | EEPROM | Analog Blocks | ROM | RAM | CPU + Logic | ALU | DES |
| Power ON | X | X | | | X | | |
| EEPROM Programming | X | | X | X | X | | |
| EEPROM Erasing | X | | X | X | X | | |
| EEPROM Execution | X | | X | X | X | | |
| ROM Execution | X | | X | X | X | | |
| ALU Execution | X | | X | X | X | | |
| DES Execution | X | | X | X | X | | |

The universal functional operations of a SC are:

| | |
|---|---|
| Power On | Switching ON of a SC product, especially the analog blocks and EEPROM. |
| EEPROM Programming | Programming of a complete EEPROM page (activate EEPROM and its logic glue for data loading). |
| EEPROM Erasing | Erasing of a complete EEPROM page. |
| EEPROM Execution | Execution of data code stored in EEPROM. |
| ROM Execution | Execution of data code stored in ROM. |
| ALU Execution | Execution of an arithmetic operation. |
| DES Execution | Execution of a cryptographic operation. |

Since the set of functional operations of a SC to consider is now established, let start to describe the verification flow for their corresponding current consumption.

## 3.1 Simulation Methodology

For both hard and digital macros, the $1^{st}$ phase in the simulation process is to retrieve the signal activities values during an operation execution. The operation is initially described in CPU assembler code, then compiled and loaded into the ROM. Thereafter, by using a netlist description of the SC product, this code is simulated by NcSIM software [6]. The signals activities values are then obtained, see Fig. 10.

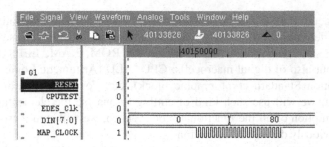

**Fig. 10.** Signals activities values with NcSIM

## Digital Blocks Simulation

The 2$^{nd}$ phase in the digital blocks simulation is to calculate the dynamic power consumption relative to these resulting signals activities values. This is realised by PrimePower software that consider specific libraries characterised for power consumption analysis [7]. Such kind of libraries results from analog electrical simulation of all the logic glue that composes the digital blocks. Transient curve of dynamic power consumption is then obtained, see Fig. 11. So, instantaneous dynamic current value $I_{OP-AC-DB}$ for the digital blocks is deduced assuming a constant $V_{DD}$.

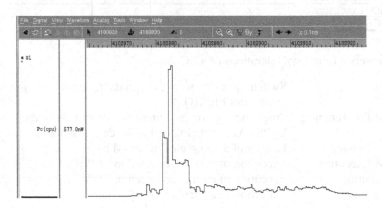

**Fig. 11.** Power consumption values with PrimePower

## Hard Blocks Simulation

The simulation process for the hard macros: ROM, RAM, EEPROM, etc., is quite similar than the one for digital blocks except that no power consumption libraries exist in this case (hard macros are not composed of logic glue). In consequence, these blocks cannot be analysed with PrimePower.

The 2$^{nd}$ phase in the hard blocks simulation process is to simulate at transistor level the dynamic power consumption of these blocks. This can be realised with conventional electrical simulators such as NanoSIM [8] or Eldo [4]. Transient curve of instantaneous dynamic current consumption $I_{OP-AC-HB}$ is then obtained for the hard blocks, see Fig. 12.

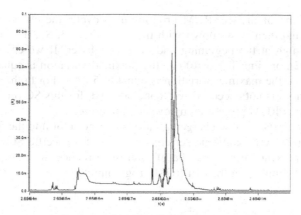

**Fig. 12.** Current consumption values with NanoSim

Then, the SC dynamic total current $I_{OP-AC}$ for a specific operation is simply the sum of the elementary dynamic currents of all the digital and hard macros, see Equation 3.

$$I_{OP-AC} = \sum_{j=1}^{DB}(I_{OP-AC-DB})_j + \sum_{k=1}^{HB}(I_{OP-AC-HB})_k . \tag{3}$$

## 3.2 SC Verification Results

The complete verification of a SC product requires the determination of current $I_{OP-AC}$ for all the possible operations of the SC. Then, for each operation, $I_{OP-AC}$ values must comply with the methodology proposed in section 2 for AC criterion.

In the following we present results obtained with this methodology applied to the starting phase of an EEPROM programming cycle, see Fig. 13. For the considered SC product, the RF interface can provide a mean current value $I_{PS} = 5$ mA for an electromagnetic field $H = 1.5$ A/m. Also, the static current $I_{OP-DC} = 1.2$ mA and recall that $T_{DIS} = 400$ ns and $I_{MAX} = 15$ mA. From equations 1 and 2, we calculate $Q_{DIS} = 4.5$ nA.s and $T = 1.6$ µs.

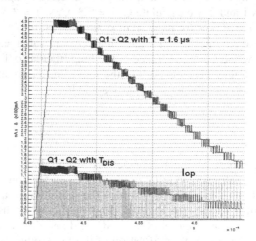

**Fig. 13.** Results for EEPROM programming

At the beginning of the EEPROM programming cycle, the charge pump runs at high frequency and then slows down with time, see Fig. 13. So, the dynamic power consumption is high at the beginning and decreases latter. If we calculate now the variation (Q1-Q2), on time $T_{DIS}$ = 400 ns the maximal variation is equal to 1.3 nA.s, on time T = 1.6 μs the maximal variation is equal to 5 nA.s. For both cases, the limit value $Q_{MAX}$ = 6nA.s is not exceeded. We conclude that, for this SC product, the starting phase of an EEPROM programming cycle is not critic.

In addition, analysis of these charge variations is very helpful to the SC designer to reduce and smooth the dynamic power consumption of a specific SC operation. For instance, in the present case, it may be of interest to reduce the charge pump clock frequency at the beginning of the EEPROM programming cycle.

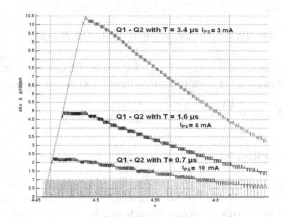

**Fig. 14.** Examples with $I_{PS}$=3mA, $I_{PS}$=5mA and $I_{PS}$=10mA

It's nothing to say that results depend directly on $I_{OP-DC}$ and $I_{PS}$ currents values. For instance, let us consider two others examples, where the RF interface provides a mean current value $I_{PS}$ = 3 mA or $I_{PS}$ = 10 mA; both for an electromagnetic field H = 1.5 A/m. From equations 1 and 2, we calculate $Q_{DIS}$ = 5.3 nA.s, T = 3.4 μs for $I_{PS}$ = 3 mA and $Q_{DIS}$ = 2.5 nA.s, T = 700 ns for $I_{PS}$ = 10 mA, see Fig. 14.

It is clear that, if the RF interface provides small current value, e.g. $I_{PS}$ = 3 mA, the time $T_{CHA}$ for charging the $C_{PS}$ capacitance is too long, then also T, and the maximal available charge $Q_{MAX}$ may be violated. On the opposite, the greater the current $I_{PS}$ will be, e.g. $I_{PS}$ = 10 mA, the smaller the time T could be.

## 4   Conclusion

The survey of power consumption in contactless SC products is essential for safe applications, and even will become critic with future specifications of new qualifying electromagnetic fields. In this paper, we propose the definition of a new AC criterion and of a dedicated methodology to check-it. This methodology uses simulations to estimate dynamic power consumption of each SC hard and digital macros during any operation execution. The complete verification of the SC product requires testing the full set of operations. We demonstrate interest of this technique with several examples including an EEPROM programming cycle. Such analysis must also help the SC designer team to improve their design to target low power consumption products.

Next step of this research will be to validate on silicon results obtained by simulation.

# References

1. Scheuermann, D.: The smartcard as a mobile security device: Electronics & Communication Engineering Journal Volume 14, Issue 5, (Oct. 2002) 205 – 210
2. Rakers, P., Connell, L., Collins, T., Russell, D.: Secure contactless smartcard ASIC with DPA protection: Custom Integrated Circuits Conference, Proceedings of the IEEE 2000, (May 2000) 239 - 242
3. ISO / IEC FDIS 14443-2000: part. 2, chap. 6, page 3
4. Mentor Graphics, Eldo,
   http://www.mentor.com/products/ic_nanometer_design/simulation/eldo/upload/eldods.pdf
5. ISO / IEC CD 7816-2004: part. 3.2, chap. 4.2.2, pages 3-4
6. Cadence, NC-SC Sim, http://www.cadence.com/datasheets/NCSC_ds.pdf
7. Synopsys, PrimePower,
   http://www.synopsys.com/products/power/primepower_ds.pdf
8. Synopsys, NanoSim,
   http://www.synopsys.com/products/mixedsignal/nanosim/nanosim_ds.pdf

# New Battery Status Checking Method for Implantable Biomedical Applications

Jong-pil Son, Kyu-young Kim, Ji-yong Jeong,
Yogendera Kumar, and Soo-won Kim

ASIC Design Lab., Dept. of EE, Korea University,
5-1 Anam-dong, Sungbuk-ku, Korea
{stardust, 90-kim, jjyjx, ykumar, ksw}@asic.korea.ac.kr
http://asic.korea.ac.kr

**Abstract.** A new scheme namely variable monitoring period scheme (VMP) is proposed to reduce the power consumption of a battery management system (BMS) used in implantable biomedical application devices. Self tuning level of reference voltage is used to make reference voltage flattened. Proposed circuit is fabricated in Samsung 0.35μm CMOS process and experimental results show that it consumes only 100nW@1.5V and total variance of reference voltage is reduced to be only 3mV over entire supply voltage range.

## 1 Introduction

In biomedical application devices such as implantable cardiac pacemakers, the energy required for the operation of the circuitry like control, sensing and pulse generation, is provided by the battery. To avoid replacement surgery of pacemakers far more often, the life span of the battery is required to be very long [1]. The lithium-iodine batteries which supply low current in μA range and last up to 10 years are appropriate choice for implantable devices. These batteries are in use for several decades due to high safety and reliability also [2]. Discharge characteristics of lithium-iodine batteries at two different temperatures are shown in Fig.1. Although, the discharge characteristics can be different at different temperatures, but generally these batteries have their output voltage level constant up to the critical voltage(Vcrit) and then fall sharply (in several months) [1][3]. The critical voltage is the highest value of low margin voltage values of all the components functioning in a pacemaker (like memory, microcontroller, voltage multiplier etc.)[4]. Low margin voltage is defined as the lowest voltage at which the circuit block can function normally.

Keeping in view the discharge characteristics, a circuit block is used in cardiac pacemakers to identify the remaining useful life of the battery. This block known as the battery management system (BMS), monitors the status of the battery and sends the alert signals before battery runs out [5]. The BMS consumes battery's power as other components do in pacemakers. To increase the life of the pacemakers' battery all components including BMS must be designed to consume less power.

J. Vounckx, N. Azemard, and P. Maurine (Eds.): PATMOS 2006, LNCS 4148, pp. 292–300, 2006.
© Springer-Verlag Berlin Heidelberg 2006

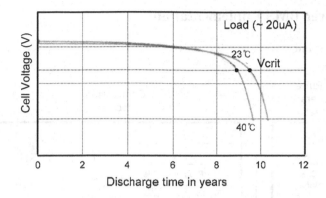

**Fig. 1.** Discharge characteristics of a lithium-iodine battery [1]

Conventionally the output voltage of the battery was measured using a resistor placed between the battery and the load [5][6][7]. But this resistor consumes lots of battery power. Also it can not be used to accurately detect the wide range of currents drawn by other components [5]. Later, the VCO and counter were used by Wong et al. [6] to measure the depleted charge from the battery. But still the power consumption of BMS was high. In the present work, a successive approximation resistor (SAR) type ADC is used to monitor the battery status. The proposed circuit operates only at regular intervals and it can be set to an idle state at other times. Also, when the output voltage of battery goes down, it can be set to monitor more frequently to avoid missing of the critical voltage. By having idle state during unwanted time intervals, low power consumption is accomplished.

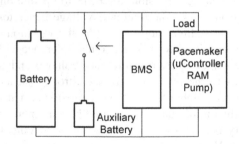

**Fig. 2.** The BMS with an auxiliary small battery

Furthermore, because of steep drop of battery output voltage, it is difficult to guaranteeing the functioning of pacemaker after the critical voltage [8]. To remove this problem, the BMS with an auxiliary small battery is also introduced in the present work. This small battery is turned on by the alert signal from BMS and it helps in guaranteeing the operation until the replacement surgery.

## 2 Low Power BMS Implementation

### 2.1 Configuration

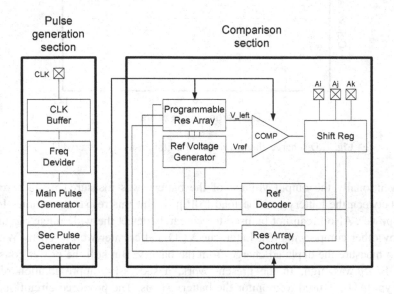

**Fig. 3.** Proposed BMS block diagram

Block diagram of the proposed BMS is shown in Fig. 3. It is divided into 2 parts, the first block is a pulse generation section which generates proper enable pulses from the signal CLK. These pulses make it possible for BMS to operate only for a short time. The other is a comparison block. The reference voltage generator generates a reference voltage (Vref) which is almost not affected by the variation of external voltage. The programmable resistance array makes another reference voltage (V_left). The following comparator compares these two reference voltages and generates a digitized output. The output goes to the resistance array control block and then generates a reference voltage (V_left) suitable for next bit comparison. This operation of comparison ends after deciding third output. All output bits are memorized and shifted by a shift register at every comparison step. These multi-bit outputs are decoded and used to tune the level of Vref according to the level of external supply voltage. (Self tuning level of reference voltage)

### 2.2 Pulse Generation Section

Fig. 4 shows the timing diagram of the BMS. As depicted, the clock frequency is just 1 Hz and it is divided into 1/n Hz by a following frequency divider. Main pulse generator makes an enable signal for the comparison section. It enables a comparison section only for 4 clock periods. The comparison section remains idle for remaining clock periods except the enabling 4 clock periods. In idle state all blocks except frequency divider remain in the stand-by mode and consume lesser power. Frequency divider remains active and awakes other blocks at the required time.

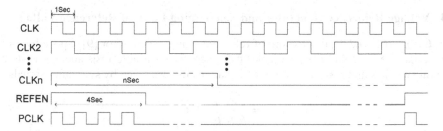

**Fig. 4.** Timing diagram of the proposed BMS

## 2.3 Comparison Section

To know the status of external supply voltage, two reference voltages are used. The one (V_left) varies its level in proportion to external supply voltage, and the other(Vref) holds its level constant regardless of external voltage. Fig. 5 shows the operation of programmable resistance array.

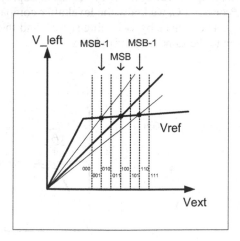

**Fig. 5.** Comparison operation

This consumes the power only if the control signal of REFEN is set enable. The REFEN is a periodic signal whose frequency is $1/n$ Hz and its enable state lasts only for 4 clock periods. The status of external voltage is represented by 3bit codes and the code of each bit is determined by comparison of two reference voltages. By controlling the switches, the level of reference voltage (V_left) is changed at every enable cycle and compared with the other reference voltage (Vref).

In the present work, total output bits are 3 and programmable resistance array is made of gate poly array. V_left is determined by the ratio of this resistance array. So it has very stable value regardless of process variation.

### 2.4 Voltage Reference Generator and Self Tuning Level of Reference Voltage

Fig. 6 (a) shows the basic structure of reference voltage generator [9]. Specially, normal resistance is replaced by variable resistance. The variable resistance consists of several switches and resistance array and changes its resistance by switching signals.

$$Vref = \frac{\sqrt{k}-1}{\beta R \sqrt{k}} + Vth \tag{1}$$

Where $k$ is multiple constant of width-length ratio, $Vth$ is threshold voltage of NMOS and $R$ is resistance of variable resistance. Equation (1) shows that the reference voltage level (Vref) is in inverse proportion to the resistance.

Because of the MOSFET's channel length modulation effect, reference voltage level (Vref) goes up slightly according to the increase of external supply voltage. Fig. 6(b) shows the scheme for compensating this effect. If the level of external voltage is known, then the resistance of variable resistance should be changed and finally the reference voltage can be flatten. In Fig. 6(b), point A shows the Vref with default resistance at low external supply voltage. As the external supply voltage level gets higher level like point B or point C, we know the level after comparison operation, the resistance array gets higher resistance by switching signals and then we can lower the level of reference voltage to the same level of point A.

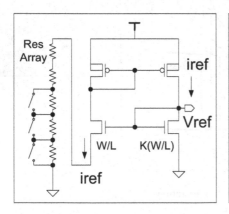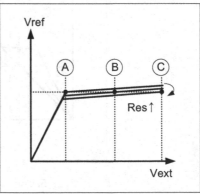

**Fig. 6.** (a) Reference voltage generator    (b) Self tuning level of reference voltage

### 2.5 Variable Monitoring Period Scheme (VMPS)

Fig. 7 shows the output voltage of a lithium iodine battery with time when output load is connected. The output voltage of battery goes down steeply when it approaches end of its life [1][3]. The BMS must notify its status before it goes under the critical volt-age (Vcrit). In the proposed scheme, the BMS does not operate at regular intervals. At higher voltage, the BMS monitors the status at long intervals. As the voltage goes down, it monitors more frequently. It is more flexible and optimized scheme which enables the BMS according to the status of previously monitored battery. In the dura-tion of steep drop of battery's output, the BMS operates at an interval of 1ts. How-ever, in the duration of maintaining relatively gentle declined output, it monitors the status at intervals of 4ts. So we can reduce the power consumption about maximum 75% by using this scheme.

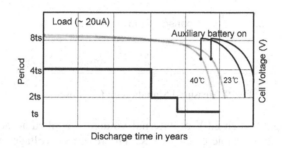

**Fig. 7.** VMPS with an auxiliary battery

Further, an auxiliary battery is used to guarantee the operation after detecting the critical voltage. This auxiliary battery is turned on by the alert signal from the BMS and helps to maintain the operation of a pacemaker.

## 3   Experimental Result

Proposed scheme is simulated and fabricated using SAMSUNG 0.35μm CMOS proc-ess.   Total chip area is 4300 μm x 600 μm and resistance array occupies 70% of total area. Fig. 8 shows the layout and fabricated chip in SAMSUNG process.

**Fig. 8.** The layout of the chip

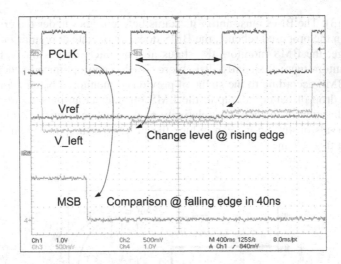

**Fig. 9.** Measured Signals with Oscilloscope

As shown in Fig. 9, when 2.0V of external voltage is applied at the input of BMS, it operates according to enable clock PCLK. The reference voltage (V_left) changes its level at every rising edge of PCLK. Then V_left is compared with the other reference voltage (Vref) at every falling edge of PCLK. Only one comparator is used for this comparison operation. To lower the power consumption, the comparator is activated by an enable pulse signal and then its output will be latched. It consumes about 4.5 μW during the enable pulse of 40ns per each comparison steps. After determining 3bit outputs, almost every block go to idle state. By having an idle state of BMS, we can accomplish the low power consumption. Total power consumption is only 100nW at 1.5V power supply.

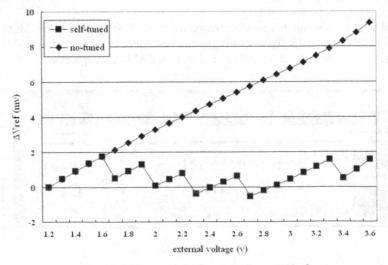

**Fig. 10.** Difference of reference voltage (ΔVref)

As illustrated in Fig. 10, when the external voltage moves up from 1.2V to 3.6V, the difference of reference voltage (ΔVref) is only 3mV by changing the resistance in reference voltage generator, while it's almost 10mV without changing the resistance. So we can get a more flat reference voltage by using this scheme. Table1 summarize the characteristics of the designed BMS.

**Table 1.** Characteristic of the proposed BMS

| Technology | SAMSUNG 0.35 μm CMOS |
|---|---|
| Area | 4300 μm * 600 μm |
| Battery range | 1.2V ~ 3.6V lithium iodine |
| Power | < 100nW @ 1.5V supply |
| Reference Voltage Difference (ΔVref) | 3mV (1.2V~3.6V) |

## 4  Conclusion

A low power battery management system based on the variable monitoring period scheme, self tuning level of reference voltage scheme and applicable in implantable cardiac pacemakers has been proposed. The VMPS is suitable for a lithium iodine battery with steep drops of output at the end of its life. A pulse generator to reduce the static current and enable time has also been used in the present scheme. A flat reference voltage with variation of only 3mV is obtained. Circuit implemented on chip using Samsung 0.35 μm CMOS process and obtained results show that proposed BMS consumes only 100nW@1.5V.

## Acknowledgment

This work is financially supported by the Ministry of Education and Human Resources Development (MOE), the Ministry of Commerce, Industry and Energy (MOCIE) and the Ministry of Labor (MOLAB) through the fostering project of the Lab of Excellency.

## References

1. Pistoia, G.: Batteries for Portable Devices. ELSEVIER (2005) 55-63
2. Greatbatch, W.: Origins of the Implantable Cardiac Pacemaker. Journal of Cardiovascular Nursing (Apr 5, 1991) 80-85
3. Atwater, T.: State of Charge indicator. IEEE MILCOM'94 Conf. Record (Oct. 2-5, 1994) Vol. 1, pp.203

4. Ryan, G., Carroll, K., Pless, B.: A four chip implantable defibrillator/pacemaker chipset. IEEE Custom Integrated Circuits Conference (1989) 7.6.1~7.6.4
5. Drori, J.: Gas Gauge Implementation. US.PATENT 6,154,012 (Nov. 28, 2000) 7-8
6. Wong, L., Hossain, S., Ta, A., Edvinsson, J., Rivas, D., Nääs, H.: A very low-power CMOS Mixed-Signal IC for Implantable Pacemaker Applications. IEEE Journal of solid-state circuits, Vol. 39, No.12 (Dec., 2004)
7. Zadeh. A: A Micro-power Precision Switched-Capacitor Charge Meter System for Implantable Medical Devices. Proc. 43$^{rd}$ IEEE Midwest Symp. On Circuits and Systems, Lansing MI (Aug 8-11,2000)
8. Renirie, A.: Long life cardiac pacer with switching power delivery means and method of alternately delivering power to respective circuit portions of a stimulus delivery system US.PATENT 4,031,899 (June 28, 1977) 6-7
9. Razavi, B.: Design of Analog CMOS Integrated Circuits Mcgraw-Hill, International edition (2001) 378-379

# Considering Zero-Arrival Time and Block-Arrival Time in Hierarchical Functional Timing Analysis*

Daniel Lima Ferrão[1],[**] , Ricardo Reis[1], and José Luís Güntzel[2]

[1] UFRGS – Universidade Federal do Rio Grande do Sul, Instituto de Informática,
Porto Alegre, Brazil
{dlferrao, reis}@inf.ufrgs.br
[2] UFPel – Universidade Federal de Pelotas, Departamento de Informática,
Pelotas, Brazil
guntzel@ufpel.edu.br

**Abstract.** Timing analysis of complex state-of-the-art designs demands efficient algorithms able to cope with design complexity. Exploring the hierarchical information generally encountered in complex designs became mandatory to perform functional timing analysis (FTA) in acceptable execution times. Although several hierarchical FTA approaches exist, only path-based hierarchical FTA is able to identify global critical paths, thus helping designers in the optimization task. In this paper we propose two versions of path-based hierarchical FTA strategies. These versions are compared to flat-mode FTA and to commercial FTA tools that operate in hierarchical mode.

## 1 Introduction

Verifying the timing constraints of current integrated digital systems is not a trivial task due to the huge number of components allowed by current fabrication technologies. Timing verification may be accomplished by circuit simulation or by timing analysis. Although providing the most accurate estimates, circuit simulation has two severe drawbacks that constrain its use only to small size blocks (around a hundred thousand transistors). The first drawback is the need for input stimuli. When looking for critical delay, the designer must determine, beforehand, which are the input stimuli responsible for the circuit critical delay operation, which is an extremely tedious task. The second drawback, and probably the most stringent one, is its long execution time.

Timing analysis, by its turn, is a partially input-independent approach that estimates the critical delay by representing each combinational block of the circuit as a weighted direct acyclic graph (DAG) with nodes representing gates and edges representing connections. The weights of nodes and edges represent the delays of gates and connections, respectively. The critical delay of each combinational block is determined by analyzing the length of the paths in the graph.

---

* This works was supported by CNPq Brazilian Agency.
** Currently with CEITEC - Center of Excellency in Advanced Electronic Technology.

J. Vounckx, N. Azemard, and P. Maurine (Eds.): PATMOS 2006, LNCS 4148, pp. 301–310, 2006.
© Springer-Verlag Berlin Heidelberg 2006

The simplest types of timing analysis algorithms disregard the logic behavior of gates, assuming the longest path delay as the critical delay of the combinational block. By doing so, the critical delay problem of a combinational block is reduced to the problem of finding the longest path in the graph, which can be solved in linear time. Such approach is referred to as static or topological timing analysis (TTA). However, there may not exist any input pattern that exercises the longest path in the circuit, and hence, the critical delay may be smaller than the delay of the topologically longest path. Paths that are never exercised (or activated) are called false paths [1][2] or unsensitizable paths.

In order to find the "true" critical delay of a circuit, and hence to avoid a possible overestimation of the critical delay, a logic-level timing analysis tool must include a sensitization check procedure. Such kind of timing analysis tool is generally referred to as functional timing analysis (FTA) tool. The existing path sensitization criteria fall into one of two types: delay-independent and delay-dependent. The most popular delay-independent criteria are static sensitization and static co-sensitization, while the most used delay-dependent ones are exact sensitization (under the floating mode) and viability [2]. The majority of existing FTA tools implicitly assume that circuits operate in the floating mode [1][2]. Under the floating mode, circuit nodes are assumed to be arbitrary, i.e. "floating", before they are settle by a single input vector $v$. Therefore, the critical delay of a circuit is the latest settling time over all possible input vectors $vi$.

The existing FTA algorithms may be classified either as "path enumeration-based" or "delay enumeration-based". Path enumeration-based algorithms operate on a path-by-path basis: beginning by the longest path, they enumerate circuit paths in a non-increasing order of delays [1]. While a path is traced, the path sensitization conditions are tested [1][3]. Normally, this process stops when the longest sensitizable path of the circuit (i.e., the true critical path) is found. Delay enumeration-based algorithms try to find a single vector or cube that leads to the critical delay of the circuit (as already mentioned, the floating mode is assumed). This class of algorithms begins by choosing a delay value and a logic value that are to be justified at the circuit output [4][5][6]. This delay value is normally set to a value slightly smaller than the topological delay of the circuit. Then, a single vector or cube that justifies this value is sought out by assigning logic values to as few circuit inputs as possible. If the algorithm fails to find such condition, then a new pair (delay, logic value) with a smaller delay is tried. This procedure continues until the algorithm succeeds to justify a pair (delay, logic value), which will be claimed as the critical delay of the circuit.

Sensitization tests may be performed by using ATPG-like techniques (e.g., [1][3][4]) or by using satisfiability - SAT (e.g., [5][6]). Path enumeration-based algorithms generally use versions of PODEM [7] or FAN [8] algorithms, modified to incorporate timing information. Delay enumeration-based algorithms may use either ATPG-like (e.g., [3][4]) procedures or SAT (e.g., [5]).

As already mentioned, the complexity of topological timing analysis (TTA) algorithms is linear with respect to the number of graph nodes. However, for circuits presenting many long false paths the difference between the delay of the topological critical path and the delay of the true (sensitizable) critical path may be significant. This is the case of carry-skip adders and some types of multipliers. Thus, to determine the true critical delay of a circuit a FTA algorithm must be used. However, comparing to TTA, FTA algorithms have much longer execution times and hence, are only applicable to circuits with up to a few tenths of thousand transistors.

One way of handling really complex circuits is to take advantage on the hierarchy derived from architectural-level descriptions. In hierarchical descriptions, each type of object (sub-circuit) is described only once but may be instantiated many times. This provides more concise circuit descriptions because redundant information is removed.

Concerning FTA, a hierarchical description offers a natural division of the problem. A hierarchical-mode tool may explore such division to reduce the computational effort by applying the FTA algorithm to smaller blocks. Also, hierarchy information helps to limit the number of sub-circuits (blocks) to be analyzed. Its means that the timing information obtained at a lower level may be re-used as many times as the number of instances of a given block. As a consequence of these two aspects, the total amount of data that must be treated may be significantly reduced if appropriate strategies are used.

Several hierarchical timing analysis strategies may be found in the literature. In [9] Blaquière and collaborators propose a multimode hierarchical method that treats circuits at various levels of abstraction. The lower levels are characterized using more accurate delay models, while higher levels are treated with less accurate models. However, path sensitization is not considered. In [10] Heo and Kim use the static sensitization criterion to identify the critical paths. However, such criterion is known to underestimate the circuit critical delay [1][3]. Kukimoto and Brayton use a SAT-based approach to characterize the logical and timing properties of circuit blocks [11]. Unfortunately, SAT is too time consuming, mainly when real-life delay models are used. Commercial FTA tools as the ones found in Cadence [12] and Synopsys [13] EDA packages, also allow hierarchical FTA. However, as detailed in the next sections, these tools present many limitations, rendering difficult their use for complex circuits.

This paper proposes and evaluates a path-based hierarchical functional timing analysis strategy to allow the analysis of very complex designs.

## 2  Path-Based Hierarchical Functional Timing Analysis

Critical path identification is still an issue of concern within the verification & optimization steps of classical design flows because circuit blocks that are traversed by critical paths are natural candidates to be submitted to timing optimization efforts. However, some of the hierarchical timing analysis approaches mentioned in the latter section are not able to identify the critical paths, mainly because they enumerate delays, instead of enumerating paths.

In this section we present two versions of a path-based hierarchical functional timing analysis method that is able to identify the critical paths of a circuit. One version assumes zero arrival times at block inputs while the other uses topological delay information to estimate block arrival times.

The proposed path-based hierarchical FTA method can be summarized by the execution flow shown in figure 1.

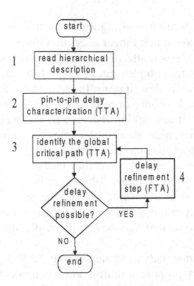

**Fig. 1.** Execution flow for the path-based hierarchical FTA method

The method begins by reading a hierarchical circuit description (step 1). Initially, we consider circuit descriptions with only three levels: the leaf sub-circuits, which are static CMOS gates, the sub-circuits made up from leaf sub-circuits only and the global circuit. The sub-circuit information read is stored in an appropriate data structure that handles a list of lists of sub-circuits, organized by the level of hierarchy. Assuming that $S_i$ is the set of sub-circuits used to describe a given sub-circuit C, the hierarchical level of C is computed by the following equation:

$$level(C) = max_i \{ \ level(S_i) \ \} + 1 \ . \tag{1}$$

This way, leaf sub-circuits are assigned to "level zero", intermediate level sub-circuits are assigned to level one and the global circuit corresponds to level two.

After storing all sub-circuits in appropriate lists according to the hierarchical levels, pin-to-pin delay characterization of sub-circuits is accomplished (step 2). Leaf sub-circuits are the first to be characterized. Although in this work we consider unitary delays for the gates, a more realistic delay model is also available in the tool prototype.

Pin-to-pin delay characterization of the sub-circuits belonging to a level higher than one consists on a topological timing analysis (TTA) procedure that determines, for each input-output pair, the maximum arrival times for rising and falling transitions. Sub-circuit characterization follows an increasing order of hierarchical level. When a sub-circuit is to be characterized, its DAG is created with the information stored in the corresponding list of sub-circuits. Time information is also granted by the same list and corresponds to pin-to-pin delay information already computed in previous steps. Remind that sub-circuits are characterized following the level order. Once all sub-circuits have been characterized, the global topological critical path is identified.

Consider the hierarchical circuit description illustrated by figure 2. If the global topological critical path traverses blocks A0, C0 and A1 of this circuit, then these blocks are candidates to be submitted to the delay refinement step. Therefore, for each of these sub-circuits a path sensitization procedure (FTA algorithm) is applied (step 4). However, in this analysis only the sub-DAG of interest must be considered. For example, in the case of instance A0, the target is to find the longest sensitizable path that begins at input $i2$ and ends at output $o3$. In the case of instance C0, the target is to find the longest sensitizable path between input $i0$ and output $o0$.

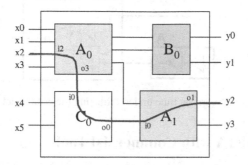

**Fig. 2.** Topological critical path in a hierarchical circuit description

After a sub-circuit passes through the delay refinement step, the critical delay with respect to the considered input/output pair is re-evaluated taking into account the sensitization conditions. Thus, the new delay estimate may be smaller than the first one (obtained by TTA). Due to that, after running the delay refinement step, the global critical path must be re-evaluated. This is gathered also by step 3 ("identify the global critical path"), which is a topological analysis that uses the most accurate delay values available at a time in the sub-circuit list.

While performing the delay refinement step, a relevant issue concerns the arrival times at the inputs of the analyzed sub-circuit. Most hierarchical FTA approaches make the naïve assumption that arrival times are equal zero or an arbitrary value. This is the case of the work of Yacin and Hayes [14] and most of commercial FTA tools as the ones found in Cadence [12] and Synopsys [13] EDA packages. However, using zero-arrival time may result in an incorrect evaluation of the sensitization conditions for a path. To understand this, consider the hierarchical circuit of figure 3. Assume that the delay of each gate of this circuit is equal 1. Consider also that we are refining the delays of the sub-circuits that are traversed by the path that begins at primary input "y" and ends at primary output "z", with logic value 0 at "y". Thus, refining the delay of block B means finding the delay of the longest sensitizable partial path that begins at input "b2" and ends at output "bout". However, if we assume zero-arrival times at inputs "b1" and "b2", then partial path {b2, ..., bout} will not be sensitizable when logic value "0" is applied to "b2". On the other hand, if we consider the topological delay of sub-circuit A as being the arrival time at "b2", then partial path {b2, ..., bout} will be sensitizable (when logic value 0 is applied to "b2").

In order to not underestimate the global critical delay, we developed a second version of our method. This version approximates the arrival times at the inputs of a given sub-circuit by using the topological delays of its fanin sub-circuits. By doing so, we avoid critical delay underestimation, hence providing a "safe" delay estimation of complex designs, still with shorter execution times than flat-mode FTA. The execution flow for this second version of path-based hierarchical FTA strategy is practically the same as the first version (showed in figure 1), except that an "arrival times estimation" step is included just before step 3 ("delay refinement step").

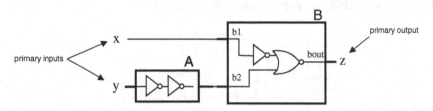

**Fig. 3.** Zero-arrival time underestimating the critical delay

## 3 Performing HFTA with Commercial Tools

Aiming to establish a comparison with state-of-the-art commercial tools, the hierarchical FTA (HFTA) flows available from two vendors, **Cadence**® and **Synopsys**®, were investigated. These flows are referred to by the vendors as "bottom-up" and "IP characterization", respectively.

The flow available from Cadence is able to consider the false path problem, but in a non-automatic way: scripts must be written to properly execute the process. The HFTA flow used in this work is available in the **Cadence Physically Knowledgeable Synthesis**® tools [12] and is represented by figure 4. Six main steps, referred by Cadence commands, are identified. The first step ("do_build_generic") receives the hierarchical netlist in Verilog format (mapped to a cell library) and the cell library description, in TLF format. Then, the project database, in ADB format, is generated. The second, third and fourth steps are responsible for circuit block (or modules, as referred by Cadence) characterization, being repeated for each block. Particularly, step "report_timing" performs FTA, generating a list of false paths of a block in format GCF. This list is loaded by command "set_false_paths", to extract a delay model for the block under analysis (using command "do_extract_model"). Thus, a delay model in format TLF is produced for each circuit block. The delay models are dependent from the adopted sensitization criterion. Finally, the fifth and sixth steps are responsible for associating the delay models obtained in the pre-characterization steps to the respective circuit instances (command "do_rebind"), and for the global analysis, when the global critical path is determined (command "report_timing").

FTA is performed during block delay characterization and uses one of the two available criteria: static sensitization and static co-sensitization (renamed by Cadence as "robust criterion"). However, it is important to highlight that although the application of these criteria lead to shorter execution times in comparison to the exact criterion, within Cadence hierarchical analysis each circuit block has to be characterized using both static sensitization and static co-sensitization, because the former criterion furnishes a lower bound estimate, while the latter furnishes an upper bound estimate.

Hence, two lists of false paths are generated for each block, one for each criterion. Therefore, the overall computational cost tends to be higher than that expected from a single step block delay characterization using the exact criterion. Another difficulty in the Cadence HFTA flow is the use of a static list of false paths of each block to guide the high level analysis. It means that once the list of false paths is determined in block delay characterization, it does not change during the whole process. However, a more appropriate procedure would be expanding the false path list while the longest sensitizable path between the considered input-output pair is not found.

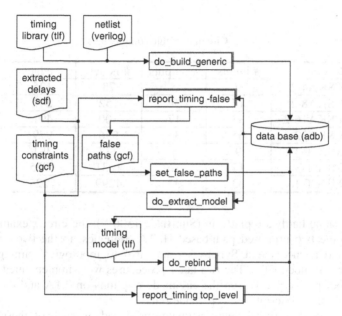

**Fig. 4.** Hierarchical FTA flow performed with Cadence tool

**Synopsys**® tools also allow false-path aware hierarchical timing analysis (HFTA). The hierarchical analysis flow belonging to **Synopsys PrimeTime**® [14] is very similar to the one of Cadence detailed in the previous paragraphs. The main steps correspond to circuit block characterization that furnishes information to the global analysis.

Unlike Cadence, FTA within Synopsys PrimeTime uses the exact floating mode sensitization criterion, but also assuming zero-arrival time for the blocks. Hence, the accuracy achieved is similar to that obtained by the first version of path-based HFTA presented in section 2.

It is important to remark that both Cadence and Synopsys HFTA flows are not automatic: in order to reduce the human interaction, scripts must be written for every circuit to be analyzed. Moreover, these flows are very restrictive, in the sense that they do not allow the refinement of block characterization. Hence, these flows spend long execution times in characterizing each block because the initial characterization remains untouched during the whole global analysis.

## 4 Comparison Results

To evaluate the accuracy and also the execution time of the two proposed versions of path-based HFTA strategies, a comparison with the HFTA flows with commercial tools described in section 3 and also with flat-mode timing analysis strategies was established. To serve as vehicle of such comparison, a set of hierarchical descriptions of carry-skip adders and multipliers was used. The carry-skip adders are made up from 2-bit ripple-carry modules. The complexities of such circuits are shown in table 1.

**Table 1.** Circuit example complexities

| Circuit | # inputs | # outputs | # nodes | # edges |
|---------|----------|-----------|---------|---------|
| CSKA4-2 | 9 | 5 | 78 | 125 |
| CSKA8-2 | 17 | 9 | 152 | 247 |
| CSKA16-2 | 33 | 17 | 300 | 491 |
| CSKA32-2 | 65 | 33 | 596 | 979 |
| MULT-4 | 9 | 8 | 237 | 391 |
| MULT-8 | 17 | 16 | 1031 | 1725 |
| MULT-16 | 33 | 32 | 4299 | 7225 |

Using the same hardware platform (SunBlade 1500™), the circuit examples were submitted to the two proposed path-based HFTA strategies, to the two commercial HFTA flows (Cadence's and Synopsys') and also to topological timing analysis (TTA) and to flat-mode FTA. The two latter procedures were implemented as part of our HFTA tool prototype. To run the circuit descriptions on TTA and on FTA, the original hierarchical descriptions were made flat.

Table 2 shows the critical delay estimates produced by each of these 5 timing analysis procedures. In this table TTA and FTA denote flat-mode topological timing analysis and flat-mode functional timing analysis, respectively. $HFTA_0$ and $HFTA_x$ denote the two versions of path-based HFTA proposed in section 2: $HFTA_0$ refers to zero-arrival time and $HFTA_x$ refers to block arrival time estimated by topological delay. $CHFTA_S$ and $CHFTA_C$ denote the Cadence HFTA flow using static sensitization and static co-sensitization, respectively. Finally, $SHFTA_x$ denotes the Synopsys HFTA flow, which uses the exact floating mode sensitization along with zero-arrival time. In these analyses the unitary gate delay model was assumed.

The first remark about table 2 concerns the accuracy obtained by the various timing analysis approaches. Delay estimates produced by TTA can be viewed as upper bounds and are often too pessimistic. On the other hand, flat-FTA furnishes tighter delay estimates and thus may be used as a reference of accuracy. In this sense, one can notice that TTA overestimated the delay of circuits CSKA8-2, CSKA16-2, CSKA32-2 and MULT-16.

From the data showed in table 2 it becomes evident the good accuracy achieved by method $HFTA_x$. It not only was successful in running on all examples, but also was able to find safe delay estimates in all cases. Moreover, in all cases it overestimated the critical delay, all other commercial tools also overestimated by the same amount.

**Table 2.** Critical delay estimates obtained from the various timing analysis strategies

|         | Flat-mode | | Hierarchical-mode | | | | |
|---------|-----|-----|-------------------|-------------------|-------------------|-------------------|-------------------|
| Circuit | TTA | FTA | $HFTA_0$ | $HFTA_x$ | $CHFTA_S$ | $CHFTA_C$ | $SHFTA_x$ |
| CSKA4-2 | 15 | 13 | 14 | 13 | 13 | 14 | 14 |
| CSKA8-2 | 27 | 17 | 26 | 17 | 17 | 26 | 26 |
| CSKA16-2 | 51 | 28* (25) | 50 | 25 | 25 | 50 | 50 |
| CSKA32-2 | 99 | 85* (41) | 98 | 41 | 41 | 98 | 98 |
| MULT-4 | 37 | 34 | 34 | 34 | 34 | 34 | 34 |
| MULT-8 | 89 | 79* (78) | 86 | 86 | 69 | 86 | 86 |
| MULT-16 | 193 | 191* (166) | 190 | 190 | † | 190 | 190 |

† Stack overflow after 5 hour executing (*core dump*).
* partial estimate, execution aborted.
(value) exact critical delay, previously known.

Differently from $CHFTA_C$ and $SHFTA_x$ commercial flows, $HFTA_x$ has shown the same precision as (flat) FTA for circuits CSKA16-2 and CSKA32-2, indicating that the proposed strategy of estimating block-arrival time tends to be more accurate than the used commercial flows. On the other hand, the four HFTA strategies that use zero-arrival time ($HFTA_0$, $CHFTA_S$, $CHFTA_C$ and $SHFTA_x$) produced pessimistic delay estimates that are close to TTA. In particular, $CHFTA_S$ strategy underestimated the delay of circuit MULT-8, what is an unacceptable result.

Table 3 shows the execution times for the considered HFTA strategies and circuit examples. It is interesting to notice that both proposed path-based HFTA ($HFTA_0$ and $HFTA_x$) methods are faster than commercial flows for almost all cases. Particularly, strategy $HFTA_x$ is not prohibitively slower than strategy $HFTA_0$, while producing more accurate estimates.

**Table 3.** Execution times for the evaluated timing analysis strategies, in milliseconds

|         | Flat descriptions | | Hierarchical descriptions | | | | |
|---------|------|-------------|-------------------|-------------------|-------------------|-------------------|-------------------|
| Circuit | TTA | FTA | $HFTA_0$ | $HFTA_x$ | $CHFTA_S$ | $CHFTA_C$ | $SHFTA_x$ |
| CSKA4-2 | 30 | 130 | 50 | 90 | 999 | 999 | 9,000 |
| CSKA8-2 | 40 | 8,600 | 80 | 330 | 1,000 | 1,000 | 9,000 |
| CSKA16-2 | 120 | 3,904,833* | 140 | 910 | 2,000 | 1,000 | 9,000 |
| CSKA32-2 | 420 | 86,400,000* | 370 | 2,630 | 5,000 | 1,000 | 9,000 |
| MULT-4 | 90 | 6,050 | 230 | 380 | 8,000 | 2,000 | 9,000 |
| MULT-8 | 1,340 | 239,972,996* | 1,040 | 3,200 | 3,235,000 | 573,000 | 9,000 |
| MULT-16 | 20,110 | 546,035* | 6,380 | 107,650 | † | 7,159,000 | 10,000 |

† Stack overflow after 5 hour executing (*core dump*).
* partial estimate, execution aborted.

It is important to notice that the time for preparing the scripts for Cadence and Synopsys tools does not appear in table 3. It is also interesting to notice that Synopsys execution time is independent from the circuit complexity.

## 5 Conclusion

This paper proposed and evaluated two versions of path-based hierarchical functional timing analysis (HFTA) that are fully automatic. One version considers zero-arrival time for the blocks while the other approximates block arrival time by using the topological delay of the fanin blocks.

The experimental results have shown that approximating the arrival time of blocks by using topological delay information produces safe delay estimates that are close to those obtained with flat-mode FTA, but with execution times orders of magnitude shorter. In particular, the proposed HFTA strategy that considers non-zero arrival times has showed to be faster and more accurate than Cadence and Synopsys tools, which assume zero-arrival time for circuit blocks.

## References

1. H.-C. Chen, D. Du. "Path Sensitization in Critical Path Problem." IEEE Transactions on CAD of Integrated Circuits and Systems, v.12, n.2, pp.196-207.
2. S. Devadas, K. Keutzer, S. Malik. "Computation of Floating Mode Delay in Combinational Circuits: Theory and Algorithms." IEEE Transactions on Computed-Aided Design of Integrated Circuits and Systems, v.12, n.12, pp.1913-1923.
3. H. Chang, J.A. Abraham. "VIPER: An Efficient Vigorously Sensitizable Path Extractor." In: 30th ACM/IEEE Design Automation Conference, 1993. pp.112-117.
4. S. Devadas, K. Keutzer, S. Malik, A. Wang. "Computation of Floating Mode Delay in Combinational Circuits: Practice and Implementation." IEEE Transactions on Computed-Aided Design of Integrated Circuits and Systems, v.12, n.12, pp.1924-1936.
5. L.G. Silva et al. "Realistic Delay Modeling in Satisfiability-Based Timing Analysis." In: IEEE Intl Symposium on Circuits & Systems (ISCAS), 1998. v.6. pp.215-218.
6. P. McGeer et al. "Delay Models and Exact Timing Analysis." In: T. Sasao, (Ed.). Logic Synthesis and Optimization. Kluwer Academic Pub., 1993. pp. 167-189.
7. P. Goel, "An Implicit Enumeration Algorithm to Generate Tests for Combinational Logic Circuits." IEEE Transactions on Computers, v. C-30, n.3, pp. 215-222.
8. H. Fujiwara, T. Shimono.. "On the Acceleration of Test Generation Algorithms." IEEE Transactions on Computers, Los Alamitos, California, v. C-32, n.12, pp. 1137-1144.
9. Y. Blaquière, M. Dagenais, Y. Savaria. "Timing Analysis Speed-up Using a Hierarchical and a Multimode Approach." IEEE Transactions on Computer-Aided Design of Integrated Circuits and Systems, v.15, n.2, pp. 244-255.
10. S. Heo, J. Kim "Hierarchical Timing Analysis Considering Global False Path" In: Proceedings of ITC-CSCC-2002, 2002
11. Y. Kukimoto, R. K.; Brayton "Hierarchical Functional Timing Analysis." In: 35th ACM/IEEE Design Automation Conference, pp. 580-585, 1998.
12. Cadence Physically Knowledgeable Synthesis® User Guide. Cadence Design Systems, Inc., 2002.
13. Synopsys PrimeTime® User Guide: Advanced Timing Analysis. Synopsys, Inc., 2004.
14. H. Yalcin; J. P. Hayes. Hierarchical Timing Analysis Using Conditional Delays. In: Proceedings of International Conference on Computer Aided Design, 1995. pp. 371-377.

# A Simple MOSFET Parasitic Capacitance Model and Its Application to Repeater Insertion Technique

Andrea Pugliese, Gregorio Cappuccino, and Giuseppe Cocorullo

Electronics, Computer Science and Systems Department,
DEIS-University of Calabria
87036 Rende, Italy
{a.pugliese, cappuccino, cocorullo}@deis.unical.it

**Abstract.** Repeater insertion is one of the most effective techniques to reduce the propagation delay related to long interconnects.

However, its application to deep submicron technologies leads to sub-optimal results if the traditional sizing rules are followed.

In the paper the Authors show the behaviour of deep-sub micron devices may differ significantly from the conventional one due to transistor parasitic capacitance. As a consequence, well-exploited assumption as linear relationship between channel width and output conductance of the CMOS gate start to fails, as well as it does optimisation techniques based upon them. A developed formula for buffer sizing is proposed based on a simplified model allowing MOS parasitic to be taken into account. Up to 50% area and leakage power saving can be obtained.

## 1 Introduction

During the last years, the role of interconnects has become without doubt the most important issue in the design of high performance CMOS circuits. This role dramatically increases with ever-increasing circuit complexity, operating speed, integration level and global communication requirements, as for system-on-chip (SOC) applications.

Thus the design and optimisation of these high-speed submicron circuits require adequate device and interconnect models in order to reduce the time-to-market avoiding costly and time-consuming fab run cycles [1]. Conventional solutions providing high accuracy, though suitable for small designs, become inapplicable to a present-day chip that contains several millions of transistors and their relative interconnects.

One of the techniques to optimise wire delay is the insertion of repeaters. However the particular area and power requirements imposed by nowadays designs dictate the need for a more accurate design of repeaters and in some cases, it implies to take in to account important phenomena previously considered as" secondary" or unimportant.

Recent studies point out the role of these "secondary" phenomena, as threshold variations, current leakage [2, 3] or device channel length modulation [4], all phenomena that may affect significantly the operations of modern nanometer CMOS.

J. Vounckx, N. Azemard, and P. Maurine (Eds.): PATMOS 2006, LNCS 4148, pp. 311–318, 2006.

However to the best of our knowledge, actual role played by parasitic capacitance on the line-driver performance remains quite unexplored.

In the paper the role of the parasitic capacitance of the buffer on the effective driving capability is highlighted.

The Authors demonstrate for usual line parameters the effective current supplied by the buffers could be 28% lower than those predicted by traditional formulas, due to the parasitic capacitances of buffer transistors. This directly affects the effectiveness of conventional buffer sizing criterions that usually take in to account only gate capacitance of the loading gate connected at the end of a line.

A novel expression that allows parasitic capacitances to be taken into account in the sizing phase of line repeater is also presented in the paper. It is based on a simplified "single-capacitor" model and it allows area delay product to be reduced by a factor 2 with respect traditional repeater sizing criterion. A significant reduction of power related to leakage currents can be also carried out.

## 2 Conventional Repeater Insertion

Repeater insertion technique has been developed to overcome the strong delay issue associated with long interconnect connecting two distinct gates of a circuit [5].

To lower the line delay (that is quadratically dependent on the line length $L$), the technique suggests to split the original interconnect, with capacitance and resistance $C_w$ and $R_w$ respectively, in $k$ segments, each of length $L/k$, as depicted in fig. 1. Each wire segment is driven by a separate repeater $h$ times greater than a minimum-sized buffer. The model commonly used in literature to carry out expressions for $k$ and $h$ is reported in fig. 2.

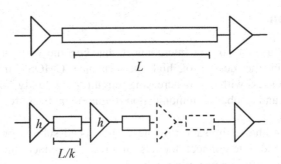

**Fig. 1.** The line of length $L$ is splitted in $k$ segments. $K$ buffers $h$-times greater than minimum sized one are used to drive each segment

$R_d$, $C_g$, $R_w$, $C_w$ being the equivalent resistance and the input capacitance of the minimum-sized buffer and the resistance and capacitance of the entire line, respectively, the expression for the 50% delay of the chain, in accord with the Elmore model [5], becomes:

$$t_{50\%} = 0.7k\left(\frac{R_d}{h}\left(hC_g + 0.5\frac{C_w}{k}\right) + \left(\frac{R_d}{h} + \frac{R_w}{k}\right)0.5\frac{C_w}{k}\right) \tag{1}$$

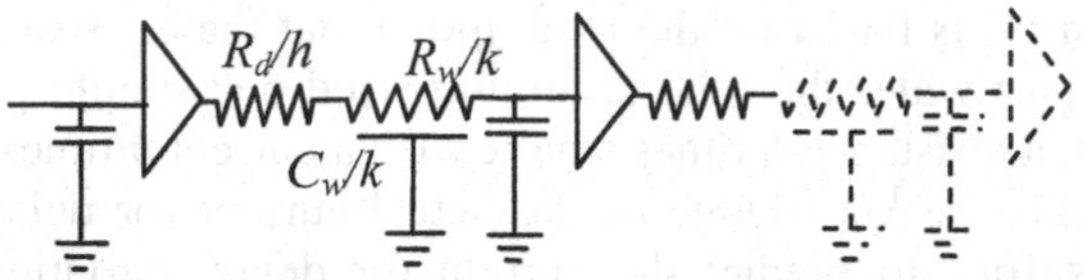

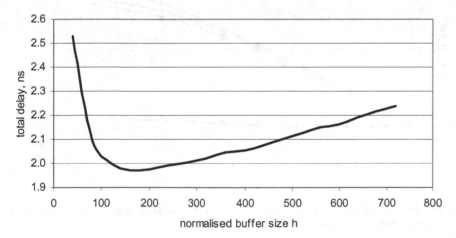

**Fig. 2.** The RC model usually used to carry out the delay of the chain of fig. 1

By setting the derivatives of $t_{50\%}$ with respect to $k$ and $h$ to zero, the optimal values for the number of segment $k_{opt}$ and the optimum buffer size $h_{opt}$ can be obtained:

$$k_{opt} = \sqrt{\frac{R_w C_w}{1.84 R_d C_g}} \quad \text{and} \quad h_{opt} = \sqrt{\frac{R_d C_w}{R_w C_g}} \tag{2}$$

These sizing rules are widely used by digital designers and their effectiveness has been proven for "mature" technologies. However their application to advanced (existing and near-future) [6, 7] CMOS processes seems not to lead to optimal results.

The plot in fig. 3 represents the overall delay of a line of length 3.6mm, split into 3 segments, as function of the repeater size. The plot refers to HSPICE simulations for a real 0.13μm CMOS technology. The wire capacitance and resistance per unit of length are 300pF/m and 30kΩ/m, respectively.

**Fig. 3.** Total delay of a 3.6mm line with 3 repeaters, as function of the repeater size

As shown, the delay reaches its minimum value (1.97ns) when buffers 170 times greater than the minimum-sized one are used. A delay of 2.52ns results when buffers with $h=246$ are used, as instead suggested by eqn.(2). This means that classical sizing rule leads to a repeater configuration that is characterised by an area-delay product that is about twice that of the best obtainable case, thus implying an enormous area and power wastefulness, a prohibitive situation most of all in complex systems.

The reason of this result has to been found in the actual effectiveness of a device widening to increase the current that the driver should supply to the line.

In fact, equation (1) is based on the assumption that the equivalent resistance $R_{out}$ of a transistor $h$ times wider than the minimum-sized one should present during the switching transient, a resistance $h$ times smaller. i.e. a current $h$ times greater.

As a consequence, the knowledge of the actual current (or delay) of a reference transistor should suffice to predict the current (or delay) variations obtainable by reducing or increasing the channel width for a specified load.

However the above mentioned assumption do not take in to account the effect that the transistor (intrinsic) parasitic capacitance may have on the effective output current when a real RC load is driven.

A great number of text-books and papers have been published dealing with circuital models for precise MOS intrinsic modelling. The counterpart to pay for their accuracy in capturing all the charge storage phenomena occurring in the devices consist in the high number of circuital elements used. It makes their application to a present-day circuit containing several millions of transistors and their relative interconnects practically unfeasible.

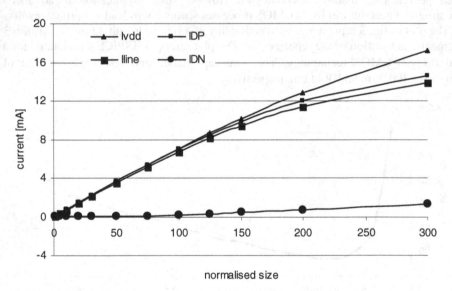

**Fig. 4.** Drain current IDP , power supply current IVDD, buffer output current Iline and the source current ISN as function of buffer normalised size

## 3 Parasitics Effect on Buffer Output Current

Plots in fig. 4 report the mean value of drain current $I_{DP}$ of a PMOS transistor during a low-to-high buffer output transition as function of buffer size with respect to the minimum-sized one (i.e. the buffer designed with minimum sized MOSFETs).

The plots refer to HSIPCE simulations for a 100nm technology. The buffer drives a 3mm long interconnect with a wire resistance and capacitance of 10k$\Omega$/m and 120pF/m, respectively. The plot also reports the mean value of the current supplied by power supply $I_{VDD}$, the current feed thought the line (i.e. the buffer output current) $I_{line}$

and the source current $I_{SN}$ flowing out from the NMOS. As shown, current effectively transferred to the line is lower than $I_{VDD}$, as well evidenced in in fig. 5, where the plot of ratio between $I_{line}$ and $I_{VDD}$ is reported for wire resistance varying from 0 (ideal wire) up 50k$\Omega$/m.

As shown, for small buffers the current supplied by the voltage supply $I_{VDD}$ is feed entirely in to the line, and the $I_{line}$ / $I_{VDD}$ ratio approaches unity. As buffer widens, the current feed thought the line decreases down to 72% of the current supplied by $V_{dd}$.

The difference between $I_{line}$ and $I_{VDD}$ is partially due to the well known short-circuit effect rises by simultaneous activation of the NMOS transistor, creating a direct path toward ground. However, by comparing the plots of fig.4, it is evidenced how short circuit current alone does not justify the difference between current $I_{line}$ and $I_{VDD}$. HSPICE simulations confirmed that a further subtraction effect to the current that should be droved into the line is given by the path created by overlap parasitic drain-gate capacitance CGD, source-gate capacitance CGS, gate-bulk capacitance as well as drain-bulk and source-bulk (diode) capacitance of each transistor.

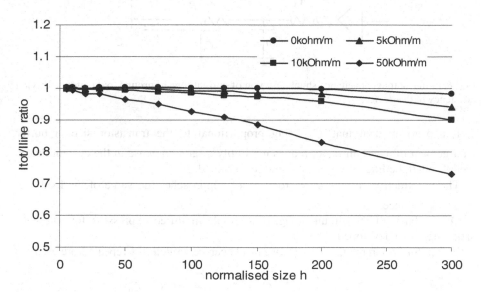

**Fig. 5.** the ratio between the current actually supplied to the line Iline and that supplied by the power supply IVDD

Even if all MOS parasitic capacitances can be easily taken into account in a small circuit analysis, a simplified model to be applied to complex circuits is needed.

On these bases a simple model has been developed and tested. The basic idea arises from the consideration that the resulting effect of all these parasitics in the case of a line driver can be seen as a unique current that is shunted to ground by means of a single capacitor of value $C_{out} = hC_0$, where $h$ represents the normalised buffer size with respect to the minimum sized one, and $C_0$ is its output equivalent capacitance, that can be carried out once and for all for a given technology and for a given range of input signal rise time.

By lumping together parasitic capacitance of both NMOS and PMOS in a single output capacitor allow first-order analysis of CMOS buffers to be easily carried out taking in to account their effect in the development of optimisation techniques as, for example, repeater insertion.

## 4  Parasitic Capacitance Inclusion in Buffer Size Formulae

As evidenced in previous sections, parasitic capacitances may play a shunting effect reducing the actual driving capability of line buffers. As results, conventional sizing criterions that neglect them may lead to non optimal sized buffers.

Fig. 6 depicts the circuits of fig 2, with the inclusion of the capacitor of value $C_{out} = hC_0$ modelling the total parasitic capacitance.

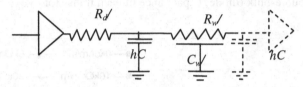

**Fig. 6.** buffer output capacitance shunt a portion of current toward ground, reducing the driving efficiency of the devices

It appears evident that $C_{out}$ being proportional to the transistor size, a buffer enlargement of a certain factor $h$ does not imply a same increase in the current that is feed through the line, as instead commonly assumed.

The "subtractive" effect is as strong as $C_{out}$ approaches the value of the load (i.e. wire) capacitance.

On the basis of the circuit in fig. 6, a simple modified expression for transistor sizing has been developed.

In fact, for the circuit, the 50% delay eqn. (1) can be written (if $k$ repeaters are used):

$$t_{50\%} = k \left[ 0.7R_d \left( \frac{C_w}{k} + C_g + C_0 \right) + \frac{R_w}{k} \left( 0.4 \frac{C_w}{k} + 0.7 \left( C_g + C_0 \right) \right) \right] \tag{3}$$

and by setting $\partial t_{50\%} / \partial k = 0$ it follows

$$0.4 \frac{R_w C_w}{k^2} = 0.7 R_d \left( C_g + C_0 \right) \tag{4}$$

From (4) the number repeaters $k_{opt}$ to achieve the minimum delay can be found:

$$k_{opt} = \sqrt{\frac{0.4 R_w C_w}{0.7 R_d \left( C_g + C_0 \right)}} \tag{5}$$

The optimal size of the buffer can be now carried out. In fact, if the 50% delay expression is re-written substituting $hC_g$, $hC_0$ and $R_d/h$ to the buffer input capacitance, output capacitance and output resistance, respectively, it follows:

$$h_{opt} = \sqrt{\frac{0.7R_d C_w}{R_w (0.4C_0 + 0.7C_g)}} \qquad (6)$$

Equation (6) applied to the line parameters of the example of fig. 3 leads to buffers with a size $h$, with respect to a minimum-sized one, equal to 178 (a value very close to the optimal value 170 carried out by simulations). HSPICE simulations show a 50% delay of 1.97ns, resulting in a speed improvement of about 28% and an area saving of 38%.

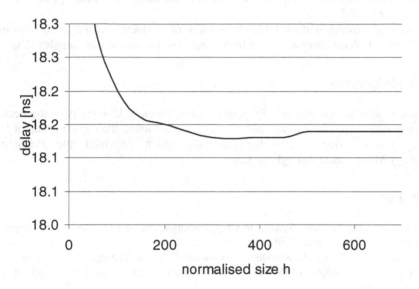

**Fig. 7.** 50% delay for a chain of repeater for a 100nm tech

The effectiveness of the proposed sizing rule has been further tested on a wide set of line parameters, using both real CMOS technology models and the Berkeley Predictive Technology Models [8].

Plot in fig. 7 reports, as example, the 50% delay for a chain of repeater as function of buffer size $h$. It refers to a 4mm long interconnect, for a 100nm technology [10], with $Rw$ and $Cw$ equal to 36k$\Omega$/m and 258pF/m, respectively. $C_g$, $C_0$ and $R_d$ equal to 0.3fF 0.45fF and 12.7k$\Omega$, respectively.

Classical sizing rules suggest a value of $h=552$, despite the value $h=406$ carried out by means of proposed sizing rule. The actual minimum delay, as shown by the plot, corresponds to a value of $h=375$. In this case the difference between delays obtained by means of the two compared expression is relatively insignificant, but the saving in terms of area is about 36%.

# 5  Conclusions

In the paper the role of the parasitic capacitances of the buffer on its effective driving capability has been highlighted.

The Authors demonstrate that the effective current supplied by the buffers could be significantly lower than those predicted by conventional buffer sizing expressions.

This degradation is as strong as parasitic capacitances approaches line wire capacitance, a common situation most of all in chip busses, where a strong line segmentation is used. As consequence, conventional optimisation expressions used to reduce chain delay may fail, leading to higher delay and most of all larger buffer then necessary. In the paper an effective developed expression for the size of CMOS repeaters is presented.

Simulation results show that the proposed formula allow area-delay product to be significantly reduced.

The reduced dimension of the buffer results also in a reduction of the power consumption related to leakage currents, a ever increasing issue for submicron complex ICs.

## Acknowledgments

The Authors want to acknowledge Prof. Eby G. Friedman, of University of Rochester, for his precious help. The Authors also want to acknowledge the device group at UC Berkeley (www.device.eecs.berkeley.edu/~ptm) which provided the Predictive Technology Models used through the paper.

## References

1. STNoC: Building a New System-on-Chip Paradigm http://www.st.com/stonline/press/news/back2005/b9014t.htm (2005)
2. Morgenshtein, A., Cidon, I., Kolodny, A., Ginosar, R. : Low-Leakage Repeaters for NoC Interconnects. Proceedings of ISCAS 2005 IEEE International Symposium on Circuits and Systems. (2005)
3. Cho, K.: Delay Calculation Capturing Crosstalk Effects Due to Coupling Capacitors.; Electronics Letters. 41 (2005) 458 – 460
4. Heydari, P., Mohanavelu, R.: Design of ultrahigh-speed low-voltage CMOS CML buffers and latches. Transactions on Very Large Scale Integration (VLSI) Systems, IEEE. Vol. 12, Issue: 10 (2004)1081 – 1093
5. Bakoglu, H.B.: Circuits, interconnections and packaging for VLSI. Addison-Wesley, Massachusetts (1990)
6. Man L. M., Banerjee, K., Mehrotra, A.: A Global Interconnect Optimization Scheme for Nano-meter Scale VLSI with implications for Latency, Bandwidth, and Power Dissipation. IEEE Transactions on Electron Devices Volume 51 (2004) 195 – 200
7. Nalamalpu, A., Burleson, W.: Repeater insertion in deep sub-micron CMOS: ramp-based analytical model and placement sensitivity analysis. Proceedings ISCAS 2000, Geneva, Swiss. 3 (2000) 766 –769
8. Cao, Y., Sato, T., Sylvester, D., Orshansky, M., Hu, C.: New paradigm of predictive MOSFET and interconnect modeling for early circuit design. Proc. of IEEE CICC (2000) 201-204

# Zephyr: A Static Timing Analyzer Integrated in a Trans-hierarchical Refinement Design Flow

Christophe Alexandre, Marek Sroka, Hugo Clément, and Christian Masson

Université Paris VI, Laboratoire LIP6, 4 Place Jussieu, 75005 Paris, France

**Abstract.** The evolution of silicon technologies has fundamentally changed the physical design EDA flow, which now has to go through a progressive refinement process where interconnections evolve seamlessly from logic to final detailed routing. Furthermore the level of integration reached makes mandatory the use of hierarchical enabled design methodologies. In this paper, we present Zephyr: an Elmore Delay Static Timing Analysis engine tightly integrated in the open academic Coriolis EDA physical design platform on which tools act as algorithmic engines operating on an integrated C++ database around which they consistently interact and collaborate. Coriolis provides high level C++ and Python APIs and a unified and consistent hierarchical VLSI data model through all the design steps from logic down to final layout. We discuss here more specifically the integration issues and concepts used to support timing analysis through the progressive refinement of hierarchical designs.

## 1 Introduction

The evolution towards nanometer silicon technologies has deeply enforced the role of interconnections in the VLSI design flow.

This has introduced fundamental changes in the physical design flow, which now has to go through a progressive refinement process in which CAD tools incrementally update an integrated central database representing the current state of the design. Within this process, interconnections evolve seamlessly from the logic view to the final detailed routing view through intermediate and more or less precise global routing steps.

Therefore it is increasingly important to have at one's disposal a flexible interconnect timing analysis tool, which is able to adapt its analysis to the changing level of precision of the routing description. Moreover, computing wire delay with an acceptable degree of precision requires to take into account the wiring topology and the distribution of resistance and capacity. This leads to the conclusion that the structure of interconnects is an information that must be continuously accessible to the timing analysis tool.

An other major problem comes from the level of integration now reached, which makes mandatory the use of hierarchical enabled design methodologies in order to handle large hierarchical netlists mixing hard IP blocks (pre-designed RAM, ROM, CPU Cores), soft IP blocks and glue control logic. Within the physical design process, this structural hierarchy may be partly lost (completely

J. Vounckx, N. Azemard, and P. Maurine (Eds.): PATMOS 2006, LNCS 4148, pp. 319–328, 2006.

lost in most place and route CAD tools which operate on the flattened netlist). However the capability to handle the physical design hierarchy while maintaining it correlated with the netlist hierarchical description makes the functional equivalence checking (through LVS, simulation or formal proof) as well as the timing and signal integrity analysis results, much easier to understand and manage by the designer.

Zephyr the Static Timing Analysis engine that we describe is designed to deal with these issues:

- It is a central component of an open academic EDA research platform (Coriolis) presented in Section 2.
- It relies on a trans-hierarchical occurrence model, a feature at the heart of Coriolis: the Hurricane database, subject of section 3.
- It is associated with an interconnect analysis engine, discussed in section 4, which estimates RC values on composite interconnects, along the refinement process.

Section 5 surveys major components and characteristics of Zephyr, and section 6 ends with the conclusion.

## 2   The Coriolis Platform

In the past ten years, the CAD community has seen the emergence of several industrial platforms. They have the common characteristic of managing a centralized design database working as a framework on which different tools can share and refine continuously the design data. By merging the logical and physical aspects of the circuits, these databases avoid inconsistencies and losses of informations due to the continuous changes in level of representation.

Cadence and Synopsys offer respectively OpenAccess and Milkyway. The main difference between them lies in their diffusion policy. While Milkyway is partially opened to Synopsys clients through the MAP-In program, Cadence is at the origin of the OpenAccess Coalition, which provides OpenAccess as a open source EDA database to registered users. Conversely, Magma's platform is entirely built around a proprietary central database whose details are not publicly available.

At the same time, a very active academic research community, mainly addressing specific algorithmic steps of the flow, shares tool implementations and common benchmarks in an open-source approach, as exemplified by the GSRC "*bookshelf*" repository [1]. However, those tools communicate only through interchange formats and the development of an integrated Physical Synthesis environment in academia was, up to now, considered as impossible [2].

Nevertheless, academic projects have recently emerged. On the one hand, the OpenAccessGear [3]: an open source development environment for physical design built on top of the OpenAccess database [4], which includes a user interface, a wrapper to the academic standard-cell placer CAPO, a set of benchmarks and a static timing analyser: OA Gear Timer.

On the other hand, Coriolis [5]: an ongoing project of the LIP6 laboratory, which provides the academic community with an open source platform (downloads under the GPL license are available through the project homepage at [6]). Coriolis is a back-end platform on which tools act as algorithmic engines operating on an integrated C++ database (named Hurricane) around which they consistently interact and collaborate. Coriolis provides a free CAD teaching and research open environment (both on design flows and algorithms) by offering both a set of core functionalities (such as a lef/def interface, a Python extension language and a graphical user interface) and a progressively enhanced suite of open-source CAD tools supporting academic VLSI design projects.

The global intent of the Coriolis project is to develop a fully integrated Physical Synthesis environment supporting progressive refinement design flows. Currently are available: a standard cell global and detailed placer, a global router and a timing analysis module, subject of this paper.

# 3   The Hurricane Database

Hurricane is a lightweight C++ object oriented database and programming platform which provides a unified and consistent modeling of hierarchical VLSI layouts through all the design steps from logic description down to detailed layout. It is outside the scope of this paper to detail Hurricane and interested readers will find documentation along with Coriolis. Here, we will summarize some concepts, with a higher focus on Hurricane hierarchy representation.

Hurricane provides a powerful object-oriented API for fast access, incremental update and consistent management of all the design views which fully relieves the application programmer from memory management issues.

It models in a unified view both the netlist and the routing (global or detailed) through "*hooking*" mechanisms which allows the seamless forward or backward transformation of a net-list into a global routing or a detailed layout (or a mix of those states), ensuring built-in consistency. For instance, segments know the contacts (or ports) on which they are anchored and the contacts (or ports) know their incident segments. Deleting some detail routing elements automatically links disconnected items by "*rubber*" fly lines, which reflects what needs to be reconnected.

Hurricane data structure embeds high performance 2D region query methods and provides a built-in high speed graphical display engine of the current state of the design, very useful for designing and debugging layout synthesis algorithms.

It provides extensibility mechanisms, notably through properties and relations which can be attached to any kind of database object (including to *occurrences*, see below).

It offers a rich (and extensible) set of powerful and generic query objects named *Collections*. *Collections* are not containers but "*set descriptors*" which provide an associated *Locator* for tracing through the corresponding set of elements. They can hide a fairly complex algorithmic trace process, visiting huge sets, but with very low memory foot print. Furthermore, *Filter* objects can be applied to a *Collection* in order to visit only the subset matching a predicate. *Collections* are very handy and flexible programming paradigms.

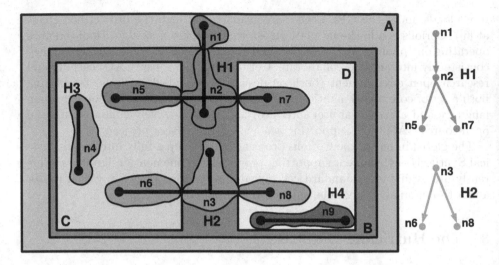

**Fig. 1.** Hypernet structure of interconnects

All modern design databases use *folded* hierarchy, in that every instance of a given cell points to the same master cell. This makes more manageable the representation of complex designs and the memory consumption. It is also easier to fix a problem in a cell and have it reflected everywhere instantly. However, there is no place in a *folded* database to attach data that would be specific to the context in which cells are instantiated.

To deal with this issue, Hurricane also represents hierarchical layout as a *folded* memory data model, but provides a **virtually unfolded** view to the tools tracing, annotating or displaying its content. For that purpose it manages the concept of *occurrences* which can refer any logical or physical item anywhere within the **virtually unfolded** design hierarchy. *Occurrences* are very light, volatile pointer pairs *<instantiation-path, item-in-the-model-cell>*, where the instantiation-path is also a compact shared object which implicitly knows the top cell, the instances composing the path and the cell master model of the lowest instance (an *Occurrence* with a NULL path refers an item of the current cell).

Two *occurrences* objects are identical if they refer to the same object of the unfolded hierarchy. If a property is attached to the first one, it becomes visible from the second one. Of course those properties are securely stored on an automatically managed hidden object which exists only if at least one property is attached to the occurrence it represents. *Occurrences* may be relative to the top cell or to some sub-cell, this allows to attach partially context dependent properties at the right level in the layout hierarchy.

*Occurrences* provide elegant ways to design algorithms for visiting, extracting and annotating hierarchical designs without the need to partially unfold the hierarchy with complex cache techniques. However this approach to annotate a *virtually unfolded* design has a memory cost which is acceptable only when the ratio of *occurrences* with attached properties (at each processing step) versus the total number of potential *occurrences* is low. This holds for most well designed layout algorithms, and more the design is hierarchic more this approach is efficient.

Combining the previously defined concepts, complex queries like: "visit all occurrences of segments on a given layer in a given area", "find all parallel adjacent segments on the same layer which may cross-talk with the segments of a net", or "visit all layout element occurrences electrically connected to a given layout occurrence" are written in few lines of code. The graphic highlighting of the visited occurrences is simply done by attaching them the "Select" property!

Thanks to the occurrence mechanism it is easy to deal with the trans-hierarchical structure of interconnect during the process of Physical Synthesis. Indeed, the *folded* design hierarchy breaks up each interconnection into a tree of net occurrences, that we name an **hypernet**. The root of this tree is the net occurrence at the highest hierarchical level, and it canonically represents the **hypernet** interconnect. This is illustrated in the figure 1.

## 4   Lightning: The Hypernet Abstraction Module

Hypernet based collections provide the capability to visit the layout elements of a virtually flattened interconnect, however this tracing process doesn't follow the tree topology of the interconnect, and is not appropriate to build a RC tree.

It is the purpose of the Lightning module to provide such a canonical method to trace routing elements of an hypernet, and offer an abstraction layer upon the real state of the design which can be either globally or detail routed, or a combination of both. It takes detailed routing data when available, while for global routing it merely follows Steiner tree topology and distances. This allows to navigate homogeneously inside hierarchical designs where hypernets may overlap globally routed glue and prerouted blocks.

Lightning builds on-the-fly a temporary lightweight data structure representing the current routing state. This is done by reading each layout element occurrence of the hypernet and converting them into nodes and edges. Nodes are factored by their coordinates and layer, they may be either bifurcation or terminals points (primary I/O or I/O port occurrences of leaf cells). Edges represent wires with a given layer and width, or layer changes through a via. Nodes and segments of global routes have no layer and width specified. Once this data model is built, the trace proceeds from the occurrence of a driver port that becomes the root of the exploration tree.

The figure 2 illustrates this trace process on a composite interconnection.

During this depth first trace process, each edge, node, branch separation at a bifurcation point or terminal which is reached triggers the call of a visitor's method: a callback which provides information about position, distance, width and layer (and also the occurrence of terminal points). A "*visitor*" is a functional object that allows the application program to specify its own operations for each step within the trace process. Notice that for logical nets the routing graph should be a tree, however if loops exist, their re-convergence points are reported (in order to manage meshed nets like clocks).

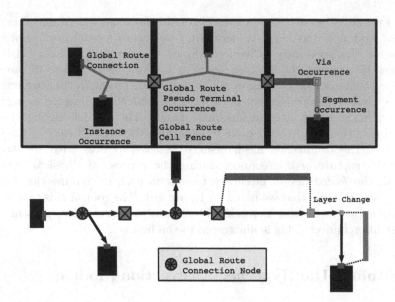

**Fig. 2.** Lightning trace process of a composite interconnection

## 5   Zephyr: The Static Timing Analyzer

Zephyr is a flexible static timing analysis engine central to the Coriolis platform and constantly accessible by optimization engines. In the current version, Zephyr is mainly intended to drive global placement and global routing engines. Therefore, the level of precision of its three internal modules (RC tree evaluator, delay calculator and static timing analyser) is adapted to this task. In the future, we consider improving progressively and jointly all Zephyr modules, in order to be able to run post Physical Synthesis precise timing analysis.
Zephyr inputs are:

- A hierarchical mixed size block and standard-cell design
- Technology timing characteristics of cell libraries in a subset of the Synopsys *"liberty"* format (*.lib*), from which we extract fixed cell delays and cell output resistances.
- User timing constraints can be provided by a subset of the *.sdc* standard format.

We will now detail Zephyr modules.

### 5.1   The RC Evaluator Module

The RC Evaluator builds a RC Forest (RCF), which associates to each hypernet a RC Tree object (RCT) whose root is attached to the hypernet driver port occurrence and whose leaf nodes are attached to the receiver ports occurrences, intermediate nodes being attached to divergence points of the hypernet Steiner tree. For multi driver hypernets, RC Trees are created for each driver.

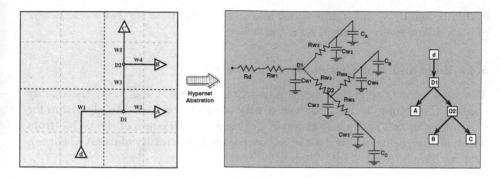

**Fig. 3.** Construction of a RC Tree

The RC Tree is built by an exploration of the hypernet through Lightning, with a *"visitor"* functional object which estimates the RC values according to the level of accuracy of the routing and the technological parameters. Currently it relies on simple estimates based on distance, width and layer, in the future it might proceed to more complex geometric queries to identify interfering wires in order to estimate capacitances more accurately, or even subcontract this task to an external RC Parasitics Extractor.

### 5.2   The Elmore RC Delay Calculator

The RC Tree object is optimised for Elmore delay computation. Each node contains the lumped capacitance of the node sub-tree as well as local resistance of the incoming wire. The delay is computed simply by back-tracking from a RCT leaf up to the root, applying either the Scaled Elmore Delay or the Fitted Elmore Delay formula [7].

### 5.3   The Static Timing Analyser Core

The Zephyr Static Timing Analysis engine, like OA Gear Timer, models the timing of the circuit as a directed acyclic graph, the Generalized Causality Graph (or GCG), which remains invariant (unless the logic is modified). In the GCG, two nodes (up and down transitions) are attached to each primary inputs/outputs or to I/O port occurrences of leaf cells, the edges representing the delays between the nodes they connect. There are two kinds of edges: those for gate internal delays (as provided by the pre-characterized cell-library - unless for registers) and those representing interconnect delays (provided by the RCT delay calculator).

Therefore the GCG is anchored on the virtually flattened view of a hierarchical design.

OA Gear Timer (according to [3]) relies on a simple wire delay model either based on the half-perimeter bounding-box of interconnections or brought through a callback function mechanism which only permits to define wire delays and capacitive loads on whole nets. Instead, Zephyr relies on its *generic* RC Tree evaluator and delay calculator which allows to differentiate the loads and delays of each driver-receiver pair of an hypernet.

## 5.4    Edge and Net Criticality Calculator

The issue of net weighting for timing-driven placement has been thoroughly studied. Tim Kong [8] has proposed a very efficient and accurate algorithm for computing an *"all path going through"* criticality for all edges of the GCG (from which net weighting can be derived as the maximum criticality of its GCG edges), that we have integrated into Zephyr.

## 5.5    The Critical Path Generator

The Timing Analysis engine is able to determine any (reasonable) amount of most critical paths in the design.

Our algorithm works by progressively expanding shared partial longest paths. They are kept ordered by decreasing slack of the most critical path going through them. Path completion lasts until the requested number of critical paths is reached. This algorithm is quite effective and requires at most $n$ operations by computed path, $n$ being the edge count of the longest path in the GCG.

To display the critical path list, the tool provides a graphical user interface composed of two windows: a critical paths list window displaying the critical paths and a critical path window detailing the different components of a given path, which can be highlighted on the layout (a screenshot showing Zephyr timing analysis on a placed and globally routed block appears on figure 4).

## 5.6    Incremental Update

Both the RC Tree and GCG nodes are anchored into the the virtually flattened design as Hurricane properties on the terminal occurrences, this allows to cross-reference them as well as notify them when a layout change occurs.

On one hand, a GCG edge can access the terminal occurrences attached to its two ending nodes, and then, to their associated RC Tree nodes for computing its delay.

On the other hand, when a layout element occurrence is modified (by route or place refinement), this is notified to the net occurrence and from then to the hypernet terminal occurrences, which in turn will invalidate the corresponding RC Tree and GCG edges. Those edges will then propagate invalidate flags in their fan-in and fan-out cones. When the next timing analysis occurs, a delay request on an invalidated GCG edge will transfer the request to its associated RC Tree, which, if it has been invalidated will initiate its re-evaluation.

## 5.7    Validation and Experimentation

The Elmore RC Delay Calculator was validated by converting the nets of a circuit into Spice models and comparing its results to Spice simulation. Comparisons

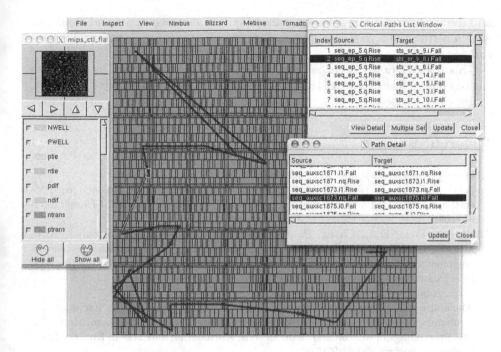

**Fig. 4.** Zephyr screenshot: critical paths list and path detail windows and a highlighted critical path

showed that Zephyr error margins do not exceed 10 percents, while for most nets, the error is below 5 percents (using Fitted Elmore Delay should improve those figures). Indeed the true source of errors is the way we approximate the RC Trees, which will require calibration through benchmarking on representative circuits in each technology used.

The critical paths, computed by the GCG, were checked against the ones given by the industrial tool TAS from Avertec [9]. The longest paths list was roughly the same in both tools, so we can rely on Zephyr to drive place and route flows.

Working with optimization engines, Zephyr has proven to be a non-critical part in terms of memory consumption and run time. For instance, we measured execution time of Zephyr on a fully placed 38k cells design. It was first globally routed in 157 seconds, the timing analysis was achieved in 8 seconds and the first 10k critical paths were computed in about one second. We are currently evaluating the speed improvement when working in incremental mode.

## 6   Conclusion

Zephyr is fully integrated in the Coriolis platform and is being experimented in a top-down progressive refinement flow for standard cell timing driven placement. This flow proceeds by a succession of interleaved phases of quadri-partitioning, global routing and static timing analysis which provides net criticality evaluation and feedback for the next refinement loop [5]. It is also used as a stand alone tool with a netlist and layout capture language, providing coarse timing estimations, early in the design process.

This demonstrates the capability of Zephyr to be seamlessly integrated in various design flows. Zephyr is already accessible to the open source community, under the GPL licence.

# References

1. http://www.gigascale.org/bookshelf/slots/
2. Adya, S.N., et al.: Benchmarking for large-scale placement and beyond. In: Proceedings of the 2003 international symposium on Physical design, ACM Press (2003) 95–103
3. Xiu, Z., Papa, D.A., Chong, P., Albrecht, C., Kuehlmann, A., Rutenbar, R.A., Markov, I.L.: Early research experience with openaccess gear: an open source development environment for physical design. In: ISPD '05: Proceedings of the 2005 international symposium on physical design, ACM Press (2005) 94–100
4. http://openeda.si2.org
5. Alexandre, C., Clement, H., Chaput, J.P., Sroka, M., Masson, C., Escassut, R.: Tsunami: An integrated timing-driven place and route research platform. In: DATE '05: Proceedings of the conference on Design, Automation and Test in Europe, IEEE Computer Society (2005) 920–921
6. http://www-asim.lip6.fr/recherche/coriolis
7. Abou-Seido, A.I., Nowak, B., Chu, C.: Fitted elmore delay: a simple and accurate interconnect delay model. IEEE Trans. Very Large Scale Integr. Syst. 12(7) (2004) 691–696
8. Kong, T.T.: A novel net weighting algorithm for timing-driven placement. In: Proceedings of the 2002 IEEE/ACM international conference on Computer-aided design, ACM Press (2002) 172–176
9. http://www.avertec.com

# Receiver Modeling for Static Functional Crosstalk Analysis

Mini Nanua[1] and David Blaauw[2]

[1]SunMicroSystem Inc., Austin, Tx, USA
Mini.Nanua@sun.com
[2]University of Michigan, Ann Arbor, Mi, USA
Blaauw@eecs.umich.edu

**Abstract.** Crosstalk analysis has become a significant part of the design cycle of high performance processors in nanometer technologies. In this paper we demonstrate that current crosstalk analysis techniques that ignore the degrading effect of multiple crosstalk events on receiver noise rejection curve filter significant number of true violations. We also demonstrate that techniques that take into account the multiple crosstalk events with traditional receiver modeling result in large number of false violations. We propose improved crosstalk analysis techniques that are multiple noise event aware (MNEA) with minimal changes to existing crosstalk analysis. We also propose enhancements to existing receiver models so they can be used with the MNEA analysis resulting in reduction of number of false violations by 68%-98% while guaranteeing identification of all true violations.

## 1 Introduction

Crosstalk in nanometer technologies has become a major concern. Technology trends such as *interconnect scaling* has resulted in an increase in the interconnect coupling capacitance and *device scaling* has resulted in faster signal transition time and smaller system cycle time. In addition, the high performance designs are larger with long interconnects further increasing the magnitude of the crosstalk pulses induced on coupled interconnects [1] [2]. Static crosstalk analysis techniques are used for identifying the interconnects that violate the signal integrity criterion as part of the physical design process of a high performance processor. This analysis is called *functional* crosstalk analysis since the violations can lead to logic failures. The analysis is required to be fast and accurate to reduce the impact on the design process time.

A typical crosstalk analysis scheme [3] [4]is illustrated in Fig. 1. The analysis can be divided in two broad categories: device modeling and interconnect modeling. The interconnects are modeled as distributed RC network. The interconnect being analyzed for signal integrity is called the *victim*. The interconnects coupled to it are called the *aggressors*. The victim-aggressor circuit is solved with accurate and efficient reduced-order and/or analytical models proposed in [5] [6]. The aggressor set is reduced based on logical constraints, timing windows and respective clock domains between the aggressors and the victim making the analysis more realistic and the circuit to be

J. Vounckx, N. Azemard, and P. Maurine (Eds.): PATMOS 2006, LNCS 4148, pp. 329–339, 2006.

analyzed smaller [4] [7]. The device modeling requires pre-characterization of the gates in the design. It comprises of: driver modeling and the victim receiver modeling. Various linear and non-linear driver models have been proposed for victim and aggressor drivers in [8] [9].

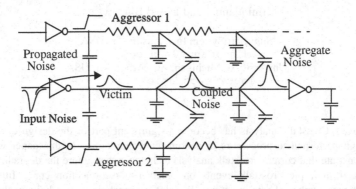

**Fig. 1.** Typical Static Noise Analysis Scheme

The victim receiver model is composed of input gate capacitance and set of *noise rejection curves* or *noise propagation tables*. If during the crosstalk analysis a victim pulse height exceeds its receiver noise rejection curve value or if the propagation through the receiver gate exceeds a predetermined threshold, the victim is said to fail the signal integrity requirements. Gate characterization for noise rejection curve is therefore, a critical step with direct impact on number of crosstalk violations.

For simple single input gates such as, inverters and buffers, the input noise rejection curve is easily computed. However, for multiple input gates, the noise limit for an input has a dependence on the state of other inputs of the gate. Current crosstalk analysis assumes that no two noise events on different inputs of a gate would align temporally (referred to as *Single Switching Bestcase*) but as the system frequency increases, the temporal alignment of multiple noise events has become a real possibility. To account for these events, current receiver models can be generated

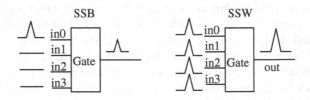

**Fig. 2.** SSB and SSW for a Comple x Gate

with the assumption that identical simultaneous noise pulses can occur on *all* inputs of a gate (referred to as *Single Switching Worstcase*). Both the SSB and SSW assumptions are illustrated in Fig. 2. The SSB analysis, though a practical assumption for low frequency designs, can filter a potential signal integrity problem in high performance design with small cycle times. The SSW approach is not a practical assumption since it results in noise rejection curves that are pessimistic by 70%, which can easily lead to 10x the real crosstalk violations and an increased system design process time. The current analysis and receiver models are therefore, only suitable for simple gates such as inverters and buffers.

In this paper, we propose modifications to traditional crosstalk analysis to make it multiple noise event aware (MNEA). We apply the new enhanced analysis to an industrial microprocessor core and design blocks in 65nm bulk CMOS technology. The results demonstrate that the proposed scheme identifies the signal integrity violations which would have been overlooked with SSB crosstalk analysis. We also demonstrate that the proposed scheme reduces the number of false violations by 68% - 98% compared to SSW crosstalk analysis.

Previous work on receiver models has concentrated on determining the dc logic values for other inputs that would yield the most pessimistic noise rejection value for an input for complex gates [4]. Modeling of different noise wave shapes has also been proposed in [10] but again the modeling assumes all inputs other than the primary input are at stable dc values. There has been no modeling which accounts for the possibility of noise events on more than one input of the receiver.

## 2  Effect of Multiple Crosstalk Noise Events

Receiver model for a gate comprises of its input capacitance and noise rejection curves (NRC) for all its inputs. The NRC is a function of input crosstalk pulse width and gate load capacitance. A sample set of NRCs are shown in Fig. 3, each curve corresponds to a constant output load. The input noise limit (y-axis) increases with reduction in crosstalk pulse width (x-axis) and increase in gate output capacitance.

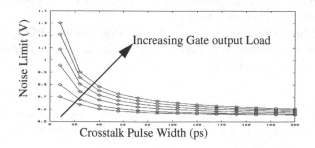

**Fig. 3.** Sample Noise Rejection Curves

A noise event is defined as *high-down* if the victim is at logic high and the crosstalk pulse results in a voltage dip on the victim. Analogous to this is the *low-up* noise event. Consider the AOI33 structure in Fig. 4, if the input *in00* of this gate is being characterized for noise rejection curves then:

1. Low-up noise of *in00* will be reduced if *in10* is also experiencing a low-up noise event,
2. High-down noise limit of in00 will reduce if one or both in01 and in02 are experiencing a high-down noise event as well.

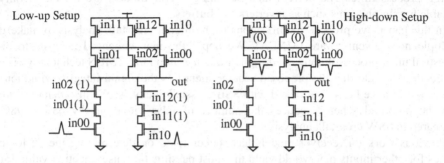

**Fig. 4.** AOI33 Circuit

The degradation is as a result of each source-drain parallel FET acting as an independent source of noise on the output. This behavior is exhibited by all FETs connected with source-drain parallel connections.

Fig. 5 shows the AOI33 *in00* high-down and low-up noise rejection curve degradation, for a given gate output load, as the number of inputs experiencing the noise evets is increased. The simulations are done assuming simultaneous identical noise pulses on all inputs. The high-up noise limit in this example degrades by 34% for two inputs with crosstalk event and further degrades by 12% when crosstalk event is introduced to the third input as well. The low-up noise limit degrades by 69% for crosstalk events on two inputs. This example illustrates three observations:

1. single switching bestcase (SSB) NRC for a receiver can degrade by a significant amount with multiple noise events,
2. single switching worstcase (SSW) assumptions degrades the NRC by a large amount,
3. as the number of inputs with a crosstalk event increases, the degradation in NRC reduces (diminishing returns).

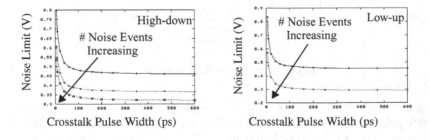

**Fig. 5.** AOI33 Noise Rejection Degradation

## 3   Crosstalk Analysis with Noise Rejection Curves

A typical crosstalk scheme using noise rejection curves is illustrated in Fig. 6. For every victim in the design a valid set of aggressors is identified. The victim-aggressor RC circuit is solved for the crosstalk pulse on the victim which is then compared to the receiver noise rejection curve for violation determination. In this normal flow the noise rejection curves are either based on SSB assumption or SSW assumption. For our proposed methodology we use SSB assumption, and further analyze the nets that are filtered for possible multiple noise event failure. Note that a violation with SSB NRC is a valid violation since multiple events would only increase the noise on the failing victim. The flow in Fig. 6, is therefore modified as follows:

1. identify the nets that are filtered from existing analysis and have receivers such as nand, nor, aoi,oai, etc.,
2. determine the number of inputs that can have a crosstalk event for every receiver by aligning aggressor timing windows,
3. degrade the noise rejection curve and determine the violation.

The problem is now reduced to determination of a model that would predict the degradation in noise rejection curve given a gate and the number of its input experiencing the noise events.

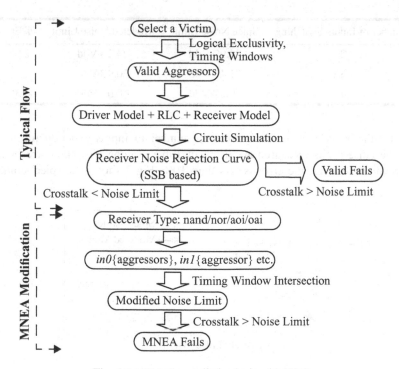

**Fig. 6.** MNEA Crosstalk Analysis with NRC

### 3.1  Noise Limit Degradation Model

For a given technology, the noise limits of gates with parallel FETs like aoi, oai, nand, nor etc. can be modeled using the noise limit with SSB assumptions. The new degraded noise limit, $V'_{NL}$ can be derived using a simple exponential formulae given by:

$$V'_{NL} = V_{NL}\left(e^{-\alpha_{nrc}N}\right)_{\ddot{\imath}} \tag{1}$$

where $V_{NL}$ is the SSB noise limit, $\alpha_{nrc}$ is the curve fitting constant ($0 < \alpha_{nrc} < 1$) and $N$ is the number of gate inputs experiencing identical noise events simultaneously.

The factor $\alpha_{nrc}$ is a constant for a circuit in a technology. It can be determined by simulating the circuit with multiple noise events during gate pre-characterization and stored in the receiver model. Determination of $\alpha_{nrc}$ has the overhead of only a single extra simulation per gate type from the current pre-characterizations. In our experiments we found that $\alpha_{nrc}$ varies with gate topology and the FET beta ratio but is independent of actual FET size. To illustrate the model accuracy we simulated a nand4 circuit in 65nm bulk CMOS technology with Spice for a noise pulse of a fixed width (600ps) and a fixed typical output load (fanout 4x).

**Table 1.** Nand4 Spice Vs Model High-Up Noise Limit

| Number of Inputs Switching | Spice Noise Limit | Modeled Noise Limit | %Err |
|:---:|:---:|:---:|:---:|
| 2 | 24.9%Vdd | 24.2%Vdd | -2.8% |
| 3 | 21.4%Vdd | 20.9%Vdd | -2.3% |
| 4 | 19.2%Vdd | 18.0%Vdd | -6.3% |

The simulation is repeated for increasing number of inputs experiencing a noise event. The noise limits measured are listed in Table 1 along with the corresponding model predicted values, the error is less than 10%. Fig 7 shows the spice simulated

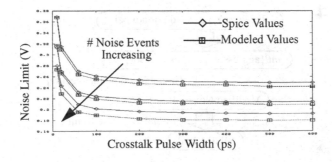

**Fig. 7.** Nand4 Noise Limit: Spice Vs. Model

and model predicted noise limit values for a nand4 for a range of noise pulse widths as the number of multiple noise events is increased. The data shows a good agreement between the model predictions and spice measurements.

### 3.2 Multiple Noise Event Aware (MNEA) Crosstalk Analysis Results

We applied the proposed MNEA crosstalk analysis incorporating the proposed noise limit model to industrial microprocessor core and blocks designed in 65nm bulk CMOS technology. The results are listed in Table 2 for original analysis with SSB and SSW assumptions, the proposed MNEA methodology and spice simulations based true violations.

As expected, a large number of violations are reported by SSW flow for all designs. The SSB analysis reports violations less than the Spice reported true violations. The MNEA analysis reduces the number of false violations (*Reduced False Violation factor*) in all cases by 68%-93% with respect to SSW. The MNEA analysis does not eliminate all false violations due to the fact that, the noise limit degradation model assumes that all multiple crosstalk events are identical, whereas in real design, different inputs would experience different crosstalk pulses. This difference is accounted for in the following sections with crosstalk flow based on noise propagation table models.

**Table 2.** MNEA Crosstalk Analysis Results

| Block | Total Nets | SSB | SSW | MNEA | Spice | %RFV |
|-------|-----------|-----|------|------|-------|------|
| Core  | 335,282   | 0   | 2295 | 741  | 454   | 84%  |
| Blk1  | 10,386    | 1   | 124  | 45   | 8     | 68%  |
| Blk2  | 103,824   | 0   | 487  | 84   | 53    | 93%  |
| Blk3  | 31,360    | 0   | 1470 | 278  | 141   | 90%  |
| Blk4  | 317,729   | 11  | 2851 | 898  | 471   | 82%  |

## 4   Crosstalk Analysis with Noise Propagation Tables

The quality of crosstalk analysis results discussed in previous section can be improved by using a topological sort scheme as illustrated in Fig 8. In this scheme all the interconnects and respective receivers in a logical path (terminating into a latch) are identified. The analysis is done such that for each interconnect, the crosstalk pulse is the aggregate of the computed crosstalk pulse and the propagated pulse along the logic path. The violation determination is done when the aggregate crosstalk pulse at the input of a latch results in changing its storage value. This scheme is complex in execution and it is difficult to correct the violations identified. A slightly modified version of this scheme utilizes propagation through the receiver and one logic stage following the receiver. This provides the benefit of attenuation through the receiver gates and hence, reduces the false violations. In addition the violations are easily identified for correction since only two stages of logic is traversed.

We propose the following enhancements to the typical SSB propagation analysis to make it a MNEA propagation methodology:

1. identify the filtered nets with receivers such as aoi, oai, nand, nor etc.,
2. for each such receiver identify the inputs that can have multiple noise events by aligning the aggressor timing windows,
3. propagate crosstalk pulse taking all noise events into account and determine violations.

Similar to NRC characterization, the gate crosstalk propagation table simulations can be done with SSB or SSW assumptions. The MNEA analysis requires determination of crosstalk propagation given more than one crosstalk pulse at the gate inputs. Analogous to NRCs, the propagation through a gate increases with multiple noise events and it also demonstrates the principle of diminishing returns with each successive crosstalk event. We propose a propagation model given the gate propagation based on SSB assumptions in the following section.

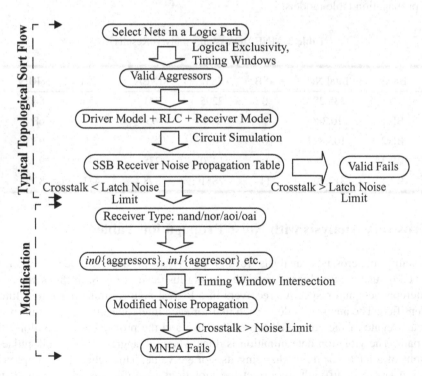

**Fig. 8.** MNEA Crosstalk with Appreciation Model

## 4.1  Noise Propagation Appreciation Model

If for a given gate the SSB propagation in known for an input then, the effect of multiple noise events on side inputs is to increase the crosstalk propagation through the gate. We propose the following formula for predicting the propagation, $V_{pknew}$ as follows:

$$V_{pknew} = \sum_{i=0}^{N} V_i \cdot e^{i \cdot \alpha_{prop}}$$  (2)

where, $V_i$ is the propagated peak for an input $i$ with SSB assumption. The constant $\alpha_{prop}$ is the curve fitting parameter. It can be obtained by simulating each gate type for a set of input pulses and propagated noise pulse. The index $i$ is obtained by sorting the input crosstalk propagated pulses such that $i=0$ corresponds to the largest crosstalk pulse width and $i=N$, the smallest. For example for a nand2 with two inputs $in0$ and $in1$, with crosstalk propagated pulses: (200mV, 500ps) and (300mV, 200ps) respectively. The new propagated pulse for $in0$ would be given by:

$$V_{pknew} = 200 \cdot e^{0 \cdot \alpha_{prop}} + 300 \cdot e^{1 \cdot \alpha_{prop}}$$  (3)

To estimate the accuracy of the model various spice simulations were done on different gate types. The crosstalk pulses on different inputs were assumed to differ in pulse height and width, the pulse width was varied from 20ps to 500ps and the noise height was varied from 50mV to 500mv. Spice simulated propagated noise and model predicted noise propagation are listed in Table 3. The error is within 10% unless one

Table 3. Multiple Noise Event Propagation Model Vs. Spice Results

| Gate | #Inputs | SSW | SSB | MSW $V_{pknew}$ | Spice $V_{pk}$ | Err |
|------|---------|-----|-----|-----------------|----------------|-----|
| nand3 | 2 | 0.982 | 0.231 | 0.265 | 0.264 | 0.3% |
| nand3 | 3 | 0.982 | 0.325 | 0.459 | 0.445 | 3% |
| nand4 | 2 | 0.640 | 0.126 | 0.150 | 0.128 | 17% |
| nand4 | 4 | 0.640 | 0.288 | 0.378 | 0.324 | 17% |
| nor3 | 2 | 0.566 | 0.410 | 0.470 | 0.468 | 0.4% |
| nor3 | 3 | 1.235 | 0.819 | 1.158 | 1.052 | 10% |
| aoi12 | 2 | 1.06 | 0.471 | 0.672 | 0.669 | 0.4% |
| oai12 | 2 | 1.02 | 0.543 | 0.966 | 0.817 | 18% |

or more crosstalk noise pulses have a very small height. The data points in Table 3.with error larger than 10% correspond to multiple crosstalk events comprising of one or more crosstalk pulses with very small pulse heights.The table also shows the corresponding SSB and SSW predicted noise propagation.

## 4.2  MNEA Propagation Crosstalk Analysis Results

A 65nm technology microprocessor core and design blocks were analyzed for crosstalk with SSB propagation, SSW propagation and the proposed MNEA propagation. The results are shown in Table 4.

**Table 4.** MNEA Crosstalk Analysis Results

| Block | Total Nets | SSB | SSW | MNEA | Spice | %RFV |
|-------|-----------|-----|-----|------|-------|------|
| Core | 335,282 | 0 | 303 | 40 | 34 | 98% |
| Blk1 | 10,386 | 0 | 7 | 0 | 0 | - |
| Blk2 | 103,824 | 0 | 60 | 5 | 4 | 97% |
| Blk3 | 31,360 | 0 | 104 | 10 | 8 | 98% |
| Blk4 | 317,729 | 0 | 159 | 46 | 34 | 90% |

The proposed MNEA analysis reduced the number of false violations by 98%, demonstrating improvement over the MNEA with NRC degradation. Note that the SSB assumption filters all real violations. Also note that the number of violations with propagation reduces when compared to NRC criterion violations in Table 2.

## 5  Conclusions

In this paper we demonstrated the need for multiple crosstalk events aware crosstalk analysis schemes due to increasing system frequency. The potential of multiple noise events aligning in time to create a functional violation is a real possibility not addressed efficiently by current crosstalk analysis and receiver models. We proposed modification to NRC and propagation based crosstalk analysis such that the false violations were reduced by 68%-98%. Our proposed changes also reported all true violations possible as a result of multiple crosstalk events.

## References

1. Caignet F., Delmas-Bendhia S., Sicard E.: The Challenge of Signal Integrity in Deep-Submicrometer CMOS Technology. Proceedings IEEE. Vol.89 (2001)
2. Heydari P., Pedram M.: Capacitive Coupling Noise in High-Speed VLSI Circuits. Transactions IEEE CAD. Vol.24 (2005)
3. Shepard K. L.: Harmony: Static Noise Analysis of Deep Submicron Digital Integrated Circuits. Transactions IEEE CAD. Vol.18 (1999)
4. R. Levy et.al.: ClariNet: A noise analysis tool for deep submicron design. DAC (2000)

5. Odabasioglu A., Celik M., Pileggi L. T.: *PRIMA:* Passive Reduced-Order Interconnect Macromodeling Algorithm. Transactions IEEE CAD. Vol.17 (1998)
6. Devgan A.: Efficient Coupled Noise Estimation for On-Chip Interconnects. Proceedings IEEE/ACM CAD International Conference (1997)
7. Krauter B., Widiger D.: Variable Frequency Crosstalk Noise Analysis: A Methodology to Guarantee Functionality from dc to $f_{max}$. Proceedings DAC (2000)
8. Tutuianu B., Baldick R., Johnstone M.: Nonlinear Driver Models for Timing and Noise Analysis. Transactions IEEE CAD. Vol.23 (2004)
9. Bai X., Chandra R., Dey S., Srinivas P. V.: Interconnect Coupling-Aware Driver Modeling in Static Noise Analysis for Nanometer Circuits. Transactions IEEE CAD. Vol.23 (2004)
10. Chen W., Gupta S. K., Breuer M.: Analytic Models for Crosstalk Excitation and Propagation in  VLSI Circuits. Transactions IEEE CAD. Vol.21 (2002)

# Modeling of Crosstalk Fault in Defective Interconnects*

Ajoy K. Palit, Kishore K. Duganapalli, and Walter Anheier

University of Bremen, FB1/ITEM, Otto-Hahn-Allee-NW1,
D-28359 Bremen, Germany
{palit, kishore, anheier}@item.uni-bremen.de

**Abstract.** The manufacturing defect in the interconnect lines can lead to various electrical faults, *e.g.* defect due to under-etching effect/conductive particle contamination on interconnect line can lead to increased coupling capacitances between the two adjacent interconnects, which, in turn, can eventually result in crosstalk fault in the DSM chips. In this paper we describe the line defect-based-crosstalk fault model that will be helpful in analyzing the severity of the defect/fault, as the crosstalk fault occasionally leads to various signal integrity losses, such as timing violation due to excessive signal delay or speed-up, logic failure due to crosstalk positive/negative glitch above/below logic low/high threshold and also reliability problem particularly due to crosstalk glitch above logic high threshold. Our crosstalk fault model accuracy is very close to PSPICE simulation results when the defect/fault is located in the middle of interconnects, whereas for the defects located at the near-end/far-end side of aggressor-victim the model accuracy differs approximately by ±5% respectively.

**Index terms:** defect-based-crosstalk fault model, signal integrity losses, aggressor-victim, ABCD-model, crosstalk-hazards.

## 1 Introduction

With the shrinking feature size or technology scaling and with ever increasing clock frequency nowadays the DSM chips are very much susceptible to various manufacturing defects. The manufacturing defect in the interconnect lines can lead to various electrical faults. For instance, breaks in interconnect line due to over-etching/cracks and scratch can cause strong, or full open (*i.e.* infinite resistance interconnect opens) and weak open (*i.e.* resistive bridges with moderate/high resistance). The open defects can eventually lead to logic faults [1, 2], because this discontinuity can completely eliminate the electrical connection between the nodes. In contrast, the under-etching effect/particle (conductive) contamination on interconnect line can lead to resistive bridging faults or increased coupling capacitances between the two adjacent interconnects which, in turn, can eventually result in crosstalk fault in the DSM chips. In this paper we describe the interconnects' defect-based-crosstalk fault model that can be utilized for analyzing the severity of the defect/fault, as the crosstalk fault due to interconnects' defect can occasionally lead to various integrity losses, such as timing

---

* CMOS12 technology data provided by Philips Semiconductors GmbH, DTC, Hamburg, Germany.

J. Vounckx, N. Azemard, and P. Maurine (Eds.): PATMOS 2006, LNCS 4148, pp. 340–349, 2006.
© Springer-Verlag Berlin Heidelberg 2006

violation (delay fault), voltage level violation/logic failure, and also reliability problems *etc*. For instance, if the victim and aggressor are driven by opposite transitions
namely, rising input transition and falling input transition respectively, then the resulting victim output transition is a delayed rising transition due to crosstalk fault. On the
other hand, if the victim and aggressor are driven respectively by static "0" and fast
rising (0→1) transition then the crosstalk positive glitch is generated in the victim's
output signal [3, 5]. If the height of crosstalk glitch happens to be larger than the upper-threshold value of logic-low voltage for the given technology, it will produce
logic failures (functionality problem), whereas for the same aggressor transition but
victim with static "1" input if the height of the generated crosstalk glitch is larger than
the upper threshold value of logic-high voltage, the crosstalk glitch will create reliability problem of the device in the long run. This is because excessive over-voltage
at the gate-input reduces the life-expectancy of the device drastically as the gate oxide
layer gradually suffers from time-dependent-dielectric-breakdown (TDDB) and hot-
carriers effect. The remaining part of the paper is organized as follows: in Section 2
we describe the defect modeling mechanism for interconnects defect which is followed by crosstalk fault model of defective pair of interconnects in Section 3. Thereafter, transient response and loss estimation from the crosstalk fault model are
described in section 4. Section 5 presents a few experimental simulation results,
whereas brief concluding remarks are presented in section 6.

## 2  Defect Modeling in Pair of Interconnects

With the aim of illustrating a real situation in nowadays DSM chips, figure 1 below
shows a particular case of two parallel defect-free interconnect lines on the same
metal layer with minimum line-spacing prescribed by the given process technology.

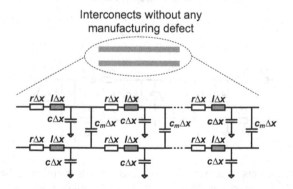

**Fig. 1.** Parallel interconnects without any defect and their equivalent electrical circuit

It is to be noted here that both top and bottom interconnects have been represented
by $n$ number of "right-$L$" distributed $RLC$ models [4] and coupling (mutual) capacitance ($c_m\Delta x$) has been added across each segment uniformly [5].

In order to characterize the behavior of a defective interconnects' pair, interconnect coupling capacitances are increased in the defective part of interconnects (see Figure 2), assuming that this particular type of manufacturing defect has little effect on the distributed resistance and inductance values of the same interconnects pair.

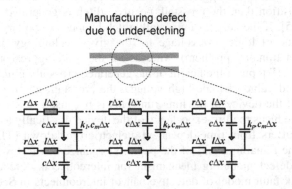

**Fig. 2.** Manufacturing defect in parallel interconnects and it's electrical equivalent circuit

Also, here, it is to be noted that manufacturing defect has affected $p$ blocks (each of length $\Delta x$) of "right-$L$" distributed $RLC$ models from both top and bottom interconnects and for these $p$ blocks the coupling capacitance values are $k_i$ times of usual coupling capacitance value ($c_m\Delta x$), where $i = 1, 2, 3, ..., p$. In the next, Figure 3 depicts the distributed $RLC$ model for full length of defective interconnects' pair.

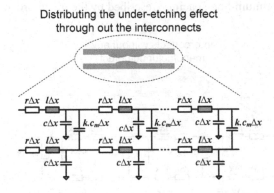

**Fig. 3.** Parallel interconnects with manufacturing defect and distribution of the effect of manufacturing defect in the electrical equivalent circuit of parallel interconnects

Note that in Figure 3 the effects of under-etching defect, *i.e.* increased coupling (mutual) capacitance values in defective $p$ blocks, have been distributed all through out the interconnects length, that resulted in $kc_m\Delta x$ value for all coupling capacitances in all $n$ blocks, where $k = \left( (n-p) + \sum_{i=1}^{p} k_i \right) \Big/ n$ .

By setting $k_i = 1$, for each $i$, results in $k = 1$, which is the situation of defect-free interconnects, whereas for $k_i > 1$, for each $i$, results in $k > 1$, which is the case of defective interconnects.

## 3   Crosstalk Fault Model of Defective Pair of Interconnects

In order to develop the crosstalk fault model of defective pair of interconnects, *i.e.* aggressor-victim interconnects, we first consider the aggressor-victim interconnect model reported in [5].

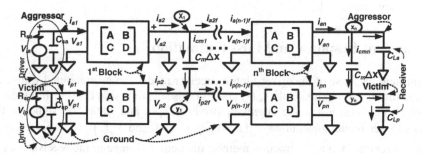

**Fig. 4.** Crosstalk fault model of defective pair of aggressor–victim interconnects

In Figure 4 the top and bottom interconnects, *i.e.* both defective aggressor and victim interconnects are represented by $n$ number of ABCD blocks and coupling capacitance $C_m = k*c_m$ across each $\Delta x$ segment of aggressor and victim interconnects where, $A = (1+ab)$, $D = 1$ and $B = a = (r + sl)\Delta x$, $C = b = (sc)\Delta x$, with $r, l, c$ be the per-unit-length resistance, self inductance, and self capacitance (with respect to ground) of the distributed right-L "*RLC*" model of both interconnects respectively and $s$ be the Laplace variable [4]. Setting $k = 1$ in $kc_m\Delta x$ coupling capacitance the model refers to crosstalk model of defect-free interconnects' pair, where $c_m$ is the per-unit-length coupling capacitance between defect-free aggressor and victim interconnects. Also note that our fault model, in addition, takes into account the linear model parameters of CMOS drivers and receivers of both aggressor and victim interconnects.

It has been shown in our previous paper [5] that the victim output from such a model can be written as:

$$V_{op}(s) = \frac{2T_1(s)}{(T_1T_4 - T_2T_3)} \cdot V_{ia}(s) + \frac{2T_2(s)}{(T_1T_4 - T_2T_3)} \cdot V_{ip}(s) \qquad (1)$$

Whereas, the corresponding aggressor output from the same model is:

$$V_{oa}(s) = \frac{-2T_3(s)}{(T_1T_4 - T_2T_3)} \cdot V_{ia}(s) + \frac{-2T_4(s)}{(T_1T_4 - T_2T_3)} \cdot V_{ip}(s) \qquad (2)$$

The fourth order approximation of $T_j(s)$ term from the numerators is:

$$T_j(s) = t_{j0} + t_{j1}s + t_{j2}s^2 + t_{j3}s^3 + t_{j4}s^4; \quad j = 1, 2, 3, 4.$$

Obviously, terms $t_{j0}$ through $t_{j4}$ are functions of interconnects', drivers' and receivers' parameters and each one is computed by summing one, or more infinite series. The terms $V_{ip}(s)$ and $V_{op}(s)$ in (1), and the terms $V_{ia}(s)$ and $V_{oa}(s)$ in (2) represent the input and output signals of the victim and aggressor respectively in $s$ domain. Also note that the crosstalk model developed in [5] was strictly for a defect-free parallel aggressor-victim model, whereas the same model has been extended and utilized here for crosstalk fault simulation of defective parallel aggressor-victim interconnects. Also note that unlike the other conventional weak coupling crosstalk model, the model considered here is a strong coupling one, implying that any change in aggressor and victim signals affects mutually the output of both interconnects through the coupling (mutual) capacitance [6].

# 4  Transient Response and Loss Estimation

The transient response of the driver-victim-receiver model can be computed when any combination of two input signals $V_{ia}(s)$ and $V_{ip}(s)$ is substituted in (1). For instance, in case of rising transition at the aggressor driver's input and static "0" signal at the victim's driver input, substituting $V_{ia}(s) = V_L \alpha / s(s+\alpha)$ and $V_{ip}(s) = 0$ respectively in (1) and thereafter, by partial fraction method the output voltage at the receiver end of the victim line can be written:

$$V_{op}(s) = \frac{2V_L \alpha}{a_8} \left[ \frac{k_{01a}}{s} + \frac{k_{02a}}{(s+\alpha)} + \frac{k_{1a}}{(s-p_1)} + \cdots + \frac{k_{8a}}{(s-p_8)} \right]$$ (3)

where, $V_L = 1.0$ or $V_{dd}$ for rising transition, $\alpha = (1/\tau_c)$, i.e. reciprocal of time constant, $p_i$ with $i = 1, 2, 3, \ldots, 8$; are the poles (solutions of characteristic equation) and $a_8 = (t_{14}t_{44} - t_{24}t_{34})$. Note that because of static "0" signal at the victim's input the second term in (1) vanishes and the voltage appearing at the victim's far end is only due to aggressor's contribution. However, for rising or falling transition as victim's driver input the second term in (1) will exist and contribute some effects (similar to right hand side term of (3)) due to victim's input itself. The partial fraction coefficients in (3) are calculated by usual procedure. Taking the inverse Laplace transform of (3) the victim's output voltage at the receiver end is computed as (4).

$$V_{0p}(t) = \frac{V_L \alpha}{a_8} \left( k_{01a} + k_{02a}e^{-\alpha t} + k_{1a}e^{p_1 t} + \ldots + k_{8a}e^{p_8 t} \right)$$ (4)

Similarly, the other signal combination can be applied as the input to the aggressor and the victim, following the procedure described in our paper [5].

## 4.1  Delay and Crosstalk Glitch Estimation

Delay is estimated by defining the delay at 50% of desired (rising/falling) signal value. Therefore, setting $V_{op}(t_d) = 0.5 \cdot V_{dd}$ in left hand side of (4) and by solving it for $t_d$ using Newton-Raphson method, the 50% delay time is calculated. If the calculated delay (50%) is greater than the nominal delay, the corresponding interconnect defect or crosstalk fault is then said to have delay timing violation (signal integrity loss). Also, crosstalk positive/negative glitch height (and it's occurrence time) can be estimated easily from (4) noting that glitch is nothing but the global maximum/minimum of victim's output signal. Thereby, setting $dV_{op}(t)/dt = 0$, at $t = t_g$ and solving for corresponding $t_g$ we can determine the occurrence time of crosstalk glitch, and thereafter substituting $t_g$ back into (4) the crosstalk glitch height can be easily determined.

## 5 Experimental Simulations and Discussion

In this section we present a few simulation experiments of our crosstalk fault model, which actually represents the defective pair of aggressor-victim interconnects. For all simulation experiments, as mentioned in Sections 3 and 4, eighth-order crosstalk fault model and distributed *per-unit-µm* interconnect *RLC* parameters were selected from Philips CMOS12 (130*nm*) technology. Both drivers and receivers parameters are also taken from the corresponding 130*nm* technology. In addition, the simulations are all carried out assuming that both aggressor and victims' drivers are having identical slew rates/strengths. The aggressor and victim interconnects' length $L= 200µm$ was selected for all simulation experiments.

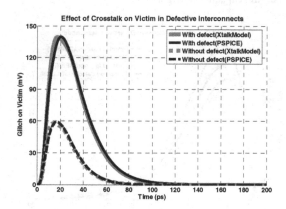

**Fig. 5.** Crosstalk effect (positive glitches) in defective/defect-free interconnects' pair

For our crosstalk fault model number of ABCD blocks considered, *i.e. n* is theoretically infinity, whereas for validation of our crosstalk fault model corresponding PSPICE simulations were performed taking into account only $n = 20$ "right-L" RLC blocks for both aggressor and victim interconnects. It has been further assumed that for PSPICE simulation out of $n = 20$ RLC blocks only six blocks are defective, i.e. $p = 6$, and correspondingly, respective coupling capacitances in the defective blocks are $k_1$, $k_2$, ..., $k_6$ times of $c_m$, where $k_1, k_2, ..., k_6$ are 5, 8, 13, 10, 6 and 4 respectively. This implies that for our crosstalk fault model the coupling capacitance value is $k*c_m$, where $k = 3$ (calculated as per section 2). The simulation experiments, depicted in Figure 5, show the crosstalk effects on the victim line, due to defective and defect-free aggressor- victim interconnects. Notice that in Figure 5 for defect-free aggressor-victim interconnects the crosstalk positive glitch obtained from our crosstalk model is approximately 58 mV and it occurs at 14.4 *ps*, whereas the both from PSPICE simulation are respectively 59 mV and 16.6 *ps*, and the corresponding per-unit-μm coupling capacitance is the usual $c_m$ value used in the Philips CMOS12 technology.

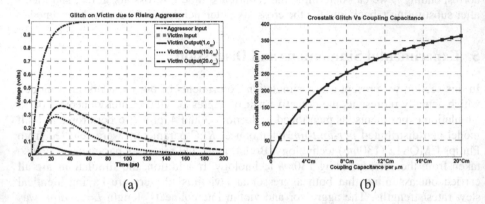

(a)                                        (b)

**Fig. 6.** Crosstalk glitch on victim due to various coupling capacitances (figure (a)) and crosstalk glitch height versus coupling capacitance (figure (b))

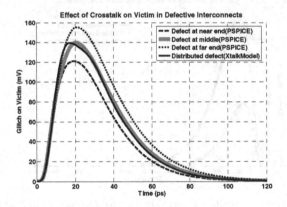

**Fig. 7.** Dependencies of crosstalk glitch height on defect location, *e.g.* at near end, middle and far end side of the pair of interconnects

Similarly, for defective pair of aggressor-victim interconnects the crosstalk glitches obtained from our fault model and PSPICE are 139.5 mV, and 139.7 mV respectively, whereas their occurrences are at 17.4 *ps* and 20.4 *ps* respectively. Note that in the latter simulation the coupling capacitance for our crosstalk fault model, *i.e.* for defective interconnects was $3c_m$. However, for PSPICE simulation of defective interconnects consecutively 6 defective blocks were selected with higher values of coupling capacitance, such as $k_i c_m$ as mentioned above. Figure 6(a) shows the various crosstalk glitches generated on the victim line due to three different coupling capacitances, implying that depending upon the severity of defect/crosstalk fault the crosstalk glitch can reach the value as high as 500 mV even, *i.e.* $0.5V_L$. Figure 6(b) shows the graph of crosstalk glitch heights (mV) versus per-unit-µm length coupling capacitances. Furthermore, figure 7 demonstrates that crosstalk glitch height can be larger, medium or smaller depending upon the location of defect between the interconnects' pair. For instance, in figure 7 largest crosstalk glitch (from PSPICE simulation) is produced on the victim line when the defect is located at the far-end side (*i.e.* close to receiver) of both aggressor-victim interconnects, whereas smallest crosstalk glitch is produced when the defect is located at the near-end side (*i.e.* close to driver) of interconnect lines. Similarly, in figure 7 crosstalk glitch of medium height (from both PSPICE simulation and our crosstalk fault model) is produced on the victim line when defect location is at the middle of interconnect lines. Also note that our fault model produces the crosstalk glitch which is closely overlapping on PSPICE simulation result except at the peak values. Simulations depicted in figures 5, 6 and 7 are all performed applying a rising transition and static "0" signal respectively at the aggressor's input and victim's input.

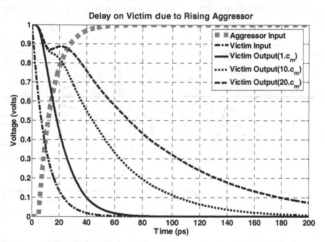

**Fig. 8.** Delayed victim's output signal due to various severities of crosstalk fault. Aggressor is shown to have skewed (5 *ps* delayed) input transition and victim has falling input transition

Figure 8 above demonstrates that when the aggressor's input is a (skewed) rising transition and the victim's input is a falling transition, due to crosstalk effect the victim's output is very much delayed and the amount of delay is highly dependent on the amount of skew (in this case 5 *ps*) in aggressor's input signal and magnitude of coupling capacitance, latter, in fact, represents the severity of the crosstalk fault (*i.e.* electrical effect of the defect), in our example. Here, larger coupling capacitance implies that fault is a severe one.

Figure 9(a) and 9(b) show respectively the 50% delay and 90% delay on victim's output due to various coupling capacitances. From the both figures it is clear that delay on the victim's output signal increases almost linearly with the increasing coupling capacitances, and 90% delay can be as large 175$ps$ when the defect leads to a coupling capacitance as high as 20 times of usual $c_m$.

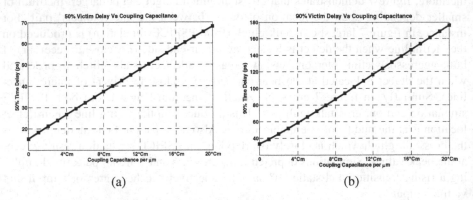

(a)                                    (b)

**Fig. 9.** Victim's delay versus coupling capacitance. Figure (a) shows (50%) delay versus coupling capacitance and figure (b) shows 90% delay versus coupling capacitance respectively.

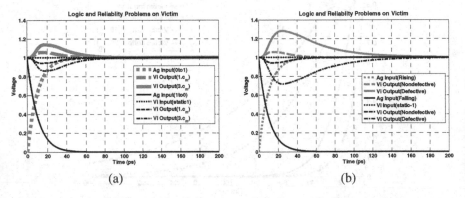

(a)                                    (b)

**Fig. 10.** Logic and reliability problems due to severity of crosstalk fault, simulations are performed with our crosstalk fault model. Figure (a) considers the severity of crosstalk fault is equivalent to ($3c_m$) and figure (b) considers the severity of crosstalk is equivalent to ($10c_m$).

Figure 10(a) and 10(b) show that, in addition to delay faults as shown in figure 9, defect can lead to both logic failure and reliability problem of device. This is because, as demonstrated in figure 10(a & b) due to falling input transition on the aggressor if the crosstalk negative glitch is produced on the victim's output, while the victim's input is static "1", it can lead to logic failure of the device if the peak value of the crosstalk negative glitch exceeds the lower threshold voltage of logic-high value.

In contrast, due to rising transition on the aggressor's input and victim with static "1" input signal if the crosstalk positive glitch, as shown in figures 10(a) and 10(b), is produced, it can cause reliability problem of the device as in this case peak value of crosstalk glitch exceeds the tolerable upper-threshold voltage of logic-high value.

# 6 Concluding Remarks

In the paper the crosstalk fault model of two on-chip defective interconnects, namely the defective aggressor and victim lines, is analyzed using a crosstalk fault model. Capacitive crosstalk coupling effect is only considered here that actually represents the interconnect defects due to under-etching/particle (conductive) contamination. It has been observed that the increased coupling capacitance due to above defect(s) can lead to timing violations (delay faults), logic failures and reliability problems, if the defect is very severe. Furthermore, it has been observed that severity of the fault is very much dependent on the location of the defects, for instance, severity of fault is maximum when the defect is located at the far-end side of the interconnects' pair whereas, it is medium and small when the defect location is at middle of the interconnects and near-end side of the interconnects respectively. Our crosstalk fault model has been validated with the PSPICE simulation results, and the accuracy of our fault model is in good agreement with the PSPICE results. However, our fault model is more flexible and much faster (at least 8 times) than the PSPICE simulation even with non-optimized MATLAB code. It is more flexible as because by changing only a few parameters, our fault model can handle all possible of combinations of input signals including the skewed one. In addition to the coupling due to mutual capacitance, our fault model can be extended to consider simultaneously the resistive bridging fault (mutual conductance) between the aggressor-victim interconnects, which is not reported here due to space restriction.

# References

1. Arumi, D., Rodriguez-Montanes, R., Figueras, J., "Defective behaviours of Resistive opens in interconnect line" Proc. of IEEE-ETS 2005, pp. 28-33
2. Chen, G., Reddy, S., Pomeranz, I., Rajaski, J., Engelke, P., Becker, B., "An unified Fault model and Test generation procedure for interconnect opens and bridges" Proc. of IEEE-ETS 2005, pp. 22-27.
3. Cuviello, M., Dey, S., Bai, X., Zhao, Y., "Fault Modeling and Simulation for Crosstalk in System-on-Chip Interconnects," Proc. of ICCAD 1999, pp. 297-303.
4. Palit, AK., Anheier, W., Schloeffel, J., "Estimation of Signal Integrity Loss through Reduced Order Interconnect Model," Proc. IEEE-SPI 2003, Siena, Italy, pp. 163-166.
5. Palit, AK., Wu, L., Duganapalli, KK., Anheier, W., Schloeffel, J., "A new, flexible and very accurate crosstalk fault model to analyze the effects of coupling noise between the interconnects on signal integrity losses in deep submicron chips," paper no. 253, Proc. of 14th IEEE-ATS'05, Calcutta, India, 18 - 21 Dec. 2005, pp. 22 - 26.
6. Young, B., "Digital signal integrity: modeling and simulations with interconnects and packages" Prentice Hall PTR, Upper Saddle River, New Jersey, 2001, pp. 98 - 101.

# Body Bias Generator for Leakage Power Reduction of Low-Voltage Digital Logic Circuits

Ji-Yong Jeong, Gil-Su Kim, Jong-Pil Son, Woo-Jin Rim, and Soo-Won Kim

ASIC Design Lab., Dept. of Electronics Eng., Korea University, Seoul, Korea
{jjyjx, joyrider1, stardust, rimwoojin, ksw}@asic.korea.ac.kr
http:// asic.korea.ac.kr

**Abstract.** This paper proposes body-bias generator for leakage power reduction of digital logic circuits which operates at low supply voltage of 0.5V. The proposed circuit adopts double charge pumping scheme to enhance the pumping gain. The proposed circuit is fabricated using $0.13\ \mu m$ CMOS process and measurement result demonstrates stable operation with body-bias voltage of -0.95V. We apply the proposed circuit to 64-bit carry look-ahead adder to demonstrate its performance. We report that the leakage power of 64-bit carry look-ahead adder can dramatically be reduced by adopting proposed substrate-bias generator. The estimated leakage power reduction is 90% (T=75°C).

## 1 Introduction

As technology scaled down, the threshold voltage ($V_{th}$) must be reduced as well as the supply voltage to satisfy system performance such as low-power and high-speed, simultaneously. However, the reduction of $V_{th}$ results in an exponentially increased leakage current, which can significantly increase total stand-by power as device dimensions and the supply voltage are continuously shrunk [1, 2]. The 2001 International Technology Roadmap for Semiconductors (ITRS) [3] predicted that in the next several processor generations, leakage power may constitute as much as 50% of total power consumption.

There have been lots of research efforts to bring focus into design techniques to control the threshold voltage and to reduce leakage power consumption. A multi-threshold voltage CMOS (MTCMOS) technique reduces the stand-by power by disconnecting the power supply from load circuits using PMOS switches and NMOS switches with high-$V_{th}$ in the stand-by mode [4]. Therefore, this technique requires extra fabrication process for PMOS switches and NMOS switches with high-$V_{th}$. A self-controllable voltage level (SVL) technique connects a lower voltage than $V_{dd}$ to source node of PMOS transistor and a higher voltage than ground level to source node of NMOS transistor, which results in leakage reduction due to the body effect [5]. But, this technique has a limited dynamic operating range for low supply voltage.

Recently, a variable-threshold CMOS (VTCMOS) scheme [6] has ensured the stable operation even at low supply voltage, whose technique increases $V_{th}$ by making the body-bias voltage either much higher than $V_{dd}$ or much lower than ground level

J. Vounckx, N. Azemard, and P. Maurine (Eds.): PATMOS 2006, LNCS 4148, pp. 350–359, 2006.

during the stand-by mode. Even though this technique has successfully been applied to a commercial DSP, it can not avoid the performance degradation due to slow conversion time and can not provide the stable substrate-bias voltage at low-supply voltage.

This paper proposes body-bias generator to reduce the leakage power of digital logic circuits. The proposed body-bias generator implemented in 0.13 $\mu m$ CMOS triple-well process requires no external power supply for the body-bias generation even at low-supply voltage, represents faster conversion time and the stable operation.

## 2  Variable-Threshold CMOS(VTCMOS) Scheme

VTCMOS is a technique that dynamically controls $V_{th}$ by body biasing of transistors. NMOS body biasing with a voltage lower than the ground level or PMOS body biasing with a voltage higher than $V_{dd}$: reverse body biasing increase the threshold voltage of transistors during the stand-by mode, while $V_{th}$ is decreased to enhance the active current due to forward body biasing during the active mode, as illustrated in equation (1)

$$\Delta V_{th} = \gamma(\sqrt{2|\phi_F|+|V_{sb}|} - \sqrt{2|\phi_F|}) \text{ (Where } \gamma = \frac{\sqrt{2\varepsilon_s qN_a}}{C_{ox}} \text{)}$$  (1)

In order to realize VTCMOS scheme, triple-well structure shown in Fig. 1 is required for independent body biasing of NMOS and PMOS. This is not a restriction since the fabrication processes of most logic circuits and memories support the triple-well structure.

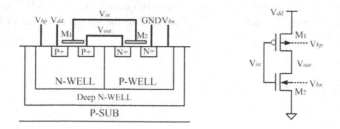

**Fig. 1.** Typical triple-well structure

By allowing both forward and reverse body biasing, one can improve process yields and reduce undesirable leakage power due to process variation. Moreover, we can obtain complete flexibility to optimally set both $V_{dd}$ and $V_{th}$ to balance between low-power and high-speed.

During the stand-by mode, it is more beneficial to minimize leakage power by body biasing as large as possible. But, during the active mode, it is not straightforward to reduce leakage power. Generally, with $V_{dd}$ scaling, $V_{th}$ must be reduced to maintain system performance, simultaneously. But, for a special operating condition, power reduction due to $V_{dd}$ scaling can be cancelled by an increase in the leakage power due to $V_{th}$ scaling. As a result, it may be more optimal to operate with higher threshold voltage if $V_{dd}$ is scaled aggressively. On the other hand, it may be optimal to operate with higher supply voltage if leakage power is dominant factor in total power consumption. Fig. 2 shows theoretical optimal $V_{dd}$-$V_{th}$ operating points for the worst case presented in [7]. This result can be used to determine both $V_{dd}$ and $V_{th}$ according to required operating frequency. While during the stand-by mode, large body biasing can minimize leakage current, but the use of such a large body biasing results in saturated leakage current as shown in Fig. 3(a) since the gate leakage current will significantly increase due to an increase of the electric field between the gate and the body terminal, while threshold voltage is nearly linear for the body bias change as shown in Fig. 3(b) [1].

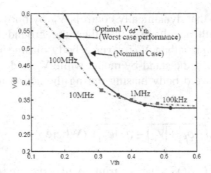

**Fig. 2.** Optimal $V_{dd}$-$V_{th}$ operating points for the worst case [7]

Since the power dissipation of digital logic circuits is proportional to the square of $V_{dd}$, it is desirable to select $V_{dd}$ as low as possible. In this work, we set to $V_{dd}$=0.5V and $V_{thn}$=0.2V to ensure the stable operating frequency over 100MHz even at the worst condition during the active mode and 0.4V in the stand by mode to reduce the leakage current.

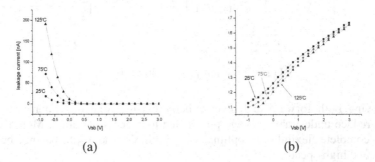

(a)                                         (b)

**Fig. 3.** Leakage current and threshold voltage as a function of body bias and temperature

Therefore, we must generate substrate-bias voltage of 0.4V in the active mode and-0.7V in the stand-by mode. Table 1 summarizes $V_{thn}$, $V_{thp}$, $V_{bn}$, and $V_{bp}$ required in the active mode and the stand-by mode, respectively.

**Table 1.** $V_{thn}$, $V_{thp}$, $V_{bn}$, and $V_{bp}$ required in the active mode and the stand-by mode

| Reqired voltages | Active | Stand-by |
|---|---|---|
| $V_{thn}$ | 0.2V | 0.4V |
| $V_{thp}$ | -0.2V | -0.4V |
| $V_{bn}$ | 0.4V | -0.7V |
| $V_{bp}$ | -0.4V | 0.7V |

# 3  Circuit Design

Positive-bias generator for body biasing of PMOS transistor has been designed by using a conventional Dickson charge pumping circuit [11]. Therefore this paper focus on the negative–bias generator for body biasing of NMOS transistor since it is difficult to generate the negative-voltage using conventional negative bias generator below -$V_{dd}$.

## 3.1  Conventional Negative Bias Generator

Charge pumping circuit has been widely used to provide the negative-bias voltage since it requires no external power supply and small power overhead.

### 3.1.1  Hybrid Pumping Circuit (HPC)

Fig. 4 shows a schematic of hybrid pumping circuit and its timing diagram [8]. In hybrid pumping circuit, transistor, M2 and M3, are PMOS and NMOS, respectively.

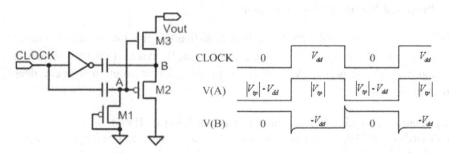

**Fig. 4.** Hybrid pumping circuit and its timing diagram [8]

When the clock is at the low level, the voltage of node A becomes $\left|V_{thp}\right| - V_{dd}$ due to capacitive coupling, which makes the voltage of node B clamp to the ground level. When the clock reaches to the high level, the voltage of node A rises to $\left|V_{thp}\right|$ due to capacitive coupling and the voltage of node B reaches to -$V_{dd}$ level. Therefore, we can ideally achieve substrate-bias voltage close to $-V_{dd}$ . However, in practical design, hybrid pumping circuit represents some voltage loss due to diode-connected transistor, M1 [9].

### 3.1.2  Cross-Coupled Hybrid Pumping Circuit (CHPC)

Cross-coupled hybrid pumping circuit [9] has been proposed to reduce the influence of some voltage loss and to improve pumping-down speed in hybrid pumping circuit. Fig. 5 shows a schematic of cross-coupled hybrid pumping circuit and output waveform of cross-coupled hybrid pumping circuit compared to that of hybrid pumping circuit. With this graph, one can see that cross-coupled hybrid pumping circuit shows a much better performance than hybrid pumping circuit in both pumping-down speed and pumping gain.

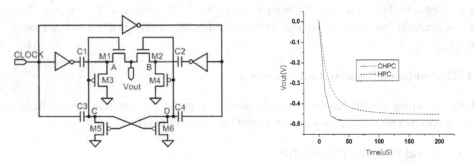

**Fig. 5.** Cross-coupled charge pumping circuit and its output waveform operating at 0.5V [9]

### 3.2  Proposed Negative Bias Generator

When we use conventional circuits [8, 9], it is difficult to generate negative voltage of -0.7V. The use of conventional pumping circuits [8, 9] makes it difficult to generate the negative voltage below $-V_{dd}$. Thus we propose a new solution to make deeper body bias voltage.

### 3.2.1  Double Hybrid Charge Pumping Circuit (Double HPC)

As described in [10], cascading N doublers can generate a voltage as large as $V_{dd} + N \cdot \Delta V$ . In the same manner, double hybrid pumping circuit as shown in Fig. 6 can be considered to obtain a voltage as twice as $V_{dd}$. Double hybrid pumping circuit supplies the negative voltage which comes from $V_{SS}$ generator instead of ground level to the drain node of transistors M4 and M5. In double hybrid pumping circuit, the output voltage of the $V_{SS}$ generator is the same as that of hybrid pumping circuit shown in Fig. 4. When the clock is at the low level, the voltage of node C becomes $2(|V_{thp}| - V_{dd})$ level, which causes the voltage of node D to clamp to $-V_{dd}$ level. When the clock rises to the high level, since the voltage of node C reaches to $2\left|V_{thp}\right| - V_{dd}$ level and it makes the voltage of node D lower to $-2V_{dd}$ level, the body-bias voltage of double hybrid pumping circuit can be achieved to $-2V_{dd}$ level which is twice as large as that of conventional hybrid pumping circuit.

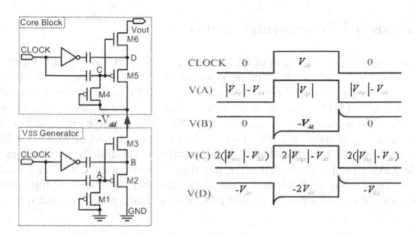

**Fig. 6.** Proposed double hybrid charge pumping circuit and its timing diagram

### 3.2.2  Double Cross-Coupled Hybrid Pumping Circuit (Double CHPC)

Remember that hybrid pumping circuit cannot reach to $-V_{dd}$ level owing to the use of diode-connected transistor shown in Fig. 4. Moreover, since during the start-up both transistors M2 and M5 are not fully turned on, this circuit has a much slower pumping-down speed than that of conventional one as shown in Fig. 7.

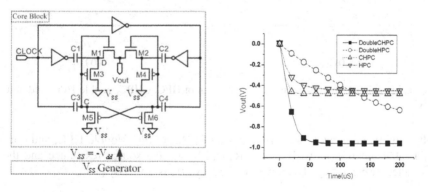

**Fig. 7.** Double cross-coupled hybrid pumping circuit and comparison of pumping-down speed and output voltage

On the other hand, this result tells us that if double charge pumping scheme is applied to some novel charge pumping circuit, one can expect to achieve a circuit with fast pumping-down speed and much deeper body-bias voltage, simultaneously. Thus, proposed double hybrid charge pumping scheme is applied to cross-coupled hybrid pumping circuit [9] shown in Fig. 5. Fig. 7 shows that body-bias voltage of double cross-coupled hybrid pumping circuit is about -0.96V, which is also twice as large as that of cross-coupled hybrid pumping circuit without degradation of pumping-down speed.

## 4 Analysis and Experimental Results

Fig. 8(a) compares pumping gain of HPC, CHPC, double HPC, and double CHPC as a function of $V_{dd}$. This comparison is done by HSPICE simulation with 0.13$um$ CMOS triple-well process. Within $V_{dd}$ range of 0.2V-0.7V, one can see that double HPC and double CHPC generate body-bias voltage as twice as those of HPC and CHPC. Fig. 8(b) shows pumping currents of HPC, CHPC, double HPC, and double CHPC. Here, $V_{dd}$ is fixed at 0.5V. Though the pumping current of HPC is a little larger than those of CHPC and double CHPC within the substrate-bias voltage range of 0.0V-0.2V, HPC begins to fall off faster than the current of CHPC and double CHPC with increasing the body-bias voltage. On the other hand, within all the body-bias voltage range, the current of double HPC is very small, which is consistent with that of Fig. 8.

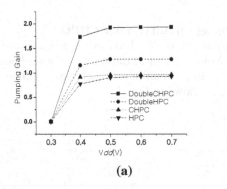 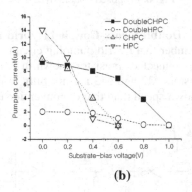

(a)                                    (b)

**Fig. 8.** Pumping gain and pumping current comparison of HPC, CHPC, double HPC, and double CHPC

Finally, Fig. 9 compares power efficiencies of HPC, CHPC, double HPC, and double CHPC as a function of $R_S/R_L$. Here $R_S$ and $R_L$ are the source resistance and the load resistance, respectively. The power efficiency ($\eta$) is given by [10].

$$\eta = \frac{(V_{out}^2/R_L)}{V_{dd} \cdot I_{dd}} \tag{2}$$

$V_{out}$ is the body-bias voltage and $I_{dd}$ represents the total supply current.

As shown in Fig. 9, one can note that as $R_L$ becomes larger, the efficiency of double CHPC increases. But the efficiency of double CHPC is a little smaller than that of

HPC and CHPC because while the power consumption of double CHPC increases twice, its pumping gain does not reach to 2.0.

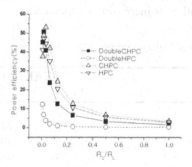

**Fig. 9.** Power efficiency comparison of HPC, CHPC, double HPC, and double CHPC

The proposed negative-bias generator (double CHPC) was implemented with a 0.13 $\mu m$ CMOS triple-well process, which represents the active area of 0.0185 $mm^2$ (0.185 $mm$ x 0.1 $mm$) including ring oscillator operating at 100MHz with 0.5V power supply. Fig. 10(b) shows measured output waveform of the negative-bias generator adopting double hybrid charge pumping scheme. The measured output voltage of the proposed circuit is about -0.95V, which is close to the simulation result. The active-to-standby mode conversion takes about 10 $\mu s$ as shown in Fig. 10(b)

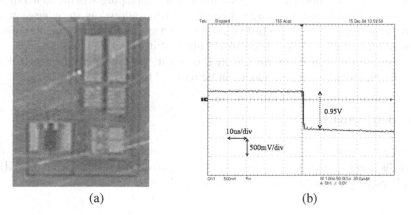

(a)                                          (b)

**Fig. 10.** Photograph of fabricated negative-bias generator and measured output waveforms

Proposed circuit was used to design 64-bit carry look-ahead adder by applying body-bias voltage of -0.95V to P-well. Moreover, positive-bias generator which provides 0.7V was connected to N-well. We have done HSPICE simulation for circuit-level using 0.13 $\mu m$ CMOS triple-well process with 0.5V power supply (T=25 °C, 75 °C, and 125 °C). Table 2 shows simulated leakage power reduction of various logic families as well as 64-bit carry look-ahead adder. With this result, one can see that during the stand-by mode reverse body biasing can significantly reduce the leakage power for all the logic families as increasing temperature.

**Table 2.** Simulated leakage power reduction of various logic families

| GATES | LEAKAGE REDUCTION | | |
|---|---|---|---|
| | 25℃ | 75℃ | 125℃ |
| 2 input NAND | 83.51% | 86.56% | 92.64% |
| 2 input NOR | 85.73% | 94.78% | 95.11% |
| 2 input XOR | 60.79% | 90.19% | 92.08% |
| D Flip-Flop | 67.97% | 91.14% | 91.93% |
| JK Flip-Flop | 69.20% | 90.92% | 91.74% |
| 16-bit Carry Look-ahead Adder | 79.34% | 94.77% | 95.92% |
| 64-bit Carry Look-ahead Adder | 79.35% | 89.53% | 91.84% |
| 2-to-1 Multiplexer (16-bit) | 70.22% | 89.89% | 93.36% |
| 4-to-16 Decoder | 65.29% | 90.61% | 91.83% |

## 5  Conclusion

In this paper, we proposed negative body-bias generator for leakage power reduction of digital logic circuits operating at low supply voltage. Our proposed circuit include the negative-bias generator which adopts double charge pumping scheme to maximize pumping gain. Double hybrid charge pumping scheme allows us to achieve much deeper negative-bias voltage with fast pumping-down speed. Our experimental results of negative-bias generator were used to design 64-bit carry look-ahead adder with dramatically reduced leakage power. With this result, we predicted that the leakage power of 64-bit carry look-ahead adder can be reduced to 90% (T=75°C).

## Acknowledgement

This work was supported by a Korea University. And authors also thank the IDEC (IC Design Education Center) for its hardware and software assistance and the KIPA (Korea IT Industry Promotion Agency) for financial support.

## References

1. A. Chandrakasan, W. Bowhill, and F. Fox: Design of High performance Microprocessor Circuits. *IEEE Press*, Location, (2000)
2. S. Borkar: Design Challenges of Technology Scaling. *IEEE MICRO*, July-August (1999).
3. SIA. *International Technology Roadmap for Semiconductors*, (2001)

4. S. Mutoh, T. Douskei, Y. Matsuya, T. Aoki, S. Shigematsu, and T. Yamada: 1-V Power Supply High-Speed Digital Circuit Technology with Multi-threshold voltage CMOS. *IEEE J. Solid state Circuits*, August (1995) 847-854
5. T. Enomoto, Y. Oka, and H. Shikano: A Self-Controllable Voltage Level (SVL) Circuit and its Low-Power High-Speed CMOS Circuit Application, *IEEE J. Solid state Circuits*, Vol. 38, No. 7, July (2003)
6. T.Kuroda, et al.: A 0.9V 150MHz 10mW 4mm2 2-D discrete cosine transform core processor with variable threshold voltage (VT) scheme. *IEEE J. Solid state Circuits*, Vol. 31, No. 11, November (1996) 1770-1779
7. A. Wang and A. Chadrakasan: Optiamal Supply and Threshold Scaling for Subthreshold CMOS Circuits, IEEE Computer Society Annual Symposium on VLSI 2003, April (2002) 5-9
8. Y. Tsukikawa, et al.: An efficient back-bias generator with hybrid pumping circuit for 1.5V DRAM's. *IEEE J. Solid state Circuits*. Vol. 29, April (1994). 534-538
9. K.S. Min and J.Y. Chung: A Fast Pump-Down VBB Generator for Sub-1.5V-V DRAMs, *IEEE J. Solid state Circuits*, Vol. 36, No. 7, , July (2001) 1154-1157
10. P. Favrat, P. Deval, and M. Declercq: A high-efficiency CMOS voltage doubler. *IEEE J. Solid state Circuits*, Vol. 33, March (1998) 410-416
11. J. Dickson: On-chip high-voltage generation in MNOS integrated circuits using an improved voltage multiplier technique, *IEEE J. Solid state Circuits*, Vol. SC-11, June (1976) 374-378
12. J. S. Shin: A New Charge Pump without Degradation in Threshold Voltage Due to Body Effect, *IEEE J. Solid state Circuits*, Vol. 35, No. 8, August (2000) 1227-1230

# Energy-Delay Space Analysis for Clocked Storage Elements Under Process Variations

Christophe Giacomotto[1], Nikola Nedovic[2], and Vojin G. Oklobdzija[1]

[1] Advanced Computer Systems Engineering Laboratory,
Dept. of Electrical and Computer Engineering, University of California, CA 95616, USA
{giacomoc, vojin}@ece.ucdavis.edu
http://www.acsel-lab.com
[2] Fujitsu Laboratories of America, Sunnyvale, CA 95616, USA
nikola.nedovic@us.fujitsu.com

**Abstract.** In this paper we present the effect of process variations on the design of clocked storage elements. This work proposes to use the Energy-Delay space analysis for a true representation of the design trade-offs. Consequently, this work also shows a comparison of clocked storage elements under a specific set of system constraints for typical corner design and high yield corner design. Finally, we show that designing for high yield can affect the choice of topology in order to achieve energy efficiency.

## 1 Introduction

The impact of process variations on Clocked Storage Elements' (CSEs) energy and delay is dependent on the sizing of the individual transistors [12]. Hence, evaluating the effect of process variations to a specific CSE topology requires a complete analysis in ED (Energy-Delay) space [15]. This analysis is then extended across a set of topologies for purpose of comparison. Several methods have been used to compare CSEs in terms of performance and/or energy [1][2][7]. The transistor tuning optimization is usually done for a given objective function or metric such as EDP (Energy-Delay Product) or Power Delay Product [1][7], and, more recently, generalized with cost function approaches [2]. However, in these cases, results are shown as a single optimum design solution and the quality of the designs is quantified using a single metric. This approach can be misleading as it fails to show all performance versus energy tradeoffs that a particular topology offers. Typically, the process of designing CSEs in mainstream high performance and low power processors starts with the choice of a topology accordingly to a rough performance and power requirements estimates. Only then, when the choice is made, transistor sizing can help meeting the energy or delay target and finally process corner variations are taken in account. In this work, the objective is to show that taking process corner variations in account can change the topology selection. This analysis reveals the impact of high yield design on an envelope of high-performance and low-power CSEs in their best energy efficient configurations.

J. Vounckx, N. Azemard, and P. Maurine (Eds.): PATMOS 2006, LNCS 4148, pp. 360–369, 2006.
© Springer-Verlag Berlin Heidelberg 2006

## 2 Efficient Energy-Delay Approach

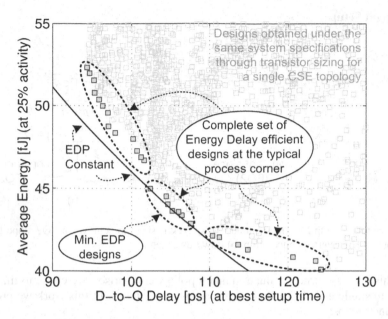

**Fig. 1.** Energy efficient designs for a single CSE topology through transistor sizing with fixed input/output load at the typical process corner

For a specific CSE topology, there is only one combination of transistor sizes that yields minimum energy for a given delay. As the entire design space is explored, a subset of combinations remains that represents the configurations that yield the smallest energy for each achievable delay. This subset is referred to as the energy efficient characteristic for a CSE [2]. Fig. 1 shows such characteristic where the D-to-Q delay represents the minimum achievable delay which occurs at the optimum setup time and the average energy is calculated for 25% data activity with a 1ns clock period. As shown in Fig. 1, from this characteristic, a wide range of ED points are possible. For the low energy sizing solutions, the delay has a high sensitivity to the transistor sizing, and for the high speed sizing solutions, the energy has a high sensitivity to the transistor sizing. Fig. 1 shows that the minimum EDP, typically used as an ad-hoc energy-performance tradeoff metric, is achieved for a range of possible configurations. Restricting the design space to EDP solutions would discard all the other potential design solutions and be misleading on the energy or delay achievable by the topology. In general case, however, the optimum design point depends on the parameters of the environment of the CSE such as the energy-efficient characteristic of the logic block used in the pipeline and target clock frequency [15]. Hence, depending on the surrounding logic the CSE design chosen may be in the high energy sensitivity region or the high delay sensitivity region (Fig. 1). In our analysis, we compare entire energy efficient characteristics of the CSEs, rather than a single energy-delay metrics. In this way, the entire space of possible designs is explored and the impact of process variations onto a topology and between topologies can be fully evaluated.

# 3   CSE Simulation Methodology

## 3.1   Circuit Setup

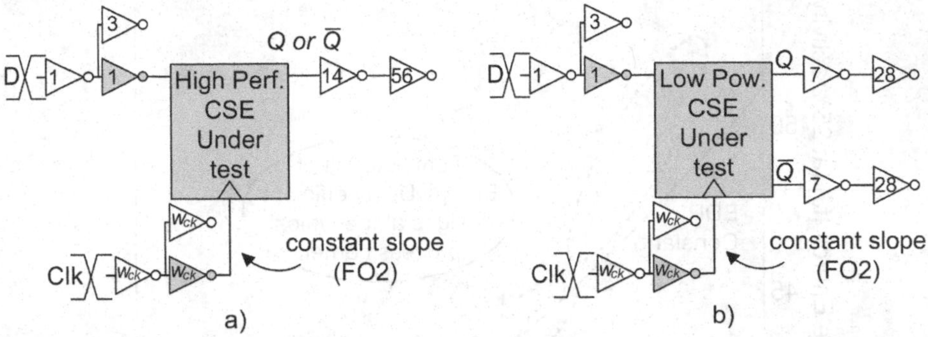

**Fig. 2.** Simulation setup for single ended CSEs, Wck is sized to achieve an FO2 slope for the clock input, a) High Performance setup, b) Low Power setup

For this process corner evaluation and topology comparison we chose to limit our analysis to single ended flip-flops and master-slave latches. In this work we propose two distinct setups:

- High performance (Fig. 2a) where one output is loaded, either Q or Qb , whichever comes first in terms of delay and a load of 14x min. sized inverters which is considered representative of a typical moderate to high capacitive load of a CSE in a critical path [1].
- Low power (Fig. 2b) where both outputs are loaded with 7x min. sized inverters. The worst case delay (D-to-Q vs. D-to-Qb) is reported for this setup.

In both setups shown in Fig. 2, the input capacitance of the CSE under test is limited to a maximum equivalent capacitance of 4 minimum sized inverters and is driven by a minimum sized inverter. These limitations restrict the scope of this comparison since load and gain have a significant impact on the ED behavior of each CSE topology. Independently, for low power designs, the simulation setup requires further restrictions on the CSE topology itself: the input must be buffered (i.e. no passgate inputs are allowed), and the output must be buffered as well (i.e. no state element on the output). Our setup requires that the slope of the clock driving the CSE must remain constant. As the configuration under test changes, the load of the clock changes as well. In order to accommodate for this variation, the size of the clock driver (Wck in Figure 2) is chosen to keep the FO2 slope characteristic.

## 3.2   Delay and Energy Quantification

The primary goal is to extract an accurate energy efficient characteristic of sizing configurations for each Flip-Flop and Master-Slave latch. These energy efficient curves must include layout and wire parasitic capacitance estimates, which are re-evaluated for each combination of transistor sizes tried. The set of H-SPICE simulations are done with a nominal 130nm process and the granularity for the transistor width is set to 0.32um, which is the minimum transistor width in this technology. The FO4 delay for this technology is 45ps. In order to accurately quantify delay for each transistor size combination and for each topology, the setup time optimization must be completed as well [1]. Nedovic et al. [6] show, in the same technology, a minimum D-Q delay zone flat for at least 10ps of D to clock variation for all CSEs presented. The granularity chosen for the simulations performed in this work was set to 5 ps, which yields a negligible D-to-Q delay error vs. setup time. The energy is measured by integrating the current necessary for the operation of the CSE, the clock driver and the data driver(s) at the nominal voltage of operation as shown by the gray elements in Fig. 2. This energy is quantified for each type of state transition ($0\rightarrow0$, $0\rightarrow1$, $1\rightarrow0$, and $1\rightarrow1$) over a 1ns clock period and combined to obtain the total energy for any desired activity factor [8]. For this technology node and the clock period we use, the offset in energy due to leakage is negligible.

## 3.3 Simulated Topologies

In this work, we examine most of the conventional single-ended topologies of the CSEs used in the industry. The CSEs are divided in two classes: High Performance and Low Power CSEs. High performance topologies consists of the Semi-Dynamic

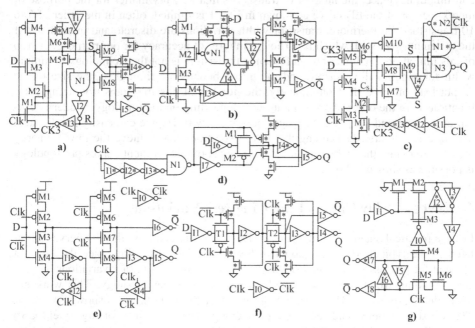

**Fig. 3.** Clocked Storage Elements: a) IPP: Implicitly Pulsed Flip-Flop with half-push-pull latch, b) USPARC: Sun UltraSPARC III Semi-Dynamic Flip-Flop, c) STFF-SE: Single Ended Skew Tolerant Flip Flop, d) TGPL: Transmission Gate Pulsed Latch, e) Modified C²MOS Master Slave Latch, f) TGMS: Transmission Gate Master-Slave latch, g) WPMS: Write Port Master Slave latch.

Flip-Flop [9] used in the Sun UltraSPARC-III (USPARC, Fig. 3b), The Single Ended Skew Tolerant Flip-Flop (STFF-SE, Fig. 3d)[6], the Implicitly Pulsed Flip-Flop with half-push-pull latch (IPP, Figure 3a) [8] and the Transmission Gate Pulsed-Latch (TGPL, Figure 3c) [7]. STFFSE and IPP are based on the SDFF dynamic structure, however STFFSE significantly improves the speed of the first stage and IPP improves energy by increasing driving capability of the second stage. The original TGPL had to be modified to fit in this comparison by adding the inverter from the input D to the pass gate in order to achieve sufficient input and output driving capability, otherwise impossible with our setup.

CSEs targeted for low power operation designs are typically static structures since they require robustness of operation under all process and system variations. The common static structures are: the Master-Slave (MS) latch used in the PowerPC 603 (TGMS, Fig. 3f)[10] and commonly referred as a low power CSE [1, 3, 8]. We also included the Modified $C^2MOS$ Master-Slave latch ($C^2MOS$, Fig. 3e) [1] and the Write Port Master-Slave latch (WPMS, Fig. 3g) [13].

### 3.4  Design Space Assumptions

As can be seen in Fig. 3, the number of transistors of a single topology varies from 18 to 32 transistors. However, a good part of these transistors are non-critical for the delay and must remain minimum size (shown as * in Fig. 3) for minimum energy consumption. Hence, the number of transistors that actually matter for the purpose of the extraction of the ED curve as shown in Fig. 1 is limited, often in the order of 5 to 10 transistors. Furthermore, transistor width variations are discrete and increments of the minimum size grid, which is sufficient in term of accuracy for our purpose. On top of this limitation, the lower bound for some transistors is not the technology minimum width for functionality reasons and the upper bounds are limited by the size of the output load of the CSE. Consequently, the number of possible transistor sizing combinations is in the order of a few thousands depending on the topology. Modern desktop computers and scripting languages combined with Hspice can easily handle such task in a few hours. By keeping the design solutions that achieve the lowest energy for a given delay, the extraction of a complete set of ED efficient curves per topology is possible as shown in Fig. 1.

## 4  Energy-Delay Curves Under Process Variations

From a practical stand point, the Energy-Delay results given by the ED curves simulated in the typical corner as shown in Fig. 1 can be misleading since they do not account for process variations. Dao et al. [14] show process corner variations and the corresponding worst cases for a single sizing solution per topology. This work extends the analysis in [14] to each design point of the ED curve, as shown in Fig. 1. The worst case delay and the worst case energy are necessary for high yield CSE design. Fast paths hazards should also be considered during implementations and we assume padding tools guarantee to cover hold times and clocking uncertainties at the same yield. In this work we assume no variability between the transistors of a single design. If transistor-to-transistor variations are taken in account, the optimization method as proposed by Patil et al. [12] has to be included as well. Effectively,

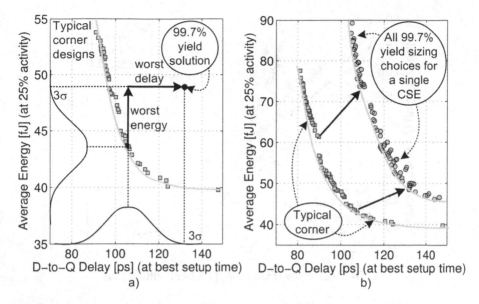

**Fig. 4.** Energy-Delay curves under process variations: a) Behavior of a single point for a 99.7% yield limit, b) Behavior of the energy efficient characteristic for a 99.7% yield limit

process variations shift the ED curves to higher energy and worse delay than the typical corner accordingly to the desired yield level in both energy and delay. This concept is shown for a single design in Fig. 4a: All of the designs at the typical corner are at the top of the distribution in the typical corner. If the process varies towards a faster corner or higher leakage corner, the energy increases. Similarly, if the process varies towards a slow corner the delay increases. Eventually, as we hit the desired yield (99.7% as example in Fig. 4a) in both energy and delay, the worst ED performance for that yield level is (48fJ ; 132ps) rather than (44fJ ; 105ps) at typical corner. To achieve the desired yield, the design must satisfy the new constraints based on the worst case delay and energy. This concept can be applied to all points of the energy efficient characteristic, thus obtaining the 99.7% yield ED-curves, shown in Fig. 4b.

## 5   High Yield and Energy Efficient CSE Designs

The purpose of this section is to show the results of an Energy-Delay space analysis for a set of CSEs under specific system constrains and to see how the results translate into high yield design space. For a complete ED space analysis, other system constraints variations such as output load and supply voltage must also be included in order to provide sufficient data for a system optimization [15].

### 5.1   High Performance CSEs

Fig. 5 shows the results of the ED analysis for the high performance CSEs. The results consist of the composite curve of the best sizings and topologies for the fixed

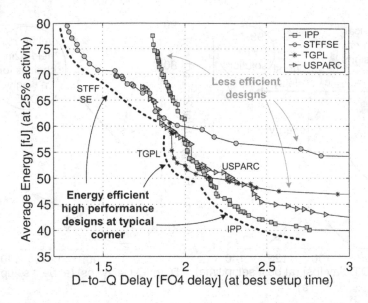

**Fig. 5.** Energy Efficient High Performance CSEs, Initial Comparison of the various topologies in the typical corner

input and output capacitance (Fig. 5). The results indicate that a subset of the IPP, TGPL and STFFSE ED characteristics constitute the best solutions, depending on the target delay. At 2.1FO4 delays and above the IPP achieve best energy efficiency and below 1.9FO4 the STFFSE achieve best energy efficiency. In between, there is a narrow section around 2FO4 in which the TGPL provides lowest energy designs. Although the USPARC flip-flop is close to the IPP and TGPL in wide range of the delay targets, in no sizing configuration it is the optimum CSE choice. It should be noted that if a smaller load is chosen in the setup (Fig. 2a), the inverter I6 (Fig. 3d) may be removed, improving the TGPL design further, and allowing TGPL to occupy wider range of the composite energy-efficient characteristic.

Fig. 6 shows the energy efficient composite characteristics extracted from Fig. 5 as well as the energy efficient characteristic for high yield, obtained as described in section 4. Designing for high yield shifts the ED curves consistently with an average of a 13% penalty in energy and a 30% penalty in delay for the STFF-SE, IPP and USPARC topologies. However, the TGPL performs worse than other studied CSE in terms of delay with a 48% penalty when process variations are taken into account. The reason for this discrepancy is the principle of operation of the TGPL. This structure relies on the explicit clock pulse to drive the pass gate (M1&M2 in Fig. 3d). Due to lower driving capability of the NAND gate N1 in Fig.3d, the pulse generator in some sizing configurations is not capable to produce full-swing clock pulse height, which further reduces the speed of the TGPL. In order to generate full-swing pulse, larger number of inverters in the pulse generator is needed. However, increasing the width of the pulse has adverse effects on the energy and on the hold time in the fast process corner.

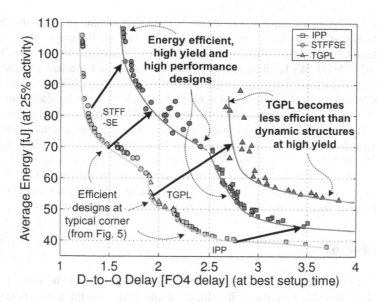

**Fig. 6.** Impact of high yield design (99.7%) on the energy efficient high performance CSEs

## 5.2  Low-Power CSEs

Static master-slave latches typically used in low power systems behave much differently than high performance topologies in term of ED performance versus sizing.

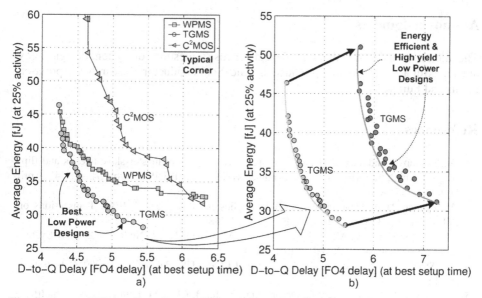

**Fig. 7.** Energy Efficient Low Power CSEs: a) Comparison of the various topologies in the typical corner, b) Impact of high yield design (99.7%) on the energy efficient low power CSEs (TGMS only)

Because the critical path from D to Q (or Qb) is similar to a chain of inverters, the ED performance is dependent on the gain specification. However, the slope of the energy efficient characteristic is dependent on the topology. For example, as shown in Fig. 7a, the energy of $C^2MOS$ MS latch increases rapidly as we move towards faster designs. This is due to the clocked transistors (M2-M3-M6-M7 in Fig. 3e), which must be large to maintain drive strength because they are stacked with the data transistors (M1-M4-M5-M8 in Fig. 3e). In the TGMS and the WPMS the "inverter – pass transistor" combination decouple the datapath inverters from the clock, hence allowing a more efficient distribution of the gain and yielding lower energy for faster designs than the $C^2MOS$ MS Latch. Fig. 7a reveals that the TGMS provides best ED results versus the WPMS and the $C^2MOS$ in all cases for the setup shown in Fig. 2b. The impact of the process variations is shown in Fig. 7b and represents a consistent 30% overhead in delay and 10% overhead in energy for all three master-slave designs.

# 6 Conclusions

This work presents the impact of process variations on the choice and design of the CSEs. We show how the boundaries in which various CSEs are the most energy efficient topologies change when the yield is taken into account. For single-ended high performance CSEs, the STFFSE, the TGPL and the IPP perform best at typical corner and only STFFSE and IPP remain efficient for high yield design. For low power designs the transmission gate master-slave latch performs best in typical corner, and it remains best for high yield design. This work reveals the impact of the process corner to the Energy-Delay characteristics for each energy efficient CSE.

## Acknowledgments

The authors would like to thank B. Zeydel for his suggestions on system design. They are thankful for the support provided by the Semiconductor Research Corporation grants and Fujitsu Ltd.

## References

1. V. Stojanovic and V. Oklobdzija, "Comparative analysis of master-slave latches and flip-flops for high-performance and low-power systems", IEEE JSSC, vol. 34, (no. 4), April 1999. p. 536-48.
2. V. Zyuban, "Optimization of scannable latches for low energy", IEEE Transactions on VLSI, Vol.11, Issue 5, Oct. 2003 Page(s):778-788
3. V. G. Oklobdzija, V. M. Stojanovic, D. M. Markovic, N. M. Nedovic, "Digital System Clocking", January 2003, Wiley-IEEE Press
4. V. Stojanovic, V. G. Oklobdzija, "FLIP-FLOP" US Patent No. 6,232,810, Issued: 05/15/2001
5. B. Nikolic, V. Stojanovic, V.G. Oklobdzija, W. Jia, J. Chiu, M. Leung, "Sense Amplifier-Based Flip-Flop", 1999 IEEE ISSCC, San Francisco, February 1999.

6. N. Nedovic, V. G. Oklobdzija, W. W. Walker, "A Clock Skew Absorbing Flip-Flop", 2003 IEEE ISSCC, San Francisco, Feb. 2003.
7. J. Tschanz, S. Narendra, Z. Chen, S. Borkar, M. Sachdev, V. De, "Comparative delay and energy of single edge-triggered and dual edge-triggered pulsed flip-flops for high-performance micro-processors", ISLPED, 2001. 6-7 Aug. 2001 Page(s):147-152
8. N. Nedovic, "Clocked Storage Elements for High-Performance Applications", PhD dissertation, University of California Davis 2003.
9. F. Klass, "Semi-Dynamic and Dynamic Flip-Flops with Embedded Logic," Symposium on VLSI Circuits, p.108-109, 1998
10. G. Gerosa, S. Gary, C. Dietz, P. Dac, K. Hoover, J. Alvarez, "A 2.2W, 80MHz Superscalar RISC Microprocessor," IEEE JSSC, vol. 29, pp. 1440-1452, Dec. 1994.
11. M. Matsui, H. Hara, Y. Uetani, K. Lee-Sup, T. Nagamatsu, Y.Watanabe, "A 200 MHz 13 mm2 2-D DCT macrocell using sense-amplifier pipeline flip-flop scheme," IEEE JSSC, vol. 29, pp. 1482–1491, Dec. 1994.Baldonado, M., Chang, C.-C.K., Gravano, L., Paepcke, A.: The Stanford Digital Library Metadata Architecture. Int. J. Digit. Libr. 1 (1997) 108–121.
12. D. Patil, S. Yun, S.-J. Kim, A. Cheung, M. Horowitz, S. Boyd, "A new method for design of robust digital circuits", Sixth International Symposium on Quality of Electronic Design, 2005, ISQED 2005. 21-23 March 2005 Page(s):676 – 681.
13. D. Markovic, J. Tschanz, V. De, "Transmission-gate based flip-flop" US Patent 6,642,765, Nov. 2003.
14. H. Dao, K. Nowka, V. Oklobdzija, "Analysis of Clocked Timing Elements for DVS Effects over Process Parameter Variation", Proceedings of the International Symposium on Low Power Electronics and Design, Huntington Beach, California, August 6-7, 2001.
15. H. Dao, B. Zeydel, V. Oklobdzija, "Energy Optimization of Pipelined Digital Systems Using Circuit Sizing and Supply Scaling" IEEE Transactions on VLSI, Volume 14, Issue 2, Feb. 2006 Page(s):122 - 134.

# IR-drop Reduction Through Combinational Circuit Partitioning

Hai Lin, Yu Wang, Rong Luo, Huazhong Yang, and Hui Wang

EE Department, Tsinghua University, Haidian District
Beijing, 100084, P.R. China*
{linhai99, wangyuu99}@mails.tsinghua.edu.cn,
{luorong, yanghz, wangh}@tsinghua.edu.cn

**Abstract.** IR-drop problem is becoming more and more important. Previous works dealing with power/ground (P/G) network peak current reduction to reduce the IR-drop problem only focus on synchronous sequential logic circuits which consider the combinational parts as unchangeable [4],[5]. However, some large combinational circuits which work alone in one clock cycle can create large current peaks and induce considerable IR-drops in the P/G network. In this paper, we propose a novel combinational circuit IR-drop reduction methodology using Switching Current Redistribution (SCR) method. A novel combinational circuit partitioning method is proposed to rearrange the switching current in different sub-blocks in order to reduce the current peak in the P/G network, while circuit function and performance are maintained. Experimental results show that, our method can achieve about 20% average reduction to the peak currents of the ISCAS85 benchmark circuits.

**Keywords:** IR-drop, circuit partitioning, Static Timing Analysis.

## 1  Introduction

With technology stepping into submicron region, circuit design for single-chip integration of more complex, higher speed, and lower supply voltage systems has made the on-chip signal-integrity (SI) problem to be a tough task. Among all the sources of SI problem, the dynamic voltage drop caused mainly by $Ldi/dt$ and IR-drop draws much attention in recent years.

As the supply voltage goes down continuously, ignoring the dynamic voltage drop through supply networks will cause run-time errors on real chips. These errors may include that transistors may not turn on with an unexpected voltage drop, and a timing constraint violation because of a delay increase of the standard gates with lower supply voltage. Some publications have already paid attention to reduce the voltage variation on P/G network for all kinds of purposes. Early publications focus directly on the optimization of the P/G network of the circuit, such as supply wire sizing [1] and P/G network decoupling capacitance (DC) insertion [2], [3] strategies. However as the technology feature

---

* This work was sponsored in party by NSFC under grants #90207001 and #90307016.

J. Vounckx, N. Azemard, and P. Maurine (Eds.): PATMOS 2006, LNCS 4148, pp. 370–381, 2006.
© Springer-Verlag Berlin Heidelberg 2006

scales down, such efforts become insufficient and suffer from the drawback of large on-chip resource occupation.

In recent years, a few researchers have focused on the optimization of the logic blocks of the circuit[4],[5]. In publication [5], a synchronous digital circuit is first divided into "clock regions" and then these regions are assigned with different-phase clocks, in this case the author tried to spread the original simultaneous switching activities on the time axis to reshape the switching current waveform and reduce the current peak.

However, those algorithms using clock as the controlling signal to distribute the switching activity have an essential defect. As mentioned in [4], these algorithms lack the ability to control combinational circuit. Even in sequential circuits, the combinational part which triggered by flip-flops works alone in one clock cycle and draw corresponding currents from power network. When these combinational parts are large enough, the current peak created by one single combinational part is quite considerable. This problem cannot be settled by algorithms dealing with clock skew assignment.

In this paper, we present our IR-drop reduction method in combinational circuits. And the paper mainly has three contributions:

1. We derive a formal problem definition of IR-drop reduction in the combinational circuits and propose a novel combinational circuit IR-drop reduction methodology using *Switching Current Redistribution* (SCR) method based on circuit partitioning.

2. We give out a combinational circuit decomposition algorithm with better circuit slack utility to support our SCR method. Combinational block is partitioned into sub-graphs based on a new partitioning criterion called *slack sub-graph partitioning* to rearrange the switching time of different parts. STA tool is used to insure the original timing constraints and critical paths, in this way the exact logic function and the highest working frequency are both preserved.

3. A simple and proper additional delay assignment strategy is proposed. Then we compare some methods which modify the decomposed circuits to redistribute the switching current while the logical function and the performance constraints of the circuit are maintained.

The paper is organized as follows. The definition of combinational circuit IR-drop reduction problem is proposed in Section 2. Our novel circuit decomposition method is presented in Section 3. In Section 4 we present the additional delay assignment and the exact circuit modification strategy to achieve the additional delay. The implementation and experimental results are shown and analyzed in Section 5. In Section 6, we give the conclusion.

## 2  Problem Definition of Combinational Circuit IR-drop Reduction

### 2.1  Preliminary

Our research focuses on gate level combinational circuits. At the gate level, a combinational circuit can be represented by a directed acyclic graph (DAG),

$G=(V, E)$. A vertex $v \in V$ represents a CMOS transistor network which realizes a single output logic function (a logic gate), while an edge $(i; j) \in E$, $i$, $j \in V$ represents a connection from vertex $i$ to vertex $j$.

We define three attributes for every vertex $v \in V$, they are , the arrival time $t_a(v)$, the required time $t_{req}(v)$, and the slack time $t_{slk}(v)$. The arrival time $t_a(v)$ is the worst case signal transfer time from the primary inputs to vertex $v$. $t_{req}(v)$ is the latest time the signal needs to arrive at vertex $v$. We define them as:

$$t_a(v) = \begin{cases} t_0 \text{ given time of arrival if } v \text{ is the primary input} \\ \max_{i \in fanin(v)} \{t_a(i) + d(i)\} \text{ otherwise} \end{cases} \qquad (1)$$

$$t_{req}(v) = \begin{cases} t_a(v) \text{ if } v \text{ is the virtual output} \\ \min_{i \in fanin(v)} \{t_{req}(i) - d(v)\} \text{ otherwise} \end{cases} \qquad (2)$$

The signal propagation delay of a vertex $d(v)$ can be respectively represented as:

$$d(v) = \frac{KC_L V_{DD}}{(V_{DD} - V_{TH})^\alpha} \qquad (3)$$

Where $C_L$ and $V_{TH}$ are the output load capacitance and the transistor threshold voltage of the gate, respectively; $K$ and $\alpha$ are technology dependent constants. The slack time of a gate v is defined as the difference of its arrival time and required time.

$$t_{slk}(v) = t_{req}(v) - t_a(v) \qquad (4)$$

The slack time of a gate $v$ represents the timing laxity of the graph at this point. The performance will not be harmed if a circuit modification still maintains the $t_{slk}(v) \leq 0$. We can call it a *slack time limitation*.

If we define a working frequency, the *critical path* of the circuits is constituted by the set of gates that has the minimum slack time value. And with the highest working frequency, this minimum slack value is zero. Our analysis focuses on the highest working frequency situation to ensure the original best performance of the circuit.

## 2.2   Problem Definition

The IR-drop $\Delta V(t)$ under a certain input can be represented as:

$$\Delta V(t) = I(V,t) \times R_{P/G} = (\sum_{v \in V} I_v(t, input_v, t_a(v), d(v))) \times R_{P/G} \qquad (5)$$

Where $R_{P/G}$ is the P/G network resistance; $I(V,t)$ is the current of the combinational circuits; $I_v$ is the switching current of the individual gate $v \in V$, which is determined by its input state $input_v$, input signal arrival time $t_a(v)$ and propagation delay $d(v)$. From the equation (5), we can modify $I_v$ through $t_a(v)$ and $d(v)$ in order to minimize the current peak of the combinational circuit. However if we adjust every gate to get the optimal result, the IR-drop reduction problem will be unacceptably difficult.

As a result, in our method the combinational circuit $G=(V, E)$ is partitioned into independent blocks $G_{sub} = G_1, G_2, , G_n$ in order to simplify the IR-drop problem. Thus the IR-drop can have an alternative definition as below:

$$\Delta V(t, G_k, D_k) = \left\{ \sum_{1 \leq k \leq n} (t, input_k, T_{a,k}, D_k) \right\} \times R_{P/G} \qquad (6)$$

Where $I_k$ is the switching current of block $G_k = (V_k, E_k)$, $G_k \subset G$ , $1 \leq k \leq n$; $input_k$ is the input state of block $G_k$; $T_{a,k} = \{t_a(v_in), v_{in} \in V_k\}$ and $D_k = \{d(v_{in}), v_{in} \in V_k\}$ are the arrival time set and the propagation delay set for all the input vertexes of block $G_k$ respectively. Therefore we only need to modify the delay value of all the input vertexes of the independent blocks to redistribute the switching current. Thus the IR-drop reduction problem of a combinational circuit can be defined as:

$$\min_{G_k, D_k} \left\{ \max_t \{\Delta V(t, G_k, D_k)\} \right\} \qquad (7)$$

while satisfies the circuit performance constraints:
$t_a(m) = 0, \forall m \in$ Primary input, $m \in V$
$t_a(u) + d(u) \leq T_{critical}, \forall u \in$ Primary input, $u \in V$
$t_a(i) + d(i) \leq t_a(j), \forall(i, j) \in E, i, j \in V$
where $T_{critical}$ is the delay of the circuit critical path.

## 2.3   Switching Current Distribution Methodology

As in the problem definition, the IR-drop reduction problem can not be easily solved. Based on circuit partition we presented our own method to solve the problem in a smart way of combinational blocks' switching current distribution.

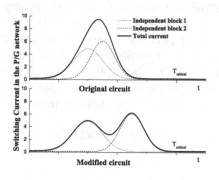 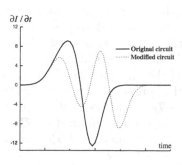

(a) Current amplitude comparison  (b) $di/dt$ comparison

**Fig. 1.** Switching current redistribution

Shown by Fig. 1, if the combinational circuit are partitioned into two independent blocks without signal dependence, their switching current can be adjusted independently, by separate the switching time of the two blocks the current peak can be considerably reduced. Moreover, as mentioned above, the $Ldi/dt$ noise is becoming significant in the P/G network. To smooth the currents waveforms in this way may also help reduce such noise when inductance of the P/G network is considered (see Fig. 1). We call this *Switching Current Redistribution*. To achieve this specific partitioning goal, we present a new algorithm combining static timing analysis (STA) information into the partitioning algorithm and make sure to maintain the critical paths after partitioning to ensure the circuit performance. And a simple and proper additional delay time assignment method is proposed to realize the redistribution of the switching current of different blocks.

## 3   Combinational Circuit Partitioning Method

The combinational circuit should be partitioned into independent blocks. These blocks should have no signal dependence between each other and their switching current can be modified independently to reduce the total switching current peak of the circuit. However, traditional partitioning algorithms [8], [9] are not capable for this specific partitioning requirement. First, traditional partitioning algorithms focus mainly on mini-cut or weighted mini-cut, while our partitioning requires awareness of signal independent characteristics of each block. Second, random assignment and element exchanging strategy in traditional partitioning algorithms can easily break critical paths of a combinational circuit. We develop our partitioning algorithm through which the critical paths are not cut off or modified in order to preserve original performance.

We first propose a concept of *slack sub-graph*. A sub-graph is called *slack sub-graph* if and only if all of its vertexes (gates) are of non-zero slack time at highest working frequency situation. And on the contrary, sub-graphs that consist of all zero slack time vertexes are defined as *critical sub-graphs*. According to this definition, *critical sub-graphs* consist of all the critical paths. If we only modify the *slack sub-graphs* under the timing constraints-all vertexes obey the *slack time limitation* discussed in the preliminary part, then the original critical paths in the circuit will not be affected, which conditionally satisfy our requirement of the "independence" characteristics between sub-graphs. Therefore our algorithm proposed a way to divide the combinational circuit into *slack sub-graphs* ($G_{SLK}$) and *critical sub-graphs* ($G_{CRI}$) which are independent under the timing constraints obtained by STA.

With the definition of *slack sub-graph*, our specific partitioning process is expressed as below:

*Combinational-circuit-partitioning (G)*
   1 Perform STA to G and get the slack time of all the vertexes;
2 $V_{CRI} = \{v \mid t_{slk}(v) = 0\}$;
3 Get all the critical edges $E_{CRI}$ ;
4 $G_{CRI} = (V_CRI, E_{CRI})$; // construct the critical block

5 $V_{SLK} = V - V_{CRI}$ ;
6 While ( $V_{SLK}$ not empty)
Begin while:
$\forall v_i \in V_{SLK}$ ; //randomly choose a vertex $v_i$
Get all the vertexes connected with $v_i$ in $V_{SLK}$, and put them in set $V_{SLK}(i)$;
Get all the edges generated by vertexes in $V_{SLK}(i)$, and put them in set $E_{SLK}(i)$;
$G_{SLK}(i) = ( V_{SLK}(i), E_{SLK}(i))$; // construct a slack sub graph
$V_{SLK} = V_{SLK} - V_{SLK}(i)$;
End while;
7 Return $G_{sub} = \{G_{CRI}, \{G_{SLK}(i)\}\}$; // return the independent blocks

Therefore, we obtain two kinds of blocks. One independent block consists of $G'_{CRI}$s, which should not be modified in order to maintain the circuit performance. We consider this block as *critical block*. And we obtain the other kind of independent blocks- slack blocks, consists of $G_{SLK}(i)'s$. The Switching Current Redistribution can be implemented through modifications of $G_{SLK}(i)'s$. From our partitioning algorithm, at least one slack block can be obtained. And always, the slack blocks whose size is comparable to the critical block are targeted to be modified, in this way we can achieve a high efficiency of current redistribution.

## 4   Strategy of Switching Current Redistribution

After circuit decomposition, it is important to modify the targeted *slack blocks* so as to redistribute their currents. Our attempt can be illustrated in Fig. 2.

For combinational circuits, there is no controlling signal like clock, so referring to equation (6), the slack block current $I(V_{SLK}, t)$ is determined by $T_{a,SLK}$, $D_{SLK}$. Thus in our method, we modify the input vertexes' delay in the *slack block* to modify the switching time of this block. We artificially delay the input signal transferring from the input to the next stage , in this way the switching time of this block is controlled. A simple and effective delay time assignment method is proposed to determine the amount of additional time that the input signal should be delayed.

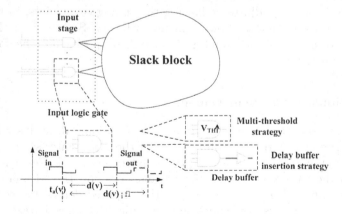

**Fig. 2.** Modify the input gates through two strategies

## 4.1    Additional Delay Assignment

Currents of different blocks are estimated using a simplified switching current estimation model similar with the one used in [10]. The switching current model of every logic gate is represented as a production of the switching activity $\alpha$ multiplied by the current waveform which is modeled as a trapezoid starting from the earliest possible switch time of the gate and ends at the latest. The trapezoid wave model is derived from the gate's original switching current waveform -a triangle representation. (see Fig. 3). The current model $I_{model}^i(t)$ for gate $i$ is presented as follow, $\alpha$ is the switching activity of gate $i$.

$$I_{model}^i(t) = \alpha I_{gi}'(t) \tag{8}$$

The total current from one slack block is the sum of all the gates' current within it. And we can easily calculate the peak when we actually store the current waveform by discrete value at each time interval.

We perform a simple but practical additional delay time assignment strategy to achieve a considerable large reduction in the switching current peak of the combinational circuit.

Here, we propose the experimental based assignment of the artificial additional delay value of input gate in every targeted sub-graph. We assign the additional delay of input vertex to the amount of its slack time to form the initial solution $SOL_{DLY}$, so that we may spread more switching current to the entire circuit switching period and reduce the overlapping of switching currents of critical block and the targeted slack blocks. Then a small nearby region search for better solution of this assignment is made based on the evaluation of $I_{peak}$. Experimental results show that little change of the initial solution is needed and this simple and practical additional delay assignment strategy can appropriately redistribute the switching current of the blocks, utilize the total circuit switching period more equably and reduce the peak current of the whole circuit to a considerably lower value.

The circuit performance is maintained since the *critical block* is not changed and the *slack blocks* are adjusted following the timing constraints. In the slack time assignment, slack information is extracted by our STA tool [7]. The final delay time information of each input gate is saved in specific data file for circuit modification procedure.

## 4.2    Additional Delay Achievement

One practical strategy to realize in circuit the additional delay insertion is to change the transistor threshold voltage $V_{TH}$ of the input gates so as to change $d(v)$ of them. Referring to equation (3), signal transfer delay of a logic gate is related to the threshold voltage of its transistors and the adequate threshold voltage can be calculated according to the required delay. However, as the threshold values of transistors can not be continuously changed in reality and are often fixed to several threshold levels in multi-threshold design due to process

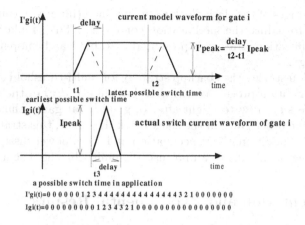

**Fig. 3.** Current model for logic gate

limitation, it is necessary to adjust $V_{TH}$ of input gates to acceptable discrete values.

Therefore, here we propose a three-level discrete $V_{TH}$ assignment to achieve the additional delay.

*Discrete $V_{TH}$ assignment*
1 Set discrete $V_{TH}$ value: $V_{THO}$, $V_{THO} + \Delta V_{THL}$, $V_{THO} + \Delta V_{THH}$;
2 Read the required additional delay $\Delta d_i$ for $v_i$, $v_i \in$ input vertexes of slack blocks;
3 $V_{input} = \{v_i \mid v_i \in input\_vertexes\_of\_slack\_blocks\}$
4 While ($V_{input}! = \phi$)
Begin while:
Random select $v_i \in V_{input}$,
$\Delta V'_{TH} =$ f($\Delta d_i$) //calculate actual $\Delta V_{TH}$ required for gate i according to equation(3)
Set $\Delta V_{TH}$: if $0 \leq \Delta V'_{TH} < \Delta V_{THL}$, $\Delta V_{TH} = 0$
if $\Delta V_{THL} \leq \Delta V'_{TH} < \Delta V_{THH}$, $\Delta V_{TH} = \Delta V_{THL}$
Else if $\Delta V_{THH} \leq \Delta V'_{TH}$
(1) Set $\Delta V_{TH} = \Delta V_{THH}$
(2) $\Delta d = d(\Delta V'_{TH}) - d(\Delta V_{THH})$ Calculate the delay difference caused by $\Delta V'_{TH}$ and $\Delta V_{THH}$;
(3) Get all the output vertexes of $v_i$, assign $\Delta d$ information to all them and put them in set $V_out$; //propagate the overflow delay to the next stage.
End while;

As in our experiment we are using TSMC 0.18m standard cell library for simulation, the three discrete $V_{TH}$ values are set to $V_{THO}$, $V_{THO} + \Delta V_{THL}$ and $V_{THO} + \Delta V_{THH}$. $V_{THO}$ is the library determining original transistor threshold voltage. And in our experiment, we set $\Delta V_{THL} = 0.2V$, $\Delta V_{THH} = 0.4V$. In reality, the actual discrete values can be determined by process limitation. First of all, the input gate is assigned one of the discrete $V_{TH}$ values that is just below the calculated value. Then, if the required additional delay exceed the maximum value that can be achieved by a single input gate, the overflow delay would be assigned to gates in the following stage of the slack block. In our experiment, we only allow two stages of the slack block to be modified (input stage and the stage following that) to reduce the modification complexity. The simulation result of this circuit modification strategy is presented in Table.1 and compared to buffer insertion strategy.

Buffer insertion strategy is a backup strategy for multi-threshold strategy, and reduces the fabrication process cost. Instead of change $d(v)$ of the input gates, specialized buffers are inserted right after original input gates, thus change the arrival time of the other gates in the slack block. However, this strategy has two major drawbacks: additional area occupation and more power dissipation. Thus we consider using it only if we can not use the multi-threshold strategy.

## 5    Implementation and Experimental Results

The implementation of our algorithm can be illustrated in Fig. 4. Our gate level netlists are synthesized using Synopsys Design Compiler and a TSMC 0.18μm standard cell library. The DAG extraction and customized circuit partitioning procedure have been implemented in C++ under a customized STA environment according to the TSMC standard cell delay library. We implemented a small tool to automatically generate the modified gate list including the delay time assignment and the two circuit modification strategies. Both the original and modified circuits are simulated using HSPICE with TSMC 0.18μm CMOS process and a 1.67V supply condition. The P/G network is modeled as RC network.

As our algorithm focuses on the redistribution of switching current from logic blocks, the architecture of P/G network model does not have much influence in

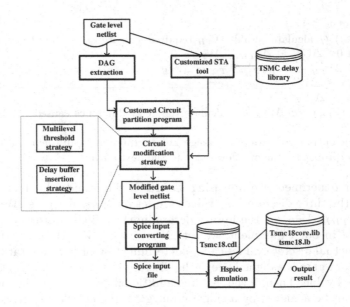

**Fig. 4.** Implementation procedure

the peak current reduction ability. We actually compared the simulation results from the circuit with simple model(single R and C) and complex model(multiple R and C connected as a mesh) of P/G network in several circuits. It shows that the detailed waveform of the current is changing slightly with the P/G network variation but the reduction rate remains approximately the same (see Fig. 5). As a result, in our simulation we simply model the P/G network as a 100 $\Omega$ resistance connected between $V_{DD}$ and the logic block, and a capacitance of 0.3pf parallel connected to the logic block to reduce the simulation complexity. We apply the proposed method to ISCAS85 benchmark circuits and all the circuits are simulated with large number of random input vectors. And we are running the program on a PC with P4 2.6GHz and 512M memory.

We show in Fig. 5 the transient on-chip current waveform in one processing cycle of the modified circuit compared with the original circuit of C1355 simulated with both simple P/G network and complex P/G network. As we expected, the current waveform of both unmodified (figures above) and modified (figures below) circuit with complex P/G network (dotted line) are different from the ones with simple P/G network (real line). However the peak current reduction rate remains approximately the same. And comparing the waveforms with the same P/G model, we can find that the current curves with single peak in one processing cycle change into curves with two or more lower swing peaks after circuit modification. Thus the switching current of the two major kinds of blocks (the *slack blocks* and the *critical block*) is actually separated and the peak current of the circuit is significantly reduced.

Table.1 shows the current peak reduction results of both multi-threshold and buffer insertion strategies. We can see that the reduction of current peak varies with the circuit structures, from 15% up to 33% by multi-threshold and from 12% up to 32% by buffer insertion, which are very impressive. The circuits with more slack to be utilized get a better optimization result through our algorithm.

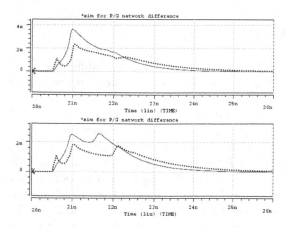

**Fig. 5.** Simulation current waveforms of C1355

**Table 1.** Comparison of the multi-threshold and buffer insertion strategies

| ISCAS85 Circuit | Original | Multi-$V_{TH}$ | | | Buffer insertion | | |
|---|---|---|---|---|---|---|---|
| | Average $I_{peak}$(mA) | Average $I_{peak}$(mA) | $I_{peak}$ Reduction | | Average $I_{peak}$(mA) | $I_{peak}$ Reduction | Area Overload ($N_{buf}/N_{totalgates}$) |
| C432 | 2.45 | 2.08 | 15% | | 2.15 | 12% | 6/160 |
| C499 | 4.27 | 2.98 | 31% | | 3.01 | 29% | 14/202 |
| C880 | 3.05 | 2.28 | 25% | | 2.31 | 24% | 38/383 |
| C1355 | 4.21 | 3.01 | 29% | | 2.85 | 32% | 22/545 |
| C1908 | 3.96 | 3.07 | 22% | | 3.04 | 23% | 31/880 |
| C2670 | 3.68 | 2.95 | 20% | | 2.98 | 19% | 49/1269 |
| C3540 | 2.78 | 2.27 | 18% | | 2.33 | 16% | 84/1669 |
| C5315 | 4.94 | 3.29 | 33% | | 3.75 | 24% | 170/2307 |
| C6288 | 4.78 | 3.87 | 19% | | 3.98 | 17% | 119/2416 |
| C7552 | 5.26 | 4.43 | 16% | | 4.46 | 15% | 201/3513 |
| average | | | 23% | | | 21% | |

Here, we comment that the algorithm would have a limit of applicability if the slack blocks have too little slack amount to be utilize, which would be very rare for functional combinational circuits. Even in that case, we suggest a circuit slow down be induced to achieve more slack utility if reducing switching current peak is the most urgent problem for a application.

Although the peak current reduction is nearly the same, the average current of the circuit shows that buffer insertion strategy induces more on-chip current besides the draw back of on chip area overload due to the insertion of buffers. Some other strategies, such as gate sizing or transistor stacking, can also be considered in order to avoid large addition current meanwhile achieve the equivalent required delay.

# 6    Conclusions

IR-drop reduction is becoming essential in deep submicron circuit design today. The efficient reduction methodology needs to be improved imperatively. In this paper, we have presented a novel methodology for IR-drop reduction in combinational circuits through circuit partitioning and switching current redistribution. The original circuit is partitioned into independent blocks and the switching time of the blocks is carefully arranged to ensure that switching current redistribution is achieved for IR-drop reduction. The additional delay assignment and insertion is achieved without affecting the circuit performance under timing constraints. The experimental results for ISCAS85 benchmark circuits show an average current peak reduction on P/G network around 20%. The only drawback of this switching current redistribution method is that as the slack in the circuit is used for current redistribution, the circuit is going to lose some tolerance ability to process variations which affect the path delay. As the statistic effect on physical design is becoming not neglectableto induce a slight circuit slow down or to maintain a certain amount of the original slack according to the specific manufacturing technique would be both applicable in order to insure a process variation tolerance ability. Since our method does not have any performance loss and do not require modifications on P/G network or circuit clock trees, it can be used with other commonly used methods such as P/G network DC insertion and clock skew assignment in synchronous circuits to achieve further reduction ability of on-chip IR-drop.

# References

1. Sheldon X.-D, Tan, C.-J, Richard Shi, Jyh-Chwen Lee: Reliability-Constrained Area Optimization of VLSI Power/Ground Networks Via Sequence of Linear Programmings. IEEE Trans. on CAD, Vol. 22, No. 12, pp. 1678-1684, 2003.
2. Mondira Deb Pant, Pankaj Pant, Donald Scott Wills: On-Chip Decoupling Capacitor Optimization Using Architectural Level Prediction. IEEE Trans. on VLSI, Vol. 10, No. 3, pp 772-775, 2002.
3. Howard H. Chen, J. Scott Neely, Michael F. Wang, Grieel Co: On-Chip Decoupling Capacitor Optimization for Noise and Leakage Reduction. Procs of IEEE ISCAS, 2003.
4. P. Vuillod, L. Benini, A. Bogliolo, G. De Micheli: Clock-skew optimization for peak current reduction. Procs of ISLPED.1996 Monterey CA USA, 1996.
5. Mustafa Badaroglu, Kris Tiri, Stphane Donnay, Piet Wambacq, Ingrid Verbauwhede, Georges Gielen, Hugo De Man: Clock Tree Optimization in Synchronous CMOS Digital Circuits for Substrate Noise Reduction Using Folding of Supply Current Transients. Procs of DAC 2002, June 10-14, New Orleans, Louisiana, 2002.
6. Amir H. Ajami, Kaustav Banerjee, Amit Mehrotra, Massoud Pedram: Analysis of IR-Drop Scaling with Implications for Deep Submicron P/G Network Designs. Procs of ISQED 2003.
7. Yu Wang, Huazhong Yang, Hui Wang: Signal-path level Assignment for Dual-Vt Technique. Procs of IEEE PRIME 2005, pp 52-55.
8. George Karypis, Rajat Aggarwal, Vipin Kumar, Shashi Shekhar: Multilevel Hypergraph Partitioning: Applications in VLSI Domain. IEEE Trans. on VLSI, Vol. 7, No. 1, pp 69-79, 1999.
9. Navaratnasothie Selvakkumaran, George Karypis: Multi-Objective Hypergraph Partitioning Algorithms for Cut and Maximum Subdomain Degree Minimization. Procs of ICCAD'03, November 11-13, San Jose, California, USA, 2003.
10. Mohab Anis, Shawki Areibi, and Mohamed Elmasry: Design and Optimization of Multithreshold CMOS (MTCMOS) Circuits. IEEE Trans on CAD, Vol. 22, No. 10, pp 1324-1342, Oct 2003.

# Low-Power Register File Based on Adiabatic Logic Circuits

Jianping Hu, Hong Li, and Yangbo Wu

Faculty of Information Science and Technology, Ningbo University,
818 Fenghua Road, Ningbo 315211, Zhejiang Province, China
Hujianping2@nbu.edu.cn

**Abstract.** In adiabatic circuits, the energy dissipation occurs during every cycle, as output nodes are always charged and discharged by power-clocks. This paper presents a low-power register file based on adiabatic logic with power-gating techniques. N-type adiabatic drivers with power-gating schemes are used to drive read bit and read data lines, while P-type adiabatic drivers with power-gating schemes are used to drive write bit lines and power storage cells. The write and read drivers for driving bit and word lines can be switched off to reduce energy losses during idle times. The energy of all nodes with large capacitances including storage cells can be well recovered without non-adiabatic loss. SPICE simulations indicate that the proposed register file achieves considerable energy savings over CMOS implementation.

## 1 Introduction

As density and operating speed of CMOS chips increase, power dissipation has become a critical concern in VLSI circuits [1]. Compared with conventional CMOS circuits, adiabatic circuits obtain low power dissipation, because they utilize AC power supplies to recycle the energy of node capacitances [2–6].

A register file is one of the most power-consuming blocks in microprocessors because it contains large capacitances on bit lines, word lines and storage cells, and is frequently accessed. Some adiabatic memories have been reported. In [7, 8, 9], adiabatic circuits, such as the efficient charge recovery logic (ECRL) [4], 2N-2N2P [2], and the pass-transistor adiabatic logic circuits with NMOS pull-down configuration (PAL-2N) [5] etc., are used to drive address lines, bit lines, and word lines. Although some adiabatic memories consume lower power than the conventional CMOS, they have large non-adiabatic energy loss on bit and word lines that include large node capacitances. In [10–12], the charge of nodes with large capacitance can be well recovered, but storage cells are still powered by a DC supply. Moreover, in the previously proposed adiabatic register files, energy dissipation occurs even if the register file is not used for read and write operations, because the output nodes of adiabatic circuits are always charged and discharged by power-clocks at all times [13].

This paper presents a low-power register file based on adiabatic logic with power-gating techniques. N-type adiabatic drivers [12] with power-gating schemes are used to drive read bit and data lines, while P-type adiabatic drivers [14] are used to drive write bit lines and power storage cells. During idle periods (the register file is not

J. Vounckx, N. Azemard, and P. Maurine (Eds.): PATMOS 2006, LNCS 4148, pp. 382–392, 2006.
© Springer-Verlag Berlin Heidelberg 2006

used for read / write operation), power-clocks to drive bit lines and word lines with large capacitances can be switched off by using the N-type and P-type adiabatic drivers to reduce energy losses. The energy of all nodes with large capacitances including storage cells can be well recovered without non-adiabatic loss. With 0.18μm TSMC process, SPICE simulations indicate that the proposed register file achieves considerable energy savings over similar implementations.

## 2 Overview of Adiabatic Drivers

A representative adiabatic logic is 2N-2N2P [2], as shown in Fig. 1 a). The buffer (inverter) consists of a flip-flop ($N_1$, $N_2$, $P_1$, and $P_2$) and the input NMOS transistors ($N_i$ and $N_{ib}$) that implement the logic function. Cascaded 2N-2N2P gates are driven by four-phase power-clocks, as shown in Fig. 1 b). A detailed description for the 2N-2N2P can be found in [2].

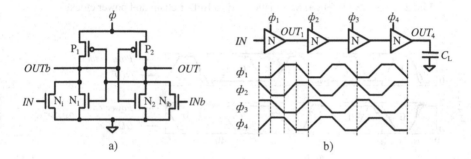

**Fig. 1.** 2N-2N2P buffer. a) Schematic, and b) Buffer chain and power-clocks

A complementary logic (2P-2P2N) [14] is shown in Fig. 2 a). Its structure and operation are complementary to the 2N-2N2P. The 2N-2N2P is a pre-discharge logic, while the 2P-2P2N is a pre-charge logic. The 2P-2P2N buffer consists of a flip-flop ($P_1$, $P_2$, $N_1$, and $N_2$) and the input PMOS transistors ($P_i$ and $P_{ib}$) that implement the logic function. The two cross-coupled PMOS transistors ($P_1$ and $P_2$) make the undriven output node clamped a DC supply $V_{DD}$. Cascaded 2P-2P2N gates are driven by the same four-phase power-clocks, as shown in Fig. 2 b).

The simulated waveforms for the two circuits are shown Fig. 3. It can be seen that they have non-adiabatic energy loss on output nodes. Energy dissipation of the 2N-2N2P and 2P-2P2N circuits includes mainly two terms: full-adiabatic energy loss that can be reduced by lowering operation frequency, and non-adiabatic energy loss that is independent of operation frequency [14]. If the clock period is much longer than the value of $RC_L$, full-adiabatic energy loss can be ignored. The non-adiabatic energy loss per cycle of 2N-2N2P can be expressed as

$$E_{\text{2N-2N2P}} \approx C_L V_{TP}^2 \qquad (1)$$

where $C_L$ is the load capacitance, and $V_{TP}$ is the threshold of PMOS transistors. Similarly, the non-adiabatic energy loss per cycle of the 2P-2P2N can be written as

$$E_{\text{2P-2P2N}} \approx C_L V_{\text{TN}}^2 \qquad (2)$$

where $V_{\text{TN}}$ is the threshold of NMOS transistors.

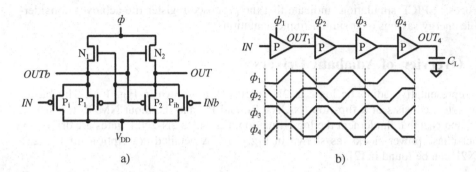

**Fig. 2.** 2P-2P2N buffer. a) Schematic, and b) Buffer chain and power clocks

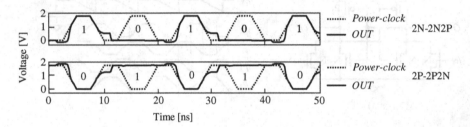

**Fig. 3.** Simulated waveforms for 2N-2N2P and 2P-2P2N buffers. The 2N-2N2P is a pre-discharge logic, while the 2P-2P2N is a pre-charge logic.

To eliminate the non-adiabatic energy loss on output loads, an N-type adiabatic driver was presented in [12], as shown in Fig. 4 a). The power-clock $\phi$ charges the output (*OUT* or *OUTb*) through $N_i$ and $P_1$ (or $N_{ib}$ and $P_2$) by control of the inputs (*IN*

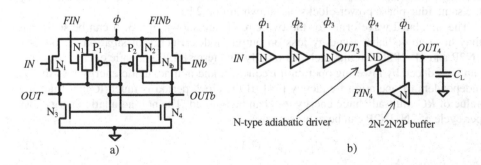

**Fig. 4.** N-type adiabatic driver. a) Schematic, and b) Cascaded buffer chain.

and *INb*). The energy of output nodes is recovered to the power-clock $\phi$ through $N_1$ and $P_1$ (or $N_2$ and $P_2$) by control of the feedback signals (*FIN* and *FINb*), which are from the outputs of the next-stage buffer. For the N-type adiabatic driver in a pipelined chain (see Fig. 4. b)), an additional 2N-2N2P buffer can be used and its outputs (*FIN₄* and *FINb₄*) control energy-recovery of the N-type adiabatic driver.

A P-type adiabatic driver is shown in Fig. 5 a) [14], and its structure and operation are complementary to the N-type adiabatic driver. The N-type adiabatic driver is a pre-discharge logic, while the P-type adiabatic driver is a pre-charge logic. For the P-type adiabatic driver in a pipelined chain (see Fig. 5. b)), an additional 2P-2P2N buffer can be used and its outputs (*FIN₄* and *FINb₄*) control energy-recovery of the P-type adiabatic driver [14].

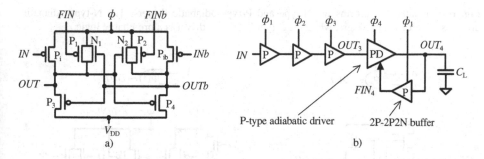

**Fig. 5.** P-type adiabatic driver. a) Schematic, and b) Cascaded buffer chain.

The simulated waveforms for N-type and P-type adiabatic drivers are shown Fig. 6. It can be seen that they don't have non-adiabatic loss on output loads. The non-adiabatic energy loss per cycle of the N-type adiabatic driver can written as

$$E_{\text{N-driver}} \approx (C_1 + C_2)V_{\text{TP}}^2, \tag{3}$$

Similarly, the non-adiabatic energy loss energy loss of the P-type adiabatic driver per cycle can be written as

$$E_{\text{P-driver}} \approx (C_1 + C_2)V_{\text{TN}}^2 \tag{4}$$

where $C_1$ and $C_2$ are the capacitance of the nodes *out₃* and *FIN₄*, respectively.

Although the 2N-2N2P and 2P-2P2N buffers have the non-adiabatic energy losses $(C_1 + C_2)V_{\text{TP}}^2$ and $(C_1 + C_2)V_{\text{TN}}^2$, this energy loss is small, because the capacitance $(C_1+C_2)$ that mainly consists of gate capacitance of the adiabatic drivers is far smaller than the load capacitance $C_L$. Therefore, they are suitable for driving large capacitances to realize power-efficient design [12, 14].

Complex logic function can be also structured for 2P-2P2N and P-type adiabatic driver. The OR gates are shown in Fig. 7. It should be pointed that their realizations are different from 2N-2N2P logic gates and N-type adiabatic drivers because of using PMOS transistors instead of NMOS.

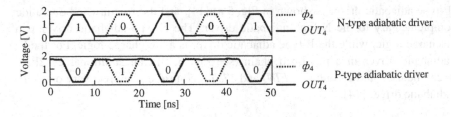

**Fig. 6.** Simulated waveforms for N-type and P-type adiabatic drivers. The N-type adiabatic driver is a pre-discharge logic, while the P-type adiabatic driver is a pre-charge logic.

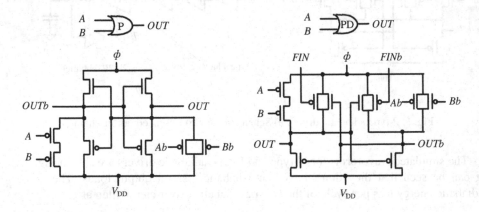

**Fig. 7.** OR / NOR gates based on 2P-2P2N and P-type adiabatic driver

## 3  Adiabatic Register File

In this session, a 32×32-bit register file using adiabatic drivers with power-gating techniques is described and simulated with 0.18μm TSMC process.

### 3.1  Storage Cell

The storage-cell structure is similar as a conventional memory cell, but the write access transistors use two PMOS ones instead of NMOS in the other implementations, as shown in Fig. 8. Another difference is that the supply of storage cells is connected to $\phi_{cell}$, which is powered by the output of P-type adiabatic driver instead of a fixed DC supply. The two pairs of access transistors ($P_W$ and $P_{Wb}$, $N_R$ and $N_{Rb}$) are enabled by *WWL* (write word line) and *RWL* (read word line) for write and read operations, respectively.

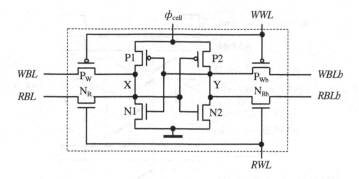

**Fig. 8.** Storage cell. It uses two PMOS write access transistors but not NMOS in the other implementations.

## 3.2 Write Address Decoder, Write Driver and Write Operation Timing

Write circuits for the register file use pre-charge logic (2P-2P2N and P-type adiabatic drivers), as shown in Fig. 9. The 3-bit addresses are pre-decoded using the 2P-2P2N OR gates. The write word lines (*WWL*) are driven by the P-type adiabatic driver.

The write driver is also shown in Fig. 9. The $\phi_{WD}$ (Power-clock for write drivers) is driven by P-type adiabatic driver. If the register file is not used for write operation,

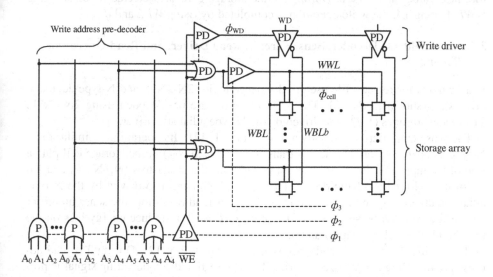

**Fig. 9.** The write address pre-decoders use 2P-2P2N circuits. The write bit lines (*WBL* and *WBLb*) are driven by the P-type adiabatic driver using power-gating approaches.

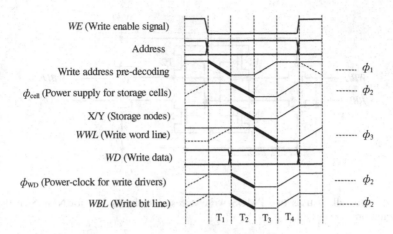

**Fig. 10.** Write operation timing

the write drivers for driving write bit lines with large capacitances can be switched off to reduce energy losses on the write bit lines, because the $\phi_{WD}$ can be set as a fixed DC voltage level ($V_{DD}$) by setting $WEb$ as '1'.

Timing diagram for write operation is shown in Fig. 10. During T1, write address pre-decoding is processed. During T2, the write address-decoding signal is produced, and the $\phi_{cell}$ is discharged, so that the charge stored in storage cells is recovered before new values are written. During T3, the storage cells are selected by discharging $WWL$. During T4, the write operation is completed by rising $WBL$ and $\phi_{cell}$.

### 3.3  Read Address Decoder, Sense Circuit, Read Driver, and Read Operation Timing

Read circuits for register file use pre-discharge logic (2N-2N2P and N-type adiabatic drivers), as shown in Fig. 11. The 3-bit addresses are pre-decoded using 2N-2N2P. The read word lines ($RWL$) are driven by the N-type adiabatic driver.

The sense amplifier is also shown in Fig. 11 [11, 12]. Its operation is similar to an N-type adiabatic driver. The access transistors ($N_R$ and $N_{Rb}$) in the storage cell play a role of the input transistors and are combined with the transistors ($N_1$–$N_4$, $P_1$ and $P_2$) to form an N-type adiabatic driver. The $\phi_{SC}$ and $\phi_{RD}$ are also driven by the N-type adiabatic drivers. If the register file is not used for read operation, the sense amplifier and read driver can be switched off by setting $RE$ as '0' to reduce energy loss on the read bit lines with large capacitances.

The timing diagram for read operation is shown in Fig. 12. During T1, read address pre-decoding is processed. During T2, The read address-decoding signal is produced. During T3, The $RWL$ (read word line) is selected and the $RBL$ (read bit line) follows the $RWL$ or stays at a ground level. During T4, the $RD$ (read data) is carried out. The register file can execute one write and one read operation within a period.

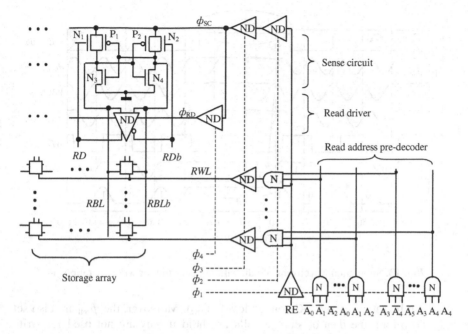

**Fig. 11.** The read address pre-decoders use 2N-2N2P circuits. The read bit lines (*RBL* and *RBLb*) are driven by sense circuits that use power-gating approaches.

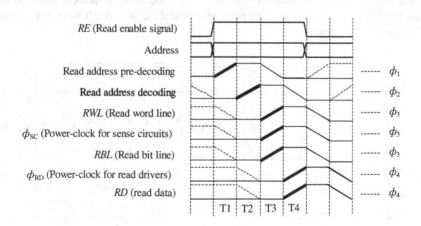

**Fig. 12.** Read operation timing

## 3.4 Simulations

The register file was simulated using ideal four-phase sinusoidal power-clocks with 0.18μm TSMC process. The simulation waveforms for write operation are shown in Fig. 13. When the register file is not used for write operation (*WEb* = '1'), the write drivers for driving write bit lines with large capacitances can be switched off because

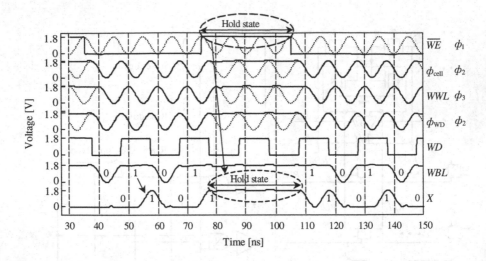

**Fig. 13.** Simulation waveforms of adiabatic register file for write operation

the $\phi_{WD}$ can be set as a fixed DC voltage level ($V_{DD}$). Moreover, the $\phi_{cell}$ are also set as $V_{DD}$. Therefore, the data of storage cells are hold if they are not used for write operation.

The simulation waveforms for read operation are shown in Fig. 14. As expected, when the register file is not used for read ($RE$ = '0') the sense amplifiers and read drivers can be switched off, thus read bit lines and read data lines don't have any charging and discharging operation.

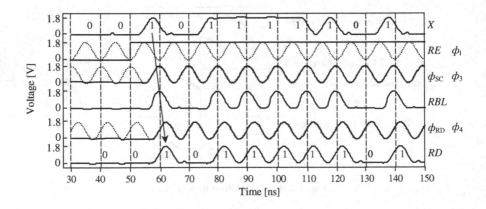

**Fig. 14.** Simulation waveforms of adiabatic register file for read operation

For comparison, a similar register was simulated using conventional CMOS logic. Energy consumption of the adiabatic and the conventional register is compared in Fig. 15. The adiabatic register achieves considerable energy savings over CMOS

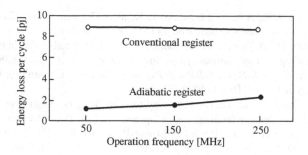

**Fig. 15.** Energy consumption of adiabatic register

implementation. The simulation results show that the energy saving on bit lines and word lines is the most significant, because of using N-type and P-type adiabatic drivers and power-gating schemes.

## 4 Conclusion

A low-power register file based on adiabatic logic with power-gating schemes is presented. The power consumption of the register file can be significantly reduced. Further comparisons with other similar implementations are required.

## Acknowledgment

This work is supported by the Zhejiang Science and Technology Project of China (No. 2006C31012), Zhejiang Provincial Natural Science Foundation of China under Grant No. Y104327, and Ningbo Natural Science Foundation (2006A610005).

## References

1. Rabaey, J. M., Pedram, M.: Low Power Design Methodologies, Kluwer Academic Publishers, Boston (1996)
2. Kramer, A., Denker, J. S., Flower, Moroney, B., J.: 2nd Order Adiabatic Computation with 2N-2P and 2N-2N2P Logic Circuits, Proceedings of International Symposium on Low Power Design, (1995) 191–196
3. Maksimovic, D., Oklobdzija, V. G., Nikolic, B., Current, K. W.: Clocked CMOS Adiabatic Logic with Integrated Single-Phase Power-Clock Supply, IEEE Transactions on Very Large Scale Integration (VLSI) Systems, Vol. 8 (4) (2000) 460–463
4. Moon, Jeong, Y., D.: An Efficient Charge Recovery Logic Circuit, IEEE Journal of Solid-State Circuits, Vol. 31 (4) (1996) 514–521
5. Liu, F., Lau, K. T.: Pass-Transistor Adiabatic Logic with NMOS Pull-Down Configuration, Electronics Letters, Vol. 34(8) (1998) 739–741
6. Chang, R. C., Hung, P. -C., Wang, I.-H.: Complementary Pass-Transistor Energy Recovery Logic for Low-Power Applications, IEE Proceedings–Computers and Digital Techniques, Vol. 149(4) (2002) 146–151

7. Moon, Y., Jeong, D. K.: A 32 x 32-b Adiabatic Register File with Supply Clock Generator, IEEE Journal of Solid-State Circuits, Vol. 33 (5) (1998) 696–701
8. Avery, S. , Jabri, M.: A Three-Port Adiabatic Register File Suitable for Embedded Applications, Proceedings of international symposium on Low power design, (1998) 288–292
9. Ng, K. W., Lau K. T.: A Novel Adiabatic Register File Design, Journal of Circuits, Systems, and Computers, Vol. 10 (1) (2000) 67–76
10. Tzartzanis, N., Athas, W. C.: Energy Recovery for The Design of High-Speed, Low-Power Static RAMs, Proceedings of International Symposium on Low Power Design, (1996) 55–60
11. Hu, Jianping, Xu, Tiefeng, Li, Hong.: A Lower-Power Register File Based on Complementary Pass-Transistor Adiabatic Logic, IEICE Transactions on Informations and Systems, Vol. E88–D (7) (2005) 1479–1485
12. Hu, Jianping, Xu, Tiefeng, Yu, Junjun, Xia Yinshui.: Low Power Dual Transmission Gate Adiabatic Logic Circuits and Design of SRAM, The 47TH International Midwest Symposium on Circuits and Systems, (2004) 565–568
13. Teichmann, P., Fischer, J., Henzler, S., Amirante, E., Schmitt-Landsiedel, D.: Power-clock gating in adiabatic logic circuits, PATMOS'05, (2005) 638–646
14. Hu, Jianping, Li, Hong, Dong, Huiying.: A low-power adiabatic register file with two types of energy-efficient line drivers, The 48TH International Midwest Symposium on Circuits and Systems, (2005) 1753- 1756

# High Performance CMOS Circuit by Using Charge Recycling Active Body-Bias Controlled SOI

Masayuki Kitamura[1], Masaaki Iijima[1], Kenji Hamada[1], Masahiro Numa[1],
Hiromi Notani[2], Akira Tada[2], and Shigeto Maegawa[2]

[1] Faculty of Engineering, Kobe University
1-1 Rokko-dai, Nada, Kobe 657-8501 Japan
numa@kobe-u.ac.jp
[2] Renesas Technology
4-1 Mizuhara, Itami, Hyogo 664-0005 Japan

**Abstract.** In this paper, we propose a new technique for higher circuit speed without increase in leakage current by using active body-bias controlling technique. Conventional body-bias controlling techniques face difficulties, such as long transition time of body voltage and large area penalty. To overcome these issues, we propose a Charge Recycling Active Body-bias Controlled (CRABC) circuit scheme on SOI which enables quick control of body voltage by using simple additional circuit. The SPICE simulation results have shown that CRABC shortens delay time by 20 %, and transition time for controlling body-bias by 98 %.

## 1 Introduction

The performance improvement of LSI's has mainly been dependent on scaling of the process technology so far. However, aggressive down-scaling with CMOS causes exponential increase in sub-threshold leakage power, due to lowered threshold voltages ($V_{th}$) in accordance with lowered supply voltages to meet performance reguirements. Hence, SOI (Silicon On Insulator) has been attracting attention as an alternative technology to replace bulk structure [1].

SOI has lower junction capacitance than bulk structure and achieves both high-performance and low-power operation owing to BOX (Buried Oxide) between transistor and substrate. In addition, the body voltage of each transistor can separately be controlled through a body contact on PD (Partially Depleted)-SOI. In contrast to bulk MOSFETs, where we have to control the voltage of whole substrate with large capacitance, PD-SOI provides quick transition of body voltage and low power operation for body-bias owing to small body capacitances [2].

The power consumption by sub-threshold leakage current ($P_{sub}$) is given by

$$P_{sub} = I_0 10^{V_{th}/S} V_{DD} \tag{1}$$

where $I_0$ is a constant, $S$ is a sub-threshold factor. As shown in Eq. (1), $P_{leak}$ depends on $V_{th}$ exponentially, and higher $V_{th}$ is effective to reduce the sub-threshold leakage current. On the other hand, higher $V_{th}$ results in performance degradation. Therfore, adaptive $V_{th}$ by active body-bias control becomes a key idea for coexistence of both

J. Vounckx, N. Azemard, and P. Maurine (Eds.): PATMOS 2006, LNCS 4148, pp. 393–402, 2006.

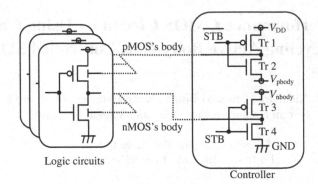

**Fig. 1.** Example of conventional ABC approach

low-power and high-performance. VTCMOS (Variable Threshold-voltage CMOS) [3] has been proposed to speed up without increase in sub-threshold leakage by controlling the body voltage. In VTCMOS technique, threshold voltage is changed in correspondence with a circuit state by controlling the body voltage. In active mode, forward body-bias lowers $V_{th}$ and enhances operation speed. On the other hand, reverse body-bias raises $V_{th}$ and reduces sub-threshold leakage current in standby mode. However, this technique has some limitations, such as very slow bias controlling operation and large area penalty due to large scale VT (Variable Threshold voltage) circuit. Although additional supply voltage shortens the time for body-bias control, the body voltages of pMOS and nMOS must be supplied separately.

In addition, reverse body-bias becomes less effective to reduce sub-threshold leakage current and increases junction leakage current as transistors are scaled down [4], [5]. Moreover, SOI degrades sub-threshold leakage reduction effect by reverse body-bias. Thus, forward body-bias for speed up becomes much more effective than reverse body-bias for leakage reduction [6].

In this paper, we propose a Charge Recycling Active Body-bias Controlled (CRABC) circuit scheme which uses the charge kept in pMOS's body for nMOS's body-bias. Although conventional active body-bias controlling (ABC) techniques require complicated control circuits or supply voltages for bias control, our CRABC scheme aims at controlling the body voltage in short transition time using simple additional circuit by charge recycling.

## 2   Charge Recycling Active Body-Bias Control (CRABC) Scheme

In Fig. 1, the conventional active body-bias controlling (ABC) technique charges nMOS's body and discharges pMOS's body by additional two supply voltages when a circuit state changes from standby mode to active mode. On the other hand, CRABC does not need additional supply voltages since it charges nMOS's body by the charge kept in pMOS's body.

In this section, we propose CRABC to achieve short transition time of body-bias without additional supply voltages. Next, we describe a configuration of CRABC and the body voltage in active mode.

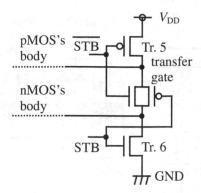

**Fig. 2.** Control circuit for CRABC

## 2.1  Configuration of CRABC

Fig. 2 shows a control circuit for body-bias in CRABC circuit scheme, employing two transistors and one transfer gate, where body-bias is controlled in accordance with the circuit state given by standby signal STB. In case STB becomes "1", Tr. 5 and Tr. 6 turn on and the transfer gate turns off. In this case, the body voltages of nMOS and pMOS in logic circuits are tied to GND and $V_{DD}$, respectively. The sub-threshold leakage current becomes smaller than that with a forward-bias. When STB changes to "0", the body is separated from GND and $V_{DD}$ and the charge kept in pMOS's body moves to nMOS's body through the transfer gate. This makes the body voltage of both nMOS and pMOS equal. The voltage finally converges on $v_{body}$, where $v_{body}$ is the voltage derived from junction capacitances, wiring capacitances and the state of logic circuits. Thus, the forward body-bias of pMOS ($V_{bs-p}$) and nMOS ($V_{bs-n}$) can be represented by

$$-V_{bs-p} = V_{DD} - v_{body} \tag{2}$$

$$V_{bs-n} = v_{body} . \tag{3}$$

Lowering $V_{th}$ by forward body-bias of each transistor speeds up logic circuits.

An advantage in CRABC circuit scheme is quick transition of body-bias since the gate to source voltage ($V_{gs}$) in the body-bias control circuit of the body-bias control circuit of CRABC is higher than the $V_{gs}$ in conventional ABC approach. Although the $V_{gs}$ of Tr. 2 or Tr. 3 in conventional ABC using two supply voltages $V_{pbody}$ and $V_{nbody}$ are $V_{DD}-V_{pbody}$ or $-V_{nbody}$, $V_{gs}$ of the transfer gate in CRABC is $V_{DD}$ or $-V_{DD}$. Thus, the lower $V_{gs}$ in conventional ABC suffers from the longer return time from standby mode due to insufficient driving power.

The proposed CRABC technique is superior to conventional ABC approach at the point that additional supply voltages are unnecessary and the transition time of body-bias is shortened. Moreover, applying PD-SOI to CRABC also contributes short transition time of body-bias and fine-grained control. A combination of CRABC and PD-SOI shortens the transition time of body-bias more and enables fine grain control of the circuit mode.

**Table 1.** Relation between $v_{body}$ and channel width

| $W_p$ [μm] | $W_n$ [μm] | $v_{body}$ [V] |
|---|---|---|
| 2.10 | 0.70 | 0.532 |
| 1.75 | 0.70 | 0.520 |
| 1.40 | 0.70 | 0.508 |
| 1.05 | 0.70 | 0.495 |
| 0.70 | 0.70 | 0.481 |
| 0.70 | 1.05 | 0.472 |
| 0.70 | 1.40 | 0.459 |
| 0.70 | 1.75 | 0.448 |
| 0.70 | 2.10 | 0.437 |

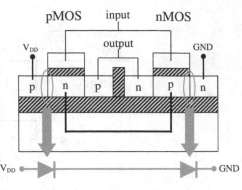

**Fig. 3.** DC-pass through two junction diodes

## 2.2 Discussion on $v_{body}$

Here, we consider a body voltage $v_{body}$ in active mode. The $v_{body}$ is fixed in GND or $V_{DD}$ in standby mode. After a state changes from standby mode to active mode, $v_{body}$ changes according to the body capacitance, a pattern of input signals and structure of logic circuit. The $v_{body}$ is decided by capacitance of controlled logic circuit and given by

$$v_{body} = \frac{C_{pbody} + C_{pwire}}{C_{pbody} + C_{pwire} + C_{nbody} + C_{nwire}} V_{DD}. \tag{4}$$

where $C_{pbody}$ and $C_{nbody}$ are the junction capacitance of the body in logic circuits, $C_{pwire}$ and $C_{nwire}$ are the wiring capacitance and the junction capacitance of each transistor in controller. As shown in Eq. (4), if both $C_{pbody}+C_{pwire}$ and $C_{nbody}+C_{nwire}$ have almost the same value, the $v_{body}$ converges to about 0.5 V when supply voltage is 1.0 V. $C_{pbody}$ and $C_{nbody}$ are proportional to total channel width. Table 1 shows $v_{body}$ of an inverter circuit applying CRABC with the supply voltage of 1.0 V when the channel width of pMOS ($W_p$) and nMOS ($W_n$) vary. We see from Table 1 that the wider pMOS channel achieves higher $v_{body}$ since $C_{pbody}$ becomes larger than $C_{nbody}$. The reason why $v_{body}$ does not become 0.5 V when $W_p$ and $W_n$ are 0.70 μm is difference in the junction capacitance of each transistor in controller.

CRABC has DC-pass which consists of two junction diodes as shown in Fig. 3 since pMOS's body is connected with nMOS's body through transfer gate in active mode. The leakage current through junction diodes is insignificant as long as $V_{DD}$ is low enough. If the supply voltage rises, two junction diodes turn on and the leakage current through DC-pass increases. As shown in Fig. 4, the leakage current through DC-pass suddenly increase with $V_{DD}$ higher than 1.2 V, while the leakage current is negligible with $V_{DD}$ less than 1.2 V. On the other hand, the leakage current in standby mode becomes out of problem since a transfer gate in DC-pass turns off.

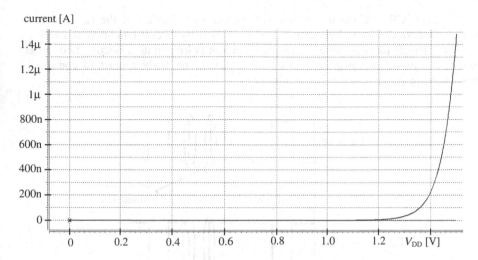

**Fig. 4.** Relation between $V_{DD}$ and current through DC-pass

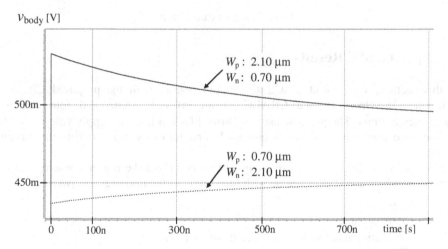

**Fig. 5.** Change of the $v_{body}$ by the leakage current

In fact, leakage current through DC-pass changes the $v_{body}$ as time passes after changing into active mode. For example, if the $v_{body}$ rises than 0.6 V, the diodes between the bodies of nMOS and GND turn on, the diode current lowers the $v_{body}$. On the other hand, if the $v_{body}$ falls in less than $V_{DD}$–0.6 V, the $v_{body}$ is raised by the diodes between $V_{DD}$ and the bodies of pMOS. As a result, the $v_{body}$ converges between 0.6 V and $V_{DD}$–0.6 V. Fig. 5 shows a change of the $v_{body}$ by the leakage current. When $W_p$ is larger than $W_n$, the $v_{body}$ becomes high. After that, we confirm that the $v_{body}$ is lowered by increase in the leakage current through diodes in DC-pass. When the $W_n$ is larger than $W_p$, the $v_{body}$ becomes low at first, and rises later.

However, CRABC circuit scheme suffers from fluctuation of the $v_{body}$ since the body is separated from GND and $V_{DD}$ and affected by circuit condition and leakage current through junction diode. This phenomenon is known as a floating body effect which causes delay variation. Floating-SOI having no body-contact to control the body voltage also has suffers from this effect.

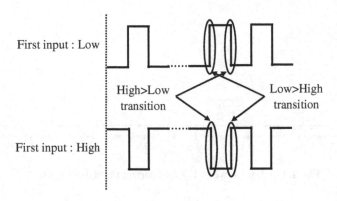

**Fig. 6.** Timing of calculation

## 3   Experimental Results

In this section, we present SPICE simuration results with the proposed CRABC technique. We have applied CRABC to an inverter circuit and four MCNC benchmark circuits. The process rule is 0.18μm PD-SOI and the supply voltage is 1.0 V. We have used wire resistances and load capacitances extracted from the circuit layout.

First, we have calculated the delay in active mode and the power consumption in both active mode and standby mode with four kinds of technique as follows:

i )     body-tied
ii )    0.5V DC-bias
iii )   conventional active body-bias controlling (ABC)
iv )    CRABC

As for conventional ABC approach , we have set $V_{pbody} = V_{nbody} = 0.5$ V using an additional supply voltage for body-bias. As the criteria for evaluation, we have defined the delay as the maximum delay at the critical path and the power as the average of 100 random input vectors at 50 MHz.

Next, we have evaluated the transition time for body-bias control between active mode and standby mode. The transition time is defined as the period from 10 % to 90 % with the body voltage.

Finally, we have evaluated the delay variation. The body voltage depends on the first input vector and transition in CRABC and floating-SOI since the body is separated from GND or $V_{DD}$ , which causes the delay variation. We have calculated

**Table 2.** Delay time and power consumption

| circuit | #Tr | technique | delay [ps] | act power [μW] | stb power [nW] |
|---------|-----|-----------|------------|----------------|----------------|
| INV | 2 | body-tied | 66 | 0.19 | 0.6 |
|  |  | dc-bias | 60 | 0.21 | 5.0 |
|  |  | ABC (conv.) | 60 | 0.21 | 0.6 |
|  |  | CRABC | 59 | 0.21 | 1.3 |
| cm82a | 58 | body-tied | 492 | 2.95 | 6.4 |
|  |  | dc-bias | 402 | 3.15 | 46.7 |
|  |  | ABC (conv.) | 403 | 3.15 | 6.4 |
|  |  | CRABC | 403 | 3.14 | 7.1 |
| cm85a | 148 | body-tied | 1,440 | 6.02 | 12.6 |
|  |  | dc-bias | 1,250 | 6.39 | 94.1 |
|  |  | ABC (conv.) | 1,261 | 6.39 | 12.6 |
|  |  | CRABC | 1,260 | 6.39 | 13.3 |
| f51m | 420 | body-tied | 2,078 | 28.98 | 50.3 |
|  |  | dc-bias | 1,650 | 31.83 | 373.7 |
|  |  | ABC (conv.) | 1,667 | 31.83 | 50.3 |
|  |  | CRABC | 1,663 | 31.83 | 51.0 |
| z4ml | 92 | body-tied | 805 | 4.84 | 9.5 |
|  |  | dc-bias | 679 | 5.14 | 71.0 |
|  |  | ABC (conv.) | 682 | 5.14 | 9.5 |
|  |  | CRABC | 682 | 5.14 | 10.2 |

differences in the delay times with an inverter circuit when the first input signal varies. For example, we have calculated the delay during High to Low transition at the point of first switching when the first input is High, and that at the point of second switching when first input is Low as shown in Fig. 6. The delay variation is defined as the ratio of the difference between the minimum delay and the maximum delay to the maximum one. We have compared CRABC and floating-SOI in terms of the delay variation.

### 3.1 Power Consumption and Delay Time

Table 2 shows the results for delay time and power consumption. CRABC, as well as 0.5 V DC-bias and conventional ABC, shortens delay time by 20 % compared with the body-tied for f51m. CRABC employs forward body-bias by connecting pMOS's body and nMOS's body, and $v_{body}$ converges on about 0.5 V with $V_{DD}$ of 1.0 V. Thus, CRABC speeds up logic circuits as well as 0.5 V DC-bias and the conventional ABC approach.

Next, we discuss power consumption. The three kinds of techniques using forward body-bias: 0.5 V DC-bias, conventional ABC, and CRABC, show 11% higher active power than the body-tied with the inverter circuit. The DC-bias technique shows 8.3 times as much standby power as the body-tied due to larger leakage current by

**Table 3.** Transition time for bias control

| circuit | circuit state | technique | transition time of body voltage [ns] | |
|---------|---------------|-----------|------|------|
| | | | pMOS | nMOS |
| INV | act > stb | ABC (conv.) | 0.09 | 0.03 |
| | | CRABC | 0.09 | 0.04 |
| | stb > act | ABC (conv.) | 0.19 | 1.13 |
| | | CRABC | 0.07 | |
| cm82a | act > stb | ABC (conv.) | 0.45 | 0.09 |
| | | CRABC | 0.48 | 0.09 |
| | stb > act | ABC (conv.) | 1.14 | 7.45 |
| | | CRABC | 0.23 | |
| cm85a | act > stb | ABC (conv.) | 0.96 | 0.19 |
| | | CRABC | 0.98 | 0.21 |
| | stb > act | ABC (conv.) | 2.46 | 18.35 |
| | | CRABC | 0.30 | |
| f51m | act > stb | ABC (conv.) | 2.65 | 0.54 |
| | | CRABC | 2.67 | 0.61 |
| | stb > act | ABC (conv.) | 6.77 | 54.64 |
| | | CRABC | 0.89 | |
| z4ml | act > stb | ABC (conv.) | 0.65 | 0.12 |
| | | CRABC | 0.62 | 0.13 |
| | stb > act | ABC (conv.) | 1.65 | 10.85 |
| | | CRABC | 0.23 | |

forward body-bias. On the other hand, CRABC shows 2.2 times as much standby power as the body-tied, since CRABC switches forward body-bias to zero-bias in standby mode. The conventional ABC approach avoids increase in standby power by controlling body-bias as well. The reason why the standby power with CRABC is larger than that of the conventional one is the leakage current through the transfer gate in the CRABC circuit. As shown in Fig. 2, only the transfer gate cuts off the path from $V_{DD}$ to GND in standby mode. In case of inverter, our approach doubled standby leakage power compared with conventional ABC approach since the transfer gate in the proposed control circuit consumes almost the same power as an inverter circuit. On the other hand, the leakage current in the control circuit of the conventional ABC approach is suppressed since the standby signal STB provides 0.5 V reverse body-bias on the gate in standby mode. Since the control circuit for CRABC can be shared for larger circuits, increase in standby power is limited to 11 % in the worst case for benchmark circuits.

### 3.2  Transition Time of Body Voltage

Table 3 shows the transition time for bias control. We have confirmed that the body voltage switches from active mode to standby mode within the order of a few nano seconds in both CRABC and conventional ABC. CRABC shortened the transition

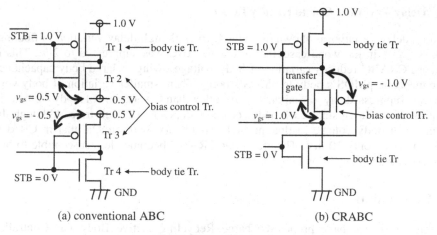

(a) conventional ABC                    (b) CRABC

**Fig. 7.** $V_{gs}$ in active mode

**Table 4.** Delay variation due to floating body effect

| circuit | technique | delay variation | |
|---------|-----------|------|------|
| | | H > L | L > H |
| INV | floating SOI | 4.7 % | 2.9 % |
| | CRABC | 0.8 % | 1.0 % |
| cm82a | floating SOI | 5.7 % | 2.4 % |
| | CRABC | 1.6 % | 0.9 % |
| cm85a | floating SOI | 5.5 % | 4.1 % |
| | CRABC | 0.7 % | 0.3 % |
| f51m | floating SOI | 1.1 % | 2.4 % |
| | CRABC | 1.5 % | 0.7 % |
| z4ml | floating SOI | 4.0 % | 2.9 % |
| | CRABC | 1.5 % | 1.0 % |

time of stb > act by 98 % compared with the conventional ABC in the best case. In contrast to CRABC, conventional ABC required 55 ns for bias control with f51m. In conventional ABC, $V_{gs}$ of bias control transistor, shown as Tr. 2 and Tr. 3 in Fig. 7 (a), is $|V_{gs}| = 0.5$ V. Lower $V_{gs}$ caused lack of driving power. Especially, transition time of nMOS's body was long due to lack of driving power in the pMOS for forward body-bias. In this case, we have to widen the width of the controller to compensate lack of driving power since the transition of the body voltage must be completed before signals input to logic circuits. On the other hand, our CRABC achieved quick transition of body voltage because of strong driving power of transfer gate, shown as $V_{gs} = 1.0$ V in Fig. 7 (b).

In this section, we have confirmed that CRABC controls circuit state faster than the conventional ABC approach. Thus, CRABC which does not require additional supply voltages nor large transistor size for bias control will ensure a speed up effect by active body-bias control.

### 3.3 Delay Variation Due to History Effect

Finally, delay variation is shown in Table 4. Even though delay variation in floating-SOI is 5.7 % in the worst case, that of our CRABC was suppressed to 2 %. This is because CRABC reduces variation of body voltage owing to large body capacitance by connecting pMOS's body to nMOS's body. Then, smaller variation of body voltage can suppress delay variation. On the other hand, variation of body voltage in floating-SOI is large since each body became independent of substrate. Although the variation of body voltage in floating-SOI was 60 mV with cm82a, that in CRABC was limited to only 10 mV. Therefore, our CRABC becomes less susceptible to history effect than normal floating-SOI.

## 4 Conclusion

In this paper, we have proposed Charge Recycling Active Body-bias Controlled (CRABC) circuit scheme in order to achieve speed up without increase in leakage current. CRABC has two advantages; one is quick control of body voltage, and the other is the simple bias controller with four transistors. According to the SPICE simulation, we have confirmed that CRABC shortens delay time by 20 %. Although conventional ABC approach required 55 ns for bias controlling due to lack of driving power of the bias control transistor, CRABC shortens the transition time by 98 % based on the enhanced driving power.

## References

1. G. Shahidi, A. Ajmera, F. Assaderaghi, R. Bolam, A. Bryant, M. Coffey, H. Hovel, J. Lasky, E. Leobandung, H-S Lo, M. Maloney, D. Moy, W. Rausch, D. Sadana, D. Schepis, M. Sherony, J. W. Sleight, L. F. Wagner, K. Wu, B. Davari, and T. C. Chen, "Mainstreaming of the SOI Technology, " 1999 IEEE International SOI Conference, Oct. 1999.
2. Y. Hirano, T. Ipposhi, H. Dang, T. Matsumoto, T. Iwamatsu, K. Nii, Y. Tsukamoto, H. Kato, S. Maegawa, K. Arimoto, Y. Inoue, M. Inuishi, and Y. Ohji, "Impact of Active Body-bias Controlled (ABC) SOI SRAM by using Direct Body Contact Technology for Low-Voltage Application,"IEDM, Tech. Dig., Dec. 2003.
3. T. Kuroda, T. Fujita, S. Mita, T. Nagamatsu, S. Yoshioka, K. Suzuki, F. Sano, M. Norishima, M. Murota, M. Kako, M. Kinugawa, M. Kakumu, and T. Sakurai, "A 0.9V 150MHz 10mW 4mm² 2-D Discrete Cosine Transform Core Processor with Variable Threshold-Voltage (VT) scheme," IEEE Journal of Solid-State Circuits, vol. 31, no. 11, pp. 1770-1779, Nov. 1996.
4. A. Keshavarzi, S. Narendra, S. Borkar, C. Hawkins, K. Roy,and V. De, "Technology scaling behavior of optimum reverse body bias for standby leakage power reduction in CMOS IC's," Proceedings of International Symposiumon Low Power Electronics and Design, pp. 252-254, Aug. 1999.
5. H. Koura, M. Takamiya, and T. Hiramoto, "Optimum Condition of Body Effect Factor and Substrate Bias in Variable Threshold Voltage MOSFETs", Jpn. J. Appl. Phys. vol. 39, pp. 2312-2317, Apr. 2000.
6. T. Hiramoto, M. Takamiya, H. Koura, T. Inukai, H. Gomyo, H. Kawaguchi, and T. Sakurai, "Optimum Device Parameters and Scalability of Variable Threshold Voltage Complementary MOS (VTCMOS)", Japanese Journal of Applied Physics, Vol. 40, Part 1, No. 4B, pp. 2854 - 2858, April, 2001.

# Designing Alternative FPGA Implementations Using Spatial Data from Hardware Resources*

Kostas Siozios, Dimitrios Soudris, and Antonios Thanailakis

VLSI Design and Testing Center, Department of Electrical and Computer Engineering
Democritus University of Thrace
67100, Xanthi, Greece
{ksiop, dsoudris, thanail}@ee.duth.gr

**Abstract.** A novel approach for efficient implementation of applications onto re-configurable architectures is introduced. The proposed methodology can applied both for designing an interconnection architecture as well as for making a thermal-aware placement. In the first case, the dominant parameters that affect performance and energy (segment length and switch boxes) are examined. This approach is based on finding the optimal wire length and then making exploration in order to determine the appropriate combination of multiple switch boxes. In the second case, a new technique for thermal-aware placement is introduced. The main goal of this technique is to spread out the power consumption across the whole device, as well as to minimize it. Both of the methodologies are fully-supported by the software tool called EX-VPR. For the purposes of this paper, the Energy×Delay Product (EDP) is chosen as selection criterion for the optimal interconnection network, while the total power consumption is the criterion for the thermal-aware routing. For the designing of the interconnection network we achieved EDP reduction by 45%, performance increase by 40% and reduction in total energy consumption by 8%, at the expense of increase of channel width by 20%. On the other hand, for the thermal-aware approach, we spread the heat and power across the whole FPGA, while we achieve about 20% reduction in total power consumption. In this case, the penalty in channel width is about 10%.

## 1  Introduction

The FPGA architecture characteristics changed and improved significantly the last two decades, starting from a simple homogeneous architecture with logic modules, and horizontal and vertical interconnections to complex FPGA platforms (e.g. Virtex-4 family [7]), which include except logic and routing, microprocessors, block RAMs etc. In other words, the FPGA architecture modified gradually from a homogeneous and regular architecture to a heterogeneous (or piece-wise homogeneous) and irregular (or piece-wise regular) structure. The platform-based design allows to a designer to build a customized FPGA architecture, depending on the application-domain

---

* This work was partially supported by the project IST-34793-AMDREL, the project PENED 03ED593 and the project PYTHAGORAS II which are funded by the European Commission and the GSRT of Ministry of Devopment.

J. Vounckx, N. Azemard, and P. Maurine (Eds.): PATMOS 2006, pp. 403–414, 2006.

requirements. The platform-based strategy changed the FPGAs role from a "general-purpose" machine to an "application-domain" machine, closing the gap with ASIC solutions. Having in mind the current trend about the design FPGA architecture, the first part of this work proposes a new software-supported methodology for selecting appropriate interconnection architecture.

Due to the fact that about 60% of an FPGA power is occupied by routing resources [4], the researchers have spent much effort on minimizing power leading to smaller devices, achieving higher frequencies and consuming less energy. A typical interconnection network of FPGA consists of: (a) the wire segments and (b) the Switch Boxes (SBs). Due to the fact that the wires have more capacitance compared to SBs, the proposed methodology targets first to minimize the impact of segments on the total power and secondly to minimize the capacitance associated with SBs.

The first goal of the novel methodology for designing a high-performance and low-energy interconnection structure of an island style-based FPGA platform is to find out the appropriate segment length, as well as the associated optimal combination of multiple SBs, taking into account the considered application-domain characteristics. The efficiency of a wire segment and SB is characterized by analyzing parameters such as energy consumption, performance, and the minimum number of required routing tracks. We made an exhaustive exploration with all the kinds of MCNC benchmarks [3] (i.e. combinatorial, sequential and FSM), to find out both the optimal segment length for minimizing the EDP of a conventional FPGA, as well as the optimal combination among three existing SBs, i.e. Wilton [1], Universal [1] and Subset [1], assuming the selected segment. Having EDP as a selection criterion, we proved that the optimal segment length is the L1&L2 for all SBs, and the SB combination "Subset-Universal" is the optimal one for the chosen segment.

As the modern reconfigurable devices consume more power compared to ASIC solutions, the researchers spent effort to tackle this issue. One of the most important defects of the power is the heat that produced within the chip. As this heat increases, a number of problems that affect the final application implementation occur. Among them, the reliability of the system, the packaging of the chip and the lifecycle of the final product are some critical issues. Moreover, as the FPGA power consumption continues to increase, low-power FPGA circuitry, architectures, and CAD tools need to be developed. The second part of the paper is focused on a novel placement algorithm development with cost function a rather "uniform" thermal distribution produced by the FPGA and its realization as a CAD tool into EX-VPR.

The paper is organized as follows. In Section 2, the proposed methodology for implementing FPGA interconnection architecture composed by longer segment wires and multiple SBs and for the thermal-aware placement, as well as the exploration procedure for specifying them is described. Section 3 presents the comparison results, while conclusions are summarized in Section 4.

## 2   The Methodology for Efficient Mapping of Applications onto FPGA Architectures

In this section, we discuss the spatial information of Switch Box (SB) connections as well as the usage of longer segments and their impact on the FPGA interconnection architecture. For that purpose, we introduce a new method for deriving special maps, each of which describes the number, as well as the location (spatial) of used transistors within a SB. In order to build these maps, MCNC benchmarks, the EX-VPR tool [2] and a Virtex-like FPGA architecture [8] were used.

The proposed methodology for determining the optimal interconnection architecture consisted of three steps (Fig.1). Detailed description of every step of the developed methodology, as well as its evaluation, will be given in the forthcoming sections. Furthermore, the methodology is software-supported by a new tool named EX-VPR, while for evaluation purposes MCNC benchmarks [11] and Virtex-like FPGA architecture [8] are used.

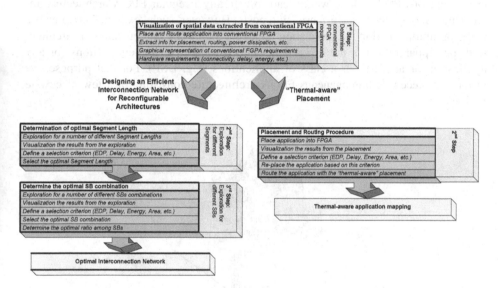

**Fig. 1.** Proposed methodology for selecting optimal application implementatio

## 2.1 Visualization of Spatial Information

The first step of the methodology is to find out the performance, the energy consumption, the connectivity and the area requirements of MCNC benchmarks. Particularly, by the term connectivity we define the total number of active connections, i.e. the "ON" pass-transistors, which take place into a SB. A specific map (or set of curves) can be created for each aforementioned design parameter, which shows the parameter variation across (X,Y)-plane of the whole FPGA device. Fig. 2 shows the total connectivity of all kinds of MCNC benchmarks of the whole FPGA, in normalized manner. Similar 3-D graphs can be derived for any application-domain specific benchmarks or applications. It can be seen that the connectivity varies from point to point of FPGA and the number of used pass-transistors (i.e. 'ON' connections) decreases gradually from the center of FPGA architecture to the I/O blocks. The connectivity requirement for more tracks in the center of the device, compared to the borders

depends on the chosen routing algorithm [5] and therefore, the interconnection resources are not utilized uniformly over any $(x,y)$ point of FPGA. Consequently, the
challenge which should be tackled by a designer is to choose only the needed hardware routing resources, considering the associated spatial information from the connectivity distribution graph. Thus, employing the appropriate amount of hardware,
significant energy consumption and delay reduction can be achieved.

Additionally, a second important conclusion draws from Fig. 2. Although a conventional FPGA architecture is a homogeneous and regular one (i.e. just repetition of
tile blocks), the actually-used hardware resources provide a non-homogeneous and
irregular picture. Ideally, we had to use different interconnection architecture at each
$(x,y)$ point of FPGA, which would lead to a totally irregular FPGA architecture increasing, among others, NRE fabrication costs. However, such "extreme" architecture
is the optimum solution for application on a specific FPGA implementations architecture, but apparently it is not a practical and cost-effective implementations for any
application or at least, for a class of applications (e.g. DSP). For that purpose, we
propose a piecewise-homogeneous FPGA architecture consisting of a few piecewise
regions.

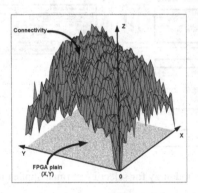

**Fig. 2.** Overall connectivity across the whole FPGA

Considering a certain threshold of the connectivity value $C_{th}$, and projecting the 3-
D diagram to (X,Y) plane of FPGA, we can create maps which depict the corresponding connectivity requirements. Assuming $C_{th} = 2$, Fig. 3 shows the connectivity
requirements of MCNC applications mapped on conventional FPGAs. The number of
distinct regions is based only on the design tradeoffs. By increasing the number of
regions, the FPGA becomes more heterogeneous, as it is consisted by more regions.
On the other hand, this increase leads to performance improvement for the device, due
to the better routing resources utilization.

Furthermore, increasing the number of distinct regions, the designer can specify in
more detailed manner the spatial distribution of energy consumption and therefore,
he/she can choose the most appropriate SB for each region at the expense of the

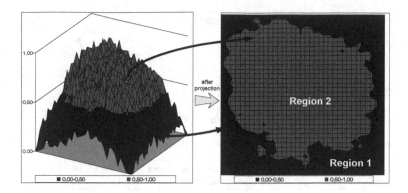

**Fig. 3.** Connectivity requirements for two regions. Each region shows the percentage of active connections.

increased heterogeneity of FPGA architecture. On the other hand, increase of the different FPGA regions has a penalty at the fabrication cost of the device. Throughout the paper, we choose $C_{th} = 2$.

Depending on the class of applications used during exhaustive exploration to visualize the spatial information of a $(x,y)$ point for various design parameters, we can derive a class-specific FPGA architecture. More specifically:

1. Performing exploration with <u>all</u> MCNC benchmarks, which are combinatorial, sequential and FSM circuits, the derived 3-D graph provides a global view to (almost) all possible applications, which can be mapped on a FPGA. Therefore, the proposed FPGA architecture with different routing features can be considered as a general-purpose FPGA platform.
2. Visualizing the spatial information of a certain application domain, for instance, DSP applications, block matching (or video compression) algorithm, we can derive an application-specific FPGA platform which is specialized and optimized under the specific constraints of the considered application-domain.
3. Depending on the fabrication costs and the volume number of chips, the proposed methodology may be used for the description of a FPGA architecture optimized for a specific application only, for instance, MPEG-2. This option might be considered as an alternative solution to Structured-ASICs.

In this paper, we provide comparison results assuming the FPGA architecture as a general-purpose platform (i.e. option (a)). Regarding with the second choice, comparison results for the DSP applications can be found in [13]. The last choice will be studied in the near feature.

## 2.2 Segment Length Exploration

The second step of the proposed methodology is to determine the most appropriate wire length of a homogeneous (conventional) FPGA, (i.e. considering the Subset

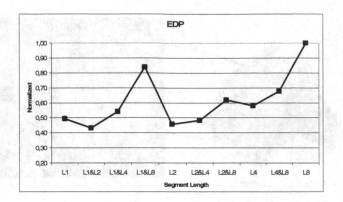

**Fig. 4.** Energy×Delay Product for different segment lengths and SBs

Wilton, and Universal SBs). The Fig. 4 shows the average value over all benchmarks for every SB architecture.

Fig. 4 gives the average variation of EDP curve for various segment lengths and the available SBs. It can be seen that the segment L1&L2 provides the minimal EDP.

### 2.3 Switch Boxes Combination Exploration

The third step of the methodology for optimal interconnection has also been studied in [13, 15]. Due to lack of space, here we provide the key results. We proved that the ratio 80%/20% of "Subset-Universal" combination minimizes the EDP value. The Subset SB is assigned to *Region_1*, while Universal SB to *Region_2* (center of FPGA). In order to support the design space exploration procedure, we used the EX-VPR tool, enhanced with the option for supporting the placement and routing of applications in FPGAs with multiple SBs and various wires lengths. The tool is based on VPR, and it is part of the MEANDER framework [6]. Extensive description of the whole design framework can be found in [2].

### 2.4 Thermal-Aware Placement

In this Section, a novel algorithm for thermal-aware placement in island-style FPGA architectures is introduced. This technique tries to minimize the total heat that produced in the chip, as well as to spread it across the whole device. Based on the visualization results from the first step of the methodology (Fig. 2), we can deduct that there is a need for higher connectivity into the center of the device compared to the corners. As the connectivity factor is proportional to the power consumption and to the heat that produced by the chip, we can deduct that the center of the FPGA device is more critical compared to the corners for minimizing all these design parameters. Taking into consideration that the thermal effect is function of the total power consumption of the device, the reduction of the heat that produced into the FPGA will lead to minimizing the power that consumed by the device.

Fig. 5 shows the proposed technique for achieving thermal-aware application mapping onto reconfigurable architectures. This approach is composed by four distinct steps:

1. Place (and route) the application onto the FPGA architecture using conventional P&R CAD tools. Most of these have as cost function the application delay. For our exploration procedure, we used the simulated annealing-based placer that described in [5]. If we also chose to route the application, the Pathfinder algorithm [14] is used. This step leads into application implementation in such a way, that the connectivity requirements (pass-transistors that are "ON") have a picture similar to Fig. 2. As mentioned above, the center of the device is crowded by active CLBs and routing tracks, while the hardware resources at the corners are less utilized.

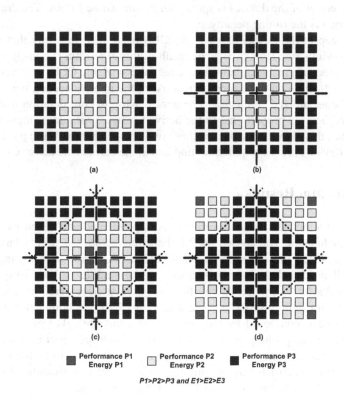

(a)

(b)

(c)

(d)

| ■ | Performance P1 Energy P1 | □ | Performance P2 Energy P2 | ■ | Performance P3 Energy P3 |

*P1>P2>P3 and E1>E2>E3*

**Fig. 5.** Thermal-aware placement technique

2. Taking into consideration the hardware components that affect the power consumption (CLB, SB, routing channels, etc.), we can deduct from Fig. 2 that the center of the device consumes much higher power compared to the corners. This means that the temperature at the center of the device is much higher compared to

the rest FPGA. The main goal of our methodology is to move resources from the center of the device, as close to the corners as possible. Due to the fact that we can not move SBs and routing channels (because these affects the final routing), we have to move CLBs. By re-routing the thermal-aware placement, the final routing resources will be utilized in a more normalized manner across the whole device. So, as our approach tries to spread the temperature across the whole FPGA, we have to apply it separately at the four quarters of the device (Fig. 5(b)).

3. The third step involves finding out the optimal Euclidean distance that each CLB have to be moved. In this work, we chose to move these components as far as possible. For this reason, we decide to flip the positions of the CLBs across the four lines that divide each quarter into two separate things (Fig. 5(c)). The criterion for the choosing of the optimal distance can be based only on the design requirements. As the CLBs are moved from the center to the corner, the power consumption (and the thermal of the device) is spread across the whole FPGA. The drawback of this approach is the timing penalty.

4. The final step of the methodology is the CLB movement in a way that described into the previous step (Fig. 5(d)). The result of this algorithm is a mapped application onto a reconfigurable architecture, where the available CLBs at the corners are fully-utilized, while on the center are rest. Also, the interconnection network in the center is better utilized compared to corners. Taking in consideration that the total power (and heat) is proportional to the active hardware resources (logic and interconnection), this algorithm separates these two components by leaving into the center of the device only the required routing and at the corners the active CLBs.

## 3   Experimental Results

The proposed interconnection architecture was implemented and tested by a number of MCNC benchmarks. The chosen MCNC benchmarks are the twenty largest ones, and they were placed and routed in an island-style FPGA array [6, 8], using the EX-VPR tool. All the benchmarks were mapped to the smallest FPGA array. Table 1 shows the results for delay and energy both for homogeneous architectures and the proposed one with multiple SBs and segment L1&L2. In the homogeneous FPGAs, the whole device is composed by only one of the available SBs (Subset, Wilton or Universal). Since our primary goal is the design of *both* high performance and low energy FPGA architecture, we choose the optimal EDP value from the exploration results (Fig. 2(a) and (b)) for our exploration results. All experiments target island-style FPGAs implemented in a 0.18μm TSMC CMOS process.

It can be seen that the proposed method achieved significant reduction in EDP of average about 45%, performance increase by 40%, reasonable gain in energy of 8%, at the expense of increase channel width by 20%. The reported gains that reported results from the average value of partial gains of the proposed architecture to each single-SB architecture. We have to point out that during the exploration procedure we used the optimal channel width for all the benchmarks and interconnection devices. It should be stressed that we achieved to design a high performance FPGA, without any negative impact on energy, although high performance circuit means high switching activity and eventually increased energy.

The results from applying the power-aware placement approach are shown in Table 2. The average gain in total power consumption, over the 20 biggest MCNC benchmarks, is about 20%. As we can deduct, this method minimizes all the parameters that affect the total power consumption of the reconfigurable architecture. It can be seen that the reduction in power that affects the routing resources is minimized about 8%, the power consumption from the logic is reduced about 34%, while the power from the clock network is almost the half (reduction about 49%).

**Table 1.** Comparison results between the proposed FPGA architecture (with multiple-SBs & L1+L2 segment) and single SB FPGA architectures in terms of delay and energy consumption

| Bench-mark | Subset | | Wilton | | Universal | | Multiple SBs L1&L2 Segment Architecture | |
|---|---|---|---|---|---|---|---|---|
| | Delay x10⁻⁸ | Energy x10⁻⁹ | Delay x10⁻⁸ | Energy x10⁻⁹ | Delay x10⁻⁸ | Energy x10⁻⁹ | Delay x10⁻⁸ | Energy x10⁻⁹ |
| alu4 | 9.77 | 5.83 | 9.74 | 5.77 | 10.9 | 5.84 | 5.38 | 4.96 |
| apex2 | 9.37 | 6.75 | 9.35 | 6.66 | 13.1 | 6.94 | 6.72 | 6.91 |
| apex4 | 8.86 | 4.17 | 8.86 | 4.17 | 10.3 | 4.24 | 6.11 | 4.24 |
| Bigkey | 7.71 | 8.05 | 6.97 | 8.04 | 6.26 | 7.87 | 3.23 | 7.06 |
| Clma | 15.1 | 11.4 | 14.8 | 10.3 | 14.9 | 10.5 | 10.20 | 9.43 |
| Des | 8.29 | 10.4 | 9.06 | 10.2 | 8.65 | 10.2 | 5.36 | 9.31 |
| Diffeq | 6.15 | 3.51 | 6.51 | 3.45 | 6.03 | 3.43 | 5.26 | 3.67 |
| Dsip | 7.99 | 7.82 | 7.93 | 7.63 | 7.93 | 7.61 | 4.85 | 7.60 |
| Elliptic | 10.9 | 12.4 | 10.9 | 12.0 | 12.3 | 12.4 | 7.12 | 10.64 |
| Ex5p | 9.26 | 4.32 | 10.6 | 4.32 | 9.55 | 4.27 | 5.38 | 4.19 |
| Ex1010 | 18.3 | 16.2 | 17.4 | 15.4 | 26.4 | 17.1 | 9.60 | 15.80 |
| Frisc | 16.1 | 12.1 | 15.7 | 11.0 | 15.8 | 11.2 | 10.60 | 9.84 |
| Misex3 | 11.7 | 5.55 | 11.8 | 5.49 | 10.1 | 5.28 | 5.81 | 5.36 |
| Pdc | 20.4 | 22.3 | 23.9 | 21.6 | 15.2 | 18.7 | 9.65 | 18.10 |
| S298 | 13.4 | 6.88 | 13.8 | 6.78 | 13.4 | 6.92 | 9.61 | 7.32 |
| S38417 | 10.3 | 22.6 | 10.3 | 22.7 | 9.91 | 22.5 | 6.89 | 19.72 |
| S38584 | 9.59 | 19.5 | 9.59 | 18.9 | 9.59 | 19.0 | 6.04 | 19.20 |
| Seq | 12.4 | 6.56 | 18.4 | 7.18 | 8.87 | 6.10 | 4.21 | 6.35 |
| Spla | 15.6 | 13.1 | 17.5 | 12.7 | 19.0 | 13.1 | 8.44 | 8.69 |
| Tseg | 5.55 | 3.18 | 6.72 | 3.19 | 6.03 | 3.15 | 4.65 | 2.13 |

A picture after a successful P&R for both the simulated annealing-based and thermal-aware placement is shown in Fig. 8(a) and 8(b), respectively. It can be seen that a existing placement algorithm does not utilize many of the available resources (logic and interconnection) in the corners of the device, while it overuses resources at the center of the FPGA. In contrary, the thermal-aware placement (Fig. 8(b)) spreads the usage both the logic and the interconnection resources across the whole device.

Projecting the 3-D curves of Fig. 9, we derive the corresponding maps shown in Fig. 10, which show the variations of the device heat for each $(x, y)$ point of the FPGA. It is apparent that the proposed thermal-aware placement algorithm achieves

**Table 2.** Comparison results for the thermal-aware placement methodology vs. the initial placement in terms of power consumption for different paramaters

| Benchmark | Initial Placement Simulated annealing based | | | | Proposed Placement Thermal-Aware placement | | | |
|---|---|---|---|---|---|---|---|---|
| | Routing (Watt) | Logic (Watt) | Clock (Watt) | Sum (Watt) | Routing (Watt) | Logic (Watt) | Clock (Watt) | Sum (Watt) |
| Alu4 | 0,0431 | 0,0054 | 0,0110 | 0,0595 | 0,0310 | 0,0033 | 0,0053 | 0,0396 |
| apex2 | 0,0503 | 0,0053 | 0,0108 | 0,0664 | 0,0394 | 0,0034 | 0,0052 | 0,0480 |
| apex4 | 0,0322 | 0,0033 | 0,0117 | 0,0471 | 0,0259 | 0,0022 | 0,0060 | 0,0341 |
| Bigkey | 0,0760 | 0,0122 | 0,0320 | 0,1203 | 0,0860 | 0,0072 | 0,0169 | 0,1101 |
| Clma | 0,1455 | 0,0150 | 0,0320 | 0,1925 | 0,1477 | 0,0129 | 0,0228 | 0,1834 |
| Des | 0,0929 | 0,0086 | 0,0249 | 0,1264 | 0,0827 | 0,0038 | 0,0082 | 0,0947 |
| Diffeq | 0,0267 | 0,0063 | 0,0152 | 0,0483 | 0,0278 | 0,0038 | 0,0077 | 0,0393 |
| Dsip | 0,0603 | 0,0088 | 0,0278 | 0,0969 | 0,0833 | 0,0061 | 0,0180 | 0,1074 |
| Elliptic | 0,0713 | 0,0110 | 0,0162 | 0,0984 | 0,0714 | 0,0075 | 0,0090 | 0,0879 |
| Ex5p | 0,0291 | 0,0029 | 0,0100 | 0,0420 | 0,0277 | 0,0022 | 0,0063 | 0,0362 |
| Ex1010 | 0,0478 | 0,0060 | 0,0172 | 0,0709 | 0,0555 | 0,0052 | 0,0100 | 0,0707 |
| Frisc | 0,0546 | 0,0073 | 0,0143 | 0,0762 | 0,0498 | 0,0053 | 0,0076 | 0,0627 |
| misex3 | 0,0420 | 0,0046 | 0,0115 | 0,0581 | 0,0325 | 0,0031 | 0,0063 | 0,0418 |
| Pdc | 0,0785 | 0,0063 | 0,0204 | 0,1052 | 0,0773 | 0,0053 | 0,0107 | 0,0933 |
| s298 | 0,0363 | 0,0053 | 0,0076 | 0,0492 | 0,0285 | 0,0039 | 0,0047 | 0,0371 |
| s38417 | 0,1459 | 0,0300 | 0,0395 | 0,2155 | 0,1114 | 0,0154 | 0,0158 | 0,1427 |
| s38584.1 | 0,1342 | 0,0294 | 0,0470 | 0,2106 | 0,1096 | 0,0138 | 0,0160 | 0,1394 |
| Seq | 0,0513 | 0,0055 | 0,0117 | 0,0685 | 0,0404 | 0,0035 | 0,0059 | 0,0498 |
| Spla | 0,0636 | 0,0060 | 0,0140 | 0,0836 | 0,0529 | 0,0045 | 0,0062 | 0,0636 |
| Tseg | 0,0314 | 0,0080 | 0,0201 | 0,0595 | 0,0247 | 0,0036 | 0,0077 | 0,0360 |

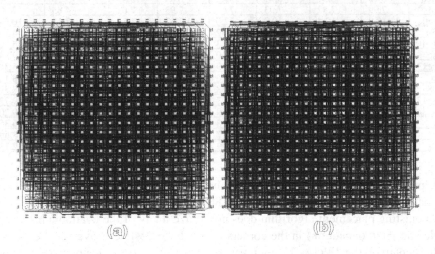

**Fig. 8.** Placement and routing with (a) simulated annealing-based and (b) thermal-aware placement

both the heat distribution in a rather uniform way across the whole device and the minimization of the maximal values of heat. In addition to that, it minimizes the total power consumption of the FPGA by a factor of 20% in average.

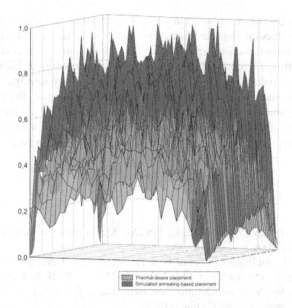

**Fig. 9.** Comparison results between the two placement algorithms in terms of heat diffusion

**Fig. 10.** Thermal distribution after P&R procedure (a) for simulated annealing-based placement and (b) thermal-aware placement

## 4    Conclusions

A novel methodology for efficient designing and implementing applications onto island-style FPGA architectures was presented. The approach is based on the appropriately usage of the spatial information of various FPGA parameters. The proposed techniques achieve both high-speed and low-energy efficient solutions (in case of designing an optimal interconnection network) or heat reduction and more uniform distribution across the whole device (in case of thermal-aware placement). The proposed routing architecture consists from the appropriate segment lengths (L1&L2) with the combination of two properly chosen SBs (Subset and Universal). The exploration results for this interconnection strategy shows reduction in EDP value about 45%, average delay reduction about 40% and average energy savings about 8%. On the other hand, the thermal-aware placement spreads the heat of the reconfigurable architecture across the whole device, giving better solutions for packaging, performance and reliability of the target system. In addition to that, it achieves power saving about 20%. Furthermore, both of the methodologies are fully software-supported by the tool EX-VPR.

# References

1. G. Varghese, J.M. Rabaey, "Low-Energy FPGAs- Architecture and Design", Kluwer Academic Publishers, 2001.
2. K. Siozios, et al., "An Integrated Framework for Architecture Level Exploration of Reconfigurable Platform", 15th Int. Conf. FPL 2005, pp 658-661, 26-28 Aug. 2005
3. S.Yang, "Logic Synthesis and Optimization Benchmarks, Version 3.0", Tech.Report, Microelectronics Centre of North Carolina, 1991
4. K. Leijten-Nowak and Jef. L. van Meerbergen, "An FPGA Architecture with Enhanced Datapath Functionality", FPGA'03, California, USA, pp. 195-204, Feb. 2003
5. V. Betz, J. Rose and A. Marquardt, "Architecture and CAD for Deep-Submicron FPGAs", Kluwer Academic Publishers, 1999
6. http://vlsi.ee.duth.gr/amdrel
7. http://www.xilinx.com/products/silicon-solutions/fpgas/virtex/virtex4/overview
8. Deliverable Report D9: "Survey of existing fine-grain reconfigurable hardware platforms," AMDREL project, available at http://vlsi.ee.duth.gr/amdrel/pdf/d9_final.pdf
9. Guy Lemieux and David Lewis, "Design of Interconnection Networks for Programmable Logic", Kluwer Academic Publishers, 2004
10. K. Poon, A. Yan, S. Wilton, "A Flexible Power Model for FPGAs", in Proc. of 15th Int. Conf. on Field Programmable Logic and Applications, pp.312–321, 2002
11. Lerong Cheng, Phoebe Wong, Fei Li, Yan Lin, and Lei He, "Device and Architecture Co-Optimization for FPGA Power Reduction", in Proc. of Design Automation Conference, pp. 915-920, June 13-17, 2005
12. A. Dehon, "Balancing interconnect and computation in a reconfigurable computing array (or, why you don't really want 100% LUT utilization), in Proc. of Int. Symp. on Field Programmable Gate Arrays, pp. 69-78, 1999
13. K. Siozios, et.al., "A Novel Methodology for Designing High-Performance and Low-Power FPGA Interconnection Targeting DSP Applications", in Proc. of IEEE Int. Symp. on Circuits and Systems, 21-24 May 2006
14. C. Ebeling, L. McMurchie, S.A. Hauck and S. Burns, "Placement and Routing Tools for the Triptych FPGA", IEEE Trans. on VLSI, Dec. 1995, pp. 473-482.
15. K. Siozios, K. Tatas, D. Soudris and A. Thanailakis, "Platform-based FPGA Architecture: Designing High-Performance and Low-Power Routing Structure for Realizing DSP Applications," accepted for presentation in RAW 2006, 13th Reconfigurable Architectures Workshop, Rhodes, April 25-26, 2006, Greece.

# An FPGA Power Aware Design Flow

David Elléouet[1], Yannig Savary[2], and Nathalie Julien[2]

[1] Laboratoire I.E.T.R, UMR CNRS 6164, Institut National des Sciences Appliquées,
35043 RENNES Cédex, France
david.elleouet@ens.insa-rennes.fr
[2] Laboratoire L.E.S.T.E.R, FRE CNRS 2734, Université de Bretagne Sud, 56321
Lorient Cédex, France
nathalie.julien@univ-ubs.fr

**Abstract.** Today and more tomorrow, electronic system design requires being concerned with the power issues. Currently, usual design tools consider the application power consumption after RTL synthesis. We propose in this article a FPGA design flow which integrates the power consideration at the early stages. Thus, the designer determines quickly the algorithm and architecture adequacy which respects the design specifications and the power budget.

## 1 Introduction

New electronic systems are extremely sophisticated, power consuming and require flexibility. Latest FPGA devices integrate processor cores, arithmetics elements, memory blocks and allow dynamic reconfiguration. Thus, FPGA becomes a design solution for complex SoC which need performances and flexibility under power constraint.

Designing a full complex system requires powerful CAD tools. At the early stages of the design flow, the designer critical problem is to define high level descriptions of the system which respect the specifications and the constraints. Recently FPGA CAD tools integrate the modular design flow, which allows the realization of complex electronics systems such as SOPC (System On Programmable Chip). As a consequence, in order to develop a new application, the designer can re-use and combine existing functional blocks called also IPs (Intellectual Properties). Although this CAD tool enhances the designer efficiency and reduces the time-to-market, it does not consider the power constraint during the early stages of the design flow.

The goal of this paper is to propose a FPGA design flow which considers the power constraint at high level. Thus, the designer can define the algorithm and architecture association which respect the power budget of the application. Therefore the proposed design flow integrates a library of components modeled in power consumption with high level parameters. This models are obtained with the FLPA methodology [8] which was first developed to model the processor power consumption. In this paper is proposed an adaptation of this methodology to FPGA.

J. Vounckx, N. Azemard, and P. Maurine (Eds.): PATMOS 2006, LNCS 4148, pp. 415–424, 2006.

The paper is organized as follows: Section 2 presents related works on power estimation and optimization on FPGA. Section 3 proposes a design flow with high level power consideration. Section 4 introduces the FLPA methodology and its adaptation to the FPGA. Section 5 illustrates how to apply the FLPA methodology to FPGA with the FIR filter IP. Finally, section 6 concludes the paper and relates the future works.

## 2   Related Works

This section relates the different methodologies which allow to lessen the impact of FPGA power issue. With the submicronic technologies, the static power consumed by the circuits becomes increasingly significant [14]. Recently, some static power reduction techniques for FPGA were developed by [5] and [1]. [5] proposes a technique of placement RCP (Region Constraint Placement) allowing to merge and to shut off the logic cells unused by the application. According to the application, the static power consumption reduction obtained goes from 20% to 40%. The static power of an application depends on this input and output logical levels. Indeed a '0' logic is more power consuming than a '1' logic. Then [1] proposes a static power reduction methodology which maximizes the application input and output number at the logic level '1'. The improvement obtained by this methodology goes from 15% to 38%. In [2], a power consumption estimator at the RTL level with an average accuracy of 16% and an algorithm which reduces the number of multiplexers during the synthesis is proposed. With this method, a power reduction of 35.8 % is obtained. A study on the dynamic power consumption of Virtex II is exposed in [13]; a dynamic model of consumption based on technological parameters is given there. A power estimator after place and route is introduced in [9]. A power supply strategy of the logic cells is proposed by [3]. The cells involved in the application critical paths are supplied with a low voltage. The improvement in consumption by this method is 11.6%. Place and Route methodologies are proposed in [15] in order to reduce the power consumed by the FPGA interconnect.

All this methodologies allow to optimize the power consumed by an application at the design flow low level. To improve the design flow effectiveness, it is necessary to consider the power constraint at the design early stages [12].

## 3   FPGA Power Aware Design Flow Framework

As figure 1 shows, usual system power estimation is obtained after design place and route, such as with Xpower. All design optimizations at this level are time consuming and are not always obvious. Moreover, this estimation is not reusable to design a new system.

The figure 2 proposes a design flow for applications on FPGA. This flow allows to design an application under power constraint with high level considerations. The design flow starts with a functional description of the application associated with a set of given constraints (frequency, area, power). The following step

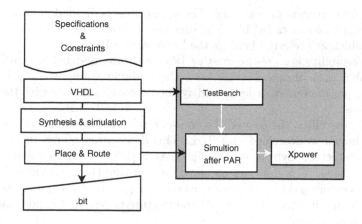

**Fig. 1.** Usual FPGA design flow power consideration

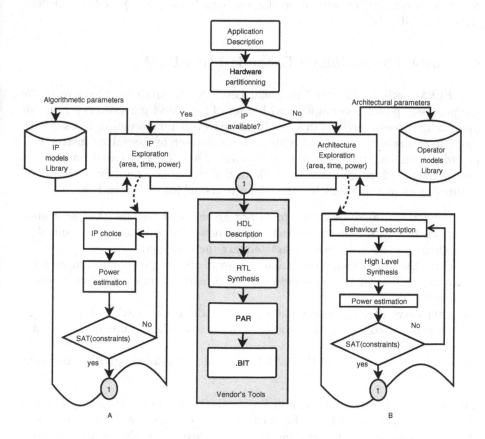

**Fig. 2.** FPGA design flow with high level power consideration

consists in an hardware partitioning. The application is divided in various hardware functional blocks called IPs. The user can be confronted with two possible scenarios which are referred here by the letter A and B.

The A possibility is to re-use existing IPs which are modeled in consumption and available in a library. In this case, the designer configures the IPs with algorithmic parameters in order to satisfy the power constraints with the design specifications.

In the B possibility, the desired IPs does not exist and requires to be designed. The IP behavior is described in VHDL. This description allows to determine, with an architectural synthesis tools like GAUT [10], the number and the kind of operators used. This information allows configuring the power models of elementary operators (adder, multiplier, memory, register, interconnection) which are available in a library. Thus, the IP architecture is designed in adequacy with the imposed constraints.

Finally, a VHDL description of the various IPs merged is obtained. This description is compatible with a vendor tools such as ISE, QUARTUS, FPGA ADVANTAGE, etc...

## 4   FLPA Methodology Extended to FPGA

The FLPA methodology, for Functional Level Power Analysis, allows to model the processor power consumption with a set of high level parameters [7]. In this approach processor architecture is divided into different building blocks. Each block is separately stimulated with a particular set of assembler instructions in order to model their power consumption. The FLPA is based on physical measurements which guarantee realistic values with good accuracy. As shown on Figure 3, this methodology has four main parts, which are given below:

- A functional analysis of the processor allows to determine the parameters which have a significant impact on the power consumption: relevant algorithmic and architectural parameters are then selected.
- Then, the power characterization step explicits the power consumption behavior (obtained by measurements) when each parameter varies independently.
- After curve fitting, the complete power model is obtained; it expresses the whole power consumption variations related to all the parameters with mathematical laws.
- Finally, the accuracy of the model obtained is validated against a measurement set.

This approach is extended for modeling both the IPs and elementary resource power consumption on FPGA. Each elementary resources or IPs will be considered as a black box with a specific granularity level. The elementary resources are defined as fine grain (B). The model obtained for elementary resources will depend on architectural parameters. The IPs are defined as coarse grain (A). The model obtained for IPs will depend on algorithmic parameters.

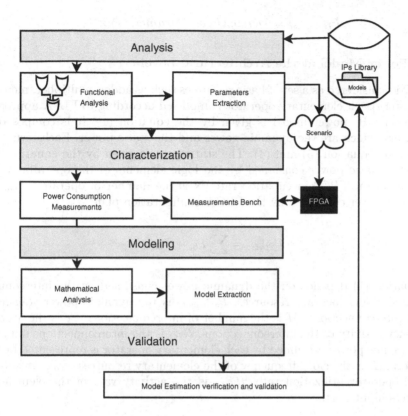

**Fig. 3.** Power characterization and modeling methodology framework

## 4.1   Power Model at the Algorithmic Level

The IP is considered as a black box. Only the high level parameters which have a significant impact on the power consumption are used in the model. The generic IP power model is given by the equation (1). It is composed of two terms, which are the dynamic power and the static power. Each of these terms are detailed by equation (2) and (3).

$$P_{Model} = P_{Dynamic} + P_{Static} \qquad (1)$$

Equation (2) is obtained by statistics analysis of power consumption measurements with no activity on the clock tree. This equation is a function of the high level parameters represented by $S(HighLevelParameters)$ and the power consumed by the FPGA configuration plan. This last part depends on the FPGA size and technology.

$$P_{Static} = S(HighLevelParameters) + P_{FPGAPlan} \qquad (2)$$

The dynamic power is deduced from the other power consumption measurements in order to obtain equation (3), which is composed of clock frequency and the different high level parameters represented here by $D(HighLevelParameters)$.

$$P_{Dynamic} = D(HighLevelParameters) \times F \qquad (3)$$

## 4.2  Power Model at the Architectural Level

The IP is considered as a set of basic resources such as adder, multiplier, memory or register. Each elementary operator is modeled according to FLPA approach. The generic IP power model is given by the equation (1). It is composed of two terms, which are the dynamic power and the static power. Each terms are detailed by equation (5) and (4). The static part is given by the equation (4). $P_{b_i}$ is the static power consumed by the logic elements of the operator which depends on the FPGA occupation rate. N is the number of operator. $P_{plan}$ is the static power consumed by the FPGA configuration plan.

$$P_{Static} = \sum_{i=0}^{N} P_{b_i} + P_{plan} \qquad (4)$$

Equation (5) depends on the dynamic power consumed by the interconnections and the elementary resources. $P_{connect_i}$ is the dynamic power consumed by the interconnections. $M$ is the number of interconncetions. $Fc$ is the average frequency activity of the interconnections. $N_{IO}$ is the interconnections number. The dynamic power consumed by each elementary operator is represented by the $P_{op_j}$ term. $F$ is the clock frequency of the elementary resources. $\tau_{op}$ corresponds to the operator utilization rate. $R_{data}$ is the activity rate of the elementary resources input port.

$$P_{Dynamic} = \sum_{i=0}^{M} P_{connect_i}(Fc, N_{IO}) + \sum_{j=0}^{N} P_{op_j}(F, \tau_{op}, R_{data}) \qquad (5)$$

## 5  Methodology Validation on FIR Filter

In this section the FLPA methodology is applied to the Xilinx Finite Impulse Response filter [16][11] on both abstraction levels. In this study case, the data size are fixed to 16 bits and the data activity rate to 50%.

The FLPA methodology is used to determine the parameters which have a significant impact on the power of the FIR filter. The significant parameters are given by the table 1 for the algorithm and architecture model. Equation 6 is given in [6] and allows to determine the parameter power sensitivity $Sens$. This metric facilitates the IP power optimization.

$$Sens(parameter) = \frac{2 \times (P(parameter_{max}) - P(parameter_{min}))}{P(parameter_{max}) + P(parameter_{min})} \qquad (6)$$

The models obtained at each level are given by the following equations. The equations (7) (8) and (9) represent the mathematical laws obtained for the IP

**Table 1.** Parameters for both models

Algorithmic Model

| Parameter level | Parameter name | Parameter description | Sensitivity (%) |
|---|---|---|---|
| Algo. | $Order$ | Filter order | 14 to 94 |
| Algo. | $D$ | Clock edges number by sample | 60 to 166 |
| Archi. | $F$ | Clock frequency | 50 to 136 |

Architectural Model

| Parameter level | Parameter name | Parameter description | Sensitivity (%) |
|---|---|---|---|
| Algo. | $Order$ | Filter order | 140 |
| Archi. | $D$ | Clock edges number by sample | 25 |
| Archi. | $F$ | Clock frequency | 113 |
| Archi. | $N_{IO}$ | I/Os number | 25 |
| Archi. | $R_{data\_mult}$ | Input activity rate of multiplier | 85 |
| Archi. | $R_{data\_add}$ | Input activity rate of adder | 8 |
| Archi. | $R_{data\_reg}$ | Input activity rate of register | 5 |
| Archi. | $\tau_{mult}$ | Multiplier utilization rate | none |
| Archi. | $\tau_{add}$ | Adder utilization rate | none |
| Archi. | $\tau_{reg}$ | Register utilization rate | none |

filters FIR by using the algorithmic approach. These laws depend on the filter order, the clock edges number by sample and the frequency for a parameter range given by (10).

$$P_{Estimate(mW)} = P_{Dynamic} + P_{Static} \tag{7}$$

$$P_{Dynamic(mW)} = (0.24 \times Order \times D^{-1.40} + 2.19 \times D^{-0.62}) \times F \tag{8}$$

$$P_{Static(mW)} = 0.57 \times D^{-1.62} \times Order + 25.118 \times D^{-0.044} \tag{9}$$

$$F \in [5_{MHz}; 45_{MHz}] \quad Order \in [5; 33] \quad D \in [1; 17] \tag{10}$$

At the architectural level, the equations (11) and (12) associated to the relations (14)(15) and (16) give the power model of the FIR filter for a parameter range given by (13). To obtain the final model $R_{data\_mult}$ is fixed to 50%. Due to the architecture FIR filter, the operators are used at each clock edge. So, $\tau_{mult}$, $\tau_{reg}$ and $\tau_{add}$ are fixed to 100%.

$$
\begin{aligned}
P_{Dynamic(mW)} = {} & 0.05 \times F \times NB_{reg} \times R_{data\_reg} \times \tau_{reg} \\
& + 1.22 \times F \times NB_{mult} \times R_{data\_mult} \times \tau_{mult} \\
& + 0.08 \times F \times NB_{add} \times R_{data\_add} \times \tau_{add} \\
& + 18.98 \times 10^{-3} \times Fc \times N_{IO}
\end{aligned} \tag{11}
$$

$$
\begin{aligned}
P_{Static(mW)} = {} & 172 \times 0.026 \times NB_{mult} + 8 \times 0.026 \times NB_{add} \\
& + 8 \times 0.026 \times NB_{reg} \quad + 9.54
\end{aligned} \tag{12}
$$

$$N_{IO} \in [0; 404] \; Fc \in [5_{MHz}; 80_{MHz}] \; Tc \in [0_{\%}; 100_{\%}]$$
$$F \in [0; 80_{MHz}] \qquad R_{op} \in [0; N] \qquad R_{data} \in [0_{\%}; 100_{\%}] \qquad (13)$$

In the case of a parallel FIR filter implementation, the number of resources (adder, multiplier and register) is determined by the equations (14)(15) and (16).

$$NB_{mult} = \left\lceil \frac{Order + 1}{2} \right\rceil \qquad (14)$$

$$NB_{add} = (Order + 1) \qquad (15)$$

$$NB_{reg} = (Order + 1) \qquad (16)$$

The model accuracy is given by the table 2. The models obtained at the algorithmic and architectural level allow to estimate with a correct accuracy the IP power consumption. Table 3 compares various power estimation given by both models and Xpower against the measurements. The algorithmic model allows to

**Table 2.** Error obtained for both models

| Abstraction level | Max. Error (%) | Min. Error (%) | Average Error (%) |
|---|---|---|---|
| Algorithmic | 34.73 | 0.03 | 12.40 |
| Architectural | -31.80 | 0.72 | 13.70 |

**Table 3.** Various power estimations compared to measurements

| Order | F | Pmeasured | Algorithmic model | | Architectural model | | Xpower | |
|---|---|---|---|---|---|---|---|---|
| | MHz | mW | Pestimate mW | Error % | Pestimate mW | Error % | Pestimate mW | Error % |
| 4 | 5 | 42.13 | 48.55 | 15.26 | 28.46 | -32.44 | 21 | 50.15 |
| 4 | 30 | 120.12 | 151.49 | 26.12 | 115.89 | -3.51 | 105 | 12.58 |
| 8 | 35 | 243.20 | 219.22 | -9.86 | 197.29 | -18.87 | 510 | 109.7 |
| 16 | 20 | 207.31 | 193.78 | -6.52 | 191.35 | 7.70 | 467 | 125.26 |
| 32 | 15 | 236.89 | 239.41 | 1.06 | 257.90 | 8.871 | 551 | 132 |

**Table 4.** Algorithmic IPs model accuracy

| IP | FPGA family | Maximum Error (%) | Average Error Error (%) | Measurement number | Parameter number |
|---|---|---|---|---|---|
| LAR space coder | Virtex II Pro | 14.51 | 4.83 | 1250 | 4 |
| Memory Block | Virtex E | 30 | 18 | 500 | 5 |
| FIR | Virtex E | 18.43 | 8.01 | 705 | 4 |
| FFT Radix 2 | Virtex II Pro | 10.88 | 3.00 | 224 | 2 |
| FFT Radix 4 | Virtex II Pro | 26.12 | 5.26 | 162 | 2 |
| FFT Pipelined | Virtex II Pro | 14.18 | 7.39 | 229 | 2 |
| MIMO encoder | Virtex II Pro | 6.39 | 1.87 | 150 | 3 |

estimate easily and quickly the IP power consumption only with a set of high level parameters. With the architectural model is necessary to proceed at a high level synthesis in order to obtained the resource number and use. The power with Xpower is estimated only after place and route. The estimation obtained with the algorithmic and architectural models are relatively reliable. Indeed, the maximum error obtained with the algorithmic model is 26% and 32% for the architectural model. Here, with Xpower the maximum error obtained is 132%.

## 6    Conclusion and Future Works

The FPGA design flow proposed in this paper allows to consider the power constraint with high level parameters. The IPs are configured at the design flow early stages in order to respect the system constraints. Thus, the time consuming in design optimization backtrack is strongly reduced. The power is estimated with a model library which is obtained with the FLPA methodology. Each model is re-usable and allows to estimate the IP or operator power consumption with a good accuracy. This approach was applied to other IPs such as Xilinx's memory blocks [4], Fast Fourier Transform, MIMO encoder and Locally Adaptive Resolution space coder. Table 4 resumes the maximum and average errors obtained with our high-level approach modeling against measurements for the different IPs on different FPGA families. Future works will consist in increasing the IPs library, in particular those dedicated to communication such as NoC.

## References

1. Anderson (J.H.), Najm (F.N.) et Tuan (T.). – Active leakage power optimization for fpgas. *FPGA'04*, vol. 28, 2004, pp. 33–41.
2. Chen (D.), Cong (J.) et Fan (Y.). – Low-power high-level synthesis for fpga architectures. *ISPLED'03*, 2003.
3. Chen (D.), Cong (J.), Li (F.) et He (L.). – Low-power technology mapping for fpga architectures with dual supply voltages. *FPGA'04*, 2004.
4. Elléouet (D.), Julien (N.), Houzet (D.), Cousin (J. G.) et Martin (E.). – Power consumption characterization and modeling of embedded memories in xilinx virtex 400e fpga. *EUROMICRO Symposium on DIGITAL SYSTEM DESIGN*, 2004.
5. Gayasen (A.), Tsai (Y.), Kandemir (M.), Irwin (M.J.) et Tuan (T.). – Reducing leakage energy in fpgas using region-constrained placement. *FPGA'04*, 2004, pp. 51–58.
6. Julien (N.), Laurent (J.), Senn (E.), Elleouet (D.), Savary (Y.), Abdelli (N.) et Ktari (J.). – Power/energy estimation in socs by multi-level parametric modeling. *Kluwer Academic Publisher*, 2005.
7. Julien (N.), Laurent (J.), Senn (E.) et Martin (E.). – Power consumption modeling and characterization of the TI C6201. *IEEE Micro VOLUME 23, Issue 5. Page(s):40 - 49*, Sept-Oct 2003.
8. Laurent (J.), Julien (N.), Senn (E.) et Martin (E.). – Functionnal level power analysis: An efficient approach for modeling the power consumption of complex processors. *IEEE DATE*, vol. 23, 2004.

9. Li (F.), Chen (D.), He (L.) et Cong (J.). – Architecture evaluation for power-efficient fpgas. *FPGA'03*, 2003.
10. Martin (E.), Stentieys (O.), Dubois (H.) et Philippe (J.L.). – Gaut : An architectural synthesis tool for dedicated signal processors. *EURO-DAC 93, Hambourg, Germany*, 20-24 sep 1993.
11. Peled et Liu (B.). – A new hardware realization of digital filters. *IIEEE Trans. on Acoust., Speech, Signal Processing, vol. ASSP-22, pp. 456-462*, Dec. 1974.
12. Rabaey (J. M.) et Pedram (M.). – Low power design methodologies. *Kluwer Academic Publisher, ISBN 0-7923-9630-8*, 1996.
13. Shang (L.), Kaviani (A. S.) et Bathala (K.). – Dynamic power consumption in virtex-ii fpga family. *FPGA'02*, 2002.
14. Sung (N.S.), Austin (T.), Blaauw (D.), Mudge (T.), Flautner (K.), Hu (J.S.), Irwin (M.J.), Kandemir (M.) et Narayanan (V.). – Leakage current: Moore's law meets static power. *IEEE Computer Magazine*, 2003.
15. Varghese (G.) et Rabaey (J. M.). – Low energy FPGAs - architecture and design. *Kluwer Academic Publisher*, 2001.
16. White (S. A.). – Applications of distributed arithmetic to digital signal processing. *IEEE ASSP Magazine, Vol. 6(3), pp. 4-19*, July 1989.

# The Design of a Dataflow Coprocessor for Low Power Embedded Hierarchical Processing

Yijun Liu[1], Steve Furber[2], and Zhenkun Li[1]

[1] The Sensor Network Group, The Faculty of Computer,
Guangdong University of Technology, Guangzhou, China
yijunliu2002@hotmail.com, zkli@gdut.edu.cn
[2] The Advanced Processor Technologies Group, The School of Computer Science,
The University of Manchester, Manchester, UK
steve.furber@manchester.ac.uk

**Abstract.** Power consumption has become one of the most important concerns in the design of embedded processor; the power dissipation of microprocessors grows rapidly as the development of CMOS technology packs more transistors per unit area. However, the potential for further power saving in microprocessors with a conventional architecture is limited because of their unified architectures and mature low-power techniques. An alternative approach to save power is proposed in this paper — embedding a dataflow coprocessor in a conventional RISC processor. The dataflow coprocessor is designed to execute short code segments, such as small loops, function calls and long equation evaluations, very efficiently. We demonstrate a factor of 7 improvement in power-efficiency over current general-purpose processors. Dataflow techniques are not new, but we apply the concept to address a new problem — to improve the power-efficiency of conventional processors.

## 1 Introduction

The drive to ever-higher performance has pushed industry to increase the complexity of microprocessors. The problem of power dissipation becomes apparent as the power consumption of processors increases with the development of CMOS technology [1]. However, further improving the power-efficiency of microprocessors is even more difficult than with other digital circuits because the architecture of microprocessors is mature and any power-saving techniques must not impact performance.

Because of its high flexibility, a 'soft'-programmable architecture, such as a von-Neumann architecture [2], is most commonly used by commercial microprocessors. However, a soft-programmable processor is normally not as power-efficient as a specifically tailored ASIC hardware. The main reason is due to execution overheads. In a conventional processor, data processing is guided by a set of 'commands' — instructions, so every data processing operation is accompanied by at least one instruction. Instructions indicate not only data values but also the addresses from where to take data values. Data processing normally

J. Vounckx, N. Azemard, and P. Maurine (Eds.): PATMOS 2006, LNCS 4148, pp. 425–438, 2006.

uses only a very small power proportion (less than 5%) of overall processor power consumption [3]. Therefore, much more power is dissipated in control flow than data processing. A RISC-like processor has a fixed instruction-length and a load-store architecture, which make it need more instructions to describe a given task (poor code-density) and spend more power in instructions fetching and data transfer than other processors.

Consequently, traditional CISC and RISC microprocessors using a conventional architecture are not efficient in terms of power consumption because of execution overheads of a soft-programmable architecture. To minimize these execution overheads, we propose an alterative architecture — embedding a dataflow coprocessor in a RISC processor.

The remainder of this paper is organized as follows: Section 2 brings forward the concept of hierarchical processing; Section 3 proposes the dataflow model of the coprocessor. Section 4 gives detailed information on a hierarchical processing architecture and the implementation of a dataflow coprocessor. Section 5 presents the experimental results on benchmarks. Section 6 concludes the paper.

## 2   Hierarchical Processing

Embedded processors differ from general-purpose processors for PCs and servers in design purposes. The success of a general-purpose processor is a selection of commercial market, for which, performance, binary compatibility with existed software and friendly programmable interfaces that attracting more software designers are the most important design issues. Therefore, the main design philosophy of general-purpose processors is to maintain the existed instruction sets while using the abundance of transistors provided by Moore's Law to increase processors' performance. For example, Intel uses hardware to translate external x86 instructions to internal RISC-like instructions for performance while maintaining the compatibility with x86 software. This approach achieves a greatly commercial success. However, it is a power inefficient approach.

The emphases of the design flow for an embedded processor are different because the characteristics of embedded applications are different from that of PC applications. Embedded processing systems often deal with infinite and continuous data streams, for which, average-performance is no longer the most important. Instead, a worst-latency constraint for real-time processing is more important. Therefore, if the overall requirements on average throughput and worst-case latency can be met, the efforts, which further increase processors' performance, are not necessary.

Another difference between PC and embedded processors comes from the support for programs. A PC processor is much more general-purpose than an embedded one, because it is impossible to know exactly what kinds of programs will be executed in a PC, and a PC processor should have the similar processing ability for all kinds of programs, introducing a lot of design efforts as well as execution overheads. Embedded processors usually deal with only a very small number of applications, and among these applications, CPU occupation rates are highly unbalanced. Embedded processors may spend most of their execution time in executing only several loops of a few programs. Therefore, a small number of important program kernels have the greatest impact on the success of an embedded processor. Moreover, since the execution and power efficiency of these important kernels are critical for overall performance and power consumption, the kernels are normally hand-optimized and provided by manufacture.

Figure 1 shows an execution segment taken from the dynamic trace of an embedded JPEG program. The JPEG program contains totally 148,040 instructions and needs 13,112,711 clock cycles to finish when running in an ARM9 processor. As can be seen from the figure, the execution segment contains several patterns having a similar shape. The x-axis of the figure shows the No. of the clock cycles (the figure totally shows 10,000 cycles), and the y-axis shows the No. of the instructions. A point means an instruction is executed in the corresponding clock cycle. If a horizon line contains more points, the corresponding instruction is executed more frequently. The lines in the rectangle are most dense (containing most points), so the corresponding instructions are most frequently executed. It can be seen from the enlarged figure that the number of the most frequently executed instruction is only 14. The 14 instructions dominate about 40% of the overall executing time, and they construct a kernel having the greatest impact on the overall power efficiency and performance. The instructions have highly imbalanced executing percentages. Most of the instructions are never executed or just executed once. It can be figured out from the analysis above that, when executing a program, an embedded processor may spend most of its time in only a small instruction segments, which can be either a tiny loop or a function call.

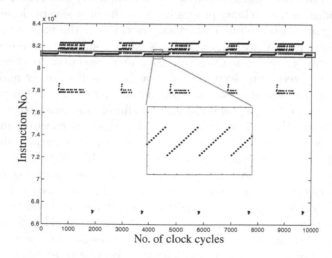

**Fig. 1.** The running trace segment of a JPEG program

Other research work also shows the executing time of an embedded processor is highly imbalanced. The design of 'loop buffer' [4] began with the observation that dynamic execution traces of embedded programs are dominated by program loops containing a very small number of instructions. Lee et. al. pointed out that about 46% of all taken instructions belong to small loops with a backward jump distance of 32 instructions or less [5].

It can be concluded from the analysis above, embedded processing has three specific characteristics:

- A embedded processor can be much less general-purpose than a PC processor because it may execute only a few programs (may be hand-optimized), so the complexity of embedded processing instruction sets can be simplified. However, some 'quirks' (such as Hamming distance for data signal processing) that can significantly improve the performance and power efficiency for the targeted kernels should be added in embedded instruction set.
- Since CPU occupation rates are highly unbalanced for different program segments and instructions, an embedded processor should bias towards the most commonly executed segments and instructions.
- The principle of locality [6] becomes apparent in embedded processing applications, especially for instructions.

Embedded processing systems can use these characteristics to increase their power efficiency and performance. However, to support general applications, abundant functionality is still a very important metrics of an embedded processor. Thus, there exists a contradiction between execution complexity and general-purpose functionality. It is very difficult to eliminate this contradiction by using a conventional unified architecture, in which, all instructions are executed in a single processor. The concept of 'hierarchical processing' is brought forward to alleviate the contradiction between complexity and functionality.

The basic idea of hierarchical processing is to include several levels of processing units (processors) in one embedded system, and the processors are not identical but have hierarchical functionalities. More complex processors support more general-purpose functionalities but have more execution overheads, thus consuming more power. Simpler processors owns a small memory and support only some commonly used instructions and addressing models, so they can be designed to be faster and more power efficient by eliminating most execution overheads. The infrequently used programs and instructions are executed in complex processors to allow the embedded system to support general-purpose functionalities. The frequently executed program segments and instructions are executed in simple processors to achieve high performance and low power consumption.

Although a hierarchical processing scheme can minimize execution overheads and maintain general-purpose functionality, it introduces other overheads, which are the communications between different level processors. Therefore, efficient and low-overhead communication is critical in the design of a hierarchical processing architecture. A multi-level hierarchical processing architecture with a lot of (instruction-level) communications and data transfers between processors is apparently not suitable. In this paper, the hierarchical processing architecture is based on a two-level CPU-coprocessor architecture, and the communications within it are not instruction-level but coarse-grained — a number of instructions are executed between two communications. In the two-level hierarchical processing architecture, the coprocessor is designed using a dataflow architecture. The design of a low power dataflow coprocessor and the communication scheme between the CPU and the coprocessor will be discussed in the following sections.

## 3   Dataflow Model of the Coprocessor

Dataflow or data-driven architecture [7] [8] was a very hot research field and considered as a likely direction for "the next generation of computer" from the 1970s to the mid 1980s. Dataflow machines optimize their hardware for fine-grained parallelization to increase throughput. However, in this paper, the dataflow coprocessor is designed specifically to improve the power-efficiency of traditional microprocessors.

The evaluation of a complex computation can be regarded as a sequence of data items flowing through data processing units (or function units) such as multipliers and adders. Figure 2(a) illustrates an evaluation circuit for the equation $x = a + (b \times c) + (d \times e)$. As can be seen from the figure, if $a$, $b$, $c$, $d$ and $e$ are valid by initialization, the output $x$ will be calculated after some time depending on the speed of the multipliers and adders used in this circuit. The sequence of the operations is not important. As long as the function units have valid inputs, they can process the operations. However, if a stream of data is to be processed, function units should synchronize with others to prevent overwriting the data values (data tokens) which are being processed. So a dataflow operation should satisfy two requirements:

- Each input port of a function unit should have a valid data token;
- Each output port (destination) of a function unit should be empty, which means the function unit which will accept the output has completed its previous calculation and sents the result(s) out.

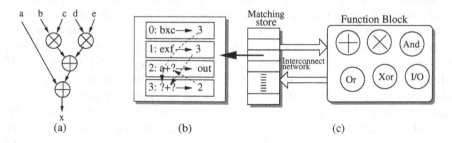

**Fig. 2.** A general dataflow architecture

Clearly, it is impossible to make a specific datapath for every possible computation such as the one illustrated in Figure 2(a). A more flexible architecture is needed which can support any computation. Figure 2(c) illustrates a basic static dataflow architecture and Figure 2(b) illustrates the mapping of the equation

$x = a + (b \times c) + (d \times e)$. There are three main components in this architecture — a matching store, a function block and an interconnect network. The matching store contains register cells which hold instructions and data tokens. The function block contains several function units where all data are processed and an Input/Output module to communicate with the outside. The interconnect network sends data tokens to the function units and returns results to the destinations in the matching store.

An instruction comprises four parts — an operation code, two operands and the destination address of the result. If an instruction satisfies the two requirements mentioned before, the instruction becomes 'active'. However, not every active instruction can immediately be processed by the function block because the number of active instructions needing a function, say multiplication, may exceed the number of 'free' function units inside the function block. Hence some instructions must wait for the execution of other instructions to get a free function unit. The interconnect network is responsible for selecting 'active' instruction; this is called 'arbitration'. If an instruction is selected by the interconnect network, the instruction is 'fired'.

Referring to the dataflow operation of figure 2(b), the question marks indicate the empty places for input tokens. Initially, both instruction0 and instruction1 are active because they satisfy the two requirements, while instruction2 and instruction3 wait for the inputs as indicated by the "question marks". If the interconnect network selects instruction0 to execute first, the output of $b \times c$ will be sent to one of the empty places in instruction3. Then instruction1 will be sent to the function block and the output will be sent to the other empty place in instruction3. Instruction3 will then become active and its result will be sent to instruction2 which in turn generates the result $x$. The sequence of instructions may be 0132 or 1032; this does not matter and is not detected outside the matching store. The outside environment only issues the operands and gets the result.

When a stream of data needs to be processed, two important details covered in the dataflow operations mentioned above have to be addressed — how to define the validation of a data token and an empty place and how to detect the state of a destination. Defining the validation of a data token and an empty place is very simple. If the interconnect network sends a result to an instruction, it also sets a valid bit corresponding to the operand to 1, indicating a valid data token. If the instruction is fired, it sets the valid bit back to 0 indicating an empty place.

Detecting the states of destinations is a problem. A straightforward solution is that the instruction requiring to send results actively polls its destinations for their states. However, this is very inefficient because the instruction may have to keep asking 'are you empty?' If the destinations are always occupied and cannot reply 'yes', it will ask forever. This is a power-hungry dynamic action. A more efficient approach is proposed called a 'negative solution'. With a 'negative solution', the receivers automatically send 'empty tokens' or 'data demands' to their senders when they are fired. Senders become active depending on the data demands from their receivers; thus in the 'negative' solution, two kinds

of tokens flow inside the processor — data tokens and empty tokens. As can
be seen from the above, operations in the proposed processor are executed in
an order determined not only by the availability of input data but also by the
requirements for data.

The basic dataflow element normally has two input arcs and one output arc,
as shown in Figure 3(a). However, the output is often sent to several different
locations and hence a 'fork' instruction is needed, as shown in Figure 3(b). A
data processing and a fork instruction can be combined into a unified instruction which has two input arcs and two output arcs as shown in Figure 3(c).
This greatly reduces the number of operations required for creating temporary
variables. Conditional instructions are indispensable for basic program segments
such as loops and branches and, to support these, another 'gate' input arc is
added to the basic dataflow element as shown in Figure 3(d). A 'fork' with a
gate control is called 'branch'; the output of a branch will be sent to the arc(s)
having the same Boolean value as the value on the gate arc. The only difference
between a 'fork' and a 'branch' is that a 'fork' simply duplicates variables and
a 'branch' sends the output depending on a conditional gate value. With the
dataflow element shown in Figure 3(d), a data token can represent two kinds of
values — a data value, which is sent to the operands arcs, and a Boolean value,
which is sent to the *gate* arc. The dataflow element illustrated in Figure 3(d)
is a unified format which combines the functions of data processing, duplication
and conditional control.

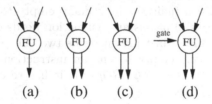

(a)      (b)      (c)      (d)

**Fig. 3.** The architectures of dataflow elements

To support the 'negative' scheme and the unified format, the structure of the
coprocessor's instructions is as shown in Table 1. The number in the bracket
after each field name indicates how many bits are needed in the respective field.
The numbers are based on a 16-bit operand length and a matching store with
32 instructions.

The function of each field is interpreted as follows:

- OPCode defines the operation to be processed, such as addition or multiplication. It also defines the types of the operands in an instruction —
  immediate data or local memory addresses for the operands (this will be
  addressed later). DorG defines whether the output value is a data value (1)
  or a Boolean gate value (0).
- OP1, OP2 and GV are three input values — operand1, operand2 and gate-
  value. Const1, Const2 and ConstG are three flags (const flags) determining

**Table 1.** The structure of an instruction

| OPCode (6) | Const1 (1) | V1 (1) | OP1 (16) |
|---|---|---|---|
| DorG (1) | Const2 (1) | V2 (1) | OP2 (16) |
| – | ConstG (1) | VG (1) | GV (1) |
| Source1 (5) | SF1 (1) | Dest1 (6) | DV1 (1) |
| Source2 (5) | SF2 (1) | Dest1 (6) | DV1 (1) |
| Source3 (5) | SF3 (1) | ETReq (1) | ETGot (2) |

whether the respective input values are constants. If an input has a const bit of 1, this input will always be valid and never be set to empty. V1, V2 and VG are three flags (operand valid bits) determining whether the respective input tokens are empty or not.

- Dest1 and Dest2 are two destination addresses for results. DV1 and DV2 are two flags attached to the output arcs. Results are sent only to the address(s) having DV equal to the gate value. If $DV1 = GV$, results are sent to Dest1. If $DV2 = GV$, results are sent to Dest2. If $DV1 = DV2$ and $DV1 \neq GV$, the instruction is a 'sink', which only absorbs input data and does not generate output. 'Sink' instructions are not very common in sequential executions, but they happen quite often at the end of a loop.
- Source1, Source2 and SourceG specify the respective addresses where the empty tokens should be sent. SF1, SF2 and SFG are three flags (source flags) deciding if empty tokens should be sent to the respective source addresses.
- The one-bit flag ETReq indicates how many empty tokens an instruction needs to become active. 0 means an instruction needs one empty token to become active; 1 means an instruction needs two. The two-bit number ET-Got indicates how many empty tokens an instruction has received. If an instruction satisfies $ETGot = ETReq + 1$, it has received enough empty token(s) to become active.

Among these bits, only a few decide the state of an instruction — the 'condition bits'. The condition bits in our architecture are Const1, V1, Const2, V2, ConstG, VG, ETReq and ETGot. Other bits indicate data values and the destinations of outputs and empty tokens. If an instruction is to be active, it should satisfy two conditions: $V1 = V2 = VG = 1$ and $ETGot = ETReq + 1$. When an instruction is fired, it clears ETGot and those operand valid bits whose const bits are 0.

Figure 4 illustrates how the state of an instruction progresses by changing the values of condition bits. Instruction0 specifies $a \times b$ with conditional control; instruction1 specifies the addition of $c$ and the output from $a \times b$; instruction2 specifies the addition of $d$ and the output from $a \times b$. Assume that $a$ is a variable and $b$ is a constant number. The diagram of the state transition of instruction0 is triggered by the events shown in the figure. The order of the numbers in this figure is <Const1, V1, Const2, V2, ConstG, VG, ETReq, ETGot>.

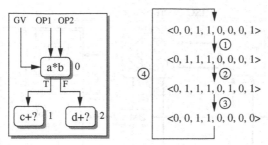

① The instruction receives input a.

② The instruction receives gate value = 1.

③ The register becomes active. After some time, it is fired and the result is sent to T branch. Valid bits and ETGot are set to zero.

④ The instruction receives an empty token sent by the instruction1

**Fig. 4.** The state transition diagram of an instruction

# 4    Architecture and Implementation

As discussed before, the dataflow machine is used as a coprocessor to process some repeatedly-used and power-hungry operations. It has no ability to fetch instructions; the main processor decides what kinds of instructions should be fed to it. The proposed hierarchical processing architecture is illustrated in Figure 5.

In the hierarchical processing architecture, the most commonly executed program segments, such as small loops and function calls, are stored in the coprocessor. To execute these program segments, the main CPU, which is a conventional embedded processor, sends data tokens to the matching store and takes results out. The coprocessor is regarded as a 'computation engine' to executed the repeatedly executed and most power hungry computations. The coprocessor supports only 16 instructions which result in a high performance and low power consumption. Because the coprocessor has a very small instruction space and a simple circuit implementation, the power overheads due to instruction fetching, decoding and complex pipeline operations are greatly saved.

The CPU and the coprocessor are designed using an asynchronous logic design [9] methodology and the communications between the two processing units are made in a way of an asynchronous request-acknowledge handshake.

The architecture of the dataflow coprocessor is different from that in Figure 2(c). The matching store is separated into two parts — the Controller and the Instruction SRAM. Only 'condition bits' are stored in the Controller because these bits determine the changes of the states of instructions. The other 72 bits of an instruction, which have no relation to the change of its state, are put in a single-port $32 \times 72$ SRAM block. The Control FSMs (finite state machines) are the basic elements of the Control and determine the states of instruction. The logic function of a Control FSM is very simple. If an FSM receives a data token it sets the respective operand valid bits (V1, V2 or VG) to 1. If an FSM receives an empty token it increases ET-

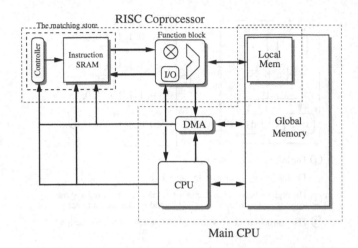

**Fig. 5.** The proposed hierarchical processing architecture

Got by 1. If $V1 = V2 = VG = 1$ and $ETGot = ETReq+1$ the FSM becomes active and sends a request signal to the interconnect network (an arbiter) which fires the FSM by sending back an acknowledge signal. The acknowledge signal clears the operand valid bits (if the respective const flag is 0) and ETGot, thus preparing for another execution. The number of Control FSMs in the Controller depends on the capability of instructions. In this dataflow prototype, there are 32 control FSMs. The acknowledge signals connect to the 32 wordlines of the instruction SRAM and the 'fired' instruction will be read out.

The scheme of separating the Controller and the instruction SRAM not only minimizes the size but also reduces the power consumption because most bits are in the SRAM block and a single SRAM is much smaller and more power efficient than a multi-port register file used in conventional processors.

The main CPU is responsible for initializing the controller and the instruction RAM. It can also start another round of computation in the coprocessor by sending valid data tokens without initializing the matching store again. The function block takes charge of data processing. The interconnect network sends empty tokens to the controller, changes V1, V2, and VG in the controller and sends computation results to OP1, OP2 and GV in the instruction RAM.

The processing of data streams is common in embedded data processing applications. In a stream-based computation, normally two memory arrays are processed and the results are put into another memory array. Since accessing a small memory is more efficient than accessing a large one, a small block of local memory is included in the dataflow coprocessor. The size of the memory depends on different applications. In the prototype design, the memory is $1K \times 16$, divided into 4 parts of the same size. Clearly, it is very inefficient if every single data item exchanged between the local and main memory moves through the function block and the main CPU. The coprocessor can control a DMA (Direct Memory Access) controller in the main processor to exchange blocks of data between the local and main memories when necessary. From the CPU's point of view, the local memory and the matching store of the dataflow architecture is just a part of the main memory which it can access. The DMA controller is also used for initializing the matching to minimize the power overhead due to coprocessor initialization.

The instruction set of the coprocessor has a unified format <OPCode, OP1, OP2, destination1, destination2> and all operands are 16 bits. OP1 and OP2 can be immediate numbers or local-memory addresses of data, depending on the two flag bits in the OPCode. The coprocessor supports memory-memory, memory-immediate and immediate-immediate instruction set architectures. At this point, the coprocessor is similar to some CISC processors that support abundant instruction set architectures. The variety of instruction set architecture reduces the number of instructions, therefore increasing the code density.

## 5  Experimental Results on Benchmarks

The coprocessor is implemented in a 0.18 $\mu$m ST CMOS technology. Under a supply voltage of 1.8 volts and a temperature of 25°C, the energy and delay characteristics of each component are shown in Table 2. (The delay of the interconnect network is included in the delays of reading and writing the matching store.)

Table 2. The characteristics of the components

| Component | Energy per operation (pJ) | Delay (ns) |
|---|---|---|
| Controller | 1.36 | < 0.3 |
| Interconnect network | 7.32 | – |
| Matching store RAM | 12.8 | 1.40 (read) |
| (1 Read and 1.5 writes) |  | 1.40 (write) |
| 16x16-bit Multiplier | 34.2 | 2.61 |
| 16-bit Adder/Logic Units | 3.17 | 0.90 |
| Local memory read | 4.18 | 1.50 |
| Local memory write | 9.86 | 1.50 |

One general program, three discrete-time signal processing algorithms and one encryption algorithm are used as benchmarks to evaluate the dataflow coprocessor:

- $SUM = \sum_{i=1}^{100} i$;
- A 5-tag finite impulse response (FIR) filter;
- A 5-tag infinite impulse response (IIR) filter;
- A fast Fourier transform (FFT) algorithm;
- The IDEA encryption algorithm.

In the dataflow coprocessor, a computation with a set of inputs and a set of outputs is called a 'computation element'. The main CPU initializes a 'computation element', such as encrypting a data item, and the dataflow coprocessor will finish the task as a single operation without the assistance from the CPU. If the main CPU wants to execute another round of a 'computation element' it does not need to initialize the task again. It just sends the coprocessor some 'seeds' to start the task. The power consumption overhead of initializing an instruction in the instruction RAM is equal to the power used to write 5 16-bit words to the memory. The power consumption overhead of starting another round of a computation element equals to the power used to write one 16-bit word to the memory. Once a program segment is initialized, it will be executed for many times, thus the initialization overhead is very small, just as what happens in a conventional cache.

The throughput of the coprocessor is higher than traditional RISC processors because the coprocessor supports only 16 instructions and the simple circuit implementation makes it faster than a general-purpose processor. By using an asynchronous control, no special effort is needed to improve the critical paths of slow circuits so long as those critical operations are rare enough that the impact on overall performance is small. The number of pipeline stages in the coprocessor is not constant. An immediate-immediate computation has three pipeline stages: reading instruction RAM, data processing and writing immediate results back; a memory-memory computation has four pipeline stages: reading instruction RAM, reading operands from the local memory, data processing and writing results back.

An attempt was made to compare the power consumption of the dataflow coprocessor with commercial microprocessors, but a realistic comparison is difficult. An estimation method is described as follows: Firstly, the same benchmarks are implemented in manually-optimized programs for a commercial processor. The programs are simulated in the software simulator provided by a microprocessor manufacturer to get the number of clock cycles needed. Then the number of clock cycles and the published energy data, such as MIPS/W and current per MHz, are used to get the estimated energy. We chose the Atmel ARM microprocessor AT91R40008 [10] for comparison. Under typical operating conditions (core voltage = 1.8v, temperature = 25°C), the power consumption of the AT91R40008 with all peripheral clocks deactivated is 0.73 mW/MHz. The estimation is based on the assumption that the execution of every instruction uses the same amount of energy, including multiplication and memory access, and each instruction takes one clock to finish. This assumption is very conservative and the actual energy dissipated is believed to be more than that estimated. The comparison of the power consumption between the dataflow coprocessor and the AT91R40008 is shown in Table 3. This table demonstrates that, compared to the AT91R40008, the dataflow coprocessor has a better power-efficiency by a factor greater than 20. The experimental results are done in a schematic level and wire capacitances are avoided. Moreover, the coprocessor uses a 16-bit datapath. The post-fabrication result on the power efficiency of a 32-bit dataflow coprocessor is estimated to be about 10,000 MIPS/W, a factor of 7.3 better than that of AT91R40008.

An interesting phenomenon shown from the experiments is that, in these applications, the function units use a large proportion of the overall power consumption. For the FIR benchmark, data processing uses as much as 40% of the overall coprocessor power consumption. Thus in the dataflow coprocessor, the power consumption due to execution overheads are greatly reduced.

**Table 3.** The power consumption between two processors

| Benchmark | SUM | FIR | IIR | FFT | IDEA |
|-----------|-----|-----|-----|-----|------|
| Clock cycles | 400 | 20 | 21 | 30 | 241 |
| AT91R40008(nJ) | 292.0 | 14.6 | 15.3 | 21.9 | 175.9 |
| Coprocessor(nJ) | 12.7 | 0.61 | 0.67 | 0.86 | 8.05 |
| Ratio | 23.0 | 24.1 | 22.9 | 25.5 | 21.9 |

The overall power saving by using the hierarchical processing scheme follows Amdahl's law [6] — the overall power saving is defined by how many percentage of the overall dynamic instructions can be stored and executed in the coprocessor. Based on the experimental results, when running the JPEG program, a main CPU spends 40% of its time in executing 14 instructions. If the 14 instructions are put and executed in the coprocessor, 34.5% of the overall power consumption can be saved.

# 6   Conclusion

In this paper, the concept of hierarchical processing is brought forward based on the observation of highly imbalance execution ratios of instructions in embedded programs. The basic idea of hierarchical processing is designing a specific data processing unit to improve the performance and power efficiency of the most commonly executed instructions while using a general-purpose processor to maintain an abundant functionality. A novel prototype architecture for low-power hierarchical processing is proposed in this paper — a dataflow coprocessor embedded in a RISC processor as a 'computation engine' to improve the power efficiency of the most repeatedly executed instruction segments. Based on the experiments of using different benchmark programs, we demonstrate that the dataflow coprocessor has the potential for about a factor of 7.3 improvement in power-efficiency over current general-purpose processors.

The reason for the power-efficiency of the dataflow coprocessor is due to its specific architecture and circuit implementation. The coprocessor has the ability to memorize several instructions so, unlike traditional RISC processors which discard instructions they have just processed and refetch them after a short period of time, the coprocessor can implement small loops and re-execute them without fetching any instructions. Similarly, frequently used instruction segments can be stored in the coprocessor as 'computation elements'. If the main processor needs to execute these programs, it just issues the inputs and the coprocessor will return the output. Thus the number of instruction fetches needed to describe these instruction segments in the main processor is greatly reduced. The low-power characteristic of the coprocessor is also due to its flexible instruction set architectures. The coprocessor supports immediate-immediate, immediate-memory and memory-memory computations. This scheme significantly improves the coprocessor's code density.

Specific circuit implementation is another factor resulting in significant power saving. The dataflow coprocessor employs an efficient 'negative' synchronization scheme. Supporting only the most frequently executed instructions helps the coprocessor get rid of most of execution overhead due to a complex instruction decoder and datapath. Splitting the matching store and using a single-port instruction SRAM block further increase the power efficiency of the coprocessor.

# References

1. D. Soudris, C. Piguet and C. Goutis (eds). *Designing CMOS Circuits for Low Power*. Kluwer academic publishers, 2002
2. A. W. Burks, H. H. Goldstine, and J. von Neumann, "Preliminary discussion of the logical design of an electronic computing instrument". *John von Neumann Collected Works*, The Macmillan Co., New York, Volume V, 34-79, 1963.
3. J. Montanaro, R. T. Witec, et al. "A 160-MHz, 32-b, 0.5-W CMOS RISC Microprocessor". *IEEE Journal of Solid-State Circuits*, VOL. 31, NO. 11, Nov. 1996.
4. R.S. Bajwa. et. al. "Instruction buffering to reduce power in processors for signal processing". *IEEE transition on VLSI*. 1997.
5. L. H. Lee, W. Moyer and J. Arends. "Instruction fetch energy reduction using loop caches for embedded applications with small tight loops", *Proceedings ISLPED'99*, Pages:267 - 269, August 1999.
6. J.L. Hennessy and D.A. Patterson. *Computer Architecture: A Quantitative approach. 3rd Edition*. Morgan Kaufmann Publishers. 2003
7. A. H. Veen. "Dataflow machine architecture". *ACM Computing Surveys (CSUR)*, Volume 18 Issue 4, December 1986.
8. I. Watson and J.R. Gurd. "A Practical Dataflow Computer". *IEEE Journal of Computer*, vol.15 no.2, February 1982, pp. 51-57
9. J. Sparsø, S. Furber (eds). *Principles of Asynchronous Circuit Design: A systems Perspective*. Kluwer Academic Publishers, 2001
10. *AT91R40008 Electrical Characteristics*, Atmel Co. 2002.

# Optimization of Master-Slave Flip-Flops
# for High-Performance Applications*

Raúl Jiménez[1], Pilar Parra[2], Javier Castro[2], Manuel Sánchez[1], and Antonio Acosta[2]

[1] Dpt. DIESIA, EPS-La Rábida, Universidad de Huelva, Cra. Huelva-La Rábida, s/n 21071-
Huelva, Spain
{naharro, msraya}@diesia.uhu.es
[2] Instituto de Microelectrónica de Sevilla/Universidad de Sevilla, Avda. Reina Mercedes s/n,
41012-Sevilla, Spain
{parra, casram, acojim}@imse.cnm.es

**Abstract.** The design of high-performance master-slave flip-flops is of crucial importance in modern VLSI. The optimization of existing structures is necessary when the requirements of the flip-flop is for low-power, high-speed or low-noise applications. In this work, the optimization via transistor sizing of a well-known master-slave flip-flop is investigated. A detailed analysis of the flip-flop structure provides information useful for optimization, giving an optimum solution for an specific high-performance application.

## 1 Introduction

Design of edge-triggered flip-flops (FFs) in current CMOS VLSI digital and mixed-signal analog-digital circuits is a key point due to several factors. On one hand, deep submicron digital designs need high-performance FFs, since their huge impact on the global performances -delay, power- of the system, mainly in heavily pipelined and parallel circuits [1]. On the other hand, FFs have a lot of importance in the reliable operation in the system, because violations in timing restrictions in FFs are usual reasons for metastable faulty operation [1]. In modern mixed-signal analog-digital integrated circuits, the switching noise injected by the digital part of the system onto the highly sensible analog part limits the performance of the global system [2, 3]. In this sense, the suited design of FFs for mixed-signal applications is of important concern, since FFs are the most important source of digital switching noise in the digital circuit, contributing every clock cycle [3]. Regarding power and delay perfor-mances of the FFs, it should be taken into account their influence on the global characteristics of the complete circuit, with especial emphasis in low power consum-ption and high speed applications.

For all the above-mentioned reasons, the design of an specific FF, or the suited choice of a memory element for an application, requires a detailed and rigorous study and analysis, specially in those design techniques where the designer can select the FF structure at a transistor level. Some implementation of different FF structures can be found in the literature [1, 4], including both new FF architectures and improvement of classical implementations.

---

* This work has been partially sponsored by the Spanish MEC TEC2004-01509 DOC, the Junta de Andalucía TIC2006-635 and the Universidad de Huelva UHU2004-06 Projects.

J. Vounckx, N. Azemard, and P. Maurine (Eds.): PATMOS 2006, LNCS 4148, pp. 439 – 449, 2006.

Within FF classification, master-slave based flip-flops (MSFFs) are widely used because of their characteristics and the suitability for high-performance applications [1, 4], yielding several modifications [5-10] of the conventional master-slave configuration shown in figure 1.

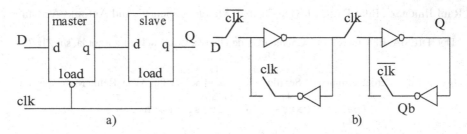

**Fig. 1.** a) Basic structure of a master-slave flip-flop. b) Static alternative.

This paper is intended for cover the optimization process of conventional MSFFs at a transistor level. In such sense, a survey of master-slave structures is presented in Section 2. Section 3 includes a characterization by HSPICE simulations of the conventional MSFF for 0.13 μm and 0.35 μm CMOS standard technologies, with especial emphasis on switching noise, power consumption and propagation delay. Section 4 presents the optimization procedure, a summary of results and some guidelines for MSFF optimization. As a final result, the most interesting conclusions are presented.

## 2 Master-Slave Flip-Flops (MSFFs) Structures

MSFFs are based on the serial connection of two latches following a master-slave configuration (figure 1). The master latch is controlled by a complemented clock phase, while the slave latch is controlled by a uncomplemented clock phase. Only in the low to high transition of clock both latches are transparent and input data D is transmitted to the output, operating as a edge-triggered flip-flop. Feedback loops in both latches ensure static storage of data, avoiding accidental discharge.

There are several modifications of the conventional master-slave configuration. In figure 2, we can find the TSPC ratioed FF [5], the GC FF [6], the conventional master-slave [8], the master-slave used in PowerPC [7], the $C^2MOS$ master-slave, used in the AMS library [8, 10], the SSTC [9] and the DSTC [9]. As a summary, in the GC FF, the switches are controlled by the input and intermediate data. In the FF used in PowerPC, the feedback switch and inverter pair are replaced by a $C^2MOS$ latch. In the $C^2MOS$ master-slave FF, the switches are replaced by two $C^2MOS$ latches. In the case of SSTC and DSTC FFs, the latches are replaced by differential structures. A full characterization of these FFs can be found in the literature [1,4,11], and it is out of the scope of this paper. Our intention is to derive the main parameters of the MSFF from the transistor and gate structure and to optimize the size of the transistors to obtain an specific target behavior concerning area, power, speed and noise.

The MSFF under consideration is shown in figure 3. It is based on the $C^2MOS$ master-slave, used in the AMS library [8, 10], including the reset circuitry. In this MSFF,

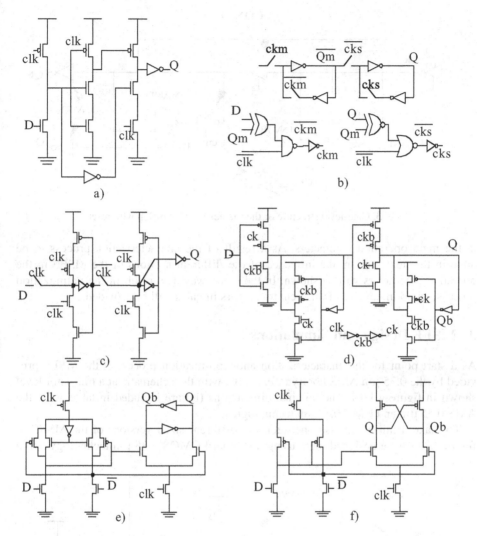

**Fig. 2.** a) TSPC ratioed [5], b) GCFF [6], c) PowerPC latch [7], d) MS-C²MOS [8, 10], e) SSTC [9] and f) DSTC [9] FFs

the switches are replaced by clocked-CMOS gates, while the reset signal is loaded in gates through the feedback loops in the latches, a C²MOS NAND in the master latch and a CMOS NAND gate in the slave latch. The MSFF with reset has been considered because of its wide usage and its more general structure.

In order to analyze the influence of the MSFF elements in the behavior characteristics, the structure has been divided into different hardware sections, as it is shown in figure 3. The C²MOS inverters (CLINVR), the C²MOS NAND (CLNAND), the NAND gate (NAND), the clock inverters (INVR1) the output inverters (INVR2) and the feedback inverter (INVR3). The reason for this classification is, on one hand, the functionality associated to the modules, and on the other, the influence of the sections

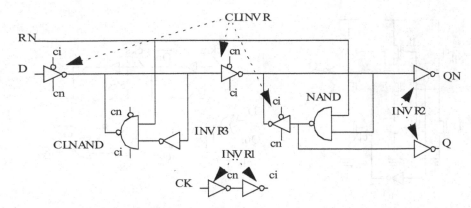

**Fig. 3.** Gate-level structure of the master-slave flip-flop with reset

in the main operation parameters. As a result of the characterization process to be done in the next section, the influence of the different sections of the MSFF in the operation parameters will be shown. In the same way as a result of the optimization process, an optimum size of different transistors in gates will be provided.

## 3  MSFF Design and Simulations

As a start point for the characterization and optimization process is the MSFF provided by the 0.35 μm AMS library (DFA cell), with the schematic at a transistor level shown in figure 4 [10]. The nominal dimensions ($t_x$) are included in table 1 for the AMS 0.35 μm and UMC 0.13 μm technologies.

To make a fair comparison between the different sized versions of the MSFF of figure 3, we have designed them using a standard CMOS 0.35 μm technology, from

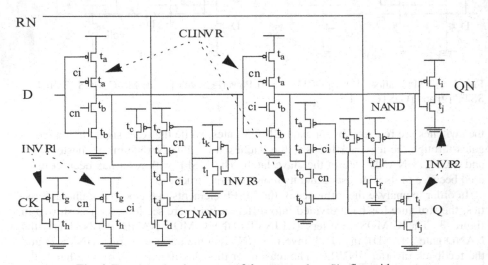

**Fig. 4.** Transistor-level structure of the master-slave flip-flop with reset

**Table 1.** Nominal dimensions W/L (in µm) for the 0.35 µm DFA AMS MSFF and for the 0.13 µm UMC MSFF version

| TECH. | clinvr | | clnand | | nand | | invr1 | | invr2 | | invr3 | |
|---|---|---|---|---|---|---|---|---|---|---|---|---|
| | $t_a$ | $t_b$ | $t_c$ | $t_d$ | $t_e$ | $t_f$ | $t_g$ | $t_h$ | $t_i$ | $t_j$ | $t_k$ | $t_l$ |
| AMS 0.35µm | $\frac{2.0}{0.3}$ | $\frac{1.0}{0.3}$ | $\frac{1.0}{0.3}$ | $\frac{1.0}{0.3}$ | $\frac{1.0}{0.3}$ | $\frac{1.0}{0.3}$ | $\frac{2.0}{0.3}$ | $\frac{1.0}{0.3}$ | $\frac{2.0}{0.3}$ | $\frac{1.0}{0.3}$ | $\frac{1.5}{0.3}$ | $\frac{1.0}{0.3}$ |
| UMC 0.13µm | $\frac{1.0}{0.12}$ | $\frac{0.5}{0.12}$ | $\frac{0.5}{0.12}$ | $\frac{0.5}{0.12}$ | $\frac{0.5}{0.12}$ | $\frac{0.5}{0.12}$ | $\frac{1.0}{0.12}$ | $\frac{0.5}{0.12}$ | $\frac{1.0}{0.12}$ | $\frac{0.5}{0.12}$ | $\frac{0.75}{0.12}$ | $\frac{0.5}{0.12}$ |

AMS, and the UMC 0.13 µm processes. The parameters used to characterize the MSFF are the power consumption, propagation delay, power-delay product, energy per transition, and switching noise (the peak of supply current as an undirected measurement), to explore their use in mixed-signal applications. The benchmark and waveforms in figure 5 have been selected for HSPICE characterization. The parameters have been measured only in the bistable, while input and output inverters simulate a realistic environment. With the simulation pattern, we have set a restrictive operation with relatively high switching activity 0.8, covering most of transition possibilities.

The most representative results obtained are shown in table 2, including the propagation delay for Q and QN outputs, the average power, the power-delay product (PDP), the energy per transition of clock and data, and the peak noise due to clock and data, always with state change. Analyzing data in table 2, we can extract valuable information for further comparison, considering only the worst case for every parameter. In this way, since delay in Q output is higher than QN, because of the NAND gate, only the average delay in Q will be considered. A similar reasoning is for energy and noise measurements: contribution of data switching is negligible when comparing to switching clock contributions, and hence, only the due-to-clock worst data contributing to energy and noise will be considered.

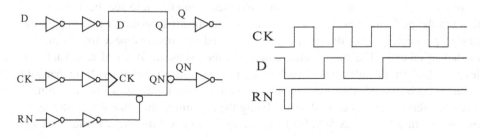

**Fig. 5.** Simulation set-up and input waveforms

**Table 2.** Results for the MSFF under optimization (AMS-0.35μm and UMC 0.13μm). Data in dashed cells will be used for further comparison

| TECH. | Average Delay (ns) | | Average Power (μW) | PDP (pJ) | Energy per Transition (fJ) | | | | Peak Noise (mA) | | | |
|---|---|---|---|---|---|---|---|---|---|---|---|---|
| | Q | QN | | | CK_r | CK_f | D_r | D_f | CK_r | CK_f | D_r | D_f |
| AMS 0.35 | 0.76 | 0.50 | 37.5 | 28.5 | 557 | 382 | 31 | 35 | 0.42 | 0.45 | 0.07 | 0.10 |
| UMC 0.13 | 0.27 | 0.17 | 2.7 | 0.73 | 33.3 | 23.1 | 1.9 | 2.0 | 0.15 | 0.16 | 0.03 | 0.04 |

# 4   Optimization Process

The start point of the optimization process is the MSFF schematic of figure 4, with the original sizes of table 1, and providing the results in table 2. Once characterized the referenced cell, we have modified the transistor sizes to explore the design space and to obtain the best results oriented towards an specific application (power, delay or noise). The design space exploration is carried out by the modification of only one subcircuit at time, to keep limited the total number of possibilities and to find out the influence of a specific block of the MSFF in the global performances. For instance, modifying exclusively the dimensions of transistors $t_g$ and $t_i$, (INVR1 block) the influence of clock inverters will be show up. In the same experiment, if an improved solution in terms of power, delay or noise is achieved, the new figures are annotated and the new dimensions are considered as a better solution. The same process is repeated for the INVR2, INVR3, CLNAND, NAND and CLINVR until an optimal solution is achieved.

A total of 12881 transient simulations have been done, sweeping the width and length of transistors $t_a$ –$t_i$ in the range 0.3, 0.5, 0.7, 1.0, 1.5 and 2.0 μm for the AMS technology, and 0.12, 0.25, 0.5, 0.75, 1 and 1.5 μm for the UMC technology. In every cases, the transistors in the same pull-up (-down) keeps the same size. With this procedure, an optimized version of the MSFF is achieved.

In a first step of the process, only one subblock is modified, to see the influence of them in the performances. In this sense, the transistor dimensions for minimizing the design parameters, with the optimized values and the improvement (in %) are included in table 3. The modifications of the dimensions are detailed at a subblock level, to find out the influence of each block in the parameter behavior. Note that data value in each row of table 3 are obtaining with the modification of only the dimensions of subblock indicated in the row, being the remaining the same that in the referenced structure (the AMS MSFF in this case). It is clear how the actuations on the dimensions of INVR2 have strong influence in all the parameters (up to a 34% of reduction in the energy per transition), while the NAND and INV3 blocks have less influence. There are also poor improvements for the delay, since the AMS MSFF

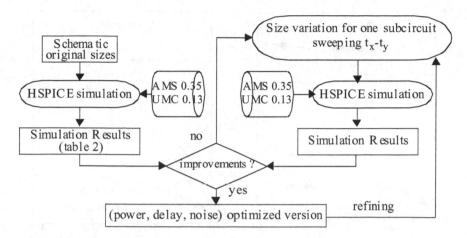

**Fig. 6.** Optimization process via resizing and HSPICE simulation

**Table 3.** Improvement in the AMS MSFF when the size of only one block is modified

| Block | TdelayQ (ns) | | Average power (μW) | | Energy per transition (fJ) | | Inoise (mA) | |
|---|---|---|---|---|---|---|---|---|
| | size (μm) | value % | size (μm) | value % | size (μm) | value % | size (μm) | value % |
| INVR1 | No improvement | | $t_g$=0.5/0.3 $t_h$=0.3/0.3 | 31.8 15% | $t_g$=0.5/0.3 $t_h$=0.3/0.3 | 508 9% | $t_g$=1.5/0.3 $t_h$=0.5/0.3 | 0.41 9% |
| INVR2 | $t_i$=0.3/0.3 $t_j$=2.0/0.3 | 0.716 6% | $t_i$=0.3/0.3 $t_j$=0.3/0.3 | 29.87 20% | $t_i$=0.3/0.3 $t_j$=0.3/0.3 | 370.4 34% | $t_i$=0.5/0.3 $t_j$=0.3/0.3 | 0.44 1% |
| INVR3 | $t_k$=1.5/0.3 $t_l$=1.0/0.3 | 0.761 1% | $t_k$=0.3/0.3 $t_l$=0.3/0.3 | 36.11 3% | No improvement | | No improvement | |
| CLINVR | No improvement | | $t_a$=0.5/0.3 $t_b$=1.0/0.3 | 35.13 6% | $t_a$=0.5/0.3 $t_b$=0.3/0.5 | 397.6 29% | $t_a$=0.3/0.3 $t_b$=1.0/0.3 | 0.39 13% |
| NAND | No improvement | | No improvement | | No improvement | | No improvement | |
| CLNAND | $t_c$=0.3/0.3 $t_d$=0.3/0.3 | 0.753 2% | $t_c$=0.3/0.3 $t_d$=0.3/0.3 | 34.8 7% | $t_c$=0.3/0.3 $t_d$=0.3/0.3 | 515.4 8% | No improvement | |

seems to be oriented towards high-speed operation. The highest level of optimization comes from the combination of modification in sizes of subblocks, as it is explained below.

Considering that the size of all the blocks can be modified simultaneously, we can find optimum solutions for an specific parameters by combining the sizes taking into account the influence of the block on the parameter. This is the difference with a random or exhaustive optimization process. As a first result of the optimization process, figure 7 shows the delay, noise, power and power-delay product values of optimized

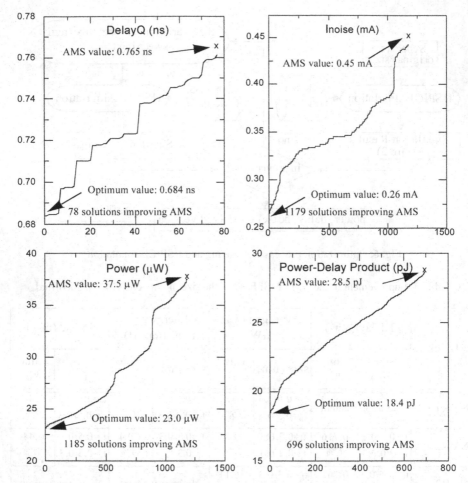

**Fig. 7.** Delay, noise, power and power-delay product values versus the number of simulated MSFFs with improved parameters when comparing to the AMS MSFF value (marked x)

MSFFs in the AMS technology. In each graphic, the parameter value is represented versus the number of MSFFs that improve the reference parameter of the AMS MSFF value, marked with x in the graphics. A detailed analysis of the graphics gives the following information valuable for the optimization process:

- The AMS MSFF presents a good behavior in terms of delay, because it is only improved by 78 solutions. However, the improvement in power and noise figures is considerable, because more than 1100 solutions show better figures. Thus a low-power and/or low-noise version of the MSFF is easily reached.

- It could be achieved an improvement of 12% in delay (from 0.77 ns to 0.68 ns), 42% in noise (from 0.45 mA to 0.26 mA), 39% in average power (from 37.55 µW to 23.07 µW), 36% in power-delay-product (from 28.5 pJ to 18.4 pJ) or 59% in worst case of energy per transition (from 557 fJ to 228 fJ).

The presence of sharp steps in the graphics of figure 7 suggests the possibility of important optimization by a slight modification of only one parameter. Additionally, the search of good solutions for several parameters is possible, as it is shown in the representation of delay, noise, average power and energy per transition versus the power-delay product of figure 8. It can be seen a set of good parameters near 20 pJ (encircled in the graphics), with all the parameters improving the data of the AMS MSFF.

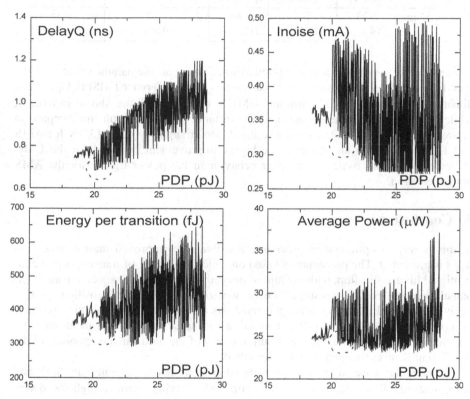

**Fig. 8.** Delay, noise, energy per transition and average power versus power-delay product for the optimized MSFFs

**Table 4.** Trade-off dimensions (in um) for the optimized 0.35 μm and 0.13 μm MSFF

| TECH. | clinvr | | clnand | | nand | | invr1 | | invr2 | | invr3 | |
|---|---|---|---|---|---|---|---|---|---|---|---|---|
| | $t_a$ | $t_b$ | $t_c$ | $t_d$ | $t_e$ | $t_f$ | $t_g$ | $t_h$ | $t_i$ | $t_j$ | $t_k$ | $t_l$ |
| AMS 0.35μm | $\frac{2.0}{0.3}$ | $\frac{1.0}{0.3}$ | $\frac{1.0}{0.3}$ | $\frac{1.0}{0.3}$ | $\frac{1.0}{0.3}$ | $\frac{0.7}{0.3}$ | $\frac{2.0}{0.3}$ | $\frac{1.0}{0.3}$ | $\frac{0.5}{0.3}$ | $\frac{0.3}{0.5}$ | $\frac{1.0}{0.3}$ | $\frac{0.3}{0.5}$ |
| UMC 0.13μm | $\frac{1.0}{0.12}$ | $\frac{0.5}{0.12}$ | $\frac{0.5}{0.12}$ | $\frac{0.5}{0.12}$ | $\frac{0.75}{0.12}$ | $\frac{0.5}{0.12}$ | $\frac{1.0}{0.12}$ | $\frac{0.5}{0.12}$ | $\frac{1.0}{0.12}$ | $\frac{0.5}{0.25}$ | $\frac{0.75}{0.12}$ | $\frac{0.5}{0.12}$ |

**Table 5.** Optimum parameters for the MSFFs and technologies of table 4. In parentheses the improvement respecting to the MSFF of reference.

| TECH. | Delay Q (ns) | Average Power (µW) | PDP (pJ) | Energy per Transition (fJ) | Peak Noise (mA) |
|-------|--------------|---------------------|----------|----------------------------|------------------|
| AMS 0.35 µm | 0.74 (2.6%) | 29.3 (21.8%) | 21.7 (23.8%) | 273 (51%) | 0.38 (16%) |
| UMC 0.13 µm | 0.23 (14.8%) | 2.2 (18.5%) | 0.64 (12.3%) | 30.1 (9.6%) | 0.15 (6.2%) |

Finally, it is possible to find an optimum solution for all the parameters and for the specific technology, improving all the parameters of the referenced MSFF. Optimized dimensions for the AMS 0.35 µm and UMC 0.13 µm MSFF are shown in table 4, while the obtained parameters are included in table 5. It is difficult the comparison between both implementations because the different supply voltage (3.3 v for AMS and 1.2 v. for UMC) and because the higher improvement in speed for the UMC technology is compensated by a better behavior in the power figures for the AMS implementation.

# 5  Conclusions

In this paper, an optimization procedure for obtaining improved master-slave flip-flops is presented. The procedure is based on a clever resizing of transistors in a conventional library flip-flop, with the aim of optimizing one or more specific parameter, namely average power, worst-case delay, worst-case energy per transition, power-delay product and switching noise generated. As a result of the optimization process, an optimum master-slave flip-flop respecting to one or more of the mentioned parameters is found. As an additional result, the way of the hardware components of the flip-flop influences the parameters is described.

As particular case, a master-slave flip-flop with reset integrated in 0.35 and 0.13µm standard technologies has been optimized, deriving it from a high-speed version to a low-power and low-noise one. As relevant information, the output inverters have more influence in power and delay, being the clock inverters more important for noise generation. An improvement of 42% in noise, 39% in average power and 12% in delay is achieved for the MSFF in 0.35 µm, if a low-noise, low-power or high-speed oriented implementation is respectively conceived. For both technologies, an optimum implementation is obtained, with higher improvements in delay for the 0.13 µm technology, being the gain in power and noise higher for the 0.35 µm MSFF.

# References

1. Oklobdzija, V. G., Stojanovic, V. M., Markovic, D. M., Nedovic, N. M., "Digital System Clocking: High-Performance and Low-Power Aspects", John Wiley & Sons, 2003.
2. Aragonès, X., González, J. L. and Rubio, A., "Analysis and Solutions for Switching Noise Coupling in Mixed-Signal ICs", Kluwer Academic Publishers, 1999.

3. Acosta, A. J., Jiménez, R., Juan, J., Bellido, M. J. and M. Valencia, M., "Influence of clocking strategies on the design of low switching-noise digital and mixed-signal VLSI circuits", International Workshop on Power and Timing Modeling, Optimization and Simulation (PATMOS), pp. 316-326, 2000.
4. Jiménez, R., Parra, P., Sanmartín, P. and Acosta, A. J., "Analysis of high-performance flip-flops for submicron mixed-signal applications", Int. Journal of Analog Integrated Circuits and Signal Processing. Vol. 33, No. 2, pp.145-156, Nov. 2002.
5. Yang, C.Y., Dehng, G.K., Hsu, J.M. and Liu, S.I., "New dynamic flip-flop for high-speed dual-modulus prescaler", IEEE J. Solid-State Circuits, vol. 33, pp. 1568-1571, Oct. 1998.
6. Strollo, A.G.M. and De Caro, D., "Low power flip-flop with clock gating on master-slave latches", Electronics Letters, vol. 36, pp. 294-295, 2000.
7. Gerosa, G., Gary, S., Dietz, C., Dac, P., Hoover, K., Alvarez, J., Sanchez, H., Ippolito, P., Tai, N., Litch, S., Eno, J., Golab, J., Vanderschaaf, N. and Kahle, J., "A 2.2 W, 80 MHz supescalar RISC microprocessor", IEEE J. Solid-State Circuits, vol. 29, pp. 1440-1452, Dec. 1994.
8. Weste, N.H. and Eshragian, K., "Principles of CMOS VLSI Design: A Systems Perspective", 2nd edition, Addison-Wesley, 1994.
9. Yuan, J. and Svensson, C., "New single-clock CMOS latches and flip-flops with improved speed and power savings", IEEE J. Solid-State Circtuis, vol. 32, pp. 6269, Jan. 1997.
10. Austria Microsystems. 0.35 μm tech. URL: http://www.austriamicrosystems.com
11. Oskuii, S. T. "Comparative study on low-power high performance flip-flops", Technical Report LiTH-ISY-EX-3432-2003, Linköping University, 2003.

# Hierarchical Modeling of a Fractional Phase Locked Loop

Benjamin Nicolle[1,2], William Tatinian[1], Jean Oudinot[2], and Gilles Jacquemod[1]

[1] Laboratoire d'Antennes Electronique et Télécommunications (LEAT)
250 Avenue Albert Einstein
Parc d'Activité de Sophia Antipolis
06560 Valbonne, France
benjamin.nicolle@unice.fr
[2] Mentor Graphics France
180 Av. de l'Europe – ZIRST Montbonnot
38334 St Ismier, France

**Abstract.** The aim of this study is to provide a multi level VHDL-AMS modeling of an analog Phase Locked Loop (PLL). Three model levels are described, analyzed and compared in terms of simulation CPU times and accuracy. The characteristic parameters of the PLL, such as the settling time, overshoot, voltage variations linked to charge pump architecture and final voltage are extracted from the intermediate level.

## 1 Introduction

RF architecture become more and more complex and the simulation time of such circuits can become critical. We show that it is possible overcome this limitation by introducing a three-level hierarchical model : structural (low level), behavioral (intermediate) and high level. The advantages and drawbacks are described.

To perform this, we used a bottom-up approach which permits to separate significant parameters to the others.

All the simulations were performed using VHDL-AMS for each model level and the high level model is also Matlab compatible.

In the second part, we describe the studied PLL more in detail, in the third part, we show how it can be modeled at each hierarchical level and finally we will show the results of each description level.

## 2 PLL Architecture

The architecture is described in Fig. 1 [1]. The input frequency is a 13MHz square signal coming from a crystal oscillator, and the output frequency must be in the range of the GSM band : 880MHz to 960MHZ divided into 200kHz-bandwidth channels. For this study, we used the PLL in the "Mobile Transmit" (GSM-TX) band, this results in frequency division ratios comprised between 67.707 and 70.369.

To perform such divisions, we need to use an N/N+1 divider, controlled by a $\Delta\Sigma$ modulator or an accumulator. The division ratios have been stored in a ROM to

J. Vounckx, N. Azemard, and P. Maurine (Eds.): PATMOS 2006, LNCS 4148, pp. 450–457, 2006.
© Springer-Verlag Berlin Heidelberg 2006

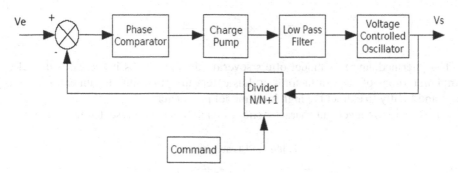

**Fig. 1.** PLL architecture

access quickly. This ROM also configures the different PLL blocks, function of the desirable divider [1].

The phase comparator includes a dead zone compensation to improve the stability of the PLL. A dead zone exists when the phase error is nearly zero. Neither the lead nor lag (from the phase frequency comparator block) signal reaches the logic '1' and the charge pump will leak off until the phase difference of the inputs is large enough for the PFD to exit the dead zone and turn on the charge pump to correct this error. The charge pump can provide currents in the range of 0.1mA to 10mA and in our case, we consider a third order $\Delta\Sigma$ with a serial topology (or accumulator) [2] and thus a third or fourth order loop filter, while in the general case the requirement is to have a filter order one degree higher than the $\Delta\Sigma$ order to efficiently remove the quantification noise [3][4].

## 3   Model Implementation

The hierarchical modeling consists in a three-level approach ; structural (low level), behavioral (intermediate level) and high level. The low level model allows to account more in detail for physical limitations such as slew rates or effects of the mismatches and offsets. This level is SPICE-like-simulator oriented, leading to simulation CPU times of about 9 to 12 hours (simulations performed on a SUNfire 280r). The PFD is a structural architecture based on two flip-flops, an AND gate and buffer for dead zone compensation.

Thanks to the intermediate model, the simulation time can be significantly lowered (about 2 to 4 hours). This can be done by adding the following changes.

The PFD, is now considered as a three state machine. This PFD architecture is only sensitive to the relative timing of edges between the reference signal and VCO output. The PFD circuit generates either lead or lag output pulses, depending on the VCO output transitions occur before or after the transitions of the reference signal, respectively. The pulses width is equal to the time between the respective edges.

The charge pump output circuitry that either sinks or sources current [5] (respectively) during those pulses and is otherwise open-circuited, generates an average output voltage-versus-phase difference. This is completely independent of the duty cycle of the input signals, unlike the classic XOR phase comparator architecture.

The LPF is taken into account by means of a Laplace transform, the division and $\Delta\Sigma$ modulator or accumulator are assumed to be ideal, while the charge pump is modeled with a behavioral equation :

$$I_{pump} = K \cdot \frac{P_{up} - P_{down}}{V_{dd} - V_{ss}}$$

The intermediate level model offers several advantages. As it decreases the CPU simulation times of about a factor 4, it thus offers the possibility to run extra simulations and finally to extract the high level model parameters.

The description level and characteristics of each block are presented in the table 1.

**Table 1.** PLL architecture

|  | *Low level (structural)* | *Intermediate level (behavioral)* | *High level (equations)* |
|---|---|---|---|
| PFD | Slew rate delay / dead zone | State machine | Fixed |
| CP | Slewrate / mismatch | Current equation | $I_{pump}$ as parameter |
| LPF | SPICE level R-C uncertainties corner model | Laplace transform | Fixed |
| VCO | Delay / transistors size, LC values | Described for GSM | Linear equation |
| ΣΔ Modulator Accumulator | Coefficients | Ideal | Fixed |
| Divider | Divider glitch Delay | Ideal | $N_{div}$ as parameter |

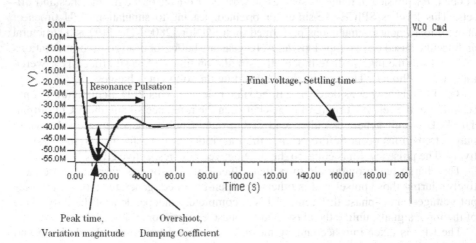

**Fig. 2.** Characteristic parameters of the PLL time response

As shown on Fig. 2, the time response of the PLL can be described with only some few parameters : peak time, overshoot, damping coefficient, resonance pulsation, final voltage, voltage variations linked to the CP architecture and the most important is settling time. All theses parameters are needed to predict the high level behavior of the PLL as a function of time. Most especially, we shall keep in mind that the voltage variations is linked to the filter order and cut-off frequency and the charge pump current. In other words, it is necessary to re-extract the high level model if those parameters are changed.

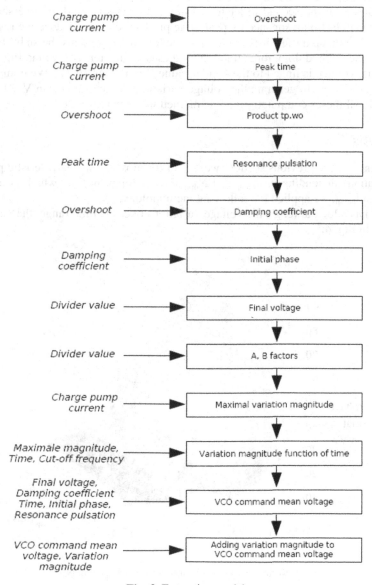

**Fig. 3.** Extracting model

For a given architecture (i. e. fixed divider command, filter and VCO), those parameters are only a function of the charge pump current ($I_{pump}$) and the division ratio ($N_{div}$).

The high level model is based on a voltage step response of a second-order loop filter, as shown in the following equation :

$$v(t)=V_{final}\cdot(1-\frac{1}{\sqrt{1-\zeta^2}}\cdot e^{-\zeta\cdot\omega_0\cdot t})\cdot\sin(\omega_0\cdot\sqrt{1-\zeta^2}\cdot t+\phi)$$

Several parameters are needed to match the intermediate level PLL response. The overshoot and peak time and their dependences are linked only to the charge pump current. Based on the second order loop filter characteristics and the overshoot, we obtained the pulsation resonance by peak time product, then we deduce the resonance pulsation. The damping factor is a function of overshoot represents the stability of the response. The methodology for extracting all theses parameters is given in Fig. 3.

The final voltage is linked to the divider value (for a given VCO). We compute the different parameters to generate the voltage variations around the mean VCO voltage command. All theses computations are explained in the results part.

## 4   Results

As explained in the previous section, we obtain for most of the characteristic parameters, variations depending on $I_{pump}$ and $N_{div}$. Except for peak time which is only dependent on $I_{pump}$, we applied the following methodology.

If one has a look at (e. g.) the voltage variations over the time range, the variations are given in Fig. 4.

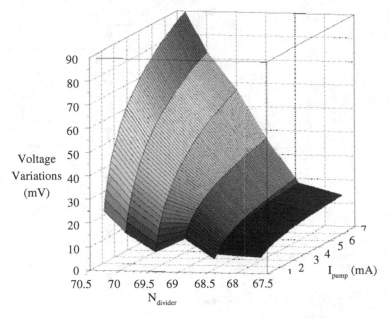

**Fig. 4.** Voltage variations as a function of $I_{pump}$ and $N_{div}$

The first step to separate the dependences on $I_{pump}$ and $N_{div}$, is to plot voltage variations on the VCO voltage command as a function of $I_{pump}$ for different $N_{div}$. Then we see that we can write (for a fixed $N_{div}$) :

$$\Delta(N_{divider}, I_{pump}) = A(N_{divider}) + B(N_{divider}) \cdot log(I_{pump})$$

With such an assumption, it becomes easy to extract the values $A(N_{div})$ and $B(N_{div})$ (second-order polynomial functions).

The results of this extraction is given in Fig. 5. We can see that the results are acceptable for high current values but the error become important for small values. To remove this effect it is also possible to develop a two section model, accounting separately for the small and high current values. The main drawback for this approach is that it can dramatically increase the extraction parameters time.

The other parameters are extrapolated in the same way. Most particularly, we express the overshoot as a sixth order polynomial function to achieve an accurate model for slight charge pump current, and the peak time as :

$$T_{peak} = \frac{a}{I_{pump}^{a}} + b$$

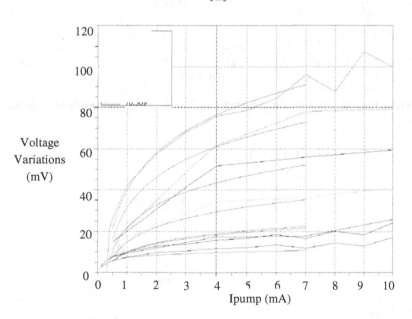

**Fig. 5.** Intermediate and high level extraction of voltage variations

We also notice some correlations between some parameters, such as product between peak time at the resonance pulsation and the overshoot that can be expressed as

$$w_{o} * T_{peak} = \frac{a}{\Delta_{overshoot}^{a}} + b$$

Such correlations greatly help to reduce the number of fitting parameters in the model and allow to reduce the use of high order polynomial functions.

Now, to show the accuracy of our extraction, we compare the simulation results for each abstraction level for $N_{div} = 70.369$ and $I_{pump} = 5mA$, in this VCO command voltage on Fig. 6 (first 20 µs) and Fig. 7 (last 20 µs).

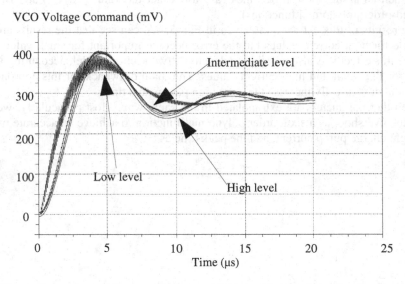

**Fig. 6.** Comparison of the simulations for each hierarchical level  acceleration phase

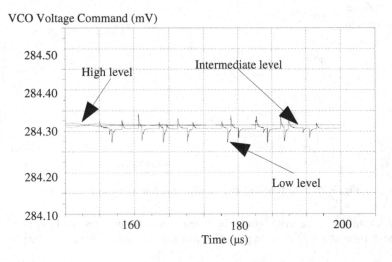

**Fig. 7.** Comparison of the simulations for each hierarchical level – stabilization phase

The difference between intermediate and high level models is only due to the approximation errors while the difference between low and higher level can be explained by the change of block, model. Most particularly, the VCO description in not detailed enough to provide more accurate estimations. The other limiting factors are removal the dead zone compensation and the fact that the fractional division (and the $\Delta\Sigma$ command) are a considered as ideal.

Despite these approximations, we obtain the same order of magnitude for the settling time in low-level and high level configurations. Another issue we have to face is to take into account the voltages variations in the stabilization phase. As we can see in Fig. 7, high level simulations do not provide these variations. So, one solution consists in extracting the variations as a function of time and add them to the previous simulation.

## 5 Conclusion

We have proposed, in this paper, a way of modeling a PLL with VHDL-AMS and we also gave the methodology for extracting the high level model parameters. We have observed a good agreement between the settling time extracted with the low-level and high-level models.

However, the main limitation is that the fitting factors of the high-level must be extracted for each filter and/or $\Delta\Sigma$/accumulator configuration. This means that a new set of intermediate-level simulations has to be run, if a parameter other than the charge pump current or division ratio is changed. This part of the work is planned so that the model can become portable.

## Acknowledgments

The authors would like to thank the CIM-PACA design platform for their support.

## References

[1] B. Nicolle et al, "VHDL-AMS modeling of a multistandard Phase Locked Loop ", *ICECS 2005 Proceeding*, p.33-36.
[2] Pamarti, Jansson, Galton, "A Wideband 2.4GHz Delta Sigma Fractional N PLL with 1Mb/s in loop modulation", *IEEE Journal of Solid State Circuits*, vol. 39, no. 1, January 2004, pp. 4962.
[3] Application notes for ADS Software "PLL Transient Response Simulation", *Tutorial*
[4] P. E. Allen, "CMOS phase locked loops" Lecture 130, 2003.
[5] E. Juarez-Hernandez and A. Diaz-Sanchez, " A novel CMOS charge-pump circuit with positive feedback for PLL applications", *Electro 2001*.

# Low Power and Low Jitter Wideband Clock Synthesizers in CMOS ASICs

Régis Roubadia[1], Sami Ajram[2], and Guy Cathébras[3]

[1] ATMEL Rousset, Avenue Olivier Perroy, ZI Rousset,
13106 Rousset, France
regis.roubadia@rfo.atmel.com
[2] E32 Parc Dromel, 13009 Marseille
sami.ajram@libertysurf.fr
[3] LIRMM, 161 rue Ada, 34392 Montpellier Cedex 5
cathebras@lirmm.fr

**Abstract.** This paper introduces two low power design techniques to improve both the jitter and phase noise of PLL frequency synthesizers used in ASICs. These techniques focus on the noise current reduction in wideband ring VCOs. Two PLLs embedding such VCOs were implemented, in $0.18\,\mu$m and $0.13\,\mu$m CMOS technologies, under 1.8 V and 1.2 V supply voltages respectively. The maximum improvement was observed for a 1.8 V PLL running at 160 MHz and consuming 1.6 mW, which phase noise was reduced from $-81.4\,$dBc/Hz to $-88.4\,$dBc/Hz.

## 1 Introduction

The design of low jitter clock synthesizers, as an embedded solution in CMOS technology usually requires a proportional increase in both die area and power consumption. In CMOS ASICs, where the required frequency range can be large (typically from several tens of MHz to 1 GHz), and where both the power consumption and die area are limiting factors, the preferred strategy for clock synthesis and management is the use of very versatile and configurable PLL-based frequency synthesizers (figure 1).

To achieve such performances, the design of wideband low jitter VCOs is required. Therefore, in terms of VCO design, the trend is oriented toward using high frequency range ring oscillators. The use of high quality integrated LC VCOs, which area is very important, and which frequency range is very short, is limited to very high frequencies (typically > 1 GHz) and very low jitter clocks, for which the power consumption is not a concern. However, special design techniques can be used to allow ring VCOs to achieve better jitter performance without increasing power consumption. Two of these techniques are presented here : the source degeneration technique, and the phase realignment technique. This paper is divided into three main sections :

- Section 2 shows the dependence of both phase noise and jitter on power consumption in ring VCOs.
- Section 3 and 4 explain the two jitter reduction techniques, and show their efficiency with PLL silicon results.

J. Vounckx, N. Azemard, and P. Maurine (Eds.): PATMOS 2006, LNCS 4148, pp. 458–467, 2006.

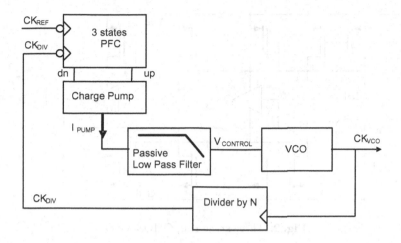

**Fig. 1.** PLL-based frequency synthesizer. Power consumption and clock jitter are mainly determined by the VCO.

## 2    Minimizing Jitter Under Constraints of Frequency and Power Consumption in Ring VCOs

Figure 2 shows the implementation of a typical three stage ring VCO. $V_{ctl}$ is the control voltage of the VCO. It is converted to a control current $I_{ctl}$ by a voltage to current converter; $I_{ctl}$ modulates the time delay of each inverter of the ring. $C_L$ is the load capacitor at the output node of each inverter. Therefore, the oscillation frequency of a N stage ring is given by [1]:

$$f_{out} = \frac{1}{2N\tau} \tag{1}$$

Where $\tau$ is the time delay of a single inverter. Assume that $V_{swing}$ is the oscillation voltage amplitude, and $q_{swing} = C_L V_{swing}$, then the rise/fall time $t_r$ is given by:

$$t_r = \frac{q_{swing}}{I_{ctl}} \tag{2}$$

As $\tau$ is proportional to $t_r$, we get:

$$f_{out} \propto \frac{I_{ctl}}{2N q_{swing}} \tag{3}$$

The ring power consumption is also proportional to $I_{ctl}$, and to the power supply voltage $V_{dd}$:

$$P = N I_{ctl} V_{dd} \tag{4}$$

Equations 3 and 4 show that, for a given $I_{ctl}$, if the number of stage $N$ decreases, $P$ decreases whereas $f_{out}$ increases. In ring oscillators, the minimum number of

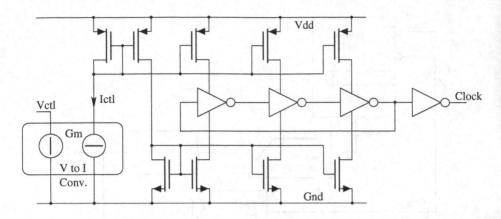

**Fig. 2.** Three stage ring CMOS VCO

stages is 3 [1]. Therefore, the three stage ring VCO offers the better trade-off between oscillation frequency and power consumption.

We will then address the problem of minimizing the jitter of a three stage ring VCO for a given oscillation frequency and a fixed power consumption. Jitter in VCOs is a parasitic variation of the oscillation period (time domain); the relation between phase error/noise and jitter is simply given by:

$$Phase\,error = 2\pi\,Jitter\,f_{out} \tag{5}$$

Phase noise is caused mainly by the electronic noises of the VCO devices. In CMOS technology, the dominant noises are flicker and thermal noises [1]. As the VCO is a loop system, these noises accumulate over time, and degrade the phase noise performance of the system [2]: this is why VCOs are usually the biggest phase noise/jitter contributors in PLLs.

To find the relation between jitter and power consumption, we will use the results of the Impulse Sensitivity Function (ISF) theory developed in Hajimiri's publications [2], [3]. The ISF is a periodic function (having the same period as the output signal of the VCO) that gives the phase shift caused by an impulse current injected in the VCO. Assume that this impulse current is a noise current, then the resulting phase shift will be phase noise. Thus, knowing the ISF and the noise currents allows to compute the VCO phase noise. For ring VCOs, the RMS value of the ISF is given by [3]:

$$\Gamma_{rms} \propto \sqrt{\frac{2\pi^2}{3N^3}} \tag{6}$$

Assuming that:
- $\Delta f$ is the frequency offset from the carrier $f_{out}$;
- $L(\Delta f)$ is the single-side-band phase noise in dBc/Hz at $f_{out} + \Delta f$;
- $\Gamma_{rms}$ is RMS value of the ISF;
- and, finally, $\overline{I_n^2}$ is the single-side-band power spectral density of the noise current in a single inverter.

Phase noise is given by [3]:

$$L(\Delta f) \propto \frac{N\Gamma_{rms}^2 \overline{I_n^2}}{8\pi^2 \Delta f^2 q_{swing}^2} \tag{7}$$

Combining equations (3), (4), (6) and (7) we get:

$$L(\Delta f) \propto \frac{N^2 Vdd^2 f_{out}^2}{3\Delta f^2 P^2}\overline{I_n^2} \tag{8}$$

Using (4), we can reformulate equation (8) in a more general form that makes the inverse of the signal to noise ratio $\overline{I_n^2}/I_{ctl}^2$ appear:

$$L(\Delta f) \propto \frac{f_{out}^2}{3\Delta f^2}\frac{\overline{I_n^2}}{I_{ctl}^2} \tag{9}$$

Equations (8) and (9) show that, when the number of stages, $V_{dd}$ and the oscillation frequency are given, the phase noise mainly depends on power consumption and current noise. It appears clearly from equation (8) that, in case of low-power design, the current noise should be minimized: the two following sections present two techniques to minimize this noise current.

# 3   The Source Degeneration Technique

Figure 3 shows the principle of the source degeneration technique. Passive resistances are connected to the sources of the transistors of a current mirror. We will now show that a current mirror with source degeneration (figure 3(b)) can have a lower output noise current than the conventional current mirror (figure 3(a)). Assuming that $g_{ma}$ and $g_{mb}$ are the respective transconductances of the

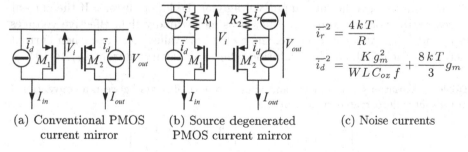

(a) Conventional PMOS          (b) Source degenerated          (c) Noise currents
    current mirror                 PMOS current mirror

**Fig. 3.** Noise sources in a conventional and a source degenerated current mirror: $i_r$ and $i_d$ are the root spectral density of, respectively, the resistor noise current and the transistor noise current. The later has two components: flicker noise and white noise. In the given formulas: $k$ is the Boltzmann constant; $T$ is the absolute temperature; $K$ is a process-dependent constant; $WLC_{ox}$ is the gate oxide capacitance of the transistor and $g_m$ is its transconductance, depending on the operating point.

transistors of figure 3(a) and 3(b), we can write down the output noise currents of the two structures as:

$$\left(\overline{i_{out}^2}\right)_a = 2\left(\frac{K\,g_{ma}^2}{(WL)_a C_{ox} f} + \frac{8kT}{3}g_{ma}\right) \tag{10}$$

$$\left(\overline{i_{out}^2}\right)_b = 2\left(\frac{K\left(\frac{g_{mb}}{1+g_{mb}R}\right)^2}{(WL)_b C_{ox} f} + \frac{8kT}{3}\left(\frac{g_{mb}R}{1+g_{mb}R}\right)^2\left(\frac{3}{2R}+\frac{g_{mb}}{(g_{mb}R)^2}\right)\right) \tag{11}$$

Clearly, these noises have a flicker and a white component. Let us call $\gamma_f$ and $\gamma_w$ the respective coefficients applied on the RMS value of flicker and white noise when switching from structure 3(a) to structure 3(b). Assuming that $(WL)_a = (WL)_b$, we have:

$$\gamma_f = \frac{g_{mb}}{g_{ma}(1+g_{mb}R)} \qquad \gamma_w = \sqrt{\frac{3}{2g_{ma}R}+\frac{g_{mb}}{g_{ma}(g_{mb}R)^2}} \tag{12}$$

Assuming a strong inversion operating point, let us call $V_{effa}$ and $V_{effb}$ the effective gate voltages $(V_{gs} - V_T)$ of the transistors. Using the classical relationship $g_m = \frac{2I_d}{V_{eff}}$, we can write:

$$\gamma_f = \frac{V_{effa}}{V_{effb}+2RI_{out}} \qquad \gamma_w = \sqrt{\frac{3V_{effa}}{4RI_{out}}+\frac{V_{effa}V_{effb}}{4\left(RI_{out}\right)^2}} \tag{13}$$

To make a valid comparison, we must design the components of the two mirrors to have the same input voltage for the same output current. Indeed, this give the same minimum voltage drop at the output of the current source. In this way, we obtain $V_{effa} = V_{effb} + RI_{out}$. Then, we can show that $\gamma_f < 1$ for all values of the $\frac{RI_{out}}{V_{effa}}$ ratio; while $\gamma_w < 1$ only when $\frac{RI_{out}}{V_{effa}} < \frac{1}{\sqrt{5}-1} \approx 0.81$. Yet, VCO current sources seldom operate at constant current defined at design time... Moreover, current dynamics can be quite large. So, let us design our two mirrors to have the same input voltage for the lower current. If the current increases, the voltage drop $RI_{out}$ increases more rapidly than effective voltages $V_{effa}$ and $V_{effb}$. As a consequence, the $\gamma_f$ and $\gamma_w$ values decrease when current increases. Table 1 shows this evolution when $I_{out}$ is varying from $I_{ref}$ to $10I_{ref}$.

**Table 1.** Variations of the flicker and white noise coefficients between a conventional and a source degenerated current mirror

| $\frac{RI_{out}}{V_{effa}}@I_{ref}$ | $\frac{1}{2}$ | $\frac{2}{3}$ | $\frac{3}{4}$ | $\frac{4}{5}$ | $\frac{8}{9}$ | $\frac{9}{10}$ |
|---|---|---|---|---|---|---|
| $\gamma_f@I_{ref}$ | 0.67 | 0.60 | 0.57 | 0.56 | 0.53 | 0.53 |
| $\gamma_f@10I_{ref}$ | 0.34 | 0.26 | 0.23 | 0.22 | 0.20 | 0.20 |
| $\gamma_w@I_{ref}$ | 1.41 | 1.15 | 1.05 | 1.01 | 0.94 | 0.93 |
| $\gamma_w@10I_{ref}$ | 0.72 | 0.61 | 0.57 | 0.55 | 0.52 | 0.52 |

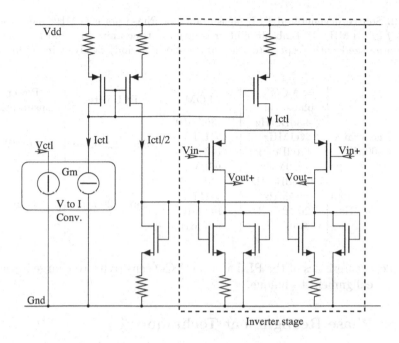

**Fig. 4.** Differential inverter stage with source degeneration

The ratio $\frac{RI_{out}}{V_{effa}}@I_{ref}$ specifies completely the design of the degenerated current source. Therefore, it appears that source degenerated current mirrors have a better noise figure than conventional ones when used with a large current dynamic. Of course this is done at the expense of a larger minimal drop voltage.

A three stage differential VCO based on this principle (figure 4) was implemented in $0.13\,\mu$m standard CMOS technology, under $1.2\,$V supply voltage. The purpose was to include this VCO in a wideband ($200$–$800\,$MHz range) low power PLL. The source degeneration technique was used for each current mirror in the ring, i.e. for the tail PMOS and load NMOS transistors of the three differential pairs.

Measurements of the VCO phase noise were done at $400\,$MHz and $800\,$MHz operating frequencies. Results given in table 2 show the improvement of figure of merit ($FOM$) at high frequencies. FOM is defined as :

$$ FOM = L(\Delta f) - 20\log\left(\frac{f_{out}}{\Delta f}\right) + 10\log\left(\frac{P}{P_0}\right) \tag{14} $$

Note : In (14), $P_0 = 1\,$mW and $FOM$ unit is dBF.

Table 2 shows that the $FOM$ improvement is about $3\,$dBF between 400MHz and 800MHz operating frequencies.

As a conclusion, the PLL jitter and power consumption performances were improved by an internal topology change of the single stage inverter in the ring VCO. The next section introduces another jitter reduction technique based on

**Table 2.** Source degenerated PLL measurements. Phase noise@1 MHz means phase noise at $f_{out} + 1\,$MHz. PLL absolute jitter is given in time units (ps) and PLL relative jitter (normalized with respect to the output clock period) is given in milliradians (mrad).

| | VCO phase noise | FOM | PLL jitter | Power consumption |
|---|---|---|---|---|
| Source degenerated PLL at 400MHz | -93dBc/Hz @1MHz -120dBc/Hz @10MHz | -136.8dBF @1MHz -143.8dBF @10MHz | 50ps/126mrad | 6.6mW |
| Source degenerated PLL at 800MHz | -93.8dBc/Hz @1MHz -120.1dBc/Hz @10MHz | -140.3dBF @1MHz -146.6dBF @10MHz | 26ps/129mrad | 14.3mW |

the loop characteristics of the PLL and the VCO sensitivity to charge injection: the phase realignment technique.

# 4   The Phase Realignment Technique

## 4.1   Phase Realignment in VCOs

The phase realignment in a VCO allows to synchronize its instantaneous phase with a sub-harmonic signal phase [4,5,6].

Figure 5 shows typical waveforms where a free running noisy VCO is periodically realigned with a reference signal. This allows a significant reduction of the PLL time response, owing to the feed-forward behavior, and a proportional increase in the PLL frequency bandwidth, which reduces both the RMS phase noise and clock jitter (see reference [4]).

It is assumed that the reference frequency is a sub-harmonic of the VCO frequency and a digital circuit allows to overcome static phase skew between the

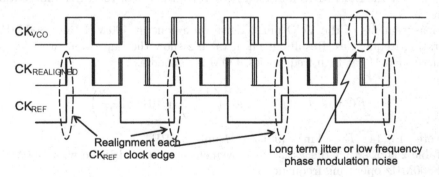

**Fig. 5.** Waveforms illustrating periodic phase realignment impact on a free running noisy VCO clock

VCO and the reference clock. The transition times of the added digital gates are also required to be negligible compared to the individual inverters that are controlled by $V_{ctrl}$.

A phase realigned VCO is based on a charge injection applied simultaneously to all ring stages in order to realize proportional phase shift of the output signal. The factor $\beta$ represents the relative phase shift of the VCO output clock $\Delta\phi$ due to realignment divided by the initial skew angle $\Delta\theta$:

$$\beta = \frac{\Delta\phi}{\Delta\theta} \tag{15}$$

The realization of a phase realigned VCO simply consists in controlling this factor $\beta$ allowing thus to determine the PLL bandwidth and loop phase margins (See references [4,5]). To achieve a stable non-null realignment factor $\beta$, it is necessary to increase the sensitivity of the ring to correlated charge injection. This requires to design inverter stages for which the rise time differs from fall time, i.e an asymmetric stage [3].

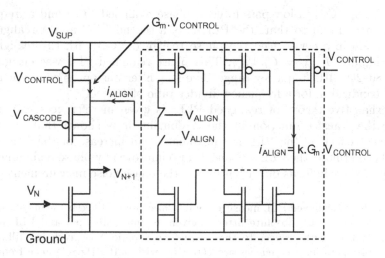

**Fig. 6.** Phase Realigned VCO single inverter

A NMOS asymmetric inverter is thus designed by controlling the bias current $G_m V_{ctrl}$ and by adding a proportional realignment feature represented by $I_{align}$ as shown in figure 6. The ring is realized with three stages and optimized to cover operating frequencies from 80 MHz to 240 MHz. This architecture provides a very stable value of realignment factor $\beta$, regardless of the process variations, and of the VCO operating frequency.

## 4.2 Phase Realigned PLL Using Phase Realigned VCO, Impact on the PLL Jitter

The implementation of the phase realigned PLL is shown on figure 7. The main loop is constituted of the main PFC (a Phase Frequency Detector), a main

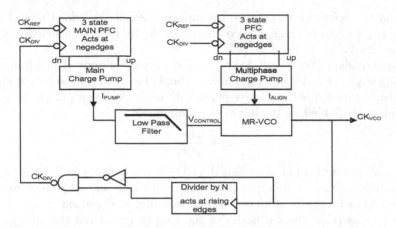

**Fig. 7.** Phase Realigned PLL

Charge Pump (CP), a low pass filter, a phase realigned VCO and a frequency divider. In addition to that, the PLL uses a second PFC and a realignment charge pump in order to feed the phase realigned VCO with the realignment current impulse $I_{align} = G_m V_{ctrl}$. This phase realigned PLL was designed to cover a 80–240 MHz frequency range. The loop filter was optimized to achieve a 100kHz bandwidth, for a frequency divider ratio of 16.

An exhaustive theory of realigned PLLs is given in references [4,5] to determine the transfer function in the Z domain: it is shown that the phase realignment effect on the PLL is equivalent to an increase of the PLL bandwidth. Furthermore, the PLL stability is also improved by phase realignment. In this paper, we only focus our attention on the phase noise measurement results

**Table 3.** Phase Realigned PLL measurements. Phase noise@100kHz means phase noise at $f_{out} + 100kHz$. PLL absolute jitter is given in time units (ps) and PLL relative jitter (normalized with respect to the output clock period) is given in milliradians (mrad). PLL operating frequencies are 160MHz (with a 10MHz reference frequency) and 240MHz (with a 15MHz reference frequency).

| | VCO phase noise | FOM | PLL jitter | Power consumption |
|---|---|---|---|---|
| Non Realigned PLL at 160MHz | -81.4dBc/Hz @100kHz | -143.4dBF @100kHz | 58ps/58mrad | 1.6mW |
| Non Realigned PLL at 240MHz | -82.7dBc/Hz @100kHz | -146.5dBF @100kHz | 36ps/55mrad | 2.4mW |
| Realigned PLL at 160MHz | -88.4dBc/Hz @100kHz | -150.4dBF @100kHz | 39ps/39mrad | 1.6mW |
| Realigned PLL at 240MHz | -88.4dBc/Hz @100kHz | -152.2dBF @100kHz | 23ps/35mrad | 2.4mW |

and on the difference between the PLL performance with or without the phase realignment.

Table 3 compares the performances of the realigned PLL, with and without the phase realignment effect. It shows that, for a phase realignment factor of 10%, the phase realigned PLL jitter is lower than the non-realigned PLL jitter. Simulations showed that, to achieve the same results as the MR-PLL with $\beta = 10\%$, the conventional PLL bandwidth should be increased from 100kHz to 200kHz. The most important result is that this jitter decrease is achieved without an increase of the power consumption: the FOM improvement is 7.4 dBF at 160 MHz and 5.7 dBF at 240 MHz when phase realignment is activated.

## 5  Conclusion

As jitter in PLLs is strongly correlated to power consumption, the design of low-power, low jitter PLLs in CMOS ASICs requires an important effort to achieve good performances, especially with the new submicronic processes, for which power supply voltage is decreasing. This paper introduced 2 examples of low-power design techniques implemented in CMOS $0.18\,\mu m$ and $0.13\,\mu m$ technologies, applied to low jitter clock synthesis. The versatility of these PLLs (wide frequency range) combined with their performances (low power, jitter, area, and voltage) make them suitable for clock management in ASIC solutions. The PLLs presented in this paper, which RMS jitter is lower than 150 mrad, are currently part of the ATMEL CMOS libraries that are used for various applications, including clock synthesis for microcontroller units, high-speed communication protocols (USB 2.0), and analog applications (reference clock for data converters).

## References

1. B.Razavi: Design of Analog CMOS Integrated Circuits. McGraw-Hill (2001)
2. A.Hajimiri, T.H.Lee: A General Theory of Phase Noise in Electrical Oscillators. IEEE Journal of Solid State Circuits **33**(2) (Feb 1998) 179–194
3. A.Hajimiri, S.Limotyrakis, T.H.Lee: Jitter and Phase Noise in Ring Oscillators . IEEE Journal of Solid State Circuits **34**(6) (Jun 1999) 790–804
4. S.Ye, L.Jansson, I.Galton: A Multiple-Crystal Interface PLL with VCO Realignment to Reduce Phase Noise. IEEE Journal of Solid State Circuits **37**(12) (Dec 2002) 790–804
5. R.Roubadia: Theory and Design of a PLL using a realigned VCO. Master's thesis, Univ. Montpellier 2 (2004)
6. R.Roubadia, S.Ajram: Multi-Phase Realigned Voltage-Controlled Oscillator and Phase-Locked Loop Incorporating the same. pending patent (apr 2004)

# Statistical Characterization of Library Timing Performance

V. Migairou[1], R. Wilson[1], S. Engels[1], N. Azemard[2], and P. Maurine[2]

[1] STMicroelectronics Central CAD & Design Solution,
850 rue Monnet, 38926, Crolles, France
[2] LIRMM, UMR CNRS/Université de Montpellier II, (C5506),
161 rue Ada, 34392, Montpellier, France

**Abstract.** With the scaling of technology, the variability of timing performances of digital circuits is increasing. In this paper, we propose a first order analytical modeling of the standard deviations of basic CMOS cell timings. The proposed model is then used to define a statistical characterization protocol which is fully compliant with standard characterization flows. Validation of this protocol is given for a 90nm process.

## 1 Introduction

With the scaling of technology, digital circuits are being designed to operate at ever increasing clock frequencies. At the same time, process fabrication uncertainties are becoming more important resulting in larger parameter variations and thus in larger timing performance variations. Within this context, the verification before fabrication of the circuit timings, which has always been a critical design step, is becoming too pessimistic and inadequate.

The common way to verify the timings of a circuit, and thus to validate it, is to use the well known multiple corner (Process, Voltage, Temperature) based approach during the static timing analysis (STA). The main drawback of such an analysis lies in its conservatism [1]. If the resulting design margins guarantee obtaining high yield values, they may induce some convergence problem during the timing optimization step. The Statistical Static Timing Analysis (SSTA) [1-4] appears as a powerful alternative to reduce these design margins and also to take inter and intra-die process dispersions into account. Intra-die variability, which has become a substantial part of the overall process variability, is not modeled, resulting in an increasing loss of accuracy.

Like the traditional timing analysis STA, the main aim of SSTA is to provide timing information allowing to guarantee the functionality of a design. The main difference between STA and SSTA lies in the nature of the information reported. Indeed, statistical analysis propagates probability density function of timing performance rather than worst case timings. This constitutes a significant advantage allowing the estimation of the manufacturing yield.

However SSTA presents some drawbacks. Firstly, the timing analysis itself is, from a computation cost point of view, more expensive than the traditional corner

J. Vounckx, N. Azemard, and P. Maurine (Eds.): PATMOS 2006, LNCS 4148, pp. 468–476, 2006.

approach. Secondly, structural correlations introduced by the logic synthesis must be captured to obtain accurate *pdf* of the propagation delays [block based]. Thirdly, it requires, at the library level, an expensive characterization step.

This paper investigates the latter problem and a solution is proposed to accurately and quickly evaluate the dispersions of standard cell timing performances. In section III, first order analytical expressions of the standard deviations of CMOS cell timings are deduced from an analytical timing representation, which is briefly introduced in section II. Section IV is then dedicated to the validation of the resulting expressions and to the analysis of their properties. These properties are then exploited to define a statistical characterization protocol of CMOS cells. Finally a conclusion is drawn in section VI. Note that to facilitate the reading, table 1 lists all the notations used in the paper.

**Table 1.**

| Symbol | Definition | Dim. |
|--------|-----------|------|
| Vdd | Supply voltage | V |
| $C_L$ | Total output load capacitance | fF |
| $T_{OX}$ | Gate oxide thickness | µm |
| $Vtn/p$ | Threshold voltage of N and P transistors | V |
| $\alpha_{n/p}$ | Velocity saturation index of N and P transistors | - |
| vs | Saturation velocity | m/s |
| L | Transistor length | µm |
| $W_{N/P}$ | N and P transistor width respectively | µm |
| $DW_{HL/LH}$ | Digital weights of a logic gate [5] | - |
| $\tau_{N/P}$ | Metrics of the timing performance of a process | ps |
| $C_{N/P}$ | Gate capacitance of N and P transistors | fF |
| $T_{HL/LH}$ | Propagation delay of a cell | ps |
| $\tau_{OUTHL/LH}$ | Falling and rising output transition time | ps |

## 2  Analytical Timing Representation

Modeling the transistor as a current generator [5], the output transition time of CMOS primitives can directly be obtained from the modeling of the (dis)charging current that flows during the switching process of the structure and from the amount of charge ($C_L \cdot V_{DD}$) to be transferred from the output to the supply rails as :

$$\tau_{outHL} = {C_L \cdot V_{DD}}\Big/{I_{MAX}} \tag{1}$$

where $I_{MAX}$ is the maximum current available in the structure. The key point here is to evaluate this maximum current which depends on the input controlling condition and also on the output load value. For that, two domains have to be considered: the Fast input and the Slow input range.

In the *Fast input ramp domain*, the high slew rate of the incoming signal forces the structure to provide all the current it can deliver [5]. As a result, the switching current has a maximum and constant value which can easily be obtained from the alpha power law model [6]:

$$I_{MAX}^{Fast} = v_s \cdot C_{ox} \cdot W_N \cdot (V_{DD} - V_{tn})^{\alpha_n} \tag{2}$$

## a. Output transition time modeling

Combining then (1) and (2) finally leads to the output transition time expression associated to the Fast input ramp range

$$\tau_{outHL}^{Fast} = \tau_N \cdot \frac{DW_{HL} \cdot Cl}{C_N} = \frac{DW_{HL} \cdot Cl \cdot V_{DD}}{v_s \cdot C_{ox} \cdot W_N \cdot (V_{DD} - V_{tn})^{\alpha_n}} \tag{3}$$

As shown, this expression captures all the sensitivity of the output transition time to process parameters such as $V_T$, Cox but also on design parameters such as $C_L$ and W.

In the *Slow input ramp domain*, the maximum switching current decreases with the input ramp duration. Extending the results of [5] to general value of the velocity saturation index, the maximum switching current flowing in a CMOS structure is

$$I_{NMAX}^{Slow} = \left\{ \frac{\left( \alpha_N \cdot v_s \cdot C_{ox} \cdot W_N \right)^{\frac{1}{\alpha_n}} \cdot Cl \cdot V_{DD}^2}{\tau_{IN}} \right\}^{\frac{\alpha_n}{1+\alpha_n}} \tag{4}$$

Where $\tau_{IN}$ is the input ramp duration (the output transition time of the controlling structure). It is usually measured between 80% and 20% of $V_{DD}$ and extrapolated on the full voltage swing. Combining (1) and (3) with (5), we finally obtain a manageable transition time expression for a falling output edge in the Slow input ramp domain:

$$\tau_{outHL}^{Slow} = \left( \frac{DW_{HL} \cdot Cl \cdot \tau_{IN}^{\alpha_n} \cdot V_{DD}^{1-\alpha_n}}{\alpha \cdot v_s \cdot C_{ox} \cdot W_N} \right)^{\frac{1}{1+\alpha_n}} \tag{5}$$

with an equivalent expression for the rising edge. As expression (3), (5) constitutes an explicit expression of the output transition time in the slow input ramp domain. To conclude with the modeling of the output transition time, one can observe that in the Fast input range the transition time only depends on the output load while in the slow input range, it also depends on the input transition time duration, and is threshold voltage independent.

## b. Propagation delay modeling

The delay of a basic CMOS structure is load, gate size and input slew dependent. Following [7-8], the input slope and the I/O coupling capacitance $C_M$ can be introduced in the propagation delay as

$$T_{HL} = \frac{\tau_{in}}{\alpha_N + 1} \left( \frac{\alpha_N - 1}{2} + \frac{V_{tn/p}}{V_{DD}} \right) + \left( 1 + \frac{2C_M}{C_M + C_L} \right) \frac{\tau_{outHL}}{2} \tag{6}$$

This expression captures all the delay sensitivity of basic CMOS structures to its environment ($\tau_{IN}$, $\tau_{out}$), and also all the sensitivity to the main process parameters through the term $\tau_{out}$.

# 3 Analytical Standard Deviation Model

Normal distributions of standard cell timing performance can be obtained from the analytical model introduced in section II. More precisely, analytical expressions of propagation delay and output transition time standard deviations can be derived from the statistical error propagation expression below:

$$\sigma^2(f) = \sum_i \left\{ \left( \frac{\partial f}{\partial p_i} \right)^2 \cdot \sigma^2_{p_i} \right\} + \sum_{i\langle j} \sum_j 2 \cdot \left( \frac{\partial f}{\partial p_i} \right) \left( \frac{\partial f}{\partial p_j} \right) \cdot cov(p_i, p_j) \tag{7}$$

where $f$ stands for the timing performance under consideration (propagation delay or output transition time, $p_i$ are the process parameters and $cov(p_i, p_j)$ is the co-variance between process parameters $p_i$ and $p_j$.

**a- Output transition time standard deviation**
The output transition time model introduced in section II clearly distinguishes two kinds of behaviours for any CMOS cell: one for fast input ramp domain, and another one for slow input ramp domain.

In the *Fast input ramp domain,* it appears following (3) that output transition time does only depend on two geometrical process parameters (W and $C_{ox}$) and one electrical process parameter (Vt). Combining expressions (7) and (3) leads to the following normalized expression of the output transition time standard deviation:

$$\frac{\sigma(\tau_{out}^{Fast})}{\tau_{out}^{Fast}} = \left\{ \begin{array}{l} \dfrac{\sigma^2(W)}{W^2} + \dfrac{\alpha^2 \cdot \sigma^2(V_t)}{(V_{DD} - V_t)^2} + \dfrac{\sigma^2(C_{ox})}{C_{ox}^2} \\[2mm] + 2 \cdot \left[ \begin{array}{l} -\dfrac{\alpha \cdot Cor(W,V_t) \cdot \sigma(W) \cdot \sigma(V_t)}{W \cdot (V_{DD} - V_t)} + \\[2mm] \dfrac{Cor(W,C_{ox}) \cdot \sigma(C_{ox}) \cdot \sigma(W)}{C_{ox} \cdot W} - \dfrac{\alpha \cdot Cor(C_{ox},Vt) \cdot \sigma(C_{ox}) \cdot \sigma(V_t)}{C_{ox} \cdot (V_{DD} - V_t)} \end{array} \right] \end{array} \right\}^{\frac{1}{2}} \tag{8}$$

where $\sigma(V_t)$, $\sigma(1/T_{ox})$, $\sigma(W)$, are respectively the standard deviation of the threshold voltage, the oxide thickness and the width of the transistor, and $Cor(p_i, p_j)$ are the correlation factors between two process parameters $p_i$ and $p_j$.
Following the same reasoning to determine the standard deviation of the output transition time in the *Slow input ramp domain,* we have obtained the following expression:

$$\frac{\sigma(\tau_{out}^{Slow})}{\tau_{out}^{Slow}} = \frac{1}{1+\alpha} \cdot \left\{ \frac{\sigma^2(W)}{W^2} + \frac{\sigma^2(C_{ox})}{C_{ox}^2} + 2 \cdot \frac{Cor(W,C_{ox}) \cdot \sigma(C_{ox}) \cdot \sigma(W)}{C_{ox} \cdot W} \right\}^{\frac{1}{2}} \tag{9}$$

Note that expression (10) does not depend on the threshold voltage standard deviation resulting in a simpler expression than (9). This was expected from (6) which is threshold voltage independent.

## b- Propagation delay standard deviation

Assuming, without loss of generality, that output load value is greater that the I/O coupling capacitance $C_M$ (see (6)), we obtained the expression of the propagation delay standard deviation in the *Fast input ramp domain*:

$$
\frac{\sigma(T)}{\tau_{out}^{Fast}} = \frac{1}{2} \cdot \left\{
\begin{aligned}
& \left[ \frac{\sigma^2(W)}{W^2} + \frac{\sigma^2(C_{ox})}{C_{ox}^2} + \left[ \frac{\tau_{IN}}{V_{DD} \cdot \tau_{out}^{Fast}} + \left( \frac{\alpha}{V_{DD} - V_t} \right) \right]^2 \cdot \sigma^2(V_t) \right. \\
& \left. + \frac{2 \cdot Cor(W, C_{ox}) \cdot \sigma(W) \cdot \sigma(C_{ox})}{W \cdot C_{ox}} \right] \\
& - \left[ \frac{\tau_{IN}}{V_{DD} \cdot \tau_{out}^{Fast}} + \left( \frac{\alpha}{V_{DD} - V_t} \right) \right] \cdot \sigma(V_t) \cdot \\
& \left( \frac{2 \cdot Cor(W, V_t) \cdot \sigma(W)}{W} + \frac{2 \cdot Cor(V_t, C_{ox}) \sigma(C_{ox})}{C_{ox}} \right)
\end{aligned}
\right\}^{\frac{1}{2}}
\tag{10}
$$

and in the *Slow one*:

$$
\frac{\sigma(T)}{\tau_{out}^{Slow}} = \frac{1}{2} \cdot \left\{
\begin{aligned}
& \left[ \left( \frac{1}{1+\alpha} \right)^2 \cdot \left( \frac{\sigma^2(W)}{W^2} + \frac{\sigma^2(C_{ox})}{C_{ox}^2} + \frac{2 \cdot Cor(W, C_{ox}) \cdot \sigma(W) \cdot \sigma(C_{ox})}{W \cdot C_{ox}} \right) \right. \\
& \left. + \left[ \frac{\tau_{IN}}{V_{DD} \cdot \tau_{out}^{Slow}} \right]^2 \cdot \sigma^2(V_t) \right] \\
& - \frac{\tau_{IN}}{V_{DD} \cdot \tau_{out}^{Slow}} \cdot \sigma(V_t) \cdot \\
& \left( \frac{2 \cdot Cor(W, V_t) \cdot \sigma(W)}{(1+\alpha) \cdot W} + \frac{2 \cdot Cor(V_t, C_{ox}) \sigma(C_{ox})}{(1+\alpha) \cdot C_{ox}} \right)
\end{aligned}
\right\}^{\frac{1}{2}}
\tag{11}
$$

## c- Discussion

In the two preceding paragraphs, we have deduced, from a first order timing representation, analytical expressions of the normalized (with respect to the nominal output transition time of the considered cell) standard deviation of both propagation delay and output transition time. If this choice may appear arbitrary, it leads to an interesting result.

Indeed, eq. (9) and (10) show that the normalized standard deviation of the output transition times does not depend on the output load and input ramp values. Similarly the normalized standard deviation of the propagation delay only depends on process parameters and on the input to output ramp duration ratio ($\tau_{IN}/\tau_{OUT}$). In other words, it is possible to extract from electrical simulations, unique normalized standard deviation curves of both propagation delay and output transition time. Since these curves are representative of the whole design space (defined by the max slew and load values) they can be efficiently exploited to speed up the statistical characterization step of library cells. Before discussing in detail the implications of this result, let us first validate it.

## 4   Validation

In order to validate the existence of these unique and representative characteristics, we extracted from electrical simulations, the standard deviations of the propagation delay and output transition time of various basic cells designed with 90nm and 65nm processes. Statistical BSIM4 model cards, in which inter-die and intra-die variations are characterized separately, were used to perform these simulations.

The simulated values, obtained for a wide range of output load ($C_L$=1fF to 660fF ) and input ramp values ($\tau_{IN}$= 1ps to 1ns), have allowed plotting the evolutions of the normalized standard deviations with respect to the input to output ramp duration ratio ($\tau_{IN}/\tau_{OUT}$). Fig.1 is typical illustration of the evolutions for various standard cells designed with 90nm process.

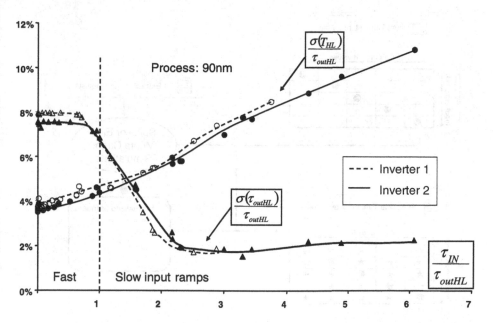

**Fig. 1.** $\sigma(T_{HL})/T_{HL}$ and $\sigma(\tau_{outHL})/\tau_{outHL}$ of two different inverters designed with a 90nm process

As expected from the preceding discussion, the normalized values of $\sigma(T_{HL})$ and $\sigma(\tau_{outHL})$ obtained, for a given inverter, and for various loading and controlling conditions belong to the same curves.

However the evolution of the output transition time standard deviation exhibits a linear behaviour (for $\tau_{IN}/\tau_{OUT}$ values ranging between 1 and 2.5) which is not captured by expressions (9) and (10). This linear behaviour corresponds to the transition from the fast input ramp domain to the slow one. Despite this lack of the model, the existence of a unique characteristic is verified by simulation validating thus the existence of unique standard deviation characteristics.

## 5  Statistical Characterization of Library Timing Performances

As mentioned in section III, the existence of these characteristic curves can be exploited to speed up the statistical characterization of library timing performances. Indeed rather than performing Monte Carlo simulations to evaluate the standard deviations of the timings for every $(\tau_{IN}, C_L)$ couple reported in the timing look up tables, one can run few Monte Carlo simulations to obtain the evolutions of the normalized standard deviations. Then, look up tables reporting the absolute values of the timing performances variability can be filled (by interpolation) from the mean values of the output transition time, usually reported in the tlf. Fig.2 illustrates the resulting characterization protocol. It goes off as explain below.

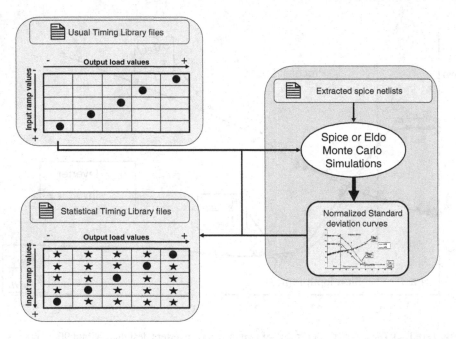

**Fig. 2.** Statistical timing performance characterization protocol

In a first step, the output load and input ramp values for which the standard cell under consideration has been characterized are extracted from the timing library format. In a second step, Monte Carlo analyses are performed in order to determine the standard deviation values for the few load values and all the input ramp values (i.e. for loading and controlling conditions identified by • in Fig.2). The choice of $C_L$ values, for which these Monte Carlo simulations are performed, is done in order to capture the minimum and maximum $(\tau_{IN}/\tau_{OUT})$ values but also the $(\tau_{IN}/\tau_{OUT})$ values ranging from 0.5 to 2.5 i.e. to properly sample the transition for the fast input ramp domain to the slow one. Note that the limit between these two domains is fully defined by the following expression [5]:

$$\tau_{IN} \geq \left(\frac{V_{DD}}{V_{DD}-V_t}\right).\tau_{out}^{Fast} \Rightarrow \frac{\tau_{IN}}{\tau_{out}^{Fast}} = \left(\frac{V_{DD}}{V_{DD}-V_t}\right) \tag{12}$$

The evolution of the normalized standard deviation is then plotted (i.e. reported in a one line look up table). Finally the statistical timing look up table is filled (by interpolation) considering the mean values of the output transition time provided by the tlf. As illustrated by Fig.2, the proposed characterization method requires 80% less Monte Carlo simulations for 5 by 5 look up tables while maintaining a high accuracy level.

The accuracy of the method is illustrated by tables 2 and 3. They give, for all inverters of 65nm library, the relative discrepancies obtained for the transition time and the delay with respect to a brute force method for which Monte Carlo simulations have been performed for all ($\tau_{IN}$, $C_L$) couples. As shown, the relative discrepancies are lower than 5% validating the proposed characterization protocol.

**Table 2.** % of error between simulated and calculated $\sigma(\tau_{OUT\ RISE})$ values

| $\tau_{IN}$(ps) / $C_L$ (fF) | 7 | 27 | 84 | 166,6 | 331,2 |
|---|---|---|---|---|---|
| 1 | 2% | 1% | 0% | 0% | 0% |
| 50 | 3% | 1% | 1% | 0% | 0% |
| 150 | 0% | 0% | 3% | 2% | 1% |
| 500 | 0% | 0% | 3% | 0% | 3% |
| 1000 | 0% | 1% | 0% | 2% | 0% |

**Table 3.** % of error between simulated and calculated $\sigma(\tau_{OUT\ FALL})$ values

| $\tau_{IN}$(ps) / $C_L$ (fF) | 7 | 27 | 84 | 166,6 | 331,2 |
|---|---|---|---|---|---|
| 1 | 1% | 0% | 0% | 0% | 0% |
| 50 | 2% | 1% | 0% | 0% | 0% |
| 150 | 1% | 0% | 1% | 1% | 0% |
| 500 | 5% | 0% | 0% | 1% | 1% |
| 1000 | 0% | 0% | 0% | 0% | 1% |

## 6 Conclusion

In this paper, we have derived from a first order analytical modeling of timing performance, a method allowing the statistical characterization of library timing performance. The proposed method presents two main advantages. Firstly, it is fully compliant with usual characterization methods and can easily be automated. Secondly, it requires a number of Monte Carlo simulations which is, in average, 80% less important than with a brute force approach, while keeping an equivalent level of accuracy (95%).

# References

[1]  C. Visweswariah. "Statistical timing of digital integrated circuits". IEEE International Solid-State Circuits Conference, CA, 2004.

[2]  A. Agarwal and al, "Statistical timing analysis for intra-die process variations with spatial correlations", ICCAD, 2003

[3]  J.Y. Le and al, "STAC: Statistical Timing Analysis with Correlation", the Design Automation Conference, June 2004.

[4]  M. Orshansky and al, "A general probabilistic framework for worst case timing analysis," DAC 2002, pp. 556-561, 2002.

[5]  P. Maurine and al, "Transition time modeling in deep submicron CMOS" IEEE Trans. on CAD, vol.21, n11, pp.1352-1363, 2002.

[6]  T. Sakurai and A.R. Newton,"Alpha-power model, and its application to CMOS inverter delay and other formulas", J. Solid State Circuits vol. 25, pp. 584-594, April 1990.

[7]  K.O. Jeppson, "Modeling the Influence of the Transistor Gain Ratio and the Input-to-Output Coupling Capacitance on the CMOS Inverter Delay", IEEE JSSC, Vol. 29, pp. 646-654, 1994.

[8]  J.M. Daga and al "Temperature effect on delay for low voltage applications", DATE, pp. 680-685, 1998, Paris.

# Exploiting Narrow Values for Energy Efficiency in the Register Files of Superscalar Microprocessors

Oğuz Ergin

Department of Computer Science
TOBB University of Economics and Technology
Sogutozu Cad. No:43, Sogutozu, 06560, Ankara, Turkey
oergin@etu.edu.tr
http://www.etu.edu.tr/~oergin

**Abstract.** Register file is a hot spot in contemporary microprocessors. As the number of instructions present in the processor at a given time increases, the size of the register file increases and it becomes a more important source of power dissipation inside the processor. Therefore it is important to pursue techniques that reduce the energy dissipation of register files. In this paper we present a technique that exploits the narrowness of the produced and consumed values in order to reduce the dynamic energy dissipation of the register file. Our technique results in 20% energy reduction in the integer register file on average.

## 1 Introduction

Modern superscalar processors use large register files in order hold the temporary values generated by the instructions. As the number of instructions inside the processor increases, the size of the register file also increases which makes it a larger source of power dissipation.

In order to exploit instruction level parallelism, superscalar microprocessors use register renaming and remove false data dependencies. Employment of register renaming technique mandates the use of large register files since every architectural register can have multiple instances. Each instruction that generates a result value allocates an available physical register at the register renaming stage of the instruction pipeline and this allocated register is released only by the instruction that renames the same architectural register [10], [11], [23]. This constraint is required in order to reconstruct the precise state in case of exceptions, interrupts and branch mispredictions. However the presence of this constraint puts more pressure on the register file since more number of registers will be needed in order to maintain high performance [22].

Contemporary microprocessors have large instruction windows (large number of instructions on flight) which put more pressure on the register file. Moreover techniques like simultaneous multithreading require more than one program states in the processor which mandates the use of more number of registers increasing the size and energy dissipation of register file even more. Therefore it is imperative to find new techniques that reduce the energy dissipation of register files.

J. Vounckx, N. Azemard, and P. Maurine (Eds.): PATMOS 2006, LNCS 4148, pp. 477–485, 2006.
© Springer-Verlag Berlin Heidelberg 2006

In this paper we propose a new technique to identify narrow values and optimize the register file to dissipate less energy when the values that require fewer bits than the full storage space of the register file are written and read.

## 1.1  Register File Energy Dissipation

Register file is build by using SRAM cells and is a major source of heat dissipation in superscalar processors. Recently, the size of the processor datapaths were increased to 64 bits widening the register files even further. In a 64-bit processor, each register file entry is composed of 64 SRAM bitcells which are in fact back to back connected inverters. Fig. 1 shows the structure of the SRAM bitcell and its connections inside the register file. The SRAM bitcell in the figure is a two ported cell; since the processor we simulated for this work is a 4 -wide P4 style machine, our register file needs 4 ports for writing and 8 ports for reading. Therefore the SRAM bitcells we used for this study are 12-ported.

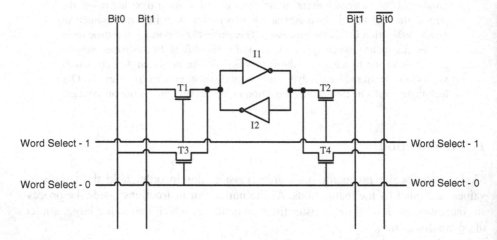

**Fig. 1.** Two-ported SRAM Bitcell

Apart from SRAM bitcells there are many components inside the register file. Register file access starts with address decoding which is done by decoder circuits (decoders). Every line has its own decoder and this decoder sends the enable signal to the word select driver if the incoming address matches the address of the entry. Once the input of the word select drivers are set, the voltage on the word select lines of the 32 bit SRAM bitcell array goes high and makes the bitcells available for either data read or a data write. If the access is for a read, the voltage on the precharged bitlines start to change and sense amplifiers pick up the small voltage difference on the bitlines. Outputs of the 32 senseamps are latched before the next clock pulse starts and the register read operation ends. If the access is for a write, bitlines are driven to corresponding voltage levels by bitline drivers. These drivers have to be strong since they may have to force the resistive voltage levels of bitcells to different values. Each of these circuit components contributes to register file energy dissipation. Especially the word line and bitline drivers dissipate a lot of energy since they have to pull a large capacitance to $V_{dd}$ level. Register file access operation is summarized in Fig. 2.

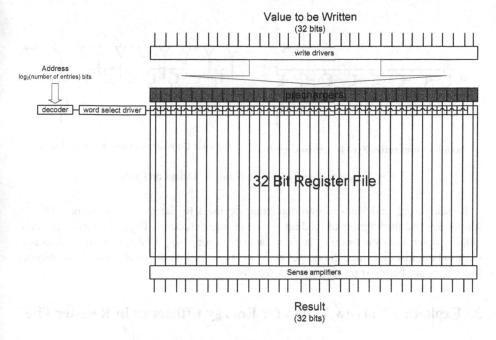

**Fig. 2.** Register File Access Chart

There are two kinds of energy dissipation in register file: leakage and dynamic. As the size of the register file increases (in terms of both number of entries and number of bits per entry) both leakage and dynamic energy dissipation increases. Exploiting narrow values can result in reduction of both static and dynamic energy dissipation. In this work we concentrate on reducing dynamic energy dissipation.

## 1.2  Narrow Values

Many produced and consumed values inside the processor pipeline contain a lot of leading zeros and ones and can be represented with less number of bits. These values store the many unneeded bits inside the 32 bit registers while wasting a lot of storage space and energy in the process. These values can be identified easily and a register file that is aware of the incoming data width can use this information for energy efficiency. The examples below show some narrow value examples, their short form and their widths:

| | | |
|---|---|---|
| 00000000000000000000000000000000 → 0 | (1 bit) |
| 00000000000000000000000000000001 → 01 | (2 bits) |
| 11111111111111111111111111111111 → 1 | (1 bit) |
| 11111111111111111111111110001010 → 10001010 | (8 bits) |

Note that the sign part of a narrow value is just compressed and it is expressed with a single bit. Since there is a bunch of these same bits in the higher order part of the value we can represent the sign part with only one bit.

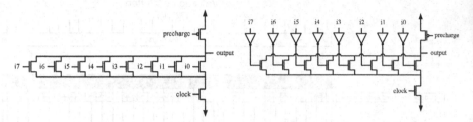

(a) 8-bit Consecutive Zero Detection Circuit    (b) 8-bit Consecutive One Detection Circuit

**Fig. 3.** Consecutive Zero (a) and One (b) Detection Circuits

Leading zero and leading one detectors are used to detect narrow values. Fig. 3 shows the circuit diagram of leading zero and one detectors. These detection circuits employ dynamic logic in order achieve fast operation. Note that n type transistors are used in both circuits since the output node has to be pulled down to ground and n-type transistors are better at passing ground signals.

## 2 Exploiting Narrow Values for Energy Efficiency in Register File

Unneeded parts of the narrow values are written to and read from the register file unnecessarily. We propose partitioning the register file and avoid wasting the energy dissipated during word selection, bit line driving and value sensing by identifying the narrow values and disabling the unnecessary part of the storage space. Once a narrow value is identified, upper order bits of the value is not written to the register file and a single bit is stored along with the value. In order to store the narrowness information a "Narrow Value Identifier" bit is added for each 32-bit stored value. This bit is set whenever a narrow value is written inside the storage space and is reset whenever a wide value is stored.

Although the register file is now divided into two parts there is still only one decoder block as shown in Fig. 4. In this example a narrow value is defined as a value that can be represented by 8 bits. Therefore the register file is divided into two parts: an 8 bit part that is always used and a 24 bit part which is used only when the stored value is wide. Every generated value is checked to determine if it can be represented with smaller number of bits. If the value is narrow, word select line of the value and the write drivers of the upper order 24 bits are not employed. This way the energy is dissipated only on the 8 bit partition which dissipates less energy on an access. The same decoder is used for both partitions but word select drivers are separate. If a value is determined to be wide, narrow value detectors provide a zero and the AND gate in the circuit enables the word select line on the 24 bit partition. There is an energy penalty when a wide value is stored since leading zero/one detectors, a multiplexer and an AND gate is added to the register file. Also the number of word select drivers are increased which increases the energy dissipation compared to the base case. However if the percentage of narrow values are significant energy savings are achieved even tough there is additional circuitry.

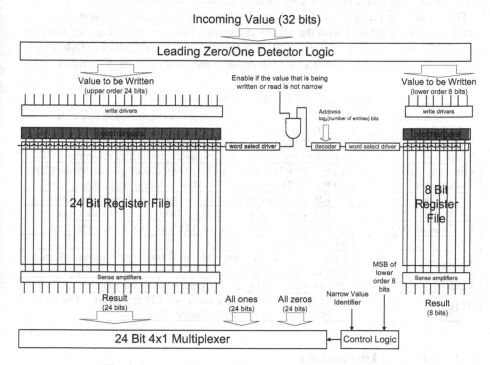

**Fig. 4.** A register file partitioned into two asymmetric parts

When a value is sought from the register file a multiplexer is used to reconstruct the stored values. If the value is wide, narrow value identifier bit is set and the control logic selects and activates the word select and senseamps of the 24 bit partition. When the narrow value identifier indicates a zero, upper order 24 bit partition is not enabled (both sensamps and word select lines are turned off), and the most significant bit of the 8-bit partition is sign-extended to find the upper order 24-bit part of the value. In order to achieve faster sign extension operation, inputs of the multiplexer is hardwired to 24-bit all ones and 24-bit all zeros. Control logic just selects the all zeros or all ones depending on the value of the sign bit in the 8-bit partition.

## 3  Simulation Methodology

In order to get an accurate idea of the percentage of narrow values inside the real processors, we used an extensively modified version of SimpleScalar simulator [3] that executes instructions in PISA format. Our simulator is mostly written in C++ and is a cycle accurate simulator that models all of the superscalar processor components.

We executed SPEC 2000 benchmarks on the simulator to observe the percentage of the narrow values in different workloads. The results from the first one billion instructions were discarded and the results from the following 200 million instructions were used. Table 1 shows the configuration of the simulated architecture.

For estimating energy dissipations inside the register file, event counts from the simulator were combined with the energy dissipations measured from actual full custom CMOS layouts of the register file. A 0.18u 6 metal layer CMOS (TSMC) technology with a $V_{dd}$ of 1.8 volts was used in order to measure the energy dissipations.

**Table 1.** Configuration of the Simulated Processor

| Parameter | Configuration |
|---|---|
| Machine width | 4-wide fetch, 4-wide issue, 4 wide commit |
| Window size | 64 entry issue queue, 64 entry load/store queue, 128–entry ROB |
| Function Units and Latency (total/issue) | 4 Int Add (1/1), 1 Int Mult (3/1) / Div (20/19), 2 Load/Store (2/1), 2 FP Add (2), 1FP Mult (4/1) / Div (12/12) / Sqrt (24/24) |
| L1 I–cache | 32 KB, 2–way set–associative, 64 byte line, 1 cycles hit time |
| L1 D–cache | 64 KB, 4–way set–associative, 64 byte line, 2 cycles hit time |
| L2 Cache unified | 2 MB , 8–way set–associative, 128 byte line, 6 cycles hit time |
| BTB | 4K entry, 2–way set–associative |
| Branch Predictor | Combined with 1K entry Gshare, 8 bit global history, 4K entry bimodal, 1K entry selector |
| Memory | 256 bit wide, 300 cycles first part, 1 cycles interpart |
| TLB | 32 entry (I) – 2-way set-associative, 128 entry (D) – 16-way set associative, 12 cycles miss latency |

## 4   Results and Discussions

Percentage of narrow values is crucial for energy savings in our technique. If the percentage of narrow values is low, energy dissipation of the register file can be increased using our technique. Luckily, as it is pointed out by many researchers before [8], [15], percentage of the narrow values in typical applications is high. Table 2 shows the percentage of narrow values. Percentage numbers are divided according to possible partitions. The column that is labeled as "1 bit" indicates the percentage of values that can be represented by 1 bit, but the column labeled as "8 bits" shows the percentage of values which are wider than 4 bits but narrower than 9 bits.

Using these percentages along with read/write statistics and the energy dissipation numbers obtained from the spice simulations of the actual circuit layouts we calculated the energy dissipated inside the register file for different register file partitions. Energy savings results are shown in Table 3. As the results reveal, there is an optimum point for the width definition for a narrow value for the best energy dissipation. As the partition becomes larger more percentage of the values are identified as narrow but the energy dissipation of the register file also increases. If the increase in partition size does not result in higher percentage of narrow values the overall energy savings starts to fade away. The optimum point seems to be 8-bits on the average while individual

**Table 2.** Percentage of Narrow Values Stored in the Register File

| # bits → | 1 bit | 2 bit | 4 bit | 8 bit | 16 bit | 24 bit | 32 bit |
|---|---|---|---|---|---|---|---|
| ammp | 8,83% | 9,17% | 1,63% | 12,87% | 13,78% | 2,97% | 50,75% |
| applu | 5,53% | 0,92% | 1,84% | 1,99% | 3,36% | 4,52% | 81,82% |
| art | 23,63% | 8,62% | 1,19% | 0,07% | 6,62% | 0,56% | 59,31% |
| bzip2 | 10,46% | 8,34% | 3,97% | 5,94% | 6,53% | 22,74% | 42,02% |
| equake | 10,65% | 8,08% | 7,43% | 9,42% | 7,78% | 5,62% | 51,02% |
| gcc | 35,74% | 0,35% | 0,10% | 1,16% | 5,34% | 0,28% | 57,02% |
| gzip | 5,20% | 5,74% | 2,81% | 19,26% | 18,10% | 12,18% | 36,71% |
| mcf | 10,53% | 12,95% | 1,32% | 6,83% | 4,57% | 3,28% | 60,52% |
| mesa | 19,10% | 4,21% | 2,11% | 2,75% | 9,53% | 8,19% | 54,10% |
| mgrid | 2,30% | 0,00% | 0,05% | 1,07% | 1,25% | 15,32% | 80,01% |
| parser | 17,84% | 4,67% | 1,73% | 11,51% | 6,70% | 9,41% | 48,14% |
| swim | 12,42% | 2,07% | 0,00% | 0,05% | 5,41% | 6,16% | 73,88% |
| twolf | 14,66% | 4,37% | 5,15% | 19,03% | 12,20% | 6,61% | 37,97% |
| vpr | 9,20% | 6,92% | 5,82% | 14,71% | 12,29% | 4,90% | 46,16% |
| wupwise | 5,58% | 0,55% | 1,11% | 0,38% | 23,46% | 30,64% | 38,28% |
| INT | 14,80% | 6,19% | 2,99% | 11,21% | 9,39% | 8,49% | 46,93% |
| FLOAT | 11,00% | 4,20% | 1,92% | 3,58% | 8,90% | 9,25% | 61,15% |
| AVG | 12,78% | 5,13% | 2,42% | 7,14% | 9,13% | 8,89% | 54,51% |

**Table 3.** Energy Savings in the Register File

| # bits | 1 | 2 | 4 | 8 | 16 | 24 |
|---|---|---|---|---|---|---|
| ammp | 8,46% | 16,69% | 16,99% | 24,12% | 22,894% | 12,181% |
| applu | 5,30% | 5,99% | 7,18% | 7,64% | 6,75% | 4,50% |
| art | 22,64% | 29,90% | 28,94% | 24,86% | 19,85% | 10,06% |
| bzip2 | 10,02% | 17,42% | 19,70% | 21,30% | 17,43% | 14,34% |
| equake | 10,21% | 17,38% | 22,65% | 26,40% | 21,45% | 12,12% |
| gcc | 34,24% | 33,47% | 31,33% | 27,72% | 21,12% | 10,63% |
| gzip | 4,98% | 10,14% | 11,91% | 24,50% | 25,28% | 15,65% |
| mcf | 10,09% | 21,77% | 21,46% | 23,47% | 17,91% | 9,77% |
| mesa | 18,30% | 21,62% | 22,00% | 20,90% | 18,65% | 11,35% |
| mgrid | 2,20% | 2,13% | 2,04% | 2,54% | 2,31% | 4,94% |
| parser | 17,09% | 20,87% | 20,98% | 26,52% | 21,00% | 12,83% |
| swim | 11,90% | 13,44% | 12,55% | 10,79% | 9,87% | 6,46% |
| twolf | 14,05% | 17,65% | 20,94% | 32,07% | 27,41% | 15,34% |
| vpr | 8,81% | 14,95% | 18,99% | 27,19% | 24,21% | 13,38% |
| wupwise | 5,35% | 5,68% | 6,26% | 5,65% | 15,37% | 15,27% |
| INT | 14,18% | 19,47% | 20,76% | 26,11% | 22,05% | 13,13% |
| FLOAT | 10,54% | 14,10% | 14,83% | 15,36% | 14,64% | 9,61% |
| AVG | 12,24% | 16,61% | 17,59% | 20,38% | 18,10% | 11,25% |

benchmarks have their own optimum points. As the table reveals, on the average across all simulated benchmarks 20% energy savings is achieved by defining a narrow value as an 8-bit value.

# 5  Related Work

Many researchers observed the presence of narrow values in some way, especially in the context of writing and reading of zero bytes [19], [21]. Also significance compression was proposed for energy efficiency by employing both hardware and compiler techniques [5], [6]. The narrowness of the values inside the processor was also used for improving performance [2], [8], [14], [15], [17]. In [16], [20], narrow values were used to reduce the complexity of the value prediction tables. Some of these works also showed that value widths are highly predictable.

Partitioning the register file, register caching and removing ports was employed to achieve energy efficiency in register file [1], [4], [7], [12], [18].

Kondo used the narrowness of the values for energy efficiency and performance by dividing 64 bit registers into 32 bit parts and allocating registers more efficiently in [13]. Each and every instruction allocates 32 bit partitions but dependents may not use both partitions when they seek the value. In some aspects our work is similar to Kondo's.

In [9], Gonzalez et al. proposed a content aware register file which is composed of multiple bank of register file. Their proposal includes 3 different register files one of which is a register file that holds the narrow values. If the register file needs to hold a wide value they use pointers from the small one to the large one.

# 6  Conclusion and Future Work

Most of the produced and consumed values inside the processor are narrow and require less space to be stored. These narrow values can be exploited to reduce the energy dissipation of data storage elements of the superscalar processors. By partitioning the register file and identifying the narrow operands it is possible to achieve 20% energy reduction in the register file. We achieved this reduction by using 8-bit narrow values.

Our analysis and approach can be used for reducing the energy dissipation of any data storage component in a processor. Some examples can be immediate field inside the issue queue and data cache. Application of our technique to these components is left for future work. Exploiting narrow values can also be used to reduce static energy of the register file by using sleep transistors on the upper order bits of the register file and turning them off when the stored value is narrow. Exploiting narrow values for static energy reduction is also left for future work.

# References

1. Borch, E., Tune, E., Manne, S., Emer, J., "Loose Loops Sink Chips", in *Proc. of International Conference on High Performance Computer Architecture (HPCA-8)*, 2002.
2. Brooks, D. and Martonosi, M., "Dynamically Exploiting Narrow Width Operands to Improve Processor Power and Performance", Proc. HPCA, 1999.
3. Burger, D. and Austin, T. M., "The SimpleScalar tool set: Version 2.0", Tech. Report, Dept. of CS, Univ. of Wisconsin-Madison, June 1997 and documentation for all Simplescalar releases (through version 3.0).

4. Butts, A., Sohi, G., "Use-Based Register Caching with Decoupled Indexing", in *Proc. of the International Symposium on Computer Architecture*, 2004.
5. Canal R., Gonzales A., and Smith J., "Very Low Power Pipelines using Significance Compression", *Proc. of the International Symposium on Microarchitecture*, 2000.
6. Canal, R., Gonzalez, A., Smith, J., "Software-Controlled Operand Gating", in *Proc. of the Intl. Symp. On Code Generation and Optimization*, 2004.
7. Cruz, J-L. et al., "Multiple-Banked Register File Architecture", in *Proc. International. Symposium on Computer Architecture (ISCA-27)*, 2000, pp. 316-325.
8. Ergin, O., et al., "Register Packing: Exploiting Narrow-Width Operands for Reducing Register File Pressure", in *MICRO*, 2004
9. Gonzalez, R., et al. "A Content Aware Register File Organization", in *ISCA*, 2004
10. Hinton, G., et al., "The Microarchitecture of the Pentium 4 Processor", *Intel Technology Journal*, Q1, 2001.
11. Kessler, R.E., "The Alpha 21264 Microprocessor", *IEEE Micro*, 19(2) (March 1999), pp. 24-36.
12. Kim, N., Mudge, T., "Reducing Register Ports Using Delayed Write-Back Queues and Operand Pre-Fetch", in *Proc. of Int.l Conference on Supercomputing (ICS-17)*, 2003.
13. Kondo, M., Nakamura, H., "A Small, Fast and Low-Power Register File by Bit-Partitioning", in *HPCA*, 2005
14. Lipasti, M., Mestan, B. R., and Gunadi, E., "Physical Register Inlining", in *ISCA*, 2004
15. Loh, G., "Exploiting Data-Width Locality to Increase Superscalar Execution Bandwidth", in *Proc. of the International Symposium on Microarchitecture*, 2002.
16. Loh, G., "Width Prediction for Reducing Value Predictor Size and Power", in First Value Pred. Wksp, ISCA 2003.
17. Nakra, T., et.al., "Width Sensitive Scheduling for Resource Constrained VLIW Processors", Workshop on Feedback Directed and Dynamic Optimizations, 2001.
18. Park, I., Powell, M., Vijaykumar, T., "Reducing Register Ports for Higher Speed and Lower Energy", in *Proc. of Intl. Symposium on Microarchitecture (MICRO-35)*, 2002.
19. Ponomarev, D., Küçük, G., Ergin, O., Ghose, K. and Kogge, P. M., "Energy Efficient Issue Queue Design", *IEEE Transactions on Very Large Scale Integration (VLSI) Systems*, Vol. 11, No.5, October 2003, pp.789-800.
20. Sato, T., Arita, I., "Table Size Reduction for Data Value Predictors by Exploiting Narrow Width Values", in *Proc. of the International Conference on Supercomputing*, 2000.
21. Villa, L., Zhang, M. and Asanovic, K., "Dynamic Zero Compression for Cache Energy Reduction", in Micro-33, Dec. 2000.
22. Wallase, S., Bagherzadeh, N., "A Scalable Register File Architecture for Dynamically Scheduled Processors", in *Proc. of International Conference on Parallel Architectures and Compilation Techniques (PACT-5)*, 1996.
23. Yeager, K., "The MIPS R10000 Superscalar Microprocessor", *IEEE Micro*, Vol. 16, No 2, April, 1996.

# Low Clock Swing D Flip-Flops Design by Using Output Control and MTCMOS[*]

Saihua Lin[1], Hongli Gao, and Huazhong Yang

[1] Electronic Engineering Department, Tsinghua University,
Beijing, China
{linsh, ggl}@mails.tinghua.edu.cn,
yanghz@tsinghua.edu.cn

**Abstract.** By using output control and MTCMOS techniques, we propose two low power low clock swing D flip-flops. Experimental results show that the leakage power of the proposed flip flops can be reduced more than an average of 59% in standby mode and in active mode the total power consumption can be reduced more than an average of 53% while the delay time stays the same. It is also show that the proposed D flip-flops can work even when the clock swing is nearly as low as $V_{dd}/3$, though the delay time is much increased.

## 1 Introduction

As feature size of the CMOS technology continues to scale down, power has become an ever-increasing important factor when designing high performance integrated circuits. The clock system is one of the most power consuming components in a VLSI system. It is reported in [1] that the clock system can consume 20%-45% of the total power dissipation in a system and in this clock system, 90% is consumed by the flip-flops themselves and the last branches of the clock distribution network which directly drives the flip-flops. As a result, reducing the power consumed by flip-flops will have a deep impact on the total power consumption.

Previously, IP_DCO_STD shown in Fig. 1 is assumed to be one of the fastest D flip-flops [2], along with a large amount of negative setup time. However, the power is large and thus makes it limited in the area of low power integrated circuit design. Thus, in [3], the authors proposed a $V_{dd}/2$ clock swing D flip flop to reduce the total power. Although considerable power can be reduced in that technique, there are glitches in the QN output of the flip-flop. Hence in this paper, we first analyze the power consumption of the flip flop and then, we propose two types of flip-flops to reduce the total power consumption. Experimental results show that the leakage power of the proposed flip flops can be reduced more than an average of 59% in standby mode and in active mode the total power consumption can be reduced more than an average of 53% while the delay time stays the same. It is also show that the proposed D flip-flops can work even when the clock swing is nearly as low as $V_{dd}/3$, though the delay time is much increased.

The rest of the paper is organized as follows. In section 2, we analyze the power consumption of IP_DCO_STD and propose the new flip flop LSM_IP_DCO and

---

[*] This work was sponsored in party by NSFC under grant #90207001.

J. Vounckx, N. Azemard, and P. Maurine (Eds.): PATMOS 2006, LNCS 4148, pp. 486–495, 2006.

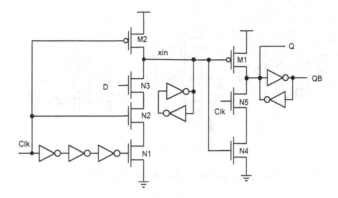

**Fig. 1.** IP_DCO_STD

S_LS_IP_DCO. In section 3, we provide the experimental results of these three flip flops and perform some discussions. Finally, in section 4, we make a conclusion of this paper.

## 2  IP_DCO_STD Analysis and Improvement

### 2.1  Power Analysis

From the BSIM MOS transistor model [4], the sub-threshold leakage current can be given by:

$$I_{DS} = I_0 e^{\left(\frac{V_{GS} - V_{th0} + \gamma V_{BS} + \eta V_{DS}}{n V_T}\right)} \left(1 - e^{-V_{DS}/V_T}\right) \tag{1}$$

where $V_T = kT/q$ is the thermal voltage, $V_{GS}$, $V_{DS}$, and $V_{BS}$ are the gate-to-source, the drain-to-source, and the bulk-to-source voltages, respectively. $\gamma$ and $\eta$ are the body effect and DIBL coefficients, respectively. $n$ is the sub-threshold slope coefficient, and $I_0 = \mu_0 C_{ox} W_{eff}/L_{eff} V_T^2 e^{1.8}$. From (1), we can find although a transistor is "off", there still exists current flowing through this transistor which results in the leakage power.

Aside from the sub-threshold leakage current in standby mode, in active mode there still exists some leakage paths. Fig. 2 shows the keeper in IP_DCO_STD. When node a is assumed to perform low to high transition, node b will perform high to low transition after the delay time of an inverter. Hence, before node b is stabilized as the low voltage 0, N0 transistor is still turned on. As a result, when node a is charged, a leakage path will exist and cause extra power consumption. Similar analysis can also be done when node a is assumed to perform high to low transition.

An even more important factor about the power consumption in IP_DCO_STD is the redundant pre-charge and discharge of the internal node xin even when the data value is constant high. For example, if D is constant high and when the first clock rising edge arrives, node xin is discharged. Then, node xin is pre-charged when the

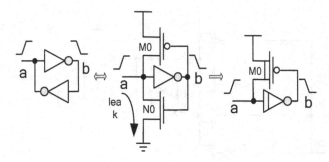

Fig. 2. Keeper Analysis in IP_DCO_STD

clock signal is low. However, since D is still high, node xin is discharge again. We can expect that if D is always high, this redundant activity can cause extra power consumption.

## 2.2  The Proposed New Low Swing D Flip-Flops

By analyzing the leakage paths of IP_DCO_STD in both active mode and in standby mode, we propose two new circuits to reduce the leakage power by using MTCMOS, as shown in Fig. 3 and Fig. 4. The inner keeper is simplified and improved for leakage reduction, as shown in Fig. 2.

For dynamic D flip-flop LSM_IP_DCO, as shown in Fig. 3, in order to eliminate the redundant switching of the internal node xin, we use the implicit conditional discharge techniques. Previously, the authors are focused on the explicit conditional discharge flip-flops and exclude the power of pulse generator for power comparison [5]. However, it is found that the pulse generator can consume considerable power and thus make explicit style of the flip flops no superior to the implicit one. What's more, if we want to use that style of the flip flops we have to design a pulse generator first, which is not very convenient. Therefore, in this paper, we propose the implicit conditional discharge flip flop.

To further reduce the total power consumption, we use the low clock swing method. Traditionally, low clock swing technique is believed to be suitable for sense amplifier based flip-flops. However, in this paper, we propose a new method so that the low clock swing is also suitable for other types of flip-flops. As shown in Fig. 3, the pre-charge transistor M2 is driven by clock traditionally. However, if the clock swing is reduced, transistor M2 can not cut off when clock is high and thus results in high leakage power. Hence, in this paper, we use the output control technique to eliminate the leakage problems. As shown in Fig. 3, the pre-charge transistor is driven by QNT now.

Although LSM_IP_DCO shown in Fig. 3 can reduce the redundant switching activity in internal node xin, many transistors are needed and thus increase the power and chip area. Hence, by analyzing the D flip-flop presented in [6] we propose a new static explicit D flip-flop, as shown in Fig. 4.

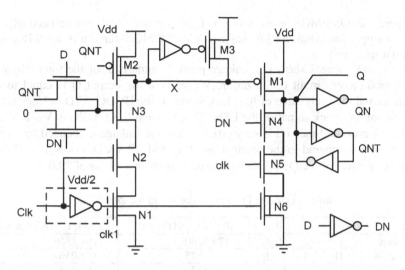

**Fig. 3.** LSM_IP_DCO

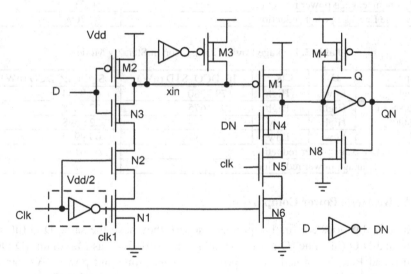

**Fig. 4.** S_LS_IP_DCO

# 3  Simulation Results

## 3.1  Standby Mode Leakage Power Comparison

The IP_DCO_STD, LSM_IP_DCO and S_LS_IP_DCO are implemented in a 0.18 μm CMOS technology and simulated using HSPICE. Two threshold voltages ($V_{th}$) are available both for NMOS transistors and PMOS transistors. High speed NMOS (PMOS) transistors feature $V_{th} = 0.1646$ V (- 0.2253 V). Low leakage NMOS (PMOS) transistors feature $V_{th} = 0.3075$ V (- 0.4555 V). The minimum length and width for high speed NMOS/PMOS transistors are 0.24 μm and 0.24 μm respectively. The minimum length and width for low leakage NMOS/PMOS transistors are 0.18 μm and 0.24 μm respectively.

Table 1 and Table 2 show the leakage power comparison of the three circuits in standby mode after circuit optimization. We assume the output Q is equal to D in these cases and the high value of the clock signal of the IP_DC_STD is $V_{dd}$ while the high value of the clock signal of the LSM_IP_DCO and S_IP_DCO is $V_{dd}/2$. We can find that the proposed method is very efficient and the leakage is reduced by an average of 59.76% compared to the original one for LSM_IP_DCO. For S_LS_IP_DCO, the leakage power reduced is even much larger, about an average of 79.07%.

**Table 1.** Leakage Power Comparison in Standby Mode

| Type | D | Clk | IP_DCO_STD (nW) | LSM_IP_DCO (nW) |
|------|---|-----|-----------------|-----------------|
| Leakage | Low | High | 179.5280 | 161.1569 |
| Power In | High | High | 191.1675 | 15.6056 |
| Standby | High | Low | 289.4279 | 15.6066 |
| Mode | Low | Low | 279.7212 | 161.1580 |
| Minimum leakage power reduction | | | | 10.23% |
| Average Leakage power reduction | | | | 59.76% |

**Table 2.** Leakage Power Comparison in Standby Mode

| Type | D | Clk | IP_DCO_STD (nW) | S_LS_IP_DCO (nW) |
|------|---|-----|-----------------|------------------|
| Leakage | Low | High | 179.5280 | 69.9954 |
| Power In | High | High | 191.1675 | 22.6688 |
| Standby | High | Low | 289.4279 | 22.6698 |
| Mode | Low | Low | 279.7212 | 69.9964 |
| Minimum leakage power reduction | | | | 61.01% |
| Average Leakage power reduction | | | | 79.07% |

## 3.2  Active Mode Power Comparison

The three D flip-flops are firstly optimized so that they have the same D-Q (hl) time (Q fall) and D-Q (hl) time (Q rise). The delay time is defined as Maximum (D-Q(hl), D-Q(lh)) and PDP is defined as the product of delay time and power. We can find LS_IP_DCO exhibits about 62.6% better performance in terms of PDP, as shown in Table 3. We also find that the proposed S_LS_IP_DCO shows an even better performance than LSM_IP_DCO in terms of PDP.

**Table 3.** Delay and Power Comparison after Optimization

| DFF | CL (fF) | D-Q(lh) (ps) | D-Q(hl) (ps) | Power (μW) | PDP (fJ) |
|-----|---------|--------------|--------------|------------|----------|
| IP_DCO_STD | 20 | 245 | 179 | 21.86 | 5.3556 |
| LSM_IP_DCO | 20 | 245 | 179 | 8.167 | 2.0031 |
| S_LS_IP_DCO | 20 | 244 | 176 | 6.877 | 1.6780 |

We further do experiments to compare the power consumptions of the three D flip-flops when different input data patterns are applied. Pattern0 represents clk = 100 MHz and D = 20 MHz, which means the typical case and the internal node xin has redundant switching activity for IP_DCO_STD. Pattern1 represents clk = 100 MHz and D = 500 MHz, which means the data changes faster than the clock signal. Pattern2 represents clk = 100 MHz and D = 50 MHz, which means the maximum switching activity of the D flip-flop. Pattern3 represents clk = 100 MHz and D = 0, which means the power is mainly due to the inverter chain. Pattern4 represents clk = 100 MHz and D = 1, which means the power is mainly due to the switching activity of internal node xin. Table 4 and Fig. 5 show the power comparison of these five cases.

From these results, we can find the new flip flops both gain an average power reduction of about 53% compared to the original one while the delay time stays the same. The minimum power reduction occurs when the input data is constant zero. In this case, the power is mainly due to the inverter chain in these flip flops. We can find that it amounts to more than one third of the total power consumption for the

**Table 4.** Power Comparison in Different Patterns

| DFF | Pattern0 (µW) | Pattern1 (µW) | Pattern2 (µW) | Pattern3 (µW) | Pattern4 (µW) |
|---|---|---|---|---|---|
| IP_DCO_STD | 21.79 | 25.43 | 28.82 | 9.975 | 2.323 |
| LSM_IP_DCO | 8.167 | 16.33 | 20.07 | 1.251 | 1.188 |
| S_LS_IP_DCO | 6.877 | 19.81 | 17.42 | 1.175 | 1.180 |
| Minimum Power Reduction for LSM_IP_DCO | 30.4% | | | | |
| Average Power Reduction for LSM_IP_DCO | 53.0% | | | | |
| Minimum Power Reduction for S_LS_IP_DCO | 22.1% | | | | |
| Average Power Reduction for S_LS_IP_DCO | 53.5% | | | | |

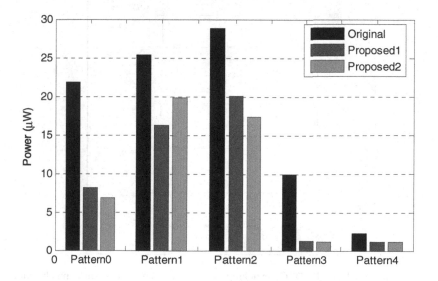

**Fig. 5.** Power consumption comparison in different data patterns

IP_DC_STD. However, by using low clock swing technique and shorten the inverter chain, the power consumed by the inverter chain is much reduced. We can also find that generally S_LS_IP_DCO shows the best performance among these three flip-flops. However, when the data frequency is larger than the clock frequency, S_LS_IP_DCO consumes more power than LSM_IP_DCO.

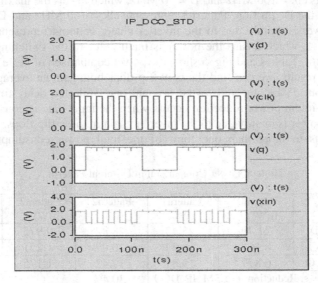

**Fig. 6.** Waveform for the IP_DCO_STD flip-flop, lots of switching activities for xin exist when D is constant high. Also some associated glitches are apparent on the output Q.

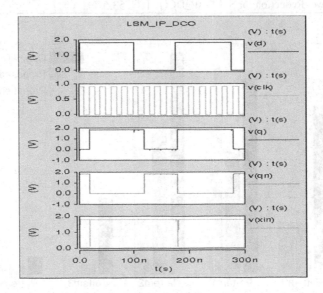

**Fig. 7.** Waveform for LSM_IP_DCO, switching activity at internal node xin is much reduced and much less glitches on output Q

Fig. 6 and Fig. 7 show the waveforms of the IP_DCO_STD and LSM_IP_DCO. We can see that the internal switching activity of LSM_IP_DCO at node xin is much less than that of the IP_DCO_STD. The glitches of the LSM_IP_DCO are mainly due to the clock feed through while the glitches of the IP_DCO_STD are due to the redundant switching activity of node xin and clock feed through.

From these figures, we can also find that the new flip-flop outputs have much less glitches than the original one when the input stays high. This is good because these glitches can cause extra power consumption of the next stage.

## 3.2   Further Discussion

As we can see, the total power consumption can be reduced if the clock swing is reduced. However, this does not mean that the total performance of the circuit can increase gradually. We will see that if the clock swing is reduced, the delay time is also increased. Hence, there are trade offs between all this factors. We will find the optimum point in the following text.

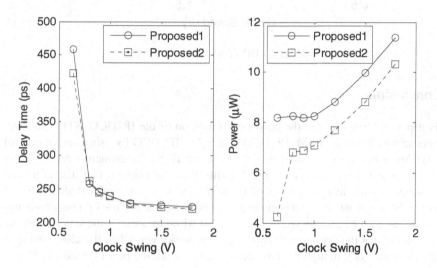

**Fig. 8.** Delay time vs. clock swing and power vs. clock swing

Fig. 8 shows the delay time and power versus clock swing respectively. As expected, as the reduction of clock swing, the power consumption is reduced and the delay time is increased. Furthermore, from Fig. 8 we can find that the delay time of LSM_IP_DCO and S_LS_IP_DCO has similar characteristic whereas the power of S_LS_IP_DCO is much less than that of LMS_IP_DCO. The lowest clock swing of the two flip-flops is 0.64 V, about $V_{dd}/3$.

When combining the curves shown in Fig. 8 we get the curve of PDP versus the clock swing as shown in Fig. 9. From this figure, it is easy to find that the minimum PDP occurs when the clock swing is around 1V but not 0.64V. Since $V_{dd} = 1.8$ V, $V_{dd}/2 = 0.9$ V is still a good point where the total performance is high in terms of PDP compared with other clock swing values.

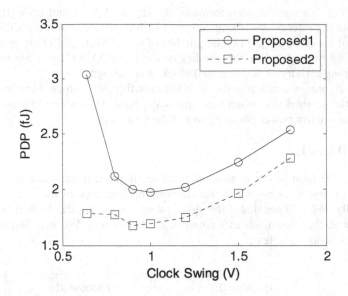

**Fig. 9.** PDP vs clock swing

## 4 Conclusion

In this paper, we first analyze the power consumption of the IP_DCO_STD and then, we propose two flip flops LSM_IP_DCO and S_LS_IP_DCO by using output control and MTCMOS to reduce the total power of the flip flop. Experimental results show that the proposed flip flops behave much better than the original one. Experimental results show that the leakage power of the proposed flip flop can be reduced by an average of 59% at least in standby mode and in active mode the total power consumption can be reduced by an average of 53% at least while the delay time stays the same. It is also show that the proposed D flip-flops can work even when the clock swing is nearly as low as $V_{dd}/3$, though the total performance is not the best in terms of PDP.

## References

[1] H. Kawaguchi and T. Sakurai, "A reduced clock-swing flip-flop(RCSFF) for 63% power reduction," *IEEE J. Solid-State Circuits*, vol. 33, pp. 807-811, May 1998.

[2] J. Tschanz, *et al.*, "Comparative delay and energy of single edge-triggered & dual edge-triggered pulsed flip-flops for high-performance microprocessors," in *Proc. ISLPED'01*, Huntington Beach, CA, Aug. 2001, pp.207-212.

[3] Saihua Lin, *et al.*, "A Vdd/2 clock swing D flip flop by using output feedback and MTCMOS,"submitted to Electronic Letters, 2006.

[4] B. J. Sheu, *et al.*, "BSIM : Berkeley short-channel IGFET model for MOS transistors," *IEEE J. Solid-State Circuits*, vol. 22, pp. 558-566, Aug. 1987.

[5] Peiyi Zhao, Tarek k. Darwish, and Magdy A. Bayoumi, "High-performance and low-power conditional discharge flip-flop," *IEEE Trans. VLSI Syst.*, vol. 12, no. 5, May, 2004, pp. 477-484.

[6] M. W. Phyu, et al., "A low-power static dual edge-triggered flip-flop using an output-controlled discharge configuration," ISCAS, 2005, pp.2429-2432.

[7] Vladimir Stojanovic and Vojin G. Oklobdzija, "Comparative analysis of master-slave latches and flip-flops for high-performance and low-power systems," *IEEE J. Solid-State Circuits*, vol. 34, no. 4, April. 1999, pp. 536-548.

[8] F. Class, *et al.*,"Semi-dynamic and dynamic flip-flops with embedded logic," in *Proc. Symp. VLSI Circuits, Dig. Tech. Papers*, June 1998, pp. 108-109.

[9] Y. Zhang, H. Z. Yang, and H. Wang, "Low clock-swing conditional-percharge flip-flop for more than 30% power reduction," *Electron. Letter.*, vol. 36, no. 9, pp. 785-786, Apr. 2000.

# Sensitivity of a Power Supply Damping Method to Resistance and Current Waveform Variations

Jürgen Rauscher and Hans-Jörg Pfleiderer

Department of Microelectronics, University of Ulm
Albert-Einstein-Allee 43, 89081 Ulm, Germany
juergen.rauscher@uni-ulm.de

**Abstract.** In this paper the influence of parameter variations to the effect of power supply noise damping in digital CMOS circuits is investigated. Splitting up the power supply path and using different additional resistors in each path combined with a slight increase of the off-chip supply voltage is found to reduce significantly power supply noise. The damping resistors are optimized using a simulated annealing schedule for the worst-case current waveform. The dependency of this approach to current waveform variations and an increased resistance due to electromigration or a higher operating temperature is examined.

## 1 Introduction

Decreased nominal supply voltage, increased frequencies, higher integration densities and limited on-chip capacitance have amplified the need for effective ways to analyze and reduce power noise. Introducing additional damping resistors in the power supply path is capable of reducing power noise [1]. This paper covers a method to insert additional damping resistors in the power supply path. For practical considerations the influence of temperature changes and electromigration (EM) has been investigated. Further the impact of switching current waveforms that differ from the ones used to optimize the damping has been investigated.

In the following a 2D signal line model is described which is used to simulate the on-chip power distribution network (PDN). An outline of the simulation method is given in Section 3. Section 4 summarizes the damping approach. The results of the sensitivity analysis can be found in Section 5.

## 2 Modeling

The whole flat on-chip PDN is modeled as a mesh of 2D signal line cells. For the further investigations an on-chip PDN is divided in 80 by 80 cells. Therefore, this results in 80 by 80 observed on-chip voltage nodes. Admittance functions $Y_x(s)$ and $Y_y(s)$ instead of lumped elements are employed to incorporate the proximity effect e.g. due to varying wire densities and widths on different metal layers as shown in figure 1. $C$ is the on-chip capacitance to ground and the

J. Vounckx, N. Azemard, and P. Maurine (Eds.): PATMOS 2006, LNCS 4148, pp. 496–503, 2006.

off-chip connection (e.g. flip-chip bump) is established with a resistor and an inductance in series which results in the current $I_{ext}$. The switching behavior of the circuit is modeled with a current source. For this purpose the current waveform of the simulated circuit block at the nominal voltage is estimated. The current waveform is then scaled linearly with $\frac{v|_{i,j}}{V_{DD}}$ which can be understood as a switching resistor model. Otherwise the simulated voltage variations would be too pessimistic because of the missing damping effect. To consider leakage currents an additional nonlinear contribution can be added up to $i_{src}$.

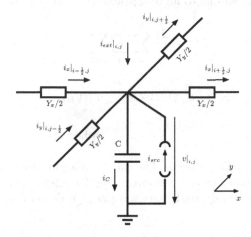

**Fig. 1.** 2D signal line cell

## 3   Simulation

Applying the modified nodal analysis on a Partial Element Equivalent Circuit (PEEC) [2] model of the on-chip PDN and using reduced order modeling [3,4] each admittance function can be written in the following form

$$Y(s) = \sum_{m=1}^{q} \frac{f_m g_m}{1 - s\lambda_m} = \sum_{m=1}^{q} \frac{I_m(s)}{V(s)}. \tag{1}$$

Thus, the $q$ first order differential equations for the currents $I_m$ can now be derived as

$$sI_m(s) = \frac{1}{\lambda_m} I_m(s) - \frac{f_m g_m}{\lambda_m} V(s) \tag{2}$$

and

$$\frac{d}{dt} i_m(t) = \frac{1}{\lambda_m} i_m(t) - \frac{f_m g_m}{\lambda_m} v(t) \tag{3}$$

respectively. The resulting system of first order differential equations for the whole PDN can be efficiently solved by discretizing the time derivatives which exhibits linear runtime behavior [4]. Since the model order $q$ is typically small (e.g. 3) the simulation time is short and enables iterative design improvements.

## 4   Damping

To reduce voltage variations to an acceptable level the following metric

$$M := \frac{\Delta t}{T} \sum_x \sum_y \sum_{t=0}^{T} m|_{i,j} \tag{4}$$

$$m|_{i,j} := \begin{cases} |(V_{DD} - v|_{i,j})|/Volts & \text{if } |(V_{DD} - v|_{i,j})| > \Delta V_{tol} \\ \\ 0 & \text{otherwise} \end{cases}$$

similar to the one in [5] is used. The safety margins for the supply voltage $V_{DD} \pm \Delta V_{tol}$ are assumed to be symmetric. Fig. 2 depicts the additional resistors $R_{damp}$ in the power supply path between package decoupling capacitance and

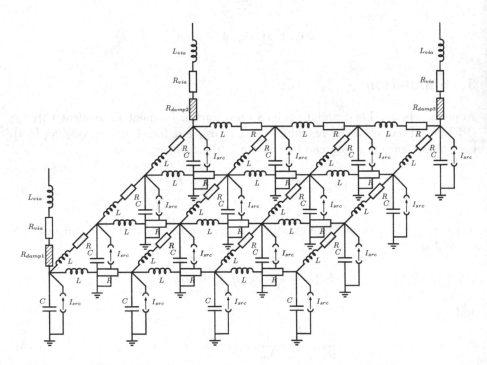

**Fig. 2.** The additional damping resistors in the model

on-chip capacitance. To overcome the additional voltage drop due to the additional resistance a slightly (e.g. 2.5%) higher off-chip voltage is necessary [6]. Since for practical purposes it is desirable to split the supply path only in a very small number of paths with different resistors, the number of different resistors is limited to three. So later it is possible to merge different off-chip connections with the same additional damping resistor. Using a simulated annealing schedule the three different values and the positions of the additional resistors are estimated so as to minimize (4) [7].

## 5   Sensitivity

The current profile A shown in figure 3 a) has been used to optimize the damping resistors. This waveform was scaled to achieve different power consumptions at specific regions of the on-chip PDN. Further, the start point of the current waveform used in the simulation was chosen randomly for such a region. In figure 4 the absolute value of the worst-case voltage variation for the 80 by 80 voltage nodes are shown. It is apparent that adding damping resistors together with a slight increase in the off-chip voltage reduces the worst-case voltage variation significantly.

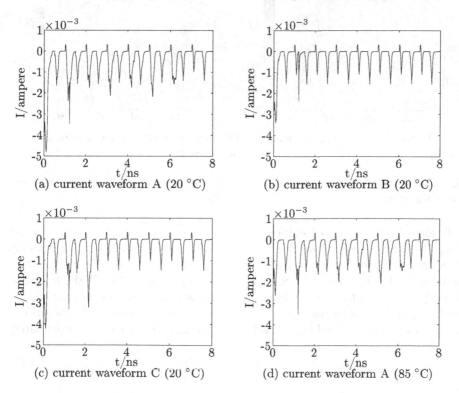

(a) current waveform A (20 °C)

(b) current waveform B (20 °C)

(c) current waveform C (20 °C)

(d) current waveform A (85 °C)

**Fig. 3.** Resulting current waveforms for the simulated circuit

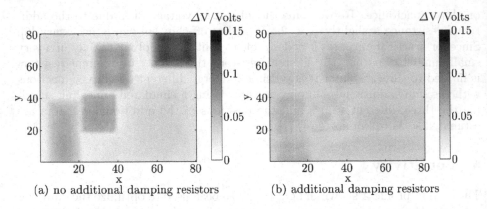

(a) no additional damping resistors

(b) additional damping resistors

**Fig. 4.** Worst-case voltage variation for the considered 80 by 80 on-chip voltage nodes using the current waveform A (20 °C)

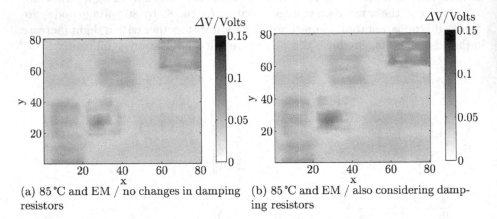

(a) 85 °C and EM / no changes in damping resistors

(b) 85 °C and EM / also considering damping resistors

**Fig. 5.** Influence of resistor variations on the damped system due to temperature and electromigration

To identify the impact of an increase in resistance due to electromigration and a high operating temperature three cases have been considered. First the on-chip PDN was optimized under the assumption that the temperature is 20 °Cand no electromigration has occurred. Second, for a temperature of 85 °Cthe temperature dependence of the on-chip interconnect resistance is included in the model. Further, a worst-case increase of the nominal metal resistance by 20% due to electromigration is considered [8]. Therefore the actual resistance is approximately given by

$$R_{\text{eff}} = R_{20\,°C}\left(1 + 4 \cdot 10^{-3}\frac{1}{°C}\left(85\,°C - 20\,°C\right)\right) \cdot 1.20 \qquad (5)$$

$$\approx R_{20\,°C} \cdot 1.5\,.$$

Additionally, the simulation for the current waveform A is repeated at 85 °C. The resulting current waveform is given in figure 3 d). Figure 5 a) shows the corresponding worst-case voltage variations. The reduction of the largest voltage variations related to the undamped system is ∼53.8% at 20 °C compared to ∼38.5% at 85 °C with electromigration. Even in the third case where the additional damping resistors vary as well the maximum voltage variation is still ∼30.8% smaller than in the undamped system (figure 5 b)). Table 1 which also summarizes the metrics, indicates that even worst-case resistance variations have limited impact to the improvements due to the additional damping.

**Table 1.** Power supply noise for the undamped and damped cases

| | Metrics | $||\Delta V/Volts|_{\max}|$ |
|---|---|---|
| no damping | 93.0 | 0.13 |
| additional damping @20 °C/no EM | $1.2 \cdot 10^{-5}$ | 0.06 |
| additional damping @85 °C/EM | 0.07 | 0.08 |
| ...also damping resistors @85 °C/EM | 0.3 | 0.09 |

Since the additional resistors were optimized for the current profile A in the following the sensitivity to discrepancies from the predicted current waveform is discussed. Figure 6 displays the voltage variations for the current waveforms B and C from figure 3 when no additional damping is provided. Using the additional damping optimized for the current waveform A results in the noise maps shown in figure 7 a) and b) respectively. In comparison to the results from the undamped model there is a reduction in the largest voltage variation by ∼44.4% for current waveform B. Examining table 2, it can be seen that the voltage disturbances here are completely within the given voltage margins (1.2 Volts ±5%). However, for the waveform C the maximum voltage variation decreases by only ∼12.5%. Optimizing the damping resistors for the waveform C results in a reduction of 18.8%. It is mandatory to use the worst-case switching pattern to estimate the damping resistors. Otherwise, the power noise might be even increased by the damping method.

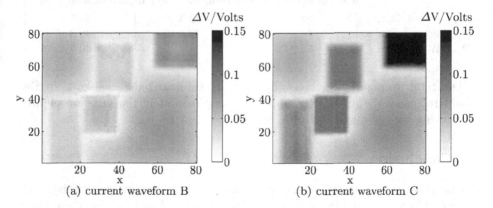

**Fig. 6.** Worst-case voltage variation for the considered 80 by 80 on-chip voltage nodes simulated with the current waveforms B and C. No additional damping.

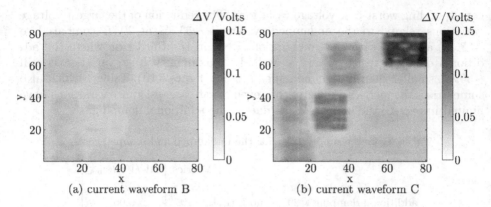

(a) current waveform B          (b) current waveform C

**Fig. 7.** Worst-case voltage variation for the considered 80 by 80 on-chip voltage nodes simulated with the current waveforms B and C. Damping resistors were optimized with current waveform A.

**Table 2.** Power supply noise results for current waveforms B and C. The additional damping resistors were optimized for current waveform A and for current waveform C.

|  | current waveform A | current waveform B | current waveform C |
|---|---|---|---|
| Metrics - no damping | 93.0 | 0.4 | 4.3 |
| $\|\Delta V/Volts\|_{max}$ | 0.13 | 0.09 | 0.16 |
| Metrics - opt. for A | $1.2 \cdot 10^{-5}$ | 0 | 1.7 |
| $\|\Delta V/Volts\|_{max}$ | 0.06 | 0.05 | 0.14 |
| Metrics - opt. for C | 0.04 | 0 | 1.5 |
| $\|\Delta V/Volts\|_{max}$ | 0.08 | 0.06 | 0.13 |

**Table 3.** Power consumption

|  | current waveform A | current waveform B | current waveform C |
|---|---|---|---|
| $P_{avg}/W$ - no damping | 54.5 | 31.3 | 43.5 |
| $P_{avg}/W$ - opt. for A | 54.6 | 29.8 | 42.3 |
| $P_{avg}/W$ - opt. for C | 52.2 | 28.8 | 40.7 |

The total average power consumptions are summarized in table 3. In the considered cases the power consumption is approximately the same or slightly lower using the optimized damping resistors.

## 6   Conclusion

The proposed damping method shows minor sensitivity to an increase of the resistance due to higher temperature and electromigration. However, the influence of current waveform variations can not be neglected in all cases. It is therefore important to choose the worst-case current waveform to determine the damping resistors.

# References

1. Waizman, A., Chung, C.Y.: Resonant free power network design using extended adaptive voltage positioning (EAVP) methodology. Trans. on Advanced Packaging **24**(3) (2001) 236–244
2. Ruehli, A.E.: Inductance calculations in a complex integrated circuit environment. IBM journal of research and development, pages 470-481 (1972)
3. Feldmann, P., Freund, R.W.: Efficient linear circuit analysis by padé approximation via the lanczos process. (1994) pp. 170–175
4. Rauscher, J., Pfleiderer, H.J.: PEEC methods in 2D signal line modeling for mid-frequency on-chip power supply noise simulations. In: 8th IEEE Workshop on Signal Propagation on Interconnects. (2004)
5. Visweswariah, C., Haring, R., Conn, A.: Noise considerations in circuit optimization. IEEE Transactions on Computer-Aided Design of Integrated Circuits and Systems **9**(6) (2000) 679–690
6. Rauscher, J., Pfleiderer, H.J.: Soc: Simulation and damping of power supply noise. In: SPIE Symp. on Smart Materials, Nano-, and Micro-Smart Systems, Sydney, Australia (2004)
7. Rauscher, J., Pfleiderer, H.J.: Power supply noise reduction using additional resistors. In: 9th IEEE Workshop on Signal Propagation on Interconnects, Garmisch-Partenkirchen (2005)
8. Mezhiba, A.V., Friedman, E.G.: Power Distribution Networks in High Speed Integrated Circuits. Kluwer Academic Publishers (2004)

# Worst Case Crosstalk Noise Effect Analysis in DSM Circuits by ABCD Modeling*

Saihua Lin and Huazhong Yang

Electronic Engineering Department, Tsinghua University,
Beijing, China
linsh@mails.tinghua.edu.cn,
yanghz@tsinghua.edu.cn

**Abstract.** In this paper, an ABCD modeling approach is proposed to model the inductive and capacitive coupling effect between the interconnect lines in DSM circuits. Then, a physical aspect model is introduced to analyze the worst case crosstalk noise effect on the delay and rise time of the driver. It is observed that the inductive coupling effect can have a great effect on the timing characteristic of the interconnect line. Experimental results show that the method proposed in this paper differs from the HSPICE simulation with an average error less than 2.5% for both the 50% delay and the rise time.

## 1 Introduction

Noise is an important parameter that has become a metric of comparable importance to area, timing, and power in digital IC design. Generally speaking, crosstalk noise has two different deleterious effects on digital circuits [1]. Firstly, when noise acts against a normally quiescent signal, it acts as a functional noise, such as undershoots, glitches. For instance, if the peak of the noise exceeds the threshold of the gate, logical errors might occur and thereby jeopardize the whole circuit's functionality and reliability. Secondly, when noise acts simultaneously or nearly simultaneously with a switching node, it acts as the timing noise, such as excessive signal delay. This increased delay may decrease the operating frequency or ultimately result in the logical error of the whole circuits. Hence, previously lots of work has been done on the crosstalk noise modeling in the DSM circuits. For instance, in [1], the authors proposed a dual-exponential noise metrics including the peak noise amplitude $V_p$, peak noise occurring time $T_p$ and pulse width $W_n$. In [3], the authors proposed a 6-node template circuit based method to calculate the noise characteristics. In [4], the authors derived a bound expression for the capacitively coupled noise voltage and in [5], the authors provided some expressions for crosstalk amplitude and pulse width in resistive, capacitively coupled lines. Recently, Ajoy K. Palit[6] proposed an ABCD modeling method to analyze the coupling crosstalk noise on the victim interconnect line in DSM chips. However, all these works do not take the inductive coupling effect into consideration whereas as the on-chip clock frequency increases, the inductive coupling effect can not be ignored any more. In [7], the authors proposed a model based

---

* This work was sponsored in party by NSFC under grand #90307016.

J. Vounckx, N. Azemard, and P. Maurine (Eds.): PATMOS 2006, LNCS 4148, pp. 504–513, 2006.

on the rigorous solution of coupled distributed *RLC* lines. However, the model is extremely complex and as such does not provide useful insight for physical design and noise optimizations.

Another problem with the pervious work is that although intensive work has been done on the crosstalk noise modeling, little is done on the crosstalk noise induced timing characteristic analysis due to its difficulty. Thus in this paper, we propose an ABCD modeling approach to model the crosstalk coupling noise on the victim interconnect line. Then, a physical model is introduced to analyze the worst case timing characteristic when considering the inductive and capacitive coupling effect.

The rest of the paper is organized as follows. In Section 2, the ABCD modeling approach to the inductance and capacitance coupled is presented. In Section 3, a novel physical model is introduced to analyze the worst case crosstalk noise effect. In Section 4, some experimental results are provided. Finally, in Section 5, we make a conclusion of this paper.

## 2  ABCD Modeling of Inductively and Capacitively Coupled Interconnects

### 2.1  ABCD Modeling Approach

Fig. 1 shows two inductively and capacitively coupled interconnect lines. The ABCD block in Fig. 1 represents the *RCG* section of $\Delta x$ -length of the interconnect line.

Considering the first ABCD block, the input-output voltage and current can be written in s-domain as:

$$\begin{bmatrix} V_{p0}(s) \\ I_{p0}(s) \end{bmatrix} = \begin{bmatrix} 1 & a \\ b & (1+ab) \end{bmatrix} \begin{bmatrix} V_{bp1}(s) \\ I_{bp1}(s) \end{bmatrix} \tag{1}$$

where $a = r\Delta x$, $b = (g+sc)\Delta x$, and $r, g, c$ are the resistance, conductance, and capacitance per unit length.

Further considering the capacitive coupling effect shown in Fig. 1, we can get:

$$V_{fp1} = V_{bp1}, I_{bp1} = I_{fp1} - c_c \cdot \Delta x \cdot s \left( V_{ap1} - V_{bp1} \right) \tag{2}$$

where $c_c$ is the coupling capacitance per unit length.

If we consider the inductive coupling effect, we get:

$$I_{fp1} = I_{p1}, U_{l1} = sl\Delta x \cdot I_{p1} + sm\Delta x \cdot I_{a1} \tag{3}$$

where $m$ is the mutual inductance per unit length, $U_{l1}$ is the voltage drop across the inductance in s-domain.

The possibilities of the input signal combinations of the aggressor line and the victim line can be grouped into three cases.

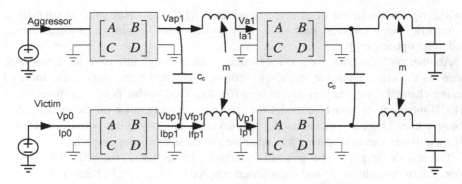

**Fig. 1.** Inductively and capacitively coupled model of an aggressor-victim system

*Case one:* Both aggressor and victim are driven by identical (synchronized) transitions i.e., both are driven by rising transitions, or both are driven by falling transitions. In such case, we can get:

$$\frac{dv_{ap1} - dv_{bp1}}{dt} = \frac{d\left(v_{ap1} - v_{bp1}\right)}{dt} = 0 \Rightarrow s\left(V_{ap1} - V_{bp1}\right) = 0, I_{bp1} = I_{fp1} \tag{4}$$

and

$$\frac{di_{a1} - di_{p1}}{dt} = \frac{d\left(i_{a1} - i_{p1}\right)}{dt} = 0 \Rightarrow sI_{a1} = sI_{p1}, U_{l1} = s\left(l + m\right)\Delta x \cdot I_{p1} \tag{5}$$

Thus when represented in the form of ABCD matrix, it follows that:

$$\begin{bmatrix} V_{fp1}(s) \\ I_{fp1}(s) \end{bmatrix} = \begin{bmatrix} 1 & s\left(l + m\right)\Delta x \\ 0 & 1 \end{bmatrix} \begin{bmatrix} V_{p1}(s) \\ I_{p1}(s) \end{bmatrix} \tag{6}$$

$$\begin{bmatrix} V_{bp1}(s) \\ I_{bp1}(s) \end{bmatrix} = \begin{bmatrix} 1 & 0 \\ 0 & 1 \end{bmatrix} \begin{bmatrix} V_{fp1}(s) \\ I_{fp1}(s) \end{bmatrix} \tag{7}$$

Thus we get the input-output voltage and current of a *RLCG* section by using ABCD representation:

$$\begin{bmatrix} V_{p0}(s) \\ I_{p0}(s) \end{bmatrix} = \begin{bmatrix} 1 & a' \\ b & \left(1 + a'b\right) \end{bmatrix} \begin{bmatrix} V_{p1}(s) \\ I_{p1}(s) \end{bmatrix} \tag{8}$$

where $a' = a + s\left(l + m\right)\Delta x$.

*Case two:* Aggressor and victim are driven by mutually opposite transitions. For example, the aggressor is driven by falling transition whereas the victim is driven by rising transition. Similarly, we get:

$$\frac{dv_{ap1} + dv_{bp1}}{dt} = \frac{dV_{dd}}{dt} = 0 \Rightarrow sV_{ap1} = -sV_{bp1}, I_{bp1} = I_{fp1} + 2c_c \cdot \Delta x \cdot sV_{bp1} \tag{9}$$

and

$$\frac{di_{a1} + di_{p1}}{dt} = \frac{d\left(i_{a1} + i_{p1}\right)}{dt} = 0 \Rightarrow sI_{a1} = -sI_{p1}, U_{l1} = s\left(l - m\right)\Delta x \cdot I_{p1} \qquad (10)$$

We can get the input-output voltage and current of a *RLCG* section by using ABCD representation at last:

$$\begin{bmatrix} V_{p0}(s) \\ I_{p0}(s) \end{bmatrix} = \begin{bmatrix} 1 & a' \\ b' & (1 + a'b') \end{bmatrix} \begin{bmatrix} V_{p1}(s) \\ I_{p1}(s) \end{bmatrix} \qquad (11)$$

where $a' = a + s\left(l - m\right)\Delta x$, $b' = b + 2sc_c\Delta x$.

*Case three:* The aggressor driver is driven by either rising or falling transition, whereas the victim line is driven by either quiescent "1", or quiescent "0". This case is more difficult because the voltage and current responses are not symmetric any more. But generally, we can still get the ABCD representation of the input-output voltage and current:

$$\begin{bmatrix} V_{p0}(s) \\ I_{p0}(s) \end{bmatrix} = \begin{bmatrix} 1 & a' \\ b' & (1 + a'b') \end{bmatrix} \begin{bmatrix} V_{p1}(s) \\ I_{p1}(s) \end{bmatrix} \qquad (12)$$

where $a' = a + s\left(l + k_1 m\right)\Delta x$, $b' = b + k_2 sc_c\Delta x$. When $k_1 = 1$ and $k_2 = 0$, this becomes the *case one* where the aggressor and the victim have synchronized identical transitions. When $k_1 = -1$ and $k_2 = 2$, this becomes the *case two* where the aggressor and the victim have the opposite transitions. For other cases, $k_1$ is an empirical parameter between -1 and 1 when considering the inductive coupling effect and $k_2$ is an empirical parameter between 0 and 2 when considering the capacitive coupling effect.

Equation (12) represents the ABCD model of the first segment of the victim line when taking into account of the inductive and capacitive coupling effect. Therefore, the entire length of the victim line can be modeled by cascading $n$ section of such ABCD blocks. As a result, the input-output voltage and current can be written as:

$$\begin{bmatrix} V_{p0}(s) \\ I_{p0}(s) \end{bmatrix} = \begin{bmatrix} 1 & a' \\ b' & (1 + a'b') \end{bmatrix}^n \cdot \begin{bmatrix} V_{pn}(s) \\ I_{pn}(s) \end{bmatrix} \qquad (13)$$

When $n \to \infty$, the ABCD matrix results in [8] :

$$\lim_{n \to \infty} \begin{bmatrix} 1 & a' \\ b' & (1 + a'b') \end{bmatrix}^n = \begin{bmatrix} \cosh\left(\gamma'd\right) & Z_0'\sinh\left(\gamma'd\right) \\ \dfrac{1}{Z_0'}\sinh\left(\gamma'd\right) & \cosh\left(\gamma'd\right) \end{bmatrix} \qquad (14)$$

and

$$\gamma' = \sqrt{\frac{a'}{b'}} = \sqrt{\frac{r + sl + sk_1 m}{g + sc + sk_2 c_c}}$$

$$Z_0' = \frac{\sqrt{a'b'}}{\Delta x} = \sqrt{\left(r + sl + sk_1 m\right)\left(g + sc + sk_2 c_c\right)} \qquad (15)$$

where $\gamma'$ is the propagation constant when considering inductive and capacitive coupling effect, $Z_0'$ is the characteristic impedance when considering inductive and capacitive coupling effect. In worst case, $k_1 = -1$ and $k_2 = 1$.

## 3  Physical Aspect Model of the Interconnect Line

In this section, we introduce a physical aspect model of the interconnect line [9]. Considering the input admittance of the interconnect line:

$$Y_{in}(s) = \frac{I_{in}(s)}{V_{in}(s)} = \frac{1}{Z_0'} \times \frac{Z_0' + Z_L \tanh(\gamma'd)}{Z_L + Z_0' \tanh(\gamma'd)} \tag{16}$$

where $Z_L = 1/sC_L$ is the load impedance. We first have to introduce two basic RLCG structures. By applying the approximation:

$$\tanh(x) \approx \frac{2x}{2+x^2} \tag{17}$$

we can expand the admittance $Y_{in} = \dfrac{q}{p \cdot Z_0' \tanh \dfrac{\gamma'd}{n}}$ into:

$$Y_{in} = \frac{1 + \dfrac{1}{2n^2}(R+sL-sM)(G+sC+2sC_c)}{\dfrac{p}{nq} \cdot (R+sL-sM)} \tag{18}$$

where $q$, $n$ and $p$ are integers.

In the viewpoint of circuit, (18) can be modeled as a RLCG parallel circuit shown in Fig. 2.

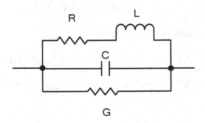

**Fig. 2.** Circuit model of (22)

Similarly, $Y_{in} = \dfrac{q}{p \cdot Z_0'} \tanh \dfrac{\gamma'd}{n}$ can be expanded into:

$$Y_{in} = \frac{\frac{q}{pn} \cdot (G + sC + 2sC_c)}{1 + \frac{1}{2n^2}(R + sL - sM)(G + sC + 2sC_c)} \tag{19}$$

where $q$, $n$, and $p$ are integers.

In the viewpoint of circuit, (19) can be modeled as a $RLCG$ circuit in series, as shown in Fig. 3.

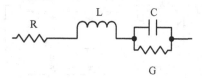

**Fig. 3.** Circuit model of (19).

By splitting (16) into two terms and further neglect the parameter $G$ in $\left(Z_0'\right)^2 / Z_L$, we can get:

$$Y_{in}(s) = \frac{1}{Z_L + Z_0' \tanh(\gamma' d)} + \frac{1}{\frac{Z_0'}{\tanh(\gamma' d)} + \frac{C_L}{C}(R + sL - sM)} \tag{20}$$

By modeling the impedance $Z_0' \tanh(\gamma' d)$ and the admittance $\tanh(\gamma' d)/Z_0'$ respectively and further using the double angle formula:

$$\tanh 2x = \frac{2 \tanh x}{1 + \tanh^2 x} \tag{21}$$

we can get the $\gamma d/2$ model of $Y_{in}$ of the $RLCG$ transmission line, as shown in Fig. 4.

By applying (17) and (21), we can get $\gamma d/4$, $\gamma d/8$...model of $Y_{in}(s)$ of the transmission line.

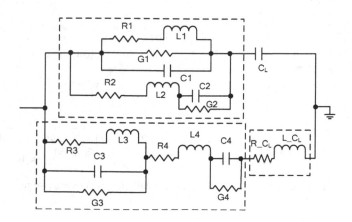

**Fig. 4.** $\gamma d/2$ model of $Y_{in}$ of the $RLCG$ transmission line

# 4  Model Verification

In this section, we first analyze the inductive coupling effect and then we provide some simulation results when the transmission lines are capacitively and inductively coupled.

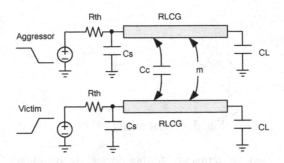

**Fig. 5.** Two coupled distributed RLCG lines

Suppose one of the interconnect line is quiescent, for example, stays at zero voltage initially. The aggressor line undergoes a rising transition. Then the crosstalk noises of the near end and the far end of the adjacent interconnect line between two models are shown in Fig. 6. The interconnect parameters are: $d = 2$ mm, $r = 1.5$ m$\Omega$/$\mu$m, $l = 0.246$ pH/$\mu$m, $c = 0.176$ fF/$\mu$m, $g = 0$, $c_s = 0$, $m = 0.0492$ pH/$\mu$m, and $c_c = 0.0176$ fF/$\mu$m.

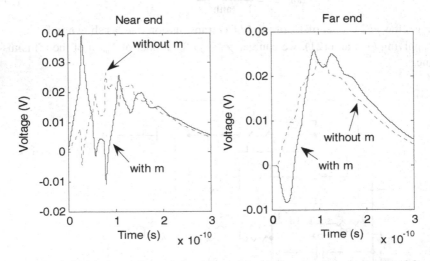

**Fig. 6.** Comparison of near end and far end crosstalk noises between two models

From Fig. 6 we can find that the inductive coupling effect has a great effect on both the near end response and the far end response of the victim line. For the near end response, this crosstalk noise can bring the nonlinear effect and the extra delay of the driver. Furthermore, this noise can be injected into the power/ground line and can affect the other parts of the whole circuit. For the far end response, if the peak of the crosstalk noise is large enough, it may result in the logical error.

**Table 1.** Comparison of 50% delay between the exact model and the $\gamma d/n$ model .The input signal parameters are $V_{dd} = 1.5$ V, $d = 2$ mm.

| $\tau$ (ps) | $R_{th}$ ($\Omega$) | $C_L$ (fF) | Exact (ps) | $\gamma d/2$ (ps) | $\gamma d/4$ (ps) |
|---|---|---|---|---|---|
| 20 | 80 | 500 | 51.22 | 53.39 | 51.98 |
| 50 | 80 | 500 | 58.29 | 58.90 | 59.10 |
| 80 | 80 | 500 | 61.44 | 62.36 | 61.24 |
| 20 | 40 | 100 | 25.50 | 24.81 | 26.24 |
| 50 | 40 | 100 | 19.25 | 19.72 | 19.43 |
| 80 | 40 | 100 | 20.19 | 20.16 | 20.17 |
| 20 | 80 | 50 | 31.56 | 33.17 | 32.08 |
| 50 | 80 | 50 | 30.85 | 30.61 | 30.88 |
| 80 | 80 | 50 | 32.39 | 32.67 | 32.63 |
| Maximum error | | | | 5.10% | 2.90% |
| Average error | | | | 2.09% | 1.07% |
| Standard deviation of error | | | | 1.68% | 0.90% |

**Table 2.** Comparison of rise time between the exact model and the $\gamma d/n$ model .The Input signal parameters are $V_{dd} = 1.5$ V, $d = 2$ mm.

| $\tau$ (ps) | $R_{th}$ ($\Omega$) | $C_L$ (fF) | Exact (ps) | $\gamma d/2$ (ps) | $\gamma d/4$ (ps) |
|---|---|---|---|---|---|
| 20 | 80 | 500 | 175.88 | 173.93 | 176.30 |
| 50 | 80 | 500 | 180.53 | 179.53 | 180.60 |
| 80 | 80 | 500 | 190.61 | 188.92 | 187.92 |
| 20 | 40 | 100 | 48.99 | 51.22 | 49.52 |
| 50 | 40 | 100 | 68.34 | 68.40 | 68.68 |
| 80 | 40 | 100 | 86.90 | 84.44 | 87.18 |
| 20 | 80 | 50 | 93.50 | 94.98 | 95.62 |
| 50 | 80 | 50 | 96.08 | 99.08 | 97.24 |
| 80 | 80 | 50 | 108.71 | 110.24 | 110.02 |
| Maximum error | | | | 4.55% | 2.27% |
| Average error | | | | 1.79% | 0.92% |
| Standard deviation of error | | | | 1.43% | 0.71% |

However, generally speaking, the peak is small and thus we mainly focus our effort on the worst case crosstalk noise effect analysis of the near end response. The interconnect parameters are: $d = 2$ mm, $r = 1.5$ m$\Omega$/$\mu$m, $l = 0.246$ pH/$\mu$m, $c = 0.176$ fF/$\mu$m, $g = 0$, $c_s = 0$, $m = 0.00492$ pH/$\mu$m, and $c_c = 0.0176$ fF/$\mu$m. The 50% delay of the near end response of the victim line is presented in Table 1.

We can find that the proposed model can maintain high accuracy when considering the worst case crosstalk effect. The results are obtained from HSPICE simulation and the exact model is assumed to be W element model in HSPICE. The highest error caused by $\gamma d/4$ model is only 2.90% while the average error is 1.07%.

We further measured the rise time of the near end response for whole waveform timing characteristic comparison. We can find that the method proposed in this paper is still very accurate when compared to the exact model. The maximum error of the $\gamma d/4$ model is 2.27% while the average error of $\gamma d/4$ model is only 0.92%.

# 5  Conclusion

In this paper, the worst case crosstalk noise effect is analyzed. At current operating frequencies, the inductive crosstalk effect can be substantial and could not be ignored any more. Thus in this paper, we propose an ABCD modeling approach to model the crosstalk noise when both considering the inductive coupling effect and capacitive coupling effect. The aggressor-victim lines are grouped into three cases according to the transition characteristics of the aggressor line and the victim line. After that, a physical model is introduced to analyze the worst case noise effect on the 50% delay and rise time. Experimental results show that the proposed method is very accurate and an average error less than 2.5% is obtained.

# References

1. A. Deutsch *et al.*, "When are Transmission Line Effects Important for On-Chip Interconnections?" *IEEE Transactions on Microwave Theory and Techniques*, Vol. 45, pp. 1836-1846, Oct. 1997.
2. Jiaxing Sun, Yun Zheng, Qing Ye, Tianchun Ye, "Worst-case crosstalk noise analysis based on dual-exponential noise metrics," in *proc VLSID'05*, pp. 348-353.
3. Li Ding, David Blaauw, and Pinaki Mazumder, "Accurate crosstalk noise modeling for early signal integrity analysis," *IEEE Trans. Computed-Aided Design of Integr. Circuits Syst.*, vol. 22, no. 5, May 2003, pp. 627-634.
4. Ashok Vittal and Malgorzata Marek-Sadowska, "Crosstalk reduction for VLSI," *IEEE Trans. Computer-Aided Design of Integr. Circuits Syst.*, vol. 16, no. 3, MARCH.1997, pp. 290-298.
5. Ashok Vittal, Lauren Hui Chen, Malgorzata marek-Sadowska, Kai-Ping Wang, and Sherry Yang, "Crosstalk in VLSI interconnections," *IEEE Trans. Computer-Aided Design of Integr.Circuits Syst.*, vol. 18, no. 12, December 1999, pp. 1817-1824.
6. Ajoy K. Palit, Volker Meyer, Walter Anheier, Juergen Schloeffel, "ABCD modeling of crosstalk coupling noise to analyze the signal integrity losses on the victim interconnect in DSM chips," *in proc VLSID'05*, pp.354-359.

7.  J. Davis and J. Meindl, "Compact Distributed RLC Interconnect Models – Part II: Coupled Line Transient Expressions and Peak Crosstalk in Multilevel Networks", *IEEE Trans. Electron Devices*, vol. 47, no. 11, Nov. 2005, pp. 2078-2087.
8.  Kaustav Banerjee, Amit Mehrotra, "Analysis of on-chip inductance effects for distributed RLC interconnects," *IEEE Trans. Computer-Aided Design of Integr.Circuits Syst.*, vol. 21, no. 8, Aug. 2002, pp. 904-915.
9.  Saihua Lin, Huazhong Yang, "A novel $\gamma d/n$ RLCG transmission line model considering complex RC(L) loads," submitted to *IEEE Trans. Computer-Aided Design of Integr.Circuits Syst.*,2006.

# A Technique to Reduce Static and Dynamic Power of Functional Units in High-Performance Processors

Guadalupe Miñana[1], José Ignacio Hidalgo[1], Oscar Garnica[1], Juan Lanchares[1], José Manuel Colmenar[2], and Sonia López[1]

[1] Departamento de Arquitectura de Computadores y Automática
[2] Ingeniería Técnica en Informática de SistemasCES Felipe II, Aranjuez Madrid
Universidad Complutense de Madrid (Spain)

**Abstract.** This paper presents a hardware technique to reduce both the static and dynamic power consumption in Functional Units of a 64-bit superscalar processor. We have studied the instructions that require an adder and we can conclude that, in 64-bit processors, there are many instructions that do not require a 64-bit adder, and that by knowing the type of operation we can also know what adder type this instruction requires. This is due that there are some types of instruction where one of the two source operands is always narrow. Our approach is based on substituting some of the 64-bit power-hungry adders by others of 32-bit and 24-bits lower power-consumption adders, and modifying the protocol in order to issue as much instructions as possible to those low power-consumption units incurring in a negligible performance penalty. We have tested four different configurations for the execution units in order to find which one obtains a higher reduction on power-consumption, preserving the performance of the processor. Our technique saves between 38,8% and a 54,1% of the power-consumption in the adders which is between 16,6% and a 23,1% of power-consumption in the execution units. This reduction is important because it can avoid the creation of a hot spot on the functional units.

## 1 Introduction

Power consumption is a main factor in the design process of high performance processors. For this reason, up to now many techniques have been explored to reduce power consumption on processors at multiple levels, such as microarchitecture, compiler, operating system and VLSI levels. Although a lot of good work had been done, there is still a long way to go. In this paper we have analyzed the use of Functional Units (FU) of Superscalar processors and we propose a microarchitecture level technique to reduce the power consumption of them analyzing which instruction is being processed.

A variety of hardware techniques have been proposed for power reduction in FUs. Brooks and Martonosi proposed to use operand values to gate off portions of the execution units [1]. Their scheme detects small values of the operand and exploits them to reduce the amount of power consumed by the execution units using an aggressive form of clock gating, disabling the upper bits of the ALUs where they are not needed.

J. Vounckx, N. Azemard, and P. Maurine (Eds.): PATMOS 2006, LNCS 4148, pp. 514–523, 2006.

A technique to exploit critical path information for power reduction was proposed by Seng et al. [2]. A set of execution units, with different power and latency characteristics is provided and the instructions are steered to these execution units based on their criticality. Specifically, the instructions predicted as critical for performance, are processed by fast and high power execution units, while the instructions predicted as not critical, are issued to slow and power-efficient execution units, thus reducing the overall power. A runtime scheme for reducing power consumption in custom logic has been also proposed in [3]. It reduces power noting that operand bit-widths are often less that the maximum data width. This technique divides the functional units into two portions - the less vs. more significant portions- and power reduction is seen if the data width fits within the less significant portion, in which case the more significant portion can be turned off, and their result bits computed by a simple sign-extension circuit instead. The work in [4] uses a similar intuition, but has different details. Haga et al. [5] presents a hardware method for functional unit assignment based on the principle that the power consumption on FUs is approximated by the switching activity of its inputs. The basic idea of this method is to reduce the number of bits whose values change between successive computations on the same functional unit.

All those methods are focused on identifying narrow-width operands. In this paper we propose a technique that reduces power consumption of the FUs using narrow operands detection. However, our technique presents one important difference from previous techniques. *Instead of checking the source operands, we look at the operation code of the instruction and sometimes, we also check just a few bits of one of the involved operands.* We have analyzed the use of 64 bit adders and we can assert that a huge amount of instructions could use a 32 bit or a 24 bit adder instead. Due to that, there are some types of instructions where one of the two source operands always is narrow. Other important question is that we propose here to *combine adders of both lengths to reduce, not only dynamic but also static power.* Experimental results shows power reductions up to 23.1% of the FU power consumption.

The rest of the paper is organized as follows. Section 2 provides an analysis of the instruction and their requirements in terms of adders. Section 3 presents our new power optimization technique. Section 4 describes the simulation methodology and tools. Section 5 presents experimental results and finally, Section 6 present some conclusions and future work.

## 2  Some Considerations About the Use of 64-Bits Adders on HPP

In this section we provide a study that shows the existence, in 64-bit processors, of a large amount of additions that do not require a 64-bit adder. We have focused on the Instruction Set Architecture (ISA) of Alpha architecture. Table 1 summarizes the subset of the Alpha architecture ISA that requires an adder. As we can see there are 7 different instructions which imply the actuation of an adder. Looking at the third column of the table we can see the length of the operand involved. From this table we can extract two conclusions. First, the operands of ARITH LONG instructions use long word data type, so they could be executed over a 32-bit adder. Second, a lot of the memory, branch and integer arithmetic instructions, where one of the source operands is either a shift or a literal constant, could be processed in a 24-bit adder instead of a 64-bits one.

Although the first idea that hints is: those instructions require a 64-bit adder because Program Counter (PC) and source registers are 64 bit width, in all of these instructions the other source operand is narrow (21 bit width for the BRA instruction type, 13 bit width for the JMP instruction type and so on). So, it is very unlike that the operation requires a full 64-bit adder, because these instructions before to be issued to the 64-bit adder, have two possibilities: The first possibility is that the operation of adding the value of the Program Counter (PC) (or Register) and the value of shift (or immediate) does not produce a carry or that if this operation produces a carry on the most significant bit of the narrow operand source (for example on 20th bit for the BRA instruction, see figure 1) it does not propagate along the whole word, until the 24th bit. In this case these instructions could be issued to a 24-bit adder. The second possibility is that this carry does not propagate along the whole word, until the 32th bit. In this other case these instructions could be issued to a 32-bit adder.

**Table 1.** Alpha processor instructions that need an adder. The third column shows the semantic of the operation.

| Instruc Type | Instruc Format | Operation |
|---|---|---|
| BRA | Branch | PC + Ext Sig(**Shift(21bits)**) |
| JMP | Memory | PC + Ext Sig(**Shift (13bits)**) |
| L/S | Memory | Rb + Ext Sig(**Shift (16bits)**) |
| LDA | Memory | Rb + Ext Sig(**Shift (16bits)**) |
| ARIT | Operate | Ra + Rb |
| ARIT_LONG | Operate | Ra(**32bits**)+Rb(**32bits**) |
| ARIT_IMM | Operate | Ra + **Immediate(8bits)** |

BRA, L/S, LDA, JMP and ARIT_IMM instructions would only require a 64-bits adder if the two following conditions are fulfilled:

1. The operation of adding the value of the Program Counter (PC) (or Register) and the value of shift (or immediate) produces a carry on the most significant bit of the narrow operand source (for example on 20th bit for the BRA instruction, see figure 1).
2. And, this carry propagates along the whole word, until the 32th bit. This happens always if the narrow operand is negative, or if it is positive and the more significant bits of the first word of the PC (or Register, depending on the operation code) are '1'. The number of significant bits depends on the operation code (for example for BRA instructions these bits are between de 21th bit and 31th bit, both include, see figure 1).

We have simulated the SPEC CPU2000 benchmark set using SimpleScalar simulator [6]. We have computed the percentage of figure 1-like cases ("special cases") for different benchmarks. These percentages are calculated regarding only to the number of additions that could be executed on a 32-bit or 24-bit adder, following the statements proposed on this paper. The average value is about *15%*. So, in order to find out the type of adder that each instruction requires, we could check the operation code and follow the next procedure:

- If the instruction is ARIT (see Table 1), it must be issued to 64-bits adder.
- If the instruction is ARIT_LONG (see Table 1), it must be issued to 32-bits adder.
- For the remaining instructions, (BRA, L/S, LDA, JMP and ARIT_IMM) we must detect the special cases of figure 1 checking the necessary bits. We have simplified the detection of the carry by checking only the most significant bit of the narrow operand and its counterpart in the other operand. This test finds more special cases than those defined on figure 1, but it is a quite simple mechanism.

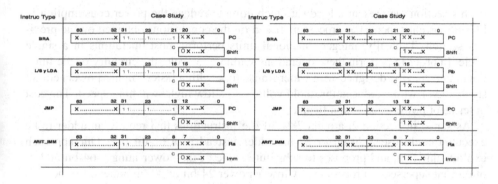

**Fig. 1.** "Special cases" when instructions cannot be issued to a 32-bit or a 24-bit adder for positive operands (left) and for negative (right). The C indicates a carry in this position and hence, the instructions cannot be issued to a small adder. X also indicates a carry.

We saw that there are a high percentage of instructions that could be executed on a 24-bit or a 32-bit adder instead of over a 64-bit adder (averaged 78,7% on both FP and integer benchmarks, 73,7% on a 24-bit adders and 4,7% on a 32-bit adder).We only would send 21,5% of the instructions to a 64-bit adder. We have observed that the percentage of instructions that could be executed on a 32-bit adder is very small, this means that if an instruction can not be issued to 24-bit adder, it can not be either issued to 32-bit adder, (only 0,4% of the instructions that can not be issued to a 24-bit adder, can be issued to a 32-bit adder). Other consideration is that ARIT_LONG instructions are only 4% of the instruction which need an adder to be processed.

Other important information that we have analyzed is the number of cycles in which there are more than one instruction that require a 64-bit or a 32-bit adder. These percentages have been calculated taking into account the total number of cycles for each benchmark. From this result we can obtain two important conclusions:

1. The averaged percentage of cycles in which there are more than one instruction that require a 64-bit is 6.2%. With this information we can try the substitution of some

of the 64-bit adders by 32-bits or 24-bit adder expecting preservation of the processors performance, except for those benchmarks with higher percentages. Anyway, we will compute all performance penalties in order to assure performance.

2. On the other hand, the averaged percentage of cycles in which there are more than one instruction that require a 32-bit is 1.5% as expected. With this information we can estimate how many 32-bit adders could be necessaries. Summing up, after analyzing those results we can establish that:

> *"although some instructions need a 64-bit adder, most of them could use a 24-bit or 32-bit adder instead with no lost of precision and these instructions can be detected by their operand code and checking a reduce number of bits".*

## 3   Power Reduction Technique

In this section we present a hardware technique to reduce the power consumption in FUs of current superscalar processors based on the conclusions obtained on the previous section. Typically, integer functional units perform most operations in a single cycle. In order to perform these operations within one cycle, the circuitry of the functional unit may be designed with wider transistors, with a faster (higher power) circuit style, and/or with a reduced threshold voltage to allow high switching speed. The cost in terms of power can be significant.

As stated in Section 2, around 78% of the instructions that require an adder to be executed could use a 24-bit or 32-bit adder instead of a 64-bit one. Our approach exploits this fact, and proposes to substitute some of the power-hungry 64-bit adders of current superscalar processors, by lower power 24-bit or 32-bit adders. We need to use the operation code of the instructions to determine the FU which will compute them. In other words, we have used a simple logic to issue an instruction to an adder.

The selection logic (arbiter), located in the issue queue, dynamically issues instructions to the available adders. In order to find out the type of adder that requires each instruction, this arbiter concurrently checks the operation code and the special cases explained on previous sections. If the adder required by the instruction is available then the instruction is issued to it. If not, the instruction is issued to the following adder available (for example, if the instruction can be executed in a 24-bit adder but there are not any of them available, the instruction is issued to 32-bit adder, if there are some of these available). We apply this policy in order to preserve performance.

## 4   Methodology

All simulations for this research were performed with a modified version of Wattch simulator [8], a framework for analyzing and optimizing microprocessor power dissipation at the microarchitecture-level. We have modified this simulator in order to calculate more accurately the power values in FUs. The changes we have implemented are:

- Wattch, in terms of consumption, considers integer execution unit just as an adder. We have included more FUs. Now the simulator models the power estimation of the integer execution unit as the addition of the power-consumption of an adder, a shifter unit, a specific unit for logic operations and a multiplier.
- The Floating Point (FP) execution unit is in the same situation. Our adaptation models power consumption on FP units as the addition of power-consumption of an FP adder and of a FP multiplier.
- We have separated total power consumption into 2 components: $P_{Dynamic}$ and $P_{Static}$. The ratio static/dynamic power-consumption is 0.33. In this way we obtain a more realistic model for current and future technologies [9].
- We have adapted clock gating in order to have the possibility of turn on/off each FU separately. For example, if a logic instruction is executing, the logic unit consumes Dynamic and Static power, while the rest of FUs consume only static power.

In order to model the effect of using 3 different adders (24-bit, 32-bit and 64-bit adders) the 64-bit adder is assigned a baseline power consumption value and the other adder power consumption are scaled down by a ratio. For the 32-bit adder we have used two reasonable ratios; $P_{32}/P_{64} = 0.5$; $P_{32}/P_{64} = 0.33$. We always consider in our simulations $P_{24}/P_{32} = 0.375$. Although these values could seem quite simplistic, we can affirm that they are correct and surely not in the best case for us. They are based on two main ideas.

First, 32-bit adder approximately dissipates half the energy than a 64-bit one (in case both adders have the same design).The origin of this reduction is the fact that in the 32-bits adder there are half the switches, –and consequently, it reduces the dynamic power-consumption– and has half the transistors –it reduces the static power-consumption–. Therefore, we can use a ratio equal 0.5. The same reasoning can be applied to $P_{24}/P_{32}$.

On the other hand, 32-bit adders are faster than the 64-bit adders (for some type of adders) [10]. However, we do not need to use the fastest 32-bit adder. In order to reduce the power-consumption even more, we can choose an adder whose critical path is very similar to the 64-bit adder critical path. This will allow us to reduce timing requirements in the 32-bit adder synthesis, and it also provides a synthesis margin to reduce the power consumption by applying two possible techniques. First, we can reduce the area, and obviously the number of gates and transistors in the design [11], or we can re-size the transistors and/or replacing some of gates by other with low-driving capabilities, so the power-consumption per gate transition is also reduced. [12]. By applying these techniques, we have estimated that a 32-bit adder could consume approximately a 33% of the 64-bit adder power consumption. So, we can use a ratio equal 0.33.

The processor model simulated can fetch 4 instructions and issue 6 instructions (4 integer, 2 FP by cycle and out-of-order. The execution unit has 4 integer ALUs, 1 integer Multiplier, 1 FP Adder and 1 FP Multiplier. Each integer ALU is made up of an adder, a shifter unit, a specific unit for logic operations.

## 5  Experimental Results

We have tested four different configurations for the execution unit in order to find which one obtains a higher reduction on power-consumption, preserving the performance of the processor. We have simulated the SPEC CPU2000 benchmarks set, with the objective of evaluate our approach. We have simulated single-sim-point regions [7] of 100M instructions, using a ref input as our default production input.

The baseline configuration has four integer ALUs, each of them has a 64-bit adder, a shifter unit and a specific unit for logic operations. Besides, there are a pipelined integer multiplier, a FP adder, and a FP pipelined multiplier. So, baseline configuration uses four 64-bit integer adders (one on each ALU). In the rest of the configuration we only have changed the number and the type of the integer adders. All of the tested configurations have at least the same number of adders as the baseline configuration in order to do not modify the performance of the processor. The rest of the configurations are:

- Conf-1: a 64-bit adder, two 32-bit adders and two 24-bit adders
- Conf-2: a 64-bit adder, one 32-bit adder and two 24-bit adders.
- Conf-3: a 64-bit adder, one 32-bit adder and three 24-bit adders.

In the Baseline configuration, all instructions that require an adder are executed in a 64-bit adder. In the rest of configurations there are instructions which exploit our proposal and they are executed in a 24-bit or 32-bits adder instead of a 64-bit one.

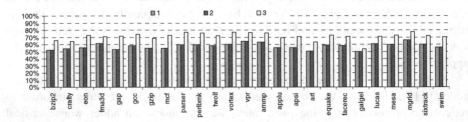

**Fig. 2.** Percentage of instructions that are executed in a 24-bits adder for every benchmark and for Conf-1, Conf-2 and Conf-3

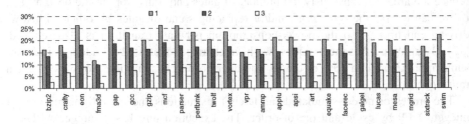

**Fig. 3.** Percentage of instructions that are executed in a 32-bits adder for every benchmark and for Conf-1, Conf-2 and Conf-3

Figure 2 shows the percentage of instructions that are executed in a 24-bit adder for every benchmark and for Conf-1, Conf-2 and Conf-3. As we can see on it, the number of accesses to 24-bit adders increases with Conf-3. This configuration shows a number of accesses to 24-bit adders very similar to the predicted one. This is because in this configuration all instructions that can use a 24-bit adder have found one available, while in Conf-1, Conf-2 there are less 24-bit adders than needed and a lot of instructions that can use 24-bit adders are finally executed in 32-bit or 64-bit adders.

Figure 3 shows the percentage of instructions that are executed in a 32-bit adder for every benchmark and for Conf-1, Conf-2 and Conf-3. As we can see on it, the number of accesses to 32-bit adders is very small in the Conf-3, as it was expected in the section 2. An important conclusion that we can obtain from this figure is that we do not need to have a lot of 32-bit adder (see Conf-3 of this graphic). It can also be observed that Conf-2 has less access 32-bit adders than Conf-1 has, whereas they have the same accesses to 24-bit adders. This is because Conf-2 uses only one 32-bit adder and the same number of 24-bit adders than Conf-1. So, some instructions that could be execute on a 24-bit or 32-bit adder are finally executed in the 64-bit adder, because they have not found one of the others available.

In order to accept any change on the cluster configuration, it is also necessary to assure that performance it is not affected. We have obtained the execution time for all benchmarks with the four different configurations, and we have observed that this technique does not affect the processor performance. The performance penalties lie between 1% and 2%.

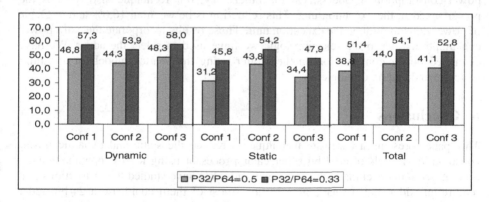

**Fig. 4.** Percentage of average Dynamic, Static and total power saved in the adders

For all the configurations, static power consumption do not depend on the benchmark, it only depends on the amount and type of adders. Obviously, all of the proposed configurations have less static power consumption than baseline configuration, because they implement only one 64-bit adder. The power consumption of the others adders is smaller. In summary, in terms of static power consumption, Conf-2 is the best configuration because it has the minimum number of 32-bit adders (one) and the minimum number of total adders (four).

With regard to dynamic power consumption in the adders, the baseline configuration has the higher dynamic power consumption because all instructions that require an adder are executed in a 64-bit adder. In the rest of configurations, dynamic power consumption is lower than the baseline configuration, because there are instructions that are executed in a 24-bit or a 32-bit adder instead of the 64-bit one. Conf-2 is the worst configuration in terms of dynamic power consumption. The reason is that, as we have say before, it has the minimum number of low power adders (one 32-bit adder and two 24-bit adders) and then, instructions that could be executed on a 24-bit or 32-bit adder are finally executed in a 64-bit adder because they have not found one of them available. On the other hand, configurations Conf-1 and Conf-3 have very similar results. It is due to: 1- the number of instructions that use 64-bits adders is the same in both configurations, 2- the difference in the number of instructions that use 24-bits adders is only 13% (see Figure 2), 3- this 13% are instructions that use 32-bits adders in Conf-1 and the difference between $P_{32}$ and $P_{24}$ it is not enough to appreciate the difference.

Figure 4 summarizes results of power-consumption saved in the adders. It shows how our technique reduces total power of the adders in all cases. Although all three configurations have very similar total power consumption figures, Conf-2 is the best for most of the benchmark. This is due to it has the smallest static consumption because the other configurations have an extra adder, and its dynamic consumption is not as far from the consumption of the other configurations. In conclusion, we can say that this extra adder contributes with more static power consumption than the amount of dynamic power consumption it saves. This is an important conclusion having in mind that static power consumption is growing on importance due to nowadays technology integration levels. Total energy saving is between an 38,8% and a 54,1% of power-consumption in adders. On the other way, our technique also reduces the power saved in the execution unit. This reduction is between an 16,6% and a 23,1% of power-consumption in the execution unit. These results incorporate the extra power consumptions due to the selection logic we have used to select the adder. We have estimated power consumption on the arbiter using the Wattch model for a similar structure and adding our logic.

## 6  Conclusions

This paper presents a hardware technique to reduce the static and dynamic power consumption in FUs of a 64-bit superscalar processor using narrow operands detection but without checking both source operands. We have studied the instructions that require an adder and we have noticed how most of them could use a 24-bit adder instead a 64-bit one, with no lost of precision. The key idea of this analysis is that we are able to know the bit-width of the adder that the instruction requires by checking the operation code of the instruction and a just few bits of one of the operands. Using this fact, we propose an approach based on substituting some of the 64-bit power-hungry adders by others with 24-bit and 32-bit lower power-consumption adders, and modifying the protocol in order to issue as much instructions as possible to those low power-consumption units incurring in a negligible performance penalty.

We have tested four different configurations for the execution unit in order to find which one obtains a higher reduction on power-consumption, preserving the performance of the system. In order to evaluate our approach we have simulated the SPEC CPU2000 benchmarks set and we have modified Wattch simulator to calculate more accurately the power values in FUs. The primary metric utilized in this paper is

Time-averaged power. Experimental Results show that our technique reduces the total power consumption of the whole execution unit. In summary, our technique saves between 38,8% and a 54,1% of the power-consumption in the adders which is between 16,6% and 23,1% of power-consumption in the execution units. Although total power is important by itself, power density is also important because if too much power is used to achieve a target delay Hot Spots can be created. So, we must also bear in mind reduction of power on functional units in order to avoid Hot Spots. We are working on applying this kind of techniques to other parts of the proceesors and we are also studying other configurations.

## Acknowledgments

This work has been supported by Spanish Government grant TIN2005-05619 of the Spanish Council of Science and Technology and UCM-Comunidad de Madrid grant 910467.

## References

1. D. Brooks and M. Martonosi. Value-based clock gating and operation packing: dynamic strategies for improving processor power and performance. ACM Transaction on Computer Systems, (2):89, 2000.
2. J. S. Seng, E. S. Tune, and D. M. Tullsen. Reducing power with dynamic critical path information. In Proceedings of the 34th annual ACM/IEEE international symposium on Micro architecture, page 114.
3. J. Choi, J. Jeon, and K. Choi. Power minimization of functional units partially guarded computation. In Proceedings of the 2000 international symposium on Low power electronics and design, pages 131–136, 2000.
4. O.-C. Chen, R.-B. Sheen, and S.Wang. A low-power adder operating on effective dynamic data ranges. IEEE Transactions on Very Large Scale Integration (VLSI) Systems, 10(4):435–453, 2002.
5. S. Haga, N. Reeves, R. Barua, and D. Marculescu. Dynamic functional unit assignment for low power. Design, Automation and Test in Europe Conference and Exhibition (DATE'03), pages 03–07, 2003.
6. T. Austin, E Larson, D.Ernst. SimpleScalar. An Infrastructure for Computer System Modelling. Computer IEEE Journal. Feb 2002, pp 59-67
7. Erez Perelman, Greg Hamerly, and Brad Calder. Picking statistically valid and early simulation points. In the International Conference on Parallel Architectures and Compilation Techniques, 2003.
8. D. Brooks, V. Tiwari, and M. Martonosi. Wattch: A framework for architectural level power analysis and optimizations. Proceedings of the 27th International Symposium on Computer Architecture, pages 83–94, 2000.
9. J. Gonzalez and K. Skadron. Power-aware design for high-performance processors. 2004 International Symposium on High-Performance Computer Architecture
10. Maldonado_Vazquez. Power-Performance Tradeoffs In Digital Arithmetic Circuits. Summer Undergraduate Program in Engineering Research at Berkeley SUPERB, Summer 2003. University of Puerto Rico- Mayaguez. Electrical Engineering.
11. S.Borkar. Desing challenges of technology scalling. IEEE Micro, (4), July 1999.
12. S.Thompson, P. Packan, and M. Bohr. MOS scaling: Transistor challenges for the 21st century. In Intel Technology Journal, 1998.

# Correct Modelling of Nested Miller Compensated Amplifier for Discrete-Time Applications

A. Pugliese, G. Cappuccino, and G. Cocorullo

Department of Electronics, Computer Science and Systems, University of Calabria,
Via P.Bucci, 42C, 87036-Rende (CS), Italy
Tel.: +39 984 494769; Fax: +39 984 494834
{a.pugliese, cappuccino, cocorullo}@deis.unical.it

**Abstract.** The nested Miller frequency compensation (NMC) for multistage amplifiers is a well-known technique used to overcome the phase margin degradation due the low-frequency poles introduced by cascading stages. The NMC exploits both the Miller capacitance-multiplier effect and the pole-splitting action. In literature NMC capacitor sizing rules have been presented to design amplifiers characterised by a third-order Butterworth unity-gain closed-loop response. In the paper, the Authors show these criteria neglecting transistor parasitic capacitances, may lead to incorrect amplifier behaviour when small load capacitances have to be driven. A developed model, allowing better pole location estimation, is also presented.

## 1 Introduction

The cascade arrangement of single amplifier stages has became more and more necessary for meeting the huge request of high-performance operational amplifiers in the present-day electronic systems. This trend is mainly caused by the unsuitability of well-established cascode design technique, which usually allows high-gain and large-swing amplifiers in CMOS low-voltage technologies [1-3]. To overcome this strong limitation, the use of a cascade of three single stages represents a solution to guarantee sufficiently-high DC gains and suitable output signal dynamic ranges with low supply voltages, limiting the power dissipation at the same time.

However, the main drawback of these amplifiers is the reduced closed-loop stability in feedback configuration for which a frequency compensation technique such as the nested Miller compensation (NMC) [1] is required. Certainly, the NMC is the reference topology to exploit the well-know Miller-effect in a multistage amplifier with more than two cascade stages. In fact, many frequency compensation techniques for multistage amplifiers proposed in literature are based on nested-Miller schemes [4].

The design of compensation network used in NMC, as well as in other compensation schemes, is usually based on simplified transfer functions of the real circuit, neglecting MOSFETs parasitic capacitances [4]. These simple functions allow primary amplifier critical aspects to be easily taken into account in the early-design stage, but

J. Vounckx, N. Azemard, and P. Maurine (Eds.): PATMOS 2006, LNCS 4148, pp. 524–531, 2006.

they may lead to inaccurate sizing of compensation network elements, with unpredictable amplifier behaviours. A typical example is the case of amplifiers driving small load capacitance, as usually occurs in discrete-time applications such as switched-capacitor (SC) circuits [5] and high speed analog-to-digital converters (ADCs) [6]. For these amplifiers classical sizing rules of compensation network elements lead to devices either with poor performance or indeed unstable. In fact, due to the small value of load capacitors imposed by speed constraint, transistor parasitic capacitances may become comparable or greater than loading one and consequently they are no longer negligible.

In this work, the design of a three-stage amplifier with NMC suitable for a SC filter is presented, showing untenability of the classical sizing criteria of the compensation network elements.

## 2  Conventional Modelling of NM Compensated Amplifiers

The scheme of a three-stage NM compensated amplifier is reported in Fig. 1.

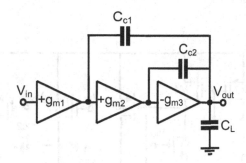

**Fig. 1.** Block diagram of three-stage operational amplifier with NMC

A study of the circuit can be found in [1]. In the latter, the multistage NMC is considered as direct extension of the two-stage Miller compensation scheme and a few of assumptions are done. First, ideal Miller integrators and a high DC gain for all stages, are assumed. Moreover, transconductance $g_{m3}$ is assumed to be greater than $g_{m1}$ and $g_{m2}$. In addition compensation capacitances $C_{c1}$ and $C_{c2}$ and load capacitance $C_L$ are supposed to be much larger than parasitic ones (these latter are related to each single amplifier stage and to inter-stage coupling). On these basis zeros introduced by feed-forward capacitor paths can be neglected (they being at higher frequency than poles) and the op-amp transfer function becomes:

$$A(s) = \cfrac{1}{\cfrac{C_{c1}}{g_{m1}}s\left(1+\cfrac{C_{c2}}{g_{m2}}s+\cfrac{C_{c2}C_L}{g_{m2}g_{m3}}s^2\right)} \tag{1}$$

In [1] the rules widely used to choose the value for compensation capacitors $C_{c1}$ and $C_{c2}$ are also presented:

$$C_{c1} = 4\frac{g_{m1}}{g_{m3}}C_L \qquad C_{c2} = 2\frac{g_{m2}}{g_{m3}}C_L. \qquad (2)$$

A so-designed amplifiers may guarantee the typical maximally flat Butterworth response in unity-feedback, with an open-loop gain-bandwidth product $GBW = g_{m1}/C_{c1}$, a phase margin of about $60°$ and two non-dominant poles with natural frequency $\omega_n = g_{mL}/\sqrt{2}C_L$ and damping factor $\zeta = 1/\sqrt{2}$.

Unfortunately, assumptions done in [1] are not always verified in real circuits. Obviously, while stage transconductances can be freely chosen on the basis of different design trade-offs (power dissipation, bandwidth, noise, maximum DC gain, and so on), load capacitance value is usually a design constraint.

For example, in discrete-time applications, amplifier typically drives a small capacitance. In this case, the role of the transistor parasitic capacitances can not be neglected with respect to the load and compensation capacitances role, as instead assumed to carry out rules (2).

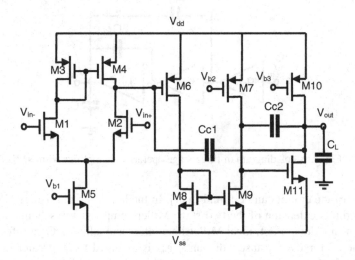

**Fig. 2.** Schematic of three-stage operational amplifier with NMC

To prove this assertion, a $0.8\mu m$ CMOS three-stage amplifier with NMC has been designed (Fig. 2). A load capacitance $C_L = 2pF$ has been considered, a typical value both for SC and ADC applications [5], [6]. The amplifier presents a total DC gain of about $103dB$ and a power consumption of $410\mu W@\pm1V$. For each stage, bias current/transconductance are $10\mu A/157\mu A/V$, $13\mu A/196\mu A/V$ and $160\mu A/1834\mu A/V$, respectively. In accord with equations (2) compensation capacitors $C_{c1}$ and $C_{c2}$ of $0.68pF$ and $0.43pF$, respectively, have to be used.

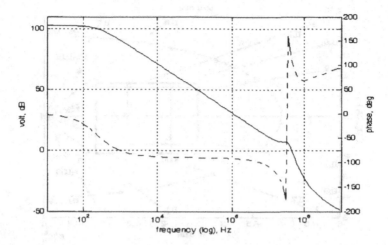

**Fig. 3.** Open-loop frequency response of the three-stage amplifier with compensation capacitances sized in accord with equations (2): magnitude plot (solid line) phase plot (dashed line)

The open-loop frequency response is reported in Fig. 3. As shown, the amplifier is unstable, resulting a negative phase margin. Evidently, the frequency compensation action carried out by $C_{c1}$ and $C_{c2}$ capacitors does not suffice to guarantee an appropriate stability margin to the amplifier in closed-loop configuration. As shown in Fig. 4, the unexpected result is mainly due to the incorrect estimation of the actual effect of compensation capacitance values on the non-dominant poles placement.

In fact, in accord with criterions reported in [1], two non-dominant poles at $\omega_n$ = 103 MHz, with a damping factor $\zeta = 1/\sqrt{2}$ and a dominant-pole in the origin exist. HSPICE simulations show instead the presence of two non-dominant poles at $\omega_n$ = 36.3 MHz, with a damping factor equal to 0.27 and a dominant pole at 253Hz .

## 3  Parasitics Inclusion in Modelling of NM Compensated Amplifiers

In the previous section, the ineffectiveness of conventional rules for sizing the compensation capacitances of NMC amplifiers driving small loads, has been highlighted. To overcome the problem, a novel model has been developed.

Fig. 5 reports the small-signal equivalent circuit of the three-stage NM compensated amplifier of Fig. 2. For each stage, transconductance, lumped parasitic output resistance and lumped load capacitance $g_{mi}$, $R_i$ $C_i$ are considered, respectively. In particular, capacitance $C_3$ includes the load capacitance $C_L$.

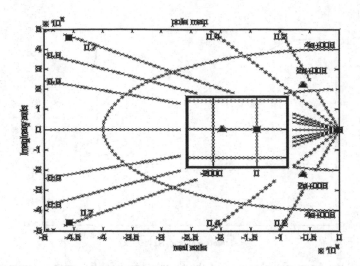

**Fig. 4.** Pole locations (rad/sec) of the three-stage amplifier with NMC (the insert in figure depicts pole locations near the origin)

■  in accord with expressions in [1]

▲  HSPICE simulation result

The circuit in Fig. 5 has a third-order transfer function given by:

$$A(s) = \frac{N(s)}{D_o(s) + C_{c1}D_1(s) + C_{c2}D_2(s) + C_{c1}C_{c2}D_3(s)} \tag{3}$$

where $N(s)$, $D_0(s)$, $D_1(s)$, $D_2(s)$, $D_3(s)$ are s-domain polynomial:

$$\begin{cases} N(s) = A_{v1}A_{v2}A_{v3} - sA_{v1}R_3(A_{v2}C_{c2} + C_{c1}) - s^2 A_{v1}R_2R_3C_{c1}(C_2 + C_{c2}) \\ D_0(s) = \Pi_{i=1..3}(1 + s\tau_i) \\ D_1(s) = s(R_1 + R_3 + R_1A_{v2}A_{v3}) + s^2(\tau_2 R_3 + \tau_3 R_1 + \tau_2 R_1) + s^3(\tau_2\tau_3 R_1 + \tau_1\tau_2 R_3) \\ D_2(s) = s(R_2 + R_3 + R_2 A_{v3}) + s^2(\tau_2 R_3 + \tau_1 R_3 + \tau_1 R_2 + \tau_3 R_2 + \tau_1 R_2 A_{v3}) + s^3(\tau_1\tau_3 R_2 + \tau_1\tau_2 R_3) \\ D_3(s) = s^2(R_2R_3 + R_1R_3 + R_1R_2 + R_1R_2A_{v3} - R_1R_3A_{v2}) + s^3(R_1R_2\tau_3 + R_2R_3\tau_1 + R_1R_3\tau_2) \end{cases} \tag{4}$$

with $A_{vi} = g_{mi}R_i$, $\tau_i = R_iC_i$ $(i=1..3)$.

The model has been developed assuming zeros introduced by feedforward capacitor paths can be neglected, as in [1]. However, despite the latter work, the proposed model allows the effects of parasitic elements of real transconductors to be taken into account.

Table 1 summarizes the values of both the output resistance $R_i$ and lumped load capacitance $C_i$, carried out by HSPICE DC operating-point analysis, for each stage of the amplifier.

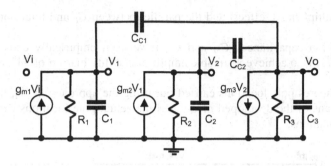

**Fig. 5.** Small signal model of three-stage NM compensated amplifier

**Table 1.** Parasitic resistances and capacitances of NMC amplifier stages of Fig. 5

| stages | $R_i(k\Omega)$ | $C_i$ (pF) |
|--------|----------------|------------|
| $1^{st}$ ($M_1$-$M_5$) | $r_{oM2}//r_{oM4} \approx 175$ | $C_{in}(M_6) \approx 0.26$ |
| $2^{nd}$ ($M_6$-$M_9$) | $r_{oM7}//r_{oM9} \approx 694$ | $(1-A_{v3})*C_{GD}(M_{11}) \approx 2.64$ |
| $3^{rd}$ ($M_{10}$-$M_{11}$) | $r_{oM10}//r_{oM11} \approx 20.6$ | $C_{out}(M_{10})//C_{out}(M_{11})//C_L \approx 2.78$ |

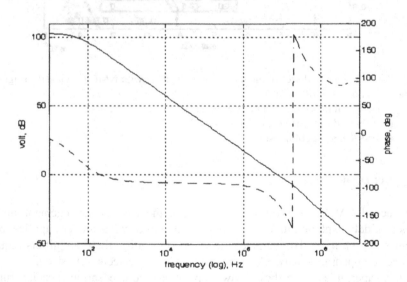

**Fig. 6.** Open-loop frequency response of the correctly compensated three-stage amplifier: magnitude plot (solid line) phase plot (dashed line)

Lumped resistance values are assumed to be the parallel of Early resistances ($r_o$) of both the driver and the load transistor of the stage.

The lumped capacitance of the first, second and last stages are, respectively, the total input capacitance of transistor $M_6$, the feedback capacitance (taking into account the Miller multiplicative effect) and the parallel between $C_L$ and total output capacitance.

Compensation capacitances $C_{c1}$ and $C_{c2}$ have been empirically chosen equal to *3.3pF* and *2.17pF* to achieve a suitable amplifier stability margin of 54°, as shown in Fig. 6.

Fig. 7 compares pole locations carried out using the approach in [1], the ones obtained by means of the developed model and the actual pole locations carried out by HSPICE simulations.

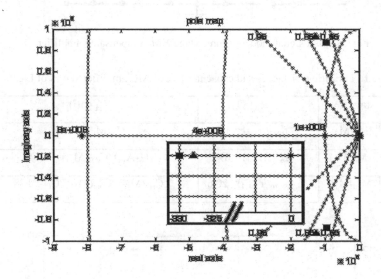

**Fig. 7.** Pole locations (rad/sec) of the three-stage amplifier with NMC (the insert in figure depicts pole locations near the origin):

   *   estimated in accord with transfer function (1)

   ■   estimated in accord with proposed model

   ▲   HSPICE simulation result

## 4  Conclusions

In the actual CMOS low-voltage technologies, the cascade arrangement of three stages is widely exploited to allow high-gain and large-swing modern application requirements to be meet. To guarantee closed-loop stability, these amplifiers require a frequency compensation network such as the NMC, to be accurately sized.

In this paper, it has been shown how conventional compensation capacitor rules of the NMC technique are inadequate when small load capacitances have to be driven, such typically it occurs in discrete-time applications.

Moreover, it has been also demonstrated that the use of a more accurate model for the amplifier allows compensation capacitors to be well-sized, achieving both stability and transient behaviour requirements.

# References

[1] Eschauzier R.G.H., and Huijsing J.H.: "Frequency compensation techniques for low-power operational amplifiers" Boston, MA: Kluwer, 1995.

[2] You F., Embabi S.H.K., and Sanchez-Sinencio E.: "A multistage amplifier topology with nested Gm-C compensation for low-voltage application", *IEEE J. Solid-State Circuits,* vol. 32, pp. 2000-2011, Dec. 1997.

[3] Eschauzier R.G.H., Kerklaan L.P.T., and Huijsing J.H., "A 100-Mhz 100-dB operational amplifier with multipath nested Miller compensation structure", *IEEE J. Solid-State Circuits,* vol. 27, pp. 1709-1717, Dec. 1992.

[4] Leung, K.N., and Mok, P.K.T.: "Analysis of multistage amplifier-frequency compensation", *IEEE Trans. Circuits Syst. I, Fundam. Theory Appl.,* vol. 48, Sept. 2001.

[5] Choi, T.C., Kaneshiro R.T., Brodersen R.W., Gray P.R., Jett W.B., Wilcox M.: "High-frequency CMOS Switched-Capacitor filters for communications application", *IEEE J. Solid-State Circuits,* vol. sc-18, pp. 652-664, Dec. 1983.

[6] Geerts Y., Marques A.M., Steyaert M.S.J. and Sansen W.: "A 3.3-V, 15-bit. Delta-sigma ADC with a signal bandwidth of 1.1 Mhz for ADSL applications", *IEEE J. Solid-State Circuits,* vol. 34, pp. 927-936, July 1999.

# Spectral Analysis of the On-Chip Waveforms to Generate Guidelines for EMC-Aware Design

Davide Pandini and Guido A. Repetto

STMicroelectronics, Central CAD and Design Solutions,
20041 Agrate Brianza, Italy
davide.pandini@st.com, guido.repetto@st.com
http://www.st.com

**Abstract.** In modern electronic products the increasing demand for greater performance and throughput often dictates the need for higher operating frequencies. The fundamental operating frequencies of microprocessors, consumer electronics, and networking applications in use today have exceed hundreds of megahertz and are rapidly approaching, and in several cases exceeding, the gigahertz range, and with the current and future technology scaling trends will continue to raise. However, with such increment in frequency often comes an increase in electromagnetic interference (EMI). Therefore, EMI and radiated emissions are a major problem for high-speed circuit and package designers, which is likely to become even more severe in the future. However, until recently, IC and package designers did not give much consideration to electromagnetic radiated emission and interference in their designs. The enforcement of strict governmental regulations and international standards in the automotive domain are driving new efforts towards design solutions for electromagnetic compatibility (EMC). In order to avoid costly design re-spins, EMC compliance must be validated before fabrication with the support of EMC-aware CAD tools and design guidelines. In this work, we propose an effective and practical approach to assess the spectral content of on-chip signals, which are one of the most detrimental sources of electromagnetic (EM) emissions, and provide valuable guidelines to focus the design efforts on reducing the high-frequency harmonics.

## 1 Introduction

Traditionally, the problem of reducing the EM emissions at the chip level has been more an art than a science, where different engineering solutions were considered, tested, and put in practice by trial-and-error, without following any systematic approach. Such avenue was mainly followed by practitioners, as there is a lack of circuit designers in the VLSI community, which also have a solid technical background on EMC/EMI. In fact, when the on-chip EM emissions exceeded the levels imposed by either the international legislation or by customers (mainly in the automotive domain), patches and workarounds could be effectively found at the PCB level by exploiting off-chip decoupling capacitances. Obviously, this approach is no longer acceptable,

J. Vounckx, N. Azemard, and P. Maurine (Eds.): PATMOS 2006, LNCS 4148, pp. 532–542, 2006.

since the international standards and regulations, the customer's requirements, and an increasingly aggressive competition in the automotive market need and dictate a deep theoretical understanding of the EMC/EMI problem, a systematic method to deploy effective and reusable solutions for a wide range of ICs and applications, and the development of an overall EMC-aware design methodology that addresses the EMI reduction during all phases of the top-down design flow.

Hence, in order to define such global and systematic approach, it is mandatory to have CAD tools helping circuit designers to promptly evaluate the effectiveness of design solutions in reducing the spectral content, specifically the high-frequency (but not only) harmonics of the on-chip signals. Since faster current variations show a larger harmonic content, it is well-known that a major critical detrimental factor impacting the EM emissions at the chip level is the simultaneous switching noise (SSN) caused by the dynamic power and ground supply voltage fluctuations. It is clear that technology scaling trends and an increasing chip complexity will require higher operating frequencies with faster clock rates. Moreover, it should also be taken into account that tighter constraints on global power consumption will demand a more aggressive use of clock gating techniques, thus increasing the amount of SSN. Because the dynamic IR-drop is a major source of EMI, one of the critical tasks to develop an effective EMC-aware design methodology is the deployment of a CAD solution that accounts for the SSN, and helps designers to reduce noise and EM emission sources by optimizing the placement of on-chip decoupling capacitors (i.e., decaps).

As ICs and packages have become smaller and more sophisticated, more devices and interconnection lines are being crowded into less space and are operating with higher clock frequencies, thus increasing probability of EM radiated emission and interference. Although smaller digital ICs and packages did not at first seem to be a serious source of EMI, their higher switching speed, combined with parasitic interconnect inductance, makes them a major source of EM emissions. Nevertheless, until recently, IC and package designers have not given much importance to EMI in their designs. However, the combination of SSN and ground bounce, fast output driver transition, transmission line reflection, and crosstalk are exacerbating these problems.

In high-performance digital designs, the high-speed clock drivers and associated circuits generate most of the EMC problems in the whole system. Hence, digital circuits are a source of broadband EM radiations due to the harmonic content of pulsed waveforms with fast transitions. The level of these radiations depends on several factors including choice of components, clock frequency, circuit layout, and shielding. So far, the relative importance of these factors has often not been adequately quantified. In this work we will investigate and analyze the spectral components of the on-chip waveforms that are critical to EMC. Quantitative knowledge of EMC factors will enable designers to make effective decisions at an early stage in the design process. If designers are able to compare the relative merits of different methods of achieving EMC, then they will be able to optimize their designs rather than be forced to apply more counter measures than may be necessary, or going through time-consuming post-layout fixes and design iterations, thus dramatically increasing the NRE costs and missing critical time-to-market windows. Moreover, in this work we will provide guidelines that designers may exploit when designing for EMC.

This paper is organized as follows: Section 2 introduces the major sources of EMI in digital circuits. Section 3 presents the spectral analysis on the typical on-chip digital signals, while Section 4 the spectral analysis of the power and ground supply fluctuations. In Section 5 some guidelines to reduce the harmonic composition of digital waveforms for EMC-aware design are proposed. Finally, Section 6 summarizes our conclusive remarks.

## 2   Electromagnetic Emissions from Digital Circuits

The more important signals contributing directly to the EM emissions of electronic systems are the clock and data signals. In high-performance microcontrollers and cores, clock rates are steadily increasing, forcing rise/fall times to decrease, and clocking to be strongly synchronous all over the chip. This means that all rising and falling signal edges occur at the same time, a goal known as "zero clock skew". Today's IC design tools support this trend. However, for reduced EM emission, clock spreading is recommended. Signal edges should be distributed over a timeslot which should be made as long as allowed by the operating frequency and circuit delay paths. Although not directly supported by the design tools, chip designers should take advantage from implementing this clock spreading concept for EMI reduction. Given the periodic nature, and the fast transition time of clock signals, their energy is concentrated in narrow bands near the harmonic frequencies [1]. To reduce the EMI from the system clock drivers and associated circuits, spread spectrum clock (SSC) techniques that modulate the clock frequency have been introduced in [2] and [3].

The impact of power and ground supply level variations on the radiated EM emissions of digital circuits was discussed in [4]. In [5] a design methodology to analyze the on-chip power supply noise for high-performance microprocessors was presented. The $L \cdot dI/dt$ noise (or SSN) is originated from package and power rail inductance, and following the increasing circuit frequencies and decreasing supply voltages, it is becoming more and more important with each technology generation [6][8][9]. The impact of SSN can be reduced by inserting decoupling capacitors in the proximity of current-hungry blocks [7]. On-chip decoupling is also an effective method of reducing radiated EM emissions, and the most powerful approach would place as much as possible on-chip decaps. However, this task can be accomplished with a significant cost both in terms of silicon area and of leakage current, since decaps are commonly implemented by means of MOSFET devices with a large channel length. As a consequence, during the floorplanning stage in order to avoid allocating excessive white space for on-chip decaps it is useful to analyze whether or not this is an effective technique to decrease the SSN and ground bounce or, in contrast, it would be much more effective to reduce the clock waveform harmonics. In [10] a systematic study to understand the effects of off-chip and on-chip decoupling on the radiated emissions was presented. It was demonstrated that off-chip decaps are effective at reducing the EM radiation in the low-frequency range, while they do not have any significant impact in the high-frequency region. In contrast, on-chip decoupling is a valuable technique to suppress the EM radiation in the high frequency region, and by a careful combination of off- and on-chip decoupling it was possible to achieve a 10dB suppression of radiated emissions over the whole frequency spectrum.

# 3  Spectral Analysis of Digital Signals

We will begin the discussion with a general overview of the spectral composition of digital signals. These waveforms are approximately trapezoidal with finite rise and fall times. Fast rise/fall times are one of the principal sources of EM emissions; hence, slowing down the rise/fall slopes is an effective technique to reduce their high-frequency harmonics. Given the periodic trapezoidal waveform typical of the on-chip clock and data signals shown in Fig. 1, its spectral content can be evaluated by means of the Fourier series [11].

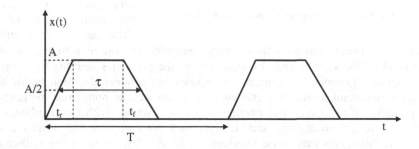

**Fig. 1.** Periodic trapezoidal pulse train (clock and data signals in digital systems)

Typically, a digital clock waveform is characterized by the following parameters: rise time $t_r$, fall time $t_f$, period $T$, amplitude $A$, and duty cycle $\tau$. In order to obtain a closed-form expression for the spectrum magnitude we assume the same rise and fall times, i.e., $t_r = t_f$. In this case, the analytical expression of the coefficients of the one-sided spectrum magnitude is given by:

$$|c_n| = A \cdot \frac{\tau}{T} \cdot \left| \frac{\sin(\pi \cdot n \cdot \tau / T)}{\pi \cdot n \cdot \tau / T} \right| \cdot \left| \frac{\sin(\pi \cdot n \cdot t_r / T)}{\pi \cdot n \cdot t_r / T} \right|. \tag{1}$$

Although (1) represents the one-sided spectrum expansion coefficients of the Fourier series of the waveform $x(t)$ depicted in Fig. 1, it is desirable to extract more qualitative and intuitive information than it is apparent from this equation. Replacing the discrete spectrum with a continuous envelope by substituting $f = n/T$ yields:

$$envelope = A \cdot \frac{\tau}{T} \cdot \left| \frac{\sin(\pi \cdot f \cdot \tau)}{\pi \cdot f \cdot \tau} \right| \cdot \left| \frac{\sin(\pi \cdot f \cdot t_r)}{\pi \cdot f \cdot t_r} \right|, \tag{2}$$

where from a careful analysis of (2) it is possible to efficiently evaluate the impact of some relevant clock parameters on the signal spectral composition. The bounds for this spectrum can be generated with the corresponding Bode plot, as illustrated in Fig. 2. While the spectral bounds do not yield an accurate quantitative measure of the signal spectrum magnitude, they are an effective tool for a fast qualitative harmonic analysis. From the plot in Fig. 2 it becomes clear that the high-frequency composition of a

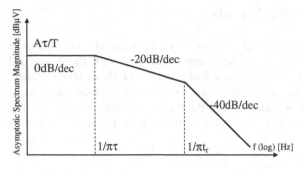

**Fig. 2.** One-sided magnitude spectrum bounds

trapezoidal pulse train is primarily due to the rise/fall times. Signals having a small (fast) rise/fall time will have larger high-frequency harmonics than pulses with larger (slow) rise/fall times. Therefore, in order to reduce the high-frequency spectrum, it is very effective to decrease the rise/fall slopes of the clock and/or data pulses.

Not only fast rise/fall times are the primary contributors to the high-frequency spectral content of the signals, and consequently, of the product's inability to meet the governmental regulatory requirements on radiated and conducted emissions, but they are also a significant source of interference. It is important to notice that the interference potential of a product and whether or not it complies with the regulatory requirements are not necessarily related: a product that complies with governmental emission requirements may cause interference. Ideally, by means of the mathematic model (2) and the corresponding Bode plots it would be possible to extrapolate some design guidelines that designers will be able to exploit to estimate the clock waveform parameters that most significantly reduce the high-frequency harmonic composition. Moreover, of interest to designers it will also be the possibility of understanding during design planning whether it is more powerful reducing the high-frequency harmonics of the clock by increasing its rise/fall time, providing the performance constraints are satisfied, or instead by changing the duty cycle, and performing a trade-off on these two techniques. Once designers can assess the effectiveness of increasing the clock rise/fall times on the high frequency spectrum, then it will be possible to generate constraints for the clock tree synthesis tool. In fact, systematically using buffers with high driving strength for the clock distribution network has a detrimental impact on on-chip EM emissions, and whenever it is possible an EMC-aware design methodology should be able to relax the performance constrains along timing non-critical paths by slowing down the digital signal rise/fall times.

## 4   Power Supply Fluctuations and Ground Bounce Analysis

Parasitic inductance and capacitance of the package and of the on-chip wires, mainly of the power rails, can introduce in a digital system a phenomenon referred to as ringing or simultaneous switching noise (SSN), along with the corresponding ground bounce. Although losses due to the wire resistance damp such oscillations around the signal steady-state values, SSN is another relevant source of EM emissions due to the harmonics generated by fast supply current variations. Today, no efficient and practical CAD tool is available to extract on-chip parasitic inductance for complex digital circuits, and obtaining accurate package models is another time-consuming task that requires 3D solver applications. Moreover, in large semiconductor companies, the

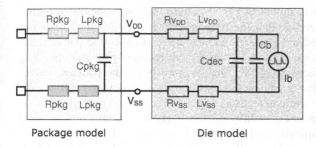

Package model        Die model

**Fig. 3.** IC model for EMC analysis

package models are usually generated in the back-end division, while the on-chip parasitic inductance estimation is under the responsibility of the front-end interconnect modeling teams, and sometimes these two tasks are not fully synchronized. As a consequence, it is not straightforward at all to obtain the complete IC model shown in Fig. 3, which designers can use for EMC analysis to assess the impact of the design techniques for EMI reduction.

The purpose of this section is to investigate the SSN effect on the spectral content of the digital signals. We will demonstrate that oscillations introduced by power and ground supply fluctuations will accentuate or enhance certain region of the spectral content of the original waveform. This factor combined with the detrimental impact on the functionality, performance, and reliability of the system requires a prevention of the ringing effects using both off-chip and on-chip decoupling capacitors as it is outlined in Fig. 3. As a consequence, for a fast evaluation of the impact of SSN on the EM emissions it is beneficial to exploit a mathematical model that captures the most important characteristics of the typical ringing waveform. Such mathematical model is given by:

$$V_{SSN}(t) = V_{peak} \cdot e^{-\alpha \cdot t} \cdot \sin(\omega_r \cdot t + \theta), \qquad (3)$$

where $\alpha$ is the damping coefficient, $V_{peak}$ is the peak oscillation amplitude, and $f_r = \omega_r/(2 \cdot \pi)$ is the ringing frequency. The SSN (and ground bounce) may show on the power (and ground) lines with the characteristic waveform illustrated in Fig. 4, which was obtained with expression (3) using typical R, L, C values from package models similar to the one represented in Fig. 3.

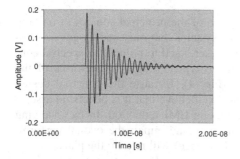

**Fig. 4.** SSN waveform

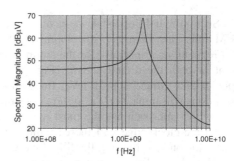

**Fig. 5.** SSN spectral content

The typical spectral content is shown in Fig. 5, where the harmonics with higher spectrum magnitude are localized around the ringing frequency (1.59GHz). It is important to point out that the package parasitic inductance dominates the parasitic inductance of the on-chip power straps, and for the current technologies and operating frequencies it is still safe to focus the EMC analysis mostly on the package inductance. However, we believe that practical CAD solutions to efficiently extract the parasitic inductance of on-chip interconnect topologies such as the power distribution network will soon become necessary following the aggressive technology scaling trends, and the increasing complexity and operating frequencies of modern System-on-Chip (SoC) designs. Moreover, the oscillations introduced by these inductive effects may also have a detrimental impact on the waveform of the typical digital signals as it is represented in Fig. 6. The spectral composition of the trapezoidal waveform with SSN is increased around the ringing frequency, as illustrated in Fig. 7. Therefore, an effective design technique to reduce on-chip EM emissions is to damp the oscillations introduced by the parasitic inductances by means of on-chip decoupling capacitances.

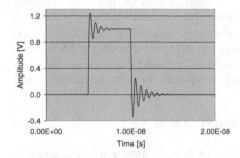

**Fig. 6.** Clock and SSN superposition

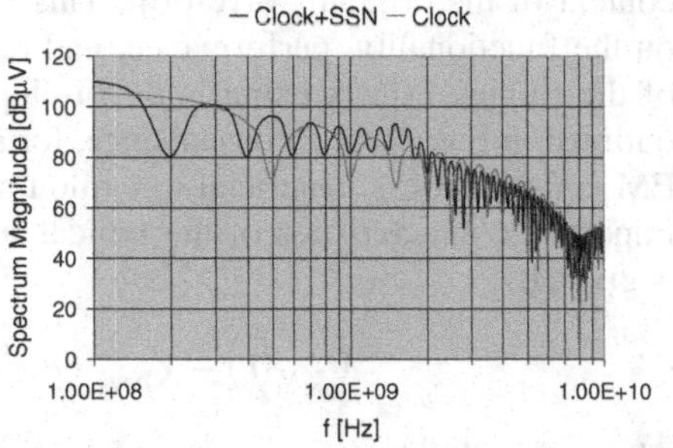

**Fig. 7.** Spectral content of clock and SSN superposition vs. simple clock

# 5   Practical Guidelines for EMC-Aware Design

In Section 3 and Section 4 we have analyzed two of the principal sources of on-chip EM emissions. Designers developing electronic systems that must satisfy governmental regulations, especially for the automotive market, need to reduce the spectral content of both the digital signals (Fig. 1), and the typical ringing waveforms of the power and ground supply level fluctuations (Fig. 4). Because the potential design solutions will impact on the system constraints, we believe that it is beneficial assessing which approach has the most relevant effect on EMI reduction. In fact, slowing down the clock edge will increase the circuit delay and impair the overall performance. In contrast, limiting the SSN (and ground bounce) will require the placement of on-chip decoupling capacitances thus increasing the final silicon area and leakage current. Consider the waveform shown in Fig. 4, represented by the mathematical model (3), and three different peak values, i.e., $V_{peak} = 0.3V, 0.2V, 0.1V$ respectively, as it is illustrated in Fig. 8. By reducing the peak of the damped oscillations, it is

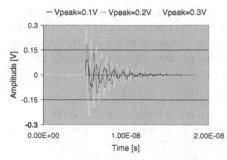

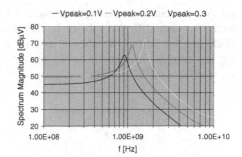

**Fig. 8.** Decap impact on SSN (time domain)

**Fig. 9.** Decap impact on SSN (frequency domain)

possible to decrease the spectrum magnitude, in particular around the ringing frequency. Moreover, since such reduction is obtained by increasing the decoupling capacitance, the ringing frequency itself is also reduced, as it is shown in Fig. 9. The overall waveform obtained by the superposition of the clock signal with the damped oscillations is represented in Fig. 6. The effect of decap increase on the ringing frequency and peak amplitude is illustrated in Fig. 10. After a spectral analysis based on the Fast Fourier Transform (FFT) [12], the harmonic composition is reported in Fig. 11. The reduction of the power and ground supply level fluctuations has a negligible impact, since the overall spectrum magnitude does not change significantly following a diminution from 0.3V to 0.1V in the peak of the oscillations.

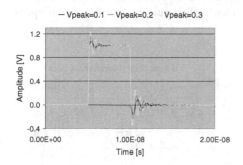

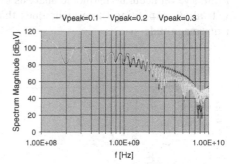

**Fig. 10.** Clock and SSN superposition

**Fig. 11.** FFT of clock and SSN

A more effective approach to reduce the high-frequency harmonics is to increase the rise/fall times of the clock signal. Fig. 12 shows the spectral content decrease corresponding to a rise/fall time increment from 250ps to 450ps for a working frequency of 150MHz, which are typical values for the 130nm technology, while Fig. 13 illustrates the high-frequency harmonic decrease corresponding to rise/fall times from 50ps to 150ps for a working frequency of 250MHz[1], which are typical values corresponding to the 90nm technology. In standard devices most switching events and current con-

---

[1]  These frequencies are typical values for automotive applications in the technologies considered.

sumption occur immediately after the clock edge. However, some skew may be introduced between different subcircuits that do not need to operate strictly synchronously. Widening the activity window is another effective technique that will allow to limiting the current fluctuations on the power distribution network, thus reducing the adverse effect on EM emissions.

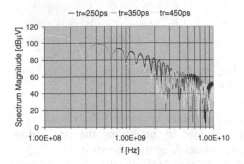

**Fig. 12.** 130nm – 150MHz clk freq

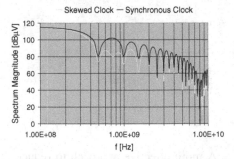

**Fig. 13.** 90nm – 250MHz clk freq

Fig. 15 demonstrates that some skew among different clock signals (Fig. 14) can reduce the overall spectral content. CAD tools should allow designers to estimate before the clock network implementation the amount of allowable skew that during the clock tree synthesis (CTS) phase will guarantee the design timing closure. A preliminary, yet accurate harmonic analysis based on the approach presented in this work will allow exploiting those techniques that most effectively reduce the signal spectrum magnitude.

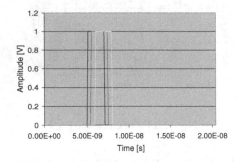

**Fig. 14.** Clock skew

**Fig. 15.** Clock skew vs. synch. clock

# 6   Conclusions

In this paper we have discussed the increasing importance of electromagnetic compatibility and electromagnetic emission reduction in electronic system design. Although EMC has been a typical requirement for the automotive market, we believe that following the technology scaling trends, the increasing complexity of SoC designs, and an aggressive demand for higher throughput, EMC will soon become mandatory also for consumer electronics, networking applications, and high-performance microprocessors, whose operating frequencies are in the range of several hundreds of megahertz up to a few gigahertzes. Hence, to develop EMC-compliant products, design techniques that reduce the level of on-chip EM radiations are necessary. However, an EMC-aware design methodology will introduce extra design cost. Therefore, we believe that it will be valuable to designers assessing during the planning phase which approach will be more effective at reducing the signal spectral content. In this work we have analyzed the impact on harmonic attenuation of three techniques:

1. On-chip decoupling capacitors for SSN and ground bounce reduction;
2. Rise/fall time increase of digital signals;
3. Clock skew introduction.

We have demonstrated that slowing down the clock rise/fall times along with some skew among different clock edges may achieve a more significant decrease in spectral content with respect to bounding the power and ground supply level fluctuations by means of decoupling capacitances. Hence, we believe that to effectively implement these solutions, CTS tools should not always exploit buffers with high driving strength in the clock distribution network. The definition of a set of constraints for the CTS tools to limit the high-driving strength buffers in the clock tree, and the subsequent relaxation of performance constraints along timing non-critical paths is an ongoing effort, and one of the most important requirements towards an EMC-aware design methodology based on the combination of circuit techniques and CAD tools.

# References

[1] H. W. Ott, *Noise Reduction Techniques in Electronic Systems*. New York N.Y.: J. Wiley and Sons, 1988.

[2] K. B. Hardin, J. T. Fessler, and D. R. Bush, "Spread Spectrum Clock Generation for the Reduction of Radiated Emissions," in *Proc. Intl. Symp. on Electromagnetic Compatibility*, Feb. 1994, pp. 227-231.

[3] J. Kim, D. G. Kam, P. J. Jun, and J. Kim, "Spread Spectrum Clock Generator with Delay Cell Array to Reduce Electromagnetic Interference," *IEEE Trans. on Electromagnetic Compatibility*, vol. 47, pp. 908-920, Nov. 2005.

[4] T. Osterman, B. Deutschman, and C. Bacher, "Influence of the Power Supply on the Radiated Electromagnetic Emission of Integrated Circuits," *Microelectronics Journal*, vol. 35, pp. 525-530, Jun. 2004.

[5] H. H. Chen and D. D. Ling, "Power Supply Noise Analysis Methodology for Deep-Submicron VLSI Chip Design," in *Proc. of Design Automation Conf.*, Jun. 1997, pp. 638-647.

[6] P. Larsson, "Resonance and Damping in CMOS Circuits with On-Chip Decoupling Capacitance," *IEEE Trans. on CAS-I*, vol. 45, pp. 849-858, Aug. 1998.

[7] S. Bobba, T. Thorp, K. Aingaran, and D. Liu, "IC Power Distribution Challenges," in *Proc. of Intl. Conf. on Computer-Aided Design*, Nov. 2001, pp. 643-650.

[8] H.-R. Cha and O.-K. Kwon, "An Analytical Model of Simultaneous Switching Noise in CMOS Systems," *IEEE Trans. on Advanced Packaging*, vol. 23, pp. 62-68, Feb. 2000.

[9]   K. T. Tang and E. G. Friedman, "Simultaneous Switching Noise in On-Chip CMOS Power Distribution Networks," *IEEE Trans. on VLSI Systems*, vol. 10, pp. 487-493, Aug. 2002.

[10]  J. Kim, H. Kim, W. Ryu, J. Kim, Y.-h. Yun, S.-h. Kim, S.-h. Ham, H.-k. An, and Y.-h. Lee, "Effects of On-chip and Off-chip Decoupling Capacitors on Electromagnetic Radiated Emission," in *Proc. of Electronic Components and Technology Conf.*, May 1998, pp. 610-614.

[11]  C. R. Paul, *Introduction to Electromagnetic Compatibility*. New York N.Y.: J. Wiley and Sons, 1992.

[12]  W. H. Press, S. A. Teukolsky, W. T. Vetterling, and B. P. Flannery, *Numerical Recipes in C*. Cambridge U.K.: Cambridge Univ. Press, 1992.

# A Scalable Power Modeling Approach for Embedded Memory Using LIB Format

Wen-Tsan Hsieh[1], Chi-Chia Yu[1], Chien-Nan Jimmy Liu[1], and Yi-Fang Chiu[2]

[1]Dept. of Electrical Engineering National Central University,
Jhongli, Taoyuan, Taiwan, R.O.C.
wthsieh@ee.ncu.edu.tw, 93521027@cc.ncu.edu.tw,
jimmy@ee.ncu.edu.tw
[2]Industrial Technological Research Institute
Chutung, Hsinchu, Taiwan, R.O.C.
yfchiu@itri.org.tw

**Abstract.** In this work, we develop two methods to improve the accuracy of memory power estimation. Our enhanced memory power model can consider not only the operation mode of memory access, but also the address switching effect and the scaling factors that use the information of physical architecture. The proposed approach is very useful to be combined with memory compiler to generate accurate power model for any specified memory size without extra characterization costs. Then the proposed dummy modular approach can link our enhanced memory power model into commercial power estimation flow smoothly. The experimental results have shown that the average error of our memory power model is only less than 5%.

## 1 Introduction

Recently, designers often use a lot of embedded memories in modern SoC designs. The power consumed by these storage units is also a large portion of the total power consumption. Since the memory is one of the major sources of total power consumption, it is also a crucial work to build its power model accurately. Designers used to generate the memory power models by using the memory compilers, which are often not accurate enough. There are two reasons that make their memory power models perform poor estimation. One is the neglect of the non-controlling signal effects. The other is the limitation of library format that limits the completeness of the memory power model. These issues will be discussed in the following sections.

Several memory power modeling approaches have been proposed in the literature [3-7]. The analytical models are proposed in [3,4]. Typically, these approaches use the detailed information of the structure to compute the energy based on the switched capacitance within the memory circuit. Other black-box approaches are proposed by [5,6]. In [5], the regression tree is built by using the clustering ability of neural network. The authors in [6] model the dependency on size parameters and control signals by using linear regression. There is an automatic model generation algorithm proposed in [7] that uses non-linear regression techniques. Although these techniques can

J. Vounckx, N. Azemard, and P. Maurine (Eds.): PATMOS 2006, LNCS 4148, pp. 543–552, 2006.
© Springer-Verlag Berlin Heidelberg 2006

improve the accuracy of traditional memory power models, the complicated models make them more difficult to be combined with current commercial power estimation flow. Due to the model complexity, their model characterization phases usually need a lot of time.

Therefore, we propose an efficient power modeling approach that includes an enhanced memory power model and the dummy modular approach. Our approach not only considers the control signals and data signals but also the specification of physical architecture to automatically adjust the power values in the power model according to the memory size. The idea is simple but useful. Our main goal is to embed our modeling algorithm into the commercial memory compiler, such that it can automatically produce the more exact memory power model in each different size. And the proposed dummy modular approach makes our power model be able to be easily combined with current EDA tools. The results have shown that we can still have high accuracy with such a simple model.

The rest of this paper is organized as follows. The preliminary about embedded memory architecture and traditional memory power model will be described in Section 2. In Section 3 and 4, our memory power modeling approach and scaling strategies are described. Finally, the experimental results will be demonstrated in Section 5 and some conclusions will be given at the end.

## 2 Preliminary

### 2.1 Embedded Memory Architecture

Memory design is typically composed of the basic storage cell array and the necessary peripheral circuitry. The typical memory architecture can be roughly illustrated as Fig. 1. It consists of a memory core, row/column decoder and a control circuit.

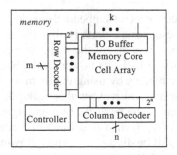

**Fig. 1.** A Typical Embedded Memory Architecture

In typical memory access procedure, the address signals are separated into m-bit row and n-bit column signals. First, the m-bit row address signals will be decoded to select one of $2^m$ rows by the row decoder. And the n-bit column address signals are decoded by column decoder to select one of $2^n$ columns. Then, the k-bit data signals in the selected cell can be read or written through the IO buffer.

## 2.2 Traditional Memory Power Estimation

A simplified memory power model has been commonly used for power estimation, where the power dissipation information for three operational modes (read, write, and idle) is provided for a compiled memory [9]. The model considers only the states of controlling signals and assumes that the accesses of a memory with the same operational mode have the same power dissipation. However, the evidence shows that even the same operation of the memory access could have quite different power dissipation values in [6]. In this kind of traditional memory power model, the results may not accurate enough because it is too simple to model the power behavior of embedded memory. It implies that considering the state of the control signals is not enough to model the power of embedded memory accurately. Although a lot of researches are proposed to improve the accuracy of traditional memory power model, the complicated model generation phase makes them more difficult to be combined with the current commercial power estimation flow.

## 3 Enhanced Memory Power Modeling Using LIB Format

In order to enhance the memory power model, we need to add some parameters that can represent the effects of non-control signals. Although more parameters can build more accurate power model, we need to consider the current library limitation to make our model be able to be combined with EDA tools more easily.

### 3.1 Dummy Modular Approach

In order to combine our memory power model into current EDA flow, the power model had better to follow the Liberty (LIB) format [1,8] which is the most commonly used in the current library format. According to the limitation of the LIB format, it only allows the signals of real I/O pins to be the indexes of the table. Therefore, the dummy modular approach has been proposed to wrap the original design into the dummy module as shown in Fig. 2. If we have any extra parameters to be added into the memory power model, we can generate the values of those parameters from the extra functional block and export them through the dummy output signals, which can be used in the library file. In Fig. 2, the *Extra_Dummy_Func* is the engine which is producing the dummy output signals. In our work, this block is implemented by using *PLI* (Programming Language Interface) Task [2].

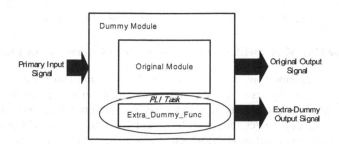

**Fig. 2.** Dummy Modular Block Diagram

Because of the discrete property of extra-dummy output signals, we choose the hamming distance (*hd*) of non-control signals, which is a popular parameter in power estimation methods, to be our additional modeling parameters. The expression of *hd* is described as below.

$$hd(X(N), X(N-1)) = \sum_i X_i(N) \oplus X_i(N-1)$$

(1)

$X(N)$: the non-control signals at the $N$-th clock cycle
$i$: the pin number of the non-control signals

The final LIB format of our memory power model will look like Fig. 3. The *hd* value is calculated by a PLI task. Compared to the traditional memory power model, the power dissipation of a memory access in our model becomes a function that considers both the control signals *CEN* and *WEN* and the hamming distance of the non-control signals: As shown in the experimental results, the estimation results can be more accurate with these extra parameters.

```
pin(CLK) {
    internal_power(){
        when : "CEN";                    //   idle mode
        power(LUT1)
        ...
    }
        internal_power(){                //   read mode
        //     hd=0:
        when : "!CEN & WEN & T0 & !T1 & ....& !T12";
            power(LUT2)
    }
        ...
    internal_power(){
        //     hd=12:
        when : "!CEN & WEN & !T0 & !T1 & ....& T12";
        power(LUT14)
    }
        internal_power(){                //   write mode
        when : "!CEN & !WEN & T0 & !T1 & ....& !T12";
        ...
    }
}
```

**Fig. 3.** Our Memory Power Model by Using LIB Format

### 3.2   Combine Our Model with Memory Compiler in Current EDA Flow

The usage of our enhanced memory power model in the simulation flow is illustrated in Fig. 4. When users request a specific size of memory to memory compiler, we can generate the enhanced power model as discussed in Section 3.1. In order to combine our enhanced memory power model with current EDA tools, we will automatically wrap the original functional module, which is also generated from memory compiler, into the dummy module with extra-dummy output pins. Then, the simulation can

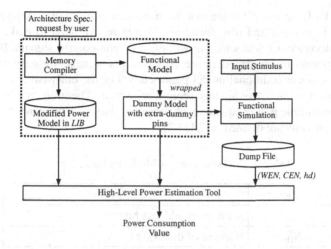

**Fig. 4.** Combine Our Model with Memory Compiler in Current EDA Flow

dump the *hd* of non-control signals information as the output signals into the dump file. In order not to perform the characterization process again and again for different sizes of memories, we will develop scaling equations to automatically adjust those power values in the power model, which are discussed in Section 4.

## 4  Scalable Model Equations

As described in Section 2, the embedded memory can be roughly divided into four functional blocks: memory core, column/row decoder and control circuit. Because these blocks do not have the same scaling ratio to the memory size on their power dissipation, it is better to model each functional block individually with the sizing parameters instead of using an unique memory power model. Therefore, we will present the derivation of our scaling strategy to each functional block in this section.

Besides, we realize that the non-controlling signal effects must be considered to increase the model precision. Therefore, we make a simple experiment at the beginning to check the non-controlling signal effects of each functional block. We measure the power dissipation of each functional block by giving the random data and address signals. The power variation of each functional block is shown in Table 1.

**Table 1.** The Variation Percentages of Each Functional Block

|                | Write mode | Read mode |
|----------------|------------|-----------|
| Memory Core    | 1.75%      | 2.65%     |
| Column Decoder | 10.28%     | 10.24%    |
| Row Decoder    | 12.71%     | 12.80%    |
| Control        | 0.11%      | 0.21%     |

According to Table 1, we can see that the most variations with varying non-control signals occur in column and row decoders. Therefore, we need to make the power equations of decoders to deal with the variation of non-control signals. Because the signals that connect to the decoders are only address signals, we only consider the address signals as our additional model parameters. For the other two blocks, the impacts of different non-control signals seem very small. Therefore, we will not add extra parameters to the power equations of those two blocks. The symbols we used in the following analysis are defined in Table 2.

Table 2. The Definitions of Modeling Parameters

| Parameter | Description |
|-----------|-------------|
| $N_A$ | Number of address bits |
| $N_D$ | Number of data bits |
| *hd* | Hamming distance of address signals |
| Col | Column number of cell array |
| Row | Row number of cell array |
| WE | Write enable, represent write/read mode |

## 4.1 Memory Core and Control Circuits

First, we want to analyze the power behaviors of memory core and control circuits. In order to demonstrate the relationship between their power dissipations and the corresponding size parameters, we made several simulations with different sizes of memory and randomly assign the input signals in both read mode and write mode. The power curves of memory core with varied size parameters are shown in Fig. 5(a). In Fig. 5(a), the solid lines represent the power behavior of those memories in write mode and the dotted lines are the cases in read mode. The same experiments are also done for the control circuits as shown in Fig. 5(b), in which the representation is the same as in Figure 5(a).

It seems that they both are logarithmic-like relationship between the number of address bits and the power dissipation of memory core. And the number of data bits can roughly exhibit the order of the amplitude in the power curve. In this work, the second-order regression will be used to obtain the most feasible coefficient matrix to fit their power behaviors. In control circuits, it seems that the relationship has similar trend of the memory core. Therefore, we will try the same model of the memory core as in the control circuit case. But we do not consider the operation mode in this case because the power behavior of control circuit is almost the same either in write mode or read mode from the simulation results shown in Fig. 5(b). The final regression equation in our work is shown in Equation (2):

$$P_{core}=P_{ctrl}=C_0+C_1N_A+C_2N_D+C_3N_AN_D+C_4N_A{}^2C_5N_D{}^2+C_6N_AN_D{}^2+C_7N_A{}^2N_D \qquad (2)$$

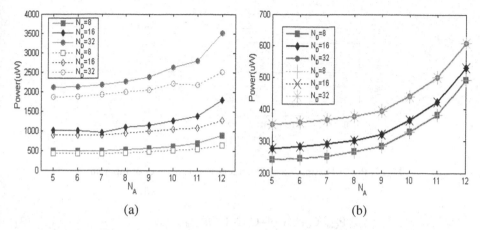

(a)                                              (b)

**Fig. 5.** Power Behavior of (a) Memory Core and (b) Control Circuits

## 4.2 Column/Row Decoder

Due to the similarity of Column and Row decoders, we will analyze only one of them to determine the model parameters of decoders. The relationship between the power behavior of row decoder circuit and the number of row address bits is shown in Fig. 6. It seems that using the number of input pins is sufficient to model the trend of decoders.

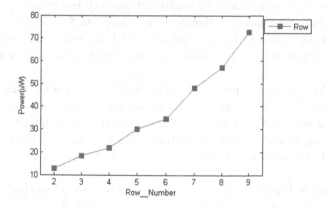

**Fig. 6.** Power Behavior of Decoder with Different Input Bits

As mentioned before, the power equation of decoders needs to consider the non-control signal effects to increase the model precision. In this work, we use the hamming distance of address signals as the additional model parameter. The power dissipation of decoders with different input hamming distance patterns is shown in Fig. 7 and the final regression equation in our work is shown in Equations (3) and (4).

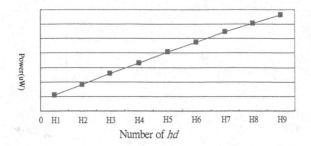

**Fig. 7.** Power Dissipation of Decoders versus number of input *hd*

$$P_{Col}=C_0+C_1Col+C_2Col \cdot hd_{Col} \qquad (3)$$

$$P_{Row}=C_0+C_1Row+C_2Row \cdot hd_{Row} \qquad (4)$$

## 5   Experimental Results

In this section, we will demonstrate the accuracy of our memory power model on a single-port SRAMs, which is generated from Artisan's Memory Compiler [9] by using TSMC 0.25 technology library and operates at 10MHz. Using the same information, the accuracy is compared with traditional memory power model, which only consider the states of controlling signals as mentioned in Section 2.2. The average power consumption estimated by our power model and traditional memory power model is also compared to the simulation results from Nanosim [10] with the same input data.

In the model construction phase, we only choose the commonly used numbers of data-bit, such as 8-bit, 16-bit and 32 bit, to characterize our model equations. We randomly generate 200 pattern pairs for these memories as the training data including both read mode and write mode. In the validation phase, each size of memory will be tested in another 600 random pattern pairs including both read mode and write mode.

The experimental results by using our memory power model and traditional memory power model are shown in Table 3. According to Table 3, the average error and standard deviation error are only 3.59% and 1.66% by using our memory power model. And the average maximum error is less than 10%. It shows that our memory power model can have higher accuracy than that of the traditional memory power model. In Table 3, there are some sizes of memory that are not chosen in the model construction phase, such as 10x6 and 10x7. For those memories, we can still estimate their power consumption accurately by scaling the values in the power models according to the size parameters.

**Table 3.** The Comparison between Our Power Model and Traditional Power Model

| Size | Traditional Memory Power Model | | | | | | Our Memory Power Model | | | | | |
|------|------|------|------|------|------|------|------|------|------|------|------|------|
| | Read Mode | | | Write Mode | | | Read Mode | | | Write Mode | | |
| | Max. (%) | Avg. (%) | Std. (%) | Max. (%) | Avg. (%) | Std. (%) | Max. (%) | Avg. (%) | Std. (%) | Max. (%) | Avg. (%) | Std. (%) |
| 5x8 | 17.03 | 8.57 | 2.71 | 26.00 | 18.95 | 2.38 | 4.76 | 1.97 | 1.15 | 10.27 | 2.91 | 2.07 |
| 6x32 | 18.10 | 10.76 | 2.07 | 7.20 | 2.68 | 2.02 | 5.63 | 1.10 | 0.92 | 7.08 | 1.72 | 1.30 |
| 7x32 | 17.60 | 10.77 | 1.98 | 10.52 | 3.26 | 2.07 | 3.83 | 1.52 | 0.89 | 8.15 | 3.03 | 1.73 |
| 8x16 | 18.57 | 10.91 | 2.19 | 17.26 | 8.56 | 2.43 | 4.19 | 0.83 | 0.66 | 8.46 | 2.26 | 1.66 |
| 9x32 | 19.69 | 13.06 | 2.08 | 17.05 | 9.21 | 2.10 | 4.22 | 1.12 | 0.85 | 7.11 | 1.61 | 1.22 |
| 10x6 | 9.94 | 2.23 | 2.83 | 11.20 | 2.47 | 3.08 | 5.56 | 3.06 | 0.91 | 7.11 | 2.17 | 1.47 |
| 10x7 | 9.40 | 2.07 | 2.63 | 9.09 | 2.29 | 2.86 | 4.99 | 2.62 | 0.86 | 6.94 | 1.83 | 1.32 |
| 11x8 | 25.62 | 14.86 | 2.87 | 13.39 | 4.72 | 2.56 | 5.10 | 2.15 | 0.93 | 11.49 | 3.54 | 2.55 |
| 12x32 | 38.03 | 31.00 | 2.23 | 14.67 | 11.73 | 1.14 | 9.54 | 5.75 | 1.07 | 7.38 | 3.28 | 1.37 |
| Avg. | 16.51 | 9.13 | 2.36 | 12.73 | 5.8 | 2.32 | 6.03 | 3.02 | 0.92 | 9.36 | 3.59 | 1.66 |

# 6  Conclusions

In this paper, we propose an enhanced memory power modeling approach. It considers not only the operation mode of memory access, but also the data switching effect and the scaling factors that use the information of physical architecture. Our memory power model is very simple and practical that can be easily combined with existing tools by using the proposed dummy modular approach. The experimental results have shown that the average error of our memory power model is less than 5% in those test cases, which is more accurate than existing power models generated from memory compilers.

# Acknowledgements

This work was supported in part by the National Science Council of R.O.C. under Grant NSC 94-2220-E-008-007 and Ministry of Economic Affairs under Grant MOEA 94-EC-17-A-01-S1-037.

# References

[1] "Library Compiler User Guide: Modeling Timing and Power Technology Libraries", Synopsys, March 2003.
[2] Swapnajit Mittra, "Principles of Verilog PLI", Kluwer Academic Publishers, March 1999.

[3]   Amrutur, B.S.; Horowitz, M.A., "Speed and power scaling of SRAM's", IEEE Trans. Solid-State Circuits, vol. 35, Feb. 2000 pp. 175 – 185.

[4]   Evans, R.J.; Franzon, P.D., "Energy consumption modeling and optimization for SRAM's", IEEE Trans. Solid-State Circuits, vol. 30, May 1995, pp. 571 – 579.

[5]   Chinosi, M.; Zafalon, R.; Guardiani, C., "Automatic characterization and modeling of power consumption in static RAMs", Low Power Electronics and Design, Aug. 1998.

[6]   Coumeri, S.L.; Thomas, D.E., Jr., "Memory modeling for system synthesis", IEEE Trans. On VLSI Syst., vol. 8, June 2000, pp. 327 – 334.

[7]   Schmidt, E.; von Colln, G.; Kruse, L.; Theeuwen, F.; Nebel, W., "Memory Power Models for Multilevel Power Estimation and Optimization", IEEE Trans. VLSI Syst., vol. 10, April 2002, pp. 106-109.

[8]   J. Olson, I. Nedelchev, Y. Lin, A. Mauskar, and J. Sproch, "STATE DEPENDENT POWER MODELING," US Patent # 5,838,579, 1998.

[9]   "TSMC 0.25µm Process SRAM-SP-HD Generator User Manual", Release 5.0, Artisan Comp., January 2002.

[10]  "Nanosim User Guide: Version X-2005.09", Synopsys, September 2005.

# Improving Energy Efficiency Via Speculative Multithreading on MultiCore Processors

Toshinori Sato[1], Yuu Tanaka[2], Hidenori Sato[3], Toshimasa Funaki[4],
Takenori Koushiro[5], and Akihiro Chiyonobu[4]

[1] System LSI Research Center, Kyushu University, 3-8-33-3F Momochihama,
Sawara-ku, Fukuoka, 814-0001 Japan
toshinori.sato@computer.org
http://www.slrc.kyushu-u.ac.jp/~tsato/
[2] Kyushu Railway Company, 3-25-21 Hakataekimae,
Hakata-ku, Fukuoka, 812-8566 Japan
yuu-ta@is.naist.jp
[3] Seiko Epson Corporation, 3-3-5 Owa,
Suwa, 392-0001 Japan
hide@mickey.ai.kyutech.ac.jp
[4] Graduate School of Computer Science and System Engineering,
Kyushu Institute of Technology, 680-4 Kawazu, Iizuka, 820-8502 Japan
{t-funaki, chiyo}@mickey.ai.kyutech.ac.jp
[5] Toshiba Corporation, 1 Komukaitoshiba-cho,
Saiwai-ku, Kawasaki, 212-8582 Japan
takenori.koshiro@toshiba.co.jp

**Abstract.** The advance in semiconductor technologies has increased the number of transistors on a die, resulting in the continuous improvement in microprocessor performance. However, the increase in power consumption and hence in power density is about to stop the progress in microprocessor performance. While supply voltage reduction is commonly known as an effective technique for power savings, it increases gate delay and thus causes performance degradation. The increasing transistors can be utilized for maintaining performance while reducing power consumption. We are considering a speculative multithreaded execution on MultiCore processors. We propose to execute only the part of the program, which has the impact on program execution time, on power-hungry cores. In order to enable this, we divide the instruction stream into two streams. One is called speculation stream, which is the main part of a program and where speculation is applied. It is executed on power-hungry cores. The other is the verification stream, which verifies every speculation. It is executed on low-power cores. The energy consumption is reduced by the decrease in the execution time in the speculation stream and by the low-power execution in the verification stream. We call this technique Contrail architecture. The paper will present the energy efficiency of a Contrail processor based on detailed simulations.

## 1 Introduction

The current trend towards increasing mobile devices requires high-performance and low-power microprocessors. Generally, high performance and low power conflict

J. Vounckx, N. Azemard, and P. Maurine (Eds.): PATMOS 2006, LNCS 4148, pp. 553–562, 2006.

with each other and it is very difficult to achieve both high performance and low power simultaneously. While power is already the first-class design constraint in embedded systems, it has also become a limiting factor in general-purpose microprocessors, such used in data centers.

The energy consumed in a microprocessor is the product of its power consumption and execution time. Thus, to reduce energy consumption, we should decrease either or both of them. As commonly known, for CMOS circuits, a power-supply reduction is the most effective way to lower power consumption. However, it increases gate delay, resulting in a slower clock frequency. That means processor performance is diminished. In order to keep transistor switching speed high, it is required that its threshold voltage is proportionally scaled down with the supply voltage. Unfortunately, however, lower threshold voltage leads to increase subthreshold leakage current. Maintaining high transistor switching speeds through low threshold voltage gives rise to a significant amount of leakage power consumption.

In order to achieve both high performance and low power simultaneously, we can exploit parallelism [3]. Two identical circuits are used in order to make each unit to work at half the original frequency while the original throughput is maintained. Since the speed requirement for the circuit becomes half, the supply voltage can be decreased. In this case, the amount of parallelism can be increased to further reduce the total power consumption. MultiCore processors are one of the solutions for high performance and low power and they have been already adopted in embedded microprocessors [6, 12, 21, 24]. Thread level parallelism is utilized for power reduction with maintaining processor performance [6]. In this paper, we propose an energy-efficient speculative MultiCore processor.

## 2  Contrail Processor Architecture

The advance in semiconductor technologies has increased the number of transistors on a die, as known as Moore's law. We propose to utilize the increasing transistors in order to maintaining processor performance while reducing its power consumption. The key idea is to execute only the part of a program, which has the impact on the program execution time, with high power. We divide the execution of the program into two instruction streams. One is called **speculation stream** and is the main part of the execution. We utilize speculation to skip several regions of the stream to reduce its execution time. In other words, the number of instructions in the speculation stream is reduced from that in the original execution. While it is executed with high power, the small number of instructions and hence the short execution time result in energy reduction. In contrast, the other stream is called **verification stream** and supports the speculation stream by verifying each speculation. Since the verification stream just performs verifications, which will not have much impact on the program execution time, it can be executed slowly. We reduce the clock frequency and hence the supply voltage delivered to the verification stream. From these considerations, its energy consumption is significantly reduced. We coined this technique Contrail architecture [20].

## 2.1 Contrail – A Speculative MultiCore Processor

We realize Contrail architecture on a MultiCore processor. Each stream is executed as an independent thread on the MultiCore processor. Each processor core has its own clock and power supply, and works at the variable clock frequency and supply voltage [7, 8, 10]. The speculation stream is executed on a power-hungry core at high clock frequency, and the verification stream is executed on low-power cores at low clock frequency. If mispredictions do not occur frequently, we expect a considerable amount of power reduction. When a misprediction occurs in the speculation stream, it is detected by the verification stream. All threads from the misprediction point to tail, including the speculation stream and any verification streams, are squashed, and processor state is recovered by the verification stream that detects the misprediction. And then, the verification stream becomes the speculation stream. In the cases, the additional power is consumed regarded as misprediction penalties.

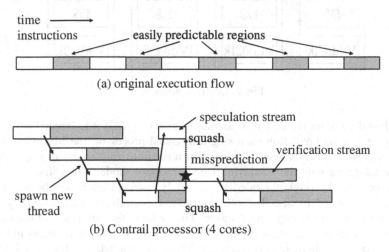

(a) original execution flow

(b) Contrail processor (4 cores)

**Fig. 1.** Execution on a Contrail processor

Fig. 1 explains how a program is executed on a Contrail processor. In this explanation, we assume that half of the regions in the original execution flow is easily predictable and is distributed uniformly as explained in Fig. 1(a). This is a reasonable assumption, since Pilla et al. [17] reported that approximately 60% of dynamic traces can be reused with the help of the value prediction. We also assume the clock frequency for the verification cores at half that for the speculation core. Under these assumptions, the execution is divided into speculation and verification streams in the Contrail processor as depicted in Fig. 1(b). The predicted regions are removed from the speculation core, and are moved into and hence are executed in the verification cores. Determining trigger points is based on the confidence information obtained from the value predictor. That is, thread partitioning is dynamically performed by hardware without any assistance of compilers. When an easily predictable region is detected, the head thread spawns a new speculation stream on the next core and it turns into a verification stream. That means only one core executes the speculative stream and the other cores execute the verification stream in a distributed manner. One of the possible implementations of the Contrail processor is a ring-connected MultiCore processor such as MultiScalar architecture [9], as shown in Fig. 2. Each verification stream stays alive until all instructions in the corresponding region re-moved from the speculation stream are executed. After that, the verification core is released for the future speculation stream.

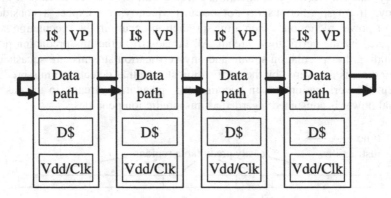

**Fig. 2.** Contrail processor

We should consider the cost of spawning a new thread. If it is larger than the cost of verifying a value prediction on a single-threaded processor, the MultiCore imple-mentation is not a good choice. However, from the following observations, we deter-mined to adopt the multithreaded MultiCore processor model rather than the single-threaded one. In the single-threaded model, only datapath alternates between high-speed and low-speed modes. The other blocks, especially instruction-supply front-end, should be always in high-speed mode. This reduces the efficiency of the variable voltage and frequency scaling technique. On the other hand, every component of each processor core can alternate two modes in MultiCore model, and thus the improve-ment in energy efficiency is expected.

## 2.2 Active Power Reduction

As shown in Fig. 2, each core has its dedicated voltage/frequency controller and value predictor. The potential effect of the Contrail processor architecture on energy-efficiency is estimated as follows: We determine the clock frequency and supply voltage for the verification cores at half that for the speculation core as used in Fig. 1. Here, we will focus on active power, and thus energy consumption is calculated as follows: For the speculation cores, energy consumption becomes half that of the origi-nal execution since the number of instructions is reduced by half. In contrast, for the verification cores, the sum of every execution time remains unchanged since the execution time of each instruction is two times increased while the total number of instructions is reduced by half. Its energy consumption is decreased due to the reduc-tion of the clock frequency and the supply voltage. It is reduced to 1/8 of the original. Thus, the total energy savings is 37.5%. It is true that the energy efficiency of

Contrail processors depends on the value prediction accuracy and the size of each region. However, we believe that the potential effect of Contrail processors on energy savings is substantial from the estimate above.

Recent studies regarding power consumption of value predictors find that complex value predictors are power-hungry [1, 16, 19]. One of the solutions for reducing power consumed in value predictors is using simple value predictors such as last-value predictor [15, 19]. However, value prediction is not the only technique for generating speculation stream. Other techniques are probably utilized for this purpose, and the key idea behind the Contrail architecture will be adopted.

### 2.3 Leakage Power Consideration

While the Contrail processor architecture has good characteristics on active power reduction, its leakage power consumption might be increased since it has multiple cores. As mentioned in the previous sections, only one core has to be fast and the remaining cores can be slow. Thus, we can reduce or even cut the supply voltage for the slow cores. Similarly, the threshold voltage of transistors for the slow cores can be raised, resulting in significant leakage reduction. There are several circuits proposed to reduce leakage current by dynamically raising the threshold voltage, for example by modulating body bias voltage [2, 13, 25]. From these considerations, we expect to keep the leakage power consumed by the Contrail processor comparable to or even smaller than that consumed by a single-core processor.

### 2.4 Related Works

Speculative multithreading [5, 9, 18, 22, 26] is very popular in microprocessor architecture. One of the differences from the previously proposed speculative multi-threaded processors is that the Contrail processor does not require any mechanism to detect memory dependence violations. Since the Contrail processor strongly relies on value prediction, any memory dependence violations cannot occur. Instead, it suffers from value misspredictions. This simplifies hardware complexity. This is because value misspredictions can be detected locally in a core, while detecting memory dependence violations requires a complex mechanism such as ARB or Versioning Cache [9]. Another difference from the previously proposed pre-computing architectures [22, 26] is that the Contrail processor architecture does not rely on redundant execution. In the ideal case, the number of executed instructions is unchanged. Another difference is that its target is the improvement in energy efficiency instead of that in performance.

## 3   Evaluation

This section explains evaluation methodology, and then presents simulation results.

### 3.1   Methodology

We implemented the Contrail processor simulator using MASE [14], a derivative of SimpleScalar tool set. Its PISA instruction set architecture (ISA) is based on MIPS ISA. The baseline processor and each core in the Contrail processor are a 2-way out-of-order execution processor. Only fetch bandwidth is 8-instruction wide. The number of cores on the Contrail processor model is 4. In the current simulator, the followings are assumed. Instruction and data caches are ideal. Branch prediction is perfect. Ambiguous memory dependences are perfectly resolved. In contrast, we model a value predictor in details. We use a 2K-entry last-value predictor [15]. For thread spawning policy, the fixed interval partitioning [5] is used, because it does a good job with load balance. The interval is 32 instructions. This value is determined based on the previous study [23]. The overhead on spawning a new thread is 8 cycles.

We evaluate a scaling for supply voltage and clock frequency based on Intel Pentium M processor [10]. The verification cores work at lower frequency and voltage (800MHz, 1.036V), and the speculation core and the baseline processor work at higher frequency and voltage (1.6GHz, 1.484V). Since leakage power strongly depends upon temperature, we should use a pessimistic assumption. We use temperature of 100°C, where the leakage power is equal to the active power [4]. This is a reasonable assumption, since it is reported that the leakage power is comparable to the active power in the future process technologies [2]. The verification cores exploit the body bias technology. It is assumed that the leakage power consumed by the cores, where reverse body bias is applied, is reduced by 2x [2]. And last, we assume that the leakage power consumed by idle cores is negligible.

We use 11 programs from SPEC2000 for evaluating general-purpose applications, 13 programs from MediaBench for multimedia application, and 3 programs from MiBench [11] for embedded applications.

## 3.2 Results

We only show the average of simulation results for three benchmark suites, respectively, due to the lack of space.

Fig. 3 presents execution cycles of the Contrail processor, which are relative to those of the baseline single-core processor. Last-value predictors have only a few contributions on single-core processor performance [15]. This is same for the Contrail processor, while performance improvement is not the goal of this architecture. The combination of value prediction and multithreading architecture achieves the improvement of around 10% in performance.

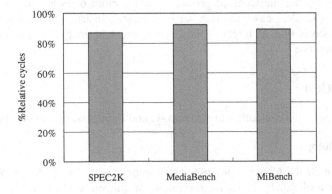

**Fig. 3.** Relative execution cycles

Fig. 4 presents the relative power consumption. Each bar is divided into two parts. The lower and upper parts indicate the average active and leakage power, respectively. As you can see, power consumption is slightly increased. This is because the execution cycle is reduced by speculation. From Figs 3 and 4, it is observed the cycle reduction rate is larger than the power increase rate. Thus, energy consumption is reduced. The results are very different from those for other low power architectures, which achieve power reduction at the cost of performance loss.

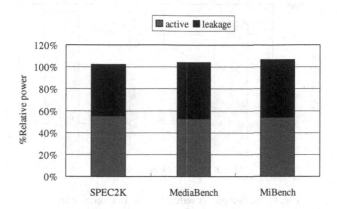

**Fig. 4.** Relative power consumption

Fig.5 shows Energy-Delay$^2$ product (ED$^2$P). The vertical line indicates ED$^2$P of the Contrail processor relative to that of the baseline single-core processor. It is observed that the improvement of 23% in ED$^2$P is achieved on average. As mentioned above, the missprediction penalties are included in the results.

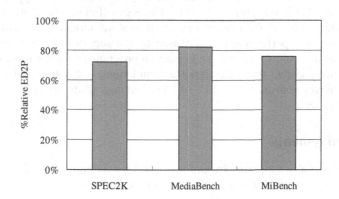

**Fig. 5.** Relative energy-delay$^2$ product

Fig. 3 shows that the Contrail processor achieves performance improvement, which is not our primary goal. Since performance improvement is not required, we can still slow down clock frequency, resulting in further power reduction. This is a hierarchical frequency scaling. A global control signal uniformly throttles every local clock, which originally has two modes; high-speed mode for the speculation core and the low-speed one for verification cores. Since the hierarchical change in supply voltage will be difficult to implement, we only change clock frequency. Under this scenario, power consumption is reduced as shown in Fig. 6, if we could ideally control the global clock. While this technique does not affect energy, the power reduction is desirable for temperature awareness.

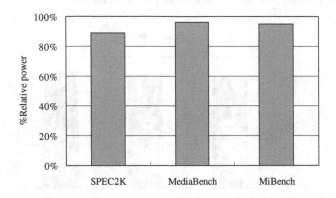

**Fig. 6.** Further power reduction via frequency control

## 4   Conclusions

The current trend of the advance in semiconductor technologies will impose the diminishing return in single-thread performance since a huge amount of the increase in power consumption and hence in power density is predicted. Multithreading and dual-power functional units will be promising techniques to reduce energy in the future microprocessors [18]. We proposed such an energy-efficient speculative MultiCore processor, which we call Contrail processor. It exploits thread level parallelism, resulting in mitigating performance loss caused by the supply voltage reduction. Only the part of the program, which has the impact on program execution time, is executed on power-hungry cores. From the detailed simulations, we found that the Contrail processor achieves approximately 23% of $ED^2P$ savings while processor performance is slightly improved.

## Acknowledgements

This work is partially supported by Grants-in-Aid for Scientific Research #16300019 and #176549 from Japan Society for the Promotion of Science.

## References

1. Bhargava, R., John, L.: Latency and energy aware value prediction for high-frequency processors, 16th International Conference on Supercomputing (June 2002)
2. Borkar, S.: Microarchitecture and design challenges for gigascale integration, 37th International Symposium on Microarchitecture, Keynote (December 2004)

3. Chandrakasan, A.P., Brodersen, R.W.: Minimizing power consumption in digital CMOS circuits, Proceedings of IEEE, 83(4) (April 1995)
4. Chaparro, P., Gonzalez, J., Gonzalez, A.: Thermal-effective clustered microarchitecture, 1st Workshop on Temperature Aware Computer System (June2004)
5. Codrescu, L., Wills, D.: On dynamic speculative thread partitioning and the MEM-slicing algorithm, 8th International Conference on Parallel Architectures and Compilation Techniques (October 1999)
6. Edahiro, M., Matsushita, S., Yamashina, M., Nishi, N.: A single-chip multi-processor for smart terminals, IEEE Micro, 20(4) (July-August 2000)
7. Fleischmann, M.: LongRun power management, white paper, Transmeta Corporation (January 2001)
8. Flynn, D.: Intelligent energy management: an SoC design based on ARM926EJ-S, 15th Hot Chips (August 2003)
9. Franklin, M.: Multiscalar processors, Kluwer Academic Publishers (2003)
10. Gochman, S., Ronen, R., Anati, I., Berkovits, A., Kurts, T., Naveh, A., Saeed, A., Sperber, Z., Valentine, R.C.: The Intel Pentium M processor: microarchitecture and performance, Intel Technology Journal, 7(2) (May 2003)
11. Guthaus, M.R., Ringenberg, J.S., Ernst, D., Austin, T.M., Mudge, T., Brown, B.: MiBench: a free, commercially representative embedded benchmark suite, 4th Workshop on Workload Characterization (December 2001)
12. Kaneko, S., Sawai, K., Masui, N., Ishimi, K., Itou, T., Satou, M., Kondo, H., Okumura, N., Takata, Y., Takata, H., Sakugawa, M., Higuchi, T., Ohtani, S., Sakamoto, K., Ishikawa, N., Nakajima, M., Iwata, S., Hayase, K., Nakano, S., Nakazawa, S., Tomisawa, O., Shimizu, T.: A 600 MHz single-chip multiprocessor with 4.8 GB/s internal shared pipelined bus and 512 kB internal memory, International Solid State Circuits Conference (February 2005)
13. Kuroda, T., Fujita, T., Mita, S., Nagamatsu, T., Yoshioka, S., Sano, F., Norishima, M., Murota, M., Kato, M., Kinugasa, M., Kakumu, M., Sakurai, T.: A 0.9V, 150MHz, 10mW, 4mm$^2$, 2-D discrete cosine transform core processor with variable-threshold-voltage scheme, International Solid State Circuit Conference (February 1996)
14. Larson, E., Chatterjee, S., Austin, T.: MASE: a novel infrastructure for detailed microarchitectural modeling International Symposium on Performance Analysis of Systems and Software (November 2001)
15. Lipasti, M.H., Wilkerson, C.B., Shen, J.P.: Value locality and load value prediction, 7th International Conference on Architectural Support for Programming Languages and Operation Systems (October 1996)
16. Moreno, R., Pinuel, L., Del-Pino, S., Tirado, F.: A power perspective of value speculation for superscalar microprocessors, 19th International Conference on Computer Design (September 2000)
17. Pilla, M.L., da Costa, A.T., Franca, F.M.G., Navaux, P.O.A.: Predicting trace inputs with dynamic trace memoization: determining speedup upper bounds, 10th International Conference on Parallel Architectures and Compilation Techniques, WiP session (September 2001)
18. Rattner, J.: Electronics in the Internet age, 10th International Conference on Parallel Architectures and Compilation Techniques, Keynote (September 2001)
19. Sam, N.B, Burtscher, M.: On the energy-efficiency of speculative hardware, International Conference on Computing Frontiers (May 2005)
20. Sato, T., Arita, I.: Contrail processors for converting high-performance into energy-efficiency, 10th International Conference on Parallel Architectures and Compilation Techniques, WiP session (September 2001)

21. Shiota, T., Kawasaki, K., Kawabe, Y., Shibamoto, W., Sato, A., Hashimoto, T., Haya-kawa, F., Tago, S., Okano, H., Nakamura, Y., Miyake, H., Suga, A., Takahashi, H.: A 51.2GOPS, 1.0GB/s-DMA single-chip multi-processor integrating quadruple 8-way VLIW processors, International Solid State Circuits Conference (February 2005)
22. Sundaramoorthy, K., Purser, Z., Rotenberg, E.: Slipstream processors: improving both per-formance and fault tolerance, 9th International Conference on Architectural Support for Programming Languages and Operating Systems (November 2000)
23. Tanaka, Y., Sato, T., Koushiro, T.: The potential in energy efficiency of a speculative chip-multiprocessor, 16th Symposium on Parallelism in Algorithms and Architectures (June 2004)
24. Torii, S., Suzuki, S., Tomonaga, H., Tokue, T., Sakai, J., Suzuki, N., Murakami, K., Hi-raga, T., Shigemoto, K., Tatebe, Y., Obuchi, E., Kayama, N., Edahiro, E., Kusano, T., Ni-shi, N.: A 600MIPS 120mW 70A leakage triple-CPU mobile application processor chip, International Solid State Circuits Conference (February 2005)
25. Transmeta Corporation: LongRun2 technology, http://www.transmeta.com/longrun2/
26. Zilles, C., Sohi, G.S.: Master/slave speculative parallelization, 35th International Sympo-sium on Microarchitecture (November 2002)

# A CMOS Compatible Charge Recovery Logic Family for Low Supply Voltages

Clemens Schlachta and Manfred Glesner

Institute of Microelectronic Systems,
Darmstadt University of Technology, Germany
{schlachta, glesner}@mes.tu-darmstadt.de

**Abstract.** In this work we will introduce an enhanced, $CMOS$-compatible adiabatic logic family based on a new diode element for charge recovery. This diode element uses bipolar transistors to reduce the diode forward voltage losses in existing charge recovery logic families allwoing the use at lower supply voltages. Based on this element the $CMOS$ compatible, static adiabatic logic familiy $biQSERL$ is introduced.

## 1 Introduction

Power consumption became a significant problem in the last years for the development of integrated logic circuits. Many concepts for reducing the power consumption, like shrinking the transistor sizes, reducing the supply voltage and optimizing the logic, have been introduced and are wide in use. Besides these another concept is still developing: the adiabatic logic. Adiabatic logic tries to reduce the power consumption on gate level by charging the nets capacitances with a better suited waveform and tries to recycle the charge stored in the nets (i.e. [Paul et al. 2000]).

In the recent years many adabatic logic families have been proposed, for example $2N$-$2N2P$, $SCAL$-$D$ or $RERL$ (i.e. [Lim et al. 2000, Kim et al. 2001]). One of the proposed concepts is the $QSERL$-logic (depicted in fig. 1) [Ye et al. 2001] or the very similar $CAMOS/ADMOS$-logic family proposed in [De et al. 1996]. These are very interesting logic families on account of to their static output levels which makes the logic compatible with standard $CMOS$. The bottleneck of these logic families are the diodes needed for decoupling the shared power clock from the already charged or discharged nets. There are some possibilities to implement diodes:

- The use of normal silicon $pn$-junctions. These kind of diodes have forward voltages (flow voltages) of about $0.6..0.7V$ which is inacceptable (20% and more of the supply voltage) in low-voltage designs with a supply voltage of $3.3V$ and less.
- The second possibility is the use of $MOSFET$s in a diode connection (gate and drain connected). In this circuit the flow voltage is mainly determined by the threshold voltage $v_{th}$ of the $MOSFET$. This leads to a voltage drop

J. Vounckx, N. Azemard, and P. Maurine (Eds.): PATMOS 2006, LNCS 4148, pp. 563–572, 2006.
© Springer-Verlag Berlin Heidelberg 2006

across the transistors that is comparable to the forward voltage of diodes. By the use of low-threshold *MOSFET*s these voltage drops can be minimized. However this will result in increased leakage currents.

– The last possibility is the use of metal-silicon junctions (Schottky-diodes), these diodes have a significant smaller flow voltage (around $0.2..0.3V$) than silicon-only junctions; but even these voltages are too large for low-voltage designs.

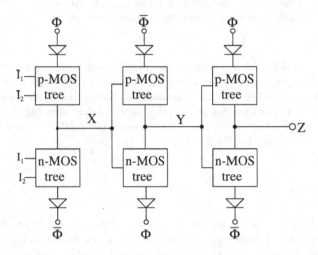

**Fig. 1.** Principle structure of *QSERL*-logic gates [Ye et al. 2001]

## 2   Bipolar Transistor Based Diode Element

Normal diodes or *MOSFET*s are not suited to overcome the physical impossibility to reduce the flow (forward) voltages of diodes to small values. A possible approach for replacing diodes is to utilize that the collector-emitter voltage of a bipolar transistor in saturation mode is less than the forward voltage of a simple silicon diode, even less than the base-emitter diode in the transistor. The difficulty in this concept is the base current generation because of the necessary circuitry in which resistors require too much effort for integration.

The idea behind the proposed diode element is that the load in a *CMOS*-design is a capacitive load. This means, that the load current is mostly depending of the change rate of the load capacitances voltage. If the base of the transistor is also connected to a capacitor, the same voltage change happens to the capacitor at the base of the transistor by the nearly constant base-emitter voltage of a bipolar transistor. If the change rate is held nearly constant, the current through the transistor and thus the voltages across the transistor will become nearly constant also. Thus the collector and the base current get into a fixed relation.

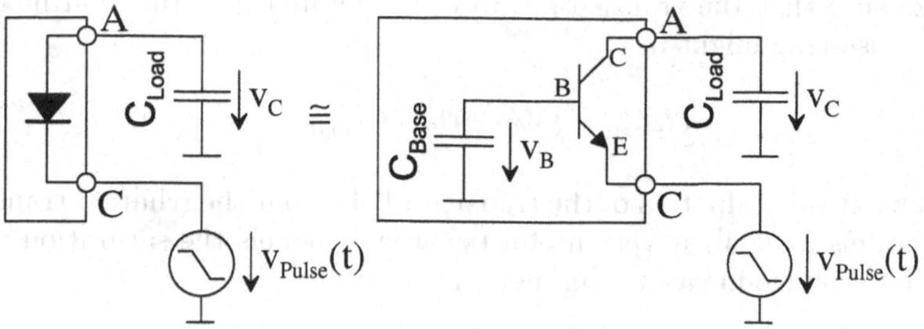

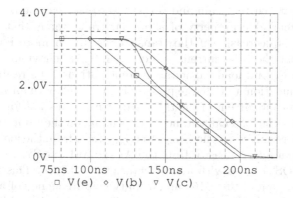

**Fig. 2.** Principle schematic of the diode element

**Fig. 3.** Voltage traces at the transistor pins for the proposed diode element. The voltage at the emitter (e, lowest trace) of the transistor is driven by the pulse source, the base (b, upmost trace) is driven by a capacitor and the load connected to the collector (c, middle trace) is capacitive. It can be seen that the collector-emitter voltage is very small after reaching the forward voltage of the base-emitter diode.

This allows to control the circuit by the emitter voltage change of the transistor as depicted in fig. 3.

Because the base-emitter connection is still a diode, this only works for negative voltage changes (with respect to ground) of the emitter voltage for a *npn*-transistor and for positive changes of the emitter voltage for *pnp*-transistor. If the emitter voltage is changed in one direction, current is flowing, if the emitter voltage is changed in the opposite direction, no current is flowing. Thus this elements acts like a diode.

The size of the base capacitor can be determined from the requirement that the transistor must be operated in saturation mode. This lead to the equation

$$C_{Load} \leq \beta_f \cdot C_{Base} \tag{1}$$

To make sure that the transistor is always operated in saturation mode, a typical dimensioning might be

$$C_{Base} \approx (5\%..20\%) \cdot C_{Load}$$

For an analytical evaluation of the transistor behaviour the (charge) transport model (i.e. [Reisch 2003]) is very useful because it models the saturation mode accurate. The voltage in saturation mode is given by

$$v_{F,Sat} = V_T \cdot \ln \left( \frac{\beta_F}{\beta_R} \cdot \frac{I_C + (1 + \beta_R) \cdot I_B}{\beta_F \cdot I_B - I_C} \right) \tag{2}$$

with $\beta_F$ as forward current gain and $\beta_R$ as reverse current gain.

The most remarkable property of a bipolar transistor is that the collector-emitter voltage is decreasing if the transistor is driven more into saturation, which means that the base current is increased. This behaviour was simulated for many slew rate and load capacitance combinations. The result is shown in fig. 4. In this simulation a discharge process is simulated with an $npn$-transistor. The collector-emitter current of the transistor is held constant for compatibility, which means that the load capacitance is depending on the ramp time. The base capacitance is determined by the $C_{Base}$ to $C_{Load}$ ratio from the load capacitance. The transistor is a $npn$-transistor from the AUSTRIAMICROSYSTEMS $0.35\mu m$ Si-Ge HBT BiCMOS process with a emitter length of $0.8\mu m$. This transistor has a typical current gain of $\beta_F = 160$ and a unity gain frequency of about $55GHz$. The process is a standard $CMOS$-process for digital logic with additional bipolar transistors to allow mixed-mode RF circuits.

It can be seen that the collector-emitter voltage is less $100mV$ in a wide range and that this element is working even for ramp times of about $1ns$.

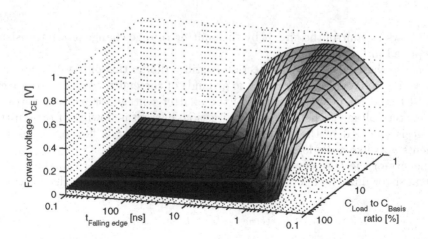

**Fig. 4.** Forward voltage in the simulated discharge process for a $npn$-transistor

# 3    Adiabatic Domino Logic

As a simple example for using the diode element introduced before, adiabatic domino logic (*ADL*) can be used. The operation of *ADL* is similar to normal domino logic, the operation cycle consists of two parts: a input value dependent charge phase and a discharge phase. In difference to standard domino logic in *ADL* the discharge phase is done via a diode to make sure that only charged nets are discharged. A possible circuit for an *ADL* gate is shown in fig. 5 (left side). The extension of the *ADL* gate with the bipolar transistor based diode element is shown in the right side of the figure.

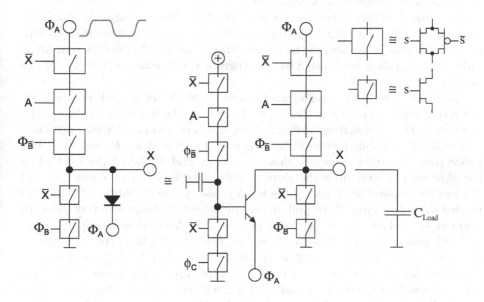

**Fig. 5.** Left side: Adiabatic domino logic. Right side: *ADL* extended with the bipolar transistor based diode element. The additional switches are required to control the base capacitances voltages, this capacitance is required for BJTs base current generation.

The idea behind the domino-logic structure is to charge the load depending on the data at the input $A$ of the stage and to discharge the load via the diode element at the end of the cycle in any case. This is comparable with normal dynamic logic except that charge recovery is used for discharging. The diode element is necessary to seperate uncharged load nets from charged load nets. In this way the discharge phase can be done after changing the input values. Because of this an *ADL* stage behaves like a register, and cascaded *ADL* stages turn into a pipeline structure with full charge recovery. In simulations (AUSTRIAMICROSYSTEMS $0.35\mu m$ SiGe-HBT BiCMOS) the *ADL* is running stable with a $166.7MHz$ power clock frequency. The phase shift is $60°$ between the stages (6 clock signals with different phases) achieving an effective data rate of $1GHz$.

# 4    An *CMOS*-Compatible Adiabatic Logic: biQSERL

Based on the diode element described in in sect. 2 a complete push-pull stage was developed. The output signal of the push-pull stage is compatible to standard-*CMOS* which allows to mix *biQSERL* and *CMOS* gates in a circuit.

The schematic of a stage is depicted in fig. 6. The stage consists of two identical halfs that operate in inverse to each other. The complementary signals are required within the stage for the pull-up/pull-down switches. The doubled structure is not a big drawback because the pass-gates in following stages need complementary control signals anyway. Furthermore, the complementary output can be used to optimize the logical circuitry.

The transistors inside the stage are used for three different purposes: The inner part with the bipolar transistors replaces the diodes in the standard *QSERL*-logic. Connected in parallel to the bipolar transistors are *MOSFET*s that allow rail-to-rail operation while using base voltages within the normal supply voltage range.

The transistors at the top and the bottom of the circuit are pull-up and pull-down transistors to charge or discharge the nets to the full supply voltage. The blocks with the ideal switches are pass-gates which perform the logical operation.

The stage uses four power clocks, $A+$ and $A-$ as well as $B+$ and $B-$. The phase pair $A$ is used as power phase to charge and discharge the load while the $B$ phase pair only drive the gates of some *MOSFET*s. The phases $B+$ and $B-$ are 90° phase shifted against the main phase $A$. These additional clocks are needed to control some of the pull-up and pull-down switches. Circuits suited to generate such clock signals have been proposed in [Athas et al. 1996].

The input signal to a stage must only be held stable within the first quarter of a clock cycle, because the state changes during that time, if necessary. In the remaining three quarters of a clock cycle the inputs can be undefined. This allows a phase shift of 90° or a quarter of a clock cycle between two stages. Thus for pipelines or other multi-stage logic the first logic stage can be clocked with a phase shift of 0° , the second stage with a phase shift of 90° and so on. This allows a high throughput while using a moderate clock speed.

In fig. 7 traces of some signals are shown. The upmost traces are the clock signals, the traces below show the input signal. The second lowest trace shows the output signal the *biQSERL*-stage (clocked with phase $A$). The lowest trace shows the base voltages within this stage. It can be seen that the base voltage is offset by the base-emitter diode voltage drop. Aafterwards this difference is compensated by the pull-up or pull-down switches. The second upmost trace shows the output of the second stage clock by phase $B$. The phase shift between phase A and phase B allows the use of the outputs of stage 0 as inputs of stage 1 without wasting a complete clock cycle.

The overall efficiency was also computed by a parametric simulation varying the frequency of the power clocks and the load capacitance. The *biQSERL*-stage

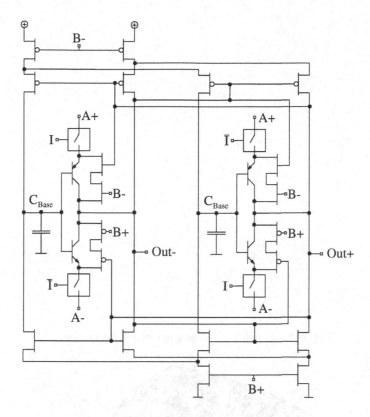

**Fig. 6.** Schematic of a stage in *biQSERL*-logic. One stage consists of two identical structures that operate in inverse to each other.

was simulated as an inverter in an inverter chain to get correct signal levels. The efficiency is calculated including the current needed by the pull-up switches.

For the simulations a fictive *pnp*-transistor was used to overcome the non-availability of a *pnp*-transistor complementary to the *npn*-transistor in the technology. Therefore the Spice-model for the *pnp*-transitor was derived from the *npn*-transistor in the used process (AustriaMicroSystems $0.35\mu m$ SiGe-HBT BiCMOS). This is not a real restriction for the concept because the non- availability of complementary transistors is an economical decision of the process designers and not caused physically.

Simulation show that an efficiency of up to 89% (11% of the power consumption of an ideal CMOS implementation) can be reached at $V_{dd} = 3.3V$ within the megahertz range. The efficiency is calculated as ratio between the energy consumed by the *biQSERL*-stage and the energy required to charge the load capacitance (both outputs) abrupt (like *CMOS*). When using only one output, the maximum efficiency would decrease to about 78%. The efficiency can be further

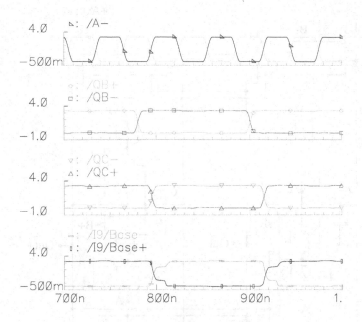

**Fig. 7.** Some voltage traces from *biQSERL* stages

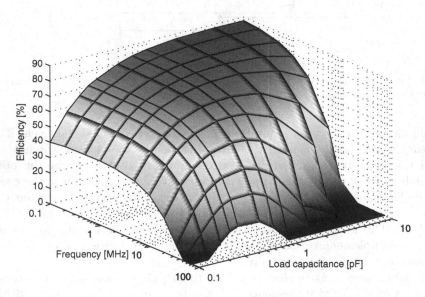

**Fig. 8.** Efficiency of the *biQSERL*-logic stage compared to abrupt charging of the same capacitance

increased by sizing the width of the pass-gate transistors to the optimum for the desired operation point. In the simulation the sizes of all transistors were constant and have been choosen to get a broad working range.

**Fig. 9.** The test ASIC manufactured in the $0.35\mu m$ Si- Ge HBT BiCMOS process from AUSTRIAMICROSYSTEMS ($7mm^2$)

## 5   Implementation Effort

Besides efficiency the implementation effort is of interest. For each half of a *biQSERL* stage ten *MOSFET*s are necessary and two bipolar transistors, this makes 20 *MOSFET*s and four BJTs in sum. Furthermore, the transistors for the pass gates are required to implement the logical function of the stage. This can be a single pass gate for an inverter or more. In account of the effort the use of *biQSERL* stages is especially usefull as line driver for large on-chip nets or buses. In this case the *biQSERL* stage acts as power driver while the logic function is implemented in a *CMOS*-gate.

The high tolerance for the base capacitor allows implementing this capacitors also as metal-metal capacitor and thus occupying no additional chip area. In the test chip ($0,35\mu m$ *CMOS*) a cell required about $54 \cdot 38\mu m$, but the size can

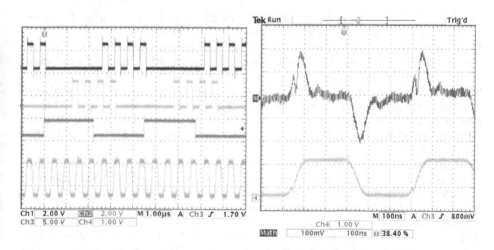

**Fig. 10.** Left side: Output traces of two inverters of the domino logic part. Right side: Current and voltage of a power phase.

be reduced by improving the layout and the use of a more advanced vertical *pnp* transistors with smaller footprint and better performance. The design was implemented in a test ASIC using the $0.35\mu m$ Si- Ge HBT BiCMOS process from AustriaMicroSystems. This process offers only a lateral-*pnp*-transistor that does not match the parameters of the vertical *npn*-transistor leading to stability problems in the test chip.

In the left picture of fig.10 the measured signals of two outputs out of one adiabatic domino logic inverter chain are shown, in the lowest trace one power phase is shown and above the input signal. The outputs are digital pads thus the sinusoidal waveform is not visible. The pulsed output is a result from the dynamic operation, the transitions from high to low level are charge recovery cycles. In the right side (upper trace) the current of one power clock is shown with the discharge and charge cycle.

## 6   Conclusional Remarks

The enhanced logic family *biQSERL* is presented. The major advantage of this logic family over the original *QSERL*-logic is the higher efficiency especially for low supply voltages. From the achieved results it can be said that the possibilities of this concept are not fully explored with this experimental design. The *CMOS* pass-gates became the bottleneck due to their limited transconductance so this design is not able to utilize the complete performance of the Si- Ge bipolar transistors. The concept shows it strength especially as driver cell for long on-chip interconnects or high fan-out nets where higher capacitive loads and moderate switching speeds are usual.

## References

[Ye et al. 2001] Yibin Ye and Kaushik Roy: QSERL: Quasi-Static Energy Recovery Logic. IEEE Journal of Solid-State Circuits, Vol. 36 (2001) 239-248.

[Lim et al. 2000] Joonho Lim and Kipaek Kwon and Soo-Ik Chae: NMOS reversible energy recovery logic for ultra-low-energy applications, IEEE Journal of Solid-State Circuits, Vol. 35 (2000) 865-875.

[Kim et al. 2001] Suhwan Kim and M.C. Papaefthymiou: True single-phase adiabatic circuitry, IEEE Transactions on Very Large Scale Integration Vol. 9 (2001) 52-63.

[Paul et al. 2000] Steffen Paul and Andreas M. Schlaffer and Josef A. Nossek: Optimal Charging of Capacitors, IEEE Transactions on Circuits and Systems I, Vol. 47 (2000) 1009-1015.

[De et al. 1996] Vivek K. De and James D. Meindl: Complementary adiabatic and fully adiabatic MOS logic families for gigascale integration, 43rd Solid-State Circuits Conference (ISSCC), 1996, Digest of Technical Papers 298-299.

[Reisch 2003] Michael Reisch: High-Frequency Bipolar Transistors, Springer Verlag, Heidelberg, 2003.

[Athas et al. 1996] W. Athas and L. Svensson and N. Tzartzanis: A resonant signal driver for two-phase, almost-non-overlapping clocks, IEEE Symposium on Circuits and Systems (ISCAS), 1996, Digest of Technical Papers, ISCAS 298 -299.

# A Framework for Estimating Peak Power
# in Gate-Level Circuits

Diganchal Chakraborty, P.P. Chakrabarti, Arijit Mondal, and Pallab Dasgupta

Indian Institute of Technology Kharagpur, India
{diganchal, ppchak, arijit, pallab}@cse.iitkgp.ernet.in

**Abstract.** This paper presents a framework for estimation of peak power dissipation in gate level circuits. This measure can be used to make architectural or design style decisions during the VLSI synthesis process. The proposed method first builds a symbolic event list for every possible input and uses this as the database for computing the peak power estimate. A novel heuristic search based method is presented which works on this symbolic event list to estimate peak power. Experimental results on ISCAS'89 benchmarks demonstrate the proposed method to be effective on moderately large circuits.

## 1 Introduction

The continuous growth in chip density, increasing complexity of designs and the advent of portable devices has created a demand for tools for fast and accurate estimates of power for various circuit implementations. Power dissipation of a circuit largely depends on propagation delays of the gates, technology parameters, circuit topology and the sequence of inputs applied on it [1]. Moreover, the total energy dissipation is not uniformly distributed over time. As a matter of fact, a sudden surge of energy or peak power may become responsible for burning of the chip. In this paper, we have addressed the general problem of estimating the peak power within a time $\delta$, where $\delta$ is an user controllable value which can be smaller than a clock period. By providing the clock period as $\delta$, this method can also be generalized to find the power for a complete transition.

There are known techniques for power estimation based on logic simulation. Exhaustive simulation is usually prohibitive even for circuits with more than 20 inputs. Consequently, researchers use either Monte-Carlo simulation or test generation based techniques [2] to find only a lower bound on maximum power. The idea of estimating maximum transition power by solving *maximum satisfiability* (Max-SAT) on gate transition conditions was first presented in [1]. This method, however, could not scale well even for circuits with more than 30 inputs and is not suitable for a non-unit delay model. A sequel to this work was presented in [4], where the authors proposed an *arithmetic decision diagram* (ADD[3]) based technique to solve Max-SAT. But ADDs also demand unreasonable space for moderate sized circuits unless used intelligently. The solution to the problem proposed in this paper also requires solving the "maximum satisfiability problem".

This paper presents a new heuristic search based algorithm to solve the problem which intelligently uses ADDs to provide a close upper bound heuristic estimate for

J. Vounckx, N. Azemard, and P. Maurine (Eds.): PATMOS 2006, LNCS 4148, pp. 573–582, 2006.

pruning. We can handle fairly large circuits which contain of the order of 60 primary inputs and latches and over 1000 gates while assuming a general delay model. Experiments with ISCAS'89 benchmarks establish the effectiveness of the proposed method.

This paper is organized as follows. In section 2 we present the proposed problem formulation. We provide an overview of the method, state the timing and power model, mathematically formulate the peak power estimation problem and illustrate it with an example. In section 3 we describe the proposed heuristic search based technique and explain it with examples. In section 4 we present results on ISCAS'89 benchmark circuits and section 5 concludes the paper.

# 2   Problem Formulation

The method presented in this paper takes a gate level netlist, previously characterized timing and power data for all elementary gates and a small time $\delta$ as input. The method outputs the value of the peak power within $\delta$ corresponding to the specific delay and power model mentioned by the user. The program also outputs an input and state vector for which the circuit is observed to dissipate the estimated peak power.

The method first builds a list of symbolic events or transitions using the method presented in [5], which will occur at different nodes in the circuit over time for all possible inputs and state transitions. This list of events is used as a database on which the proposed peak power estimation method is applied. In the next few subsections we explain the event list generation method and the peak power estimation method and illustrate them with examples.

## 2.1   Symbolic Event List Generation

In [6] timing analysis of combinational circuits was performed using event propagation. [5] provides a method which is completely symbolic and adaptable for use in sequential circuits. Using the method described in [5] we generate lists of symbolic events in all circuit nodes, which is explained by the following example.

Fig 1 illustrates the event list generation method for a small circuit. Each event is denoted by a 3-tuple $(c, t, v)$. $c$ is the **event propagation condition**, **event time** (t) is the timepoint at which the event occurs and $v$ is the **binary value** at the node after the event occurs. The event propagation condition is a Boolean function over the present state and next state of the flip flops and the primary inputs. The event propagation condition is stored as a Binary Decision Diagram (BDD). In order to construct the event propagation condition, we first insert two variables for each flip flop and one variable for each primary input in the circuit. For each flip flop $i$, we have 2 variables $i$ and $i'$, where $i$ denotes present state and $i'$ denotes next state. If the values of $i$ and $i'$ differ, it is considered as a transition, and if they are the same then it denotes a no-change at the flop output. $i.\overline{i'}$ denotes a falling transition, $\overline{i}.i'$ denotes a rising transition, $i.i'$ denotes fixed logic 1 and $\overline{i}.\overline{i'}$ denotes fixed logic 0. Primary inputs can only stay at a fixed logic 1 or a fixed logic 0.

Initial node values are represented by events with time -1. Events at flip flops have a time $t = 0$. All other events at intermediate nodes in the circuit have a positive event

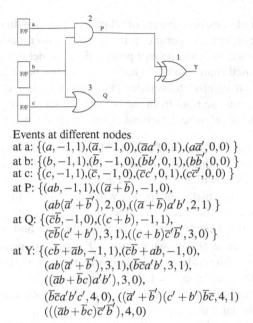

Events at different nodes
at a: $\{(a,-1,1),(\bar{a},-1,0),(\bar{a}a',0,1),(a\bar{a}',0,0)\}$
at b: $\{(b,-1,1),(\bar{b},-1,0),(\bar{b}b',0,1),(b\bar{b}',0,0)\}$
at c: $\{(c,-1,1),(\bar{c},-1,0),(\bar{c}c',0,1),(c\bar{c}',0,0)\}$
at P: $\{(ab,-1,1),((\bar{a}+\bar{b}),-1,0),$
$\qquad (ab(\bar{a}'+\bar{b}'),2,0),((\bar{a}+\bar{b})a'b',2,1)\}$
at Q: $\{(\bar{c}\bar{b},-1,0),((c+b),-1,1),$
$\qquad (\bar{c}\bar{b}(c'+b'),3,1),((c+b)\bar{c}'\bar{b}',3,0)\}$
at Y: $\{(c\bar{b}+\bar{a}b,-1,1),(\bar{c}\bar{b}+ab,-1,0),$
$\qquad (ab(\bar{a}'+\bar{b}'),3,1),(\bar{b}\bar{c}a'b',3,1),$
$\qquad ((\bar{a}b+\bar{b}c)a'b'),3,0),$
$\qquad (\bar{b}\bar{c}a'b'c',4,0),\ ((\bar{a}'+\bar{b}')(c'+b')\bar{b}\bar{c},4,1)$
$\qquad (((\bar{a}b+\bar{b}c)\bar{c}'\bar{b}'),4,0)$

**Fig. 1.** Example1: Event list generation

time which is the delay after which an event at a flip flop propagates to the intermediate node. All flip flop transitions are assumed to take place at time $t = 0$. Initial lists of events at flip flop output nodes a,b and c are shown in Fig. 1.

Once the event list for the input lines of a gate is constructed, the event generation algorithm in [5] can check whether these events can propagate to the gate output. An event on an input of a gate can propagate to the output of that gate only if the other inputs stay at noncontrolling values. In case an event satisfies this condition, an event with proper timing and event propagation condition is inserted at the gate output. This way event lists for the gate outputs are constructed. For example, a rising transition event $(\bar{a}a',0,1)$ at time $t = 0$ at node a will propagate to output of the AND gate at node P at time $t = 2$ if either node b remains at fixed logic 1 or it has a rise transition $(\bar{b}b',0,1)$ at the same time $t = 0$. This way all events at node P, Q and Y are symbolically generated as listed in Fig. 1. Please refer to [5] for detailed explanation of this event generation method.

## 2.2 Peak Power Estimation

This section contains the timing and power models that are used for generating event lists. Mathematical formulation of the peak power problem is provided thereafter.

**Power and Delay Model:** Power dissipation of a circuit is directly related to the number of events that occur. The total transition power of a gate is characterized by the formula $P = 0.5CV_{DD}^2N_G$ [1], where C is the output capacitance for the gate and $N_G$ is the number of events within unit time at the output of the gate. The transition power of a circuit is the sum of transition powers of all gates. Since, we do not have data for power values, we have conducted experiments using a unit power model, where each event or transition is assumed to consume unit power. But, a general power model can also be used in the proposed framework. We have replaced the basic gates (AND, OR, NOT, XOR etc.) in the circuits by characterized cells taken from a technology library. Delay values for these gates are read from the library. We have also conducted experiments using a unit delay model, where each gate is assumed to have the same delay.

**Peak Power Within a Time $\delta$: (PP($\delta$)):** This is the maximum possible power dissipation that can occur within a $\delta$ time interval. Here, we illustrate computation of peak power within unit time with the example circuit depicted in Fig. 1.

We show how to calculate peak power within time $t = 3$ to $t = 4$. We consider only events which can occur between this time, that is, all events at node $Q$ and $Y$. Solving Max-SAT on these event propagation conditions we find that under the transition $(a\bar{a}'b\bar{b}'c\bar{c}')$ one event at $Q$ and two events at $Y$ occur. So, peak power between times $t = 3$ and $t = 4$ is 3. Similarly we calculate peak power for all other time windows between $t = 0$ and $t = 1$, between $t = 1$ and $t = 2$ and between $t = 2$ and $t = 3$, etc. We find out that 3 is the maximum for all such time windows of unit length. So, 3 is returned as peak power within unit time.

If $E_{(t,\delta)}$ is the set of all events at all nodes occurring within time $t$ and $t + \delta$, $prop(e)$ is the propagation condition for event $e \in E_{(t,\delta)}$, then the set of clauses of Max-SAT is $C = \cup_{e \in E_{(t,\delta)}} prop(e)$. The maximum transition power among the events in $E_{(t,\delta)}$ ($MTP(t,\delta)$) is found by solving the Max-SAT over set of clauses $C$. Mathematically, it can be written as: $MTP(t,\delta) = MaxSAT(\cup_{e \in E_{(t,\delta)}} prop(e))$ and peak power within $\delta$ time can be written as:

$$PP(\delta) = Max_{t \in Set\ of\ different\ event\ times}\ MTP(t,\delta)$$

## 3    Heuristic Search Based Solution

The decision version of Max-SAT is NP-complete. Therefore, no algorithm with subexponential running time is known for this problem. It has also been proved that approximating Max-SAT for a lower bound within a factor of more than $7/8$ is also NP-Hard [8,9]. However, there are polynomial time algorithms with a performance guarantee of $3/4$ [7]. Now, we discuss the exact algorithms used by us for solving Max-SAT.

### 3.1    Max-SAT Via ADDs and Its Problems

In our symbolic method, we have chosen ADDs as the data structure to represent weighted clauses. The propagation condition for each event is taken and a 0-1 ADD (conversion from BDD to ADD) is constructed out of this, so that in the resultant ADD, a zero valued leaf is reached when the event condition is false and a leaf with value one is reached when the event condition is true. Once we get ADDs for each event, we can build an ADD-sum out of them. The ADD-sum [10] is the ADD based method to compute the total number of events under every possible input and flip flop transitions. Thus the maximum leaf value of this ADD will estimate the maximum power. The algorithm is shown as Algorithm 1. Refer to [10] for understanding ADD-based operations.

**Algorithm 1.** ADD based Max-SAT solution

  **Input:**
  $E$ = set of events at all nodes in the circuit.
  $\delta$ = a small time window provided by the user.
  **Initial:** $maxLeaf = 0$.
  **for all** time instance $t$ **do**
    $E_t \subseteq E$ : set of events occurring within $t$ and $t + \delta$.
    $maxPow$ = constant 0 ADD. (no event for every state transition)
    **for all** $e \in E_t$ **do**
      $B$ = BDD of the propagation condition for $e$.
      $O$ = 0-1 ADD representation of $B$.
      $maxPow = ADD\_sum(maxPow, O)$
    **end for**
    $maxLeaf = max\{maxLeaf, ADD\_maxLeaf(maxPow)\}$
  **end for**
  **output:** $maxLeaf$.

If we use single ADD to solve the problem, we usually face space limitations. The number of events in a circuit being very large, a single ADD that contains sum of event powers will become too large to handle.

## 3.2 A Heuristic Search Based Method

In order to address the space explosion problem with ADDs we propose a method based on symbolic ADD manipulation and heuristic search [11]. ADDs are very efficient for solving the Max-SAT problem for a small set of clauses. But it can not handle larger number of clauses due to its space complexity. So, we propose a mixed technique in which we break the whole set of clauses into disjoint subsets. These subsets have to be small enough so that we can easily solve them using ADDs and then construct a solution for the whole problem using a heuristic search technique.

**State Space and Connectivity.** The state space of the heuristic search problem is a partial or complete assignment to all variables corresponding to the primary inputs, flip flop present states and next states in the circuit. The variables are ordered. Each state can either have no children or have two children. If the state has two children then they are the states which can be formed by appending the partial assignment of the parent with an assignment of the next variable to 0 or 1. This way, the state space is connected as a binary decision tree.

Fig 2 shows part of the search tree. Circles denote search nodes, letters outside the circles are the name of variables which are to be assigned next. Each edge emanating from the search nodes lead to a state where a new partial assignment is formed by appending the partial assignment to its parent with an assignment to the next variable to either 0 or 1. Leaves to this tree are complete assignments to all variables. The objective of the search is to find a leaf corresponding to the variable assignment that leads to maximum number of events in the circuit. The numbers enclosed within the circles in Fig. 2 denote the heuristic estimates of the search nodes as described later.

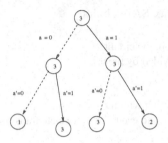

**Fig. 2.** Part of search tree

**Heuristic Estimate.** The heuristic value of a search node is an upper bound on the maximum number of events that can occur if the events are restricted to the partial assignment corresponding to the search node. In order to compute the heuristic value for all search nodes, we first group the event propagation conditions in groups of size $p$ and solve their Max-SAT using ADDs. ADDs have the same variable ordering as that of the search tree. Given a search node, we perform a graph traversal in each of the ADDs to find the top most nodes which satisfy the partial assignment corresponding to the given node. The sum of maximum leaf values (ADD_maxLeaf) of all these nodes is taken as the heuristic value of the search node.

Computation of the heuristic values are shown with an example below. Here, we consider events at node $a$, $b$ and $P$ only from Fig 1. We group events at node $a$ and $b$ together and the events at node $P$ are grouped separately. The resultant ADDs are shown in Fig 3.

Suppose we are computing the heuristic value for a partial assignment $a = 1$ and $a' = 1$. If we traverse the ADD in Fig 3(i) from the root along the path $a = 1$, $a' = 1$, we reach a

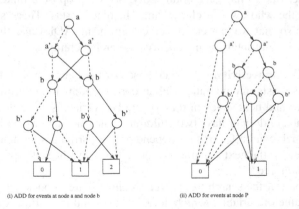

(i) ADD for events at node a and node b          (ii) ADD for events at node P

**Fig. 3.** ADDs for event groups: (i) ADD for events at node a and node b (ii) ADD for events at node P

node for which the subgraph rooted at that node has a maximum leaf value of 1. Similarly, for the ADD in Fig 3(ii), if we traverse the ADD from the root along the path $a = 1, a' = 1$, we reach a node for which the subgraph rooted at that node has the maximum leaf value of 1. This makes a total of $1 + 1 = 2$, which is an upper bound for maximum power on nodes a,b and P under the condition $a = 1$ and $a' = 1$. Heuristic values of the search nodes are shown as the numbers enclosed within the circles in Fig. 2.

**Search Strategy.** We have developed an A* search technique [11] which explores the search tree nodes in the decreasing order of their heuristic estimate.

# 4   Experimentation and Results

For our experimentation, we took ISCAS '89 benchmark circuits [12]. These circuits are sequential and we have assumed that only the flip flops can change values simultaneously

**Table 1.** Peak Power of ISCAS'89 Benchmarks using a General Delay and Unit Power Model

| Circuit | Peak Power | Peak Power $\delta = 2$ ns | | Peak Power | Peak Power $\delta = 1$ ns | |
|---|---|---|---|---|---|---|
| | | memory for CUDD(MB) | CPU Time (seconds) | | memory for CUDD(MB) | CPU Time (seconds) |
| s27 | 6 | 4.54 | .5 | 3 | 4.54 | .5 |
| s208 | 41 | 4.7 | .6 | 23 | 4.7 | .7 |
| s298 | 58 | 7.5 | 2.5 | 44 | 6.9 | 1.7 |
| s344 | 55 | 103 | 295 | 36 | 84 | 141 |
| s349 | 53 | 104 | 293 | 36 | 86 | 140 |
| s382 | 61 | 36 | 21 | 41 | 33 | 13.2 |
| s386 | 30 | 5.5 | 1.3 | 24 | 5.3 | 1 |
| s400 | 65 | 38 | 22 | 44 | 25 | 11.7 |
| s420 | 79 | 5.1 | 1.7 | 45 | 5.2 | 1.6 |
| s444 | 74 | 19 | 10.5 | 45 | 16.3 | 6.3 |
| s499 | 48 | 8.3 | 3.9 | 26 | 7.8 | 3.4 |
| s510 | 56 | 558 | 2482 | 35 | 447 | 1189 |
| s526 | 97 | 39 | 21.5 | 62 | 33 | 10.7 |
| s526n | 97 | 41 | 22.6 | 63 | 35 | 73 |
| s641 | 36 | 105 | 218 | 24 | 85 | 112 |
| s635 | 125 | 6.9 | 22.2 | 63 | 6.5 | 20 |
| s713 | 34 | 60 | 41 | 19 | 55 | 32 |
| s820 | 79 | 31 | 54 | 61 | 30 | 27 |
| s832 | 80 | 31 | 56 | 62 | 30 | 21 |
| s838 | 155 | 6.7 | 11.3 | 89 | 6.6 | 10.3 |
| s953 | 74 | 149 | 297 | 43 | 132 | 165 |
| s967 | 73 | 227 | 639 | 38 | 211 | 330 |
| s1196 | 30 | 48 | 14 | 18 | 41.5 | 10.3 |
| s1238 | 30 | 53 | 15 | 18 | 52 | 15.7 |
| s1488 | 121 | 11 | 20 | 76 | 14.7 | 11 |
| s1494 | 121 | 15 | 21 | 76 | 14.6 | 12 |

whenever a clock arrives. The inputs are treated as fixed values. However, transitions at primary inputs can also be inserted using the same framework.

We have performed our experiments on a general delay and unit power model. The basic gates from the ISCAS benchmarks are mapped to gates taken from a proprietary library, which has the same number of ports and similar functionality. For example, 2-input AND gates are replaced by one of the many 2-input AND gates of the library having different delay values. Then, these delay values are used for generating symbolic event lists. So, this is a general delay model. We have assumed unit power on each transition. We have also conducted experiments for unit delay and unit power frame work, so that the results can be reproduced without the proprietary library.

We implemented our algorithm on a Xeon Server with 4 GB RAM. The popular CUDD [10] package was used for BDD and ADD manipulation.

Table 1 shows the peak power estimate within 2 nano seconds and 1 nano second respectively for all benchmark circuits for the general delay model. All gate delays are

**Table 2.** Peak Power of ISCAS'89 Benchmarks using a Unit Delay and Unit Power Model

| Circuit | Peak Power | Peak Power δ = 2 unit | | Peak Power | Peak Power δ = 1 unit | |
| | | memory for CUDD(MB) | CPU Time (seconds) | | memory for CUDD(MB) | CPU Time (seconds) |
|---|---|---|---|---|---|---|
| s27 | 7 | 4.54 | .5 | 6 | 4.5 | .5 |
| s208 | 51 | 4.7 | .7 | 39 | 4.7 | .65 |
| s298 | 88 | 7.7 | 2.0 | 75 | 7.2 | 1.84 |
| s344 | 89 | 104 | 268 | 64 | 91.5 | 172 |
| s349 | 89 | 103 | 268 | 64 | 91.6 | 164 |
| s382 | 105 | 20.9 | 8.8 | 76 | 20 | 6.1 |
| s386 | 51 | 5.74 | 1.2 | 40 | 5.5 | 1.0 |
| s400 | 112 | 20.9 | 9.9 | 82 | 19.2 | 6.8 |
| s420 | 105 | 5.2 | 1.3 | 77 | 5.1 | 1.3 |
| s444 | 116 | 18.6 | 7.9 | 84 | 17.7 | 5.6 |
| s499 | 55 | 6.34 | 1.7 | 48 | 6.2 | 1.53 |
| s510 | 78 | 442 | 1756 | 56 | 432 | 1255 |
| s526 | 131 | 34.6 | 20.7 | 112 | 29.2 | 16 |
| s526n | 133 | 38.2 | 18.9 | 113 | 35 | 14 |
| s635 | 158 | 6.8 | 15.9 | 125 | 6.8 | 14 |
| s641 | 63 | 97 | 230 | 44 | 79.7 | 142 |
| s713 | 49 | 57.8 | 40 | 34 | 55 | 31 |
| s820 | 132 | 35 | 38.9 | 105 | 32 | 25.5 |
| s832 | 132 | 34.4 | 41 | 106 | 32 | 25.7 |
| s838 | 213 | 6.7 | 5.7 | 153 | 6.7 | 5.4 |
| s953 | 119 | 139.3 | 241 | 84 | 135 | 181 |
| s967 | 113 | 217 | 523 | 79 | 210 | 326 |
| s1196 | 42 | 62.4 | 17.1 | 30 | 51.2 | 14.3 |
| s1238 | 42 | 61.9 | 18.1 | 30 | 51.4 | 14.3 |
| s1488 | 219 | 15 | 14 | 152 | 15 | 10 |
| s1494 | 214 | 15.5 | 14.5 | 147 | 15 | 10 |

real numbers which vary between 2 to 6 nano seconds. The first column contains the name of the circuit from ISCAS'89 benchmarks. Columns 2 to 4 show the data for peak power within 2 nano seconds, where column 2 shows the peak power estimate, column 3 shows the memory usage in MB and column 4 shows the CPU time required in seconds. Similarly, columns 5 to 7 show the data for peak power within 1 nano second.

Table 2 shows the result for peak power for the unit delay model. Here, column 1 is the name of the circuit. Column 2 to 4 are the peak power estimate within 2 unit of time, the memory usage in MB and the CPU time in seconds, respectively. Columns 5 to 7 show the peak power estimate within 1 unit of time, the memory usage in MB and the CPU time required in seconds.

We have found out that the proposed method can handle some circuits with 32 flip flops and 35 primary inputs (e.g s838) in reasonable time without memory explosion.

# 5  Conclusion

We have shown that symbolic event generation along with heuristic search techniques can be used efficiently in computing peak power dissipation in circuits. Our experiments on ISCAS benchmarks indicate that inspite of being an exact algorithm, we are able to solve problems of reasonable size.

# References

1. Devadas. S., Keutzer. K., White. J, "Estimation of Power Dissipation in CMOS Combinational Circuits Using Boolean Function Manipulation", IEEE Transactions on Computer Aided Design, vol. 11(3), pp. 373-383, March, 1992.
2. Wang.C., Roy.K. and Chou.T., "Maximum Power Estimation for Sequential Circuits Using a Test Generation Based Technique", Custom Integrated Circuits Conference, 1996., Proceedings of the IEEE 1996. pp. 229-232.
3. Bahar. R et al, "Algebraic Decision Diagrams and their Applications", Formal Methods in System Design, 1997, Vol 10, No. 2-3, pp. 171 - 206.
4. Manne. S., Pardo. A., Bahar. R., Hachtel. G., Somenzi. F., Macii. E., Poncino. M., "Computing the Maximum Power Cycles of a Sequential Circuit ", Proceedings of the 32nd ACM/IEEE conference on Design automation, 1995, pp. 23-28.
5. Mondal. A., Chakrabarti. P.P, Mandal. C.R, "A New Approach to Timing Analysis using Event Propagation and Temporal Logic", Design, Automation and Test in Europe Conference and Exhibition Volume II (DATE'04) p. 1198-1203.
6. Yalcin.H, Hayes.J.P, "Event Propagation Conditions in Circuit Delay Computation", ACM Transactions on Design Automation of Electronic Systems (TODAES), Vol. 2, No. 3, July 1997, pp. 249-280.
7. Bergman.S and Lozinskii. L. Eliezer, "A Fast Algorithm for MaxSAT Approximation", Proceedings of the Sixth International Conference on Theory and Applications of Satisfiability Testing, Portofino, Italy, 2003, pp. 424-431.
8. Hstad. J.,"Some Optimal Inapproximability results", Proceedings of the twenty-ninth annual ACM symposium on Theory of computing, 1997, pp. 1-10.
9. C. H. Papadimitriou and M. Yannakakis., "Optimization, approximation, and complexity classes.", Journal of Computing and System Sciences, 43:425–440, 1991.

10. Somenzi. F., Department of Electrical and Computer Engineering, University of Colorado at Boulder (Fabio@Colorado.EDU), "CUDD: CU Decision Diagram Package Release 2.4.1", "http://vlsi.colorado.edu/ fabio/CUDD/cuddIntro.html"
11. Nilsson, N.J., Artificial Intelligence : A New Synthesis, ELSEVIER, 1998.
12. Brglez, F., Bryan, D., and Kozminski, K. 1998. Combinational profiles of sequential benchmark circuits. In Proceedings of the IEEE International Symposium on Circuits And Systems, 1929–1934.

# QDI Latches Characteristics and Asynchronous Linear-Pipeline Performance Analysis

Eslam Yahya[1,2] and Marc Renaudin[1]

[1] TIMA Laboratory, CIS Group
46 Av. Félix Viallet, Grenoble, France
{Eslam.Yahya, Marc.Renaudin}@Imag.fr
[2] Banha High Institute of Technology, Banha, Egypt

**Abstract.** Asynchronous logic is a hot topic due to its interesting features of power saving, low noise and robustness to parameters variations. However, its performance analysis is relatively complex. In fact, the handshaking protocol strongly influences the performance of the pipelined architectures. This paper introduces verified Standard-Logic schematics for QDI asynchronous latches and analyzes their characteristics. Buffering capacity and protocol gain are defined and analyzed. Based on this analysis, reduced performance equations are first introduced. By means of the dependency graphs, a new formal method is then proposed to analyze the performance of asynchronous linear-pipeline. This methodology is used to derive general equations for each latch type. Contrarily to previously proposed methods, this method can be applied to any asynchronous linear-pipeline without restrictions on its functional block delays. Therefore, the contributions of this paper enable the designers to understand the benefits brought by the different asynchronous latches, to compare them and make the right choice according to their design constrains....

## 1 Introduction

Integration capacity of the recent chips is gradually increasing. This increasing introduces many problems especially in power consumption, robustness against environment-parameters variations and Electro Magnetic emission. Asynchronous circuits seem to be a practical solution for such problems [Mar 03], [Pet 02]. Research and industry are increasingly motivated towards the asynchronous circuits due to the following interesting features [Jac 03], [Jen 01], [Van 99]: (1) Low power consumption, (2) No global-signal distribution problems, (3) High security, (4) Low emitted EM noise and (5) Tolerance against environment parameters change. In case of asynchronous circuits, latches are complex compared to the synchronous Latches/Registers. Asynchronous latches not only memorize the data, but also implement the communication protocol between different system-blocks. As a result, the system performance is strongly affected by the handshaking protocol. The exact performance equations for the latches are essentials but never had been derived before. This paper discusses this idea in the context of linear-pipeline. Non-linear pipeline will be considered in another paper. Fig.1 shows the structure of asynchronous linear-pipelines used in the paper.

J. Vounckx, N. Azemard, and P. Maurine (Eds.): PATMOS 2006, LNCS 4148, pp. 583–592, 2006.
© Springer-Verlag Berlin Heidelberg 2006

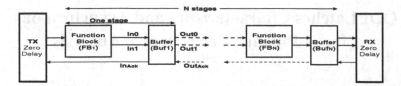

**Fig. 1.** Structure of an Asynchronous Linear-Pipeline

We faced difficulty in reading many papers concerning the asynchronous logic because the used conventions are not clearly defined. This paragraph defines the conventions used in this paper. The word buffer will be used instead of latch for consistency with the literature. The *Linear-Pipeline* can be defined as "simple pipeline structure that contains no fork or join". It can contain any number of stages, each *Stage* consists of "One function block, which is transparent to the acknowledgment signals, and one asynchronous buffer". The *Function Block* "Is composed of logic elements those perform the required processing". Asynchronous buffer has two channels, input channel and output channel. The *Channel* used here is a dual rail channel, which expresses each bit using two wires (0=01, 1=10, Reset=00) and a third wire is used for the acknowledgment. After Reset, all outputs hold Reset value '00', and the acknowledgment is high. The buffer at stage$_i$ 'Buf$_i$' receives its input from function block 'FB$_i$' and sends its output to block 'FB$_{i+1}$'. The communication protocol used in this paper is the four-phase protocol, which is a *Return-to-Zero protocol* (RTZ) [Jen 01], [Mar 03]. In RTZ protocols, the individual *Data Pattern* consists of two tokens. The *Evaluation Token* "which expresses the data (01 or 10)" and *Reset Token* "which resets the logic to prepare it for the next evaluation". The token becomes a *Bubble* if the Acknowledgement signal, confirming that the following stage does not need the token any more, is received. *Buffer Cycle Time Pn* is "The time needed by the buffer at stage$_n$ to process a complete data pattern". The starting point of the pipeline is the *Transmitter* (TX), where the ending point is the *Receiver* (RX). TX and RX are considered zero-delay, which means that TX produces a new token as soon as it has the acknowledgment and RX produces the acknowledgment as soon as it has a new token. This assumption isolates the pipeline from the environment effects. There are plenty of asynchronous buffers [Ste 96], [And 95]. This paper concerns WCHB (Weak-Conditioned Half Buffer), PCHB (Pre-Charged Half Buffer) and PCFB (Pre-Charged Full Buffer). These buffers are originally introduced as pre-charged buffers [And 95]. However, their handshaking protocols can be used in any circuit regardless the logic type. The same naming conventions are used in this article because they are well known, although the proposed architectures are based on standard gates not pre-charged gates. We suggest changing these names to express the protocol regardless the implementation scheme. We reviewed the schematics of these buffers and realized that verified schematics are in need. A complete design and verification process is proposed in [Esy 06]. The paper is structured as two main parts; the first part introduces a verified schematic for each buffer type, discusses the different characteristics of each buffer and proposes reduced performance equations based on structural analysis. The second part discusses the formal methods of asynchronous buffer performance-analysis and proposes a new method that produces general equations those can be applied to any asynchronous linear-pipeline.

## 2 Buffering Capacity

*Buffering capacity* is defined as "The number of cascaded tokens the buffer can simultaneously memorize". Tokens here mean the unacknowledged tokens, and cascaded tokens can be in any order (Evaluation+Reset, Reset+Evaluation). Compared to static spread and cycle time which are properties of the pipeline (buffers and functional blocks), buffering capacity characterizes the buffer itself regardless the pipeline parameters. The following figures show the schematics for the three buffers.

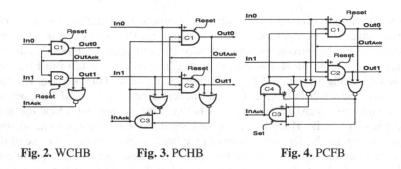

**Fig. 2.** WCHB          **Fig. 3.** PCHB                    **Fig. 4.** PCFB

### 2.1 WCHB Capacity and PCHB Capacity

Fig. 2 and Fig. 3 show WCHB and PCHB circuit diagrams respectively. The two Muller gates C1 and C2 in both buffers can only hold either an Evaluation token or a Reset token at a time. After receiving the acknowledgment signal on the output side, the token becomes a bubble and the buffer is ready to memorize another token. Consequently, WCHBs and PCHBs have a buffering capacity of one token. They can only memorize half of the data pattern, so they are called half buffers.

### 2.2 PCFB Capacity

PCFB circuit appears in Fig. 4. In all papers, this buffer is proposed as a full buffer, which is not actually accurate. Analyzing the circuit diagram shows that PCFB is something between half buffer and full buffer. Suppose that the buffer $Buf_i$ is empty, it receives an evaluation token, memorizes the token inside the Muller gates C1 and C2, and then responds by putting the InAck low. That means the outputs of C3 and C4 are low. If $FB_{i+1}$ is slower than $FB_i$ then, $FB_i$ sends the reset token. This makes C3 going high giving InAck high, which means that the channel is free and $FB_i$ can send the next token. Now the buffer is memorizing the evaluation token in (C1 and C2) and memorizing the reset token by two things, the low output of C4 and the high output of C3. In that case, PCFB is memorizing the two tokens, Evaluation then Reset, simultaneously. Thus, this buffer now behaves as a full buffer. Suppose now, $FB_{i+1}$ acknowledges the memorized Evaluation token by putting OutAck low, C1 and C2 go low, which makes C4 going high. Because C3 is high, $FB_i$ sees the channel free and it sends a new Evaluation token. Now the buffer memorizes only one token, the reset token, and it has unacknowledged Evaluation token at its inputs. Can the buffer acknowledge this new token as it is expected to do? As a full buffer the answer should be yes, but the real answer is no. This is because it has no real memory elements at its inputs. The conclusion is that, PCFB behaves as a full buffer when it memorizes an Evaluation token followed by a Reset token. However, it behaves as a half buffer when it memorizes a Reset token followed by an Evaluation token. Hence, PCFB sometimes has a buffering capacity of two tokens, other times it has a buffering capacity of one token.

## 3  Protocol Gain

Each asynchronous buffer defines a different protocol for handling the relation between two adjacent function blocks. What is meant by *Protocol Gain* is "How much decoupling the buffer introduces between two adjacent function blocks". Analyzing the behavior of any buffer shows that, at $stage_i$, $Buf_i$ receives data from $FB_i$, memorizes this data, sends the data to $FB_{i+1}$ and acknowledges $FB_i$. This behavior is ruled by two facts. The first fact is that, $Buf_i$ cannot accept a new token until $FB_{i+1}$ acknowledges the previous token. The second fact is that, $Buf_i$ cannot out a new token until this token is sent by $FB_i$. These two facts are logical, but they enforce some sequential relations between the buffer sides. How can we break these two facts, or one of them, to add some concurrency between the two sides? The first fact can easily, but costly, be broken, simply by adding more buffering capacity to $Buf_i$. The more buffering capacity we add, the more $Buf_i$ can accept tokens which have no place at $FB_{i+1}$. What about the second fact? The answer lies in the question: what does $Buf_i$ expect from $FB_i$? It expects data pattern that consists of two cascaded tokens, Evaluation and Reset. Because $Buf_i$ cannot predict what evaluation token (01, 10), will be sent by $FB_i$, then it must wait for this token. On the contrary, if $Buf_i$ receives an evaluation token, it knows that the coming token is a Reset one (even before $FB_i$ sends it). Here we can gain some concurrency if $Buf_i$ generates the Reset token for $FB_{i+1}$ before receiving it from $FB_i$. Subsequently, two kinds of gain can be defined. The first one is the *Extra Buffering Gain* (EBG) "Which results from adding more buffering capacity to the buffer". The second type is the *Token Expectation Gain* (TEG) "which appears when $Buf_i$ is able to generate the Reset token for $FB_{i+1}$ before receiving it from $FB_i$".

### 3.1  Gain of Each Buffer Type

Let us first consider WCHB, this protocol adds a single memory space between two-cascaded blocks. As a result, in a continuous-flow pipeline, if $FB_i$ is in the evaluation phase then $FB_{i+1}$ is in the reset phase and vice-versa. Suppose that the Evaluation is longer than the Reset and $FB_i$ is evaluating, then $FB_{i+1}$ finishes its reset and Acknowledges $Buf_i$ asking for the new Evaluation token, but $Buf_i$ is waiting for $FB_i$ to evaluate. Later $FB_{i+1}$ will be in the Evaluation phase, $FB_i$ finishes its Reset and sends a request to $Buf_i$ which is waiting $FB_{i+1}$ to evaluate. Hence, the cycle time will be twice the Evaluation time (the worst between Evaluation and Reset). Consequently, we have:

$$P_{WCHB} = 2 * MAX [ T_{Eval}, T_{Reset} ]. \tag{1}$$

By recalling Figure 3, it is obvious that PCHB has more concurrency than WCHB. How can we exploit this concurrency? Suppose that the function blocks have reset time longer than evaluation time. Hence, while $FB_i$ is resetting, $FB_{i+1}$ finishes its evaluation and waits for the reset token. Here the key advantage of PCHB appears. It generates the reset token for $FB_{i+1}$ causing an overlapping between the reset phases of both sides (benefits of TEG). This reduces the total delay from twice the worst of Evaluation and Reset to the summation of Evaluation and Reset times. On the contrary, if the Evaluation time is the longest, then PCHB performance will be the same as WCHB. In this case, while $FB_i$ is evaluating, $FB_{i+1}$ finishes its reset and asks for the new evaluation token which can not be predicted by the buffer. Therefore, we have:

$$P_{PCHB} = T_{Eval} + MAX\ [\ T_{Eval},\ T_{Reset}\ ]. \tag{2}$$

PCFB has the ability to generate the Reset token for $FB_{i+1}$ before receiving it from $FB_i$ (TEG). In addition, it can memorize two tokens at a time with the order mentioned before (EBG). Hence, its performance gains from the unequally Reset and Evaluation times not only when the Reset time is larger but also when the Evaluation time is.

$$P_{PCFB} = T_{Eval} + T_{Reset}. \tag{3}$$

## 3.2 Simulation Results of Zero-Delay Buffers

A test circuit, as in Fig. 1, is designed using the different buffer types and identical function blocks in all stages. Its simulation results are compared with the expected results from the equations. This is done in order to insure the consistency of the equation with the circuit behavior. The buffer internal delays are neglected in order to concentrate on protocols differences regardless the differences in circuitry. Table 1 summarizes the simulation results and shows that they are coherent with equations (1), (2) and (3). It is obvious from the table that, WCHB has the same performance in both cases. PCHB gains when $T_{Eval} < T_{Reset}$. However, PCFB gains in both cases.

**Table 1.** Simulation results of Zero-Delay Buffers

| $T_{Eval} < T_{Reset}$ | WCHB | PCHB | PCFB | $T_{Eval} > T_{Reset}$ | WCHB | PCHB | PCFB |
|---|---|---|---|---|---|---|---|
| 100/300 | 600 | 400 | 400 | 300/100 | 600 | 600 | 400 |

## 4 Formal Performance-Analysis

Although the above equations give good estimation of the buffers performance, more formal and detailed equations are needed. Designers need exact equation to choose the suitable buffer for their circuits. One of the formal methods that can be used is the *Dependency Graph* method. It is a graph-based method where the nodes of the graph correspond to specific rising or falling transitions of the circuit components, and the arcs depict the dependencies between signals transitions [Ted 94], [Ted 90]. If all the stages have the same function blocks, the graph can be folded. Buffers Unfolded and Folded dependency-graphs are shown in Fig. 5.

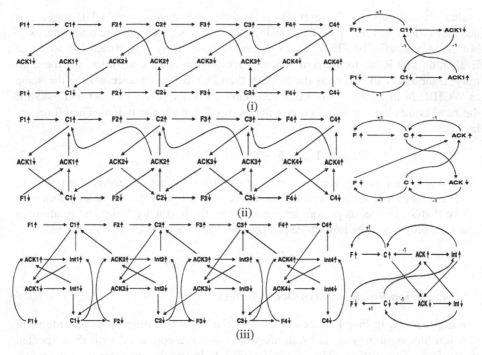

**Fig. 5.** (i)WCHB, (ii) PCHB and (iii) PCFB Unfolded/Folded Dependency Graphs (C: Buffer output, F: Function-Block output, Ack: Acknowledgment Signal, ↑/↓: UP/Down Transitions)

## 5 Performance-Analysis Using Folded Dependency-Graphs

This method is based on the folded graphs, and can be summarized into two steps. From the Folded dependency graph, classify all loops in which the summation of stages-indices (represented by I) is less than, greater than and equal to zero in three subsets. After that, obtain the Cycle Time "P" as the Max Latency of loops combinations in which (I = 0). More details can be found in [Ted 94], [Ted 90].

### 5.1 Buffers Performance-Analysis Using Folded Dependency-Graphs

WCHB folded dependency-graph is shown in Fig.5.i. From this figure, the loops with index-sum greater than Zero are, [C↑, F↓], [C↓, F↑], their index-sum is (+1). Concerning the loops with index-sum less than Zero, there is only one loop [C↑, Ack↓, C↓, Ack↑] with index-sum of (-2). There is no loop with index-sum of Zero; it will be a composition of the other loops. WCHB equation is shown in eq.4. Note that, the second part of the equation is multiplied by 2 to obtain total index sum of Zero. Applying the assumption of zero-delay buffer ($T_{C\uparrow} = T_{Ack\downarrow} = T_{C\downarrow} = T_{Ack\uparrow} = 0$) where $T_{F\uparrow}/T_{F\downarrow}$ are $T_{Eval}/T_{Reset}$ respectively, then the exact equation (4) confirms the estimated one (1).

$$P_{WCHB} = (T_{C\uparrow} + T_{Ack\downarrow} + T_{C\downarrow} + T_{Ack\uparrow}) + 2\,\text{Max}\,[\,(T_{C\uparrow} + T_{F\downarrow}),\,(T_{C\downarrow} + T_{F\uparrow})\,].\qquad(4)$$

The folded graph of PCHB is shown in Fig.5.ii. Due to its concurrency; the extraction of the loops subsets is more complicated. The possible loops in this circuit are (F↑, C↑) with index-sum of (+1), (F↓, Ack↑, C↑, Ack↓, C↓) with index-sums of (+1, 0, -1) and (C↑, Ack↓, C↓, Ack↑) with index-sums of (0, -1, -2). There are some ambiguity in extracting the loops and assigning their indices sums. The last two loops have three index-sums, which is ambiguous especially when the cycle time is being calculated. For example, the last loop index sum depends on the chosen path between (Ack↓, C↓) and between (Ack↑, C↑). If the zero arcs are chosen, then the total sum is zero. On the contrary, if one of them is zero and the other is (-1), the total sum is (-1). Finally, if both paths are through the (-1) arcs then the resultant sum is (-2). It is ambiguous for us to calculate the cycle time using the above loops and very hard to formulate an equation to express the cycle time.

Concerning the PCFB circuit, it has an internal memorized signal; it is the output of C4 in Fig. 4. We called this signal (Int). It appears in the folded graph in Fig 5.iii. The possible loops of this buffer are, (F↑, C↑), (F↓, Ack↑, Int↑, Ack↓, Int↓, C↓) with index of (+1) and (Ack↑, C↑, Ack↓, Int↓), (Ack↑, C↑, Ack↓, C↓, F↓), (Ack↓, C↓, Int↑), (Ack↓, C↓, Int↑, C↑), with index of (-1). Finally, the loop (F↓, Ack↑, Int↑, Ack↓, C↓) has an index of (0). The resultant cycle time equation is shown in eq.5. Where eq.6. shows the cycle time after applying the zero-delay buffer assumption. Eq.6. is not the same as eq.3. In addition, neither eq.5 nor eq.6 can explain the performance gain in PCFB when TEval is lower than TReset.

$$P_{PCFB}=Max\ [(T_{F\downarrow}+T_{Ack\uparrow}+T_{Int\uparrow}+T_{Ack\downarrow}+T_{C\downarrow}),(Max[(T_{F\uparrow}+T_{C\uparrow}),(T_{F\downarrow}+T_{Ack\uparrow}+T_{Int\uparrow}+ \quad (5)$$
$$T_{Ack\downarrow}+T_{Int\downarrow}+T_{C\downarrow})]+Max[(T_{Ack\uparrow}+T_{C\uparrow}+T_{Ack\downarrow}+T_{Int\downarrow}),\ (T_{Ack\uparrow}+T_{C\uparrow}+T_{Ack\downarrow}+T_{C\downarrow}+\ T_{F\downarrow}),$$
$$(T_{Ack\downarrow}+T_{C\downarrow}+T_{Int\uparrow}),\ (T_{Ack\downarrow}+T_{C\downarrow}+T_{Int\uparrow}+T_{C\uparrow})])].$$

$$P_{PCFB} = Max\ [T_{F\uparrow},\ T_{F\downarrow}\ ] + T_{F\downarrow}. \quad (6)$$

# 6  Performance-Analysis Using Unfolded Dependency-Graphs

The *Total Cycle Time* $P_{Total}$ is "The total time the circuit takes to completely process a complete data pattern". Hardness of calculating the cycle time comes from concurrency of the circuit events. However, in any circuit, regardless how much its events are concurrent, there is an event-transition where all the circuit events are requisites. As a result, this event-transition directly or indirectly synchronizes all the other events; which insures that, all parallel event-sequences are allowed to start after this transition. We call such a transition, the *Main Synchronization Event-Transition*. Starting from this transition and tracing the circuit until returning back, while considering the longest of any parallel event-sequences, should give the correct cycle time. This section proposes a methodology based on the unfolded-graphs, this methodology can be summarized as: 1) Draw the unfolded-graph of your circuit. 2) Define the main synchronization event-transition. 3) From this transition, going up for example, trace the circuit until reaching the dual transition considering the longest of any parallel event-sequences. This forms the first part of the equation. 4) Returning back to the main synchronization event-transition, considered in step 3, while considering the longest of any parallel event-sequences, forms the second part of the equation. Note, *starting and ending event-transitions should be considered once.* Because the ending transition of the equation first part is the starting transition of its second part etc. then, either starting or ending transition is considered every time. This prevents from adding the same transition twice. Contrarily to the other method, this method has no restriction on the function blocks. Each stage can have a different function block with different delay values, which makes the methodology a realistic solution for linear pipeline. The following subsections apply this method to each buffer type to extract a general stage equation (Pn). In all of these equations 8, 9 and 10, the performance of any stage depends on the previous, current and next stages. Subsequently, the total cycle time will be the maximum of these stage equations and it can be obtained by the general equation of eq.7. Where n, is the stage index, N is the total number of stages and Pn is the general stage equation of each buffer in the linear pipeline.

$$P_{Total} = Max_{(n=1 \text{ to } n=N)} [ Pn ]. \tag{7}$$

### 6.1  Buffers Performance-Analysis Using Unfolded Dependency-Graphs

WCHB unfolded-graph is shown in Fig.5.i. The main synchronization event lies in the outputs of C1&C2 in Fig.2. This event appears in the graph as $C\uparrow\&C\downarrow$. Starting from $C\uparrow$, we write down the first part of the equation, Max $[(F\uparrow,C\uparrow,Ack\downarrow,C\downarrow)$, $(Ack\downarrow,C\downarrow,F\downarrow, C\downarrow)]$. $C\uparrow$ is considered as the starting transition and we choose not to include it while including the ending transition. It is important to note that we navigate from $C\uparrow$ of a stage to $C\downarrow$ in the same stage. From $C\downarrow$, we return back to $C\uparrow$ for writing the equation second part, Max $[(F\downarrow, C\downarrow, Ack\uparrow, C\uparrow), (Ack\uparrow, C\uparrow, F\uparrow, C\uparrow)]$. The final cycle time equation is as follows:

$$Pn_{WCHB}=Max[(T_{F(n+1)\uparrow}+T_{C(n+1)\uparrow}+T_{Ack(n+1)\downarrow}+T_{C(n)\downarrow}),(T_{Ack(n)\downarrow}+T_{C(n-1)\downarrow}+T_{F(n)\downarrow}+T_{C(n)\downarrow})] \\ +Max[(T_{F(n+1)\downarrow}+ T_{C(n+1)\downarrow}+T_{Ack(n+1)\uparrow}+T_{C(n)\uparrow}), (T_{Ack(n)\uparrow}+T_{C(n-1)\uparrow}+T_{F(n)\uparrow}+T_{C(n)\uparrow})]. \tag{8}$$

In fact, this equation is equivalent to eq.4 if all stages have similar buffers. By applying the zero-delay buffer assumption, this equation gives eq.1.

The new procedure is applied on PCHB unfolded-graph, Fig.5.ii. The output transitions of Muller gates C1&C2 are the main synchronization event and $C\uparrow$ is the starting transition. This gives the cycle time equation appears in eq.9. The assumption of zero-delay buffer makes eq.9 same as eq.2. By using the new method, this is the first time we have performance equation for PCHB.

$$Pn_{PCHB} =Max[(T_{F(n+1)\uparrow}+T_{C(n+1)\uparrow}+T_{Ack(n+1)\downarrow}+T_{C(n)\downarrow}),(T_{Ack(n)\downarrow}+T_{C(n)\downarrow})]+ \\ Max[(T_{F(n+1)\downarrow}+T_{Ack(n+1)\uparrow}+T_{C(n)\uparrow}),(T_{Ack(n)\uparrow}+Max[(T_{C(n-1)\uparrow}+T_{F(n)\uparrow}+T_{C(n)\uparrow}),(T_{C(n)\uparrow})])]. \tag{9}$$

Concerning PCFB unfolded dependency graph, Fig.5.iii, the same procedure is applied while taking the main synchronization event at the outputs of C1&C2 and $C\uparrow$ is the starting transition, which gives eq.10. Unlike eq.5, the zero-delay buffer assumption makes eq.10 similar as eq.3.

$$Pn_{PCFB} = Max[(T_{F(n+1)\uparrow}+T_{C(n+1)\uparrow}+T_{Ack(n+1)\downarrow}+T_{C(n)\downarrow}),(T_{Ack(n)\downarrow}+T_{Int(n)\downarrow}+T_{C(n)\downarrow})] \\ +Max [ (T_{F(n+1)\downarrow} + T_{Ack(n+1)\uparrow} + T_{C(n)\uparrow}), (T_{Int(n)\uparrow} + T_{C(n)\uparrow}) ]. \tag{10}$$

## 6.2  Simulation of Assumed-Delay Buffers with Random Function-Block Delays

A ten-stage linear-pipeline circuit, like in Fig.1, is simulated. Buffers are modeled in VHDL using assumed internal delays. These delays are around the expected delays of a 130 nm cmos process. Using the assumed delays, Table 2 shows the values of the equation-parameters for each buffer type. Function block delays are randomly chosen to confirm the generality of the proposed method. Table 2 shows these values with the total cycle time calculated from the equations and obtained from simulation.

**Table 2.** Buffer Equation-Parameters, Function-Block Delays and Total Cycle Times

| WCHB | | PCHB | | PCFB | | |
|---|---|---|---|---|---|---|
| $T_C=150$ | $T_{Ack}=30$ | $T_C=200$ | $T_{Ack}=130$ | $T_C=200$ | $T_{Ack}=160$ | $T_{Int}=130$ |
| Stage:$T_{Eval}/$ $T_{Reset}$ | 1: 500/900 | 2: 2/1.5 ns | 3: 300/100 | 4: 10/1 ns | 5: 5/6 ns | |
| Stage:$T_{Eval}/$ $T_{Reset}$ | 6: 60/100 | 7: 2/9 ns | 8: 1/12 ns | 9: 7/4 ns | 10: 390/130 | |
| WCHB Total Cycle Time | | PCHB Total Cycle Time | | PCFB Total Cycle Time | | |
| Eq/Sim: 21.66/21.66 ns | | Eq/Sim: 16.06/16.06 ns | | Eq/Sim: 13.92/13.92 ns | | |

From the above table, it is obvious that the equation results are coherent with the real performance. Moreover, these equations can generally be applied to linear-pipelined architectures. Fig.6 A, B and C show the stage cycle times for WCHB, PCHB and PCFB respectively. It is clear from the figure that no buffer type is the superior in all cases. For example in stages 1 and 3, WCHB is the best buffer. In stage 7, PCHB is the best solution. On the other hand, PCFB is superior to the others in many cases.

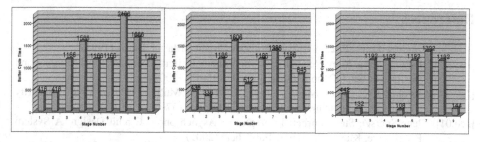

**Fig. 6.** (A)WCHB, (B)PCHB and (C)PCFB Stage Cycle Times, the time unit is ten-picoseconds

## 7  Conclusion and Future Work

This paper has introduced verified standard-logic schematics for WCHB, PCHB and PCFB. As far as we know, these are the first schematics in standard logic for these buffers, which enables the use of standard libraries instead of special ones. The buffering capacity of each type is defined and the variable capacity of PCFB is explained. Moreover, this paper proves that PCFB is not really a full buffer as mentioned in all previous works. The protocol gain is defined and classified into EBG and TEG, these parameters are useful guidelines for designers to understand how to compare between buffering protocols and choose the suitable one according to their circuit conditions.

Formal performance analysis using the folded-graph method has been done. It is found that this method is not suitable because it gives some ambiguity and even incorrect results. Moreover, this method is not generic; it is only applicable on linear pipeline with similar function blocks in all stages. The unfolded-graph method is proposed then used to derive general performance equations for each buffer type. Obviously, this method is working with all tested buffers. In addition, it is applicable to any linear pipeline with no restriction on the delays of the function blocks. Such general performance equations are new contributions in the area of performance analysis. WCHB performance is the worst of the all, where it cannot gain from the unbalanced Evaluation and Reset times of the function blocks. PCHB gains in case of longer Reset time. PCFB is the superior, where its performance gains in case of unbalanced Evaluation and Reset times regardless which is the longest.

An important conclusion is that, no buffer type is absolutely the best; it depends on the circuit conditions, if all functional blocks are identical with symmetric Evaluation and Reset times, then WCHB is the best. However, PCHB will be better if the Reset is longer in all blocks. PCFB is recommended when the evaluation is longer, but it works also with longer Reset. In case of randomized block delays, PCFB is expected to achieve the best results in terms of the total delay. However, mixing between the different types can achieve the best results in terms of area as well as performance, but it should be done very carefully. The general equations introduced in this article constitute a theoretical basis for design automation. If these equations are integrated inside a tool like our TAST tool, then the tool can automatically select the best buffer type according to the circuit conditions. More study for mixing between different types is in progress. In addition, extending these equations to be applied to nonlinear pipeline is in the phase of study.

# References

[And 95]  Andrew Lines: Pipelined Asynchronous Circuits. Master Thesis (1995)
[Esy 06]  Eslam Yahya, Marc Renaudin: Asynchronous Buffers Characteristics: Molding and Design. Research Report, TIMA-RR--06/-01--FR (2006)
[Jac 03]  Jacques J.A., Simon Moore, Huiyun Li, Robert Mullins, George Taylor: Security Evaluation of Asynchronous Circuits. CHES, pp. 137-151 (2003)
[Jen 01]  Jens SparsØ, Steve Furber: Principles of Asynchronous Circuit Design. A System Perspective. Kluwer Academic Publishers (2001)
[Mar 03]  Marc Renaudin, Joao Leonardo: Asynchronous Circuits Design: An Architectural Approach. (2003)
[Pet 02]  Peter A. Beerel: Asynchronous Circuits: An Increasingly Practical Design Solution. Proceedings of ISQED'02, IEEE Computer Society (2002)
[Ste 96]  Stephen. B. Furber and Paul Day: Four-Phase Micropipline Latch Control Circuits. IEEE Transitions on VLSI Systems, 4(2):247-253, (1996)
[Ted 90]  Ted Williams: Latency and Throughput Tradeoffs in Self-Timed Speed-Independent Pipelines and Rings. Technical Report No. CSL-TR-90-431 (1990).
[Ted 94]  Ted Williams: Perfoemance of Itrative Computation in Self-Timed Rings. Journal of VLSI Signal Processing, 7, 17-31 (1994).
[Van 99]  C.H. (KEES) Van Berkel, Mark B. Josephs, Steven M. Nowick: Scanning the Technology. Applications of Asynchronous Circuits. Proceedings of the IEEE, Vol. 87, No 2 (1999)

# Power Modeling of Precharged Address Bus and Application to Multi-bit DPA Attacks to DES Algorithm

M. Alioto, M. Poli, S. Rocchi, and V. Vignoli

DII – Dip. di Ingegneria dell'Informazione, Università di Siena,
v. Roma n. 56, I-53100 – Siena, Italy
{malioto, poli, rocchi, vignoli}@dii.unisi.it

**Abstract.** In this communication, a model of the precharged bus power consumption in digital VLSI circuits is developed. This model is used to analytically evaluate the result of a multi-bit Differential Power Attack (DPA) to the address bus of cryptographic ICs running the DES algorithm. This attack to the address bus is based on the observation of its power consumption, and is well known to be a major threat to the security of the confidential information stored or processed by SmartCards. The results allow to achieve a quantitative model of the DPA attack effectiveness, and is useful as a theoretical basis to understand the trade-offs involved in DPA attacks. This deeper understanding is useful to identify the cases where a SmartCard under attack is weaker with respect to DPA attacks, i.e. when the power consumption reveals the maximum amount of information. Cycle-accurate simulations on DES encryption algorithm running on a MIPS32® architecture are used to validate the model and the underlying assumptions.

## 1 Introduction

In the last decade, a considerable interest has been growing in storage, processing and transmission of confidential data, due to the diffusion of electronics devices such as SmartCards and PDAs [1]-[2]. Unfortunately, the secrecy of the confidential data is no longer guaranteed by the adoption of only cryptographic techniques, since their circuit implementation always leaks information due to the physical interaction with the external environment [3]. Indeed, cryptographic circuits are open to *side-channel* attacks that are based on the observation of some physical quantity (e.g. running time, Electromagnetic emissions, power consumption) which is somehow related with the processed data (including the secret information). Among the side-channel attacks, the Differential Power Analysis (DPA) is currently regarded as one of the most dangerous threats to the information security [3]-[4]. Indeed, DPA attacks require a rather inexpensive equipment and a very limited knowledge of the implementation, and no IC tampering is needed.

DPA attacks are based on the observation of the instantaneous power consumption of an IC during the encryption (decryption) of a known plaintext (ciphertext) with an assigned (but secret) cryptographic key [4]. Since the power consumption of an IC is strongly related to the processed data (including the secret key), the analysis of power

J. Vounckx, N. Azemard, and P. Maurine (Eds.): PATMOS 2006, LNCS 4148, pp. 593–602, 2006.

waveforms through statistical techniques allows for easily extracting several bits of the secret key, thereby greatly reducing the space where the key can found with an exhaustive search [3]-[4].

As is well known, in digital ICs most processed data are transferred on busses, whose power consumption is strongly data-dependent and is the dominant contribution to the overall power consumption of any IC [3]-[6]. In particular, the address bus is by far the most critical block in terms of resistance to DPA attacks [5]. Thus, it is essential to deeply understand and model the address bus power consumption and the result of a DPA attack [3]-[6].

Until now, DPA attacks to busses have been discussed in some papers, among which the most successful are the so-called *multi-bit attacks* [3], [6]-[7]. However, this kind of attack is not so well understood in the case of busses, since no rigorous analysis of the power consumption and the attack result is available in the literature, excepting a few intuitive considerations [3], [6]-[7].

In this paper, a quantitative model of the precharged address bus power consumption and the application to DPA attacks is discussed. This model allows for developing an in-depth understanding of the trade-offs involved in multi-bit DPA attacks to the address bus, and to comparatively evaluate their effectiveness. The deeper insight that is gained through the analysis allows for identifying the cases where attacks are more successful, i.e. where the address bus of an Integrated Circuits running the DES algorithm leaks the maximum amount of information. In turn, this allows for identifying the most critical conditions in which cryptographic ICs should be tested to measure their DPA resistance, as well as to elaborate novel countermeasures. To validate the theoretical results, DPA attacks were carried out on an implementation of the DES cryptographic algorithm running on an MIPS32® architecture simulator.

## 2   Review of Single-Bit DPA Attacks

In general, a DPA attack starts from the acquisition of $N$ power consumption sampled traces $PC_i$ (with $i=1...N$), each of which consists of $M$ samples $PC_i(j)$ (with $j=1...M$) that are measured from the chip performing the encryption (decryption) algorithm by applying a well known input sequence $I_i$.

### 2.1   DPA Attacks with $N \to \infty$

In a single-bit attack, the knowledge of a single intermediate bit $D$ (e.g. an intermediate output signal of the algorithm) which is actually evaluated by the digital circuit when running the algorithm is required. In general, $D$ depends on known data (such as the input $I_i$) and a part $k$ of the secret key according to a known *partitioning function f* [4]

$$D = f(I_i, k) \tag{1}$$

whose correct value is not known because $k$ is secret, but is physically evaluated by the circuit performing the algorithm at some value $j^*$ of $j$. It is worth noting that function $f$ can be easily selected from the knowledge of the algorithm, regardless of its specific circuit implementation.

Since in practical circuits the power consumption also depends on $D$, the generic power trace $PC_i$ is affected by the value of $D$ at $j=j^*$, whereas it is not at $j \neq j^*$. In other words, the average power consumption $A_0$ in (2) among all traces $PC_i$ having $D=0$ at $j=j^*$ is different from the average $A_1$ in (3) among the traces having $D=1$ at $j=j^*$

$$A_0(j) = \frac{\sum PC_i(j)\big|_{D=0}}{N/2} \tag{2}$$

$$A_1(j) = \frac{\sum PC_i(j)\big|_{D=1}}{N/2} \tag{3}$$

where inputs were assumed sufficiently random to make the number of traces with $D=0$ and $D=1$ equal. Now, let us define the differential power trace $\Delta$ as $A_0$-$A_1$, whose value $\Delta_{N \to \infty}$ for when an infinite number of traces is equal to

$$\Delta_{N \to \infty}(j) = E[PC_i(j)|D=0] - E[PC_i(j)|D=1] = \begin{cases} \varepsilon & \text{if } j = j^* \\ 0 & \text{if } j \neq j^* \end{cases} \tag{4}$$

where it was observed that the average $A_0$ ($A_1$) tends to the mean value of the power consumption $E[PC_i(j)|D=0]$ ($E[PC_i(j)|D=1]$) for $D=0$ ($D=1$), and that $E[PC_i(j)|D=0]=E[PC_i(j)|D=1]$ for $j \neq j^*$ (since $PC_i(j)$ does not depend on $D$), otherwise it is equal to a non-zero value $\varepsilon$. These results rely on the assumption that the power traces can be correctly grouped into two sets according to the known value of $D$: in this case, from (4) it is apparent that a spike appears in the differential power trace $\Delta$.

## 2.2  Intra-signal and Inter-signal *SNR* in DPA Attacks with Finite *N*

When $N$ is finite, from the Central Limit theorem it is well known that $\Delta$-$\Delta_{N \to \infty}$ at a given $j$ is a random variable with zero mean and a standard deviation equal to $\sigma/N^{1/2}$ (being $\sigma$ the standard deviation of $\Delta$-$\Delta_{N \to \infty}$ in a single power trace) [4], [8]. Accordingly, $\Delta$ consists of the signal $\Delta_{N \to \infty}$ in (4) and an additive noise signal $\Delta$-$\Delta_{N \to \infty}$, which tends to mask the spike $\varepsilon$. Thus, to detect the spike, $N$ must be sufficiently high to make $\varepsilon$ much greater than the noise standard deviation $\sigma/N^{1/2}$. To this aim, an Intra-Signal Signal-to-Noise Ratio $SNR_{INTRA}$ is defined as [3]-[4]

$$SNR_{INTRA} = \frac{\varepsilon}{\sigma}\sqrt{N} \tag{5}$$

which is in the order of 10-20 in typical conditions where the spike is reliably detected [6]. Under an assigned value of $SNR_{INTRA}$, the number of traces (and thus the effort to perform the attack) to recognize the spike is easily found by inverting (5).

These considerations hold if the power traces are correctly classified into the two sets according to the actual value of $D$. Since inputs $I_i$ are known, from (1) this means that the part of the secret key $k$ is correctly guessed. On the other hand, when the guess of $k$ is incorrect the power traces are classified according to the wrong predicted value $D_{wrong}$ in (1). In the ideal case where $D_{wrong}$ is statistically independent of the actual value $D_{correct}$, the power traces $PC_i$ (which are affected by $D_{correct}$) do not depend on $D_{wrong}$, thus $E[PC_i(j)|D_{wrong}=0]=E[PC_i(j)|D_{wrong}=1]$. In other words, under a wrong guess of $k$, the differential power $\Delta$ is equal to zero for every value of $j$ (including $j^*$), i.e. no spike appears.

The above considerations justify the typical DPA attack procedure [4], which after the acquisition of the power traces evaluates $\Delta$ for all possible[1] guesses of $k$. When a spike with an adequate amplitude (i.e. with $SNR_{INTRA}$ sufficiently high) is found, the guessed $k$ of the corresponding power trace is equal to the correct secret value. Iteratively proceeding in the same way, the complete key is easily recovered.

Actually, $D_{wrong}$ and $D_{correct}$ are never completely independent, hence spikes will appear even if a wrong guess is made, hence in this case the spike amplitude is lower than that for the correct guess. Therefore, the key recovery requires the detection of the maximum spike among all the possible key guesses. This is possible if a sufficiently high values of the Inter-Signal SNR in (6), $SNR_{INTER}$, is obtained

$$SNR_{INTER} = \frac{\varepsilon(D = D_{correct})}{\max[\varepsilon(D = D_{wrong})]}.$$
(6)

## 3   Multi-bit DPA Attacks to Precharged Busses: $SNR_{INTRA}$ Evaluation

The single-bit attack can be generalized to the multi-bit attack by introducing a partition function which predicts the value of $m$ bits (usually lower than the bus width $n$), which is a very effective technique to attack busses [6]. In the case of a precharged bus which is analyzed in this paper, the power dissipated by the $m$ bus lines under attack is proportional to the number of zeroes transferred on the same lines [9], thus it is equal to $(m-w)$ being $w$ the bus weight and assuming a unity proportionality constant with no loss of generality. Accordingly, the partition function in (1) classifies the power traces depending on $w$ [6], according to (7)

$$D = \begin{cases} 0 & \text{if } 0 \le w \le L-1 \\ 1 & \text{if } m-L+1 \le w \le m \end{cases}$$
(7)

where $L$ is a variable ranging from 1 to $m/2$ which must be properly set by the attacker. From (7), the power traces with weight lower than $L$ (greater than $m-L$) is assigned to the power traces set with $D=0$ ($D=1$), whereas the other waveforms are discarded, as depicted in Fig. 1. In the following, a model of $SNR_{INTRA}$ and criteria to optimally set $L$ to maximize it (i.e. to enhance the attack effectiveness) are discussed.

By substituting the power $(m-w)$ into (2)-(3) and assuming $N \to \infty$, the spike $\varepsilon$ in the differential power (4) is given by

---

[1] An exhaustive search is possible since $k$ is not the entire key, but only a limited set of its bits.

$$\varepsilon = E[w(j)|D=1] - E[w(j)|D=0]$$
$$= E[w(j)|w=m-L+1,...,m] - E[w(j)|w=0...L-1]$$ (8)

thus $\varepsilon$ is the difference of the average weight in the subset in Fig. 1 of power traces having $(m-L+1) \le w \le m$ and the average weight in the subset having $0 \le w \le (L-1)$.

To evaluate the average weights in (8), let us assume that all symbols are approximately equally likely, which is reasonable in a cryptographic circuit which exhibits the features of confusion and diffusion in every operation involving the key [10]. Accordingly, the average weight for $D=0$ and $D=1$ results to

$$E[w(j)|w=m-L+1,...,m] = \sum_{i=m-L+1}^{m} i\binom{m}{i} \Big/ \sum_{i=m-L+1}^{m} \binom{m}{i}$$ (9)

$$E[w(j)|w=0,...,L-1] = \sum_{i=0}^{L-1} i\binom{m}{i} \Big/ \sum_{i=0}^{L-1} \binom{m}{i}$$ (10)

where it was observed that the number of $m$-bit symbols with weight $i$ is $\binom{m}{i}$ [11], and the number of power traces in the set $D=0$ ($D=1$) is $\sum_{i=0}^{L-1}\binom{m}{i}$ ($\sum_{i=m-L+1}^{m}\binom{m}{i}$). Now, it is possible to evaluate the $SNR_{INTRA}$ in (5) by observing that the actual number of power traces used to evaluate the averages is lower than $N$, since the power traces with weight ranging from $L$ to $(m-L)$ are discarded, according to Fig. 1. Due to the assumption of equally likely symbols, the fraction $v$ of useful traces compared to the number of acquired traces is equal to the fraction of symbols which are not discarded over the $2^m$ symbols

$$v = \left[ \sum_{i=0}^{L-1}\binom{m}{i} + \sum_{i=m-L+1}^{m}\binom{m}{i} \right] \Big/ 2^m .$$ (11)

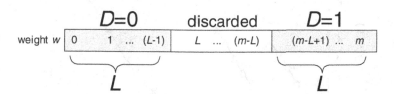

**Fig. 1.** Classification of power traces according to the weight $w$ in multi-bit attacks

By substituting (8)-(10) into (5), replacing $N$ by $N \cdot v$, and performing some simple analytical manipulations, $SNR_{INTRA}$ turns out to be given by

$$SNR_{INTRA} = \varepsilon \cdot \sqrt{v} \cdot \frac{\sqrt{N}}{\sigma} = g(m,L) \cdot \frac{\sqrt{N}}{\sigma}$$ (12)

$$\text{where } g(m,L) = \frac{\sum_{i=0}^{L-1}(m-2i)\cdot\binom{m}{i}}{\sum_{i=0}^{L-1}\binom{m}{i}}\cdot\sqrt{2\frac{\sum_{i=0}^{L-1}\binom{m}{i}}{2^m}}. \tag{13}$$

From (12)-(13), it is apparent that $SNR_{INTRA}$ strongly depends on parameter $L$, as confirmed by intuition. Indeed, according to Fig. 1, if $L$ increases the average weight for $D=1$ ($D=0$) decreases (increases), due to the additional contribution of symbols with a lower (greater) weight. Thus, from (8) $\varepsilon$ tends to decrease, thereby reducing $SNR_{INTRA}$ in (5). However, if $L$ increases the number of discarded traces decreases (i.e. $v$ in (11) increases), thereby increasing $SNR_{INTRA}$. According to the above considerations, a trade-off between two opposite phenomena exists when considering the dependence of $SNR_{INTRA}$ on $L$.

Eqs. (12)-(13) is useful to understand this trade-off, as well as to identify the value of $L$ which maximizes $SNR_{INTRA}$, or equivalently function $g$ in (13). By numerically maximizing (13), it is found that the optimum value of $L$ that maximizes $SNR_{INTRA}$ is approximately equal to $m/2$, thus *the DPA attack is most effective when L is set to its maximum allowed value*. For example, this is shown by the plot of $g$ as a function of $L$ for $m$ equal to 8, 16, 32 and 64 in Fig. 2.

According to eqs. (12)-(13) and Fig. 2, $SNR_{INTRA}$ increases as increasing $m$, thereby confirming the usual assumption that *attacks to a greater number of bits are more effective* [3], [6]-[7]. It is worth noting that these results are not affected by the $n$-$m$ bus bits which are not under attack, since they are independent of $D$, thus they give the same contribution to $A_0$ and $A_1$, i.e. a zero contribution to their difference $\Delta$. For example, the eventual constant bits in memory accesses representing a memory offset do not affect $\Delta$.

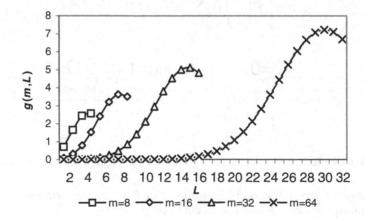

**Fig. 2.** Plot of function $g$ in (13) versus $L$ for $m$=8, 16, 32, 64

## 4   Multi-bit DPA Attacks to Precharged Busses: $SNR_{INTER}$ Evaluation

To evaluate the inter-signal $SNR$, according to (6) it is necessary to evaluate the spike $\varepsilon$ associated with the correct and the wrong keys. Since the spike amplitude depends on the partition function, in the following the attack to the address bus in a processor running the DES algorithm is discussed, as it is regarded a major threat to information security [5], [7]. In DPA attacks, it is well known that it is convenient to attack the S-BOX function which is a fundamental block in the DES implementation [4], [7]. This function is implemented with a look-up table stored in memory due to its large size. To access the table elements, an $n$-bit address is transferred to the address bus that consists of $m=6$ bits identifying the element, other than $n-m$ bits which represent the table address offset [1], [2]. The 6 bits are obtained by XORing a 6-bit sub-key $k$ with 6 bits of the plaintext [1], [2].

When considering the attack under the correct sub-key, the spike $\varepsilon$ obtained by substituting (9)-(10) into (8) is reported in Table 1 versus the parameter $L$, which can range from 1 to $m/2=3$.

When considering the attack under a sub-key having only one wrong bit at a given position, the predicted S-BOX address bits are correct excepting that at the same position, due to the XOR operation. Under this assumption, the bus weight predicted with the wrong key differs from the actual weight by $\pm 1$, which has two effects: 1) the predicted average weight is different from the actual average weight, 2) some power traces are incorrectly classified[2]. As a consequence, the spike $\varepsilon$ differs from the value under the correct key, and is evaluated in the following by assuming $L=3$ and, without loss of generality, that the wrong key bit is the last one. Under this assumption, the correspondence between the predicted and the actually transferred value is reported in Table 2. In this case, assuming again equally likely symbols, the average weight of the power traces which are predicted to belong to the set $D=0$ is

$$E\left[w(j)|D=0\right] = \sum_i i \cdot n_i \Bigg/ \sum_{i=0}^{2}\binom{6}{i} = \sum_i i \cdot n_i \Big/ 22 \qquad (14)$$

where $n_i$ is the actual number of bus values having weight $i$. An analogous relationship holds for the average weight in the set with (predicted) $D$ equal to 1. In (14), $n_i$ with $D=0$ can be evaluated by considering the actual values in Table 2 which are classified into the set $D=0$, i.e. associated with predicted values with weight equal to 0, 1 or 2. In regard to $n_0$, it is equal to 1 because the only value with weight 0 (i.e. (000000)) is actually transferred, even though it is predicted to be (000001) due to the last bit error. In regard to the $n_1$ values with weight 1, there are five (i.e. (100000),(010000),...(000010)) that are incorrectly predicted to have a weight of 2

---

[2] Indeed, some actual values with weight equal to $L-1$ $(m-L+1)$ that should be assigned to the set $D=0$ $(D=1)$ will be predicted to have a weight of $L$ $(m-L)$ and thus discarded according to Fig. 1. Analogously, some values with weight $L$ $(m-L)$ that should be discarded will be predicted to have a weight $L-1$ $(m-L+1)$, and thus assigned to the set with $D=0$ $(D=1)$.

(i.e. (100001),(010001),...(000011)) and one (i.e. (000001)) that is incorrectly to have a weight of 0 (i.e. (000000)), thus $n_1=6$. In regard to the $n_2$ values with weight 2, there are five (i.e. (100001),(010001),...(000011)) that are incorrectly predicted to have a weight of 1 (i.e. (100000),(010000),...(000010)), thus $n_2=5$. Regarding the $n_3$ values with weight 3, there are ten (i.e. (110001),(101001),(100101),(100011), (011001),(010101),(010011),(001101),(001011),(000111)) having a weight 3 that are predicted to have a weight 2 (i.e. (110000),(101000),(100100),(100010),(011000), (010100),(010010),(001100),(001010),(000110)), thus $n_3=10$. It is worth noting that ten values with actual weight 2 (i.e. (110000), (101000),(100100),(100010), (011000),(010100),(010010),(001100),(001010),(000110)) are incorrectly discarded since the are predicted to have a weight of 3 (i.e. (110001),(101001),(100101), (100011),(011001),(010101),(010011),(001101),(001011),(000111)). By substituting the above values of $n_i$, the resulting average weight in (14) is 46/22, and by iterating the same procedure for the set with $D=1$ it is obtained that its average weight is 86/22, thus the difference magnitude $\varepsilon$ results to 40/22≈1.8, as reported in Table 1.

The above evaluated spike $\varepsilon$ (under a key with only one wrong bit) is lower than the value 2.7 under the correct key in Table 1, due to the incorrect classification of power traces, as expected. Obviously, when considering the attack under a sub-key having more than one wrong bit, the classification of power traces is affected by more significant errors[3], thus an even lower value of $\varepsilon$ is expected, as was confirmed by simulations. Thus, from (6) to evaluate $SNR_{INTER}$ it is only necessary to know $\varepsilon$ under the correct key and that with only one wrong bit, hence other keys will not be considered. The resulting $SNR_{INTER}$ in (6) (i.e. the ratio of the $\varepsilon$ with correct and wrong key) is reported in Table 1. Finally, by reiterating the above procedure for $L$ equal to 1 and 2, the results in Table 1 are easily obtained.

**Table 1.** Spike amplitude vs. $L$ for a correct and a wrong key (differing by 1 bit)

| | $\varepsilon$ (correct key) | | $\varepsilon$ (wrong key) | | $SNR_{INTRA}$ (eq. (6)) | | |
| $L$ | predicted | simulated | predicted | simulated | predicted | simulated | % error |
|---|---|---|---|---|---|---|---|
| 1 | 6 | 6 | 4 | 4 | 6/4=1.5 | 1.5 | 0% |
| 2 | 30/7≈4.3 | 4.24 | 20/7≈2.9 | 2.72 | 4.3/2.9=1.5 | 1.56 | 4% |
| 3 | 60/22≈2.7 | 2.67 | 40/22≈1.8 | 1.74 | 2.7/1.8=1.5 | 1.53 | 2% |

## 5　Validation, Final Remarks and Conclusions

The power model above derived was validated by running the DES algorithm on a MIPS32® cycle-accurate simulator, which is a widely adopted microprocessor architecture in SmartCards [2], [12]. In this architecture, DPA attacks were performed by monitoring the address bus power consumption in $N=1,000$ encryptions and attacking

---

[3] This is not true in the particular case with 6 wrong bits, in which the predicted values are the complement of the actual bus values, due to the XOR operation. Thus, the two sets are exchanged and $\varepsilon$ has the same amplitude and opposite sign compared to the correct key.

the *S-BOX* function, as usual [4], [7]. As an example, the resulting differential power trace $\Delta$ for $L=3$ is plotted in Figs. 3a-3b versus time $j$ under the correct key and a key with only one wrong bit, respectively. The simulated values of the spike amplitude $\varepsilon$ and $SNR_{INTRA}$ are reported in Table 1, and the resulting model error is always within 4%. This confirms the good model accuracy and the validity of the introduced approximations that were intuitively justified above.

At the best authors' knowledge, the proposed power model is the first quantitative analysis of DES multi-bit attacks to address busses, which is a theoretical basis to better understand the information leakage through the address bus. The proposed model is also useful to understand how to enhance the effectiveness of DPA attacks in terms of Intra-Signal and Inter-Signal *SNR* by properly setting the parameter $L$ which can be freely chosen by the attacker. In particular, from (12)-(13) it was shown that the Intra-Signal *SNR* is maximized by setting $L$ to the maximum value $m/2=3$. In regard to the Inter-Signal *SNR*, from Table 1 it is apparent that it is not affected by parameter $L$, but it is always equal to 1.5 regardless of the specific $L$. Accordingly, the choice of L must be made by only considering the Intra-Signal *SNR*. This is an interesting result, which means that the effectiveness of DPA attacks to the address bus of the DES algorithm is maximized when $L$ is set to 3. This means that micro-processors running the DES algorithm should always be tested by setting $L=3$ to evaluate the resistance to DPA attacks of their address bus, as well as to verify the effectiveness of novel countermeasures.

**Table 2.** Correspondence between the predicted value and the actual value with $L=3$ for a key with a wrong last bit

| predicted value | actual value | predicted value | actual value | predicted value | actual value | predicted value | actual value |
|---|---|---|---|---|---|---|---|
| 000000 | 000001 [c] | 010000 | 010001 [d] | 100000 | 100001 [d] | 110000 | 110001 |
| 000001 | 000000 [a] | 010001 | 010000 [b] | 100001 | 100000 [b] | 110001 | 110000 [f] |
| 000010 | 000011 [d] | 010010 | 010011 | 100010 | 100011 | 110010 | 110011 |
| 000011 | 000010 [b] | 010011 | 010010 [f] | 100011 | 100010 [f] | 110011 | 110010 |
| 000100 | 000101 [d] | 010100 | 010101 | 100100 | 100101 | 110100 | 110101 |
| 000101 | 000100 [b] | 010101 | 010100 [f] | 100101 | 100100 [f] | 110101 | 110100 |
| 000110 | 000111 | 010110 | 010111 | 100110 | 100111 | 110110 | 110111 |
| 000111 | 000110 [f] | 010111 | 010110 | 100111 | 100110 | 110111 | 110110 |
| 001000 | 001001 [d] | 011000 | 011001 | 101000 | 101001 | 111000 | 111001 |
| 001001 | 001000 [b] | 011001 | 011000 [f] | 101001 | 101000 [f] | 111001 | 111000 |
| 001010 | 001011 | 011010 | 011011 | 101010 | 101011 | 111010 | 111011 |
| 001011 | 001010 [f] | 011011 | 011010 | 101011 | 101010 | 111011 | 111010 |
| 001100 | 001101 | 011100 | 011101 | 101100 | 101101 | 111100 | 111101 |
| 001101 | 001100 [f] | 011101 | 011100 | 101101 | 101100 | 111101 | 111100 |
| 001110 | 001111 | 011110 | 011111 | 101110 | 101111 | 111110 | 111111 |
| 001111 | 001110 | 011111 | 011110 | 101111 | 101110 | 111111 | 111110 |

[a] actual weight 0/predicted weight 1      [b] actual weight 1/predicted weight 2

[c] actual weight 1/predicted weight 0      [d] actual weight 2/predicted weight 1

[e] actual weight 2/predicted weight 1      [f] actual weight 2/predicted weight 3

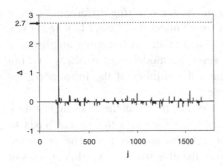     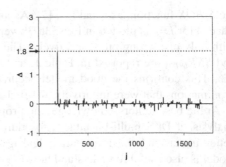

**Fig. 3a.** Differential power under the correct key

**Fig. 3b.** Differential power under the key with only one wrong bit

# References

1. A. Menezes, P. Van Oorschot, S. Vanstone, *Handbook of Applied Cryptography*, CRC Press, 1997.
2. W. Rankl, W. Effing, *SmartCard Handbook*, John Wiley & Sons, 1999.
3. T. S. Messerges, E. A. Dabbish, R. H. Sloan, "Examining Smart-Card Security under the Threat of Power Analysis Attacks," *IEEE Trans. on Computers*, vol. 51, no. 5, pp. 541-552, May 2002.
4. P. Kocher, J. Jaffe, B. Jun, "Differential Power Analysis," *Proc. of CRYPTO'99*, pp. 388-397, 1999.
5. X. Zhuang, T. Zhang, S. Pande, "HIDE: an infrastructure for efficiently protecting information leakage on the address bus," *Proc. of ASPLOS'04*, pp. 72-84, Boston (USA), Oct. 2004.
6. T. S. Messerges, E. A. Dabbish, R. H. Sloan, "Investigations of power analysis attacks on SmartCards," Proc. of USENIX Workshop on Smartcard Technology, pp. 388-397, Chicago (USA), 1999.
7. C. Clavier, J.-S. Coron, N. Dabbous, "Differential Power Analysis in presence of hardware countermeasures," Springer-Verlag, LNCS 1965, pp. 252-263, *CHES'00*, 2000.
8. A. Papoulis, *Probability, Random Variables, and Stochastic Processes*, McGraw-Hill, 1965.
9. J. Rabaey, *Digital Integrated Circuits (A Design Perspective)*, Prentice Hall, 1996.
10. C. Shannon, "Communication Theory of Secrecy Systems," *Bell Systems Technical Journal*, vol.28, 1949, pp.656-715.
11. R. B. Lin, C. M. Tsai, "Theoretical analysis of bus-invert coding," *IEEE Trans. on VLSI Systems*, vol. 10, no. 6, pp. 929-935, Dec. 2002.
12. MIPS Technologies Inc., *http://www.mips.com*

# Adaptive Coding in Networks-on-Chip: Transition Activity Reduction Versus Power Overhead of the Codec Circuitry

José C.S. Palma[1], Leandro Soares Indrusiak[2], Fernando G. Moraes[3],
Alberto Garcia Ortiz[2], Manfred Glesner[2], and Ricardo A.L. Reis[1]

[1] PPGC - II - UFRGS - Av. Bento Gonçalves, 9500, Porto Alegre, RS – Brazil
{jcspalma, reis}@inf.ufrgs.br
[2] MES – TU Darmstadt – Karlstr. 15, 64283 Darmstadt – Germany
{lsi, agarcia, glesner}@mes.tu-darmstadt.de
[3] PPGCC - FACIN – PUCRS - Av. Ipiranga, 6681, Porto Alegre, RS – Brazil
moraes@inf.pucrs.br

**Abstract.** This work investigates the reduction of power consumption in Networks-on-Chip (NoCs) through the reduction of transition activity using data coding schemes. The estimation of the NoC power consumption is performed with basis on macromodels which reproduce the power consumption on each internal NoC module according to the transition activity on its input ports. Such macromodels are embedded in a system model and a series of simulations are performed, aiming to analyze the trade-off between the power savings due to coding schemes versus the power consumption overhead due to the encoding and decoding modules.

## 1 Introduction

The advances in fabrication technology allow designers to implement a whole system on a single chip, but the inherent design complexity of such systems makes it hard to fully explore the technology potential. Thus, the design of Systems-on-Chip (SoCs) is usually based on the reuse of pre-designed and pre-verified intellectual property core that are interconnected through special communication resources that must handle very tight performance and area constraints. In addition to those application-related constraints, deep sub-micron effects pose physical design challenges for long wires and global on-chip communication. A possible approach to overcome those challenges is to change from a fully synchronous design paradigm to a globally asynchronous, locally synchronous (GALS) design paradigm [1]. A Network-on-Chip (NoC) is an infrastructure essentially composed of routers interconnected by communication channels. It is suitable to support the GALS paradigm, since it provides asynchronous communication, scalability, reusability and reliability [2].

The growing market for portable battery-powered devices adds a third dimension (power) to the previously two-dimensional (speed, area) VLSI design space [3]. Power consumption is directly related to battery life as well as costly package and heatsink requirements for high-end devices [4]. In order to ensure the final system complies to

J. Vounckx, N. Azemard, and P. Maurine (Eds.): PATMOS 2006, LNCS 4148, pp. 603–613, 2006.

the desired function, thermal and cost requirements, the power consumption issues must be addressed during the design of all subsystems in a SoC, including the interconnect structure. One problem related to power consumption in busses is the capacitances induced by long wires. Such problem is minimized in NoCs, since point-to-point short wires are used between routers. However, NoCs consumes power in routers, diminishing the apparent advantage in terms of power when compared to busses.

The power consumption in a NoC grows linearly with the amount of bit transitions in subsequent data packets sent through the interconnect architecture [5]. Using the Hermes NoC architecture [6] as case study we could show that bit transitions affect the power consumption up to 370% for interconnect lines, 180% for router input buffers and 16% for router control logic. One way to reduce power consumption in NoCs, in both wires and logic, is to reduce the switching activity by means of coding schemes. [7]. Several schemes were proposed in the late 90's, all of them addressing bus-based communication architectures.

The main contribution of this work is the evaluation of such schemes in the context of NoC-based systems. The trade-off between power savings versus the power consumption overhead due to additional circuitry is presented.

This paper is organized as follows. Section 2 reviews coding schemes aiming to reduce power consumption in bus-based systems. Section 3 introduces the coding in NoCs. Section 4 presents the power consumption model for Networks-on-Chip. In Section 5 the analysis on power consumption is explained. Section 6 presents some experimental results and Section 7 presents the conclusions and future works.

## 2   Coding Schemes

Based on the observation that it is possible to reduce the power dissipation on bus drivers by reducing the average number of signal transitions, several coding schemes have been previously proposed. Some of these schemes exploit spatial redundancy, increasing the number of bus lines, while others exploit temporal redundancy, increasing the number of bits transmitted in successive bus cycles. There are also few schemes that do not rely on spatial nor temporal redundancy [7].

Some of these schemes require *a-priori* knowledge of the statistical parameters of the input traffic, but in this work we focus on schemes that do not require such knowledge as we intend to apply them on general-purpose NoC-based systems.

Bus-Invert [8] is an example of such schemes. It uses an extra control bit (an extra line) called *invert*, which indicates when the data value in the communication lines are inverted or not. The data value is inverted when the Hamming distance (the number of bits in which they differ) between the present value and the next data value is bigger than half of the number of lines.

In [7] the authors propose an Adaptive Probability Encoding scheme which does not require any *a-priori* knowledge of the input traffic and its statistics. It is capable of on-line adaptation of the encoding to the stream statistic behavior. This scheme operates bit-wise, according to its actual and the last value.

The encoding is done with basis on approximate statistical information collected by observation of the bit stream over a window of fixed size S. The authors claim that a window size with S = 64 offers a good compromise between complexity and accuracy.

The statistical information concern the four joint probabilities for a single bit ($P_{0,0}$, $P_{0,1}$, $P_{1,0}$ and $P_{1,1}$). In order to deal with integer values and simplify the hardware, the authors use the occurrence frequencies $N_{00}$, $N_{01}$, $N_{10}$ and $N_{11}$ instead of probabilities. Since the sum of the four occurrence frequencies is known ($N_{00} + N_{01} + N_{10} + N_{11} = S$ -1), not all the four occurrences are actually required. Considering that $N_{01}$ and $N_{10}$ must be balanced over the observation window (they can differ by 1 at most), it is sufficient to consider only $N_{00}$ and $N_{11}$ joint probabilities, since their knowledge implies the other two. Considering $N_{01} = N_{10}$, the symbol $N_T$ is used to denote them.

Such scheme uses four different encoding functions $F(x(n), x(n-1))$. The function selection is done according to the JPD (*joint probability distribution*) of the current window. The decision is taken as follows:

a) y(n) = x(n)                    when $N_{00} > N_T > N_{11}$
b) y(n) = x(n)'                   when $N_{11} > N_T > N_{00}$
c) y(n) = x(n) xor x(n-1)         when $N_T < \{ N_{11}, N_{00} \}$
d) y(n) = x(n) nxor x(n-1)        when $N_T > \{ N_{11}, N_{00} \}$

When the most probable pair of symbols is 00, it is reasonable to leave the bits unchanged, since a zero in the stream will result in no transition. Similarly, when $N_T$ is the most probable symbol, the transitions are eliminated by XOR-ing two consecutive bits. This yields a sequence of ones that are complemented before being sent through the communication channel.

## 3  Adding Coding Modules into NoCs

In Networks-on-Chip the data is transmitted in packets, which are sent through routers, from sources to targets. These packets are composed by a header (containing routing information) and a payload (containing the data to be transmitted). In Hermes [5], the header is composed by two flits[1], comprising the target address and the packet length. Thus, an approach merging coding schemes and a Network-on-Chip should not encode the packet header, since it must be used by routers in every hop[2] through the Network-on-Chip.

By this way, encoding and decoding operations must be done in the source and target cores only, converting the original data to the encoded (and transmitted) one and vice-versa. In this work the encoder and decoder modules are inserted in the local ports of the routers, that is, between the cores and the NoC interconnect structure. It is important to say that this method is general, since it does not change the NoC structure.

Fig. 1 shows an IP core connected to a local port of a Hermes router. The incoming data packets pass through the decoder module, while outgoing data packets pass

---

[1] Smallest data unit transmitted over the network-on-chip.
[2] Hop is the distance between two routers in a network-on-chip.

through the encoder module. The remaining ports of the router must be connected to other routers according to the network topology.

This figure also shows the internal modules of a Hermes router: a switch control (SC) responsible for arbitration and routing functions and FIFO buffers for the input channel of each port (North, South, East, West and Local). The input and output channels are simplified in the figure, since they are composed of groups of signals. For example, the input channel is composed of *data_in*, *tx* and *ack_tx* signals in a handshake flow control configuration, or *data_in*, *tx* and *credt_in* in a credit-based configuration.

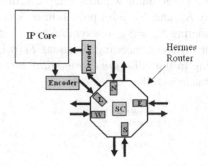

**Fig. 1.** Encoder and Decoder modules location

## 4   NoC Power Consumption Model

The power consumption in a system originates from the operation of the IP cores and the interconnection components between those cores. It is proportional to the switching activity arising from packets moving across the network. Interconnect wires and routers dissipate power. As shown in [5], several authors have proposed to estimate NoC power consumption by evaluating the effect of bits/packets traffic on each NoC component.

The router power consumption is estimated splitting it into the buffer power consumption and the control logic power consumption. It is also important to estimate the power consumption in the channels connecting a router to another one, as well as in the channels connecting a router to its local core. In this paper, wire lengths of 5 mm for inter-router links and 0.25 mm for local links were considered.

The conducted experiments employ a mesh topology version of Hermes with six different configurations. The parameters were obtained varying flit width (8 and 16 bits), and input buffer depth (4, 8 and 16 flits). For each configuration, 128-flit packets enter the NoC, each with a distinct pattern of bit transitions in their structure, from 0 to 127.

Considering an approach with data coding, it is also necessary to compute the power consumed in the encoder and decoder modules. These modules were also simulated with 128-flit packets with different traffic patterns. However, until now in this work only the encoder and decoder configurations for 8-bit flit width were used.

The flow for obtaining power consumption data comprises three steps. The first step starts with the NoC VHDL description (without coding scheme) and traffic files, both obtained using a customized environment for NoC configuration and traffic generation [9]. Traffic input files are fed to the NoC through the router local channels, modeling local cores behavior. A VHDL simulator applies input signals to the NoC or to any NoC module, either a single router or a router inner module (input buffer or control logic). Simulation produces signal traces storing the logic values variations for each signal. These traces are converted to electrical stimuli and later used in SPICE simulation (third step).

In the second step, the module to be evaluated (e.g. an input buffer) is synthesized within LeonardoSpectrum using a technology-specific cell library, such as CMOS TSMC 0.35µ. The tool produces an HDL netlist, later converted to a SPICE netlist using a converter developed internally for the scope of this work.

The third step consists in the SPICE simulation of the module under analysis. Here, it is necessary to integrate both, the SPICE netlist of the module, the electrical input signals and a library with logic gates described in SPICE. The resulting electric information allows the acquisition of NoC power consumption parameters for a given traffic.

After that, this process was repeated with a new version of the NoC which uses a coding scheme. In the case of Adaptive Encoding, the encoder and decoder modules were also developed in VHDL, synthesized to CMOS TSMC 0.35µ technology, converted to a SPICE netlist and simulated with different traffic patterns. In the case of Bus-Invert, it is necessary a new analysis of all NoC modules, since this scheme requires the insertion of a control bit in all modules, increasing the power consumption of them.

## 4.1 Model Definition

Average power per hop ($APH$) is used here to denote the average power consumption in a single hop of a packet transmitted over the NoC. $APH$ can be split into three components: average power consumed by router ($APR$); average power consumed in a link between routers ($APL$); and average power consumed in a link between the router and the system core attached directly to it ($APC$). Equation (1) gives the average power consumption of a packet transmitted through a router, a local link and a link between routers.

$$APH = APR + APL + APC \qquad (1)$$

Moreover, the analysis presented in [5] shows that a better understanding of the average power consumption in the router ($APR$) can be achieved by dividing it into its buffer ($APB$) and control ($APS$) components. This is because the bit transition effect on power consumption at the router control is much smaller than its effect on the power consumption at the router buffer. Fig. 2a illustrates this effect for a 16-word input buffer and for the centralized control logic of an 8-bit flit width Hermes router. The graph depicts power as a function of the amount of bit transitions in a 128-flit packet (100% = 127 bit transitions in each one of the 8 input bits). Clearly, power consumption increases linearly with the increase of bit transitions in a packet.

In regular tile[3]-based architectures (cores are placed inside a limited region, which is usually called tile), tile dimension is close to the average core dimension, and the core inputs/outputs are placed near the router local channel. Therefore, APC is much smaller than APL, as showed in Fig. 2b.

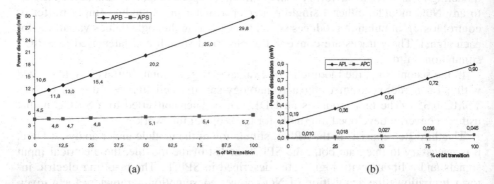

(a)                                                         (b)

**Fig. 2.** (a) Analysis of the bit transition effect on the power consumption for a 16-word input buffer and for the centralized control logic of an 8-bit flit width Hermes router. (b) Analysis of the effect on local and inter-router links. Each tile has 5 mm x 5 mm of dimension, and uses 8-bit links. Data obtained from SPICE simulation (CMOS TSMC 0.35µ technology).

Based in these results, APC may be safely neglected without significant errors in total power dissipation. Therefore, Equation (2) computes the average router-to-router communication power dissipation, from tile $\tau i$ to tile $\tau j$, where $\eta$ corresponds to the number of routers through which the packet passes.

$$RRP_{ij} = \eta \times (APB + APS) + (\eta - 1) \times APL \qquad (2)$$

Considering now an approach with data coding in the NoC local ports, two new parameters may be introduced to Equation (2): APE and APD (encoder and decoder average power consumption, respectively). Fig. 3 illustrates the analysis of the effect of bit transitions on power consumption of the encoder and decoder modules, both with 8-bit width. As showed in this figure, power consumption also grows linearly in these modules as the amount of bit transitions is increased.

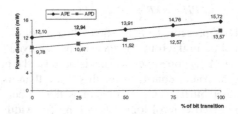

**Fig. 3.** Analysis of the effect of bit transitions on the power consumption of 8-bit encoder and decoder modules of Adaptive Encoding scheme

---

[3] Cores are placed inside a limited region, which is usually called tile.

Based on the described analysis, it was possible to build macromodels for the several parts of the proposed model – APB, APS, APL, APE and APD - representing the power consumption in the different modules of a NoC. For sake of simplicity, the macromodels estimate the average power consumption of a module without considering its internal state (power consumption is function of the transition activity on the module's inputs only). Such simplification incurs on error, but our experiments have shown that the error is relatively small. For instance, in the case of the encoder and decoder modules, the simplification leads to an error of 5% in the power estimation (about ±0,6 mW).

Note that all modules (buffer, control, encoder and decoder) and also the communication channels consume power even with 0% of bit transitions on the data. This occurs due to static power consumption, switching of internal signals, internal state update and clock. In communication channels, this power consumption is due to clock and flow control signal activity. We refer it as Po in the subsequent analysis (see Table 1). The remaining of the power consumption grows linearly with the bit transition rate (the slope is referred as R).

**Table 1.** Macromodel for the NoC and Adaptive Encoding modules ($AP = Po + \%T * R$)

| Module | Po | R |
|---|---|---|
| Buffer (APB) | 10,61 | 19,19 |
| Control (APS) | 4,39 | 0,72 |
| Encoder (APE) | 12,1 | 3,62 |
| Decoder (APD) | 9,78 | 3,79 |
| Inter-roter channel (APL) | 0,19 | 0,71 |

Considering a NoC with the Bus-Invert coding scheme, the power consumption must be calculated with basis on a new macromodel, which takes into account the extra bit of this scheme in all NoC modules (see Table 2).

**Table 2.** Macromodels for the NoC and Bus-Invert modules ($AP = Po + \%T * R$)

| Módulo | $P_0$ | R |
|---|---|---|
| Buffer (APB) | 11,49 | 22,13 |
| Control (APS) | 4,39 | 0,98 |
| Encoder (APE) | 1,16 | 3,88 |
| Decoder (APD) | 0,55 | 0,25 |
| Inter-roter channel (APL) | 0,19 | 0,8 |

Equation (3) computes the average router-to-router communication power dissipation, from tile $\tau i$ to tile $\tau j$, passing through $\eta$ routers and using a coding scheme.

$$CodedRRPij = APE + \eta \times (APB + APS) + (\eta - 1) \times APL + APD \qquad (3)$$

## 5  NoC Power Consumption Analysis

As stated in Section 4, the average power estimation depends on the communication infrastructure (here assumed to be a Hermes NoC) and on the application core traffic. This Section shows the method to compute the average power consumption in a NoC with and without coding schemes.

The average power consumption analysis is done with different traffic patterns. Some of these traffics are synthetic (generated by a traffic generation tool) and others are real application data which was packetized and transmitted over the NoC.

In order to fully evaluate the traffic resulting from real application data, experiments must be performed with realistic amounts of data. However, the simulation times for hundreds of packets in a SPICE simulator are really large. So, a better alternative was taken, exploring the possibility to embed the macromodels into a higher abstraction model, which was simulated within the PtolemyII environment [10]. Such abstract model include a model of an encoder, a section of the NoC interconnect and a decoder. These models are used to track the percentage of bit transitions in each traffic pattern and, based on the energy macromodels, calculate the average power consumption for such traffic patterns.

Considering for instance a synthetic traffic pattern with 2000 8-bit flits, the maximum amount of bit transition is 15992 (1999 x 8 = 100%). After the system simulation, the amount of bit transitions computed was 11994, corresponding to 80% of the maximum possible switching activity. Thus, the average power in the buffer and control logic must be calculated with base in the rate of 80% of bit transitions.

$$APB = Po + \%T * R \qquad APS = Po + \%T * R \qquad APL = Po + \%T * R$$
$$APB = 10{,}6 + 0{,}8 * 19{,}2 \qquad APS = 4{,}39 + 0{,}8 * 0{,}72 \qquad APL = 0{,}19 + 0{,}8 * 0{,}71$$
$$APB = 25{,}96 \text{ mW} \qquad APS = 4{,}97 \text{ mW} \qquad APL = 0{,}76 \text{ mW}$$

Using the Equation (2) it is possible to calculate the average power of a packet passing through only one router as follows:

$$RRP_{ij} = APB + APS + APL \quad \rightarrow \quad RRP_{ij} = 25{,}96 + 4{,}97 + 0{,}76 = 31{,}69 \text{ mW}$$

Considering now that using the Adaptive Encoding scheme the amount of bit transitions was reduced to 3998 (30%). In this case the energy consumption in the NoC is:

$$APB = 10{,}6 + 0{,}3 * 19{,}2 \qquad APS = 4{,}39 + 0{,}3 * 0{,}72 \qquad APL = 0{,}19 + 0{,}3 * 0{,}71$$
$$APB = 16{,}36 \text{ mW} \qquad APS = 4{,}6 \text{ mW} \qquad APL = 0{,}4 \text{ mW}$$
$$RRP_{ij} = 16{,}36 + 4{,}6 + 0{,}4 = 21{,}36 \text{ mW}$$

It is also necessary to include in this computation the power consumed by the encoder and decoder modules. In this example the original traffic pattern has 80% of bit transitions. In this case, the power consumption in the encoder module is:

$$APE = 12{,}1 + 0{,}8 * 3{,}62 \quad \rightarrow \quad APE = 14{,}99 \text{ mW}$$

However, the power consumption in the decoder module must be calculated with base in the encoded traffic with 30% of bit transition, as follows:

$$APD = 9{,}78 + 0{,}3 * 3{,}79 \quad \rightarrow \quad APD = 10{,}91 \text{ mW}$$

The power reduction in the Network-on-Chip in this example was 10,33 mW (31,69 - 21,36). On the other hand, the coding scheme consumes 25,9 mW (14,99 + 10,91). Considering a power save of 10,33 mW in each hop, we can assume that after 3 hops the power consumption of the coding scheme can be amortized, since the encoding and decoding occur only once in a transmission.

# 6  Experimental Results

This section presents experimental results obtained by system level simulation within Ptolemy II, using the macromodels described in Section 4, for a number of traffic patterns (both real application data and synthetically generated traffic).

Table 3 shows the results obtained with Adaptive Encoding scheme. The first column describes the type of traffic. The second column reproduces the reduction of transition activity reported by Benini et al. in [7] (when available) and the third column presents the reduction of transition activity found on our experiments by reproducing the coding techniques proposed in [7]. Both cases report the results in terms of reduction in the number of transitions with respect to the original data streams. The fourth column shows the power consumption (*APH*) without use of data coding techniques, while the fifth column shows the same measurement when coding techniques are used. Finally, the sixth and seventh columns present the power consumption overhead due to the encoder and decoder modules (*APE + APD*) and the number of hops which are needed to amortize this overhead.

The results presented in the second and third column show some differences between the results obtained in [7] and in the present work. This can be caused by the relation between consecutive flits sent through the NoC. In [7] the authors use a 32-bit *flit* channel. Thus, the transition activity is computed between bytes in the same position of consecutive *flits* (sending 4 bytes in each *flit*). In this work we use 8-bit *flit*, and the transition activity is computed between consecutive bytes.

Experiments with the transmission of synthetically generated streams showed that the use of coding techniques can be advantageous if the average hop count for packages is larger than three (so the overhead of encoding and decoding is amortized). However, different examples like sound (.wav) streams showed that the encoding and decoding overhead can be amortized only after 21 hops (power reduction of 1,14 mW/hop). In some other cases, the encoder increases the number of transitions, increasing the power consumption of the system.

Table 4 presents the experimental results with Bus-Invert. The third column is calculated with basis on the macromodel of the normal NoC (without coding scheme), while de fourth column is calculated with basis on the macromodel using Bus-Invert (with 1 more bit in all modules).

**Table 3.** Experimental results with Adaptive Encoding

| Stream | Bit transition reduction (reported in [7]) | Bit transition reduction (simulated within the scope of this work) | NoC Average Power consumption without coding (APB+APS+APL) | NoC Average Power consumption with coding (APB+APS+APL) | Coding modules power consumption (APE + APD) | # of hops |
|---|---|---|---|---|---|---|
| HTML | 9,3 % | 5,5 % | 18,26 mW | 18 mW | 23 mW | 88 |
| GZIP | 16,3 % | 8% | 20,34 mW | 19,7 mW | 23,65 mW | 37 |
| GCC | 15,6 % | 4 % | 19,93 mW | 19,7 mW | 23,5 mW | 102 |
| Bytecode | - | 9 % | 19,32 mW | 18,93 mW | 23,29 mW | 61 |
| WAV | 2,1 % | 21,95 % | 20,36 mW | 19,22 mW | 23,52 mW | 21 |
| MP3 | - | - 2,17 % | 20 mW | 20,11 mW | 23,63 mW | - |
| RAW | - 3,4 % | - 10,98 % | 18,7 mW | 19,1 mW | 23,2 mW | - |
| BMP | - | - 0,5 % | 20,24 mW | 20,27 mW | 23,7 mW | - |
| Synthetic 1 | - | 75 % | 22,62 mW | 17,02 mW | 23,52 mW | 4 |
| Synthetic 2 | - | -27 % | 18,45mW | 19,34 mW | 23,21 mW | - |

**Table 4.** Experimental results with Bus-Invert

| Stream | Bit transition reduction (simulated within the scope of this work) | NoC Average Power consumption without coding (APB+APS+APL) | NoC Average Power consumption with coding (APB+APS+APL) | Coding modules power consumption (APE + APD) | # of hops |
|---|---|---|---|---|---|
| HTML | 6,2 % | 18,26 mW | 19,41 mW | 2,32 mW | - |
| GZIP | 18,7% | 20,34 mW | 20,93 mW | 2,73 mW | - |
| GCC | 17,9% | 19,93 mW | 20,68 mW | 2,65 mW | - |
| Bytecode | 12 % | 19,32 mW | 20,28 mW | 2,5 mW | - |
| WAV | 18,8 % | 20,36 mW | 20,93 mW | 2,7 mW | - |
| MP3 | 17,4 % | 20 mW | 20,68 mW | 2,66 mW | - |
| RAW | 14,6 % | 18,7 mW | 19,56 mW | 2,4 mW | - |
| BMP | 18,2% | 20,25 mW | 20,86 mW | 2,71 mW | - |
| Synthetic 1 | 50,7% | 22,62 mW | 20,3 mW | 3,15 mW | 1 |
| Synthetic 2 | 2,45 % | 18,45 mW | 19,76 mW | 2,36 mW | - |

Table 4 shows that the power consumption in the NoC increases with the Bus-Invert scheme applied over real traffic, regardless of the fact that the bit transition was reduced. This is due to the inclusion of the extra bit in all NoC modules, increasing their power consumption. Even so, this scheme was efficient with one of the synthetic traffics. It is important to point out that these results concern the NoC configuration used in this work, using $0.35\mu$ technology.

In both schemes, the power savings in inter-router channels are much smaller than in the router logic. However, in new technologies the power consumption in channels will be more relevant [11]. In that scenario, the encoding schemes may be advantageous, since they were developed to communication channels.

## 7 Conclusions

This work investigated the reduction of power consumption in Networks-on-Chip through the reduction of signal transition activity using data coding techniques. Power macromodels for various NoC modules were built and embedded in a system-level model, which was simulated with a series of real and synthetic traffic.

Our experiments have shown that the effectiveness of the coding is dependent of the transition activity patterns. By synthesizing a variety of traffic patterns, we could see that the power savings with Adaptive Encoding range from -1 to 15 mW/hop. However, the coding modules of this scheme present high power consumption. Bus-invert modules are economic in power consumption, but are not efficient in an 8-bit *flit* NoC.

Our results point the direction for further research addressing the use of multiple coding schemes to better match the transition activity patterns, and the use of NoC configuration to help the decision whether a packet should be encoded or not (for instance, sending encoded packets to neighbor cores won't pay off). Encoded packets could carry an identification bit in their header.

Future work includes the evaluation of coding schemes in NoCs implemented using state-of-the-art technologies, where the power consumption in channels becomes more relevant due to relative increase in wire capacitance.

# References

[1]  Iyer and D. Marculescu. "Power and performance evaluation of globally asynchronous lo-cally synchronous processors". 29th Annual International Symposium on Computer Ar-chitecture (ISCA), pp. 158-168, May 2002.

[2]  W. Dally and B. Towles. "Route packets, not wires: on-chip interconnection networks". Design Automation Conference (DAC), pp. 684–689, June 2001.

[3]  D. Singh, J. M. Rabaey, M. Pedram, F. Catthoor, S. Rajgopal, N. Sehgal and T. J. Moz-dzen. "Power conscious cad tool and methodologies: A perspective". Proc. IEEE, vol.83, pp. 570-594, Apr. 1995.

[4]  M. Pedram. "Power minimization in IC design". ACM Trans. Design Automat. Electron. Syst., vol. 1, no. 1, Jan. 1996.

[5]  J.C. Palma, C.A. Marcon, F. Moraes, N.L. Calazans, R.A. Reis, A.A. Susin. "Mapping Embedded Systems onto NoCs - The Traffic Effect on Dynamic Energy Estimation". In: 18th Symposium on Integrated Circuits and Systems Design - SBCCI 2005. New York: ACM Press, 2005. pp. 196-201.

[6]  F. Moraes, N. Calazans, A. Mello, L. Möller and L. Ost. "HERMES: an infrastructure for low area overhead packet-switching networks on chip". The VLSI Journal Integration (VJI), vol. 38, issue 1, pp. 69-93, October 2004.

[7]  L. Benini, A. Macii, E. Macii, M. Poncino, R. Scarsi. "Architecture and Synthesis Algo-rithms for Power-Efficient Bus Interfaces". Computer-Aided Design of Integrated Circuits and Systems, IEEE Transactions on Volume 19, Issue 9, Sept. 2000 Page(s):969-980.

[8]  M. R. Stan, W. P. Burleson. "Bus-Invert Coding for Low-Power I/O". VLSI Systems, IEEE Transactions on Volume 3, Issue 1, March 1995 Page(s):49-58.

[9]  L. Ost, A. Mello; J. Palma, F. Moraes, N. Calazans. "MAIA - A Framework for Networks on Chip Generation and Verification". ASP-DAC, Jan. 2005.

[10]  Brooks, E.A. Lee, X. Liu, S. Neuendorffer, Y. Zhao, H. Zheng. "Heterogeneous Concur-rent Modeling and Design in Java (Volume 1: Introduction to Ptolemy II,") Technical Memorandum UCB/ERL M05/21, University of California, Berkeley, CA USA 94720, July 15, 2005.

[11]  Sylvester, D.; Chenming Wu; "Analytical modeling and characterization of deep-submicrometer interconnect". Proceedings of the IEEE. Volume 89, Issue 5, May 2001 Page(s):634 – 664.

# A Novel Methodology to Reduce Leakage Power in CMOS Complementary Circuits

Preetham Lakshmikanthan and Adrian Nuñez

VLSI Systems Design and CAD (VSDCAD) Laboratory,
EECS Department, Syracuse University,
Syracuse, New York - 13244, U.S.A.
{plakshmi, anunezal}@syr.edu

**Abstract.** Leakage power loss is a major concern in deep-submicron technologies as it drains the battery even when a circuit is completely idle. The subthreshold leakage current increases exponentially in deep-submicron processes and hence is a crucial factor in scaling down designs. Efficient leakage control mechanisms are necessary to maximize battery life. In this paper, a novel technique that achieves cancellation of leakage effects in both the pull-up network (PUN) as well as the pull-down network (PDN) for any CMOS complementary circuit is presented. It involves voltage balancing in the PUN and PDN paths using sleep transistors. Experimental results show significant leakage power savings (average of 54X at a temperature of 27°C) in CMOS circuits employing this sleep circuitry when compared to standard CMOS circuits. At any given temperature, using our methodology the leakage power loss increases linearly with increasing circuit complexity and hence the leakage loss can be predicted for any CMOS complementary circuit.

## 1 Introduction

Battery-powered electronic systems form the backbone of the growing market of mobile hand-held devices used all over the world today. With miniaturization, power dissipation has become a very critical design metric. Minimizing power is presently an extremely challenging area of research. For deep-submicron processes, supply voltages and threshold voltages for MOS transistors are greatly reduced. This to an extent reduces the dynamic (switching) power dissipation. However, the subthreshold leakage current increases exponentially thereby increasing static power dissipation. Leakage current is the current that flows through a transistor when no transactions occur and the transistor is in a steady state. Leakage power depends on gate length and oxide thickness. It varies exponentially with threshold voltage and other parameters. Equation 1 approximates the subthreshold leakage current [1] of a MOSFET.

$$I_{sub} = A.e^{\theta}.\left[1 - e^{\left(\frac{-qV_{DS}}{kT}\right)}\right]$$

(1)

J. Vounckx, N. Azemard, and P. Maurine (Eds.): PATMOS 2006, LNCS 4148, pp. 614–623, 2006.

where,

$$A = \mu_0 C_{ox} \frac{W}{L} \left( \frac{kT}{q} \right)^2 e^{1.8}$$

and,

$$\theta = \left[ \frac{q}{n'kT} \left( V_{GS} - V_{th_0 - \gamma' V_s + \eta V_{DS}} \right) \right]$$

$\mu_0$ is the carrier mobility, $C_{ox}$ is the gate oxide capacitance, W and L denote the transistor width and length, $\frac{kT}{q}$ is the thermal voltage at temperature T, $n'$ is the subthreshold swing coefficient, $V_{GS}$ is the gate to source voltage of the transistor, $V_{th_0}$ is the zero-bias threshold voltage, $\gamma' V_s$ is the body effect where $\gamma'$ is the linearized body effect coefficient and $\eta$ is the drain induced barrier lowering (DIBL) coefficient. $V_{DS}$ is the drain to source voltage of the transistor.

$$P_{leak} = \sum_i I_{sub_i} . V_{DS_i} \tag{2}$$

Equation 2 gives the total leakage power for all the transistors.

Design styles [2] play a key role in determining the power dissipation, performance and supply/threshold scalability of a circuit. Dynamic circuits achieve high levels of performance (speed) and utilize lesser area. However, they require two operation phases - pre-charge and evaluate, cannot be scaled easily due to their low noise immunity and require keeper circuits to restore logic levels. On the other hand fully complementary (CMOS) styles are usually robust, dissipate low power, have fully restored logic levels and are easily scalable. In general, they require more area (2X transistors when compared to X+2 in the case of dynamic circuits). Also, for large fan-in gates they have lower performance.

Cell phones and pocket PCs have burst-mode type integrated circuits which for the majority of time are in an idle state. For such circuits it is acceptable to have leakage during the active mode. However, during the idle state it is extremely wasteful to have leakage as power is unnecessarily consumed for no useful work being done. Given the present advances in power management techniques [1],[3],[4],[5] leakage loss is a major concern in deep-submicron technologies as it drains the battery even when a circuit is completely idle. By the year 2020, leakage is expected to increase 32 times per device [6] and is a major challenge in scaling down designs. This motivates the need for efficient leakage control mechanisms to minimize power overheads in deep-submicron circuits.

The focus of this paper is to present a novel implementation strategy to reduce leakage power in CMOS complementary circuits. Figure 1 on the next page shows subthreshold leakage power trends [7] in accordance with Moore's law. Clearly with deep-submicron processes, chips will leak excessive amounts of power. Our methodology significantly reduces leakage power, with savings of 54X (on an average) for circuits designed with 180 $nm$ technology.

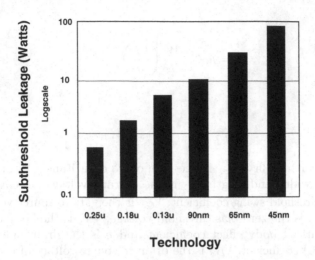

**Fig. 1.** Projected Subthreshold Leakage Power [7]

The organization of the paper is as follows. Section 2 outlines some related research work in the area of leakage power minimization. The architecture and working of the sleep-circuitry embedded CMOS cells, which is the core of this research, is explained in Section 3. Section 4 provides experimental results of leakage power reduction for standard CMOS complementary circuits showing the effectiveness of our approach. A comparison of our sleep-circuitry embedded approach with the traditional power-gating methodology is also done here. Finally, the conclusions drawn from this work and the scope for future research is detailed in Section 5.

## 2   Review of Prior Research

A lot of interesting research work has been done in trying to minimize leakage power. Listed below are some publications related to our work :

Kao et al [8] used Multi-Threshold CMOS (MTCMOS) for power gating. Here, low threshold (low-$V_T$) transistors that are fast and leaky are used to implement speed-critical logic. High threshold (high-$V_T$) devices that are slower, but, having low subthreshold leakage are used as sleep transistors. Multi-threshold voltage circuits have degraded noise immunity when compared to standard low threshold voltage circuits. The sleep transistor has to be sized properly to decrease its voltage drop when it is on. A method to size sleep transistors based on a mutual exclusion discharge pattern principle is described. However, using this principle at the gate level is not practical for large circuits.

Ye et al [9] show that "stacking" of two *off* devices significantly reduces subthreshold leakage compared to a single *off* device. These stacks are series-connected devices between supply and ground. (Eg : PMOS stack in NOR or

NMOS stack in NAND gates). Their technique enables leakage reduction during standby mode by input vector activation. It involves extensive circuit simulations in order to install a vector at the input of the circuit, so as to maximize the number of PMOS or NMOS stacks with more than one *off* device.

Narendra et al [10] present a full-chip subthreshold leakage current prediction model. They also use a stack-forcing method to reduce subthreshold leakage. This is achieved by forcing a non-stack transistor of width '$W$' to a series-stack of two transistors, each of width '$\frac{W}{2}$'. This effective method does not affect the input load and the switching power. However, there is a delay penalty to be incurred as a result of this stack-forcing. Hence this technique can only be used on devices in paths that are non-critical.

Kursun et al evaluate the subthreshold leakage current characteristics of domino logic circuits in [11]. They show that a discharged dynamic node is preferred for reducing leakage current in a dual-$V_T$ circuit. Alternatively, a charged dynamic node is better suited for lower leakage in a low-$V_T$ circuit. The keeper and output inverter need to be sized in a dual-$V_T$ domino circuit with a high-$V_T$ keeper in order to provide similar noise immunity as that of a low-$V_T$ domino logic circuit. [12] employs these techniques coupled with sleep transistor switches for placing idle domino circuits in a low leakage state. A high-$V_T$ NMOS sleep transistor is is connected in parallel with the dynamic node of domino logic circuits. In the standby mode of operation, the pull-up transistor of the domino circuit is off, while the NMOS sleep transistor is turned on. The dynamic node of the domino gate is discharged through the sleep transistor, thereby significantly reducing the subthreshold leakage current.

## 3    Sleep Circuitry Embedded CMOS Complementary Circuits

The sleep transistor concept used for dynamic circuits in [12] was adapted and modified to work for leakage reduction in static CMOS complementary circuits. A combination of high-$V_T$ and standard-$V_T$ sleep transistors are used in our implementation, to provide a well balanced trade-off between high speed and leakage loss. Our technique facilitates in the creation of an ultra-low power standard cell library built with sleep circuitry embedded components.

Figure 2 on the next page is the topology of a generic CMOS complementary circuit with sleep transistors embedded in it. We refer to such circuits as VSDCAD sleep-embedded CMOS circuits for the remainder of this work. There are 'n' inputs $in_1, \ldots in_n$ feeding the *Pull-Up Network* (PUN) as well as the *Pull-Down Network* (PDN). The sleep circuitry consists of three transistors - two PMOS devices $\{P_0$ and $P_1\}$, and one NMOS device $\{N_0\}$. Transistors $P_0$ and $N_0$ are standard-$V_T$ devices, while $P_1$ is a high-$V_T$ device.

$P_0$ is connected in parallel with the PUN, one end connecting to the source $(V_{dd})$ and the other end to a common point $X_1$. $N_0$ is connected in parallel with the PDN, one end connecting to the *gnd* and the other end to a common point

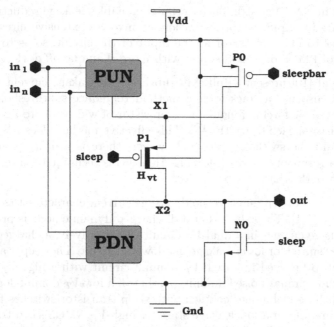

**Fig. 2.** Block Diagram - Generic CMOS Complementary Circuit

$X_2$. The high-$V_T$ transistor, $P_1$, connects between the two common points $X_1$ and $X_2$ and behaves like a transmission gate. Two input signals 'sleep' and its complement 'sleepbar' feed transistors $\{P_1, N_0\}$ and $P_0$ respectively. The output of the CMOS circuit, 'out', is drawn from the common point $X_2$.

The working of the VSDCAD sleep-embedded CMOS circuit is now explained. In the normal operating mode, 'sleep' is off and 'sleepbar' is on. This causes transistors $\{P_0, N_0\}$ to turn off and transistor $P_1$ to turn on. The circuit now behaves exactly as a normal CMOS complementary circuit should. The sleep operating mode is a little more involved. In this mode, 'sleep' is on and 'sleepbar' is off. Hence transistors $\{P_0, N_0\}$ turn on and transistor $P_1$ turns off. Since $P_0$ is on, common point $X_1$ is also at voltage $V_{dd}$. The PUN is now between two points at equal voltage potential ($V_{dd}$) and hence no leakage current should flow through the PUN. Similarly, $N_0$ is on and common point $X_2$ is grounded. The PDN is now between two points at equal voltage potential ($gnd$) and hence no leakage current should flow through the PDN. Since 'out' is connected to $X_2$, during the sleep mode the output value will always be '0'. The leakage loss occurring during the sleep mode will be only through transistor $P_1$ which is turned off, but, connected between points $X_1$ and $X_2$ that are at different voltage potentials.

## 4    Experimental Results

Experiments using the VSDCAD sleep-embedded methodology were conducted on a variety of CMOS complementary circuits. They include simple NOR2,

NAND2, AND2, XOR2, XNOR2, NOR3 and NAND3 gates and more complex MUX2X1, HALF-ADDER, FULL-ADDER, 8-BIT ADDER and 4-BIT ARRAY MULTIPLIER circuits. These circuits were implemented using TSMC's 180 $nm$ technology [13] with a supply voltage ($V_{dd}$) of 1.8V. The transistors in all the circuits were unit sized.

**Table 1.** Leakage Power Measurements @ Temp. = $27°C$ (Avg. Power Savings = 54X)

| CMOS Complementary Experimental Circuit Name | Standard Mode Leakage Power Loss (Average) | Sleep Embedded Mode Leakage Power Loss | Power Savings (C3/C4) |
|---|---|---|---|
| NOR2 | 44.90 $pW$ | 0.89 $pW$ | 50X |
| NAND2 | 43.73 $pW$ | 0.89 $pW$ | 49X |
| OR2 | 100.36 $pW$ | 1.78 $pW$ | 56X |
| AND2 | 81.51 $pW$ | 1.78 $pW$ | 46X |
| XOR2 | 174.99 $pW$ | 2.67 $pW$ | 66X |
| XNOR2 | 174.94 $pW$ | 2.67 $pW$ | 66X |
| NOR3 | 33.12 $pW$ | 0.89 $pW$ | 37X |
| NAND3 | 33.04 $pW$ | 0.89 $pW$ | 37X |
| MUX2X1 | 214.35 $pW$ | 3.56 $pW$ | 60X |
| HALF ADDER | 256.51 $pW$ | 4.45 $pW$ | 58X |
| FULL ADDER | 843.25 $pW$ | 14.24 $pW$ | 59X |
| 8-BIT ADDER | 6.73 $nW$ | 0.1139 $nW$ | 59X |
| 4-BIT ARRAY MULTIPLIER | 8.77 $nW$ | 0.1602 $nW$ | 55X |

First, standard CMOS circuits were simulated and leakage power measured using SPECTRE[1] at a temperature of 27°C. For every circuit (excluding the 8-BIT ADDER and 4-BIT ARRAY MULTIPLIER), all possible input combinations were applied and leakage power loss measured in every case. Column 3 (C3) from Table 1 lists the average leakage power loss for all standard CMOS circuits tested. Next, the VSDCAD sleep circuitry was introduced and all circuits simulated again, but, in the sleep mode of operation. Column 4 (C4) from Table 1 lists the leakage power loss for all 13 circuits in the sleep (standby) mode of operation. Column 5 from Table 1 gives the leakage power savings of the sleep mode when compared to the standard mode of operation. It can be observed that savings vary from 37X to 66X for the various experimental circuits listed. These are significant power savings given the massive leakage power values predicted in circuits designed using deep-submicron processes (as shown in Figure 1).

Certain trends can be observed from the results. First, the sleep mode leakage power loss of the VSDCAD sleep-embedded circuit was 54X (the average of

---

[1] TM - Cadence Design Systems, Inc.

Column 5, Table 1) lesser than the leakage loss of the standard CMOS circuit. These power savings can be achieved by turning the sleep circuitry on or off appropriately. Secondly, in the sleep mode the leakage power loss through every cascade stage is constant. It is basically the leakage loss through the high-$V_T$ PMOS transistor acting like a transmission gate (Eg: P1 from Figure 2) and this value is 0.89 $pW$. Hence from Column 4 of Table 1 on the previous page, it can be observed that for circuits with one cascade stage (NOR2, NAND2, NOR3, NAND3) the leakage power loss is 0.89 $pW$. For circuits with two cascade stages (OR2, AND2), the leakage power loss is 1.78 $pW$. Similarly, XOR2/XNOR2 gates have three stages (the actual XOR2/XNOR2 CMOS circuit and two inverters for complementing the inputs) and hence its leakage power loss is 2.67 $pW$. This shows that at any given temperature, using our methodology the leakage power loss increases linearly with increasing circuit complexity and can be predicted for any CMOS complementary circuit.

**Table 2.** Leakage Comparison - VSDCAD (vs) Power-Gated Circuits

| CMOS Circuit Name | Power-Gated Circuit Leakage (pW) | VSDCAD Sleep-Embedded Circuit Leakage (pW) | Improvement (C2/C3) |
|---|---|---|---|
| NOR2 | 2.23 | 0.89 | 2.5X |
| NAND2 | 4.18 | 0.89 | 4.7X |
| OR2 | 6.67 | 1.78 | 3.7X |
| AND2 | 7.88 | 1.78 | 4.4X |
| XOR2 | 12.10 | 2.67 | 4.5X |
| XNOR2 | 14.31 | 2.67 | 5.4X |
| MUX2x1 | 17.61 | 3.56 | 4.9X |
| FULL ADDER | 74.08 | 14.24 | 5.2X |
|  |  | Average | 4.4X |

Since power-gating is the most commonly used technique for reducing leakage power, we compare it with the VSDCAD sleep-embedded methodology. In our power-gated CMOS circuit implementation, a high-$V_T$ PMOS transistor connects between the power source ($V_{dd}$) and the PUN acting as a switch. A 'sleep' signal controls this high-$V_T$ PMOS transistor. In the standby mode of operation, 'sleep' is on, thus cutting off power from the CMOS circuit. 8 experimental power-gated CMOS circuits - NOR2, NAND2, OR2, AND2, XOR2, XNOR2, MUX2x1 and FULL ADDER were implemented for comparison against similar VSDCAD sleep-embedded circuits. TSMC's 180 $nm$ technology with a supply voltage ($V_{dd}$) of 1.8V was used. All transistors (including the high-$V_T$ power-gate device) were unit sized. SPECTRE was used to simulate the power-gated circuits in the standby mode ('sleep' is on) at a temperature of 27°C and their leakage power measured. Column 2 (C2) of Table 2 gives the leakage power loss for each of the power-gated cells. Column 3 (C3) of Table 2 lists the leakage power loss for each of the VSDCAD sleep-embedded cells in the standby mode of operation (calculated previously and tabulated in Column 4 of Table 1). The leakage loss of the power-gated cells (C2) when compared to that of the VSD-CAD sleep-embedded cells (C3) is expressed as a ratio in Column 4 of Table 2 on the previous page. The leakage improvement using the VSDCAD sleep-embedded methodology across all the experimental circuits is 4.4X (on an average). This significant improvement over the traditional power-gating technique shows the effectiveness of the VSDCAD sleep-embedded methodology.

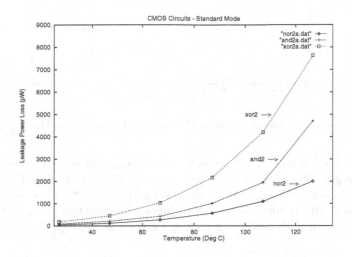

**Fig. 3.** Temperature Effects On Leakage Power - Standard Mode

Prior research [1], [14] shows a much larger leakage power loss occurring at higher temperatures. This is due to the fact that subthreshold leakage current is exponentially dependent on the temperature, as seen from Equation 1 in Section 1. Experiments to study the temperature effects on leakage current were conducted on three CMOS circuits - NOR2, AND2 and XOR2 gates. Circuit simulations were performed using SPECTRE at six different temperature values : 27°C, 47°C, 67°C, 87°C, 107°C and 127°C respectively. All three circuits were first simulated in the standard mode of operation. Figure 3 is a graph showing the leakage power loss for the NOR2, AND2 and XOR2 gates at various temperature values. The XOR2 gate being a larger circuit than the other two, exhibits the largest leakage power loss at all temperatures.

Next, the VSDCAD sleep circuitry was introduced and these circuits were again simulated in the standby mode of operation. Figure 4 on the next page shows the graph of the leakage power loss at various temperatures for all three circuits in the sleep mode. Even at higher temperatures, significant leakage power savings are seen using our methodology when compared to the standard mode of operation.

A preliminary study was done to see the area and delay penalty occuring due to the extra sleep transistors added in the standard circuitry. We noted an area

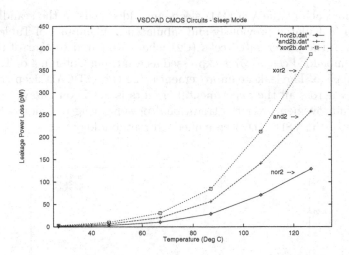

**Fig. 4.** Temperature Effects On Leakage Power - Sleep Mode

increase of 1.5X (on an average) as well as a propagation delay increase of 1.5X (on an average). This nominal delay overhead is offset by the significant power savings seen. Designers/Synthesis tools could add the VSDCAD sleep-embedded combinational cells in *non-critical paths*, thereby not affecting the overall circuit delay, while significantly saving on leakage power loss.

## 5   Conclusions

A novel technique employing a combination of high-$V_T$ and standard-$V_T$ sleep transistors to cancel leakage effects in both the PUN and PDN paths of CMOS complementary circuits is presented. It effectively reduces standby leakage power. With our methodology, at any given temperature the leakage power loss increases linearly with increasing circuit complexity. Hence the leakage loss can be predicted for any CMOS complementary circuit. At a temperature 27°C, experimental results on circuits designed using TSMC's 180 $nm$ technology show an average of 54X leakage power savings in CMOS complementary circuits employing this VSDCAD sleep circuitry when compared to standard CMOS circuits. In deep-submicron processes, these power savings are significant given that leakage power loss drains the battery even when the circuit is idle.

Some directions for future research would include building and characterizing an ultra-low power standard cell library (combinational + sequential cells) containing these VSDCAD sleep-embedded components. The temperature effects on leakage current need to be further studied. Preliminary efforts as a consequence of this research show large leakage savings at higher temperatures. The effect of leakage power loss associated with 90 $nm$ and smaller deep-submicron process technologies needs to be studied in depth. New techniques to address those issues should be incorporated in future methodologies.

# References

1. K. Roy and S. Prasad. *Low-Power CMOS VLSI Circuit Design.* Wiley-Interscience, New York, USA, 2000.
2. J. Rabaey, A. Chandrakasan, and B. Nikolic. *Digital Integrated Circuits - A Design Perspective.* Prentice Hall Publishers, New Jersey, USA, second edition, 2002.
3. M. Pedram and J. Rabaey. *Power Aware Design Methodologies.* Kluwer Academic Publishers, Massachusetts, USA, 2002.
4. L. Benini, G. D. Micheli, and E. Macii. Designing low-power circuits: Practical recipes. *IEEE Circuits and Systems Magazine,* 1(1):6–25, January 2001.
5. F. Fallah and M. Pedram. Standby and active leakage current control and minimization in cmos vlsi circuits. *IEICE Transactions on Electronics, Special Section on Low-Power LSI and Low-Power IP,* E88-C(4):509–519, April 2005.
6. International technology roadmap for semiconductors (itrs-05). http://www.itrs.net/Common/2005ITRS/Design2005.pdf.
7. Shekar Borkar. Gigascale integration. http://www.intel.com/cd/ids/developer/asmo-na/eng/strategy/182440.htm?page=2.
8. J. Kao and A. Chandrakasan. Dual-threshold voltage techniques for low-power digital circuits. *IEEE Journal of Solid-State Circuits,* 35(7):1009–1018, July 2000.
9. Y. Ye, S. Borkar, and V. De. A new technique for standby leakage reduction in high-performance circuits. In *IEEE Symposium on VLSI Circuits Digest of Technical Papers,* pages 40–41, June 1998.
10. S. Narendra, V. De, S. Borkar, D. Antoniadis, and A. Chandrakasan. Full-chip subthreshold leakage power prediction and reduction techniques for sub-0.18-$\mu$m cmos. *IEEE Journal of Solid-State Circuits,* 39(2):501–510, February 2004.
11. V. Kursun and E. Friedman. Node voltage dependent subthreshold leakage current characteristics of dynamic circuits. In *Proceedings of the 5th International Symposium on Quality Electronic Design,* pages 104–109, March 2004.
12. V. Kursun and E. Friedman. Energy efficient dual threshold voltage dynamic circuits employing sleep switches to minimize subthreshold leakage. In *Proceedings of the IEEE International Symposium on Circuits and Systems,* volume 2, pages 417–420, May 2004.
13. Tsmc processes through mosis. http://www.mosis.org/products/fab/vendors/tsmc.
14. L. He, W. Liao, and M. Stan. System level leakage reduction considering the interdependence of temperature and leakage. In *Proceedings of the 41st Design Automation Conference,* pages 12–17, June 2004.

# Techniques to Enhance the Resistance of Precharged Busses to Differential Power Analysis

M. Alioto, M. Poli, S. Rocchi, and V. Vignoli

DII, Università di Siena, v. Roma, 56
I-53100 SIENA – Italy
Phone: ++39-0577-234632; Fax: ++39-0577-233602
{malioto, poli, rocchi, vignoli}@dii.unisi.it

**Abstract.** In this communication, different techniques to improve the resistance to Differential Power Analysis (DPA) attacks of precharged busses are discussed. These statistical attacks rely on the observation of the power consumption, and are very effective in recovering confidential information that are stored or processed in SmartCards running cryptographic algorithms. Accordingly, a few techniques to improve the information security by reducing the effectiveness of DPA attacks are discussed. These techniques are statistically analyzed and compared in terms of DPA resistance, power and area overhead. Finally, these techniques are mixed to improve the robustness to DPA attacks. Cycle-accurate simulations on DES encryption algorithm running on a MIPS32® architecture are used to validate the discussed techniques.

## 1 Introduction

Nowadays, the massive usage of electronics devices storing and communicating confidential data (e.g. SmartCards, PDAs and SmartPhones) has increased the interest of designers in information security [1], [2]. Although several countermeasures have been developed to protect stored information, most devices are vulnerable to implementation (or side-channel) attacks based on the information leakage due to the physical interaction with the external environment [3]-[4].

In the last decade many type of implementation attacks were developed. Among them, the analysis of the power consumption have been shown to be a major threat to the security of confidential data [5], [6]. In particular, the Differential Power Analysis (DPA) is a non-invasive powerful attack since it is independent of the algorithm implementation and does not require complex or expensive equipment [5]. The DPA attacks exploit the correlation of the power consumption with the processed data, and are based on statistical techniques to recover the latter from the observation of the former. Accordingly, in the last years several countermeasures to DPA attacks were proposed that aim at reducing the dependence of the power consumption on the processed data (including the confidential ones).

In any IC, the most critical blocks in terms of DPA resistance are those presenting a power consumption which is large and strongly dependent on the input data. For this

J. Vounckx, N. Azemard, and P. Maurine (Eds.): PATMOS 2006, LNCS 4148, pp. 624–633, 2006.
© Springer-Verlag Berlin Heidelberg 2006

reason, busses are regarded as the most dangerous source of information leakage [3]-[6], and thus should be properly protected. To this aim, in this communication precharged busses are first modeled in terms of power consumption statistics. Then, two strategies to improve the resistance to DPA attacks are introduced and analyzed, and the trade-off with power and area is discussed. Then, the two strategies are mixed to further improve the immunity to DPA attacks. Finally, the theoretical results are validated carrying out DPA attacks on an implementation of the DES cryptographic algorithm running on an MIPS32® architecture simulator.

## 2   Differential Power Analysis Attacks: A Brief Review

The DPA attacks aim at recovering the value of a portion of a secret key $k$ used in a cryptographic algorithm, by measuring the information leakage due to the power consumption variations caused by the data manipulation. A DPA attack is based on the collection of $N$ power consumption sampled traces $PC_i$ (with $i=1...N$), each of which consists of $M$ samples $PC_i(j)$ (with $j=1...M$) measured from the chip performing the encryption (decryption) algorithm on a well known input sequence $I_i$.

Let us assume that the cryptographic algorithm under attack evaluates an intermediate bit $D$ which depends only on known data (such as the input $I_i$ and a portion of the secret key $k$) through a proper partition function $f$

$$D = f(I_i, k) \tag{1}$$

where function $f$ can be derived from the algorithm since by observing that $D$ is physically computed by the circuit at some time value $j^*$ (for example, it could be an intermediate output of the algorithm, which is evaluated by some digital block). More details on the choice of function f in precharged busses will be given in Section 2.2.

In practical circuits, the power consumption $PC_i$ also depends on the processed data $D$, i.e. the power consumption is affected by the value of $D$ at $j=j^*$, whereas it is not at $j \neq j^*$. Thus, a proper analysis of $PC_i$ allows for identifying $D$, which in turn from (1) reveals the value of the secret information $k$, as discussed in the following.

### 2.1   DPA Attacks Under Simplified Assumptions

In a DPA attack, the power traces are first classified into two sets according to the value of $D$ at $j=j^*$, which for now is assumed to be known. Then, the average power consumption $A_0$ ($A_1$) is evaluated in the set with $D=0$ ($D=1$) among all traces $PC_i$, whose expression is given in eq. (2) (eq. (3))

$$A_0(j) = \frac{\sum_{i=1}^{N/2} PC_i(j)\big|_{D=0}}{N/2} \tag{2}$$

$$A_1(j) = \frac{\sum_{i=1}^{N/2} PC_i(j)\big|_{D=1}}{N/2} \tag{3}$$

where inputs were assumed sufficiently random to make the number of traces with $D=0$ and $D=1$ equal. When an infinite number of traces $N$ is assumed, $A_0$ in (2) ($A_1$ in (3)) is equal to the power consumption mean value $E[PC_i(j)|D=0]$ $(E[PC_i(j)|D=1])$ under condition $D=0$ $(D=1)$. Due to the power consumption dependence on $D$ at $j=j^*$, $A_0$ is different from $A_1$ only for $j=j^*$, thus their difference $\Delta$ for $N\to\infty$ results to

$$\Delta_{N\to\infty}(j) = \lim_{N\to\infty}\Delta(j) = \lim_{N\to\infty}[A_0(j) - A_1(j)] =$$

$$= E[PC_i(j)|D=0] - E[PC_i(j)|D=1] = \begin{cases} \varepsilon & \text{if } j = j^* \\ 0 & \text{if } j \neq j^* \end{cases} \quad (4)$$

which is usually referred to as the *differential power*. The result in (4) relies on the assumption that the power traces are correctly grouped into two sets, assuming that $D$ is known. In this case, from (4) it is apparent that a spike $\varepsilon$ appears in the differential power trace $\Delta$.

Actually, the correct value of $D$ is not known because $k$ is secret, thus the latter must be necessarily guessed. When the guess of $k$ (and thus of $D$) is incorrect, (4) no longer holds. This can be explained by observing that the power consumption is determined by the actual $D$, $D_{actual}$, and not by the guessed $D$, $D_{guess}$ (since it is not physically evaluated by the circuit). To be more specific, assuming $D_{actual}$ to be statistically independent of $D_{guess}$, the power consumption is also independent of $D_{guess}$, thus $E[PC_i(j)|D_{guess}=0]=E[PC_i(j)|D_{guess}=1]=E[PC_i(j)]$ for every value of $j$. As a consequence, the differential power $\Delta$ is equal to zero for every value of $j$. Accordingly, an adversary can recognize the correct guess of $k$ from the occurrence of peaks in the differential power trace $\Delta$, whereas the wrong keys lead to a flat differential power trace. For this reason, in DPA attacks the secret portion of the key $k$ is found by exhaustively guessing its values (this is computationally feasible only for a portion of the key at a time) and selecting that leading to peaks into the differential power trace.

## 2.2  Practical DPA Attacks to Precharged Busses

The analysis in the previous subsection is based on two hypotheses which are not satisfied in practical cases. First, a finite number $N$ of power traces is actually collected, thus from the Central Limit theorem $\Delta - \Delta_{N\to\infty}$ at a given $j$ is a random variable with zero mean and a standard deviation which is proportional to $1/\sqrt{N}$ [7]. Accordingly, $\Delta$ can be thought of as the sum of the signal $\Delta_{N\to\infty}$ in (4) and an additive noise signal $\Delta - \Delta_{N\to\infty}$ which tends to mask the spike $\varepsilon$. Thus, $N$ must be sufficiently high to reduce the noise standard deviation below $\varepsilon$, in order to detect the spike. This is possible when a sufficiently high signal-to-noise ratio is achieved, which is usually referred to as the Intra-Signal Signal-to-Noise Ratio $SNR_{INTRA}$ [3].

Furthermore, the second hypothesis that the actual and guessed $D$ are statistically independent, and thus that spikes do not appear in wrong guess, is not completely correct. Intuition suggests that under a wrong guess the spike amplitude is lower than that for the correct guess [5]. Therefore, the correct value of $k$ is recovered by identifying the maximum spike among all the possible key guesses. This is possible only if the spike $\varepsilon_{correct}$ under the correct $k$ is significantly greater than the maximum spike $\varepsilon_{wrong}$ under wrong guesses, i.e. if the Inter-Signal signal-to-noise ratio $SNR_{INTER}=\varepsilon_{correct}/\varepsilon_{wrong}$ is sufficiently greater than unity.

Finally, in DPA attacks to $n$ bits of a precharged bus, the partition function $f$ in (1) is a function of all the bus lines values (and not of a single bit) as in (5) [3], [6]

$$D = \begin{cases} 0 & \text{if } 0 \le w \le n/2 - 1 \\ 1 & \text{if } n/2 + 1 \le w \le n \end{cases} \tag{5}$$

which partitions the bus power traces according to the weight $w$ (i.e. the number of lines set to 1) of the corresponding data transferred on the bus. This choice is easily justified by observing that the power dissipated by the $n$ precharged bus lines is proportional to the number of transferred zeroes [8], thus it is proportional to $(n-w)$. Accordingly, the partition function in (1) classifies the power traces leading to a "high" power consumption (i.e. with a large number of zeroes) to the set with $D=0$, and to a "low" power consumption (i.e. with a small number of zeroes) to the set with $D=1$.

## 3  DPA Resistance and Statistical Analysis of Precharged Busses

The immunity of a generic circuit to DPA attacks can be improved by reducing its power consumption dependence on the processed data [5]. For example, in the limit case of a constant (i.e. data-independent) power consumption, no peak could be observed in the differential power trace. In general, a lower data dependency of the bus power consumption can be achieved by reducing its variations, which from a statistical point of view means that the power consumption variance should be kept as small as possible. Accordingly, in the next subsections the power consumption of precharged busses is first statistically modeled, and two techniques aiming at reducing the power consumption variance are then discussed.

### 3.1  Precharged Busses: A Statistical Analysis

In a generic $n$-bit precharged bus, each bus line is first precharged to the logic state 1 and then set to the value to be transferred, thus a transition occurs only if the transferred data is equal to zero [8]. Without loss of generality, in the following it is assumed that each bus line transition gives a unity energy contribution to the overall power consumption, making the latter proportional to the number $\overline{w}$ of bus lines transferring a zero. In general, the precharged bus power consumption mean value $\mu_{PC}$ and variance $\sigma_{PC}^2$ depend on the transferred data statistics, and under the usual assumption of uniformly distributed and statistically independent data, result to [9]

$$\mu_{PC} = E[\overline{w}] = \sum_{i=0}^{n} i \cdot \Pr(\overline{w} = i) = 2^{-n} \cdot \sum_{i=0}^{n} i \binom{n}{i} = \frac{n}{2} \tag{6}$$

$$\sigma_{PC}^2 = E[(\overline{w} - \mu_{PC})^2] = \sum_{i=0}^{n} i^2 \cdot \Pr(\overline{w} = i) - \mu_{PC}^2 = \frac{n}{4} . \tag{7}$$

where it was considered that the probability of having a number of zeroes equal to $i$ is

$\Pr(\overline{w} = i) = 2^{-n} \binom{n}{i}$ [9].

## 3.2  Bus-Invert Coding Approach to Reduce the Power Consumption Variance

The Bus-Invert coding approach is a well-known low-power technique that is used to reduce the bus activity [10]. In this technique, the data value is transferred on the bus if $\overline{w} \leq n/2$, whereas its bit-wise complement is transferred if $\overline{w} > n/2$. To correctly decode the bus value, an extra invert line $inv$ is added to the bus and is set to 0 if $\overline{w} > n/2$ and to 1 otherwise. This limits the maximum value of $\overline{w}$ to $n/2$, thereby reducing the average power consumption [9]-[11]. Interestingly, this technique can be used to enhance the bus immunity to DPA attacks, since it also reduces the power consumption variance, as shown in the following.

To evaluate the mean value and variance of the power consumption with Bus-Invert coding, it is necessary to consider the power contribution invert line. To this aim, the probability that $inv=1$ is easily found to be given by [9]

$$\Pr(inv=1)=\Pr\left(\overline{w}\le\frac{n}{2}\right)=\sum_{i=0}^{n/2}\Pr(\overline{w}=i)=\frac{1}{2}+2^{-(n+1)}\binom{n}{n/2} \tag{8}$$

where $n$ was assumed to be even, as usual. Assuming uniformly distributed and statistically independent data, the power consumption mean value $\mu_{PC,inv}$ normalized to $\mu_{PC}$ and the variance $\sigma^2_{PC,inv}$ normalized to $\sigma^2_{PC}$ are easily found to be given by [9]

$$\frac{\mu_{PC,inv}}{\mu_{PC}}=\frac{n+1}{n}\left[1-2^{-n}\binom{n}{n/2}\right] \tag{9}$$

$$\frac{\sigma^2_{PC,inv}}{\sigma^2_{PC}}=\frac{n+1}{n}\left[1-2^{-2n}(n+1)\binom{n}{n/2}^2\right] \tag{10}$$

that are respectively plotted in Figs. 1a-1b versus $n$.

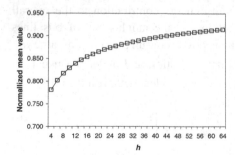
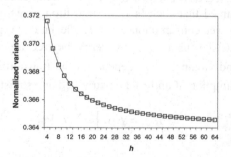

**Fig. 1a.** Bus-Invert coding: power consumption mean value vs. $n$

**Fig. 1b.** Bus-Invert coding: power consumption variance vs. $n$

From Fig. 1a, the normalized mean value of the power consumption is always lower than unity, thus the Bus-Invert coding approach always leads to a power saving in the order of 10-15% for n ranging from 16 to 64. From Fig. 1b, the normalized variance is approximately equal to 0.36 regardless of the bus width n, thus a 3X reduction in the power consumption variance is achieved by adding an invert line, which makes the bus more resistant to DPA attacks, as previously anticipated. Summarizing, the Bus-Invert coding approach is able to reduce the power consumption and its variance, at the expense of an additional line which determines a negligible area overhead.

### 3.3  Addition of Balance Lines to Reduce the Power Consumption Variance

In a $n$-bit bus, an alternative approach to reduce the power consumption variations is to add $h$ extra lines, called Balance lines, that must be properly controlled to minimize the power consumption variance. This can be done by keeping the power consumption as close as possible to the mean value in (6). To this aim, the number of zeroes $\overline{w}_h$ in the Balance lines must be chosen to minimize the difference of the overall number of zeroes $\overline{w} + \overline{w}_h$ in the bus/Balance lines and the mean value $n/2$ in (6). To this purpose, when $h<n/2$ it is apparent that $\overline{w}_h$ must be set to 0 if the number of the bus zeroes $\overline{w}$ is greater than $n/2$, to the maximum value $h$ if $\overline{w} <n/2-h$, and to the difference $n/2-\overline{w}$ in the intermediate case. Accordingly, the normalized power consumption mean value is equal to the sum of the three contributions associated with the three cases, which after some tedious analytical manipulations can be rewritten as

$$
\frac{\mu_{PC,h<n/2}}{\mu_{PC}} = \frac{E[\overline{w}+\overline{w}_h]}{n/2} = \frac{2}{n}\left[ \sum_{i=\frac{n}{2}+1}^{n} i \cdot \Pr(\overline{w}=i) + \sum_{i=\frac{n}{2}-h+1}^{\frac{n}{2}} \frac{n}{2}\Pr(\overline{w}=i) + \sum_{i=0}^{\frac{n}{2}-h}(h+i)\Pr(\overline{w}=i) \right]
$$

$$
= 2^{-n}\left[ 2^n\left(\frac{h}{n}+1\right) + \frac{h}{n}\binom{n}{n/2} - \frac{2}{n}\sum_{i=0}^{h}(h-i)\binom{n}{n/2-i} \right]
$$

(11)

whereas the normalized variance results to

$$
\frac{\sigma^2_{PC,h<n/2}}{\sigma^2_{PC}} = \frac{E\left[(\overline{w}+\overline{w}_h)^2\right] - \mu^2_{PC,h<n/2}}{n/4} = \frac{4}{n}\left[ \sum_{i=n/2+1}^{n} i^2 \Pr(\overline{w}=i) + \right.
$$

$$
\left. + \sum_{i=n/2-h+1}^{n/2}\left(\frac{n}{2}\right)^2 \Pr(\overline{w}=i) + \sum_{i=0}^{n/2-h}(h+i)^2 \Pr(\overline{w}=i) - \mu^2_{PC,h<n/2} \right] =
$$

(12)

$$
= \frac{h^2+n(n+1)}{n} + \frac{2^{-(n-2)}}{n}\sum_{i=0}^{h}(h-i)\left[i+h2^{-n}\binom{n}{n/2}\right]\binom{n}{n/2-i} +
$$

$$
- \frac{2^{-2(n-1)}}{n}\left[\sum_{i=0}^{h}(h-i)\binom{n}{n/2-i}\right]^2 - \frac{4}{n}\left[\frac{n}{2}+h2^{-(n+1)}\binom{n}{n/2}\right]^2
$$

Analogously, when $h \geq n/2$ $\overline{w}_h$ must be set to 0 if the number of the bus zeroes $\overline{w}$ is greater than $n/2$, and to the difference $n/2-\overline{w}$ otherwise. Accordingly, the normalized power consumption mean value and variance are equal to the sum of the two corresponding contributions, which after some tedious analytical manipulations result to

$$\frac{\mu_{PC,h\geq n/2}}{\mu_{PC}} = \frac{E[\overline{w}+\overline{w}_h]}{n/2} = \sum_{i=n/2+1}^{n} i\cdot\Pr(\overline{w}=i) + \sum_{i=0}^{n/2}(h+i)\Pr(\overline{w}=i) = 1 + 2^{-(n+1)}\binom{n}{n/2} \quad (13)$$

whereas the variance results to

$$\frac{\sigma_{PC,h\geq n/2}^2}{\sigma_{PC}^2} = \frac{E[(\overline{w}+\overline{w}_h)^2] - \mu_{PC,h\geq n/2}^2}{n/4} =$$

$$= \frac{4}{n}\left[\sum_{i=n/2+1}^{n} i^2 \Pr(\overline{w}=i) + \sum_{i=0}^{n/2}(h+i)^2\Pr(\overline{w}=i) - \mu_{PC,h\geq n/2}^2\right] = \frac{1}{2} - n2^{-2(n+1)}\binom{n}{n/2}^2. \quad (14)$$

To better understand the effect of Balance lines on the bus power consumption, the normalized mean value in (11) and (13) and the normalized variance in (12) and (14) are respectively plotted in Figs. 2a-2b versus $h$ for the typical case with $n=32$. From Fig. 2a, the addition of Balance lines increases the power consumption by only a few percentage points (at most 7% for high values of $h$). In regard to the variance, from Fig. 2b it is reduced by a factor of 3 for $h$ in the order of $n/4$, and a further increase in

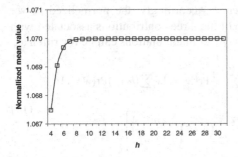

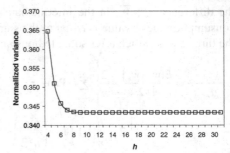

**Fig. 2a.** Balance lines technique: power consumption mean value vs. $h$ for $n=32$

**Fig. 2b.** Balance lines technique: power consumption variance vs. h for n=32

$h$ does not give a significant advantage. It is worth noting that this variance reduction is almost the same as that obtained with the Bus-Invert coding approach discussed in the previous subsection. As far as the area is concerned, for $h=n/4$ a 25% area overhead is paid.

## 4   Mixed Approach to Minimize the Power Consumption Variance

According to Section 3, the Bus-Invert coding and the Balance lines approaches are able to reduce the power consumption variance by a factor of 3 with a reasonable area and power overhead. However, by mixing the two approaches, the variance can be further reduced, or equivalently the power consumption can be kept close to its mean value $n/2$ in (6). Indeed, according to Section 3.2 the Bus-Invert coding allows for making the number of zeroes $\overline{w}$ (i.e. the power consumption) not greater than $n/2$, and the $h$ Balance lines permit to keep $\overline{w}$ closer to $n/2$.

As an interesting particular case, the variance can be even reduced to zero by adding one invert line, which makes $\overline{w} \leq n/2$, and $n/2$ Balance lines which make the resulting $\overline{w}$ always equal to $n/2$ for any transferred data. In this case, the power consumption variance is equal to zero, hence the bus is completely secure with respect to DPA attacks while keeping the mean power consumption equal to the case without any protection in (6). In other words, the mixed approach with one invert line and $n/2$ Balance lines makes the bus resistant to DPA attacks with no power overhead. This very interesting result comes at the cost of 50% greater area, due to the increase in the overall number of bus lines to the value $(3n/2+1)$.

The above limit case privileges the DPA resistance at the cost of an area increase. However, different trade-offs can be achieved by reducing the number $h$ of Balance lines, which determines a lower area cost but a greater variance (and thus a lower DPA resistance). In the typical case with $n=32$, the normalized mean value and variance for some values of $h$ are reported in Table 1, whose results are obtained by generating 10,000,000 random data and transferring them through the bus coded with the mixed approach above discussed (closed-form analysis is extremely complicated). From Table 1, for $h=n/4$ the variance is strongly reduced by 4 orders of magnitude compared to the bus without protection. In other words, a significantly better immunity to DPA attacks is achieved with a 25% area increase and no power overhead.

**Table 1.** Mixed approach: normalized mean value/variance of power consumption

| $h$ | normalized mean value | normalized variance |
|---|---|---|
| 1 | 0.932 | 0.267 |
| 4 | 0.992 | 0.035 |
| 8 | $\approx 1$ | 3.4 E-4 |
| 16 | 1 | 0 |

# 5   Evaluation of the Mixed Approach: DPA Attacks to a MIPS32

To validate the proposed techniques, DPA attacks to the 32-bit data bus of the widely adopted MIPS32 architecture running the DES algorithm were performed [12]-[13]. To this aim, a cycle accurate simulator of the MIPS microprocessor was implemented. The correct operation of the DES algorithm on the MIPS architecture was verified by extensive comparison with public test vectors [14]. To derive the differential power trace, the well-known attack to the first round S-BOX function output transferred on the data bus was carried out [5].

To evaluate the resistance to DPA attacks, the minimum number of power traces $N_{min}$ needed to detect the spike (i.e. to achieve a reasonable Intra-Signal of 10 and Inter-Signal signal-to-noise ratio of 2 [6]) was evaluated. Obviously, for $N>N_{min}$ an even better *SNR* is achieved, as discussed in Section 2.2. A random power contribution was added to model the contribution of other logic blocks whose power consumption is not affected by the bus partition function value in (5). The average value of this random power was set equal to that of the unprotected bus, i.e. assuming that half of the chip power consumption is due to the data bus. This is a conservative assumption, since the bus power consumption is usually a small fraction of the chip power consumption, thus a larger noise level (i.e. more difficult attacks) occurs in practical cases. This does not limit the generality of the results, since we are interested in the comparative evaluation of the techniques, and not on the absolute value of $N_{min}$.

The resulting value of $N_{min}$ and that normalized to the value obtained in the unprotected bus (in brackets) is reported in Table 2. In this table, $N_{min}$ is reported for the Bus-Invert technique, the Balance lines technique and the mixed approach. By inspection of Table 2, the Bus-Invert coding technique allows for increasing $N_{min}$, and thus the resistance to DPA attacks, by a factor 45, which is an interesting result. Instead, the Balance lines technique gives a lower increase in $N_{min}$ (up to 6.76), compared to the unprotected bus. As discussed in Section 3, the Balance lines technique leads to a much greater area penalty, thus the Bus-Invert coding should always be preferred in applications where a moderate security level is required.

When a very high level of security is required, the mixed approach should be adopted. Indeed, from Table 2 it allows a greater $N_{min}$ increase, even for low values of $h$ in the order of some units. Due to the very high computational effort required to evaluate the differential power trace, the number of power traces $N$ was limited to

**Table 2.** Number of power traces needed for a targeted *SNR* (without/ with additional noise)

| Unprotected bus | Bus-Invert | Balance lines | | | Mixed | | |
|---|---|---|---|---|---|---|---|
| | | $h=1$ | $h=4$ | $h=16$ | $h=1$ | $h=4$ | $h=16$ |
| 10,428 | 467,475 | 10,744 | 28,440 | 70,468 | >600,000 | >600,000 | $\infty$ |
| (1) | (45) | (1.03) | (2.73) | (6.76) | (>57.5) | (>57.5) | |

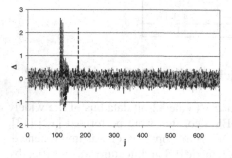

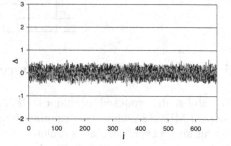

**Fig. 4a.** Differential power trace with $N=$ 30,000 for the unprotected bus

**Fig. 4b.** Differential power trace with $N=$ 30,000 for the mixed technique with $h=4$

600,000, which is much greater than the typical values adopted in practical DPA attacks, which are in the order of some thousands [5]-[6]. For these typical values of $N$, it is impossible to detect any spike if the mixed approach is adopted. For example, the differential power trace for $N=30,000$ in the unprotected bus and in the mixed technique for $h=4$ is reported in Figs. 4a and 4b, respectively. It is apparent that in the second case the power trace is essentially a random noise, whereas the bus without protection leads to a well-defined spike. An even better result is obtained for $h=16$: according to considerations in Section 4, simulations confirm that the bus never leaks any information on the key, due to the perfectly constant power consumption.

# References

1. A. Menezes, P. Van Oorschot, S. Vanstone, *Handbook of Applied Cryptography*, CRC Press, 1997.
2. W. Rankl, W. Effing, *SmartCard Handbook*, John Wiley & Sons, 1999.
3. T. S. Messerges, E. A. Dabbish, R. H. Sloan, "Examining Smart-Card Security under the Threat of Power Analysis Attacks," *IEEE Trans. on Computers*, vol. 51, no. 5, pp. 541-552, May 2002.
4. P. Kocher, "Timing attacks on implementations of Diffie-Hellman RSA, DSS, and other systems," *Proc. of CRYPTO'96*, pp. 104-113, 1996.
5. P. Kocher, J. Jaffe, B. Jun, "Differential Power Analysis," *Proc. of CRYPTO'99*, pp. 388-397, 1999.
6. T. S. Messerges, E. A. Dabbish, R. H. Sloan, "Investigations of power analysis attacks on SmartCards," *Proc. of USENIX Workshop on Smartcard Technology*, Chicago (USA), 1999.
7. A. Papoulis, *Probability, Random Variables, and Stochastic Processes*, McGraw-Hill, 1965.
8. J. Rabaey, A. Chandrakasan, B. Nikolic, Digital Integrated Circuits (A Design Perspective), Prentice Hall, 2003.
9. R. B. Lin, C. M. Tsai, "Theoretical analysis of bus-invert coding," IEEE Trans. on VLSI Systems, vol. 10, no. 6, pp. 929-935, Dec. 2002.
10. M. R. Stan, W. P. Burleson, "Bus-invert coding for low-power I/O," IEEE Trans. on VLSI Systems, vol. 3, no. 1, pp. 49-58, Mar. 1995.
11. M. R. Stan, W. P. Burleson, "Low-power encodings for global communication in CMOS VLSI," IEEE Trans. on VLSI Systems, vol. 5, no. 4, pp. 444-455, Dec. 1997.
12. MIPS Technologies Inc., http://www.mips.com.
13. Federal Information Processing Standards Publication (FIPS PUB) 46-3, *http://csrc. nist.gov/publications/fips/fips46-3/fips46-3.pdf*.
14. National Institute of Standards and Technology (NIST) Special Publication 800-17 *http://csrc.nist.gov/publications/nistpubs/800-17/800-17.pdf*.

# Formal Evaluation of the Robustness of Dual-Rail Logic Against DPA Attacks

Alin Razafindraibe, Michel Robert, and Philippe Maurine

Microelectronics Department - LIRMM
161 rue Ada, 34392 Montpellier, France
razafind@lirmm.fr

**Abstract.** Based on a first order model of the switching current flowing in CMOS cell, an investigation of the robustness against DPA of dual-rail logic is carried out. The result of this investigation, performed on 130nm process, is a formal identification of the design range in which dual-rail logic can be considered as robust.

## 1 Introduction

It is now well known that the Achilles' heel of secure ciphering algorithms, such DES and AES, lies in their physical implementation. Among all the potential techniques to obtain the secret key, side channel attacks are the most efficient. If there are a lot of different side channel attacks, DPA, introduced in [1] is nowadays considered as one of the most efficient since it requires only few skills and material to be successfully implemented.

Because of it dangerousness, many countermeasures against DPA have been proposed in former works [2, 3]. Recently, synchronous [4] or asynchronous [5, 6] dual-rail logic has been identified as a promising solution to increase the robustness of secure applications. However some experiments have shown that the use of basic dual-rail structures is not sufficient to warrant a high level of robustness against DPA. To overcome this problem, specific dual-rail cells [4, 7, 8] and ad hoc place and route methods [9] have been developed. Nevertheless, none formal evaluation of the intrinsic robustness of dual-rail logic has been proposed. This paper aims at introducing an analytical evaluation of the robustness of dual-rail logic against DPA attacks.

The remainder of this paper is organized as follows. In section II, the basics of DPA are briefly summed up and the claimed benefits of dual-rail logic are reviewed. The identification of the masked assumptions supporting these claims is also done in this section. In section III, an analytical model of the switching current waveform of CMOS cells is developed and validated on a 130nm process. This model is then used, in section IV and V, to identify the design range on which the dual-rail logic can be considered as robust against DPA. The latter is done through the development of design criteria (section V) that can be used to increase the robustness against DPA attacks of dual-rail circuits. Finally a discussion about the use of dual-rail logic against DPA attacks is proposed and a conclusion is drawn in section VI.

J. Vounckx, N. Azemard, and P. Maurine (Eds.): PATMOS 2006, LNCS 4148, pp. 634–644, 2006.
© Springer-Verlag Berlin Heidelberg 2006

## 2  DPA and the Dual-Rail Countermeasure

Differential Power Analysis attacks rely on the fact that the power consumption of basic CMOS cells, and therefore of CMOS circuits, is data dependent. With this consideration, it is possible to retrieve the secret key of a secure application by measuring the statistical correlation between the power consumption and the manipulated data according to some assumptions made on the secret key. Roughly speaking, the higher is the correlation value, the closer the guess key is from the correct secret key.

Consequently, to secure a circuit against such attacks, the first to be made is to break DPA attacks assumption in making power consumption independent of the manipulated data. With this intention, lots of solutions have been proposed [1] at all level of abstraction. It is clear that most of them aim at reducing the correlation between the data and leaking syndromes. Dual-rail logic is one of these proposed solutions.

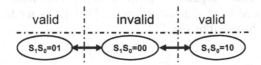

**Fig. 1.** Dual-rail encoding

First, the main advantage of dual-rail logic lies in the associated encoding used to present logic values. Fig.1 gives the return to zero encoding considered in the rest of this paper. In the dual-rail encoding, each data bit is represented by two wires. As shown on Fig.1, a rising transition on one of the two wires indicates that a bit is set to a valid logic 'one' or 'zero', while a falling transition indicates that the bit is set to an invalid value which has no logical meaning. Consequently, the transmission of a valid logic 'one' or 'zero' always requires switching a rail to $V_{DD}$. Therefore, the differential power signature of dual-rail circuits should be significantly lower than the one of single rail circuit.

However, this claim is valid if and only if both the power consumption and the propagation delay of dual-rail cells are data independent. Since usual dual-rail cells, such as DCVSL or asynchronous DIMS logic [16] do not have balanced power consumption nor data independent propagation delays, a lot of effort [4, 7, 8] have been devoted to define fully (power and delay) balanced dual-rail cells. In its seminal paper [7], K. Tiri for example has introduced the Sense Amplifier Based Logic as a logic style with constant power consumption. Afterwards, dynamic current mode logic has also been identified in [10] as an alternative to SABL while secured dual-rail CMOS schematics are given in [7] and [4].

Even if all these formerly proposed solutions appear efficient to counteract the DPA, they are all based on three crude assumptions. More precisely, in all the above mentioned works it is assumed that:

- **Assumption n°1:** all the inputs of the gate under consideration are controlled by identical drivers, i.e. that the transition times of all the input signals have the same value,
- **Assumption n°2:** the switching process of the gate under consideration starts always at the same time,
- **Assumption n°3:** the differential output nodes are loaded by capacitance of identical value ($C_1 = C_2$).

Considering that both the power consumption and the propagation delay of CMOS gates strongly depend on the transition time of the signal triggering the gate switching, and on the output capacitance switched, one can wonder about the validity domain of the three above mentioned assumptions.

## 3   Switching Current Waveform Model

In order to evaluate this validity domain, the modelling of the switching current waveform of CMOS dual-rail gate is of prime importance. Considering that any single rail gate can be reduced to an equivalent inverter [11], let us model any dual-rail cell by two inverters as illustrated by Fig.2 (a).

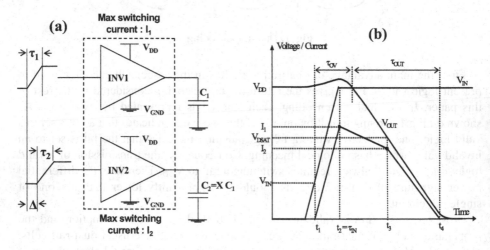

**Fig. 2.** (a) Reduced equivalent model of a dual-rail cell , (b) Typical waveforms observed during the switching of a cell

With such a reduction procedure, the modelling of the switching current waveform of dual-rail gates comes down to the one of basic cmos inverters. A great effort has been dedicated to the modelling of the inverter switching process [11, 12]. For typical loading and controlling conditions (Fast input ramps [11]), the switching current waveform of a CMOS gate can be modelled by a piece wise linear function as illustrated in Fig.2 (b). For more details, one can refer to [11, 12].

In Fig.2 (b), $I_1$, $I_2$ and $t_1$, $t_2$, $t_3$ and $t_4$ are the characteristic points to be modelled. $I_1$ and $I_2$ are respectively the maximum current values that can deliver the considered inverter ($V_{GS}=V_{DD}$) while its drain to source voltage is equal to $V_{DD}$ and $V_{DSAT}$ respectively. By taking into account the effects of the channel-length modulation [14, 15], we can deduce expressions (1) and (2) of $I_1$ and $I_2$ respectively.

$$I_1 = \frac{K}{DW} \cdot W \cdot (V_{DD} - V_T) \cdot (1 + \lambda \cdot V_{DD}) \tag{1}$$

$$I_2 = \frac{K}{DW} \cdot W \cdot (V_{DD} - V_T) \cdot (1 + \lambda \cdot V_{DSAT}) \tag{2}$$

In the above expressions, K, W, $V_{DD}$, $V_T$, $\lambda$ and DW are respectively the transistor conduction factor, the transistor width, the supply and threshold voltages, the channel length modulation factor and finally the logical weight (DW=1 for inverters). The latter takes into account the reduction of the gate to an equivalent inverter.

Considering the characteristic points $t_i$, $t_1$ and $t_2$ are defined as the time values at which the input signal reaches the voltage values $V_T$ and $V_{DD}$ respectively. These definitions lead to:

$$t_1 = \frac{V_{TN}}{V_{DD}} \cdot \tau_{IN} \tag{3}$$

$$t_2 = \tau_{IN} \tag{4}$$

The characteristic time value $t_3$ corresponds to the time value at which the output voltage crosses the $V_{DSAT}$ value while $t_4$ is the time value at which the switching process ends. Thus, time values $t_3$ and $t_4$ can be expressed by:

$$t_3 = \tau_{ov} + \frac{V_{DSAT}}{V_{DD}} \cdot \tau_{OUT} \tag{5}$$

$$t_4 = \tau_{OV} + \tau_{OUT} \tag{6}$$

where $\tau_{ov}$ is the time value at which the overshooting ends [12] and $\tau_{out}$ is the output transition time measured between 80% and 20% of $V_{DD}$ and extrapolated on the full voltage swing. For a fast input rising edge, an expression (7) can be found in [11] while the expression (8) of the $\tau_{ov}$ can easily be obtained by solving the differential equation governing the behaviour of the inverter.

$$\tau_{OUT} = \frac{DW \cdot C_L \cdot V_{DD}}{K \cdot W \cdot (V_{DD} - V_{TN})} \tag{7}$$

$$\tau_{OV} = \tau_{IN} + \frac{C_M}{I_1} \cdot V_{DD} \tag{8}$$

In the above expressions $C_L$ and $C_M$ stands respectively for the total output load capacitance and the I/O coupling capacitance. Afterwards, in order to validate the first order model of the switching current waveform of CMOS gate, we did compare for various cells, calculated current waveforms to those obtained with Eldo (a spice level tool). Fig.3 gives an illustration of the results obtained. It represents the switching current waveforms of a cmos inverter (130nm) loaded by $C_L$= 4fF for different controlling conditions ($\tau_{IN}$ ranging from 20ps to 100ps).

As shown, the calculated current waveforms are quasi-similar to those obtained with Eldo simulation tool. Afterwards, the proposed model (implemented in matlab tool) can be exploited to evaluate the contribution of any CMOS cell to the DPA attacks signatures of any dual-rail circuit.

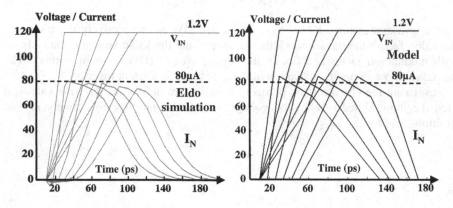

**Fig. 3.** Simulated and calculated I,V waveforms of an inverter

# 4    Switching Current Imbalance Model

The DPA signature of a dual-rail circuit or logic block is, as established in [6], the sum of all the contributions of the standard cells constituting it. The key question is then what is the contribution of a single cell to the global signature of a circuit?

Neglecting the structural correlations introduced by the schematic of the logic block under consideration, the contribution of a cell is just the difference between the current profiles obtained respectively while the gate settles a valid '1' and a valid '0' on its differential output. In order to determine in paragraph V the validity domain of the three assumptions supporting the claim that the dual-rail logic is intrinsically robust to DPA, let us model the maximum amplitude of the difference $I^S_{MAX}$ between the current profiles associated to the settling of logic '1' and '0' for different loading and controlling conditions.

## 4.1    Unbalanced Output Loads (Assumption n°3)

Considering for simplicity the reduced dual-rail cell representation of Fig.2 (a), we have first evaluated the effects of having unbalanced capacitance ($C_1$ and $C_2$) values on the two differential output nodes. More precisely, we have evaluated the maximum amplitude $I^S_{MAX}$ of the difference between the current profiles associated to the settling of logic '1' and '0' respectively. Depending on the $C_2/C_1$ ratio, we have obtained two different expressions for $I^S_{MAX}$:

$$I_{MAX}^S = \frac{I_1(1-\beta)}{\left(\dfrac{V_{DD}}{V_{DSAT}}-1\right)} \cdot \left(\frac{C_2}{C_1}-1\right) \quad \text{if} \quad 1 < \frac{C_2}{C_1} < \frac{V_{DD}}{V_{DSAT}} \tag{9}$$

$$I_{MAX}^S = I_1 \cdot \left(1 - \frac{\beta.V_{dd}}{V_{dsat}} \cdot \frac{C_1}{C_2}\right) \quad \text{if} \quad \frac{C_2}{C_1} > \frac{V_{DD}}{V_{DSAT}} \tag{10}$$

Where $\beta$ is the ratio between $I_1$ (1) and $I_2$ (2).

In order to valid our model, we have simulated the structure of Fig.2 (a) on a 130nm process and implemented expressions (9) and (10) in Matlab software. With respect to different values of $C_2/C_1$ ($C_1$=4fF), we have obtained waveforms in Fig.4 (a). Note that the considered transition time value of the input signal triggering the switching was 50ps. By looking closely at Fig.4 (a), one can conclude that the accuracy of expressions (9) and (10) is satisfactory.

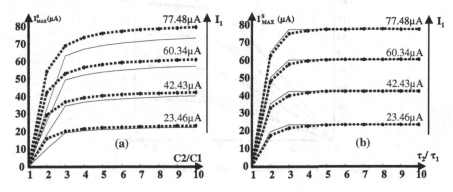

**Fig. 4.** Simulated and calculated values of $I_{MAX}^S$: (a) vs. $C_2/C_1$, (b) vs. $\tau_2/\tau_1$

### 4.2 Unbalanced Input Transition Time Values (Assumption n°1)

In a second step, we did investigate the effect of unbalanced input transition times, i.e. on unbalanced values of $\tau_1$ and $\tau_2$ (Fig.2 (a)). Following the same reasoning than in the preceding paragraph, we have obtained the expression of $I_{MAX}^S$:

$$I_{MAX}^S = \min\left\{ K \cdot \frac{W}{DW} \cdot V_{DD} \cdot \left(1 - \frac{\tau_1}{\tau_2}\right); I_1 \right\} \tag{11}$$

In expression (11) $\tau_1$ and $\tau_2$ are the transition time values of the signal driving INV1 and INV2. To illustrate the validity of expression (11), we have plotted in Fig.4 (b) the simulated and calculated evolutions of $I_{MAX}^S$ with respect to $\tau_2/\tau_1$ values for cmos inverters designed in a 130nm process ($\tau_1$=50ps, $C_1$=$C_2$=4fF). As shown, one can note that the accuracy of expression (11) is satisfactory.

### 4.3 Unbalanced Arrival Time Values (Assumption n°2)

In a last step, we did investigate the effect of unbalanced input signal arrival times (input transition times and output loads being perfectly balanced: $\tau_1=\tau_2$ and $C_1=C_2$). As in the two preceding paragraphs, we have deduced from the modelling of the switching current waveform the expression of $I^S_{MAX}$: (12).

$$I^S_{MAX} = \min\left\{ K \cdot \frac{W}{DW} \cdot \left(\frac{V_{DD} \cdot \Delta}{\tau}\right); I_1 \right\} \qquad (12)$$

where $\Delta$ is the difference between the arrival time values of the input signals controlling INV1 and INV2. We have plotted on Fig.5 the simulated and calculated evolutions of $I^S_{MAX}$ with $\Delta/\tau$. As shown the difference between the simulated and calculated values is low, validating thus expression (12).

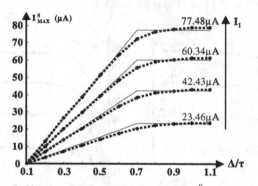

**Fig. 5.** Simulated and calculated values of $I^S_{MAX}$ vs. $\Delta/\tau$

## 5  Design Criteria and Discussion

Up to this point, we have developed a first order model of the switching current waveform. Then, we have deduced expressions of the maximum amplitude of the difference $I^S_{MAX}$ between the current profiles associated to the settling of logic '1' and '0' respectively. Let us now exploit these expressions to determine (quantify) the validity domain of assumptions 1 trough 3.

Defining $I_{TH}$ as the smallest current imbalance that can be monitored with a given amount of current profiles measures, it is now possible to quantify the imbalances that can be tolerated at both the input and the output of a dual-rail gate.

### 5.1  Unbalanced Output Loads (Assumption n°3)

Equating expressions (9) and (10) to $I_{TH}$, it is possible to define the critical ratio value $(C_1/C_2)$Crit below which the induced current imbalance can be successfully captured by a differential power analysis (if $I_1 > I_{TH}$):

$$\left.\frac{C_1}{C_2}\right|_{Crit} = \min\left\{\left(\frac{I_{TH}}{I_1} \cdot \frac{\frac{V_{DD}}{V_{DSAT}} - 1}{(1-\beta)} + 1\right)^{-1} ; \frac{V_{DSAT}}{\beta \cdot V_{DD}}\left(1 - \frac{I_{TH}}{I_1}\right)\right\}$$ (13)

Fig.6 (a) illustrates the calculated and simulated evolutions of $(C_1/C_2|_{Crit})$ with respect to $I_1$ for different $I_{TH}$ values. For the simulated values we have used the experimental setup of Fig.2 (a) in which inverters are replaced by nand2 gates and afterwards by latches. As shown the accuracy of expression (13) is satisfactory. For instance let us consider the case of an inverter characterized by a value of $I_1$ equal to 150µA. Assuming that the input transition values are identical and $I_{TH}$=100µA, we may conclude, accordingly to (13), that the output loads imbalance must not be smaller than 0.45. Note that the grey part of the figure is a direct illustration of the benefit of dual-rail logic over single rail one (for $I_{TH}$=20µA).

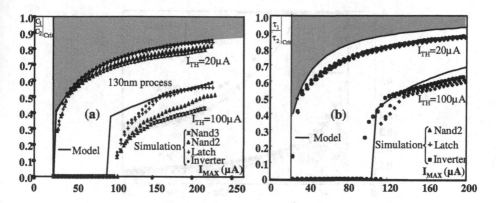

**Fig. 6.** (a) $C_1/C_2|_{Crit}$ vs. $I_1=I_{MAX}$ , (b) $\tau_1/\tau_2|_{Crit}$ vs. $I_1=I_{MAX}$ for two different $I_{TH}$ values

Considering the validity of **<u>assumption n°3</u>**, one can conclude that there is no absolute value of $C_1/C_2$ ratio above which all dual-rail gates can be considered as robust. However according to (13) one can note that the more current ($I_1$) a gate can deliver, the closer from one is $(C_1/C_2)_{Crit}$, i.e. the less robust to DPA the gate is.

### 5.2 Unbalanced Input Transition Time Values (Assumption n°1)

Following the same reasoning than in the preceding paragraph, we have deduced expression (14), the transition time imbalance that can be tolerated at the gate input.

$$\left.\frac{\tau_1}{\tau_2}\right|_{Crit} = 1 - \frac{I_{TH} \cdot (V_{DD} - V_T)}{I_1 \cdot V_{DD}} \text{ if } I_1 > I_{TH}$$ (14)

Fig.6 (b) shows the calculated and simulated evolutions of $(\tau_1/\tau_2)_{Crit}$ with $I_1$ for different $I_{TH}$ values. The simulated values have been obtained for inverters, nand gates and latches. As shown, the accuracy of expression (14) is satisfactory. As in the preceding paragraph, expression (14) allows concluding that the more current ($I_1$) a gate can deliver, the less robust to DPA it is.

### 5.3 Unbalanced Arrival Time Values (Assumption n°2)

The arrival time imbalance that can be tolerated at the input of a dual-rail cell has been obtained following the same reasoning than in the two preceding paragraphs:

$$\left|\frac{\Delta}{\tau}\right|_{Crit} = \frac{I_{TH} \cdot (V_{DD} - V_T)}{I_1 \cdot V_{DD}} \text{ if } I_1 > I_{TH} \tag{15}$$

where $\tau = \tau_1 = \tau_2$ is the input transition time value of all the incoming signals. Note that in this expression $\Delta$ may have value ranging from $[-\tau$ to $+\tau]$.

Fig.7 represents the calculated and simulated evolutions of $(\Delta/\tau)_{Crit}$ with $I_1$ for different $I_{TH}$ values. As shown the accuracy of expression (15) is satisfactory.

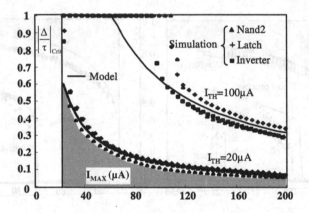

**Fig. 7.** $\left|\Delta/\tau\right|_{Crit}$ vs. $I_1 = I_{MAX}$ for two different $I_{TH}$ values

Considering expression (15), it appears that **<u>assumption n°2</u>** is really a crude assumption. Let us consider the case of a nand2 gate characterized by a value of $I_1$ equal to 80μA. Assuming that the outputs loads ($C_1$ and $C_2$) are identical, we may conclude, accordingly to (15), that the arrival time imbalance must not be greater than 0.8 times the transition time value of the incoming signal ($I_{TH}$=100μA). This is quite small considering that typical $\tau$ values are ranging from 20ps to 200ps.

### 5.4 Discussion

From the preceding results and expressions, it appears that there is really a design range within which dual-rail logic can be considered as robust to DPA attacks. However, this design space appears for the 130nm process under consideration quite narrow since the tolerable load, input transition and arrival time imbalances are quite small, especially for the arrival time imbalance.

Previously we have often concluded that the smaller is the current value ($I_1$), the more robust is the dual-rail cell against DPA attacks. Consequently, one possible solution to enlarge this secure design range seems to work with reduced supply voltage values since it induces smaller current values ($I_1$). However such an approach imposes to manage properly the power (security) versus timing (speed) trade off.

Considering once again the narrowness of the secure design range, it appears mandatory to develop dedicated tool and/or design solutions to properly balance not only the parasitic capacitances introduced during the place and route as proposed [9], but also tools and/or design solutions to properly balance the transition and arrival times. Within this context, expressions (13) to (15) constitute clever design criteria to evaluate the dangerousness of a dual-rail cell within a dual-rail circuit.

# 6  Conclusion

In this paper a first order switching current model has been introduced. Based on this analytical model, an investigation of the dual-rail logic robustness against DPA has been carried out. It has allowed identifying the design range in which dual-rail logic can be considered as robust. For the 130nm process under consideration, the identified secure design range appears to be quite narrow for the nominal supply voltage value. However the results obtained suggest that it is possible to significantly enlarge it by using reduced supply voltage values.

# References

[1]  P. Kocher and al. "Differential power analysis". CRYPTO'99, Lecture Notes in Comp. Science, vol. 1666, pp. 388-397.

[2]  D. Suzuki and al. "Random Switching Logic: A Countermeasure against DPA based on Transition Probability", Cryptology ePrint Archive, 2004/346, http://eprint.iacr.org/complete/

[3]  D. Sokolov and al. "Design and Analysis of Dual-Rail Circuits for Security Applications," IEEE Trans. on Computers, vol. 54, no. 4, pp. 449-460, April, 2005.

[4]  S. Guilley and al. "CMOS structures suitable for secured hardware". Design, Automation and Test in Europe Conference and Exposition.

[5]  J. Fournier and al. "Security Evaluation of Asynchronous Circuits", Workshop on Cryptographic Hardware and Embedded Systems, 2003.

[6]  G. F. Bouesse and al. "DPA on Quasi Delay Insensitive Asynchronous Circuits: Formalization and Improvement," Design, Automation and Test in Europe, pp. 424-429, Vol. 1, 2005.

[7]  A. Razafindraibe and al. "Secured structures for secured asynchronous QDI circuits" in XIX Conference on Design of Circuits and Integrated Systems, Nov. 24-26, 2004.

[8]  K. Tiri and al. "Securing encryption algorithms against DPA at the logic level: next generation smart card technology", Cryptographic Hardware and Embedded Systems Workshop, September 8-10, 2003.

[9]  K. Tiri and al. "A VLSI Design Flow for Secure Side-Channel Attack Resistant ICs," date, pp. 58-63, Design, Automation and Test in Europe (DATE'05) Volume 3, 2005.

[10] F. Mace and al. "A dynamic current mode logic to counteract power analysis attacks", DCIS 2004.

[11] P. Maurine and al, "Transition time modeling in deep submicron CMOS" IEEE Trans. on CAD, vol.21, n11, pp.1352-1363, 2002.

[12] K.O. Jeppson. "Modeling the Influence of the Transistor Gain Ratio and the Input-to-Output Coupling Capacitance on the CMOS Inverter Delay", IEEE JSSC, Vol. 29, pp. 646-654, 1994.

[13] T. Tsividis. "Operation and Modeling of the Mos Transistor", Oxford University Press, 1999.

[14] T. Sakurai and al. "Alpha-power law MOSFET model and its applications to CMOS inverter delay and other formulas", IEEE J. Solid-State Circuits, vol. 25, pp. 584-594, April 1990.

[15] Jens Sparso and al. "Principles of Asynchronous Circuit Design: A Systems Perspective", Kluwer Academic Publishers.

# A Method for Switching Activity Analysis of VHDL-RTL Combinatorial Circuits

Felipe Machado, Teresa Riesgo, and Yago Torroja

Universidad Politécnica de Madrid, E.T.S.I. Industriales, División de Ingeniería Electrónica
C/ José Gutiérrez Abascal, 2. 28006 Madrid, Spain
{fmachado, triesgo, ytorroja}@etsii.upm.es

**Abstract.** The analysis of circuit switching activity is a fundamental step towards dynamic power estimation of CMOS digital circuits. In this paper, a
probabilistic method for switching activity estimation of VHDL-RTL combinatorial designs is presented. Switching activity estimation is performed through
the propagation of input signals probabilities and switching activities by means
of BDDs (Binary Decision Diagrams). In order to avoid the BDD memory explosion of large circuits, an automatic circuit partition is performed taking advantage of the specific characteristics of some VHDL statements that permit the
circuit division in exclusive regions. In addition, a reduced representation of
switching activity BDDs is proposed. The method is implemented in a CAD
tool, which, besides the signal probabilities and switching activities, offers
abundant information and means for circuit exploration.

## 1 Introduction

Power consumption of VLSI circuits has become a major concern not only due to the
proliferation of mobile devices, which require larger autonomy with limited battery
weight, but also due to the excessive power densities of high performance circuits.
This trend is expected to worsen with the continuous scaling of the technology, and
may threaten its evolution in the future [1]. Historically, the power dissipation due to
the switching activity of circuit nodes has been the main source of power dissipation.
Nowadays, the static power dissipation is gaining importance because of the effects of
non-ideal scaling. In order to reduce the total chip dissipation, balance between both
static and dynamic sources of power dissipation has to be found [2]. Therefore, new
tools and methods are needed to estimate all the sources of power dissipation.

The average dynamic power consumption of a CMOS digital circuit can be approximated to the following formula:

$$P_{avg} = \tfrac{1}{2} \cdot f_{clk} \cdot V_{dd}^2 \cdot \Sigma_x \left[ C_x \cdot a_x \right] \tag{1}$$

Where $f_{clk}$ is the clock frequency; $V_{dd}$ is the supply voltage; $C_x$ and $a_x$ represent, respectively, the load capacitance and the switching activity at the output of any gate $x$
of the circuit.

Consequently, switching activity estimation is a fundamental stage towards the estimation of dynamic power; in addition, signal probability calculation constitutes a

J. Vounckx, N. Azemard, and P. Maurine (Eds.): PATMOS 2006, LNCS 4148, pp. 645–657, 2006.

previous step for switching activity when probabilistic methods are used. Besides, switching activity may be useful for reliability analysis [4], [5]; and signal probability may be useful for leakage power estimation, due to its dependence on the gate input vectors [6], [7].

In this paper, we present a method, and an automated tool based on it, for signal probability and activity estimation of VHDL-RTL designs. Signal probability and activity are propagated through a circuit model that extracts the Reduced Ordered Binary Decision Diagram (ROBDD [3] just BDD henceforth) of the combinatorial part of the circuit. To avoid the BDD memory explosion of large circuits, the tool previously divides them in smaller independent regions. Consequently, the propagation is not performed through a global BDD, but through various steps over smaller BDDs. We also present an efficient representation of the BDD involved in the activity computation.

The design exploration made to extract the BDDs reports plenty of information about the circuit internal nodes, which may be employed to estimate the other parameters of the dynamic power estimation formula: area and capacitance, and to analyze the circuit power behavior in order to optimize it.

This paper is structured as follows: in the next section some of the related terminology will be defined; then, some of the previous works in this field will be summarized; section 4 will explain the proposed method, both for signal probability and switching activity; section 5 will show how the method is implemented in an automated tool; section 6 will illustrate some results; and to finish, conclusions and future work will be exposed.

## 2  Definitions

In this section some of the terminology related to the topic will be presented:

- *Signal probability*, $P_x$, is the probability that node $x$ evaluates to logic one. $P_x;^-$ is the probability of node $x$ to be zero. $P_x;^- = 1 - P_x$
- *Transition probability*, $P(x_{i \to j})$, is the probability that node $x$ experiments a transition from $i$ to $j$ ($i, j \in \{0, 1\}$), in two consecutive time steps. $P(x_{0 \to 1}) = P(x_{1 \to 0})$
- *Switching activity* (or signal activity), $a_x$, is the probability that node $x$ experiences a transition that implies a change of value from one time step to other.

$$a_x = P(x_{0 \to 1}) + P(x_{1 \to 0}) = 2\,P(x_{0 \to 1}) . \tag{2}$$

- *Signal inactivity*, $a_x;^-$, is the probability of node $x$ to remain in the same state from one time step to other.

$$a_x;^- = 1 - a_x = P(x_{1 \to 1}) + P(x_{0 \to 0}) . \tag{3}$$

The activity of temporally independent (ti) signals can be directly calculated from its signal probability by (4), but for temporally dependent this formula may lead to wrong results.

$$a^{ti};_x = 2 \cdot P_x \cdot (1 - P_x) \tag{4}$$

Because only combinatorial circuits are considered and the circuit inputs are supposed to be strict-sense stationary, therefore, all the circuit signals are strict-sense stationary, i.e. their characteristics do not change as time varies. As a consequence:

$$P^0;_x = P^T;_x \tag{5}$$

Where $P^0;_x$ and $P^T;_x$ are the probabilities of signal $x$ at time 0 and $T$ respectively.

## 3  Previous Work

Methods to estimate the power consumption of gate and register transfer level designs are commonly classified in dynamic (or simulative) and static (or probabilistic). The dynamic method uses simulation to capture the internal nodes statistics. The circuit is stimulated with a *typical* sequence of input vectors and, with the purpose of avoiding excessive large simulation times, several methods have been developed to shorten the input vector length [8], [9].

The contribution of this paper is oriented to the probabilistic method, in which, user-defined input probabilities are propagated through a circuit model. The probabilistic method is faster, but for large circuits, accurate models may involve great complexity and computational resources. Therefore, circuit partition and efficient computation methods are needed. A large number of methods have been proposed to solve this question.

One of the earliest works in this field was presented by Parker [10], where a polynomial representing each gate output probability was generated; afterwards these polynomials were propagated through the gates. Structural correlations were considered but they did not compute switching activities. The method is simple and general, but the worst-case complexity is exponential.

An extension of the previous method to compute switching activity was presented by Costa [11]. Temporal correlations and arbitrary transport delays were also taken into account. In order to simplify the calculations, those structural correlations deeper than a certain level $l$ were neglected. The calculation of the switching activity ($a_y$) was made performing an XOR of the output function ($y$) at two consecutive time steps: $a_y = y^0 \oplus y^T$.

Looking for handling temporal correlations, simultaneous transitions and structural dependences, Schneider [12] introduced Markov chains, Shannon expansion and reconvergence analysis. Computations were implemented using BDDs, whose sizes were controlled by a maximum depth value of the combinatorial logic considered in structural dependences. Switching activity was also calculated by xoring the output, and was represented in a TFBDD (Transition Function BDD), in which each variable in time 0, $x^0$, is followed by itself at the following time step $x^T$, (fig. 4).

In a similar way, Marculescu [13] also used Markov chains to deal with spatiotemporal correlations; but additionally they handled spatial correlations for the primary inputs (only pairwise correlations). To propagate the switching activity and the signal correlations they use BDDs through a dynamic programming.

A model proposed by Theodoridis [14] suggests the usage of timed boolean functions, adopting a real-delay model to handle the influence of glitches.

Recently, Bhanja [15] has proposed the use of cascaded Bayesian networks to partition the circuit and to handle correlated inputs.

All these methods perform gate-level probabilistic estimation, in the present article we move up a step in the description level and consider RTL primitives such as multiplexers, which permits better circuit partitions and BDD variable orders. We also propose an optimized representation of activity BDDs.

# 4   Proposed Method

The proposed method builds a zero-delay model that works with VHDL-RTL combinatorial designs, considering structural dependences and temporal correlations. To address the complexity problem of the model for large circuits, we propose a method to divide the circuit in smaller regions. Some particularities make the signal activity calculation different from the signal probability calculation, and the BDD size for the activity computation entails even more serious difficulties. Therefore, in the next sections, the probability and activity calculations will be exposed separately.

## 4.1   Signal Probability Calculation

BDDs are widely used for signal probability computation. Having a BDD, its logical function is obtained adding all the paths leading to node 1. Each path is mutually disjoint, and therefore their probabilities can be evaluated separately. Individual signal probabilities can also be evaluated separately if spatial independence at the circuit inputs is assumed. All these steps are summarized in figure 1.

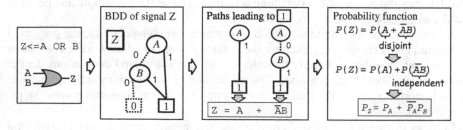

**Fig. 1.** Obtaining the probability function of a Boolean function through BDDs

Large circuits should be partitioned in order to reduce the BDD size. Partitioning must consider circuit reconvergences to avoid computation errors due to signal dependencies at their inputs. In many of the previous works, reconvergence analyses were accomplished to get smaller regions with mutually independent inputs [9], [11], [12]. But, having mutually independent inputs is not a necessary condition for the proper calculation of signal probabilities. Signal probabilities can be correctly computed with mutually dependent inputs when they are mutually disjoint [16].

We propose to take advantage of disjoint signals produced by some high-level language statements, e.g. the alternative paths of *if* and *case* statements. Although they may be mutually dependent, they always are disjoint events, i.e., they can never occur at the same time. This property applies only for the alternatives; the condition must remain independent respecting to the alternatives.

Figure 2 shows the reconvergence region obtained from mutually independent inputs, which covers the whole circuit. Both alternatives of the *if* statement (*H*, *I*) depend on signal *C*, consequently the circuit could not be partitioned there, and independent signals must be searched back.

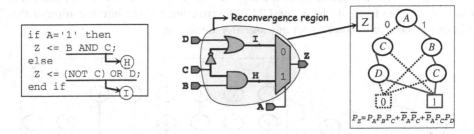

**Fig. 2.** Reconvergence region from mutually independent inputs and the resulting BDD for *Z*

But considering the disjoint events property, the alternatives *H* and *I* can divide the reconvergence region because the *if* statement produces events that can never simultaneously occur (figure 3). For this small example, the reduction in BDD nodes for signal *Z* reaches a 40% (from 5 to 3 nodes). Note that in both cases, the BDDs for the intermediate signals (*H*, *I*) have to be constructed in order to compute their individual probabilities.

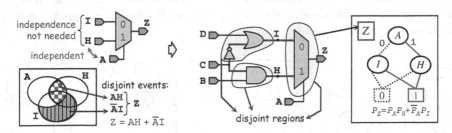

**Fig. 3.** Partition resulting from *if* statements disjoint events

Another advantage of the applied method to VHDL-RTL designs is related to the variable order of the resulting BDD. Its size depends on the variable order, and following the process own structure, going from the outer conditions to the inner conditions and assignments, is an efficient way to arrange the BDD.

## 4.2 Switching Activity Calculation

Switching activity computation implies that signals have to be considered in two time steps. Usually, signals are temporally correlated, thus (4) cannot be used to calculate their switching activity, instead, xoring two consecutive time steps of the signal is a extensively employed alternative [11], [12]. This operation increases severely the BDD size and further minimizations of the BDDs are needed.

Schneider [12] proposed to use TFBDDs to represent the activity function. The TFBDD structure considers signals ($x$) in consecutive time steps $x^0$, $x^T$: the XOR is performed on the same function BDD in two consecutive times $(0, T)$. The BDD variable order is maintained, but the variable at time 0 is followed by itself in time $T$. TFBDDs have to be evaluated considering their basic structure, formed by the node pairs $(x^0, x^T)$. On figure 4, the general TFBDD structure and the interpretation of the all possible node arrangements for any signal $A$ are shown.

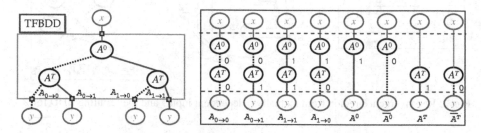

**Fig. 4.** General TFBDD structure, and interpretation of all of its node arrangements of signal $A$

To clarify these concepts, the TFBDD construction for an OR gate and its activity function computation is shown in figure 5. After performing the XOR of the probability BDDs in two consecutive time steps $(Z^0 \oplus Z^T)$, the TFBDD representation of the activity is obtained $a_Z$. On the right, all the paths leading to node 1 are extracted to get the activity formula, when nodes of the same signal in different times appear together they have to be evaluated jointly.

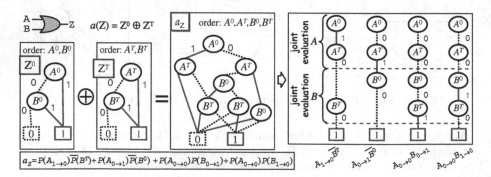

**Fig. 5.** OR gate TFBDD construction and its activity equation extraction

With the purpose of reducing the BDD size, we suggest a different representation from the TFBDD. Rather than using a representation based on time steps: $x^0$, $x^T$; we utilize a representation based on activity and inactivity: $a_x$, $\overline{a_x}$; and then, on transition probabilities, which have been named *activity BDD* (aBDD). In aBDD variable order, the activity node $a_x$ is always followed by its variable node $x$. On the left of figure 6, the general aBDD structure is represented, on the right, we can see the interpretation of all node arrangements that can be found in a path for any variable $A$. Note that when in the same path, both the activity and the signal node $(a_A, A)$ appear, they should be jointly evaluated.

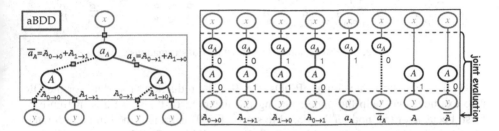

**Fig. 6.** General aBDD structure, and interpretation of all of its node arrangements

An operator has been defined to directly transform the probability BDD into an aBDD. The resulting aBDDs are simpler than TFBDDs; for this small example a reduction of 3 nodes out of 7 has been accomplished. Figure 7 shows the aBDD for an OR gate, and how the activity function is obtained accounting all the paths leading to node 1. As well as the inactivity equation, for which all paths leading to 0 are taken.

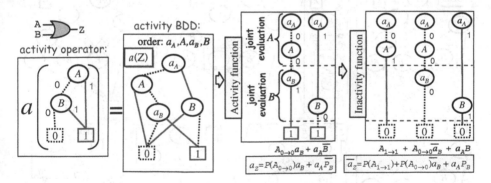

**Fig. 7.** Creation of aBDD and Activity and inactivity equation extraction from the aBDD

Figure 8 shows the equivalence between various TFBDD and aBDD structures. t1 is the general case of a TFBDD structure, whose aBDD equivalent is a1. The TFBDD structure t2 is very common; note how its aBDD equivalent (a2) has one node less. Even greater reductions are accomplished respecting to t3 and a3. Finally, because there is no distinction between $P^0{}_{;A}$ and $P^T{}_{;A}$ in aBDDs, both structures t4 and t5 have a unique equivalent a4, what also helps to reduce the final aBDD size.

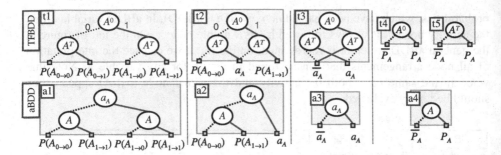

**Fig. 8.** TFBDD and aBDD structure transformations

TFBDDs can be reduced into aBDDs (fig. 9). The reduction procedure for the OR gate example may help the understanding the meaning of the structures in figure 8. First, because of (5), node $B^0$ (squared in step 1 fig. 9) is transformed in node $B$ (step 3), this node can be transformed because it has no children $B^T$ to be jointly evaluated. Accordingly, the edge going form $A^T$ to $B^T$ (step 3) has been moved to the new node $B$ (step 4). The squared structure in step 5, is transformed into $a_B$ (step 7) because $B_{0 \to 0}$ and $B_{1 \to 1}$ ($a_B$; ‾) finish in node 0, and $B_{0 \to 1}$ and $B_{1 \to 0}$ ($a_B$) finish in node 1 (step 6). The squared structure in step 7 is transformed into the squared structure in step 8, both $A_{0 \to 1}$ and $A_{1 \to 0}$ lead to the same node, therefore they can be joined into the activity $a_A$ (see equation 2).

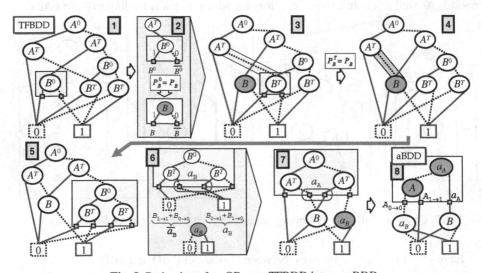

**Fig. 9.** Reduction of an OR-gate TFBDD into an aBDD

With the purpose of giving more examples and exposing the node reduction achievements, figure 10 compares them for some primitives. Similar results are obtained from more complex circuits, usually reducing the nodes between 30-40% and the number of BDD paths more than a half.

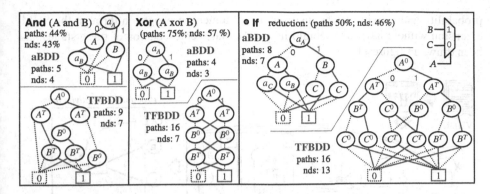

**Fig. 10.** Comparison between TFBDDs and aBDDs

The benefits of this representation can be added to the proposed circuit partition, although the mutually disjoint events property is not totally exact for activity computation as it is for signal probability, the experimental results shows that error in activity can be neglected (section 6, fig. 13.b).

## 5 Implementation in an Automated Tool

The method has been automated in a preliminary version. The program uses the Simplified Hardware Model (SHM)[17] developed in Ardid [18]. SHM is a hardware-oriented extension of the intermediate format of a VHDL description, where VHDL signals and statements are associated according to their hardware relationships. It is a schema halfway between the intermediate format resulting of compilation and the synthesized circuit, where the memory elements are located but the combinatorial logic is not totally defined. The developed program automatically extends SHM with additional information in order to facilitate the probability and activity computations.

First, all the combinatorial regions of the circuit are studied separately, and a combinational depth is assigned to each signal in order to know how far the signal is from the primary inputs (input ports and memory elements). Signals are selected according to their combinational depth, consequently no signal is chosen if its sources have not been processed yet.

Then the signal region is delimited, making use of the disjoint event property already explained. The BDD structure of the region is generated and annotated into SHM. Next, the BDD structure is translated into the BuDDy BDD package [19] to calculate the signal probability numeric value.

Once the Boolean function of the signal is represented in a BDD, the aBDD is created performing using the activity operator. It leads to the numerical calculation of the signal activity. Both signal probability and switching activity numeric values are annotated in the SHM and may be used in further calculations for other signals.

The process starts again with another signal with the same or higher combinational depth. At the end, the SHM extension is saved; therefore any change in the inputs probability and activity values just requires a numeric propagation through the SHM extension without having to rebuild it. A schematic representation of these stages has been drawn in figure 11.

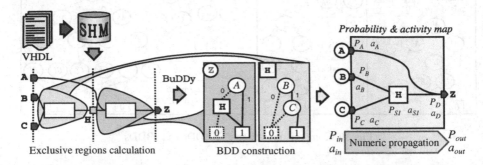

**Fig. 11.** Schematic view of the stages carried out by the tool

Besides, all the information annotated in the SHM can be used to explore the design space. There is plenty information on signals, expressions and other internal nodes that may help the designer and reviewers. For each of these nodes, probability and activity values, immediate and primary sources, common dependences, limits of their disjoint regions and corresponding BDDs, are available among other data.

Figure 12 shows some screenshots of the tool working in a small example. The *Activity Browser* permits the navigation through the design, letting the user know the signal probabilities and switching activities of the internal nodes, the demarcation of the disjoint regions and their dependences. In addition, both signal probability and switching activity BDDs can be visualized thanks to the integration of Graphviz [20] in the tool. Links to the VHDL code are also available.

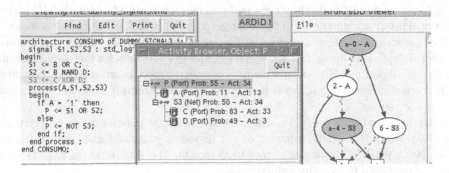

**Fig. 12.** Activity browser, activity BDD viewer and VHDL back-annotation windows

All these complementary information given by the tool have demonstrated its usefulness for the improvement of the design quality. During the accomplishment of the tests described in next section, the analyses provided by the tool revealed that some code did not describe any useful hardware and some signals that apparently were dependent, actually were not. For example, many of the VHDL code of the example in figure 12 are useless. Port $P$ just depends on signals $A$, $C$ and $D$. Note also how $S3$ divides the circuit into two smaller regions and the way it is represented in the activity browser.

# 6   Results

With the purpose of validating the method, results have been contrasted with zero-delay simulations of several academic VHDL circuits. The input sequences have been randomly generated constrained to the signal probability and switching activity values; then, the observed internal node probabilities and activities of the simulation have been compared with the results of the proposed probabilistic method.

For the tested circuits, in figure 13 has been plotted the distribution of number of nodes with a certain absolute error (multiplied by 100) for signal probability (fig. 13.a) and switching activity (fig. 13.b). No error have been found larger than 0.015. The absolute mean error for signal probability for all the circuits is 0.0031 and for switching activity 0.0013, the maximum mean error for a circuit was 0.0034 and 0.0018 for switching activity, having a standard deviation of 0.0043 and 0.0037 respectively.

An average of 35% in node reduction has been achieved using the proposed activity BDD representation, while path reductions were higher than 55%. aBDDs always reduces the number of nodes and paths respecting to TFBDDs. As an example figure 14 shows the node reductions achieved for each signal in two circuits (without partitioning), similar results are obtained for other circuits.

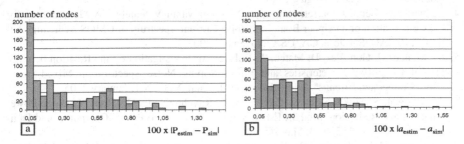

**Fig. 13.** Number of nodes with an absolute error for signal probability and switching activity

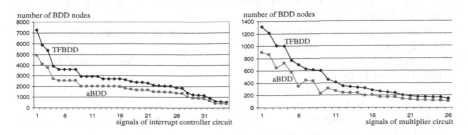

**Fig. 14.** Number of nodes in the TFBDD and aBDD representations of two sample circuits

# 7 Conclusions

A method to reduce the size of the reconvergent regions and the BDDs used to propagate signal probability and switching activity of VHDL-RTL combinatorial circuits has been presented. The method calculates exact signal probability using input disjoint signal properties and it is accurate enough for switching activity. Computations are performed in a zero-delay model without spatial correlations among the circuit input ports.

A BDD representation to compute the switching activity has been also expounded. Important reductions on the BDD size are accomplished, which in addition, benefits from the reductions obtained in the previous reconvergence analysis.

A first version has been implemented in an automated tool aiming to help designers to explore the design space. Although the whole synthesisable VHDL subset is not considered yet, there is work in progress to extend it; special effort is done to extend the method for sequential circuits, input correlations and glitch analysis. The potential of the method extends further than power estimation, quality analysis and other estimations, such as area and testability are prospective applications of our tool.

# References

1. International Roadmap for Semiconductors, 2005 Edition. http://public.itrs.net
2. M. Horowitz, E. Alon, D. Patil, S. Naffziger, R. Kumar: "Scaling, Power, and the Future of CMOS". IEEE Int. Electron Devices Meeting, Washington DC, USA, December 2005
3. R. Bryant: "Graph-Based Algorithms for Boolean Function Manipulation". IEEE Trans. on Computers, V. 35, N. 8, August 1986
4. A. Nardi, H. Zeng, J. Garret, L. Daniel, A. Sangiovanni-Vicentelli: "A Methodology for the Computation of an Upper Bound on Noise Current Spectrum of CMOS Switching Activity". ICCAD, San Jose, CA, USA, November 2003
5. M. Méndez, J. González, D. Mateo, A. Rubio: "An Investigation on the Relation between Digital Circuitry Characteristics and Power Supply Noise Spectrum in Mixed-Signal CMOS Integrated Circuits". Microelectronics Journal, V.36, N.1, January 2005
6. A. Agarwal, S. Mukhopadhyay, C.H. Kim, A. Raychowdhury, K. Roy: "Leakage Power Analysis and Reduction: Models, Estimation and Tools". IEE Proc. - Computers and Digital Techniques, V. 152, N. 3, May 2005
7. A. Ferré and J. Figueras: "On Estimating Leakage Power Consumption for Submicron CMOS Digital Circuits", PATMOS, Belgium, September 1997
8. D. Soudris, C. Piguet, C. Goutis, "Designing CMOS circuits for low power", Kluwer Academic Publishers, 2002
9. F. Najm: "A Survey of Power Estimation Techniques in VLSI Circuits". IEEE Trans. on VLSI Systems, V. 2, N. 4, December 1994
10. K. Parker, E. McCluskey: "Probabilistic Treatment of General Combinational Networks". IEEE Trans. on Computer, V.24, June 1975
11. J. Costa, J. Monteiro, S. Devadas: "Switching Activity Estimation Using Limited Depth Reconvergent Path Analysis", ISLPED, Monterey, CA, USA, August 1997
12. P. Schneider, U. Schlichtmann, B. Wurth: "Fast Power Estimation of Large Circuits". IEEE Design & Test of Computers, spring 1996

13. R. Marculescu, D. Marculescu, M. Pedram: "Probabilistic Modeling of Dependencies during Switching Activity Analysis". IEEE Trans. on CAD of ICs and Systems, V.17, N.2, February 1998
14. G. Theodoridis, S. Theoharis, D. Soudris, C. Goutis: "Switching Activity Estimation under Real-Gate Delay Using Timed Boolean Functions", IEE Proc. - Computers and Digital Techniques, V. 147, N. 6, November 2000
15. S. Bhanja, N. Ranganathan: "Cascaded Bayesian Inferencing for Switching Activity Estimation with Correlated Inputs", IEEE Trans. on VLSI Systems, V.12, N.12, Dec. 2004
16. V. Agrawal, S. Sheth, "Mutually Disjoint Signals and Probability Calculation in Digital Circuits", Great Lakes Symposium on VLSI, Lafayette, LA, USA, February 1998
17. Y. Torroja, F. Casado, F. Machado, T. Riesgo, E. de la Torre, J. Uceda: "Using a Simplified Hardware Model to Analyse the Quality of VHDL Based Designs", DATE (User Forum), France, March 2000
18. — "Ardid: A Tool and a Model for the Quality Analysis of VHDL Based Designs", Virtual Components: Design & Reuse, Kluwer, 2001
19. Buddy: http://buddy.sourceforge.net
20. Graphviz: http://www.graphviz.org

# Nanoelectronics: Challenges and Opportunities

Giovanni De Micheli

EPFL

The scaling of CMOS technology is coming soon to an end, and yet it is unclear whether CMOS devices in the 10-20 nanometer range will find a useful place in semiconductor products. At the same time, new silicon-based technologies (e.g., silicon nanowires) and non-silicon based (e.g., carbon nanotubes) show the promise of replacing traditional transistors. In this scenario, there are multiple challenges to face, like the production of nanoscale CMOS with reasonable yield and reliability, the creation of newer circuit structures with novel materials as well as the mixing and matching of older and newer technologies in search of a good balance of costs and benefits.

Within this rich set of possibilities, opportunities will be driven by the ability of designing complex circuits with these technologies. Unprecedented problems related to defect density, failure rates, temperature sensitivity compensate the availability of an even larger number of devices. Our ability to define the right design technology and methodology will be key in the realization of products of these nanotechnology, and on the direction that the semiconductor road will take after the inevitable curve that is on the horizon.

J. Vounckx, N. Azemard, and P. Maurine (Eds.): PATMOS 2006, LNCS 4148, p. 658, 2006.
© Springer-Verlag Berlin Heidelberg 2006

# Static and Dynamic Power Reduction by Architecture Selection

Christian Piguet[1], Christian Schuster[2], and Jean-Luc Nagel[1]

[1] CSEM Centre Suisse d'Electronique et de Microtechnique, Jaquet-Droz 1
2000 Neuchâtel, Switzerland
[2] IMT Institut de Microtechnique, University of Neuchâtel,
2000 Neuchâtel, Switzerland

**Abstract.** As leakage power and total power is a more and more dramatic issue in very deep submicron technologies, this paper explores new design methodologies for designing leakage tolerant digital architectures, based on architectural parameters like activity, logical depth, number of transitions for achieving a given task and total number of gates. Various architectures for a same logic function are compared at very low Vdd and Vth that define the optimal total power consumption of each architecture. The first proposed design method selects the best architecture out of a set of architectures (baseline, sequential, parallel, pipelined, etc..) at optimal Vdd and threshold voltages Vth, while a second design method takes Vdd and threshold voltages Vth as given constraints.

## 1 Introduction

Starting from 0.18 μm technologies, static power consumption, due to leaky "off" transistors, is now a non negligible source of power dissipation even in running mode [1]. Thus, the total power consumption (i.e. dynamic plus static power) has to be optimized instead of simply reducing dynamic power, the latter being due to switched capacitance charge/discharge.

Many research efforts aim at reducing the static power consumption at the device level using for instance MTCMOS, VTCMOS, Gated-Vdd, or DTCMOS [2]. Conversely very few papers considered the joint static-dynamic power optimization at a higher level, namely at system and architectural levels.

This paper therefore gives a survey of different tools and methodologies targeting the optimization of total power consumption at the architectural level.

## 2 Problem Formulation

For a given architecture, reducing the supply voltage Vdd leads to a reduction of the dynamic power consumption, whereas it also results in a decrease of performance or speed. To compensate this effect, the threshold voltage Vth should be reduced too. Unfortunately, lowering the Vth exponentially increases the static power consumption,

J. Vounckx, N. Azemard, and P. Maurine (Eds.): PATMOS 2006, LNCS 4148, pp. 659–668, 2006.

as shown by formula (1). At a certain point, this increase in static power consumption becomes larger than the gain in dynamic power and the total power consumption becomes larger.

$$I_{off} = I_0 e^{-\frac{Vth}{n*U_T}} \tag{1}$$

with $I_0$ being the current at $VG=V_{th}$.

Therefore, between all the combinations of Vdd/Vth guaranteeing the desired speed, only one couple will result in the lowest power consumption (Fig. 1). These working conditions will be called optimal working point or ideal working point. The location of this optimal working point and its associated total power consumption are tightly related to architectural and technology parameters.

As can be observed in Fig. 1 the ratio of dynamic (Pdyn) over static (Pstat) power at the minimum of total power consumption is not constant and depends on some parameters, e.g. the activity as illustrated in Fig. 1, but also on the logical depth, working frequency, etc. Without loss of generality we can write:

$$Pdyn^{opt} = k_1 * Pstat^{opt} \tag{2}$$

where $k_1$ is expected to depend in a complex fashion on architectural parameters.

A first approximation [3, 4] was obtained by considering that the optimum of the total power consumption is obtained with the same amount of static and dynamic power ($k_1=1$). From the results shown in Fig. 1, this approximation is clearly too rough. The parameter $k_1$ can be obtained by searching the minimum of Ptot(Vdd). The value of $k_1$ is roughly located between 1 and 5 as shown in [6].

Fig. 1 illustrates the fact that reducing the activity allows reducing Ptot, whereas it tends to increase the optimal Vdd and Vth. As architectural modifications will change simultaneously several factors (not just the activity), it is necessary to develop a methodology to evaluate the influence of such transformations on Ptot. The original-ity of this methodology is that at this optimal point there is a given ratio between dynamic and static power, which is strongly correlated to the ratio between Ion/Ioff of the technology. Moreover, due to the increase of the leakage current in the modern technologies, this ratio Ion/Ioff is becoming smaller and smaller. On the other hand, the optimal ratio Ion/Ioff is dependent on architectural parameters, which are the activity **a** and the logical depth **LD** (number of gates in series). An approximation for Ion/Ioff is given by:

$$Ion/Ioff = k_1 * LD/a \tag{3}$$

Note that $k_1$ is itself depending on architectural parameters such as LD and a.

If the Ion/Ioff ratio is small (100 to 500), one can see that LD has to be small and activity quite large! This can lead to a paradigm shift, as activity reduction has until now been a primary goal, due to the fact that only dynamic power was considered. By optimizing both static and dynamic power, the goal of a low-power design methodol-ogy is obviously not always to reduce as much as possible the activity. In fact, very inactive gates or transistors doing nearly nothing are still leaky devices. So it is not optimal to have too many gates or transistors with an extremely low activity. On the other hand, if the reduction of activity is not due to an increase in the number cells but rather to a reduction of the number of transitions, both nominal and optimal total power will benefit from it.

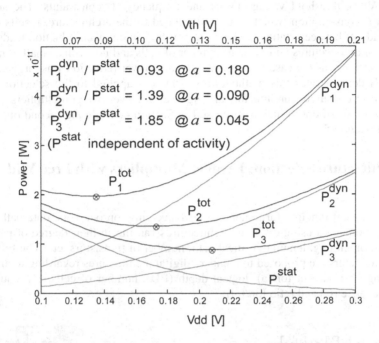

**Fig. 1.** Total power consumption of a square transistor for the UMC 0.18 um technology. The optimal working point is marked by the cross mark.

## 3  Design Constraints

Different design constraints can be applied when searching for the best set of architectural parameters (activity, logical depth, number of cells) in terms of total power consumption, which depend on how the optimal working conditions can be modified.

1) Vdd and Vth can be freely (and precisely) modified. Whereas the supply voltage is in general easily controllable, it is harder to modify the threshold voltage as body back-biasing becomes less and less efficient in very deep submicron technologies. In [5] a new design methodology is proposed for designing leakage tolerant digital architectures, based on architectural parameters like activity, logical depth, number of transitions and total number of gates for achieving a given task. Various architectures for a same logic function are compared at very low Vdd and Vth corresponding to their optimal total power consumption. In [6] the methodology aims at selecting the one with the minimum total power consumption by simultaneously optimizing static and dynamic power dissipation. This optimal power has been estimated for eleven 16-bit multiplier architectures. When a precise modification of Vth is not allowed, it may be possible to select a technology that matches as closely as possible the Vth requirements.

2) Vdd and Vth are fixed by the application. This methodology allows us to compare several architectures (or micro-architectures) performing the same function and to select the one presenting the smallest total power consumption under fixed supply voltage (Vdd), threshold voltage (Vth) and frequency (f) constraints. The smallest total power consumption, which is closely related to the architecture, results clearly from a tradeoff between static and dynamic power. Static power reduction leads to the selection of architectures with a small number of cells and not with a small number of transitions, as it was the case when only dynamic power reduction was targeted. Reference [7] demonstrates this methodology, which is applied to the selection of the lowest power consuming architecture among a set of eleven 16 bit multipliers.

The first type of constraints is discussed in Section 4, while the second one is discussed in Section 5.

## 4   Architecture Selection: Parallel Multipliers with Free Vdd and Vth

The same logical function (arithmetic, filter banks, microprocessors, data paths, etc.) can be implemented using different architectures varying in their degree of parallelization and pipelining, length of critical path, number of transistors, etc. The following design parameters are proposed to compare digital architectures regarding total power and leakage: activity factor (a), logical depth (LD), number of cells (N), equivalent cell capacitance (C) and ratio Ion/Ioff.

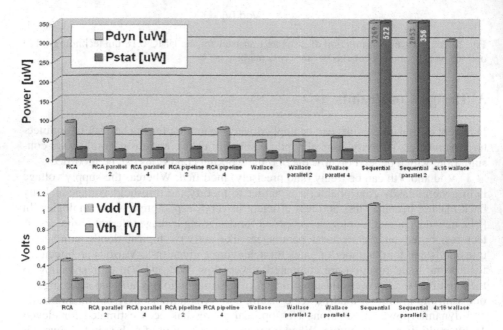

**Fig. 2.** Optimal total power and corresponding Vdd/Vth couple for eleven multiplier architectures at their optimal working point. (UMC 0.18 μm, 31.25MHz).

Eleven 16 bit multipliers architectures have been described and synthesized. Their power consumption was analyzed using the same stimuli for all circuits and the optimal Vdd and Vth were computed.

All circuits work at 31.25 MHz, and were synthesized with Synopsys in the UMC 0.18μm technology. The various architectures are the following: *Ripple Carry Array* or RCA (basic, pipelined 2, pipelined 4, parallel 2, parallel 4), *Wallace Tree* (basic, parallel 2, parallel 4) and *Sequential* (basic, 4x16 Wallace, parallel) [6].

The architecture providing the lowest total power consumption is the structure based on the Wallace tree, operating at very low Vdd and Vth. As could be expected at these low Vdd and Vth, the Ion/Ioff ratio for optimal total power consumption is rather small, approximately between 100 and 1'000 (compared to several million at nominal Vdd). Moreover, the percentage of static power over the total power is between 15% and 30%, i.e. $k_1$ between 3 and 6, far from $k_1=1$. Ion/Ioff being very close to $k_1*LD/a$, shows that (3) is a good approximation.

**Table 1.** Number of cells, activity, Vdd, Vth, k1 and optimal total power for the 11 multiplier architectures (UMC 0.18 μm, 31.25MHz)

| | Area [$*10^3 \mu m^2$] | # of cells | # of cell transitions | a | LD | k1 | $k_1LD/a$ | $I_{on}/I_{off}$ | Vdd [V] | Vth [V] | Pdyn [μW] | Pstat [μW] | Ptot [μW] |
|---|---|---|---|---|---|---|---|---|---|---|---|---|---|
| RCA | 23 | 577 | 171 | 0.20 | 46 | 3.8 | 856 | 919 | 0.43 | 0.21 | 92 | 24 | 116 |
| RCA parallel 2 | 47 | 1156 | 181 | 0.11 | 23 | 3.6 | 761 | 740 | 0.35 | 0.24 | 76 | 19 | 94 |
| RCA parallel 4 | 92 | 2316 | 208 | 0.06 | 12 | 3.5 | 660 | 452 | 0.31 | 0.25 | 70 | 22 | 92 |
| RCA pipeline 2 | 27 | 641 | 187 | 0.21 | 31 | 3.3 | 497 | 448 | 0.35 | 0.21 | 73 | 25 | 98 |
| RCA pipeline 4 | 33 | 769 | 220 | 0.21 | 24 | 3.1 | 350 | 278 | 0.31 | 0.21 | 75 | 29 | 104 |
| Wallace | 25 | 755 | 199 | 0.20 | 16 | 3.1 | 254 | 226 | 0.29 | 0.21 | 43 | 15 | 58 |
| Wallace parallel 2 | 50 | 1506 | 208 | 0.11 | 8 | 3.1 | 237 | 147 | 0.27 | 0.23 | 45 | 18 | 63 |
| Wallace parallel 4 | 97 | 3017 | 238 | 0.06 | 4 | 3.3 | 218 | 112 | 0.27 | 0.25 | 54 | 21 | 75 |
| Sequential | 10 | 257 | 654 | 2.23 | 192 | 6.2 | 530 | 439 | 1.06 | 0.14 | 3269 | 522 | 3792 |
| Sequential 4x16 wallace | 14 | 355 | 255 | 0.59 | 100 | 3.8 | 646 | 432 | 0.53 | 0.17 | 302 | 84 | 386 |
| Sequential parallel 2 | 16 | 325 | 502 | 1.28 | 160 | 5.6 | 701 | 634 | 0.91 | 0.16 | 2053 | 356 | 2409 |

Figure 2 shows the results in total power consumption for these eleven multiplier architectures as well as the corresponding optimal Vdd and Vth. Table 1 adds the number of cells, activities, LD number of transitions and the k1 ratio. Particular cases are now discussed.

Parallelizing the RCA (i.e. dividing its LD and a) shows improvements to total power. Similarly, using a two-stage pipelined RCA (i.e. dividing its LD, but keeping a almost constant) reduces the total power compared to the basic RCA, as could be expected. However, the register overhead becomes too important with a four-stage pipeline leading to a poorer solution. Although increasing the parallelism of the RCA was beneficial, increasing the parallelism of the Wallace structure does not lead to a better solution. In fact, the total power consumption becomes a little bit higher due to the increased number of cells, which are inactive and leaky. Despite a quite small number of cells, sequential architectures implemented using the add-shift algorithm, present a very large total power due to their lack of speed, requiring a very high Vdd and a very small Vth to fulfil the speed requirements.

Comparing the four-time parallel RCA and twice parallel Wallace, it can be observed that the first is composed of 2316 cells, while the second has only 1506 cells, the ratio of areas being over 1.8. Still, both architectures present 208 cell transitions for executing a 16x16 multiply, showing that various architectures with a quite different number of cells can achieve their function with the same number of transitions. Fig. 3 reports both architectures under the same conditions (Vdd = 0.31 V and Vth = 0.25 V). The architecture containing fewer cells still presents a larger activity and a smaller leakage but it also reports a smaller dynamic power (second bar in Fig. 3, for the same Vdd and Vth). Moreover, this architecture can be supplied with smaller Vdd and Vth thanks to its smaller LD (third bar in Fig. 3) to meet the same speed performances than the RCA parallel 4, with better results in total power consumption. Accordingly, an attractive goal to reduce the total power consumption would be to have fewer transistors to perform the same logic function, i.e. with the same number of transitions but more activity.

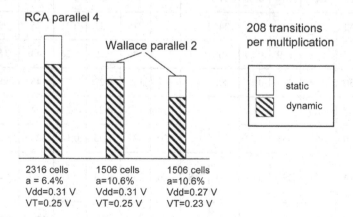

**Fig. 3.** Comparison of two multiplier architectures (RCA parallel 4 and Wallace parallel 2) showing the same number of transitions per multiplication but different total power

# 5   Architecture Selection with Fixed Vdd and Vth

The proposed design methodology provides the minimal total consumption considering fixed supply voltage and fixed threshold voltages. In practice, this hypothesis is most of the time valid because the designer can rarely chose optimal supply voltages for different blocks of the circuits. All the architectures in the implementation set share the same Vdd, Vth and f, but present different values for a (activity) and N (number of cells). One has to compare a couple of architectures before selecting the best one. The design methodology is presented in details in [7]. Tables 2 and 3 show the winner in different situations. Firstly with Vdd=1V and Vth=0.3V showing the RCA as the best architecture (Table 2) and then with Vdd=1V and Vth=0.1V reporting Sequential 4_16 as the best choice (Table 3). In both cases the working frequency is 31.25 MHz.

**Table 2.** Consumption of the eleven multipliers in μW for Vdd = 1 V, Vth = 0.3 V and f = 31.25 MHz

| RCA | RCA parallel 2 | RCA parallel 4 | RCA pipeline 2 | RCA pipeline 4 | Wallace Tree | Wallace parallel 2 | Wallace parallel 4 | Sequential | Sequential 4_16 | Sequential parallel 2 |
|---|---|---|---|---|---|---|---|---|---|---|
| **501** | 624 | 752 | 594 | 785 | 511 | 629 | 767 | - | 1067 | - |

**Table 3.** Consumption of the eleven multipliers in μW for Vdd = 1 V, Vth = 0.1 V and f = 31.25 MHz

| RCA | RCA parallel 2 | RCA parallel 4 | RCA pipeline 2 | RCA pipeline 4 | Wallace Tree | Wallace parallel 2 | Wallace parallel 4 | Sequential | Sequential 4_16 | Sequential parallel 2 |
|---|---|---|---|---|---|---|---|---|---|---|
| 3350 | 6136 | 11405 | 3924 | 5077 | 3655 | 6807 | 12900 | 4382 | **2843** | 4606 |

## 6 Total Power Consumption Formula

An approximated closed-form total power consumption equation for circuits working at their optimal supply and threshold voltage can be found in [8]. Comparisons of this formula to the numerical calculation show an error less than 3% on a set of thirteen 16 bit multipliers (eleven of them reported in Table 1). Starting from this equation, the influence of architecture transformations (including pipelining, parallelization and sequentialization) on the optimal total power can be discussed and predicted without having recourse to numerical computations. Finally, by a similar approach, the impact of the technology choice on achievable power saving can be considered, showing how a moderated trade-off between leakage and speed is the key characteristic of a good low power technology.

## 7 Technology Selection

The 0.13μm ST Microelectronics technology exists in three different flavors, namely High Speed (HS), Low Leakage (LL) and Ultra Low Leakage (ULL). The optimal total power was calculated for the eleven thirteen 16 bit multipliers.

As shown in Figure 4, the optimal total power of the parallel version of the Wallace multiplier is higher than that of the basic one when using the HS process whereas it is the opposite for ULL and LL processes. This can be explained by the fact that parallelization (where the number of cells is more than doubled) is more penalized-with technologies presenting a very high leakage. Moreover speed gain resulting from a logical depth reduction of an already fast structure in "fast" technologies is often extremely limited.

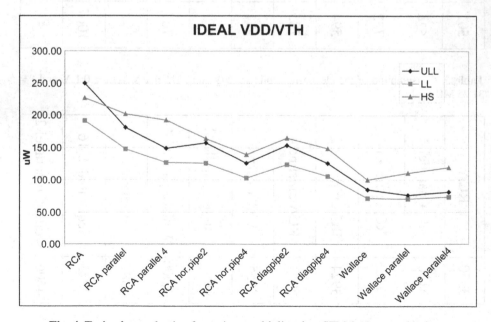

**Fig. 4.** Technology selection for various multipliers in a STM 0.13 μm technology

Similarly, the optimal total power for ULL is always larger than for LL in corresponding architectures. This can be explained by the slow ULL technology. This corresponds to a higher optimal Vdd (higher dynamic power) and lower Vth (higher static power).

From these examples, it appears that under such conditions (circuits working at 31.25MHz) the technology presenting the lowest optimal power consumption is the LL, showing that extreme technology flavors (ULL and HS) are penalized.

Starting from these observations, we can understand that a more advanced technology node with ultra-high speed and large leakage might consume more than a previous but LL or ULL technology node at its optimal working point when considering the same performances.

# 8 Conclusion

Total power consumption resulting from the sum of the static and dynamic contribution shows an optimum corresponding to very low Vdd and Vth. As illustrated in this paper, this minimum is characterized by a dynamic power somewhat larger than the static power (between 3.1 and 6.2 times in the considered multiplier architectures). The optimal ratio Ion/Ioff is also discussed and reported to be related to the architectural parameters LD and a. This relationship has been demonstrated for eleven 16 bit multipliers showing optimal values of Ion/Ioff between 100 and 1000.

Parallelization and pipelining can improve the power consumption when this leads to a reduction of Vdd and an increase of Vth (e.g. with RCA multiplier) but are not interesting for structures where the increase in static power does not allow this reduction (e.g. Wallace structure).

The choice of a circuit architecture can also been performed with fixed constraints like fixed Vdd and fixed Vth. In this case, dependent on their values, a sequential or a parallel architecture has to be selected.

Another interesting choice is the technology and it can be performed using this methodology to obtain the optimal total power.

# Acknowledgment

This work was supported by the Swiss National Science Foundation (SNSF), under grant 105619. The authors would also like to thank TIMA for providing the STM libraries.

# References

1. M. Belleville, Olivier Faynot, "Evolution of deep submicron bulk and SOI technologies", Chapter 2, in "Low Power Electronics Design", edited by C. Piguet, CRC Press, 2005
2. K. Roy, A. Agarwal, C. H. Kim, "Circuit Techniques for Leakage Reduction", Chapter 13, in "Low Power Electronics Design", edited by C. Piguet, CRC Press, 2005
3. R.W. Brodersen, et al.,"Methods for True Power Minimization", Proceedings of the Int'l Conf. on Computer Aided Design, (2002) November, pp. 35-42. San Jose, California

4. K. Nose, T. Sakurai, "Optimization of Vdd and Vth for Low-Power and High-Speed Applications", Proceedings of the Asia and South Pacific Design Automation Conference, (2000) January 25-28, pp. 469-474, Yokohama, Japan
5. C. Piguet, C. Schuster, J-L. Nagel, "Optimizing Architecture Activity and Logic Depth for Static and Dynamic Power Reduction", Proc. of the 2nd Northeast Workshop on Circuits and Systems – NewCAS'04, June 20-23, 2004, Montréal, Canada
6. C. Schuster, J-L. Nagel, C. Piguet, P-A. Farine, "Leakage reduction at the architectural level and its application to 16 bit multiplier architectures", PATMOS '04, September 15-17, 2004, Santorini Island, Greece
7. C. Schuster, J-L. Nagel, P-A, C. Piguet. Farine, "An Architecture Design Methodology for Minimal Total Power Consumption at Fixed Vdd and Vth", Journal of Low-Power Electronics (JOLPE), Vol. 1, No. 1, pp. 1-8, April 2005.
8. C. Schuster, J-L. Nagel, C. Piguet, P-A. Farine, "Architectural and Technology Influence on the Optimal Total Power Consumption", DATE 2006, March 6-10, 2006, Munchen, Germany

# Asynchronous Design for High-Speed and Low-Power Circuits

Peter A. Beerel

USC Viterbi School of Engineering

Asynchronous design is emerging as a practical alternative to synchronous design for both low power and high performance applications. Moreover, ASIC flows that support asynchronous design are becoming complete, including many that leverage existing front-end and back-end synchronous-oriented tools. This talk will review the different design styles and flows and highlight some of the on-going commercialization efforts in this area. Special attention will be paid to the single-track circuit families developed at USC that provide ultra high performance and low power characteristics. We will review the associated standard-cell libraries and flows that have been developed as well as the recent chip design efforts that demonstrate the benefits of this technology.

J. Vounckx, N. Azemard, and P. Maurine (Eds.): PATMOS 2006, LNCS 4148, p. 669, 2006.
© Springer-Verlag Berlin Heidelberg 2006

# Design for Volume Manufacturing in the Deep Submicron ERA

Robin Wilson

STMicroelectronics

The deep sub-micron technologies of today present us with new opportunities and challenges. On one hand the level of integration and available process options enables the development of fully integrated high performance systems (digital, mixed signal and RF) , while on the other hand we have the challenge of designing with increasing manufacturing variation and new electrical /reliability effects to consider. New design tools and methodologies are required. Looking to the past and even the present can give clues for the direction to take for the future. This talk , will describe through concrete examples the challenges overcome in developing design platforms for volume manufacture in the most recent technology nodes, including discussing the most imminent challenges to solve to maximize the benefit from forthcoming technologies.

J. Vounckx, N. Azemard, and P. Maurine (Eds.): PATMOS 2006, LNCS 4148, p. 670, 2006.
© Springer-Verlag Berlin Heidelberg 2006

# The Holy Grail of Holistic Low-Power Design

F. Pessolano

Philips Semiconductors

The power density has been steadily increasing with technology scaling, while die sizes have not shrunk accordingly due to cost reasons. The combination of these two trends has resulted in a constant increase in power consumption for integrated circuits. This situation further worsens when we also look at the application from its power/performance requirements point of view. Most of the products, that consumers want, already have hard power budgets as either the final device is expected to run on batteries for weeks or due to the increasing cost of energy. These trends lead to power as our primary foe along the path dictated by Moore's law.

No longer being able to rely on the inherent low-power performance of underlying semiconductor processes, new ways must therefore be found to reduce power consumption. At present the challenge is mainly about reducing active power consumption, but as the contribution of leakage currents to overall power dissipation in next-generation deep sub-micron processes increases, it will be just as important to cut static power as well. A solution in this direction requires the development of a low-power approach or, most likely, a set of application specific approaches spanning from technology to software in a combined way. Furthermore, this problem is not purely technical; we will show in this presentation how low-power design is as much a technical problem as a managerial and mindset issue. Therefore, the "holy grail of a holistic low-power approach" must be a combination of a (vertical) technical solution as well as a solution for changing the mindset and alleviate its managerial consequences.

J. Vounckx, N. Azemard, and P. Maurine (Eds.): PATMOS 2006, LNCS 4148, p. 671, 2006.
© Springer-Verlag Berlin Heidelberg 2006

# Top Verification of Low Power System with "Checkerboard" Approach

Jean Oudinot

Mentor Graphics

Low power management is a critical design front for complex wireless systems. Not only different natures of the blocks required different power supplies (1.5V, 2.5V). Blocks are switched on and off sequentially during the duty to save power. A simple connection error can damage or destroy a block. Top level verification of such a complexity is required to guaranty the quality and the robustness of the final product.

Since chips are too complex to allow full transistor level top verification, the idea is to mix multi-level abstraction trade-offs to overcome the simulation speed performance issue. We call this approach a "checkerboard methodology". Instead of running the complete chip at the transistor level, specific blocks are switched down to transistor level while the rest of the chip remains at a high level of abstraction. Power up and down is therefore verified on specific blocks successively one after another to guarantee their functional performance within the complete system. The idea is to divide-and-conquer to achieve high functional coverage. Breaking down the test process like this also has the advantage of allowing parallel simulation on computer farms.

As a result, designers should not spend time trying to reduce each test down to a critical path. Instead, they simply need to define, for each test, a specific set of stimuli and a specific netlist configuration defining which blocks to be switched to transistor level (active blocks) and which ones should remain at behavioural. Such tedious preparation phase is supported by a graphical cockpit ADVance VCB from Mentor Graphics.

J. Vounckx, N. Azemard, and P. Maurine (Eds.): PATMOS 2006, LNCS 4148, p. 672, 2006.
© Springer-Verlag Berlin Heidelberg 2006

# The Power Forward Initiative
## Charting the Industry's Course to Achieving Enhanced Power Management Solutions for Advanced Process Geometries

Francois Thomas

Cadence

As the electronics industry continues its move towards advanced process geometries, significant challenges have emerged that cannot be met by the existing design infrastructure. Across the design and manufacturing chain, a need has emerged for a power-aware infrastructure that will benefit design teams; ASIC, library, IP, and tool vendors; equipment providers; and manufacturing facilities alike.

Current limitations in the existing design infrastructure prevent power-related aspects of design intent from being specified across the design chain. These limitations are preventing companies from initiating profitable low-power projects due to high levels of risk and uncontrollable design costs. In the recent past, isolated efforts to lower power consumption have been made. However, in order to effectively address the larger challenges posed by power consumption at the advanced process nodes, an urgent need for a broad new industry alliance has emerged: the Power Forward Initiative.

The Power Forward Initiative's primary goal is to remove the barriers to automation of advanced low power design, and to provide a pathway towards the development of a standards-based solution.

To achieve these goals, ongoing work on the Common Power Format is being considered within the larger industry frame of reference. Looking to satisfy the needs of the broad constituency of chip design teams and providers of tools, equipment, IP, silicon, manufacturing, test and services, the Common Power Format has been created to deliver a comprehensive solution to the challenges posed by today's advanced power requirements. The Common Power Format is being architected for future support of new design techniques and materials breakthroughs, including architecture, hardware and software system modeling, as well as analog and mixed-signal design.

J. Vounckx, N. Azemard, and P. Maurine (Eds.): PATMOS 2006, LNCS 4148, p. 673, 2006.
© Springer-Verlag Berlin Heidelberg 2006

# Author Index

# Lecture Notes in Computer Science

For information about Vols. 1–4071

please contact your bookseller or Springer